JOSEPH P. KENNEDY

THE MOGUL, THE MOB,
THE STATESMAN, AND
THE MAKING OF
AN AMERICAN MYTH

TED SCHWARZ

WILEY

John Wiley & Sons, Inc.

CONTENTS

ACKNOWLEDGMENTS

THE WRITING OF JOE KENNEDY'S LIFE WAS NEVER ANTICIPATED when I first became involved with the Kennedy family. I was writing about Special Olympics, the Kennedy family program that brings the retarded and severely disabled together for athletic events. I was writing for publications ranging from *Family Circle* to city magazines such as *Phoenix*. I visited Washington, D.C., and the office of Special Olympics. I also talked with family members, including Joan Kennedy, now the ex-wife of Senator Ted Kennedy.

As I worked on stories that were all positive concerning the group and the participants, I was troubled by stories of Rosemary Kennedy's past; of her father, Joe; and of her relationship with her mother after Rosemary was given a prefrontal lobotomy. I also was surprised to hear a different story from a staff member of Special Olympics than the story from the Kennedys themselves.

Eventually I began interviewing individuals who were intimate with family members, often including Joe Kennedy. I went to the Kennedy Library to do research several times. I went to the National Archives. I obtained documents from the Roosevelt Library. And I found people who were involved with the 1960 election and the Kennedy men in Hollywood as I researched books on those around the family (e.g., *The Peter Lawford Story*, which I wrote with the actor's widow, Patricia Seaton Lawford).

Then I worked with Barbara Gibson, a brilliant woman who, over the years, had worked on Capitol Hill, for the FBI, and for the ten years prior to Rose Kennedy's stroke, as the personal assistant to Mrs. Kennedy. Barbara knew the entire family, including Joe Kennedy. She had watched the trysts, the lies, the deaths, the glories, and all else that occurred with the family in Hyannis Port and Palm Beach. More important, as we completed both the biography of Rose Kennedy and the story of the third generation of Kennedys, Barbara helped me meet the invaluable "invisible" people.

The very rich have staff members the more foolish among the employers ignore. These are almost entirely individuals with strong moral principles, an intense work ethic, and a willingness to serve without personal attention. They observe and record what takes place, yet never say anything, never give interviews to the tabloid press. They are sometimes rewarded and sometimes victimized by their employers, yet whichever way their lives go, they remain quiet. Gossip, and it occurs, is shared only among themselves and those whom they come to implicitly trust.

Barbara Gibson was an invisible witness and a friend to the invisible. The family knew her and recognized that there were times when she was the conduit to their mother or grandmother. The family included her in circumstances expected by Rose, who was always called by the deferential "Mrs. Kennedy."

Eventually Barbara left and told the true story of the family. It was Barbara who rescued Rosemary Kennedy's personal diary from the trash and tried to arrange for it to go to the Kennedy Library. The problem was that the diary was proof of the dyslexia, not retardation. The diary showed a girl growing into young womanhood—the black sheep of the family by Joe's standards, perhaps, but not someone who needed to be brutalized by a surgeon who literally destroyed a portion of her brain. It was a book explosive in its revelations within a family preferring the maintenance of myth over reality, and that was why the Kennedy Library refused to take it for their collection.

Rose Kennedy told Barbara Gibson to throw the diary in the trash, which Barbara did, setting it out as required, then taking it from the trash can and keeping it. Barbara's work with the FBI had made her aware of a number of test cases relative to the ownership of discarded information. The courts had ruled that once something is in the trash and set out for collection, anyone may take and keep it. This was the approach used when mob leader Joe Bonanno wrote his autobiography in Sicilian, thinking he would like to have his story published. The book was believed to contain details of crimes that either would be resolved because of what he said or for which the statute of limitations had not run out and for which he could be charged. Bonanno had second thoughts, though, and set it in the trash, where FBI agents, dressed as trash collectors, took it for possible leads.

Barbara's ownership of Rosemary's diary was legal, the way she obtained it quite proper. It also was the key lead to the search for the truth about Rosemary's real condition.

Eventually a series of calls to Massachusetts doctors led to the discovery that one of the doctors who had been on the protocol committee for determining who would and who would not get a prefrontal lobotomy in 1940s Boston was alive. He was over ninety, his body deteriorating rapidly, but his mind so sharp that he was still teaching part time. Dr. Robert Eiben was interviewed, and he recalled Joe's early efforts before taking Rosemary to St. Elizabeth's Hospital in Washington, D.C. He also confirmed that there was no retardation, nothing that warranted the surgery Kennedy planned to buy wherever he could.

Problems with the financial aspects of publishing royalty payments Barbara and I faced with earlier books led to her decision never to write again despite great editorial success. Since a book like this is the result of a combination of everything that has come before (articles, books, interviews, and the like) and what new material can be located through aging politicians, mob figures, businesspeople, family members, and the like, I must give Barbara Gibson the credit she often fails to receive from other Kennedy family biographers. She was an important source. But even more, she was the key to locating the invisible people who told about others, invisible and reachable, dead, albeit with families who kept personal letters and diaries, and alive for interviews.

1

MR. AMBASSADOR

THEY STOOD TOGETHER IN THE OVAL OFFICE—JOE KENNEDY AND Jimmy Roosevelt—supplicant and sponsor—waiting for the president to speak. It was 1937, and Franklin Roosevelt was in the midst of his second term in office. Adolf Hitler had taken firm control of Germany, and the German people were lauding the idea of National Socialism— the Nazi Party—and the domination of the Aryan race. Britain was facing the possibility of a war in Europe that would ultimately be fought, in part, on their island soil. At the same time, the British government was encouraging hostility between a small number of fascist Arab leaders and the Jewish people within Palestine to keep previously friendly Arabs and Jews from uniting against British occupation. The Japanese were moving into China. It had become obvious that the world was facing the possibility of simultaneous violence in Europe, Asia, and the Middle East. The men who would be chosen to represent the U.S. government in the world's capitals would have to be selfless, creative, possess analytical minds, and have the ability to adjust to rapidly shifting international alliances. As President Roosevelt saw it, his representatives would have to be everything Joe Kennedy was not.

Kennedy recognized Franklin Roosevelt's hostility. That was why he had spent several years cultivating Jimmy's friendship. He knew the young man was as weak as his father was strong. All three men were womanizers, but the older two had learned how to balance their public and private lives so they would never experience a public scandal.

Joe Kennedy was the bolder of the two. His West Coast relationships with movie stars had become so well known at home in Massachusetts that his wife, Rose, was likely to be humiliated. Some residents suspected the truth. Any man of wealth and power, away from his family and surrounded by beautiful women seeking employment in his films, might willingly share a bed with some of them. Certainly the news stories told of the deals he was making with women such as Gloria Swanson, the best-known screen star of her day. Maybe it was all business and maybe it was not.

There was reason to gossip about Joe because of the family into which he married. His father-in-law, former Boston mayor John Fitzgerald, had been scandalously improper with women in public and had been driven from office for suspicion of what he did privately with one Toodles Ryan. Perhaps Joe was like Rose's father despite the fact that the couple had nine children, supposed proof that their ardor for each other had not waned.

Anticipating the gradually more openly spoken gossip that was being fueled by stories from Hollywood and New York about Joe's lunch-hour business meetings with Swanson, Kennedy boldly confronted those who might think him unfaithful by bringing home his mistress. The action was brilliant. No man would be foolish enough to have his mistress and her daughter living in the guest rooms of the house he shared with his wife and children. The feat was so outrageous that his neighbors recognized their imaginations had gotten the better of them. With Swanson in her home, Rose could hold her head high, envied by many within the Irish Catholic community for having a husband who was so devoted and successful, and for having so famous a houseguest.

Franklin Roosevelt also had learned to be circumspect with longtime lover Lucy Mercer, who would be by his side at the moment he died. Eleanor knew of Lucy, though she at first thought the affair ended when she confronted him about the relationship in 1918. She had chosen to stay married to Franklin, a man whose work and ideals she respected. They had become close working partners over the years, and she was a trusted adviser. At the same time, he was fearful enough of her public openness in areas with which he disagreed, or that could reveal an aspect of his character he wanted hidden, that he was known to edit some of the extensive freelance writing she sold during the White House years.

Franklin Roosevelt had another concern during the White House years. He was a robust man with great stamina, in excellent health, and able to work effectively for many hours at a time. However, he could not walk. Adult-onset polio, first discovered in August 1921, confined him to wheelchairs created to meet his needs at home, at work, and while traveling. Painful leg braces and a subtly helping hand were used to give the illusion that he could stand or walk. The disability was not a handicap for running the nation, but a photograph of the president in a wheelchair probably would have cost him his reelection.

Jimmy Roosevelt, eighteen years younger than Joe, thought he had become close friends with Kennedy during the 1932 election. Jimmy overindulged in casual sex and alcohol, and was seemingly always looking for a way to gain enough money and prestige to warrant his father's unconditional love. His mother had no patience for his weaknesses and his various get-rich-quick ventures, which had proven successful only when others interceded. His father had no illusions about the young man, yet delighted in his company and would trust him to be his assistant throughout his presidency.

Joe understood the family dynamics as well as the ways the Roosevelt name could benefit him in his own business pursuits. Unlike Jimmy, he also knew that it was dangerous to become indebted to another man. When Jimmy's presence with Joe on a 1933 business trip to England had helped ensure liquor-importing rights for Kennedy, he rewarded the youth by having Jimmy Roosevelt's insurance company protect the shipments. He also helped Jimmy obtain some of Ford Motor Company's insurance business.

Two years later, in 1935, Joe had helped Jimmy become president of the National Grain Yeast Corporation of Belleville, New Jersey, a company benefiting from the return to beer manufacturing. He also arranged for Jimmy to work as Samuel Goldwyn's assistant at MGM Studios in Hollywood.

Ultimately Jimmy was unsuccessful with all his various work ventures, but his father did not care. Franklin appreciated his son's discretion concerning his father's work and adultery.[1]

In Joe's mind, it was Jimmy Roosevelt, indebted to Kennedy for past favors, who was the key to his own dreams. Jimmy seemed to agree, having arranged for this meeting at the White House. It was the meeting in which Joe would officially ask to be made ambassador to the Court of St. James, arguably the most important American diplomatic post in the days before all of Europe erupted in war. It also was a post for which Kennedy was singularly unqualified by temperament, experience, and lack of understanding about international relations. As Jimmy later admitted, his father laughed so hard at the absurdity of the idea that he almost fell off his wheelchair when the young man suggested his father consider such an appointment prior to bringing Joe to this meeting.

Had anyone else requested a meeting between the president and Joe Kennedy, the request would have been denied. Only Jimmy could convince his father to welcome Joe to his office. Kennedy knew this and had called in the first marker.

Jimmy Roosevelt and Joe Kennedy arrived at the White House at the appointed time. The meeting would be a private one among the three of them. There would be no other staff members present, no advisers, no cabinet officers or members of Congress. Drinks were not served. Food was not offered. The atmosphere was formal, and Joe stood before his longtime enemy, a man who had obtained the political position Kennedy himself still coveted. The high-profile ambassadorship to England was a way to achieve several of his own dreams.

It is impossible to know what Joe was thinking as he waited for Franklin Roosevelt to speak. He undoubtedly felt certain that the job was his. He may have imagined the headlines that would so please Rose, a woman who continued to influence his life even as he repeatedly cheated on her. He knew that it would help his oldest son, Joe Jr., who was considering a political career and an eventual run for governor of Massachusetts. And as he had told Jimmy, "I'm intrigued by the thought of being the first Irishman to be ambassador from the United States to the Court of St. James."[2]

Perhaps Joe, a longtime business associate of such organized-crime figures as Al Capone and Frank Costello, felt that the appointment would at last appease his first humiliation by Roosevelt. Joe had grudgingly supported Roosevelt in his 1932 bid for the White House, but only because of the Depression and his belief that Roosevelt was the best man for business. He had arranged for the writing of a book titled *I'm for Roosevelt* to explain to other business leaders why they should look to a Democrat most of them personally disliked. However, he never forgot an incident that happened years earlier.

The Great War—World War I—was beginning in Europe, and most of Joe Kennedy's former classmates were enlisting. Joe either had to put on a uniform, something he was loath to do, find himself an important Stateside position, or be branded a coward. He managed to use the political connections of both his father and his father-in-law to become an assistant manager to Bethlehem Steel chairman Charles Schwab, who was working from the company's Fore River shipyard in Quincy, Massachusetts.

At the same time that Joe was at Fore River, Franklin Roosevelt was assistant secretary of the navy. He had negotiated with Argentina to have the Fore River plant drastically repair and restore two battleships for the Argentine navy. When they were finished, Roosevelt wanted them released immediately, a request he made to Kennedy. Joe allegedly refused, explaining that his boss insisted that payment be made in full before the vessels went to sea. Schwab eventually sent Joe to Washington to make the request for payment more personal.

Kennedy was extremely confident. He was certain that he would triumph, thus ingratiating himself with the wealthy, powerful Schwab in ways that would benefit his future business endeavors. Instead, Roosevelt was adamant. He had no intention of respecting Schwab's request, and he considered Kennedy nothing more than a self-centered young man who had much to learn about life. Kennedy left the meeting so frustrated that he later recalled bursting into tears when he was alone. Roosevelt sent two navy tugs filled with armed marines to take the battleships from Fore River and send them down to Argentina. Payment would be made later.[3]

Two decades had passed since the Fore River incident. Joe Kennedy had become wealthy and influential, while Franklin Roosevelt had ascended to the presidency of the United States. Ironically Jimmy, the beloved son, idolized Roosevelt's nemesis because he failed to understand the subtle way Joe was manipulating him for Joe's own ends. The president did understand what was happening, which was why he became inwardly outraged when he learned that Jimmy had said that he considered Joe almost as a foster father.

Finally the three men were together in a room that was decidedly Roosevelt's territory. It was more than just the president's office. It also was filled with decorations relating to the sea, a world beloved by Franklin. The desk had his ever-present ashtray, his small animal statues, and other items he enjoyed. A lifetime of personal keepsakes filled most of the space, only some of the furniture having served previous White House occupants.

Joe had gained the private audience through a long series of maneuvers and behind-the-scenes lobbying with Jimmy. He had exploited his relationship with the president's son, gained the desired payoff from the youth, and now expected to benefit from Franklin as well. Instead he was told to take a few steps back from the president's desk, move closer to the fireplace, and then drop his pants.

Both Joe and Jimmy were stunned. Kennedy asked the president to repeat his request, certain he had heard incorrectly. He hadn't. Joe was to drop his pants.

It is impossible to know the reason for the humiliation Franklin demanded. He died without writing about it. The only primary source was Jimmy, who discussed it in interviews and in the biography of his parents he wrote after their deaths.

Most likely FDR made the request without knowing how Joe Kennedy would react. Perhaps he would become indignant, recognizing that he was being exposed to ridicule, and would refuse to continue his relationship with the White House. Perhaps he would recognize that his demands had exceeded the president's willingness to work with him.

At the same time, it is possible that Roosevelt hoped Joe would comply with the request. He may have wanted to show Jimmy his longtime nemesis's obsession with power and prestige, the way in which he would go to any extreme, including allowing himself to be humiliated, to obtain his goals. All that is certain is that Joe hesitated, then slipped off his suspenders and dropped his pants. As Jimmy later related, his father said, "Joe, just look at your legs. You are just about the most bowlegged man I have ever seen. Don't you know that the ambassador to the Court of Saint James has to go through an induction ceremony in which he wears knee britches and silk stockings? Can you imagine how you'll look? When photos of our new ambassador appear all over the world, we'll be a laughingstock. You're just not right for the job, Joe."

Kennedy did not show whatever emotions he was feeling. Instead he asked for time to get the British government's permission to substitute a cutaway coat and striped pants for the traditional knee britches.

The president, certain that the British would stay with tradition, gave Joe two weeks to get written approval. At the end of that time someone else would be offered the appointment.

Joe agreed, pulled up his pants, straightened his clothes, and left. Two weeks later the White House announced the appointment of Ambassador Joseph P. Kennedy. He did not know that he was about to be placed in the spotlight of the world's stage. He could not foresee how revealing public life would be, even in those times of press discretion and respect for a man's position even when his personal life was held in disdain. He could not know that for the rest of his life he would pay dearly to keep the American people from seeing the suddenly illuminated flaws that tainted every future triumph with pain, anguish, and humiliation.

2

COMING TO AMERICA

PATRICK JOSEPH KENNEDY MAY HAVE PASSED DOZENS OF FRIENDS and relatives as he walked the six miles from his home in Duganstown, County Wexford, to the port community of New Ross in 1848. The fortunate ones still had homes—hovels that offered shelter from the rain and a place in which to sleep. The Kennedys were blessed with four rooms in their cottage, though how long they could maintain such relative wealth was unknown. They were tenant farmers working twenty-five acres of land with diverse enough crops, sheep, and cattle to have avoided the hardships that were destroying so many of their fellow Irish. However, the British absentee landlord was regularly raising their rent. Patrick, as the youngest son, knew he would never inherit what few possessions his family retained. And with the cost of farming rising, he would probably never be able to marry and have children.

Others had lost even the most rudimentary shelter through the restrictive laws imposed on the Irish by the British government or the ever-higher rents for tenant farmers. They survived as best they could, their brief lives filled with infections, illness, hunger, and often painful early death. They sat and stared at anyone passing by, too weak to do more than wave or speak briefly with the still-strong youth who dared to hope for a better future.

For many years even the poorest among the Irish had been able to survive on the vitamin-rich potato that grew in abundance like manna—the secretion found on the tamarisk tree—eaten by the Hebrew people during the great Exodus. Then, in 1845, everything changed. A fungus appeared in the potato fields, diminishing the crop. It seemed to be a one-time problem, short-lived, and only mildly troublesome to the economy. By the following year, American newspapers, running articles of interest to their Irish readers in Boston and elsewhere, mentioned that the 1846 potato crop was expected to be unusually good, a fact that would assure adequate money for the poor farmers.

The newspaper stories were wrong. The fungus returned, and by the fall there was almost no crop, no money, and many in Ireland were facing slow starvation.

The winter also was unusually harsh. There were snowstorms that made travel impossible. There was icy rain. Laboring jobs that were normally available to the people were almost nonexistent that year. People who still had homes burned their possessions to stay warm. Those living outdoors often starved or froze to death. Many thousands died. Many others used what little money they could find to try to reach other countries, including the United States. Between 1846 and 1849, an estimated 1 million people would eventually try to flee to North America. At least the same number, and probably more, died in Ireland.

As Patrick Kennedy made his six-mile walk after receiving a blessing from the priest at his home church at Ballykelly, he saw what appeared to be the last throes of the Irish Catholic community. The lack of food was accomplishing what the muskets and swords of the British government's occupational force of soldiers had failed to do.

Ironically, the starvation was not all that evident to the visitor casually passing by scenes that undoubtedly horrified Kennedy. The body's response to too little food can be a misleading one. The obese child stuffed with abundance may look little different from the famished toddler whose stomach is bloated as death approaches. The difference is often seen only in the listlessness of the starving child and in the eyes that seem to be controlled by a rheostat turning increasingly dimmer with each passing day.

A casual visitor might not see once-vibrant individuals when he looked at the lethargic beings resting by the road. He would not see formerly proud, hardworking men and women now too weak to do anything except sit outside their homes, praying for better times, yet knowing they would be visited by death long before their lot would improve. And they did not understand what Patrick knew—the voyage to the United States was not a trip to some promised land. He was not seeking streets "paved with gold" of the myth motivating other emigrants from throughout Europe. He was gambling that he would stay alive to find work and a future, knowing that the reality might be a death far swifter than he would experience at home.

Americans frequently talk about the horrors of the middle passage—the journey of enslaved Africans to the United States. Psychologically the middle passage was one of the world's most blatant examples of man's inhumanity to man. African men and women who were captives of either their own country's leaders or the leaders of enemy communities were sold to white merchants whose commodity was human flesh. From that initial betrayal—the sale of one person by the leadership of his or her country—to the resettlement on a plantation ruled by the owner, much was done to keep the living cargo reasonably healthy. The slaves were locked in holds. Often they were chained together while below, side by side, the weak with the strong, the living with the newly dead. They endured darkness and terror, the greatest freedom they were allowed being periodic exercise times on the deck, where they were "danced" and sometimes instructed in out-of-context Bible passages. Illness was rampant. Fear was a constant companion. And the kindest among the ship's captains still kept the Africans in hell.

Captains running the middle passage might have been amoral or brutal, but they had an incentive to keep their cargo as healthy as possible. The men and women they brought to the colonies and, later, to the States had to be resold. A person who was too weak to work, to breed, or otherwise to benefit a plantation owner could not be sold. This meant a loss of income to the captains and the people for whom they worked.

How so many Africans survived is uncertain. Some of the captured men were former warriors, losers in battle and sold by those who defeated them. Their bodies may have been honed for battle and able to recover from prolonged deprivation and abuse. Or their survival may have had to do with the land, a place where everyone walked or ran, food was plentiful, and good health was normal. Again, the ravages of the voyage may have been lessened because of how well they were at the start of their ordeal.

The Irish were different. Many of the emigrants were suffering from malnutrition and a forced sedentary existence before they boarded the ships. No one cared, though, because they voluntarily paid in advance to travel to the United States. There would be no resale upon landing. Once the captain pocketed the $20 fee, he would not predictably benefit again. A passenger dying en route meant one less body to keep on board the ship.

The most comfortable travelers were sometimes the people who had managed to scrape together extra money for living expenses in America but had brought inadequate food for the crossing. Too often the food supplies of the immigrants would spoil while the better-preserved food eaten by the crew would remain safe. Families with what seemed to be adequate food but too little money to buy more often found themselves going hungry in the midst of rot. Families with cash and possessions

could buy food from the stores kept by the crew. The prices were exor-
bitant, though, if they ran out of cash, the captain would accept barter.
In some instances, the wealthiest families making the crossing would
arrive in Boston or some other destination with nothing but the clothes
on their back. Yet the parents and children would be healthier than the
others traveling in steerage.

The availability of clean, safe drinking water was another concern.
Most captains made certain there was adequate good water, properly
stored, for himself and his crew. This did not mean that it was pleasant
to drink, though. Often it became foul on the journey, the crew adding
vinegar to the water barrels to cleanse the liquid and keep it safely
drinkable.

A few captains felt that money could be saved by using new barrels
for the crew's water and less expensive, used barrels for the passengers.
The latter had previously held wine and were never meant for recycling.
Chemical reactions eventually made water in used barrels undrinkable.
Some of the passengers would consume it anyway, risking illness or
death. Others chose to avoid it if they thought they could survive the
time between when the water began to cause illness and when the ship
was expected to dock. For them, the last hours of the voyage were made
with the agony of dehydration.

By the time Patrick Joseph Kennedy had the $20 needed for steer-
age passage to England and the United States, it is likely that he and
the others making the trip understood the potential hardship they were
facing. Surviving friends and relatives sent word back from Boston, and
the deadly statistics were well understood. One in three of the passengers boarding a packet ship going directly to the United States might
die. Kennedy was increasing his chances of surviving by going first to
Liverpool, England, and from there to the United States. Two shorter
voyages were less traumatic than the more direct single crossing. Still
the voyage would be forty days, and many on board were likely to have
what might be a deadly disease.

Accurate information concerning how many men, women, and children died the previous year trying to reach Boston was not known.
However, thirty-eight thousand people lost their lives trying to reach
Canada, on voyages with similar hardships. The deaths were so great
that the people watching the packet ships such as the one Kennedy
would take often referred to them as coffin ships.

By contrast, the middle passage deaths are estimated at between one
in five and one in seven for the enslaved Africans being transported to
America. The world awaiting the Africans was one of a lifetime of hor-

ror in captivity, a future the Irish emigrants would never confront. However, on the voyage to America, it was actually the Irish who were more likely to die.

Perhaps the crossing to America would have been more enticing had Patrick Kennedy held the fantasy that the country was the land of hope. There is an American myth that, except for African slaves and white indentured servants, immigrants came seeking streets paved with gold. Stories abounded of a society in which a poor man with intelligence, a willingness to work hard, and a mind eager for education could learn to raise himself to the top. America was far from classless, but the myth held that the servant girl could marry the master, the newspaper boy could become a titan of industry, and the difference between being the lowest-level employee in a great house and the owner of a similar mansion could be just one generation.

The real opportunity for upward mobility was never that simple. The biases of the dominant class in any community determined how much an immigrant might rise in his or her adopted country. And a few cities had a social elite that particularly hated Irish Catholic immigrants, their children and grandchildren, such as the ruling "Brahmins" of Boston—the city's most highly educated, conservative, and bigoted wealthy upper class.

Patrick Joseph Kennedy did not understand the world he was facing nor how it eventually would shape the dynasty he was to found. For him it would be enough to survive the voyage, find a job, find a wife, and create a family.

The unusual forces that came to influence the lives of Patrick Joseph Kennedy, his family, and his descendants can be traced back to twelfth-century England. King Henry II sent soldiers to Ireland because he felt that the Irish people were an undisciplined lot who needed to more strictly adhere to his ideas of law and order. Ironically, many of these same ideas would come into play several hundred years later, in the relationship between the Massachusetts Bay Colony and the British crown. But bigotry and hatred lack historical perspective, so the irony of the Irish experience at the hands of the British and its relationship to the American colonists' problems exists only in hindsight.

The Irish briefly prevailed against the British invaders, and then were subject to separate attacks ordered by Edward III and Richard II in the fourteenth century. Always the kings wanted to challenge the Irish practices, quite foreign to the British culture, but not go to the trouble and expense of keeping a long-term occupying force. The latter thinking changed under King Henry IV, who, along with his son Henry VII, placed a permanent occupying force in Ireland. Soldiers would rotate in and out of duty on the island, but the British presence was to remain forever.

The Irish people did not accept the British rule, and numerous rural communities had residents who lived their lives in ways that did not meet with British government approval. The rebellion was subtle until the frequently married Henry VIII decided that divorce was better than murder when changing wives. He announced that the Church of Rome was no longer the highest religious authority. Instead, the ruler of England would be the head of the Church of England. The monarch would have greater power than the Pope.

Irish Catholics were outraged. The exact nature of papal authority had been and would continue to be an evolving theological concept. However, the Pope was still believed to be the successor to Peter, Jesus' "rock" on which was built the foundation for what became church leadership. Jesus also spoke about the separation of God and civil rulers when he said that a person should give to Caesar what belonged to Caesar, and should give to God what belonged to God. Catholics saw this as a clear delineation between religious authority through the Pope and civil authority through the king. For Henry VIII to try to usurp the power that Jesus taught belonged solely to the religious side of life was an abomination the Irish Catholics could not tolerate.

By the time James I came to the British throne, relations between the British government and the Irish Catholics were at their lowest point. In 1605 a handful of Irish Catholic fanatics led by Guy Fawkes, acting without the awareness of either the church hierarchy or the vast majority of the laity, decided to bomb the leaders of the British government. Fawkes was stopped before both royalty and civil leadership could be destroyed, but the British refused to believe that a small group of terrorists was able to act on its own. Instead, they saw a plot sponsored directly by the Pope. Irish Catholics were obviously part of a vast subversive army out to destroy the rightful leadership of Britain.

The Guy Fawkes "Gunpowder Plot," as it came to be known, reinforced the idea that the Irish Catholics, in supporting the Pope, were backing Roman rule. In the theology of the time, Rome, having been the occupying force in Jerusalem whose leadership arranged for the death of Jesus, was akin to the ancient city of Babylon. Rome, like Babylon, was accused of being the mother of all that was obscene on earth. The leadership of Rome came to be viewed as the source of all human hostility against God and His people. By the early 1600s, anyone who belonged to the Catholic Church was viewed by many Protestants in both Britain and Ireland to be a supporter of Rome (the Roman Catholic Church)—the seventeenth-century personification of the Whore of Babylon. As to the Pope, since his theology was counter to that of the monarchy in England, the king or queen always being the titular head of the Church of England, the Catholic leader must be the Antichrist.

The oppression of the Irish increased. James I arranged for Scottish and English Protestants to move to regions of Northern Ireland under strict military control. By the time of Oliver Cromwell in the mid-1600s, Irish Catholics were being forced from their land. Ulster and other areas of Northern Ireland were to be Protestant strongholds, ideally with the majority of the citizens not being Irish natives. Many former residents were murdered. Others lost everything they owned and were forced to live a nomadic existence in the forests.

Brief relief seemed to come when Cromwell died and Charles II, a Catholic in exile in France, was invited to return to London to wear the crown. By then Protestants dominated both Dublin and the Irish House of Commons. The minority controlled the majority, the country divided in ways that would continue to present times.

All of this came to a head in 1685 when Catholic James II took the throne, then was removed in favor of his Protestant daughter Mary and her husband, William of Orange. Catholics formed their own army, declared loyalty to James II, and sought the help of France's Catholic king Louis XIV. However, on July 1, 1690, the British defeated the bulk of the Irish forces. The war was essentially over, and in 1691 all property was taken from Irish Catholics and given to Scottish and English Protestants. Further punitive actions in the form of the Penal Laws assured that Catholics were denied all civil rights as well as the right to teach their language.

The Penal Laws denied the Catholics the right to attend universities, to enter the field of law, to serve on juries, to work for the government, or otherwise to be in positions where they might be able to influence the country. Punishment for violations was severe and frequently included the death penalty. Later the Irish would not be allowed any form of education, leading to secret teachings in secluded areas. A highly literate population was reduced to poverty and illiteracy in one generation.

It is within the context of this overwhelming hatred that Good-woman Glover's story unfolded in Boston. It was a story that would reflect loathing that would be little changed 150 years later, when the potato famine forced Patrick to walk to New Ross and the life that awaited him if he survived the ocean voyage.

Goodwoman Glover would not have been hanged if she had been born a man. Goodwoman Glover would have been a respected elder had she been born both a man and a Puritan. Instead, the woman known as Goody Glover was declared both a "hag" and a witch, her wrists bound, a rope placed around her neck, and her life ended.

The story of Goody Glover has been told many times and in many different ways. The basic facts are quite simple.

Goody Glover had passed menopause in a culture that venerated women only when they were in their childbearing years. Other cultures looked upon elderly women as having gained wisdom that added value to the community. Many Indian tribes looked upon old age as the natural blessing of the Great Spirit, for example. Only families whose members violated a cultural taboo might have someone die young. But in the mind of Cotton Mather, both a physician and a Puritan minister, a woman's value came from having and raising children. Older women, especially those outside his religion, were "hags." In Goody Glover's case, the name was reinforced by her late husband's attitude. They had been emotionally estranged prior to his death, and he had called her a "witch." The term was meant in a derogatory manner, not as a reflection of her religious practices. But the fact that he had angrily used the name was well known among his friends and acquaintances.

Goody Glover's other sin was having been born in Ireland, where the recently outlawed Gaelic was her native tongue. She spoke English adequately enough to get by in the British colony, but her speech betrayed her origins. Worse, she was a Catholic who practiced her faith as best she could in the absence of clergy and churches. This meant engaging in such rituals as saying the rosary in front of a statue of the Virgin Mary.

It was for her reverence that Goody Glover would be hanged. She prayed in Gaelic, and according to the bias of Cotton Mather and other leaders of Boston, that meant she was "cursing" Mary in the "Devil's tongue." Worse, when asked to recite the Lord's Prayer, she said it flawlessly in Latin, the language of the Catholic Mass, but stumbled on the words in English. In the mind of Cotton Mather, considered one of the most learned men in Boston, her failure to use English, the language God intended, confirmed that she was inherently evil. He ignored the fact that English was her third language, not her first.

The ultimate "proof" that Goody Glover was a witch came from thirteen-year-old Martha Goodwin. The young teenager falsely accused her family's washerwoman of stealing clothes that had been hanging outside to dry. The washerwoman denied it and her mother, Goody Glover, who also did washing for a living, quickly came to her daughter's defense, cursing Martha for her malice. She knew the teenager was a lying troublemaker, a fact that would be reinforced as the story of the Goodwin family progressed. She would not tolerate the false accusations, cursing the child. She did not expect that her justifiable anger, her age, and her native tongue would be used to have her arrested, tried, and executed.

Cotton Mather could never admit his hatred of an Irish Catholic. That would rightfully imply that her death was the result of his bigotry, not the justifiable end to which all witches must succumb. However, when word of Goody Glover's execution reached Ireland, those who heard about it understood. It was one more example of extreme British Protestant hostility, this time in colonial America.

The rest of the story of Goody Glover and the Goodwin family has been told in different ways. Two conclusions can be drawn from what seems to be the best factual information. The first is that Cotton Mather used Martha Goodwin, the oldest of the children, to reinforce his fantasies about possession and demonic influence. The second is that the younger Goodwin children, like many of the "victims" of witchcraft, had physical ailments affecting their behavior. The most likely was encephalitis lethargica, an epidemic of which passed through Salem during this time.[1]

There were other factors coming into play during this era. Indian wars were a constant, and the public lived in terror of the violence that was a daily part of their lives. They were a superstitious people in a strange land. Their parents' lifestyles were quite different from the more sophisticated existence they had enjoyed in England. Everything was new and unfamiliar. And adding to all this was an awareness that among some Christians, especially Spanish Catholics, there was the belief that Armageddon, the last battle between good and evil, would be fought in this New World. While such beliefs did not relate to where they were living, the times were frightening.

The Goodwins were considered a pious family, whose importance to Cotton Mather was increased because they were members of his church.

There were six children in the family, but the four afflicted children ranged from ages five to thirteen.

Under ordinary circumstances today, the odd behavior of victims of physical ailments that affect the body's central nervous system would result in hospitalization. In the days of Cotton Mather, such behavior was not understood by everyone in a medical context. Rather, many of the adults worked with physician/ministers like Mather, seeking answers within their own theology. It was only in the larger cities such as Boston that there was a better understanding of illness and the use of what were called "simples"—a variety of herbal medications.

The Goodwins did turn to the more sophisticated men of Boston, but they chose four ministers, as well as a fifth, from Charlestown. The five, who fit the summoning of the elders to pray for healing as defined in the New Testament Book of James, held a day of prayer in the Goodwin house. It was a triumph, according to the records. The youngest afflicted child, a boy, was "miraculously cured."

The truth did not matter. The possibility of illness did not matter. The parents and Mather had convinced themselves that the cause was spiritual. The proof was in the change of the boy, though it was no more accurate than someone sick with influenza who takes antiviral medication, aspirin, and chicken soup eaten with the "lucky spoon" missing from the kitchen during the two weeks prior to the onset of the illness. If the parents believe that the "lucky spoon" has been responsible for the child's health since birth, when it was given as a present, all the other factors will be ignored. The flu came because the spoon was missing, and it ended when the spoon was found. The fact that the disease ran the course expected is ignored. The fact that the medication selected was known to have an impact on similar cases is ignored.

Cotton Mather and the Goodwin children's parents were convinced by the "cure" that what happened was related to both possession and demonic assault. Then some of the children, especially Martha, added their own stories of victimization that were both dramatic and unwitnessed by an adult.

Cotton Mather was the most gullible. He was convinced, based on the reports of the children, that the devil controlled them. He would write that they could fly like geese, flapping their arms and traveling as much as twenty feet without their toes touching the ground. He also spoke of, and was presumably a witness to, their purring like cats and barking like dogs. The fact that all children are likely to make such sounds during play did not matter to him. The cat and dog imitations occurred after the curse of Goody Glover and thus represented possession.

Mather decided that further studies were in order. John Goodwin, the children's father, initially blamed himself for the erratic behavior of his children. Rather than thinking them possessed, he decided that he had been an inadequate father and lacking in his relationship with God. The idea that the children might be possessed because of the curse of an Irish Catholic woman was a blessing to him, and he readily agreed to let his oldest daughter, the original "victim," live with Cotton Mather.

Martha Goodwin was no more possessed than any other rebellious adolescent. She understood his prejudices and used them against him. For example, Mather's library contained writings by members of other religious faiths. These were books he used to "prove" the errancy of their faith. He also believed that Satan could cause one of his possessed to be able to read the texts with ease, then have difficulty reading the books of the one "true faith"—his own. One of his first tests of Martha Goodwin was to hand her a book written by one of the hated Quakers, a book she read aloud with ease.

Intrigued by Martha's actions, Mather handed her a book written by a Catholic author. Again she had no trouble with the text. Finally he gave the girl a copy of the Anglican Book of Common Prayer, another tome by a hated religious group. This time, knowing the feuds among the British royalty, she not only read the book with ease (Martha had the standard education of the day, and since literacy was stressed from early age, she had no problems with the texts, all of which were in English), she also declared it to be more meaningful than the Bible.

Finally Mather handed Martha the Bible translation then in use by the Puritans.[2] This time she claimed to be unable to read it.

There were other tests as well. Each time Martha determined what Mather did not wish to hear from her, then used those words to upset him.

Mather never wavered in his belief in witches during this period. The community knew that giving the otherwise learned man a description of the devil, a witch, or a "poppet" used for rituals (a poppet was a puppet similar to a voodoo doll) would delight him. He was a prolific writer, documenting everything he learned, and justifying acts of extreme cruelty to those he condemned. And though several other trials would follow the 1688 hanging of Goody Glover, the frenzy reaching its greatest height in 1692 in Salem, where fifteen "witches" were executed, news of the Glover murder shocked the Irish. The hatred they had endured from the British apparently knew no territorial limits.

By 1700, the Irish Catholics in Massachusetts were viewed as a military and political threat. The French were primarily Catholic, and it was felt that the Irish in Massachusetts were likely to unite with the French against the British, an alliance based solely on religion. Since the teaching order of the Jesuits was working with local Indian tribes, some thought that a military alliance of disparate forces was about to be achieved. That was why, in June 1700, a law was passed banning all Catholic priests from Massachusetts. Any priest caught in the colony would be jailed for life. Any priest caught in the colony who escaped jailing would be executed once hunted down and recaptured.

The fear of a terrorist force waiting to be unleashed continued to frighten the Puritans of Massachusetts. The citizens were convinced that a conspiracy involving the Indians, the French, and the Irish Catholics was about to take many lives. As a result, on September 22, 1746, a law was passed allowing a three-man committee to regularly look into the actions and personal lives of Irish Catholics living in the area. Within one more generation, the start of myths about the Catholic Church was under way.

Among the early myths many people took as truth was that all Catholics were taught that any head of state who had been excommunicated could be removed from power. Anyone classed as a "Heretick" could be killed without mercy, according to town leaders as they prepared an 1872 ordinance continuing to deny rights to Catholics.[3] Church members were dismissed as followers of "popery," an evil so insidious that Protestants who did not denounce it were considered either suspect or fools.

The violence against Catholics and the suspicions concerning an evil plot continued into the years just before the potato famine forced Patrick Kennedy to flee his homeland. Many believed that the Catholics were secretly trying to overthrow the U.S. government. Additional "proof" of the threat came in the form of the parochial school system that was being developed. Eventually the hatred became so great that a type of pornographic literature was developed to further the anti-Catholic thinking. The literature, always written by women or under a woman's byline, described the secret lives of women in Catholic orders. The writers were supposedly either nuns who went over the wall and escaped the horrible abuse or were young women destined for a horrible life who managed to flee the captors who were "training" them.

Awful Disclosures was one of the first of these books. The author, ironically named "Maria Monk," was allegedly in the Hôtel Dieu Nunnery in Montreal, Canada. She told of the sexual violence and debauchery that she claimed was part of her daily life.

Another author was Rebecca Reed, who was said to have fled the Ursuline convent in Charlestown, Massachusetts. Again the work was pornography described as autobiography.

In the years that followed there would be variations on this theme. Some women wrote books about being held captive by one Indian tribe or another in the mid-nineteenth century. And during the Cold War, magazines such as *Blue Book for Men* would run stories about heroism in World War II by American GIs saving women from torture by German SS soldiers. The stories were fairly straight action-adventure, but the drawings illustrating the stories showed scantily clad women in bondage, their clothing torn from beatings and other abuse.

What made the "escape from a convent" stories different was their intent to inflame emotions against a contemporary group. The writers wanted to make money by combining titillation with the reinforcement of the accepted hatred of Catholic leaders, including longtime nuns. Tragically, men who used the stories to justify their own violence often took the pornographic fantasies as truth.

The fate of the Ursuline convent about which Reed wrote was an example of the impact of this type of pornography. The real school was highly respected as a training ground for wealthy Catholic girls. It was quite similar to the finest Protestant schools for women attended by many of the daughters of the men who bought Reed's book. However, Reed probably knew none of this when she wrote the best-selling *Six Months in a Convent*, a book she at least had the courage to call "fiction," knowing her readers would think it to be based on fact. Ten thousand copies sold the first week it was on the market, and twenty times that number were sold by the end of the first month. By August 1834 the bigots, their hatred fueled by Reed's fantasies, could take no more. They attacked the convent, ordered all the nuns and students to leave, and then set it on fire.

With intolerance so rampant and the danger of physical violence a constant concern, the immigrants tended to stay together, creating their own culture—a hybrid of Irish traditions, pubs, and jobs available only among limited trades and within limited sections of Boston. Because of the British sanctions, the people were generally illiterate despite being in the midst of a community where the dominant Protestants considered intellectual skills to be of utmost importance in life. Instead of recognizing that the immigrants had endured years of oppression that had turned a country renowned for its writers, poets, and storytellers into a place where education was banned and storytelling was carried out in secret, the Protestant elite considered the people stupid.

The hatred of the people for their illiteracy was compounded by the disdain for the pub-centered form of Irish entertainment. They did not understand that, in Ireland, the inability of families to support themselves caused young people to delay marriage. The sexes engaged in separate activities, and males were encouraged to expend their energies in often raucous activities. It was a nineteenth-century version of year-round sports being promoted for young men so they don't get into "trouble" with females. Instead of midnight basketball in school gymnasiums, the center of such activity was always the pub.

The pub culture did not change when the Irish came to America. They had little money. They faced hatred by the Boston elite that was similar to the British hostility. The jobs available to them were usually clustered in areas where they also found cheap housing. And the one place they were welcome to talk, drink, and share their problems was the pub. It was the most comfortable place to spend their time when they weren't working or spending time with family.

Prior to Patrick Kennedy's arrival in Boston, there had been efforts to remove the Irish. Some leaders wanted them to move West and become farmers, a lifestyle no longer familiar to them. Catholic bishop Joseph Fenwick envisioned a utopian community of Irish Catholics moving to their own land in another section of New England where they would have their own church, school, and living arrangements, again revolving around the land.

None of the ideas interested the Boston Irish. They had abandoned their homeland for survival. Now that they were getting by, albeit in abject poverty, they would go no farther. They were neither farmers nor homesteaders. They would continue to stake their futures within major cities, such as Philadelphia, Cleveland, and Chicago. Many worked for the railroad, settling in cities along the lines. For many years they dominated the Teamsters Union.

Politicians were the first "outsiders" to understand and exploit the Irish culture. They recognized that the best way to reach the men, whose votes would one day sway election campaigns, was to spend time in the pubs. Soon aggressive politicians paid men to meet the immigrants, first at the docks and then in the pubs to which they steered them. There the men would be given assistance with housing, jobs, education, and health needs. The cooperative pub owners were rewarded with a growing customer base, the newly disembarked usually developing a loyalty to the saloon in which they were helped. And the politicians would gain votes or other backing as needed. It was an arrangement that was the start of machine politics—an often corrupt exchange of favors that would affect regional and national elections manipulated, in part, by the heirs of Patrick Joseph Kennedy, whose packet ship from Liverpool docked at Noddles Island in East Boston.

Jobs for unskilled and semiskilled laborers were plentiful in East Boston. Kennedy found work as a cooper—one of the men who built barrels to hold whiskey, among other liquids. It was a job in an industry that had exploded in importance between the time the potato famine was recognized and when Patrick arrived. There were 1,200 licensed liquor dealers in Boston in 1849 as Kennedy settled into his new life. Three years earlier there had been only 850.

Kennedy was fortunate in another way. The immigrants landed without knowledge of the locations where they might be docking and having to build their new lives. Some came to the North End. Some landed in the East End. Like the counties they left, and to which they expressed deep loyalty, there were radical differences in the lifestyles. The North End had the greatest concentration of extreme poverty. Much of the housing was so overcrowded that men, women, and children, often strangers to one another, found sleeping space in rooms where their bodies lay touching. Typical was attic housing, where floor space ran a dollar a week, paid in advance. A single outhouse served all the residents. Food waste was often tossed out the windows. Rodents and insects abounded. Disease was prevalent. Nevertheless, survival was easier than in Ireland, but not by much.

By contrast, the East End, which included Noddles Island, had jobs that paid enough for a man to marry and raise a family. This was the center of the whiskey trade, among other businesses. An iron refinery was built in East Boston. A sugar refinery was constructed. There was food and shelter for all, and though it was expensive and overcrowded— often a large, multiroom house or a mansion carved into so many rooms that extended families shared the same bed—it was still a place to build a better future. The Boston Brahmins looked on the area as a slum riddled with disease not seen for more than a century. But the immigrants understood that they were no longer going to bed hungry. They were no longer facing an early death, devoid of the pleasures of a spouse and children. The establishment's hell was the immigrants' new beginning.

With a steadier income than he had been able to dream about in his native Ireland, Patrick began looking for a wife. His choice would be made in a manner similar to the way other Kennedy men picked their wives in America. He found someone recommended by friends who was strong-willed, hardworking, and comfortable dealing with whatever unplanned event might alter the life she had planned to lead.

Bridget Murphy had not wanted to leave Ireland. She had been raised to be the ideal wife in a community that no longer existed. She knew how to cultivate potatoes and other small crops. She could milk cows. She was skilled in the myriad chores needed to raise a family and help a husband. What she lacked was family money. Her parents, like those of her friends, were too poor to provide a dowry, and without the dowry, marriage would not take place.

Most young women leaving Ireland to start a new life on their own journeyed to England. The trip was shorter, safer, and cheaper than the one to America. There were jobs for women working in factories, and there were jobs as servant girls in the homes of the wealthy. Both positions paid adequately and allowed the young girls to meet men who might take a fancy to them without concern for their family's wealth.

Bridget had other ambitions. She wanted to travel to the United States despite the risks of the voyage. She knew she would still be working as a servant in a wealthy family's home. However, the women who had made the voyage before her had often told their parents, relatives, and friends back in Ireland how well they were treated after they arrived. They had adequate food to eat, a clean room in which to live, and fair treatment if they did their jobs as required.

Bridget sailed from Liverpool on March 20, 1849. She was two years older than Patrick, with friends in East Boston. They were the ones who introduced her to the hardworking Patrick Kennedy,[4] and six months later, on September 26, 1849, the couple, along with mutual friend Ann McGowan and Bridget's cousin Patrick, traveled by ferry to Boston, where Patrick and Bridget were married.

Patrick and Bridget Kennedy, like most of the Irish in Boston, adored children. There is a myth that large families were obligations expected by the Catholic Church or that children were born to help their parents through old age. But the Irish Catholics in Boston saw children as neither a duty nor as a form of Social Security. They simply loved children, devoting their lives to the betterment of the next generation. They often worked multiple jobs, exhausting themselves and weakening their immune systems, in an effort to give their families a better life. Despite this, more than 60 percent of all children born to first-generation Irish Catholics in Boston at this time would die before reaching age five.

The Kennedys were luckier than many of the couples their age. Their first two children—Mary and Johanna[5]—thrived. However, when their third child, a son named John, was born, he developed juvenile-onset cholera (cholera infantum) and died on September 24, 1855, when he was just twenty months old.

There would be two other children: a daughter named Margaret, and a son, Patrick Joseph, called "P. J.," who was born on January 8, 1858. The four surviving children all thrived. Patrick Kennedy Sr. did not. He had worked hard, frequently moving his family from residence to residence, eventually taking in a boarder to supplement pay that was often $1 for fourteen hours of work. By the time P. J. was born, Patrick Sr. was exhausted and susceptible to the cholera that took his life shortly after P. J.'s birth.[6]

3

THE BARKEEP

THE WIDOW BRIDGET KENNEDY BEGAN LOOKING FOR WORK, FIRST finding employment in a notions shop on Border Street near the ferry landing. Travelers, businesspeople, and laborers all passed the area, and though the money was adequate, she later took a better-paying job as a hairdresser for the Jordan-Marsh department store.

Bridget Kennedy understood the importance of education for her children and used what little money she could spare to have them attend the neighborhood school run by the Sisters of Notre Dame. There was intense conflict between the church-run schools and the public institutions. Not only was there the history of prejudice that resulted in signs such as NO IRISH NEED APPLY and IRISH AND DOGS NOT ADMITTED, but also the teachers in public schools often taught about the evil machinations of both the Pope and the Spanish Catholics who, it was alleged, were looking to conquer other territory. The Boston Catholic Church leadership, by contrast, declared that attending public school was an occasion for sin. Each system had leaders who exaggerated the evils of the other, but the bigotry against the Irish was so extreme that most Irish families did not wish to consider public education.

The Kennedy children had helped their mother when she worked in the notions shop, and P. J. recognized that when he was big enough, he would have to leave school to get a job. His mother and siblings needed the extra income a strong young man could bring in, and there were neither child labor laws nor mandatory education requirements to prevent his taking a job. Barely literate, he eventually found work as a stevedore. The pay was adequate for both helping his mother and setting aside some savings, but such work was of low status in a city where every group had its social hierarchy.

The Brahmins—the Boston Protestant elite—looked down on those among the Protestants they felt were undereducated. All the Protestants held the Catholics in disdain, and the Irish Catholic immigrants were ranked the lowest in the Protestants' social order. Then came the class order of the Irish Catholic community, where status and friendships were based on the county from which a man emigrated. Those from County Cork hated those from County Mayo, for example. This could lead to jovial arguments in the pubs, but it was a problem for laborers, whose workdays were determined by foremen who gave hiring preference to workers from their home county.

There were other status symbols as well. East End Boston residents were considered to be better than those from the North End. A civil service laboring job had higher status than the identical work for a private sector employee. And as the Irish again became an educated people, those Irish Catholics who could attend Harvard College gained higher status than those who attended other institutions, regardless of national reputations. Harvard was where the children of the Protestant elite went to make contacts that would assure the "right" marriage, often to a classmate's sister, and the "right" job, often from a classmate's father who expected his own son to gain a job offer from the father of some other classmate.

His home county, his job as a dockworker, his background as the son of a widow who had been married to a cooper, and his East End residence determined P. J. Kennedy's status among Irish Catholics. He was considered only a little better than the North End tenement dwellers.

P. J. had no interest in a life of manual labor, though not because of its lack of status. He seems to have never given thought to anything other than becoming an entrepreneur. He could hold his own on the docks, but he saw what happened to men like his father who worked their bodies to exhaustion and an early grave. At the same time, he was keenly aware of the money to be made in the liquor trade. The working poor used the pubs as frequently as those with better jobs. And the Protestant elite enjoyed liquor, though they drank in higher-class establishments.

Young Kennedy decided that the way to upward mobility was through buying a bar and parlaying its success. He began looking around, apparently using friends of his late father for advice. When he learned of a bar for sale in Haymarket Square, he purchased it with a combination of his own savings and a loan from his mother.

Kennedy enjoyed the world of the pub. He was a tall, gregarious man with a compassionate heart and a delight in being a power broker without selling out the immigrant community to special-interest groups. He rarely drank. He knew when to keep his mouth shut. And he liked listening to the stories of the immigrants, their families, and their children's families. He knew when men were out of work despite doing their best to find employment. He knew when politicians were making moves against one another, and he knew when there were problems of local concern that needed resolving.

Kennedy, like other bar owners, found that men would quietly approach him at times when they needed help. A week's groceries, fuel to get through a harsher than anticipated winter, a place to live or a loan of rent money, and other assistance were available for the asking. P. J. knew what it was to struggle, but he also instinctively understood that favors done today could reap rewards later. He just had to be certain that he did favors for everyone trustworthy and owed no man himself. Then, when he felt it was in his best interest to support one politician or another, or one side of a community issue or another, he could call in favors and assure the needed voter turnout. Kennedy showed his customers that they benefited from the support they provided, including voting many times each on election day, as the politicians did favors in exchange for the votes. He also showed the politicians that unless they did him favors, he would be capable of supporting a rival. The arrangement was corrupt yet beneficial for all.

Kennedy's influence became greater as he joined with others in investing in two more establishments, including one within Maverick House, a hotel first built in 1835 and reincarnated in different forms over the years. It always served travelers and upscale businesspeople with lodging, a prestigious meeting location, and fine food. Being owner of the bar meant not only steady profits but also a chance to broaden his contacts, to meet and work with people who would never wish to be seen in any of the Irish Catholic workingman pubs of Greater Boston.

P. J. also added to his wealth by opening a wholesale liquor distribution business. From an office on High Street he handled both the importation of liquor and the sale of a wide variety of alcoholic beverages throughout the community. He profited both from his own three locations and from the success of his competitors.

Eventually P. J. did what other immigrant groups felt the need to do: he helped start a neighborhood bank, called Columbia Trust. This was one time when he was in complete agreement with Mayor John Fitzgerald, who had railed at the heads of the Boston banks for not having any Irish as executives. He told the bank presidents that they had Irish depositors helping to make the banks successful and the presidents financially well off, but they had no Irish employees.

The bank presidents explained that many of the banks had one or two tellers whose families were from Ireland. It was the type of hatred and condescension that would be experienced by blacks, Italians, and other groups who were minorities in cities throughout the nation.

P. J. Kennedy, with the mayor's blessing, joined with others to form Columbia Trust, a bank that was little more than a credit union, the type of institution many immigrant groups formed after discovering that they were considered pariahs by the establishment. Such institutions primarily provided loans to depositors. The amounts were small, and because the people using the institutions were neighbors and friends, the default rates were low. However, Columbia Trust had only approximately $200,000 and served a low-income clientele. The men who owned it, such as P. J. Kennedy, found such institutions a better way to help people than through the personal loans requested in their businesses.

The value in such small institutions was that the customers were loyal, and though shareholders rarely benefited, there was usually a modest profit that made them desirable for acquisition by "real" banks in the neighborhood. More important, the larger facilities knew that the customer base they had ignored had become so loyal to the small institution that they would remain depositors. As their incomes increased or their children reached adulthood and gained better jobs, there would be growing deposits and a real profit.

It was inevitable that P. J. would be asked to enter politics, not just work behind the scenes. He had common sense, compassion, and the loyalty of men who were willing to vote as many times as he desired. He chose to run for a seat in the Massachusetts House of Representatives and, in 1886, won by a landslide. Six years later he won a seat in the state Senate. However, he found that he did not like making speeches and carrying out the public obligations of an elected official. He had more fun and seemingly greater power by working behind the scenes. He decided not to continue in public office.

While all this was taking place, P. J. was falling in love. The woman's name was Mary Augusta Hickey, and in the stratified Boston social structure, she was not someone he would normally have been permitted to date. Her father was a prominent businessman whose sons had been raised with privilege, growing into manhood in ways that placed them at the top of the community. One son, John, was a physician who graduated from Harvard Medical School. Another son, Jim, was a police officer who quickly rose to the rank of captain. And the third son, Charles, was making his fortune as a funeral director and would eventually become mayor of Brockton, Massachusetts.

Mary Hickey was an educated woman, having graduated from Notre Dame Academy. While P. J. was known to be an avid reader, she had the formal education few first-generation Americans of Irish Catholic descent had experienced. She had never had to labor in other people's homes. She had never known the need for herself or her brothers to financially contribute to her parents' survival while they were growing up. But she knew, when she and P. J. were married in 1887, that he loved her for herself. He was not a social climber. He was a man who was self-made, with power and influence, beloved in the community and moving into a position that the sons and daughters of Irish Catholic immigrants had never experienced. What she could not comprehend was that when she gave birth to their first child on September 6, 1888, the infant the couple named Joseph Patrick Kennedy would dramatically alter the next century's business, entertainment, and political environment, both personally and with the sons he would produce.

P. J. and Mary Kennedy began raising their family—Joe, Loretta, and Margaret, with a second son dying in infancy—from a modest house on Meridian Street, a business district near one of P. J.'s saloons. Everyone knew the location, and though P. J. attempted to keep his evenings free for family and reading, men would occasionally stop by seeking the same type of assistance he had long offered from his bars.

It was the election of 1894 that would have a profound impact on the lives of the Kennedy family, including young Joe. The political situation once feared by those who hated the influx of Irish immigrants had come to pass. In the almost fifty years since the potato famine began, the number of Boston Irish residents had reached a critical mass for influencing elections. Seven years earlier, Hugh O'Brien had been elected as the first Irish mayor of Boston. But he had been wise enough to work for the city, keeping himself as distanced as he could from just being identified by his country of origin. He wanted to be seen as a product of Boston and the United States, not the country of his birth.

O'Brien had little choice other than adopting the political posture that helped put him in office. The state legislature did not trust what was happening in Boston. They decided to eliminate the patronage that was so critical to a politician's establishing a long-term, intensely loyal following. They passed the first civil service laws to assure that critical jobs with the police department, the fire department, and even the granting of liquor licenses all fell under control of a special commission, not a city's mayor.

The legislation was obviously aimed at Boston, a city in transition in many ways. Boston had been the financial center of the United States, but New York was overtaking the city in that area. The early leaders whose families were wealthy, isolated by their bigotry, and set in their ways became custodians of the past. However, even with the changes, new leaders were rising, mostly from the Irish Catholic community, and they were seeking ways to save the city. They wanted it expanded in ways that would take advantage of the waterfront, the ease of shipping, and even the potential with banking if the funds of the upwardly mobile Irish Catholic were considered. New jobs would give laborers a chance to own their own homes and educate their children. Inheritance would help their children assure a better life for their grandchildren. The new financial elite would come from benefiting those who had been held in disdain.

As a result of the changes being legislated in the state's capital and demanded by Irish Catholic political upstarts, 1894 was different. The twenty-five ward leaders were suddenly critical for delivering the ballot for any politicians, and the Brahmins realized that they would often have to find a compromise individual who was acceptable to all residents of the city. And among the ward leaders, the three most important were the East End's P. J. Kennedy, now known more widely as Patrick or Pat; the North End's John F. Fitzgerald; and the West End's Martin Lomasney. The latter was so powerful and sophisticated in political maneuvering that he was nicknamed "the Mahatma."

The Irish Catholic rivals developed political clubs to assure community support. The clubs existed to support political candidates, usually starting with the founder. Lomasney had one of the first, with his Hendricks Club. John F. Fitzgerald had the Jefferson Club. Later, when a man named James Michael Curley was making his political move, he created the Tammany Club for Roxbury's Ward 17. With or without a club, the community was divided into a series of wards, ward communities, captains, lieutenants, ward heelers, and volunteers. Their actions would vary with the needs and changes in the ward. Sometimes they would look for jobs for their residents. Sometimes they would work to bring new immigrant groups into the fold, such as the influx of East European Jews who were coming to the city. And sometimes they would get votes the old-fashioned way—through multiple voting on election day.

Ironically, as the feared growing power of the Irish Catholics was becoming obvious, they were also being seen as more mainstream than members of other groups. These were at least the first- or second-generation Boston citizens born in the United States. They spoke the language. They earned their living in a variety of businesses. And they were Americans in every other way except for their ancestors' country of origin and the Gaelic some still spoke with the elderly. This was quite different from the growing number of other Irish, Orientals, Orthodox Jews, Greeks, Poles, blacks, and others. As a result, there was a backlash, which ranged from the American Protective Association chapter, which fought all rights for Catholics, to the 1894 creation of the Immigrant Restriction League of Boston. Such prominent men as Congressman Henry Cabot Lodge belonged to the Immigrant Restriction League, which wanted to apply special tests to assure that no inferior aliens were allowed in the country.

Two years later, John F. Fitzgerald, Patrick Kennedy, Joseph Corbett, and James Donovan formed the Board of Strategy. They were determined to control the remaining political spoils and to blunt the power of the West End's Martin Lomasney.

It was in this world of power, business success, and public service that Joe Kennedy was being raised. At the same time, through his father, he was becoming aware of John Fitzgerald, who was making a move to become the mayor of Boston upon the death of then Mayor Patrick Collins, who died in office on September 14, 1905.

Thomas Fitzgerald of County Wexford had come to the United States in 1845, an unskilled man who had the misfortune to land in the poorest section of Boston. His early years in the city were stereotypical of the day—working as a farm laborer and then as a street peddler. Even his marriage, to Rosanna Cox, a cleaning woman, or "Bridget" as such individuals were called, fit the pattern for what the Protestants viewed as his "class." The couple settled into a tenement, and eventually Thomas went into business with his brother James, opening a small grocery store, where James did most of the work.

John Fitzgerald, the third of nine sons (two daughters did not survive infancy), was different from his family. He had to go to school barefoot, but he did not mind. He accepted his family's poverty, taking whatever jobs he could find as he grew older, including selling newspapers. Eventually, because of his good mind and the location of his family's home, he was able to attend Boston Latin School. This was considered the finest public school in the United States. It had been founded in 1635, educating such early leaders of the community and the nation as Cotton Mather, Benjamin Franklin, John Hancock, and John Adams. Ralph Waldo Emerson was a graduate, as were numerous leaders in finance, philosophy, business, and the arts. The school had many of the sons of the elite who realized that the education was superior to that in most private institutions. It also had the children of families with little money like the Fitzgeralds.

John thrived at Boston Latin. His grades were so good that he was accepted to the 1884 freshman class of Harvard Medical School.

There was no question that young Fitzgerald would be a success. He was a tiny man of great athletic skill and power. He was brilliant and cunning, and he had a sense of responsibility that he would carry over into ward politics.

The one setback for Fitzgerald came with the death of his father when he had been in medical school just nine months. His mother had died six years earlier, but his father and John's two older brothers kept everyone together. When his father died, the two older brothers were on their own and either could not or would not help with the six boys younger than John. He took control of the family, dropping out of school to take a job with the Custom House that would pay enough money for the brothers to have a housekeeper.

Given Fitzgerald's extroverted nature, it was not surprising that he would be drawn to a woman who was shy and retiring. Mary Josephine "Josie" Hannon was a farm girl in South Acton, a village several miles from Boston. It was an isolated community often shut off from the outside during harsh winters. However, they had a good school in the area and she, like John at Boston Latin, made the honor roll.

Josie's shyness came from an incident that occurred when she was eight years old. It was a warm winter day, and though there was still ice on the nearby Fort Pond Brook, it was breaking up. She was delighted to get outside to play, and though she was told to watch her four-year-old sister Elizabeth, as well as a friend of her sister, she was easily distracted, in the manner of all eight-year-olds. When the two younger girls went down near the water's edge, Josie paid little attention. She never expected them to try to step on the ice.

Both little girls slipped beneath the water. By the time Josie realized what had happened and called to her father, it was too late. He carried the lifeless corpses to the kitchen, overcome with grief. The incident had been her parents' fault for expecting an eight-year-old to be responsible. But they could not handle their own emotions. They could not admit that they had any part in the incident. Josie would be raised with their constantly reminding her of her failings. She turned inward, thriving in book learning while withdrawing from others.

John Fitzgerald first met his second cousin, Josie Hannon, in 1878. He was fifteen years old at the time and had been invited into the country to pick apples from the Hannon trees. She was two years younger, appearing briefly, then fleeing from this strange boy she knew was a relative.

Fitzgerald had never met anyone like Josie. He thought her beautiful and her extreme shyness intriguing. He began returning to the farm to see his cousins, gradually winning Josie's trust. She would spend time with him, listening to his stories about life on the streets of Boston, a city completely foreign to her.

For eleven years John returned to the farm. After he had won Josie's friendship, he quietly began a slow courtship. He would later claim that he knew he had to marry her from the moment he met her. Given his tendency to have affairs after their marriage, it is likely that he "practiced" with other girls when he was in the city.

Josie began to see John Fitzgerald as an escape from the sameness of life on the farm and as a chance to stop being reminded of her "failing" when she was eight. The idea of Boston was exciting to her. John was an aggressive youth, earning his way in the world, becoming part of politics, a man with a future. Whether she loved him or what he could do for her did not matter. He cared about who she was, not an incident sixteen years earlier. And he genuinely seemed to want to spend the rest of his life with her. The latter was surprising because she had nothing to offer him other than herself. She had no money. She had no skills for the city. Even her education was limited, although she had been at the top of her class.

The Hannons were impressed, but they also understood one possible impediment. Both Josie and John had the same great-grandfather, James Fitzgerald. At the time, the Catholic Church required that no related couple should marry until they were at least four generations removed from their common ancestor. It was believed that the marriage of cousins three generations from a common ancestor or closer was the same as incest.

The issue was not a risk of birth defects, as has long been a concern when first cousins marry. Even the incest taboo was handled in a pragmatic way at the end of the nineteenth century. The couple had to have a member of the clergy inform them that the second-cousin relationship was a "minor impediment," something that could be overcome through dispensation. The pragmatic priests would then provide that dispensation if the couple would donate a sum of money—usually a dollar, the equivalent of a day's pay for many of the poor—to an approved charity.

John Fitzgerald went from priest to priest, each of whom provided a letter showing that John had overcome the minor impediment in the eyes of the church. He would dutifully show the letters to the Hannons, who remained unconvinced that such a marriage was not incestuous. Or so the family legend states.

The truth about Josie and John may have been more complex. Rose was always under the impression that her grandparents feared birth defects in any offspring. Given the family dynamics and the way Josie was raised, it is equally likely that the Hannons did not want to give up a daughter who was otherwise likely to become a spinster. Josie would be able to continue to work the farm with her parents if she failed to find a husband. She would be able to care for them in their old age. They had always held her in disdain, and it was likely that John was a shocking intrusion on their unspoken expectations.

John Fitzgerald finally gained the Hannons' approval and made his dollar donation to Boston's archbishop John Joseph Williams on September 7, 1889. The couple was married on September 18 in St. Bernard's Catholic Church in Concord, Massachusetts.

The Fitzgeralds' first children were Rose Elizabeth and Agnes. Rose was born on July 22, 1890; her sister, two years later. Four other children would follow. The family lived at 4 Garden Court Street in Boston's North End. It was from there, at about the time of Agnes's birth, that John moved aggressively into politics. He became the Democratic ward boss for the North End and a state senator with ambitions. This meant that he spent most of his time away from home, leaving the raising of his daughters to his wife. It was a necessary arrangement that estranged him from Josie but brought him closer to Rose.

Rose was the first child and the daughter with whom John spent the most time before politics and community meetings kept him away from home until late most nights. Each time he would come in the house, if Rosie was awake he would lift her in his arms and "fly" her through the air. His absences made the time together all the more exciting. She came to want to be with him when he campaigned, to be with him at work, to share his life as much as a child could do so.

Josie was always too shy for politics. She and John understood that she would not campaign, not make appearances as his wife. Unlike Bridget Kennedy, who accepted the constant comings and goings of neighbors in need, Josie insisted that the Fitzgerald home would have no one coming in who was not invited as a guest. There would be no ward meetings. There would be no patronage planning. People seeking the state senator's help could meet him away from home.

The few times Josie left the house with her husband were for formal social events where a wife's presence was mandatory. She may or may

This rare photo shows the shy Josie Fitzgerald and her husband, John, the parents of Rose Fitzgerald Kennedy. (Cleveland State University Library, Special Collections)

not have enjoyed such activities, but she did take pride in dressing properly for them.

The couple was short. John was five feet, six inches tall with the cockiness of a bantam rooster strutting to show the ladies how unfortunate they had been to pick someone else for a mate. Josie was three inches shorter than her husband, but she had the regal bearing of a woman of money, of breeding, and of flawless genetics. The gowns she wore made her appear tall and aristocratic. Her quiet reserve was not recognized as shyness. Instead, she seemed somewhat mysterious, as though she were intellectually and socially far superior to those attending such events as the Boston College Ball. They did not realize that she was uncomfortable in the midst of so many people and saddened by her husband's constantly leaving her side. He would shake hands with the men, dance with the women, and work the room for votes. He was

always campaigning, always seductive. His endless chatter and willing-
ness to burst into song led to his friends and detractors calling his style
"Fitzblarney," and he became known first as "Johnny Fitz" and later as
"Honey Fitz." He was the darling of every woman except his wife.

Josie never showed public displeasure with her husband's antics.
Married life was better than life on the farm. Divorce was not a consideration, and John was a good provider. However, as Rose grew into
young womanhood, she took over the duties of attending political functions with her father, reveling in the sometimes tawdry, sometimes
sophisticated atmosphere.

It was 1905 when Honey Fitz made his most important political
move. He was forty-two years old and aggressively seeking the mayor's
office that had become available with the death of Collins. He was
working alone, both the South End's Jim Donovan and the East End's
Patrick Kennedy having agreed to support Lomasney's candidate, city
clerk Edward J. Donovan.

Honey Fitz had his own carefully honed political machine revolving
around the Jefferson Club. It was sophisticated and capable of bringing
out the vote throughout the city. But with the three rival Democrats
aligned against him, he had the appearance of the odd man out, an
image the Irish Catholics loved. He was able to beat Donovan by 3,700
votes in the primary. Then he reunited the Strategy Board alliances and
the massive numbers of voters they could assemble.

Honey Fitz had another weapon. He purchased the *Republic*, a weekly
newspaper that was financially profitable but that also could be used to
present his platform. It was a vehicle to give him a political voice, whether
for his own campaigns or to support others.

Lomasney was disgusted, throwing his support behind the Republican candidate, a man named Louis Frothingham, who had previously been the Speaker of the Massachusetts House of Representatives.
Frothingham was the better-financed, better-known, and more desired
candidate who would have beaten Honey Fitz had there not been an independent candidate. Municipal Court judge Henry M. Dewey, a Republican, decided to run without party affiliation on the assumption that he
might do well. What he did not count on was being a "spoiler" for
Frothingham. By Dewey taking votes the political analysts felt would
have gone to the Republican, Honey Fitz was able to win. He had 44,171
votes, slightly over 8,000 more than Frothingham. Since the judge had
more than 11,000 votes, it was obvious that Frothingham lost solely because of the three-way race.

On January 1, 1906, John Fitzgerald became Boston's first Irish Catholic mayor. He vowed to make the type of improvements that would provide a broad base of opportunity for the residents. He would seek to develop factories, the waterfront, the schools, and all other aspects of the city other than the financial world, which had been its early strength. He was obviously speaking in ways that would benefit the immigrants, and the residents knew that Boston would never be the same again. He also had attained a social status that elevated his daughters to the elite among Boston Irish Catholic society.

4

THE BARKEEP'S BOY AND
THE POLITICIAN'S DAUGHTER

THE YOUNG JOE KENNEDY DID NOT GRASP THE SOCIOPOLITICAL
situation in Boston. He had no tolerance for the neighbors who regularly interrupted the family's dinner to meet with his father. He had no interest in the way Mayor Fitzgerald had subtly expanded the number and form of city workers to get around the civil service regulations. He did not realize how closed a community the world of the Brahmins remained, how much an Irish Catholic man gained power, influence, and respect solely through actions within the immediate vicinity. A man of substance was expected to take care of a man with need, but the man with substance was never expected to become obviously too rich, too successful. Where and how he lived determined whether he was accepted within the community.

Despite his father's example, Joe didn't understand the world of the first-, second-, and third-generation Irish Catholic immigrants. Joe thought you gained respect by what you had, whom you married, and where you lived. He believed that the closer he could come to being like the Brahmin society leaders, the greater the respect he would earn from the oppressed Irish who could not consider such a leap of caste.

Pat Kennedy knew better. He understood that the Boston Irish were always willing to elevate a man who was down and always willing to put down a man whom the community sensed had achieved too much. They wanted to perceive even the most successful as people who were basically like themselves, living in the same neighborhood, drinking in the same pubs, just luckier and with fewer worries.

Ironically, Mary encouraged Joe's social climbing in the same way that Pat delighted in his son's entrepreneurial efforts, his hustle, and his competitive spirit. She wanted her son to straddle the two worlds of Boston. She never realized that ultimately such actions would cause him to be estranged from both.

One of the reasons why Pat Kennedy encouraged his son's moneymaking efforts was because of the way other sons of wealthy fathers behaved. They no longer shared the work ethic of the typical immi-grant male offspring. Instead they were spoiled, expecting to be given things that their parents and grandparents had to earn through hard work that often had shortened their lives.

Not that Joe knew just how successful his father had become. The elder Kennedy quietly invested in a variety of businesses, including Suf-folk Coal and Sumner Savings Bank in addition to the liquor businesses and Columbia Trust. As a political leader he arranged numerous con-tracts with the city so he would gain a piece of the action from the work being done.

Over time, as Pat proved himself a loyal friend to the working poor, he changed some of his ways. He hired servants to help care for the family home, justifying the action by not only giving jobs to those with limited skills but also for using their labor to free himself to help oth-ers. He also took his family to Europe, again an acceptable expenditure because love of the ancestral home was also a source of community pride. Ultimately Pat bought a yacht, hired a man to captain the vessel, and purchased a second home, in Palm Beach, where he could spend the winter. But by then he had earned enough respect to weather any criticism.

By the time he died, Pat's estate was worth the present-day equiva-lent of well over $750,000. From that sum Joe first knew just how suc-cessful his father had been in his business deals.

Oddly, during his early school years Joe Kennedy always was drawn to friends who came from lower-income families. These were boys whose parents could not provide the essentials of food, clothing, and a permanent home unless their sons worked before and/or after school. The boys constantly needed to find ways to make extra money, and Joe joined them in their pursuits to retain their friendship. Over time he did everything from selling newspapers, a job where the boys often had to fight rivals for the best corner, to helping the Orthodox Jews on holy days and the Sabbath. The Orthodox had a strict set of rules concerning what constituted work and what did not, and among the tasks they felt were sinful to perform were lighting stoves and gaslights. They paid neighborhood Catholic and Protestant boys to enter their homes and do what their rabbis defined as work. When the boys grew older, some of the Orthodox shopkeepers hired Gentiles to keep their stores open on the Sabbath, observing the twenty-four hours from sundown Friday to sundown Saturday as their day of rest, then working on Sunday, when their employees were expected to observe the Christian Sabbath. In this way they could be obedient to God, make certain their employees were obedient, and still keep their businesses functioning seven days a week.

One of the earliest stories about Joe Kennedy's business sense was originally told by a friend of the late Ronan Grady,[1] a youth who raised pigeons to sell for roast squab. The pigeons were kept in coops, their breeding and diet carefully controlled. The birds were healthy and plump, and they were safer to cook because they had spent their lives in captivity.

Joe teamed up with Grady in an effort to sell more pigeons at lower cost, splitting the increased profits. Throughout part of one summer, the two boys would take the tame pigeons, hide them under their shirts, then go to the Boston Common, where wild pigeons were in abundance. They would release their tame birds, then return to Grady's coops to wait for the birds. Invariably at least two additional birds would be added to the coops and sold for dinner.

Pigeon buyers recognized that wild birds could be disease-ridden and dirty. They counted on suppliers like Joe to have only tame birds. The customers would have been outraged by the deception had it ever been discovered.

Another source of income was derived from Joe's skills as a local sandlot baseball player, not to mention that he owned the best bat, ball, and glove, a situation guaranteed to make him team captain. He then used his father's position in the community and his own salesmanship to raise the money to buy his friends uniforms. He and the other boys were attending the Church of the Assumption, so they named their team after the church, another gimmick guaranteed to get contributions. Working-class Irish Catholics felt a moral obligation to support anything involving the church. They mistakenly thought that the priest was encouraging the baseball team and gave generously.

Having been successful in outfitting the team, Joe decided to see if he could make a profit from the regular games. Between the family members of the players and the church members who wanted to support "their" Assumptions, Joe felt there was the potential for a paying crowd of spectators. He arranged to rent an enclosed ball field on Locust Street, charged admission to the games, and made a profit at the end of the first season.

Joe may have been genuinely successful at the box office, but he was less so on the playing field. He was the best batter on the team and one of the best all-around players only because he faced no real competition. The truth was that Joe was like the contemporary basketball player who is a legend on the neighborhood playground and leads an average team to victory in contests with below-average players. However, he would not have his comeuppance until college, when he was forced to compete with far more skilled young men, some of whom were capable of turning professional.

Pat Kennedy understood the way his son had manipulated the Irish Catholic community and the people connected with both the Church of the Assumption and Assumption School. He probably took pride in the youth's success, but he and Mary wanted Joe to understand life outside of the narrow world of church and parochial schools. This was especially true for Mary, who decided that their son should go to public school before attending college. She chose Boston Latin School, the one Rose's father attended as a teenager. Unlike Honey Fitz, Joe was not ready for the rigorous educational demands he encountered when he was enrolled in the seventh grade on September 11, 1901. He failed three of his classes, barely passed several others, and eventually would have to repeat a grade before he graduated.

Boston Latin was important in other ways for young Joe. It took him out of the closed world of the Irish Catholic community, just as it did the man who would one day be his father-in-law. However, whereas Honey Fitz used the experience to find a way to consolidate power among disparate social and political groups, Joe developed a longing for a world that would forever be denied him.

Joe Kennedy may have had limited involvement with his father, but he was similar to Pat in both temperament and ethics. They were ruthless men who would take whatever action was necessary to achieve or maintain power. At the same time, they learned how to manipulate others in ways that would keep them from being beholden to any man. They would always do favors in exchange for a future payback rather than asking for help from someone who could later claim their assistance.

Pat Kennedy may have been the role model for the way Joe would conduct business, but Mary Kennedy fueled his dissatisfaction with the society in which he was raised. She not only encouraged him to have the type of education experienced by many of the Brahmins, she also wanted him to learn how to pass as part of the Protestant elite. For example, Mary taught her son to avoid saying his full name when doing odd jobs at the bank in which his father had invested. Instead he introduced himself as "Joe." There would be no "Kennedy" to instantly alert the customer that he was of Irish descent. Just "Joe."

Although Joe would use his Irish Catholic heritage whenever mentioning it would be of help, as he grew older he would have himself and his sons referred to by whatever titles they had achieved. Joe would be known as "the ambassador." Not "Mr. Kennedy" or "Ambassador Kennedy," both of which stressed the family name. It was just "the ambassador," as his sons would become known as "the congressman," or "the senator," or "the attorney general," or "the president."

While Joe was learning life lessons that would color his early sports and business efforts, he continued to not do well academically. The only subject in which he achieved adequate marks at Boston Latin was mathematics, and that success probably was due to the teaching skills of Patrick T. Campbell.

Campbell was an innovative educator who eventually would be named superintendent of the Boston public schools. He had a reputation for working with each student in whatever manner the youth needed to master a subject. He undoubtedly tutored Joe until he understood what would eventually become critical to Joe's early business career. In all other classes Joe was so poor a student that he was regularly reprimanded by Headmaster Arthur Fiske,[2] then had to repeat his senior year, graduating after his original class.

What Joe lacked in intellectual ability he made up for in personality. He was always well liked and was voted president of his senior class the year he failed to pass. This was an honor under the best of circumstances, but given how few Irish Catholics attended Boston Latin and his poor academic record, it was a unique experience. It also gave Joe the idea that he could leave the world of immigrants and ethnic politics and achieve power and respect among the Brahmins.

Joe was a member of the Boston Latin baseball team the four years he attended the school, and he was captain for two of those years. The tribute did not reflect his ability, though. The more popular Walter Elcock, a superior all-around athlete, was the youth expected to captain the team. However, Elcock was from a poor family with barely enough to eat. When Joe befriended him, he assured that Elcock would be beholden to him in the future by frequently treating his classmate to steak dinners.

Elcock did feel beholden to Joe, and backed him as team captain. He felt that the rewards of Joe's friendship and the fact that he was already captain of the school football team overrode any sense of loss that came from giving up the baseball team position.

Young Kennedy did have some athletic skills, though they were exaggerated by being compared with the poor quality of many of the opponents he faced during his high school years. In Joe's senior year, for example, he managed a .667 average for hitting (he successfully hit the baseball two out of every three times at bat) and was awarded the Mayor's Cup for the feat. However, while he was always gracious as a winner, he was known to be unable to accept any criticism on the field, no matter how deserved. He regularly fought with the umpires, creating scenes that were an embarrassment to his teammates. It was a weakness he never overcame, though he learned to keep his anger more controlled, to seek revenge in subtle ways rather than the yelling fits that upset too many baseball games.

It was during a 1906 Democratic outing in Old Orchard, Maine, that Joe Kennedy met Rose Fitzgerald in a meaningful way. The two had known about each other, and they had been part of a two-family outing in Maine that was recorded in a photograph at least a decade earlier. Neither remembered their encounter when they were small. Neither forgot their encounter during the party activities.

Joe and Rose had long been aware of each other's parents, of course. Pat Kennedy could not discuss the city's politics with his son without mentioning John Fitzgerald. As for Honey Fitz, he was always in the difficult position of having his own political agenda yet needing Pat to deliver votes critical to the mayor's success.

As for Rose, Joe undoubtedly read about her in the paper. With Josie remaining shyly behind the scenes, Rose acted as her father's first lady at events Pat and Mary Kennedy also attended. This meant that the mayor's daughter would be in the paper with almost the same frequency as an adult. It was the Old Orchard outing that triggered Joe's looking more seriously at Rose Fitzgerald.

There has been much written about the relationship between Joe Kennedy and Rose Fitzgerald, much of it Kennedy family myth. There have been stories about love at first sight. There have been stories about their many years of wedded bliss. And there has been a tendency to make the couple something they weren't.

Rose was not a respectable young lady by contemporary standards. She was a teenager exposed to an adult world that she wanted to embrace with a passion that could be embarrassing to her family. She liked Joe, liked his looks and his attentions, though he was both her intellectual and social inferior. She was delighted to be asked by Joe to attend the first dance of the year at Boston Latin, and she was angry when Honey Fitz told her that she could not go with the Kennedy boy. John Fitzgerald understood the character of both Kennedy father and son, and he wanted his daughter kept apart from it. He did not realize that the idea of forbidden love delighted Rose's sense of romantic fantasy.

Rose began arranging times to be with Joe, if only for a few stolen moments together. Frequently the couple met at the Boston Public Library right after some of Joe's baseball games, or they might come together in a mutual friend's house. The first time they were openly together was when Honey Fitz reluctantly gave his daughter permission to have Joe be her escort to the afternoon dance for graduating seniors at Dorchester High School.

Rose, at sixteen, was a year younger than most of the graduating seniors. She had a love of learning and an excellent mind. She hoped to attend Wellesley College and would have been embraced by the faculty had her father agreed to her first choice for higher education.

Wellesley was a unique institution in its day, as dedicated to the full education of women as Harvard was dedicated to the social advancement of men. Wellesley students had no time for learning the domestic skills that were a common part of most women's college curricula. They also had little or no interest in the marriage potential of the brothers of their classmates. Instead, they came because the faculty included internationally respected scholars teaching science, mathematics, psychology, languages, business, and the arts. One of the faculty members was Emily Green Balch, a woman who dedicated herself to abolishing the sweatshops that employed many low-income women in Boston, New York, and elsewhere. Balch worked to better the lives of those who would have to labor for survival, and so successful were her efforts that eventually she was awarded the Nobel Peace Prize.

A Wellesley College student received an education that would enable her to become a doctor, lawyer, physicist, corporate CEO, or enter any other field still perceived to be appropriate only for a man. The faculty looked only for ability and proven intellectual success when accepting a student, and Rose Fitzgerald met their criteria.

Joe was delighted to be wanted by a girl who was sensual, brilliant, and from the most prominent Irish Catholic family in the city. Being wanted by a girl you find attractive is a natural aphrodisiac for any adolescent boy, of course, but Joe saw Rose as a chance to gain power and social position that a barkeep's boy could otherwise never enjoy. Joe came from earned wealth, but he needed a young woman like Rose to achieve his greater ambitions.

The problem for Honey Fitz was that he saw in Joe his own character flaw—a delight in womanizing. Joe was one of the young men known as "stage-door Johnnies." These were youths from wealthy families who would stand at the back door of theaters while the showgirls changed back into their regular clothes. When the girls emerged, the men would offer them a night on the town. The women gained access to expensive restaurants and nightclubs, and some of them became serious enough about the youths to marry them. Others either thanked their dates and went home, or chose to repay the kindness with a more intimate experience in the bedroom. While no names have ever been revealed, if Joe Kennedy remained a virgin throughout his years at Boston Latin and later in college, it was not for want of trying to correct this situation.[3]

The other problem for Joe was that the mayor had a special relationship with his daughter that increased the influence he had in her life. John Fitzgerald was frequently away from home, but he made every effort to include his oldest daughter in his life. Rose would go with her father to polling places on election day, smiling at the men as they approached, then handing each a cigar wrapped in a dollar bill to get them to vote repeatedly for her father.[4] Rose attended balls, not only for young women her age but also for civic and social groups where she was the youngest person present. She was part child, part woman, thrust into a world where she was center stage, yet where her father always was present. Agnes undoubtedly felt neglected, and Josie resented her husband's frequent absences. But in Honey Fitz, Rose saw the perfect father. She also recognized that she was only filling in for her emotionally withdrawn mother. In her mind, had Josie Fitzgerald been willing to do so, she would be Honey Fitz's constant companion. That was the right way for a couple to go through life together, and eventually she would be shocked to learn that her father, so seemingly faithful to his wife, probably had one affair after another in the privacy of his office and various women's bedrooms.

By contrast, Joe saw his parents as being uninvolved with his life. Mary Kennedy delighted in the social world her husband's wealth and prominence allowed her to experience. She cared deeply about her son, guiding him in ways she thought would make his future more successful. But neither Mary nor Pat, both of whom were proud of their son's achievements, made extra time for him growing up. Seemingly as a result, Joe became selfish, seeking pleasures when and how he desired them, with little or no thought to the ultimate consequences of his actions. This was most blatant in his relationships with women. He could be passionately aggressive, then walk away to pursue someone else with the same intensity. He was loyal to a handful of male friends, but only because they were more intelligent than he was and so lacking egos that they were happy to work in the background, letting him take credit for their work.

Joe was not good husband material for Rose Fitzgerald or any other young woman. Honey Fitz knew this. What he did not understand was that the only way to stop his daughter was to break her spirit, and even then she would still have her way.

Rose began plotting to be with Joe Kennedy, and her friends delighted in assisting with the illicit romance. They held small parties that her father approved her attending, the only unmentioned guest being Joe Kennedy.

There also were larger social events both youths legitimately attended. The mayor could not stop his daughter from being part of the elite Irish Catholic social scene just because the equally prominent Kennedy family was from this world. However, his protection for his daughter was based on the dance card each girl kept and took home to show her parents.

Each young lady was given a decorated, folded card with a hole punched through one end so a ribbon, tied through the hole, could be suspended from her wrist. The card would have numbers corresponding to the numbers of songs the orchestra would play throughout the evening. Boys would come over and sign their names so the girl would mingle with what were usually as many males as there were dance numbers. A special boy might get the first and last dance, but only the most serious or daring of couples would spend the evening together.

A father concerned about his daughter's social life could check the dance card at the end of the evening. That was how Rose and Joe conspired to fool him.

Joe's name would be on the card for the first dance so that Honey Fitz would not be suspicious. Then they would write the names of other boys, usually fictitious, for the various numbers when Joe would dance with Rose. Their favorite was "Sam Shaw," a boy who not only did not exist but who also served as their "beard." They had him appear three or four times during some of the dances they attended together so the mayor would think his daughter had a growing new love interest.

Honey Fitz became most concerned about his daughter when she graduated from high school. He sensed that the situation with the Kennedy boy had not changed as he thought. He also was having arguments with his wife over their daughter's education.

The Fitzgeralds were devout Catholics, but Honey Fitz understood the benefits of a public school education both from his experience at

Boston Latin and because, as mayor of Boston, he did not want to be seen turning his back on the Protestant majority. Josie hated the idea of their daughter having had to attend Dorchester and did not want her finishing her formal education at the Protestant Wellesley. Her husband disagreed, but felt it was best to compromise by arranging for Rose to study at two schools—the New England Conservatory of Music, where she would study the piano, and also the College of the Sacred Heart on Commonwealth Avenue in Boston.

Rose hated the plans being made for her. She loved learning music, and many New England Conservatory of Music graduates worked professionally in the field. However, part of being a "proper" young lady in early-twentieth-century Boston was to be able to competently play the piano. Since her personal ambitions did not include the concert stage, she knew that her studies would be viewed as a sophisticated form of learning domestic arts.

Likewise, the College of the Sacred Heart had nuns who believed that any woman who chose a secular life rather than the vocation of nun was being right with God solely when her focus was the home. She would not work outside her house or church. She would have as large a family as the Lord might allow, and her vocation would involve caring for her husband and raising children. Rose, who understood the rough-and-tumble world of city politics as well as any man, would be expected to abandon a world of glamour, power, and influence.

The Sacred Heart curriculum reinforced a world Rose did not wish to endure. There were more piano lessons, the study of French and German, and a variety of domestic science programs. Always it was clear that a woman was secondary to a man. Always it was clear that she would go from the loving care of her father to the loving care of her husband. Independence, whether that meant having her own apartment or having a career outside the home, was inappropriate for a good Catholic woman as defined by the Sisters of the Sacred Heart.

John monitored his daughter's progress, watching for changes in her attitude toward Joe. He thought that conforming to traditional Catholic teachings might help tame Rose. When he realized that she was still infatuated with the young man, the only thing he could think to do was to send her abroad to finish her education.

The Sacred Heart nuns operated schools throughout the world. Among them was a convent school in Blumenthal, Holland, so far away that Joe Kennedy could not follow. Honey Fitz enrolled Rose in the school, and then, as if to head off further trouble, he enrolled his younger daughter, Agnes, as well.

The Sacred Heart nuns in Holland were a disturbingly odd group of women quite different from those in other schools, including the Boston school Rose had attended. Some of the sisters felt that the greatest joy in life was to share in the pain of Jesus crucified. They wore bracelets and other items that were designed to poke the skin and inflict pain as they moved. The devices were a little like those sold for masochists in contemporary businesses specializing in fetish wear.

Other nuns stressed the enduring of suffering as the greatest spiritual blessing. They did not inflict pain on themselves. However, their joy came from whatever problems life held for them. Always the focus was on Jesus Christ crucified, a concept not shared by other Catholic orders whose focus was on the teachings and the love of Jesus.

The nuns in Holland were unusual because so many had a background as victims of political violence and social upheaval in European countries headed toward what would be called the Great War and, later, World War I. The Catholic Church was viewed as a political entity. It was little more than a generation earlier, in 1869, that the Pope had come to be viewed as infallible in his pronouncements of matters of faith. This meant that in a conflict between the teachings of the church and the head of state of a country, a Catholic would be expected to follow the Pope. In the turmoil of the times, the church leaders sometimes were seen as dangerously subversive.

Priests found themselves being imprisoned, tortured, and/or murdered by some European leaders. Nuns were occasionally raped, then banished. Among the nuns of the Convent of the Sacred Heart in Blumenthal were women who had endured such brutality. Their fear, bitterness, and what would today be called posttraumatic stress occasionally led to rigid actions, hatred of men, and a determination to protect the young women in their care in ways that were seemingly inappropriate. However, they recognized that the students were not going to enter the religious life, so they had to be prepared to endure the even more troubled world of society at large.

Sacred Heart's curriculum was designed to assure that the students would become "good" Catholic wives and mothers in a manner that seemed to make it more of a discipline than a loving relationship. To achieve this end, the nuns created a rigid two-year course of study and discipline. There were rules, regulations, and rituals carefully detailed and to which the girls were expected to adhere. The girls were expected to participate in the classroom as required but to be silent much of the rest of the time. Those who hated the environment and wished to be taken home discovered that their pleas for parental help were never received.

The nuns opened all letters before passing them through the post office. Those that did not meet with their approval were returned to the girls.

Some of the students quickly recognized that they were in a spiritual jail from which only graduation would release them. Others, like Rose, decided to rise to the challenge being offered. Her letters to her parents were generally innocuous and went through the censors with ease. Always she stressed her love for Blumenthal. However, she also suggested that if it were necessary to be home to help with her father's reelection campaign, she and Agnes would suffer the loss of another year in Holland. They would make the "sacrifice" out of love, so strongly did they wish to stay.

Whether Rose thought her father really would want her by his side, or whether she thought her father might recognize that his favorite daughter was unhappy, is unknown. He did not bring her home.

Separate from the letters sent as required by the convent, Rose periodically wrote to Joe, knowing that he could not reply. She found ways to sneak them past the censors, sending what she could when she could.

Other than writing to Joe and attempting to coerce her father into letting her come home, Rose looked upon the school as a competitive event she was determined to win. Each week there were group meetings during which award cards were given to the girls who had best met all the rules and regulations. Some cards were noted with the French for "very good." Other cards were noted with "good." Each girl anxiously waited to hear her name called because there were those who had not earned a card, and to have to sit without being honored was humiliating. Rose made certain she was always honored, ultimately winning the school's highest honor—a Child of Mary.

The attitude toward women was obvious in the reason the Child of Mary honor was the highest award the nuns could give. It had nothing to do with academic ability or achievement. The worst student in all classes could still be so honored.

The award was also not given based on work in the community at large. These were not sisters who dedicated themselves to the greater society, helping the poor, the sick, and those in need, as was common with other orders.

Instead, the honor was for the students who mastered all the rituals of worship and prayer. It was through ritual that the Sisters of the Sacred Heart believed that true piety could be achieved. They also expected those who were called a Child of Mary to continue those rituals in their daily lives for so long as they lived.

Rose Fitzgerald still sought Joe Kennedy in her life, no matter how distant he might be. She defied both her father and the nuns by finding ways to sneak out letters as often as possible, not knowing if he ever received them, though taking comfort in the fact that the sisters never found them. Rose never lost the spark of rebellion against authority, but the Blumenthal nuns broke her spirit in ways that would be apparent only when she experienced crises in her marriage. This was why the pain she would experience upon learning of Joe's adultery would be worn almost with pride. She did not deny him her body, for a woman would never let her anger toward her husband interfere with her fulfilling her sacred duty to have children. She never would contemplate divorce, even when Joe secretly arranged for one of their daughters to have a needless surgical procedure that left the young woman with the mind of a child.

Rose Fitzgerald would care for her children, care for Joe, and honor the sacred place of family in life. She also would attend daily Mass, observing the rituals even when her personal life at times seemed counter to the moral and theological teachings of the church. Rose would never be part of a church community. She would not share with others in the parish life and activities. Instead, she would go to Mass, say her prayers, receive communion, and leave. She said her rosary, went to confession, and did all the other things considered mandatory to be a Catholic. She followed the rules, and though she often told her children and grandchildren that when someone receives much in life, much is expected from them, she did not live accordingly. For Joe Kennedy, this would make her the perfect mate.

When Joe finally graduated in 1908, Pat made another decision to go against the tradition for the Irish Catholic community. Instead of going to one of the area Jesuit institutions, as was standard for those families who had the money, Joe would attend Harvard College.

It is important to understand the reality of Harvard's undergraduate program when Joe was enrolled. Today Harvard has the reputation of being one of the nation's elite universities. Harvard professors have included the winners of major prizes in literature, science, medicine, economics, and other fields. Entrance to Harvard is limited to those high school students with outstanding academic and extracurricular records. Both their grades and their test scores are among the highest in the nation.

The Harvard of 1908 was quite a different matter. It was a school that catered first and foremost to the social and financial Protestant elite of Greater Boston. Young men attended, not so much with the thought of gaining a superior education but for the contacts they could make. They understood that they would be meeting the sons of prominent business leaders. They would be dating the sisters of their classmates. And when they graduated, there was a good chance they would be engaged to marry a friend's sister and have a fast-track management job from the same youth's father.

There was no attempt to disguise the reality of Harvard's system. While a broad range of youth might be accepted, including token Catholics and Jews, the president evaluated the students entering as freshmen and then created an unwritten but strictly adhered-to caste system. What was their parents' social standing? What jobs did they hold? How much money did they make? Were they properly Protestant, attending the right churches?

The president's analysis was then used to determine how the students would be treated in all activities, beginning with the start of their freshman year. The students would eat in the order of their ranking, process to activities in that same order, and sit in chapel accordingly. There would be no moving up the ranks based on academic achievement, service to the university, or anything else that might single out a man for honors at a different institution. The only hope for young men who wanted to break through this arrangement, such as Joe Kennedy, was to attempt to befriend youths at the head of the line. They would still be relegated to the original order for all school activities, but at least they would gain slightly greater standing by being seen with the elite in casual relationships.

Joe suddenly found himself in a world he could not manipulate. He might as well have been branded for the four years of his college education. Even worse, the defiant act of going to Harvard instead of a Jesuit institution meant that he was considered an outsider by both the Brahmins and the Boston Irish Catholics.

The Boston archbishop, William Cardinal O'Connell, was the leader in the moral stance against Harvard. He told Catholic families that they were endangering their souls by exposing themselves to ideas (e.g., Protestant theology) that were inherently morally wrong. As a result, it was only because Joe was the barkeep's boy, the son of one of the most respected business and political leaders in the community, that he was not shunned by the families whose children had once been his friends and baseball teammates.

Joe Kennedy further isolated himself by living on campus. Most of the boys from the area, Protestants as well as the handful of Catholics and Jews, commuted from their homes. Harvard was their city school, and though most of the parents were well off, few could or would afford tuition, room, and board.

The one place where Joe hoped to gain recognition was in athletics. But even on the playing field, he never quite achieved his goals. Harvard was a football school. Many of the athletes came from preparatory schools where playing football received greater emphasis than classroom work. The parents were rich. Their children would inherit. Education was secondary to proving your toughness, courage, and resiliency on the playing field. They took the same pride in their sons being accepted at Harvard that they might have taken if the National Football League had existed to draft the boys. In fact, on a percentage basis, the Harvard football team drew the same size audience that professional sports would achieve decades in the future.

This is not to say that baseball wasn't important. Baseball players gained respect, though they were always second to football players. Only the youths who played both sports, which Joe did not, were held in highest esteem.

Baseball was simply too common. Young men could play it anywhere. Football required special uniforms padded to reduce injuries during the violent encounters among linemen, intense workouts, and skilled coaching. Any child with a ball, a bat, and a glove could play baseball. At Harvard, it was the sport of those who couldn't make the football team, and the prestige came only when you were a varsity player regularly on the field.

Joe Kennedy felt he could overcome the bias against baseball. He saw himself as triumphing in his first year as he had in high school, and for that first year at Harvard he did prove himself a team standout. The sportswriters for the school newspaper felt that Joe Kennedy would assuredly be first-string varsity. They did not anticipate major changes on the team that would relegate Joe to benchwarming.

The Harvard freshman team baseball competition was little more skilled than the players Joe had faced in high school. Also, he was twenty, at least a year older than many of the freshmen. He had the edge of an extra year of practice in high school. And he had gained additional experience the summer before his freshman year, when he played in the White Mountain League. In addition, he had learned the benefits of relying on the anonymous skills of another person to gain the image of being a writer.

The resort hotels, seeking to enhance the entertainment they could offer tourists and summer visitors, sponsored teams of high school graduate and young college baseball players. There was no pay, though room and board were provided. Each player was housed according to his ability. The weakest team members, as decided by the manager, would stay in the least expensive hotels. The team manager stayed in the best hotel, sometimes with the star player or players. As long as no cash exchanged hands, the players were considered amateurs and allowed to play for their college teams during the academic season.

Henry J. "Harry" O'Meara was the manager of the Bethlehem team, on which Kennedy was asked to play for the ten-week season. He also had recruited John Conley, one of Joe's classmates.

O'Meara, who was planning a business career, made the best team deal that summer. Both he and the players would live in the Uplands, considered to have the finest food and accommodations available in the region. He also had agreed to help the *Boston Globe* find a stringer among the college students, someone who could supply articles on both sports and the society people staying in the White Mountain resorts.[5]

The stringer job would pay as much as $30 a week, depending on how many usable articles the freelance writer supplied. This was more than enough money for a man to support a family, and very much in line with what some staff jobs paid. Thus it was a serious position, and the clippings of published articles written during the ten-week period could easily help a young man win a full-time job on a major city paper.

Joe Kennedy wanted the paycheck but not the work. He was not a writer. He was incapable of the creativity, the hard work, the discipline, and the quality needed to please the readers of Boston's largest paper. Fortunately, his fellow player John Conley did want to be a journalist and was willing to practice his craft under the eyes of experienced editors without taking credit or getting a check. His ego was satisfied with seeing his words in print. Any editing would serve as real-world education. They were valuable enough rewards for him to let Kennedy take the byline and all the money. The *Globe* editor never knew the difference and was delighted to print what he thought were articles by the son of a prominent Boston Irish Catholic politician.

Joe Kennedy's clippings were so impressive that the *Globe* offered him a full-time reporter's job at the end of the summer, but he modestly declined. He never admitted the truth, and though Conley was obviously ready to begin the successful career he eventually enjoyed, he had to find other ways to prove his worth in the newspaper business. As Joe knew, his friend said nothing about the arrangement.

As for Joe, years later, when he paid writers to create books that bore his byline (and eventually that of his son John), he felt that achieving the image of an intellectual was worth whatever the cost might be in cash and moral integrity.

The freshman year at Harvard was difficult, the caste system galling. Joe Kennedy had to fall back on his political heritage, finding ways to make both the students and the professors feel beholden to him whenever possible.

The professors were rather simple. His father was a liquor importer, wholesaler, and retailer. A bottle of the most popular Scotch—Haig & Haig Pinch Bottle Scotch—provided to those from whom there was no other way to gain a passing grade assured that he would always be promoted. Manipulating his classmates was quite a different matter.

Joining the football team was not a consideration for Joe. He also could see that he was not being welcomed by the leaders of the various social clubs[6] that could assure a man's success no matter what the president's ranking. That was why he focused on baseball and gaining the friendship of two of the elite members of his class, as defined by the student body standards.

The first person Joe befriended was Robert Fisher, a youth who would be named an All-American for his football skills. Fisher, though from an extremely poor family, was otherwise the Harvard ideal. He was both highly intelligent and an outstanding team player. He lived at home, commuting to school until Joe arranged for him to share his room at Perkins Hall. It was an unusually generous gesture that created both a bond of friendship and a sense of being obligated to young Kennedy.

Joe also befriended two other youths. Tom Campbell was an outstanding football player and preparatory school graduate. Unfortunately, he also was a Catholic, and though he was considered of greater prominence than Joe because he wasn't Irish, his religion kept him from being ranked with the prestige he would have had as a Protestant.

Robert Sturgis Potter, the other young man, was the one friend Joe sought from the baseball team. Harvard's president had placed Potter in the finest dormitory on campus in recognition of the youth's old-money, Philadelphia family. With the three youths a part of his life, Joe thought that he could focus on the baseball season, generally ignore academics, and still move up in status.

His hopes were buoyed at the end of the freshman year when the baseball team won all but two games—one a loss and the other a tie.

The student newspaper, the *Harvard Crimson*, noted that Joe probably would move to first base during his second year. As it turned out, he would never be first string again. An influx of players with greater skill and the addition of a former professional player as a more demanding coach led Joe to become a benchwarmer. There were new players coming to Harvard and returning players whose skills had been better honed than Joe's over the summer. The new coach created A and B teams. The former played; the latter suited up for the games, then sat in reserve in case of injuries to A team players. Joe made only the B team.

Joe, severely depressed, would have quit the team entirely, but his low social standing, his failure to be invited to join any of the elite clubs, and his poor grades meant that being able to claim he was on the varsity was his only distinguishing success at Harvard.

The greatest humiliation for someone in Joe's position came with the threat of losing his letter sweater. All the members of the baseball team were given sweaters with the Harvard "H," which they proudly wore around campus. A baseball player may have lacked the prestige of football players, but there were few enough varsity athletes that anyone having the letter was respected. The problem Joe had was that he had to play in at least one game during his junior year to retain the sweater as a senior.

To make matters worse, Joe had done poorly in all his courses. His interest in both history and economics led him to apply himself to those two areas, earning his highest marks. But had all his grades matched the two fields of interest, Joe still would have been a relatively poor student. His parents were regularly apprised of his shortcomings, further adding to his humiliation.

Joe had hoped that his friendship with Bob Fisher, who had made the elite Porcellian Club, would enable him to be accepted by the sons of the old, wealthy, influential Protestant families. Again he was wrong.

Joe had been typecast as new-money Irish Catholic by the president of Harvard when he first started classes. This placed him in the lowest pecking order—below old-money Brahmin, new-money Brahmin, and Jews. There was no one lower accepted in the school. Joe could learn the social customs of the Brahmins from Fisher, but he could not move within their circle. His only hope for any status lay with his winning the permanent right to wear his Harvard H in his senior year, and that meant playing, if only for a couple of minutes, in one of the games during his junior year. He also knew that this would not take place through honest means.

*   *   *

Joe made his move for a letter in the 1911 Harvard-Yale game by planning strategy well before game day. Senior captain and pitcher Charles "Chick" McLaughlin was a man interested in the new industry of silent movies. He saw this form of entertainment as part of the future of the nation. At the time the industry was fragmented, some men owning studios, some distribution networks, and others the theaters. This would change—ironically, under Joe Kennedy's guidance—but that change was years ahead. A man living in the East hoping to make his fortune in the movie business bought theaters. However, to be able to open such a business, he needed a license.

The Brahmins like McLaughlin learned the hard way what the Irish and other immigrant groups had figured out by their second generation in the United States. Maybe you couldn't have the type of corporate job that would bring you power and wealth, but you could obtain a position that would make others beholden to you. This was why the civil service and government employment were critical for ambitious men like P. J. Kennedy and John Fitzgerald. This also was a world that young Joe planned to reject in the future, yet was quite willing to use when it suited his needs.

Joe Kennedy's father was politically connected with the people who awarded business licenses, including those for the new motion picture theaters. McLaughlin was told that the price for the license would be Joe Kennedy's winning a letter. This meant that he had to go against the coach's decision about who would play.

McLaughlin pitched the game until there was no chance that the addition of a relatively weak player would hurt the score. Harvard was ahead, 4 to 1. It was the top of the ninth. Yale had two outs. Then he signaled to Joe to take over first base.

The action undoubtedly shocked the coach. Joe had not played in competition for two years. It was one thing for him to dress in uniform and sit on the bench. He should not have been brought into the last game of the season, during which the mayor and his daughter were in the stands. The coach had placed him on the bench. The pitcher, as team captain, could call Joe in to play, but it was so unusual that the coach must have been surprised. He would not override the decision, though. That would create a potential problem best handled away from the playing field.

The moment proved to be the last hit of the last game. The Yale batter hit a pop-up down the first-base line and into Joe's glove. McLaughlin was the hero to all except those who, years later, heard Joe's epic retelling and saw Kennedy's possession of the ball routinely awarded to the winning pitcher. These later acquaintances didn't know that Kennedy pocketed the ball instead of tossing it back to Chick. He had coerced the captain into letting him play long enough to keep his letter. Then he had scorned the young man by stealing the ball, knowing the real star had already sold his soul for the theater license.

Every Harvard man present that day who saw Joe pocket the ball understood what he had done. It was only to Rose that young Kennedy was a hero, but that was good enough. As much as Joe wanted to be like the Brahmins, and as many Protestant women as he would later seduce, he never wanted anyone other than Mayor Fitzgerald's daughter to be his wife. It was the one aspect of his life where he could never escape his culture and the social order of Irish Catholic Boston with which he would have an enduring love/hate relationship until his death.

What mattered to Joe was that he had his letter in sports, a reputation as a newspaper writer, and an adequate social club membership for the senior year he would barely pass. He left behind a trail of enemies, but after one more mediocre academic year he would always be able to tell the world that he was a Harvard man.

Years later, when trying to explain about his baseball career at Harvard and why he sat out his senior year, Joe claimed that he had been scouted by professional teams until the big Harvard-Navy game. Joe was pitching against Navy, he claimed, determined to lead his team to victory. So enthusiastic was he that he overdid it, injuring his pitching arm severely enough to effectively end his career.

There was another side to Joe Kennedy that led him to explore the idea of what made a man respected. He had long gone into Boston to attend the popular shows, sometimes dating showgirls, sometimes buying the sheet music from musicals, then going to a friend's house to stand around the piano, singing. He also attended matinee concerts of classical music, developing a lifelong love for the great symphonies. He acquired a large collection of records and would privately listen to works he could not discuss with friends. He felt they would think less of him for his one intellectual pleasure.

Joe also discovered the world of books at Harvard. He never would be an avid reader. He seemed to have little interest in the content of literature. Instead he was fascinated with the respect writers received. He held in near reverence those whose names were on the jackets of books.

He thought that the true measure of a man's worth came, in part, from writing books or at least in having other people think you had achieved so important an accomplishment. He had started to establish such a reputation the summer before his freshman year when he accepted the unearned byline as a newspaper writer.

It was another O'Meara who foiled what Kennedy hoped would be his most lucrative scheme during the summer after his sophomore year in college. Kennedy and his friend Joe Donovan spent approximately $600 to buy a tour bus to allow them to take advantage of the tourists who flocked to Boston every summer. There were already several sightseeing bus companies in the area, and it was not hard to see which routes were the most lucrative. You could tell by the location of the hotels and other businesses catering to visitors which stands had the most people wanting to use the services. The best was South Station, where a company was already operating.

Joe was arrogant enough to think that since the mayor had honored him for his baseball prowess before he went to Harvard, and since he was friends with the mayor's daughter, John Fitzgerald would help him get the stop he wanted. He did not realize that use of the stop was determined by the commissioner of police, one Stephen O'Meara. This O'Meara, unlike Joe's friend, hated both P. J. Kennedy and John Fitzgerald. Denying the barkeep's boy a chance to have an exclusive business was a way he could get back at both men. Since the existing tour bus operator was a friend of the commissioner, revenge was all the more to be enjoyed.

Joe Kennedy was told he would have to share South Station, a reaction that was anticipated. He explained that he had worked out a schedule during which each bus would have exclusive use of the stop. The plan Joe had created would assure equal access to business throughout the day.

The truth was that the two Joes had analyzed the rhythm of South Station. There were times of day when traffic was consistently light. There were times of day when people were standing in line, eager for a chance to see the sights. Joe Kennedy drew up a schedule that evenly split the day. However, the rival company's bus was expected to use the stop only during the weakest hours for customers.

Commissioner O'Meara did not know exactly what Kennedy and Donovan were trying to do, but he knew it was not honest. When Joe Kennedy told the commissioner that the routes were created to have the exact same number of passengers, O'Meara expressed his satisfaction with the arrangement. Then he told the youths that he was reversing them. Since they were identical, they could operate during the hours they had given to the rival bus operator.

The end result was what Joe anticipated, though not with the revenues he had fancied. His schedule, now being used by a rival, proved extremely lucrative. The schedule he thought his rival would have to follow was so limited in passengers that Joe probably did not break even that first year.[7]

While Joe hustled his way through Harvard, Rose Fitzgerald returned from the Convent of the Sacred Heart's Holland school a radically changed woman. She still lusted for Joe Kennedy, perhaps all the more because he remained moderately forbidden fruit. She also expected that life would be hers for the taking, since she was now one of the most worldly young women in Boston, albeit undereducated for her intelligence and interests. She planned on working with her father, becoming a social leader among Boston's elite Irish Catholic women, and eventually marrying Joe. At the same time, she had been ingrained with the philosophy of the Sacred Heart schools as stated in numerous documents of the time:

> The child of the Sacred Heart understands that her role is central to the design of creation. If she is not among those few called to the perfect life of religion, it will be her task to guide the souls of her own children. Her special influence depends upon her distinctively feminine qualities: tact, quiet courage, and the willingness to subordinate her will to another's gracefully and even gaily. Filled with the tranquility of inner certitude, she does not disperse her energies in pointless curiosity, in capricious espousal of new theories, in the spirit of contention. Long years of silence, of attention to manners and forms, have instilled in her that self-control without which order and beauty are impossible. Her bearing is the outward shape of that perfect purity which is her greatest beauty, and which models itself on the ideal womanhood found in the Mother of God. She who can bear the small trials of daily discipline will not falter at those crises in life which require firmness and fortitude.

The words were believed with an intensity that would dominate Rose's life. But when she returned to young Joe, newly graduated from Harvard and attempting to find success in business that would impress her father, she never expected a life where the belief would be challenged. With Josie still unable to attend many public functions, Rose Fitzgerald, a veteran world traveler, fluent in two languages, financially comfortable, and with an outgoing personality, was about to serve as de facto first lady of Boston. She also was establishing the equivalent of an Irish Catholic Junior League, creating a social order that would be coveted by the elite daughters of the most prominent men in the community. It was the Irish Catholic equivalent of the networking possible for the Protestant men of Harvard, a world Joe desperately wanted to share.

Rose Fitzgerald started her takeover of Boston Irish Catholic society with her debut. Honey Fitz not only wanted to introduce his daughter, he also wanted to show the power and influence the family had achieved. To this end, he invited slightly more than 450 people, and those attending included the governor of Massachusetts, all the members of City Council, and two congressional representatives. In addition, the day was declared an official holiday.

Protestant women of importance coming out in Boston would be besieged by invitations from various Protestant social clubs. Each would represent families of wealth and power, and the club to which the debutante pledged established the world in which she would live. The man she married would likely come from one of these families. Where she lived, where her husband worked, where they traveled, all would be similar to the lives of the other young women who were members. But Rose was a Catholic, and no matter how important and wealthy she might be, she would never be tolerated by the Protestant social clubs.

Rose may have hoped that she would be able to unite Catholic and Protestant society through joining a Protestant club, but the rejections did not surprise her. When no one called on her, she joined the Cecilian Guild, the Boston Irish equivalent of the Junior League. Then she created the Ace of Clubs. Membership was limited to those young women who had studied overseas and were reasonably fluent in French. At first Rose was pretentious enough to demand that only French be used for Ace of Clubs meetings. However, the other girls, all of whom were part of Irish society, refused to go along with such nonsense, and that requirement was dropped.

Wellesley graduates were better educated, and the Protestants among them were eligible for well-established social clubs. But the Wellesley women lacked the experience and often the family money of those Irish Catholic women who had gone to school in Europe. Each group had reason to both respect and deride the other.

The Boston newspapers treated the Ace of Clubs with the same respect they previously held solely for the elite Protestant organizations.

No matter how their parents earned their money, the young women who were members had achieved something that gave them an elite status. They were likely headed toward being the wives and mothers of men who would have a great impact on the city, state, and nation, men who might become as illustrious as past figures such as Benjamin Franklin and Cotton Mather.

Ironically, it was Rose who quickly tired of the club she created. The high point of the group's activities was an annual ball held in the luxurious Somerset Hotel. Rose always would lead the grand march of attending couples. Everything was beautiful, formal, and rather boring.

Part of the problem was that as Rose matured into womanhood, she accompanied her father when he promoted the port of Boston. Sometimes the trips were legitimately for business. Sometimes they were perquisites of being mayor and in a position to influence business decisions that made money for others. A trip to the Panama Canal and Latin America was meant to increase Boston business, but the United Fruit Company, a firm that would most benefit from the relationship, paid for it.

Rose also met numerous dignitaries. For example, when Irish-born Sir Thomas Lipton, the wealthy, middle-aged, bachelor head of the Lipton Tea family, was visiting Boston, he was guest of honor at a party in the Copley Plaza Hotel. Josie Fitzgerald had no interest in attending. Rose, by contrast, was thrilled to meet the lusty millionaire, whose sexual adventures—real or rumored—led gossips to wonder if he would ever commit to a wife. This question was raised during the party, at which time Sir Thomas announced that his bride had been decided upon and was in the ballroom. He then told Rose Fitzgerald to stand for all to see.

Rose delighted in the joke, loudly turning him down. "I won't accept you, Sir Thomas," she was later quoted as saying. "I think you are altogether too fickle."[8]

Later, while visiting England in 1911, Rose and her father saw the royal yacht and, a little farther in the water, Sir Thomas Lipton's vessel *Erin*. The king and queen were visiting the wealthy Sir Thomas, so Honey Fitz managed to get some of the royal yacht's crew to take Mayor Fitzgerald and his daughter out to Sir Thomas's vessel. It is not known what he said to convince them, but when the mayor arrived, climbing the ladder to the deck, Sir Thomas was delighted to greet him. It was the first time Rose met royalty, a heady experience for someone whose ancestry was always considered inferior by the British.

By contrast, Joe Kennedy's first trip to Europe was not until 1913, when he and some friends decided to see Germany and France. He was determined to appear sophisticated, asking everyone he knew who had made such a trip what to do and how to do it. He also assembled letters of introduction that could be used for business. However, the trip was all pleasure, including a visit to the Folies Bergère followed by dancing at the Dead Rat nightclub, a popular Paris nightspot for American expatriates.

Joe Kennedy graduated from Harvard certain only that he wanted to make money. Since his father was one of the investors in a local bank, Joe thought banking might be an interesting business to enter. However, he knew nothing of the industry other than basic accounting and some knowledge of the banking laws he had gained while at Harvard.

There was little sophistication to the banking industry, and men hired as assistant examiners did not have to have a background in the field. The pay was $1,500 a year, less than the stringer pay for the *Boston Globe*, and the hours were long. However, the men who held the position could learn on the job, and the knowledge they gained was better than a degree in the field.

Each new bank Joe visited enabled him to learn how an institution established loan creditworthiness of individuals and businesses. He was able to see if the trust placed in the individuals had been valid or if a person or business had defaulted. He learned from the repeated success and glaring failures of others, coming to understand how to run an institution.

Joe also looked into the real-estate industry, though in a manner that would remain somewhat mysterious over the years. He is known to have invested in real-estate companies twice in his life, the first being Old Colony Realty, for which he was named treasurer while working full-time as a bank examiner. The second, at the end of his life, was a company whose primary income prior to its collapse appeared to be money laundering. However, the latter was never proven.

Old Colony Realty revealed a toughness in Joe that was similar to the intensity of John Fitzgerald's career as a ward heeler. During the period when he was learning politics and working his way up in the Democratic Party, Honey Fitz spent some election days watching polling place checkers. The checkers were aware of the way each man voted, and the ward heelers, like John Fitzgerald, made certain the men holding patronage jobs voted for the candidate designated by the ward boss.

The vote check was an accepted practice, albeit an improper one. Whenever the candidate was important to the ward boss's personal future, any man who was told to vote for the candidate and chose to vote for someone else would be in trouble. A minor infraction that would not affect the outcome of a close race would lead to the voter being beaten. A major infraction costing the ward boss's candidate his job would lead to the voter being fired from his patronage position.

Each time Fitzgerald turned in an errant voter, he was destroying a man's ability to feed and shelter his family. The punishment was of no concern to Fitzgerald, who coldly believed that any man who did not follow the party line had no business benefiting from whoever was in office. Honey Fitz's future son-in-law showed the same indifference to the potential suffering of others when he was with Old Colony Realty, a three-way partnership started by Harry O'Meara, the manager of the Bethlehem baseball team.

Boston laborers desired to own their own homes, working long hours to achieve their dream. These were small shelters of little value except to the families who owned them. Yet despite their modest size and cost, many of the men fell behind in their payments whenever laboring jobs became scarce.

Joe Kennedy and his partners understood that certain jobs were cyclical. There would be good months, when the workers were flush with money, and bad months, when they had to delay paying the mortgage. Over the years, the men were always able to meet their obligations. When they couldn't, many institutions would give them short-term loans, almost always repaid, to get them through the crisis, or they would be allowed to miss payments, then pay extra each month until they caught up.

Old Colony took a different approach. The business targeted the owners of multifamily dwellings—duplexes, triplexes, and small apartments—who had fallen behind because all the tenants were in the same business and there was a seasonal downturn. They would buy the property for a fraction of its value, evict the families living there, send in work crews to at least cosmetically improve the multifamily dwellings, then resell them to other laborers with the dream of home ownership. The buildings never were idle long because they had the allure of being both a man's home and his income property. The new buyers would invariably pay more than the market value warranted, not realizing the mistake until they, too, got into trouble and lost their investment. Then the cycle would repeat itself.

Ironically, it was at Old Colony that Joe Kennedy showed a rare moment of compassion. He was never a generous man. Even when he became wealthy, he did not establish foundations or engage in secret philanthropy, as some rich Americans chose to do.[9] Yet there is one known instance when he was with the real-estate company that an all-too-seldom side of him was revealed.

Harry O'Meara told of a time when a man named Henry Siegal stopped by the real-estate office to see if he could get the partners to contribute money to a man in crisis. In a short period of time, the man had lost his job, been unable to pay his rent, faced eviction, and had his child die. The child's death, which occurred the day before Siegal's visit to Old Colony, was especially traumatic. Without the funds for burial, the boy was wrapped in a sheet and left in the front room of the apartment from which the man would soon be forced out.

O'Meara knew Siegal well enough to trust the man's judgment of the need. He did not ask the name of the person to be helped. He did not ask where he lived. He simply wrote a check for $50 as Joe Kennedy arrived, hearing the end of the story.

Kennedy, according to O'Meara,[10] was livid. He felt that $50 was not enough to sustain anyone with so many problems. He tore up the check and said that the man either should be helped or ignored. He then told Siegal to bring the man to his office so he could evaluate him for himself.

The man was close in age to the Old Colony business partners. He was a Catholic who had been an altar boy at the same time and in the same church as O'Meara. By the time they saw him, though, he looked much older, disheveled, and was wearing clothing that was near to rags.

Joe Kennedy gave the man $150 and told him to get decent clothing and a haircut. He called the funeral home and arranged for the proper burial of the child. He called the landlord and arranged for the rent to be paid. Then he gave the man a job as salesman for Old Colony, which eventually went into land development and the construction of new housing.

Other than having the title of treasurer, there are no records as to what duties Kennedy performed. All that is known for certain was that when Joe and his two partners dissolved the company during World War I, Joe gained $25,000 in assets.

The business venture that truly impressed Honey Fitz was also in finance. Joe decided to use his father's investment and influence in Columbia Trust to become a bank president.

Joe Kennedy felt that his age, which made him among the youngest bank presidents in the nation, was what was important. He liked being the first, the youngest, the best, regardless of the truth. But the requirements of the job were little more taxing than the bank examiner's position had been. The approximately $200,000 in assets the bank contained made it small by the standards of the day. By having less than from $1 million to $5 million in assets, it was little more than a small business or a small, one-sponsor credit union might be today.

Once again Joe Kennedy lucked into a situation that had more to do with the times than the reality of the bank or his personal skills. In 1913, banks began increasing their deposits and depositors by merging with one another. Services could be increased, but nothing changed when it came to bias against the Irish and others. If anything, fewer jobs were going to minorities after the mergers. In addition, small neighborhood banks could become branches deemed unnecessary, removing them from the neighborhood. This meant that people whose loans were based on personal trust by friends and neighbors working at the bank would possibly be denied by strangers making the decisions following the merger. Joe had gained enough knowledge in the eighteen months he worked as an assistant examiner that the board of directors of Columbia Trust felt comfortable having him take control. It was not a big job and could not compare with heading a larger institution. However, it was a bank, he was president, and no one in the state held such a position at so young an age.

Rose Fitzgerald was delighted with Joe's achievement, knowing that her father would think better of the youth she wanted to marry. What she did not fully grasp was that her father was in serious trouble as a politician as well as a husband. He was no longer in a position to object to any relationship his daughter wanted to have. And the reason was "Toodles."

5

SCANDAL AND MARRIAGE

NO ONE OTHER THAN HONEY FITZ AND ELIZABETH "TOODLES" RYAN ever knew the extent of the relationship they shared. What is certain is that given the morals of the time and the political sensitivity of the mayor, the open displays of affection that led the mayor to being black-mailed almost certainly reflected a private, adulterous affair.

The truth was that Rose's father was no more flamboyant than men like James M. Curley, who was planning to challenge Honey Fitz for the mayor's race. Both men treated every man and woman they met as though the person were a beloved yet seldom seen family member. And both men, like the vast majority of the politicians of the day, had scandals in their pasts. The most serious for Curley was the time he spent in federal prison in 1904 when he took the postal service exam for another man. Such a crime was forgiven by the voters because it was committed in a seemingly selfless manner—to get someone else a job. There was undoubtedly a payoff or a kickback, but the action was a quiet one, out of sight of everyone except the government agents who arrested him.

Honey Fitz also helped others get jobs, though he utilized a combination of patronage and creative hiring, often in exchange for more obvious kickbacks and payoffs. One man went on the Boston city payroll as a tree climber. He was not a tree surgeon or gardener. He did not rescue helpless kittens and hapless children. He just climbed trees. He was rarely busy.

Another Boston man worked repairing rubber boots. Whenever someone employed by the city needed a rubber boot repaired, the man did the work. He, too, rarely had to do more than sit and wait.

A third man was paid to warm tea. And a fourth man, a dermatologist the mayor liked, was the official Boston dermatologist.

The mayor's biggest problem was how blatant he was. Other mayors took payoffs in exchange for special favors. Others arranged for "ghost" employees—men and women who were on the payroll of one department or another, collecting their wages week after week yet never showing up for work. Since every mayor was under press scrutiny from the moment he left his house in the morning until he returned home late at night, Honey Fitz's actions were better known than those of his political opponents. To make matters worse, his often innocent flamboyance included flirting with every woman in a room and dancing with as many as possible at every social event. When one of the women was the Ferncroft Inn's cigarette girl, Elizabeth Ryan, the same age as the mayor's popular daughter Rose, people looked closer. What they saw implied a more intimate relationship and a scandal in the making.

Miss Ryan, nicknamed "Toodles," was a loose-moraled young woman who earned a portion of her income by enjoying the companionship of any man willing to pay for her time and attention. This meant most of the wealthy and powerful politicians and businessmen of the day.

Honey Fitz was one of the politicians who never denied that Toodles was his special friend; he just did not explain what that meant. He engaged in blatant public displays of affection, frequently dancing with her or openly giving her a kiss. Yet no one ever suspected the mayor was paying for her time and attention, a fact that implied possible adultery.

Given the era, either the mayor was enjoying a joke on the press and his rivals, never doing more than they witnessed, or he was privately engaging in far greater intimacy. Either way this might not have affected Honey Fitz's career had Toodles not been used by a political rival who revealed himself only when the mayor was most vulnerable.

Toodles Ryan always managed to separate the pleasure of business from the business of pleasure. She also practiced her own version of monogamy by regularly returning home to her longtime lover, Henry Mansfield, the wealthy owner of the Ferncroft Inn, a popular lodging featuring excellent food, dancing, and an upstairs gambling area. The latter was illegal yet allowed to operate unhindered, since some of the customers were men responsible for enforcing the law.

Toodles, then still known as Elizabeth Ryan, had met Mansfield when she came to Boston from New York to see the 1907 Harvard-Yale football game. She was a department store model determined to conquer the big city after being raised on a Connecticut farm. When her friends suggested she accompany them to Boston for a couple of days, she was delighted.

The group stayed in the Lenox Hotel on the first day, then moved to the Ferncroft Inn, a more expensive location where the illicit gambling was a major attraction. Instead of the roulette table, the attractive, blond-haired Elizabeth Ryan met Mansfield. He was forty years old, but though he was many years her senior, she found the fact that he not only owned the inn but also two other businesses more than enough incentive to look beyond the difference in their ages.

Mansfield began his affair with Toodles the first night she was there, and then hired her for a variety of tasks. She was a cashier and a cigarette girl, the work she was doing when Mayor Fitzgerald met her. She was also a shill for the gambling operation, flirting with wealthy men until she convinced them to accompany her to the gaming room on the second floor.

Elizabeth Ryan's nickname was apparently invented by Mansfield instead of something friends had called her before they met. He seemed to want the name of "Elizabeth" Ryan to be unsullied. She was "Elizabeth" when she was his monogamous companion and "Toodles" when she played for pay with any man who wanted to afford the price. Mansfield eventually proposed marriage to Elizabeth, then kept putting off the date. He was conflicted over the Madonna/whore image she lived both in his fantasies and in his real life.

Toodles had a different perspective. She simply saw a rich guy getting what he wanted from her, then trying to play her for a sucker.

Toodles may have been outraged as she claimed. She also simply may have recognized that the game she was playing could not continue forever in Boston. She was getting older, possibly losing her appeal, and needed to secure her future. Whatever the case, she went to attorney Daniel Coakley, a man who hated the mayor, and asked him to represent her in a breach-of-promise suit. She was deeply "hurt" by her continuing single status after Mansfield convinced her they would be married. Her heart was broken. Her future was shattered. And only the payment of $50,000 could enable her to again hold her head high in society at large.

Coakley probably determined the proper payoff. He was a master at finding just the right amount of money to restore a young lady's reputation. While no one is certain whether he was involved in such activities at the time he met Toodles, Coakley and Suffolk County district attorney Joseph Pelletier would both eventually be disbarred for their efforts on behalf of underage women of an unusually friendly nature.

In the latter scam, Coakley had women lure wealthy men to a hotel room. The couple would undress, get into bed, and be in the midst of whatever activity the man desired when a police officer would angrily enter the room. It was against the law for an unmarried couple to engage in sex, the officer would announce. Then he would be further "outraged" to discover that the young lady was a minor. Fortunately for the unclad "cad," the sympathetic Coakley, representing the "victim," would have a word with the justice-seeking Pelletier. Together they would determine an appropriate sum of money to assure that all charges would be dropped. Naturally the police officer, who invariably would fail to file a written report with his superiors, received a piece of the action for his efforts at law enforcement.

It is uncertain whether Mansfield paid off. From what is known, it can be presumed that some form of financial arrangement was made, the attorney getting paid and Toodles benefiting enough to be willing to go along with a new scam. It is doubtful that Mansfield spent as much as $50,000 to rid himself of the young woman. Her revelations could hardly disgrace a man everyone knew was involved with prostitution and gambling. What is known is that the lawyer must have seemed a fair business partner to Toodles, for she was willing to work with him in his own scams.

There were several ways Curley knew he could use Toodles against the mayor, but they all came with a degree of risk. Honey Fitz was a popular politician who had long taken care of his constituents. There was no physical evidence or eyewitnesses to any sexual affair between the mayor and Toodles. There was no hotel front desk registration form or maid's whispered testimony that she had seen the mayor sneaking in, sneaking out, or inside any hotel room. The Toodles affair was limited to the public's awareness of kissing, close dancing, and endless rumors.

Going public with the Toodles charge also would mean openly hurting Josie Fitzgerald. Politicians knew that lies, innuendos, and even worse, the truth, always would be a danger, and they were hardened to such attacks. The voters, by contrast, wanted negative campaigning to be limited to public figures, not a withdrawn, almost reclusive wife. A public attack by Curley could result in a voter backlash against the spreader of bad news. That was why he decided to work privately, sending a letter to Josie to warn her that the mayor's reputation was about to be destroyed. The letter was rimmed in black, a technique that was similar to a funeral announcement. It also would not be made public. Voters who might be horrified by such an action would remain unaware that he had taken it.

No one knows what Josie believed about Toodles and her husband. Josie's relationship with John Fitzgerald was a close one, but much of his life was spent away from home. He could have had an affair. He could be sexually involved with a woman no older than their beloved Rose. But even if he wasn't, Honey Fitz had been forced into a position he knew Josie would not tolerate. They had always understood that no matter how dirty politics became, he would never bring his world into their home. The letter sent to Josie meant she was becoming an intimate part of his public life, something she would not and could not tolerate.

Honey Fitz's first reaction was to challenge Curley. Let him prove there was an affair. Let him bring forth witnesses. Let him reveal whatever "facts" he had about Mansfield's kept woman. The mayor knew that if he made the challenge in public, the allegations would lead nowhere. Curley had neither proof nor witnesses. He could only damage his own career.

The problem with such a strategy was the letter Josie received. She would not tolerate any possible further invasion of her family's privacy.

Rose Fitzgerald understood some of what was happening with her father. Her daughters would one day laugh about how sexually naive their mother was, though whether they were talking about her knowledge of various positions or her refusing to face the idea of adultery in her own marriage or that of any other family member is uncertain. Certainly Rose knew that a politician's too-varied sex life had been successfully used against him by his enemies, including her own father when he was campaigning.

Rose did not take the Curley/Toodles attack seriously. She understood rough-and-tumble Boston politics, where a frequently repeated lie was almost as good as the truth. She also had spent so much time with her father that she could not imagine him with another woman. She probably did not see where the family or her father's career would be hurt by the charges if he fought back. But she also did not understand how deeply her mother's convictions ran about where politics and home life had to remain separated.

While Honey Fitz weighed his decision, the public attacks continued. One often-repeated poem used by the more literate of his detractors included this line: "A whiskey glass and Toodles' ass made a horse's ass out of Honey Fitz."

Honey Fitz knew he was through, yet there was enough of the competitor in him that he wanted to find a way to leave office without admitting he had been politically outmaneuvered. He found the excuse by accident when the Arcadia caught fire the night of December 2, 1913.

The Arcadia began life as a flophouse, a place where men who would today be living on the streets could spend a few cents to get a room for the night. Such businesses had one fee for a chair, a second rate for a room with a bed, and sometimes a third rate for at least a semiprivate bath area. The alcoholics and mentally ill paid by the day. The aged poor, living without income, pension, or family, often tried to rent by the week. In the case of the Arcadia, the original use had been abandoned as local do-gooders converted the South End building into a mission for detoxing alcoholics. On the night of December 2, twenty-eight former drunks were asleep when the smoke and flames overcame them.

Honey Fitz was horrified by both the enormity of the tragedy and the sad reality that the dead men had been trying to get their lives together. He tried to help the fire department, then worked with inspectors to determine the cause of the fire. It was an accident he did not want to see repeated anywhere in the city.

James Curley's people made a brief stab at further attacking the mayor by claiming that one of the dead drunks had been Honey Fitz's brother. They stopped when they realized the sympathy was with the dead.

The seriousness of the mayor's concern about not repeating such a tragedy became evident over the next two days. He went from building to building in the South End, personally checking every room, talking with every resident, and examining all the possible fire hazards. There was no one in Boston who doubted his emotional commitment to the least among the residents as he worked.

The endless walking tour took the mayor into places "nice" people, including Honey Fitz before those days, never saw. The staircases he climbed had been stained by urine and excrement, the smells of which never disappeared. There was vomit left by drunks who sometimes died in their own waste. And there was the odor of coal gas that seemed to hang over the streets.

On December 4, an exhausted and nauseated John Fitzgerald was inside a rescue mission whose rooms were filled with the coal gas odor. He collapsed, falling down a few steps, and was rushed to the hospital. The injuries were not serious, but they occurred during an effort to help the least successful of Boston's citizens, and even James Curley dared not criticize him for the moment. Mocking a man's alleged adultery was one thing. Attacking him for caring about the community was quite another.

The recovered Honey Fitz announced that he was not well enough for another term in office. He withdrew a community hero, planning to run again in 1917.

As Honey Fitz waited out the time between elections, he became more involved with *The Republic*, giving himself an extra voice in governmental affairs. Usually the paper reported the news as it happened. However, when James Curley, who easily won the election from which the mayor withdrew, felt that he needed to allow an antiwar demonstration days after the nation entered what would eventually be called World War I, the newspaper's editor attacked him. The paper stated that Curley was unpatriotic, that no one should be allowed to speak if he or she was challenging the nation in wartime.

Curley responded that he felt he had to support the constitutional right to free speech. He also decided to use the paper's attack to counter what was rumored to be a Honey Fitz return to politics. Curley announced that the editorial against the antiwar speakers was a means of "stifling free speech in general, as a measure of personal protection from the truth, which in its nakedness is sometimes hideous though necessary.

"I am preparing three addresses which, if necessary, I shall deliver in the fall, and which, if a certain individual had the right to restrict free speech, I would not be permitted to deliver.

"One of these addresses is entitled 'Graft, Ancient and Modern,' another, 'Great Lovers: From Cleopatra to Toodles,' and last, but not least interesting, 'Libertines from Henry VIII to the Present Day.'"

Mayor Curley's counterattack worked. It would be another twenty years before John Fitzgerald openly returned to politics.

The person who benefited most from John Fitzgerald's problems was Joe Kennedy. If the mayor knew Joe's tendency to enjoy the young showgirls of Boston and New York, it did not matter. Joe might have been cheating on his daughter's fantasies, but he was a single man. He was not committing adultery. Besides, just as Honey Fitz could excuse his failure to seek reelection on his endangered health, so he could justify Joe Kennedy as a son-in-law because the young man was a bank president. The fact that he thought Joe Kennedy was the lowest type of Irish and not worthy of his family's social standing went unmentioned.

The impact of Honey Fitz's hatred for Joe and the Kennedy family was evident in the way the wedding took place. A wedding was meant to show off the bride's family, its importance in the community, its wealth, and the friends it attracted. It always was to have a larger guest list than attended the daughter's presentation to society. However, while Rose's father invited 450 people when she had her debut, her wedding breakfast only had 75 in attendance. William Cardinal O'Connell officiated at the ceremony, a nod to the Fitzgerald family prominence, but the mayor made certain the public knew who mattered. When the *Boston Post* photographer posed the happy family for the next day's paper, the picture showed John and Josie Fitzgerald and Rose Fitzgerald Kennedy standing together. Joe Kennedy, the groom who should have been routinely included in all such photos, was conspicuously absent from the newspaper's image.

For those who understood the family dynamics, Honey Fitz was telling his world that Rose was married to the man she loved. It was too bad she didn't have better taste.

In the years that followed, there were stories told of even greater problems that day. Allegedly Joe and Honey Fitz argued during the reception. Rose, outraged by the actions of her new husband, was said to have taken off her wedding ring, set it on the mantel, then walked over and stood by her father. While such an aggressive defense of someone she loved was typical of Rose's strength, it is doubtful that this battle, and its supposed outcome, ever took place.

First there was Joe, a weak man of great ambition who had just achieved the high point of social success through marriage. He would not consider either jeopardizing his new situation or embarrassing the cardinal by acting in the manner described.[1] It is also doubtful that Rose, the proud Child of Mary, would have publicly stood against her new husband.

Joe Kennedy never fully appreciated his new bride—her experiences, connections, and intellect. She was just twenty when she joined the Boston Public Library's board that selected children's reading materials. Her selection was believed to have been based on ability, not family connections. She never bragged about the achievement, accepting it as important work she was pleased to be allowed to handle. She also taught Sunday school in two different churches, one of which, in the North End, was undergoing a transition from an Irish immigrant congregation to an Italian immigrant congregation.

Rose was a woman who could help him achieve his financial and political goals, but he was too proud, too blind, or too foolish to use her. He also had no intention of allowing her to live near her father's world. Instead, Joe borrowed $2,000 to make a one-third down payment on a $6,500 house in Brookline. It was a moneyed community, supposedly one of the wealthiest in the United States. It was home to members of the Protestant elite, yet once again Joe could not match up. The house, at 83 Beals Street, had nine rooms, but it was not one of the better houses on one of the better streets. Still, Brookline was not the North End, and the neighbors' ancestry was mostly British, not Irish.

Joe was deeply in debt when the couple made their move into what, for Rose, would be isolation. He had purchased a two-carat diamond engagement ring, a wedding ring, invested in the bank, bought a house, and soon would purchase a Ford car he managed to wreck not long after acquiring it. Even worse, Rose became pregnant either on the couple's honeymoon at the Greenbrier Hotel in White Sulphur Springs, West Virginia, or shortly thereafter.

Adding to the troubled early days of Joe's marriage were the sexual issues Rose's pregnancy raised that would never be resolved for the couple or their children. For example, after actor Peter Lawford married Joe and Rose's third oldest daughter, Patricia, he complained that having sex with his wife was like being involved with some sort of sacred ritual. While Lawford delighted in all but the missionary position, his sex life ranging from the almost routine to the kinky and fetishistic, he later told both friends and his fourth wife, Patricia Seaton Lawford, that Pat Kennedy got on her knees to pray before intercourse. Her actions, he believed, resulted from her mother's influence from the time she was old enough to be educated about sex.

Rose had three problems affecting her intimate relations with Joe and her teachings to her children. First there was the attitude of the Catholic Church. Sex was stressed as a joyful, almost sacramental way for procreation. Couples were encouraged to have sex regularly, loving the children with whom God might bless them. Birth control was considered wrong. Only abstinence during a woman's most fertile period was approved (the "rhythm method").

At the same time, Rose's time in the Blumenthal convent school had led to her being taught a warped view of male/female relations. Sex was not encouraged except as a duty for having children. And the teachings came from women who not only had agreed to a celibate life—some also had been raped during a time of political upheaval, a horror for which there is no record of efforts at counseling.

The third problem was the popular attitude toward sex. This was the tail end of the Victorian era. The sexual revolution of the flapper era had not begun. Little was understood about human sexual physiology, and studies of sexuality were nonexistent.

Rose Kennedy sits with her first three children—Joe Jr. (left), John (right), and infant Rosemary. (Cleveland State University Library, Special Collections)

Among the popular beliefs reflected in magazines was that a man's abilities were affected by the frequency with which he had intercourse. Frequent sex by a man decreased his efficiency on the athletic field and in business. He could not think so clearly, run so fast, and generally perform at his best if sex were enjoyed more often than once or twice a month. The central nervous system also could be affected, the man being left disabled with a neuromuscular condition.

A woman also had problems from frequent intercourse. She could easily become too exhausted to function as expected when caring for husband and family.

Joe probably recognized that the notion of sex as debilitating was nonsense, and if he believed it was possible, he seemed to console himself with the fact that his virility allowed him to enjoy frequent intercourse without consequence. Rose, however, read the popular literature of the day and was determined to help her husband in any way she could. He refused to allow her to be an intimate in his business, as she had been with her father's political career. She hoped she could at least keep him at his "peak" in business by denying him sex during most of the months of each of her pregnancies.

This sacrifice for her husband became most evident after the birth of the couple's first child, Joseph Patrick Kennedy Jr., on July 25, 1915. Joe was enthusiastically welcomed in the nuptial bed before each new pregnancy, then denied sexual favors as much as possible thereafter. It was a practice that eventually led to one of Joe's own. Whenever he had a serious, longer-term affair with another woman, he would prove his "faithfulness" to her by pointing out that Rose was not pregnant during the time they were together.

But that was all in the future. What mattered was that Joe and Rose had their first boy, the special son, as their first daughter would be special in the raising of the family.

Rose firmly believed that the oldest child of each sex was to be the leader of the younger siblings. As long as the child was of normal intelligence, abilities, and emotional stability, he or she would experience the excitement of life, then share the experience with the next-older same-sex sibling.

Joseph Jr. would serve this leadership role for the boys, and their third child but first daughter, Rose Marie (called Rosemary), would be the leader of the girls. In the years to come the family would be forced to deny the truth of their children's upbringing. They would be forced to create a myth about their second son, the disabled-from-birth John Fitzgerald Kennedy, as well as their dyslexic but otherwise perfectly healthy first daughter. But when Joseph Patrick was born, both Rose and Joe still felt their lives had a foundation of blessings on which to build their future.

6

THE ADVENTURE BEGINS

HONEY FITZ MAY HAVE BEEN A LAME DUCK, BUT THE BIRTH OF HIS grandson and his son-in-law's ambitions gave him much to do in his last days as mayor. First there was the matter of introducing Joseph Patrick Kennedy Jr., a healthy, ten-pound boy, to the world. He immediately called the press, and the next morning's *Boston Post* contained the quote "I'm sure he'd make a good man on the platform one day. Is he going into politics? Well, of course he is going to be president of the United States; his mother and father have already decided that he is going to Harvard, where he will play on the football and baseball teams and incidentally take all the scholastic honors. Then he's going to be a captain of industry until it's time for him to be president for two or three terms. Further than that has not been decided. He may act as mayor of Boston and governor of Massachusetts for a while on his way to the presidential chair."

Rose, by contrast, became further frustrated with her lifestyle as she faced being a young mother. She had no interest in directly involving herself with the care of the baby. Instead, she became an executive mother, a role she would continue to play as her family grew in the next few years. There would be file cards for each child with all shots, illnesses, and other details carefully listed. The action would be similar to Lillian Gilbreath, the efficiency expert who developed the science of adapting industrial jobs to the interests and abilities of the workers. She also had twelve children (immortalized in the book *Cheaper by the Dozen*), whom she raised with scientific theories best suited for the workplace. Most of them grew to be as troubled with substance abuse as would some of Joe and Rose's children.

Years later, when speaking with Barbara Gibson, her assistant for the ten years prior to her totally debilitating stroke, about the birth of her first son, Rose Kennedy showed little emotion. Instead, what she remembered most was the cost—$125 to Dr. Frederick L. Good for prenatal care, delivery service, and immediate postnatal care. Also, $25 was paid for the delivery assistance of Dr. Edward J. O'Brien, the anesthetist/

assistant who sedated Rose with ether to ease the pain. And another $25 per week was spent for a nurse who tended to Rose throughout her final days of pregnancy.

The use of ether was the first instance of Joe and Rose utilizing often-dangerous quackery in seeking medical care, a folly they passed on to their children. Their second son, John Fitzgerald Kennedy, would eventually take a dangerous combination of vitamins and amphetamines in shots given to him by a man known among New York's rich and foolish as "Dr. Feelgood."

Contemporary doctors understood that the use of ether for childbirth was exceedingly dangerous for both mother and child. Ether often complicated the birth process, ultimately creating more trauma for the mother. Worse, the ether occasionally killed the babies when the amount used for the mother was an overdose for the infant still attached to the umbilical cord. Rose should have been aware of these concerns, both from her avid reading and from the normal precautions provided expectant mothers by their physicians.

Once the children were born, Rose oversaw the child-rearing staff. She spent a total of $10 a week to employ both a maid/cook and a hospital-trained nursemaid.

Joe undoubtedly approved of the way his wife was handling the chores of the new baby. He seemed to enjoy the children, though usually he was working in some other city, writing to them, calling them, or encouraging them in various athletic competitions. He was not a man prone to physical contact with the boys and girls he sired, though that was not unusual for the Brahmin families he sought to emulate.

The wealthy still believed in the adage that children should be seen and not heard. They paid others to raise the children, bringing them to the parents only when properly cleaned and dressed. Their homes would have a cook, a maid, a liveryman, perhaps a butler, and others to handle the structured manner of feeding and caring for children taught in the various child-rearing books of the day.

The lower classes were equally concerned with adhering to contemporary child-rearing beliefs, but they had to handle the nurturing themselves. The husbands went to whatever job they held, and the wives worked alone with the children until they were ready for school. Often, those who had to work had the children with them. Their relative poverty often made for a better home life and children who grew into emotionally healthier adults.

Before John Fitzgerald left office, he felt obligated to help boost his son-in-law's career. He didn't have to like the young Kennedy to help him. Any politician in Boston would extend help to family, no matter how distasteful he might otherwise find such an individual.

In Joe's case, the help was of questionable value. Joe was appointed director of the Collateral Loan Company, a position that was both high-profile and where he would work with men who represented both the city of Boston and the state of Massachusetts. This was an era of loan sharks in the housing market. Men would give loans and charge interest so high that they knew the borrower eventually would be unable to make his payment. Then they would foreclose, own the house, and sell it to someone else at a far higher percentage than was routinely requested for traditional loans.

The Collateral Loan Company was meant to stop such practices. It was supposed to be run much like a credit union, treating the people fairly. What neither Honey Fitz nor Joe realized was that the men in charge had been ignoring their duties, and an embezzler had taken $26,000 from the organization. Joe spent five months trying to handle the scandal during which several individuals, including the president, were let go. Then he himself quit, hoping to live down the first bad publicity he had ever received.

Eventually Joe was able to gain a position on the board of trustees of the Massachusetts Electric Company. The work was relatively mean-ingless, an oversight service with little power and little need. However, it had long been a position given to one or another of the powerful Brah-mins, and Joe delighted that he was the first Irish Catholic to hold it.

Joe did not make the social and business contacts he anticipated with the Massachusetts Electric Company, but he did become known to attorney Guy Currier. Currier was everything Joe Kennedy wanted to be—rich, ruthless, and so seemingly unassuming that many people, even in Boston, had no sense of what he had accomplished. They also did not know the subtlety of his power.

Currier was trained as both an engineer and a lawyer, then entered politics, serving in both the state House of Representatives and the state Senate. Like Joe's father, he found he preferred the power of the back room to being in public office. He went into an unofficial partnership with several men who acted as lobbyists and dealmakers for some of the wealthiest men in the area. Although a Democrat, Currier had the sense to team with Republican boss Charlie Innes, along with Jakey Ward-well, a man who represented banking, insurance, and railroad interests. The fourth man in the group was Arthur Russell, vice president of the New Haven Railroad. Together they represented businesses that made Boston famous. They also worked with young politicians and rising businessmen, seducing them with lavish dinners, political favors, and any-thing else necessary to gain their loyalty. Then they helped them rise in power, calling in favors as needed.

Currier also understood how to live well, a lifestyle Joe would eventually emulate. Currier married the famous Shakespearean actress Marie Burroughs, then built a home for her in New Hampshire. The couple also lived at 65 Mount Vernon Street on Beacon Hill, a home so large that there was a full ballroom on the top floor. The residences enabled them to lavishly entertain the rich and powerful, including presidents William Howard Taft and Calvin Coolidge. They also enabled Currier to have relations with a number of beautiful women, an adulterous life that only a few of his closest friends knew existed.

Currier helped Joe Kennedy get a position on the Massachusetts Electric Company. The attorney had connections with both James Curley and Martin Lomasney. Currier knew he could enhance his power through favors that would be owed if he added the man who was the son of Pat Kennedy and son-in-law of Honey Fitz to the list of people he had helped. There might never be a use for young Kennedy, but if there were, a favor would be granted to eliminate the favor owed. What Currier did not expect was to claim Joe's personal indebtedness when Currier kept Kennedy out of military service.

Joe Kennedy realized that the United States was going to become involved with the impending war in Europe at the same time as most American youths—with the 1915 German sinking of the passenger ship *Lusitania*. It was an act of war against noncombatants, and it was followed by the creation of a four-week civilian training camp to prepare citizens who might need to become soldiers. The camp, in Plattsburgh, New York, was under the command of Harvard graduate and career military man General Leonard Wood.

The first training camp had 1,200 men. They were not on active duty, nor were they comfortable with just a civilian status. This was a way to be one step ahead of world events, almost-trained soldiers who could move more comfortably into boot camp and a leadership position when war finally arrived. Most came from moneyed backgrounds, and a third, like General Wood, were Harvard graduates. They paid their own way but trained in the manner of professional soldiers. Many of Joe's former classmates attended the camp. Joe did not.

Both the federal government and the youth of the nation liked the idea of being prepared for battle. A dozen camps similar to the one

General Wood ran were developed the following year, with 16,000 men participating. They did not realize the full scope and horror of the war until the British engaged in the Battle of the Somme. It was only when word of the results of that 1916 battle made its way back to this nation that the public learned that just 50,000 men out of the 110,000 combatants survived the attack against the German lines.

The war that was unfolding was the last of the so-called noble wars of history. It was the last war that would be almost exclusively waged on the ground. It was the last war in which men would throw themselves against one another in human waves that left thousands dead, wounded, or disabled for life. Many youth were still convinced that such sacrifice was an important test of manhood. No one enlisted to die, but many enlisted to see if they could handle the rigors of combat for the glory of their nation. It was "the war to end all wars," and a victory for the forces of good would save future generations from enduring such slaughter. Or so many of the young men fantasized.

Joe Kennedy, by contrast, did not want to die. He did not want to wear the uniform of his nation. He did not want to test his bravery. He did not want to join his former classmates and friends in what many thought would be a great adventure. He just wanted to make enough money to be a millionaire by the time he was thirty-five, and real life was throwing him off schedule. Fortunately there was one more favor his father-in-law could do for him.

Rose did not realize that Joe Kennedy was a draft dodger. She had become pregnant with their second child, John Fitzgerald "Jack" Kennedy, who was born on May 29, 1917, and undoubtedly she saw her husband as a man who was torn by a sense of duty for his country and the demands of working in business to help his growing family. It would be the kind of moral dilemma her church teachings would tolerate. She remained too much in love to sense the weaknesses that would forever drive him to successes he never could enjoy.

One each of Rose's brothers and sisters heeded the call to serve. Seventeen-year-old Eunice Fitzgerald joined the Red Cross, spending her days helping the organization prepare to give assistance and her evenings at the Red Cross facility on the Boston Common. The latter was a variation of the type of work for which the United Service Organization (USO) would become known one generation later. The young men of the city who were preparing to fight in Europe could come by to talk, dance, sing, and eat with young ladies who had been their neighbors, classmates, or friends.

Tom Fitzgerald enlisted with the American Expeditionary Forces, and all of Joe's friends from Harvard enlisted, including those with young families such as his own. The Harvard men took officer training in Plattsburgh, New York, the same location where many went to General Wood's preinduction camp, and looked forward to leading the troops to victory.

It is not known how Honey Fitz felt about his son-in-law's failure to try to serve the country any more than it is known how he felt about his son risking his life abroad. What is certain is that when he realized that Joe did not want to go to war and Rose was happiest with him at home, he called in a favor.

It was 1914 when John Fitzgerald, no longer mayor but still politically powerful, went to the wealthy Charles Schwab, the head of Pennsylvania's Bethlehem Steel Corporation, to convince him to buy the Fore River Shipyard in Quincy, Massachusetts. Fore River employed a large number of men who were skilled shipbuilders, some living in Boston and others in Quincy. The economy was down, and many were out of work. There was talk that Fore River would close entirely, creating an economic recession that would seriously damage the region's economy. However, Honey Fitz recognized that war was imminent, and when it came, Fore River would be extremely profitable for the new owner.

Schwab understood. He saw that most of the current shipbuilding was being done in the nearby Boston Navy Yard. More men were employed, and wages were higher. However, Boston had little room to expand production. By buying Fore River, he was guaranteed to make large sums of money when the war effort forced full production.

Honey Fitz waited until the orders started coming in and nine thousand men were working full time at Fore River before he approached Schwab with a personal request. His son-in-law needed a job that would keep him out of the military. Could Schwab use a businessman who knew nothing about shipbuilding, the management of large numbers of employees, and tended to be a loner? Schwab felt he could, offering Joe $15,000 a year to be assistant general manager. Joe felt his skills had been recognized with the extremely high salary he was being given. Schwab felt that the money was a payback to Honey Fitz, and a small one at that, given the profits he was beginning to make. If Joe could actually handle himself effectively, so much the better, though Schwab had no false hopes.

There was already trouble at Fore River when Joe arrived. To keep the workers happy during the period when there was little work, the men signed a contract agreeing to work for low wages until business improved. Then their wages would be raised to match the higher-paying amount provided by the Boston Navy Yard.

The money was expected to begin to be paid on October 15, 1917, at the same time Joe arrived. It was a period of full employment and seemingly unlimited work to build ships for war, and the men knew the additional money was available. However, Schwab and his management team ignored the agreement, paying the men their previous lower scale. Five thousand of the workers went on strike, and Joe was told to handle the matter.

Ruthlessness had worked for Joe when he was in real estate, and he saw no reason not to use a hard-line approach. The shipbuilding jobs were draft-exempt. Joe told the men he would fire the strikers and replace them with other men from the community who would be glad to have work that would keep them from the front lines while feeding their families. The union was livid, as was the U.S. government. Joe was willing not only to endanger the livelihood of a community of skilled workers, he also was openly speaking as though everyone shared his lack of patriotism and honor. Assistant Secretary of the Navy Franklin D. Roosevelt was sent to Fore River to talk with the union organizers.

Roosevelt understood what Kennedy did not. First, any delays in meeting the war needs endangered the nation. Second, any wholesale firing would eliminate the most skilled among the available workers. New men could be hired, but they would have to be trained. There would be a period when they would make mistakes more experienced men would not. They would be slower in production as they tried to master unfamiliar skills. There could not be a labor problem, and there certainly could not be wholesale firing of more than half the men.

Equally important, the workers understood that they were not draft dodgers. Their skills were more valuable on the home front. Most of the workers, if of appropriate age, would have enlisted had they not known the critical nature of their work.

"There is probably no one plant in the Country whose continuous operation is more important to the success of this Country in the war, than that at Fore River. As a patriotic duty the Department urges both sides to sink all minor differences and to get together for the sake of the success of our Country in this war at once," Roosevelt said. Then, privately, he told the union that they were right. There was a signed contract that had been violated by not providing the pay increase.

Schwab had no intention of letting the assistant secretary of the navy be angry with him. Instead he demoted Kennedy to a job with little responsibility and no supervisory duties. Since he wasn't one of the men who actually built the ships, the loss of job status (with no decrease in pay) led to Joe's losing his draft deferment.

Joe refused to go without a fight. He learned that there was a certain amount of war profiteering taking place in the shipyard. The money was being taken by or going through Joseph Powell, the vice president of Bethlehem Steel. Joe went to him and explained that either Powell would write a letter to his draft board, assuring the men that Kennedy was performing a critical wartime service for the nation, or Joe would reveal the secret. Powell immediately contacted a powerful friend, Emergency Fleet Corporation's Industrial Service Department chief Meyer Bloomfield, to intercede with District 5 Board on behalf of Joe. The telegram, sent February 25, 1918, stated:

MR. KENNEDY WHO IS ASSISTANT GENERAL MANAGER OF FORE RIVER PLANT TELLS ME THAT HE HAS BEEN PLACED IN CLASS I OF THE DRAFT IN SPITE OF MY PERSONAL APPEAL TO THE BOARD STOP THERE ARE NOT OVER SIX MEN IN THIS ESTABLISHMENT WHOSE LOSS AT THIS TIME WOULD BE FELT AS MUCH AS KENNEDY'S AND FOR HIM TO BE PUT IN CLASS I IS INEXCUSABLE FROM ANY POINT OF VIEW STOP WHAT CAN YOU DO TO HELP US OUT STOP[1]

The ruse worked. Joe Kennedy remained.[2]

Based on surviving documentation, Kennedy may have become a "hero" in the draft board's files, but he was of limited value in the plant. The greatest surviving documentation of the time is related to the plant baseball team and how it was doing in competition with other teams in related industries. There were many professional ballplayers who were of an age to work in wartime industries rather than going into battle—men such as Babe Ruth and Shoeless Joe Jackson—that the competition among amateur teams could be fierce. Here Joe was in his element, and much of his most important work involved organizing, restructuring, and finding training time for the ball team.

The one incident that would forever outrage Joe Kennedy had to do with what must be considered rather slipshod original work on a pair of destroyers that had been built for Argentina well before the war. There are several versions of the story as it relates to the original payment for the ships by the Argentine government. All that is certain is that by the time Joe was working at Fore River, the two ships had been rather massively repaired to correct problems that should not have occurred so early in the lives of the vessels.

The Argentine government said that it should not have to pay for the work that was completed, since it should not have had to be done in the first place. Charles Schwab did not argue about whether the needed repairs had had to be made considerably earlier than normal use should have required. He just said that Joe Kennedy should tell the Argentine government the ships would not leave the shipyard without payment.

Once again Franklin Roosevelt was outraged. Argentina needed to remain as strong a military power as possible. It also needed to feel itself aligned with the United States. He told the Fore River personnel to release the two ships. He would handle the issue of payment later.

Joe was constantly frustrated by his failures. At the height of the war production, the interrelated steel and shipbuilding businesses were breaking all records for Charles Schwab. Thirty-six destroyers were produced in twenty-seven months; submarines were being made faster than once thought possible. So many workers were earning large incomes that Joe opened the Victory Lunchroom, a cafeteria that put additional money in his own pocket. It was built as Joe arranged for housing for the area workforce that eventually reached twenty-two thousand. However, there was a difference between making money and overseeing aspects of the newly booming economy, and meeting the business interests of his employer.

Assistant Secretary of the Navy Franklin Roosevelt tried to find a compromise, but none of the suggestions involved immediate payment. He adamantly refused all the arguments Joe made on behalf of Schwab. Instead of impressing his boss with his competence and skill as a negotiator, he was in tears, he recalled years later, as he left Roosevelt's office. Then he had to watch helplessly as tugboats filled with armed U.S. marines took the vessels from the shipyard.

In the midst of Joe's work at the shipyards and his desperate effort to once again win the approval of a wealthy, powerful Brahmin, Rose again gave birth. This time the child was a daughter, Rose Marie "Rosemary" Kennedy. She, like her older brother Jack, would become the focus of Kennedy family myth.

Jack had been born with a number of problems, including a bad back that would prove painfully disabling his entire life. He would technically be unfit for military service and eventually be so ill that, in the White House, his personal physician made clear to the family that he would not live to complete his second term. But all that was in the future. Joe knew that his second child was not as vigorous as the first.

Rosemary was the child whose beauty and independence exceeded that of her sisters, and whose rebellious streak reminded Joe of his wife when she was young. Bright, personable, and mature enough to meet Queen Elizabeth the year she became a debutante, she was also dyslexic. She had difficulty learning to read, a problem that was readily corrected as an older teen when she was able to study in England with teachers well versed in her special needs.

Many years later, the family required yet another myth. Joe feared the truth, feared being little more than an ordinary man with a ruthless streak, a knack for business, and the desire to have his family become honored as much for their cleverly disguised failings as for their legitimate successes.

Rose was more honest, but only within the family. She shared Joe's lies, reinforcing them with details that did not always match her own earlier version of "the truth." That was why she would one day explain that Rosemary had been damaged at birth.

The story that would be told to fuel the new myth was that Rose knew the baby was coming when her obstetrician, Dr. Good, was not able to rush to her side. The year was 1918, and a massive epidemic of influenza was ravishing the nation. Joe was exhausted because the shipyard was always shorthanded with men off the job because of illness, men dying from illness, and men trying desperately to work when so sick that they occasionally collapsed on the job. Dr. Good was handling anyone in need and could not provide a wealthy young mother with special attention prior to childbirth.

A nurse was in attendance. She was trained in childbirth, and the procedure was simple in almost every instance. Certainly Rosemary's delivery was routine. However, according to Kennedy family myth, Rose was under orders to wait for the doctor before having the baby. The doctor was paid his high fee only if he was present. The nurse's pay would have been much lower. As she later explained to her personal assistant, Barbara Gibson, "the nurse held my legs together [to stop the birth until the doctor arrived], and we always thought that was the reason for Rosemary's retardation."[3]

Eunice Kennedy Shriver later contradicted her mother's statement. She told author Larry Leamer that the birth story was speculation. The family had no idea why Rosemary was retarded. What no one would admit was that she was perfectly normal except for the dyslexia, a common problem well understood today. Numerous highly successful individuals, from business executives to screenwriters, have the same problem. The only reason for the retardation was the surgery Joe would insist she have when she reached young womanhood.[4]

Rosemary quickly displayed one additional trait that upset Joe Kennedy. He spent little time with his children. At least from the time Rosemary was born, he increasingly was having sexual affairs. His business had often kept him away from home until extremely late at night, and during problems at the shipyard, Joe might have to sleep in his office for two or three days. Rose had adjusted to Joe's coming into the house either long after she had gone to sleep or finding that he was too tired to do anything but rest. Since she did not expect regular sex, especially during her pregnancies, she did not grow suspicious that anything was wrong.

It was shortly after Rosemary's birth that Rose discovered Joe's adultery. Exactly how and when are uncertain, but their relationship became strained after that. However, as a Child of Mary and follower of the Sacred Heart ideals she was taught, she never let on to Joe. She never denied him the marital bed except when trying to keep him at maximum alertness for business. So far as he was concerned, nothing changed.

The children had far less attention from Joe than did Rose. Desperate to please him, to get whatever attention he might provide, they respected his demands to be competitive. They learned that they were expected to be aggressive in all activities, whether against strangers, friends, or family members. It was a ridiculous idea, especially the encouragement of competition within the family where their age differences made them inherently unequal. As a result, there developed both a fierce loyalty to one another when faced with outside attack and a sibling rivalry that would eventually lead to what was almost certainly the wartime suicide of Joe Jr.

Unfortunately for her future, Rosemary was the one child who could not be manipulated, who did not care about her father's family values.

Rosemary was always the independent Kennedy. She was the dreamer, the loner, the child most likely to go adventuring on her own. She could ignore her parents' wishes and advice, never worrying about possible consequences.

This lack of competitiveness was a factor in Rosemary's being slower to develop than the other children. However, this was a judgment call made by parents whose other children would do anything to gain Joe's approval. Neither Rose nor Joe ever compared Rosemary's progress growing up with children from other families. "Normal" children did not matter. Joe was developing a concept of how a Kennedy was to behave.

On those rare occasions when they were all in church together, Kennedys would be more pious than any other family. On the playing field they would be more aggressive, willing to win at all cost. In politics they would use anyone who might help their cause. And when their limitations might become obvious if they tried too hard, he found men who could be bought to shape the family "history." Such men would write his books and those of his sons. They would tell Kennedy myth as truth. And whenever a Kennedy was still rejected, the family would believe that it was the result of jealousy over their superiority, not a reflection of their inadequacies.

Rose Kennedy would prove little better than her husband in this regard. She treated Rosemary as she would any firstborn daughter of the founder of the Ace of Clubs. Rosemary would learn the basics for acquiring knowledge no matter how hard Rose had to work to battle against the not-yet-understood dyslexia. "Oh, I worked so hard with her to get her to read and write," she later told her assistant Barbara Gibson. "The reason my handwriting looks as though it's partially printing was so that she could imitate it."[5]

The education process would be difficult, but all other aspects of raising her daughter to be a leader would not. Rosemary would travel the world in the two decades of normal life Joe allowed her. She would be presented to the queen of England. She would chaperone her younger sisters as appropriate. And the only frustration for either parent was that her eventual institutionalization meant that they had wasted their time working with her growing up.

That was why Rosemary would one day have to be called retarded from birth. That was why her dyslexia was a weakness not to be revealed, even though Nelson Rockefeller rose to great heights in business and politics, ultimately becoming vice president of the United States, while admitting to his own fight with dyslexia.

A mere Rockefeller could have dyslexia; a Kennedy could not.

7

ADJUSTING TO PEACETIME

WAR HAS ALWAYS BEEN GOOD FOR THE ECONOMY. THERE ARE HIGH-paying jobs in war-related industries, extensive overtime, and new oppor-tunities for businesses that support the workers. Restaurants, automotive repair businesses, laundries, apartment owners, and others all experience demand that is unprecedented in peacetime. Civilians have an easy time finding jobs, yet the diversion of various materials for use in the war effort limits the availability of many consumer goods. Personal savings increase, and when the troops at last return home, the desire to buy the latest clothing and labor-saving devices and to experience new forms of entertainment result in a postwar boom for retailing.

The shipbuilding industry was one of the few exceptions to the new prosperity that followed the Great War. It was a fate Joe Kennedy and others at Fore River had anticipated and tried to avoid.

As the war was ending, the shipyard was tooled up to handle vessels designed to hunt down and kill the enemy. There would be a glut of such ships when the fighting stopped, just as there was already a surplus of serviceable cargo ships, the vessels needed in peacetime. Any business that required a vessel to move freight could find one at a reasonable price or could continue using its existing corporate fleet.

At first Joe hoped he might sell the services of Fore River to poten-tial peacetime users despite his own inability to discern a meaningful market. His one weakness as an entrepreneur was his tendency to get comfortable within one industry. He would hesitate to change, even when the times made such change essential. That was when he needed an outsider to jump-start his career.

The Fore River job may have been a temporary opportunity to avoid serving in the military, but when the war was over, Kennedy could not face leaving. That was why he eventually made an appointment with broker Galen Stone in the hope that there still might be a chance to bring peacetime work into Fore River so he could retain his position.

Stone, in partnership with Charles Hayden, had achieved the wealth and influence that Joe Kennedy coveted. Each recognized the weaknesses within himself and the strength within his partner. Each recognized that together they could achieve success in ways that neither would be able to do on his own.

Charles Hayden was a man who loved the action of business, the buying, selling, and manipulation of companies, whether running them, investing in them, or both. Everything was a challenge to be surmounted. Everything had a potential for greater wealth.

Galen Stone was a writer who looked at business with the emotional distance required of his profession. Upon arriving in Boston in the 1880s, Stone worked first for the *Commercial Bulletin* and then for the *Boston Advertiser.* Having no stake in the businesses or the business community itself, he learned to analyze companies, their products, their marketing, and their competition. He saw what made one company successful and a rival fail to hold its own. He could be coldly objective, yet he also understood the back room, where business and politics intertwined.

Hayden, Stone, and Company was formed in 1892. Each man wanted to utilize the skills of the other, though they decided that it was most practical for them to work from two different cities. Boston was no longer at the center of the American financial universe. Banking, insurance, the stock market, numerous corporate headquarters, and the like were on the move to New York City. Boston still had old money and too many businesses to ignore. By having Stone stay in Massachusetts and Hayden operate from New York, they could commute by train to confer as needed while always being available for any opportunities that might come along. Unfortunately for the longtime friends, the separation exaggerated the differences in their personalities, and they gradually found themselves acting increasingly autonomously.

Galen Stone had always been drawn to aggressive men in business. He saw in them a trait that he lacked. They could move decisively, instinctively, and usually correctly in a fraction of the time that he himself would take. Stone was the analyst, the man who needed to know everything to write a story during his days as a reporter, and still was uncomfortable if he did not have all the details to make a reasoned decision.

What went unsaid as Hayden, Stone became respected not only for its ability to invest in new businesses, helping it to great success, but also for its stock market purchases, was that Stone was a man for whom laws would be written. He was a variation of an insider trader, the type of man who gets rich through knowledge others are unable to obtain. All other stockholders were at a disadvantage, especially the small buyer who was becoming increasingly active in the years leading up to what would become the Great Depression.

Stone used all his reporter's training to gain contacts in businesses in which he was interested or where he already had an investment. Then he would learn where the business was headed. For example, if a company was introducing a new product line, Stone would learn from marketing personnel if there were large orders pending or if the company was discovering that no one cared about the idea the owners thought would make them rich. Then he would buy stock if the company was going to prosper and quietly arrange to sell his stock if he thought the price was going to drop. More important, he did not share this information with the majority of his customers, encouraging them to buy what later would prove to be his own holdings, driving up the market value just before the problem was revealed and the stock price drastically declined.

Stock market manipulation through the use of still-secret corporate knowledge was not yet illegal, though the public did not understand how the game was played and how their holdings were being endangered. Eventually such insider trading would become illegal, but stock manipulation was merely unethical, a game a "gentleman" did not play, when Joe decided to make an appointment to see Galen Stone.

Joe Kennedy probably reminded Galen Stone of his longtime friend and business partner. Joe was familiar with Stone both because of his fame and because his father-in-law regularly worked with the company. Honey Fitz may have been run out of politics but not out of backroom deals. He knew everyone who mattered in Massachusetts. He knew who had behind-the-scenes power. He knew who could make deals and what value they would place on them. He also knew that most business executives expected to pay a price for access, for contracts, and for anything else that brought them profit. Sometimes this was in the form of a kickback. Sometimes this meant giving unqualified or underqualified men jobs. Sometimes this meant the use of ghost employees. Whatever the case, Honey Fitz still could act as a broker of information, access, power, and jobs, and he knew Galen Stone quite well.

Joe Kennedy approached Stone's Boston office in what Kennedy realized was a last-chance effort to make Fore River have postwar business and keep his own job. Galen Stone, in addition to his firm's work, was chairman of the Atlantic Gulf and West Indies Steamship Line. Joe hoped he would need new vessels now that the war was over, though a little research on his part would have revealed that more ships were as unnecessary for Stone's fleet as they were for every other company of any size.

Galen Stone's secretary arranged a fifteen-minute appointment, then canceled it at the last minute because Stone decided to go to New York to meet with his partner, Charles Hayden. Stone was already in a cab on his way to the train station when the secretary informed Joe that he was not important enough for Stone to delay his commute.

Kennedy, desperate and again stung by rejection, rushed outside and took a cab to the train station. The Boston to New York train still had seats, so he bought himself a ticket, boarded, and walked the cars until he found Stone. Then he sat down next to him, planning to pitch his business during the four-hour ride.

Stone enjoyed the nerve of Kennedy. The youth, like Hayden, was a natural salesman, especially since Kennedy had a product no one wanted. Bemused at the end of the trip, he left Joe at the station with neither an order for Fore River nor any hope of getting one.

Discouraged, Joe returned home, where Honey Fitz again interceded. Joe had been a failure in the shipbuilding business, but he could genuinely say he had been an administrator. He was a hustler and knowledgeable about business and banking. Honey Fitz quietly worked with men who both knew Galen Stone and owed him favors—Guy Currier and Frederick "Buck" Dumaine, treasurer of a large cotton mill operation—to talk with Stone about hiring Joe to work in the stock brokerage division of the company.

Stone went along with the hiring of Kennedy. In July 1919 Joe began work as a broker to gain an understanding of the base business, then was moved to manager of the Boston office's stock market at a salary of $10,000 a year.

Hayden was furious about the hiring. Joe may have impressed his partner with the aggressiveness he showed in taking the Boston to New York train, but he was inexperienced. Hayden, Stone was a manipulator of the market, not just a company that bought and sold as orders came in.

Hayden was correct about Joe Kennedy's inexperience. What he did not realize was how frightened Joe had become. He could not accept the fact that most of his success had come through the hard work or intervention of others. The only successful business he had created and run was the cafeteria he developed to feed the instant city of workers created through wartime hiring. He was ready to admit defeat, not in the sense of discussing his failures but in being willing to learn from a man he was convinced was an innovator.

Stone taught Kennedy two important lessons almost from the start. The first was to know any business in which you were likely to invest.

When he financed a new company, gaining a position on its board and taking a percentage of the profits, he made certain he did more than read a prospectus. He went to the business and talked with the lowest-level employees, the men who understood what was happening day to day and often had greater insight than the men at the top. He treated every employee with respect, and once he was involved with a company, he routinely walked among the workers, talking with them. They quickly saw that he wanted to learn what they were doing, where they were successful, and where they were frustrated. He could see the future in their words, and he never made a mistake with those investments.

By contrast, the stock market was a game that could be manipulated only so far. There were always forces outside of any single individual's control that could enable you to make or lose a fortune on any given day.

The most blatant example was with changes in postwar America. Charles Schwab was warning all his friends to invest in nothing. There would be fallout with the change from wartime to a peacetime economy. There would be a demand for consumer goods, but there also would be a tremendous loss of jobs. No one could safely predict consumer spending.

Stone did not listen to Schwab. Stone's income-tax bill for 1919, a year when taxation was extremely low, reached $1.5 million. The following year, when Stone continued to work the market, he paid no income taxes. He was still an extremely rich man, but the market prevented him from amassing further wealth. However, as he pointed out to Joe, he was not worried. He invested in carefully selected stocks in companies he well understood. He knew that by holding the stocks for the long term, he would eventually profit beyond what was possible with any other investment he might make. He continued to make quick deals from insider information over the years, but he considered that a separate activity from serious investment.

Joe Kennedy had amassed just enough money that he decided to impress his new employer by taking advantage of a tip. Buck Dumaine, the man Honey Fitz had asked to help his son-in-law get the Stone job, was the treasurer of Amoskeag Mills in New Hampshire. Joe heard from someone who allegedly knew Dumaine well that the Amoskeag Mills stock was about to split four to one. This meant that every share Joe bought before the news was made public would result in his owning four shares in the same company after the split was declared.

Kennedy fancied himself a young version of Stone, utilizing insider information to make his killing. He bought as many shares as he could afford for $160 each, the current selling price. Within days the stock had dropped to $80 a share. As Joe again felt foolish for losing half his money while trying to impress yet another wealthy Brahmin, he met Buck, who laughed at him for trying to manipulate his wealth. There was no plan for a stock split of any type.

Fearing the stock loss could be greater than he had already endured, Joe sold what had become half-price shares. Then the stock split as the rumor had indicated.

Joe had been suckered. Worse, in his mind, was the fact that Dumaine had taken the action because he could. Joe Kennedy would later claim it was the last time he ever tried to take advantage of insider information, another of the Kennedy Wall Street myths. He would always use all opportunities to make money, regardless of ethics.

It was from his substantial loss, as well as from Galen Stone's guidance, that Joe Kennedy began to look at interrelated businesses. This was a period in business history when businesses had not yet discovered the success possible from merging companies that routinely sold to one another. Today a manufacturing company might also own businesses that make the parts needed for product assembly, the warehouse operations needed for storage, the shipping companies used to transport the merchandise, and sometimes even the retail operation. Each business can help reduce the cost of the parent company's products, or the businesses can be spun off and sold for their assets when cash flow warrants.

Henry Ford had just started thinking about integrating businesses when Joe was looking to recover his lost money. Ford was best known as an automobile manufacturer, but he also owned steel mills to make the raw product. He realized that every ton of coal he used for his blast furnaces meant a profit for someone else. He decided to buy the Pond Creek Coal Company to reduce his eventual expenses.

Galen Stone was a visionary who had invested in Pond Creek and was chairman of the board before its purchase by Ford was a consideration. He was majority stockholder and was happy to make a profit by selling his shares to Ford. When the deal was about to be completed, he told Joe Kennedy to buy as many of the outstanding Pond Creek Coal Company shares as he could afford. He told other friends as well, wanting all of them to benefit.

Kennedy realized that there were subtle differences in insider trading. He had acted upon a rumor that anyone could have started to manipulate the price of stock. It was a technique he would use himself, and one that would eventually be appropriated by "short" buyers. These were investors who sold stock they did not own, knowing that the law allowed them a week to give the shares to the buyer. During that week they would spread whatever rumors they could to assure that the public lost faith in the company. Shares would be sold, the price would drop, and the short seller would buy the same number of shares he had sold the week before. His profit would be the difference between the "sell" price he had received and the "buy" price he paid after the stock dropped.

The Ford deal was a simple transaction. The business arrangement was completed. It just had not been announced. The men Galen Stone tipped off quietly acquired as many shares in Pond Creek as they could afford at the selling price of $16 a share (Joe borrowed enough money to buy fifteen thousand shares). Then, when the purchase arrangement was announced, the outstanding stock shares rose in price to $45 each. Joe did not wait to see if the price would rise still further. He sold, making a profit of $29 a share.

There was another business opportunity that presented itself to both Joe Kennedy and his father. This was the Volstead Act, which went into effect at midnight on January 16, 1920, the same year that Joe and Rose were prosperous enough to move to a twelve-room house on Naples Road in Brookline.

Prohibition of alcohol was an odd experiment in forced social change. The use of alcohol had always been limited in the United States. Orthodox, Conservative, and some Reform Jews used wine with their meals, especially the seder, which celebrated Passover. This was also true to a lesser degree among those Christians who recognized the Jewish heritage of the religion and knew that the Last Supper of Jesus was a seder meal. However, the idea was to use the alcohol in moderation. The idea of drinking for recreation with the thought of getting drunk went against the culture. It was considered wrong to lose control.

Other groups used alcohol as part of their social fabric. This was especially true of the immigrant Italian workers in Chicago and the immigrant Irish workers in Boston. Saloons and pubs were places to talk, to complain, to be among friends who shared your hardships and joys. Again, while alcoholism was frequently a problem, the alcohol usually was enjoyed slowly and in moderation, the main attraction of the bars being the camaraderie of people often oppressed or held in disdain by the elite of the community.

Alcohol use at parties was the prerogative of the wealthy. Again, while there were abusers, most drinkers handled their drinking in moderation. There was status to being able to buy what was suddenly illegal.

Prohibition changed everything. The youthful rebellion of the 1920s, a backlash against the staid values of Queen Victoria's era, led to the desire for excess as a way of blatantly defying parental values. Women went in public without escorts, and many sought jobs they desired for self-esteem, not income. A sexual revolution was taking place with the creation of sensual dances and new ways to look at marriage.

Drinking was also in transition. In upscale portions of major cities and in smaller communities across the nation, alcohol was available almost exclusively in restaurants prior to Prohibition. The major exceptions were sections with immigrant groups who used bars and pubs as social centers.

Few people, including law enforcement officers, thought of bootlegging as a serious crime. In New York City, there were fifteen thousand legal locations for obtaining alcoholic beverages before the Volstead Act went into effect. After Prohibition was the law, thirty-two thousand speakeasies were selling liquor. Again, suppliers were critical.

And in Boston, Joe Kennedy and his father understood the new opportunity for making money. They had established sources for liquor coming from Canada and other parts of the world. They had established clients. They understood the ongoing demand from the neighborhood bars where the locals held enough political clout so that limited payoffs to city officials and law enforcement would allow their operations to continue. And they saw that in wealthy, Protestant society the serving of alcohol was about to become a status symbol. That was why contacts were made and men such as Al Capone began working with Kennedy and others to handle the deliveries.

In the years to come, the Kennedy family would try to deny that Joe was a bootlegger. However, it is not known if the denial was based on their not being comfortable with some of the earliest family money coming from criminal activity or if it was because the mythic image of such men was that of violent, machine-gun-toting criminals killing rivals without conscience. Murder was a part of the business, but rarely for either the men at the top or those who tracked them down.

It was into this world, the one without violence to outsiders, that Joe Kennedy moved quietly. He didn't personally deliver the liquor. He didn't check on the daily operations of the various nightclub owners. He took orders and found ways to import whatever he could to move through the system run by others. For example, he was a close friend of William Randolph Hearst and Hearst's mistress Marion Davies whom he visited in their castle in San Simeon. Hearst never drank, a trait he shared with Joe. Marion and most of Hearst's guests enjoyed alcohol, as Joe well knew.

Each time Joe was with Marion, she would give him a liquor order. Joe would obtain the bottles, usually through his Canadian sources, and then have them dropped at a point where Capone's men would retrieve them. Capone's men would then deliver to their various clients throughout the United States.

Marion hid the bottles in various parts of the first floor of the house. Guests were served while Hearst was changing into evening clothes in his upstairs bedroom. The guests also knew where some of the bottles were hidden should they want an additional drink during the evening. And the original source was always Joe Kennedy.

What is less certain is how Joe met Marion and Hearst. This was before Joe entered the movie business. He may have known Marion from her days on Broadway. The dating he did while in Harvard had never stopped, and it may be through the women he knew in the entertainment field that he encountered Davies.

More likely Joe came to know Hearst through the growing newspaper coverage he received. The Hearst papers found Joe to be good copy, and Hearst routinely sought out men who were of growing importance, as well as those colorful characters he enjoyed having around. His parties were famous for having everyone from actors to physicians, a disparate gathering that made them lively and a desired invitation if you were anywhere on the West Coast. Hearst went so far as to run limousines from Los Angeles to San Francisco for those guests who worked in Hollywood or were visiting there on business.

There was also legal alcohol during Prohibition, and Joe may have been a part of that world as well. Medicine was limited in 1920. Hospitals were places people feared because they often were the resting places of last resort for the terminally ill. The medicines that treated the afflictions of those days were limited and often no better than Coca-Cola syrup for upset stomachs, and alcohol for most other things. Aspirin had been in common use for two decades, though little else. Surgical procedures, though safer than in the past because of the knowledge of antisepsis, were little different from what the Roman doctors were attempting in the first century A.D. As a result, doctors often prescribed alcohol in one form or another, and pharmacists could legally both stock and sell what would be illegal elsewhere. Naturally, many men and women attempted to convince their physicians that they were afflicted with whatever liquor might "cure," and many doctors could be bribed to prescribe liquor "just in case" it would help.

Author Laurence Leamer[1] learned from Christopher Kennedy, one of Joe's grandsons, that an audit of Joe's estate had been conducted in the early 1990s. Christopher was quoted as saying, "He [the Wharton M.B.A. auditor] transcribed to the dollar every source of income and use of cash, and every dollar is accounted for." The implication is that Joe Kennedy could not have been a bootlegger. Of course, the fact that Joe was unlikely to maintain publicly available records concerning criminal activities seems to have been overlooked by Christopher.

The family also has not been able to argue with the memories of the men present at the tenth reunion of Joe's Harvard graduating class. Joe arranged to obtain Canadian liquor through his father's supplier. The class contributed to the cost—$302 for 26½ gallons of liquor.

It is not known what Joe expected to gain from supplying the liquor. Alcohol was often a part of Irish jokes, the drinking one of the stereotypes. It would seem that Joe was simply encouraging hate. At the same time, he was one of the more financially successful members of his class, and at least one of his classmates sought a loan from Columbia Trust, Joe seemingly delighting in making certain his classmate had adequate collateral. Joe enjoyed reminding the young Brahmin that he, Kennedy, was more successful than someone he perceived as the higher-born man.

Most likely Joe supplied the alcohol both because he could and because his classmates would be beholden to him. There would come a time when he would need a favor, and since they were already in his debt, the favor would cost Joe nothing.

There have been other sources concerning the bootlegging who have spoken out over the years. Patty Barham was one of the most credible direct witnesses, since her father, a physician, also was Hearst's business partner. Among their joint ventures was the *Los Angeles Herald Examiner* and an insurance company, and Dr. Barham frequently took his daughter to San Simeon gatherings. Mob figures also have discussed this era, such as Owen Madden, who mentioned his bootleg work with Joe to his attorney, and Thomas Jefferson McGinty of Cleveland, whose business concepts eventually were used to plan some of the early Las Vegas casinos.

Bootlegging was profitable, but it was simply one more business venture for Joe. He was not involved on a daily basis. The money was excellent, and aspects of the liquor business would supply the family with large sums of money long after it was again legal. Joe's primary work still was with Galen Stone. Just as Joe had used his work as an assistant bank examiner to learn the banking business, now he used his job in the brokerage house to begin studying new businesses and ways to form them, such as the Ford/Stone transaction. Among these was the motion picture industry, which he first learned about when Max Mitchell of Cosmopolitan Trust Company decided to back one of the new films.

The film industry was still in its infancy in those days. Eastern businessmen owned most of the companies, and many of the productions were being made in the Southwest. The producers ranged from men who had grown up in the "rag trade"—a term used for everything from the buying and selling of scrap fabric material to some phase of manufacturing or retailing clothing—to those who owned theaters and entertainment businesses. The idea of a businessman backing a movie was an oddity, but Mitchell took the risk for a client, a man who had been successful in retailing.

This was a time when the film industry was not yet concentrated in one city or in the hands of a small number of companies. Anyone with adequate money and a script could make a movie using local actors, since all the films were silent. There were several parts of the country where small production companies were churning out film after film, hoping to regularly earn more than they spent. There were also independents that hoped they understood distribution well enough to profit from the showing of what often was a single film. It was for one such company that Mitchell risked $120,000 to shoot, edit, and print for distribution *The Miracle Man*. The investment was a wise one, with the film grossing $3 million.

Mitchell and the producer went into a partnership to produce other movies, certain the industry was a simple one to dominate. They failed to realize that *The Miracle Man* was a rare exception, and the company quickly went bankrupt. They offered Joe Kennedy the business.

Kennedy recognized that he knew nothing about film production, nor did some of the "experts" who, like Mitchell, may only have enjoyed a little luck. What he did understand was business, and while the movies presented a risk, the theaters that showed the product of the emerging industry did not. He formed an investment group and bought the Maine–New Hampshire Theaters, Inc., chain of thirty-one small movie houses. He stayed with a portion of the investment for more than forty years. During that span, twenty-three were sold singly as personal economics necessitated or a better opportunity arose, the remaining eight being retained.

In 1923 Joe also bought a movie house in Stoneham, Massachusetts, near Boston. Then he bought the rights to a number of British films so he could show them in his chain.

Each movie theater owner paid a fee to the distribution firms for the right to show the films they represented. Part of the money went to the distributor and part to the production company. The rental amount was based on the number of theaters in a chain, the seating capacity of each theater, the duration of the showings, and similar details. Joe began to understand the subtleties of the industry, such as the type of films that have the greatest draw and the length of time a film has an appeal in a community. He realized that by understanding the reasons why a movie did well or poorly in each community's theaters, a movie could be written and produced for a specific audience with the reasonable expectation of a predictable return. Movies could be produced for general audiences, but they also could be produced to appeal to a small-town, midwestern U.S. audience, a big-city audience, or whatever else might work. However, at that moment he was not interested in being more involved in the film industry than owning a theater chain.

Joe next turned to both the liquor business, as Prohibition became the law of the land, and the highly lucrative stock market, where the techniques for investment and manipulation he learned from Hayden, Stone would hold him in good stead. That manipulation involved the creation of a pool of seemingly unconnected investors working together to alter the price of a stock in a company that was of little interest to investors, a fairly priced stock that neither rose nor fell. The shareowners tended to hold it for the long term, taking whatever dividends might be paid.

The pool approach involved the increased buying and selling of the shares of the stock in ever-increasing amounts. A pool might be created locally, regionally, or nationally. The Hayden, Stone pool members were in the New England area for easy coordination of purchases. The men would buy and sell among themselves to create the illusion of growing activity in the stock.

Gradually other stockbrokers would notice what was happening and mention the change to their clients. Then outsiders to the pool, unaware of the manipulation, would begin to buy the stock, helping it continue its rise. The fact that it was overvalued by the conservative investment standards of the day meant nothing to the new buyers. They saw a stock on the rise and wanted a piece of the action. Neither they nor their brokers realized the pool was manipulating it until the stock reached a prearranged price ceiling, at which the pool members sold to an eager market. The purchases briefly increased the price still higher, and then the new investors realized there was no further action. The stock began dropping to its original value or lower, and the members of the pool pocketed thousands of dollars in profits.

In those early days of market manipulation there were men who were considered gamblers and those who were deemed speculators. The difference was subtle. Joe considered himself a speculator because he took calculated risks, manipulated the prices himself, and coordinated the selling to assure a likely profit. He had no interest in the companies except as vehicles for making money. If he hurt their business expansion or reduced their ability to operate because of a drop in stock, it was of no concern.

By contrast, a gambler, in Kennedy's mind, was someone who enjoyed the action. A gambler wanted to win. A gambler wanted to make money. But a gambler first sought the excitement of being in the game. He would often stay too long with a "winner," being forced to sell after the price reached its peak and was on the way down. Or he would stay too long with a "loser," watching the price continue to drop after he expected it to hit bottom and start a recovery.

The proof of Joe's self-analysis came in April 1924. That was when he tackled the problem of a short-selling raid on Yellow Cab.

Joe Kennedy was no longer a part of Hayden, Stone, and Company except as a location for his office. Galen Stone had retired in 1922, and though Joe would continue to consult with him, respecting his investment advice, he decided to leave the firm but set up his own office at the same address. He was thirty-four years old and eager for deals. He also returned to the title he felt afforded him the greatest opportunity— Joseph P. Kennedy, banker. And it was in this capacity, coupled with his experience as a broker, that Yellow Cab approached him approximately two years after Joe started his new business.

Kennedy had no interest in Yellow Cab, though he did have a friend named Walter Howey, who apparently had overinvested his limited resources in the company. Howey worked for William Randolph Hearst, traveling from newspaper to newspaper to correct editorial problems and boost circulation through livelier-reading papers as Hearst requested. Howey had formerly worked in Chicago with Charles MacArthur, the husband of actress Helen Hayes. During his tenure in Chicago, Howey had been part of the new breed of newspaperman. He was a man who wanted his staff, less educated than newspeople a generation earlier, to do anything for a sensational story.

One of the reporters who worked for Howey was given $100 to pay for the life story of a death row inmate on his way to be executed. The money was to help the man's family after his death.

The Chicago reporter gained permission to meet with the prisoner. He interviewed him, then suggested that since they had time before the execution, he might want to play a game of cards to get his mind off what he was facing. The man quickly agreed, the reporter suggested a small wager, and then proceeded to win back the money he had paid.

Howey had been thrilled with the story and never reprimanded the reporter. However, MacArthur was so bemused by the incident that he and a friend, Ben Hecht, wrote a play about the paper and the unusual characters who worked there. Howey was the model for the editor, and the reporter was the model for one of the characters who hides a killer from the police until a full story can be obtained. The outrageous comedy was called *The Front Page* and went on to be both a perennially produced play and a series of feature films under a variety of names, including *His Girl Friday*, with Cary Grant playing the Howey character.

Joe met Howey in 1922 when he had been assigned to work in Boston. Hearst wanted new ideas to invigorate his property there, but Howey had made a tactical error by suggesting that the paper stop covering political news. Kennedy explained how the city worked. He showed the editor that political news in Boston was the only news that mattered to many people. Howey returned to the old ways of running the paper, and the two men became friends.

In March 1924 Howey felt himself financially well off with stock in Yellow Cab. The price was averaging $85 a share, and the company was headed by John Hertz, a man whose many ventures included working for newspapers.

A month later, Yellow Cab stock had dropped to $75. It was not a major change, but neither Hertz nor his friend Howey could see any reason for the change. Then came another loss of money, with the stock dropping to $50 a share. It was obviously being manipulated, and if the short sellers did anything more to further cause the price to drop, the company could go out of business.

Hertz understood how the stock market game was played and contacted friends in the business to see where the action in Yellow Cab stock was coming from. The bulk of the action was traced to the New York firm of Block, Maloney, and Company. A livid Hertz went to New York to challenge the brokers, and Howey wanted Joe to meet him there.

Joe loved the challenge he was facing. By then Rose had given birth to five children—Joe, Jack, Rosemary, Kathleen, and Eunice—with a sixth, Patricia, about to be born. She wanted her husband present, but childbirth was both routine and an inconvenience for Joe, who summoned his assistant Eddie Moore and left on the next available train.

The pool idea was perfect to counter the actions of Block, Maloney, and Company. The Yellow Cab stock could be manipulated from a variety of cities without the rival brokerage realizing what was happening until it began climbing again. Joe would tackle the action from a suite in the Waldorf-Astoria, and he would utilize $5 million that Hertz obtained from such friends as William Wrigley and Albert Laker. The former had made his fortune in chewing gum. The latter was a major figure in advertising. They felt confident that they would ultimately profit from the venture, and they did not mind risking their capital.

The Waldorf-Astoria staff provided Joe with a suite customized to include a bank of telephones and a stock ticker, a device used to keep track of the ongoing buying and selling of stock on the New York Stock Exchange. Each day Joe took a sheet of paper and wrote out a pattern of buy-and-sell orders that seemed random in nature but was designed to confuse the short sellers. He sensed that the idea of those who were trying to profit from short selling was to keep the stock dropping below $50 a share. In fact, the stock reached a low of $48 a share as Joe started his maneuverings. On May 9 it would again drop below $50, to $46 a share. But aside from those two incidents, Joe was able to be in control.

Slowly the stock rose over the first day or two, and then began fluctuating. Joe constantly monitored the activity, including the reactive buying and selling of everyone from shorts to the smaller investors. An unprecedented ten thousand shares were traded at the end of April, helping to bring the stock to $62 a share when the market reopened. The May 9 volume was double what had occurred in April, and though the price dropped as noted, it returned to a level above $50, and the shorts abandoned their manipulation.

At the time, no one comprehended what Kennedy had done. The raiders did not realize the effort that had gone into stopping their activity, an important secret, since it kept them from trying again. Officially the market changed because the company changed, the third-quarter 1924 profits being lower than the profits for the same quarter the year before. However, the company *was* profitable, even as the stock fluctuated.

The only questionable aspect of the manipulation was whether Kennedy ever personally profited from his controlled manipulation. Rumor spread that he briefly went against the company he was working to bolster his income as a "tip" for his hard work. While it was in line with Joe's character, and Hertz later wanted nothing further to do with the man who saved his company, Joe was able to assure the return of the funds provided for the manipulation.

8

HOLLYWOOD BECKONS

IT WAS AN ODD LITTLE BRITISH AUTOMOBILE BUSINESS WITH A quirky president whose background was as a blacksmith and wheelwright. Robertson-Cole, a partnership of H. F. Robertson and Rufus S. Cole, were the distributors of the British Rohmer Automobiles in the United States. They also acted as importers and exporters of motion pictures produced by others.

The motion picture side of Robertson-Cole began to dominate the company's business, the result more of good fortune than an understanding of how to be part of the industry. Certain they could become producers as well as distributors, the partners went to the Hollywood Cemetery Corporation and bought some of its unneeded land on Gower Street near Melrose. There they constructed a studio complex that was opened in 1920. Two years later the partners left the company, and Patrick A. Powers, an ex-blacksmith, took over the presidency of what was renamed the Film Booking Office of America (FBO).

Powers, who had the administration building named for himself, understood the movie industry better than his predecessors. Another of his ventures had been creating the Universal Film Manufacturing Company. But he did not understand how to obtain financing, and soon the company was in trouble. Graham's of London, a banking firm, took control of FBO and placed Major H. C. S. Thomson in charge. It cost the company $7 million for the acquisition, and it rapidly proved an error of business judgment. By 1925 the company was going under solely because of management's lack of understanding about financing, a fact that came to the attention of Joe Kennedy. He decided that he could do better because his background gave him an understanding of the one side of the business where the others had failed.

Joe's part ownership of the motion picture theater chain had taught him a harsh lesson about the movie industry. There were several separate businesses interdependent on one another, but it was the distribution of the films where money was made and power was held. The theaters paid to show each movie, the fee based on numerous factors, including the size of the potential audience and whether rights were being bought for a single house or a group of them.

While the movie companies considered all talent to be contract labor, some actors were proving more popular than others. Likewise, while some of the writers and producers thought that elaborate stories, often the cinematic equivalent of "great literature," should be produced, smaller communities delighted in Westerns and other action films. A distribution company could charge a theater more money to rent a movie the theater owner knew would draw a large crowd.

The distributors also were beginning to understand that they could offer a package of films, including some that would not have a large draw, for a price that would be slightly higher than normal for the unpopular work. The theater owners were willing to pay the extra money to assure getting those films they knew would fill the seats.

Joe saw that as a theater owner he was always dependent on the movie studios. Their product was the basis for controlling the business. It was fine to think that the movie companies needed theaters to assure a profit. The reality was that the product controlled the marketplace, and Joe Kennedy wanted to invest where he would have the most control.

The specific problems of the British film company are not known. All that is certain is that Joe Kennedy, working with a consortium of investors who included Guy Currier, Joe's father-in-law John "Honey Fitz" Fitzgerald, Filene's Department Store head Louis E. Kirstein, and Frederick H. Prince, who made his money in railroads, bought the firm for $1 million.

The investment group was the last one Joe would assemble with old Protestant money. Frederick Prince was the son of the last Brahmin mayor of Boston. His father served two terms, then watched as the Irish came to dominate the city.

The mayor's son was actually part of the change that was coming in Boston. He had gone to Harvard, but left after his freshman year to take a job as a stockbroker. In his new job he went to Maine on behalf of a client, examining a small branch railroad as an investment. He then bought the railroad himself. Some say he made the purchase because he recognized the value of the business, and they probably are accurate in their evaluation. Others say that he purchased it for a client without the client's authorization. When the client told the heads of the brokerage house that he had no intention of paying, Prince had to keep it.

Such business serendipity is unlikely, though, especially since Prince ultimately acquired forty-four railroads, the Armour Company, and the Chicago Union Stockyards. The purchase was probably shrewdly calculated, as was his joining the consortium that was buying into a key element of the movie business.

There were numerous changes taking place in the lives of the Kennedys as Joe made his move into the film industry. Bootlegging was a continuous source of money, yet one Joe rarely needed to handle personally. He also did not believe in drinking but was upset that Rose did not use alcohol. "I think it's stupid," Mrs. Kennedy later told her assistant Barbara Gibson. "My husband used to say I was terrible because he made a lot of money from liquor and I never drank any."[1]

Years later, when her children were grown, Rose worried about the staff drinking liquor and didn't want it in the house. She never realized that one of her sons, at least two of her daughters, and one of her daughters-in-law were alcohol abusers. One of her grandchildren eventually died from a drug habit shared with some of his siblings and cousins.

Drinking aside, Rose wanted to be involved with her husband's business life as she had been with her father's political career. Although the children were coming almost one after the other, she hired staff to care for the added burdens of Rosemary being followed by Kathleen in 1920, Eunice Mary in 1921, Patricia in 1924, Robert "Bobby" Francis in 1925, with Jean in 1928 and Edward "Teddy" Moore in 1932. She and Joe moved into larger and larger homes and hired more servants, so she was always free to share a life with her husband, even though he was more comfortable pursuing ventures on his own. Sometimes this was because women were not welcome, sometimes it was because women were too welcome and he didn't want Rose to discover his cheating.

Years later the children would complain about their parents. Joe was more accepted because many of his friends had fathers who were also in business. A man's absence while working long hours meant loneliness, but they understood from their friends that fatherhood was a part-time activity. Their mother's use of surrogate caretakers was quite a different matter. As adults, both Jean and Jack Kennedy would talk about the fact that they themselves were lacking in emotional sensitivity to intimates. The only time they enjoyed physical touch was during sex. And for Jack, at least, there was no connection between sex and commitment. The former was solely biological. The latter was something he never experienced for very long.

Joe's various ventures frequently involved his moving away from the family for prolonged periods of time. Not long after the birth of Joe Jr., Kennedy was wealthy enough to bring Rose and the children on his various prolonged business trips. He never considered the possibility, though. Instead, he isolated Rose, frustrating her to the point where eventually she left him.

Rose's brief separation from her husband occurred in 1920. It was early January. Rose was pregnant with her fourth child, and two of the other three were sick. There was a nursemaid handling the illnesses and a maid caring for the rest of the household chores. Joe was away on a business trip, and Rose had no purpose other than to sit around with a swollen belly, feeling unloved, unwanted, and frustrated by her inability to utilize her many skills. She decided to return to her father's house, though she knew she might be less than welcome there. While her father adored her, and her mother would be glad to see her, Rose's youngest sister, Eunice, for whom she would name one of her children, was dying of tuberculosis. Eunice was still physically active, but her health was obviously declining a little each day, and the doctors explained that she would never recover. Having a runaway bride and four grandchildren suddenly appear on the Fitzgerald doorstep while Eunice was in her last days or weeks was not something the family was certain to desire.

Honey Fitz continued to be a man of energy and wit, but there was sadness all around as well. Still, there seemed to be more life for her in the midst of her parents' dealing with the impending death of her youngest sister than there was in the home she and Joe shared on Beals Street in Brookline.

In another time, in another society, Rose Kennedy would have divorced her husband. She knew he was a philanderer. He did not flaunt his women as yet. He did not come home with someone else's lipstick, his clothing bearing someone else's scent. He did not yet date where other wives would see and talk. He was discreet but not discreet enough. For reasons that have never been recorded, Rose knew that her husband was unfaithful, a situation she could not quite relate with her education about sex and male business success. Because she loved him so much that she denied him sex except for procreation so he could concentrate on his work, she did not comprehend how he could seek women who thought so little of his business needs that they gave him their bodies with what presumably was uncontrolled abandon. A man of his education and business attainments should have remained celibate except when he and his wife were attempting to enlarge their family. The greatest pain came from his straying. The confusion came from why he would act in so cavalier a manner toward his work.

It was Rose's attitude toward society that brought an accommodation between Rose and Joe. The Ace of Clubs was having its annual ball, an event that had been missed during the war. Rose, eight months pregnant, was the organizer, working with Miriam Finnigan, the new president. Rose had experienced enough childbirth to know that there were no serious limitations on her activity before she went into labor. Moreover, the black gown she purchased disguised her pregnancy so the other young women would not criticize her.

Agnes and Eunice also wore elaborate gowns, the three Fitzgerald sisters delighting in what they knew might be the last social event they would ever share. Even Josie Fitzgerald attended, an act that might have been the greatest love she could show her daughters, given both her past and the relatively recent humiliation over the Toodles incident.

Most important, though, was Joe in formal attire. No one knew they were not sharing a bed or even a house at that moment. He was as attentive as any husband, knowing when to quietly move back to give his wife the spotlight.

Later that week, Honey Fitz sat with his daughter to explain the facts of life as he saw them. He had never liked Joe Kennedy. He had been against the marriage. He had seen in Joe a mirror of his own philandering. He had also sensed the youth's coldness and lack of integrity.

Marriage had not changed Joe Kennedy, nor did it guarantee his father-in-law's approval. But a marriage was a commitment everyone had to respect, including Rose and her father. That was why Honey Fitz helped Joe, and Joe was being a good son-in-law when he shared investment opportunities with Fitzgerald. Yet the two men were still at odds, just as Rose was having trouble forgiving what he had done.

Regardless of personal feelings and regrets, a cardinal had sanctified the marriage. Divorce was unthinkable. The bond was sacred even if the couple no longer shared the passion that brought them together. Rose was advised to do whatever would make her life easier, from taking more time for herself to hiring a larger household staff. Joe was wealthy and could afford any luxury his wife desired. She should take advantage of everything the marriage had to offer, fulfill her obligations, and never leave Joe again.

Rose recognized in the life she would lead what the Sisters of the Sacred Heart had trained her to endure. The marriage might be strained, but she would endure. She was wealthy enough to leave the care of her children to others, acting as supervisor of the house with her meticulous records, constantly updated, then placed in card files. She would travel on her own. She would embrace happily what time she and Joe shared where he truly gave himself to her, and she would not deny him the marital bed in the ways they both agreed were "proper." She also would never ask too many questions, because a question could lead to an answer she did not wish to know.

By 1923 Rose and Joe's accommodations with each other assured her support of his involvement in the movie industry. This was true despite the fact that the Catholic Church and other religious groups were still trying to decide the values of motion pictures as well as the moral risks of attending the new films.

Books, including the Bible, had stories of moral depravity. Wars, murder, adultery, and other acts were common themes in literature, on the stage, and in opera.

Theatrical works occasionally created controversy. The opera *Salome* was promoted by some touring performing companies as having a nude scene. However, how and where the scene was included varied with the city in which the singers were appearing. Both self-censorship and the fact that only adults attended the performances assured limited controversy in any community.

Books relied on the imagination. A child reading a love scene would not have the erotic understanding of an adult capable of experiencing the same emotions. The same passage might bore one reader and prove intensely erotic for another.

Movies left nothing to the imagination. A book about a pirate kidnapping a maiden and threatening her virginity would be no more graphic than the fantasy of the reader. A movie might show the woman being terrorized, beaten, bound, and her clothing torn from her body. The excitement on the face of the villain, the terror on the face of the heroine, and the re-created violence would all be reality for the viewer.

Likewise, a woman cheating on her husband would be shown, not with shame but in the midst of experiencing pleasure. She might pay a price at the end, or she might be seen in the vanguard of youth shedding the strictures of the past to lead a more liberated lifestyle.

Nothing like this had ever existed before. Would men imitate such depravity? Would women abandon modesty, chastity, and appropriate decorum? Would the immoral become acceptable? Or would people put it in context, see it as entertainment, and not change their lives?

Either way, should there be limits placed on the industry? Should certain types of films be considered inappropriate for anyone? Worse, if a book was accepted as great literature, yet graphic in its depiction of sex and violence—*The Iliad* or *The Odyssey*, for example—could the story be safely viewed in film form?

The industry writers grappled with this issue as they faced the wrath of church leaders and other critics.

Perhaps the classic letter, only partially facetious, was the one writer Herman Mankiewicz sent to his friend Ben Hecht when he asked the broke Hecht to come to Paramount Pictures as a $300-per-week screenwriter. Hecht was a "serious" writer, the editor of the *Chicago Literary Times,* and a novelist of works such as *Erik Dorn.* The Hollywood money would make him solvent, and he hopped a train to Hollywood. His first eighteen-page outline for the first of his works Paramount would film brought him a bonus of $10,000. He also had the Mankiewicz note, stating:

> I want to point out to you . . . that in a novel a hero can lay ten girls and marry a virgin for the finish. In a movie this is not allowed. The hero, as well as the heroine, has to be a virgin. The villain can lay anybody he wants, have as much fun as he wants cheating and stealing, getting rich and whipping the servants. But you have to shoot him in the end. When he falls with a bullet in his forehead, it is advisable that he clutch at the Gobelin tapestry on the library wall and bring it down over his head like a symbolic shroud.[2]

The movie industry that Rose encountered was in the midst of a self-censorship that would eventually be codified, not only in Hollywood but also in individual states. What should have been a new art form, revealing human society in all its aspects, wrestling with issues for which there were only gray areas—war, unpunished violence against good people, the depth and breadth of interpersonal relations, and the like—became clichéd. The writers, including Hecht when he decided to make his fortune in Hollywood, created a mythological nation and a mythological people. In many of their minds, what they were doing was creating a nonexistent Christian ideal. Worse, because the movies seemed as real to viewers as life itself, many Americans thought that what were actually their normal lives were, instead, exceptions. The writers were providing misinformation and making it public "truth," an accusation that proved justified a few years later, when film biographies became popular. Even the least noble individuals took on heroic and/or humanitarian qualities, or the depth of the person was left unstudied. They were film versions of children's biographies, the equivalent of the work of writers such as the nineteenth-century Reverend Weems, who created the myths of the cherry tree and total honesty on the part of George Washington.

Rose's visit to Hollywood convinced her that though glamour was combined with titillation, the movies always seemed to show good triumphing over evil, a proper moral message. Instead of being concerned that leaders of the Catholic Church continued to condemn the new industry, she delighted in thinking that her Joe would further the production of good films with proper endings. That she was also seduced by the glamour of it all and the fact that she would indirectly be in the midst of it went unsaid.

Joe's plans solidified in 1926. He made his first move to change the way his business handled film when he began to look at the takeover of Film Booking Office of America, Inc., the distribution division of Robertson-Cole Pictures. He and his lawyer went to London in August 1925 to meet with Lloyd's and Graham's Trading Company, the parent organization of the movie company. However, not everyone in the British company wanted to work with the brash American investor. They wanted him to have a proper introduction to their world, something that a few joked would take a royal act to move things along.

Joe understood the game being played against him. He also realized he could handle matters by making contact with the prince of Wales, heir to the throne of England, who was vacationing in Paris.

Joe sailed for France, then went to what the press was calling the prince's favorite restaurant. Joe bribed the maître d' to place him near where the prince routinely sat. Then, when the prince came to dinner, Joe, who had never met the prince, walked over and shook his hand, explaining that he was delighted to see him once again. Joe enthusiastically talked of the time they spent together at the Myopia Hunt Club party of Bayard Tuckerman.

Tuckerman, a Brahmin, had never met Joe Kennedy, and even if he had, he would not have invited him to a party. Irish Catholic businessmen were lower than dogs in the Tuckerman social circle. However, not only was the prince's attendance at the Tuckerman party big news in the newspapers, the coverage also made clear that it was too large a gathering for the prince to be likely to remember more than a small number of those present. Joe was counting on the prince's inherent politeness and tact when he shook his hand. As he expected, the prince was delighted to be with Joe "again."

The prince asked why Joe was in Paris, and Kennedy explained that most of his work was actually being done in London, where he was having trouble meeting with the bankers. The prince of Wales offered to help Joe with a letter of introduction. It was a document that assured that Joe's consortium could buy the film company, beginning Joe's career in Hollywood.

Honey Fitz, who put up some of the investment money, did not wish to give his son-in-law credit. In February 1926 he telephoned an editor at the *Boston Post* to let him know what he had accomplished with his son-in-law. The story was carried under the headline "Fitzgerald a Film Magnate." Eleven years later, in December 1937, the former mayor gave a series of interviews about his life and family. Among the stories he told was how Joe and his friends were preparing to travel to Florida for a vacation. While some went to the train station, Joe responded to a tip that Lord Inverforth was in Boston representing a number of British bankers. Joe rushed to the hotel and put together the final details of the film deal. Then, according to Honey Fitz's story to the writer, half an hour later Joe alerted the friends that the vacation was off. "I've just bought a motion picture company," Joe was said to have exclaimed.

With all the success, Joe still could not feel comfortable. He and Rose used their growing wealth to buy a summer home in Cohasset, a town on the Atlantic Ocean fifteen miles southeast of Boston. Cohasset was dominated by old-money Boston Protestants. The area was so expensive, exclusive, and so long limited to families who lived there year after year and generation after generation that all newcomers were greeted with hostility. That one of the newcomers was both new money and Irish did not sit well in the community. They couldn't block the Kennedys from buying, but they did deny them membership in the Cohasset Country Club. As was later explained, "The women in Cohasset looked down on the daughter of 'Honey Fitz'; and who was Joe Kennedy but the son of Pat, the barkeeper?"[3]

That was the Kennedy family story about the bias Joe and Rose endured. However, years later some of the members said that the vote went against Joe because they found him dishonest. They weren't concerned with his family history. He was simply a crooked man, and they didn't want him around. Most likely there is some truth in both stories.

It was time for Joe to resettle his family in another state before personally moving to Hollywood to see if he could become a mogul. He purchased a house in Riverdale, a luxury section of the Bronx in New York City. Then he rented a private railroad car, loaded Rose, the children, and several of the servants, and took them to their new home in style. He claimed he needed the larger city to operate more effectively. In truth, he had never been able to receive the respect he desired in Boston. He knew that Rose, whose life had revolved around daily Mass, overseeing the caretaking staff for the house and children, and going shopping, enjoyed more respect than he did. She had been educated abroad. She had founded the Ace of Clubs. She had become politically savvy through working with her father. She might be an Irish Catholic woman, but in Boston Joe would always be second to his wife, and his wife would never know the respect of a less-educated, less-skilled Brahmin.

A new business, a new home, a new city, and a new state just might jump-start Joe's chances to be looked up to in his own right.

9

GOING HOLLYWOOD

JOE KENNEDY MADE HIS MARK IN HOLLYWOOD WHEN THE MOVIE industry had transformed itself into the dominant force of American popular culture. Only the wealthy still scorned the medium in favor of literature, theater, and occasionally burlesque. They lacked an understanding of the impact movies were having on society, perhaps the reason that even contemporary Americans tend to think of those early silent films as little more than bawdy comedies, slapstick, and action pictures.

Certainly there was plenty of base entertainment. Mack Sennett's bathing beauties, the Keystone Kops, chase pictures such as *Teddy at the Throttle* with Teddy the Great Dane and Pepper the cat, and the Tons of Fun have all been etched in the contemporary American mind. This may be because such films have a universal appeal that led to their later reuse as part of children's television programs and late-night cable fare. What has not survived to the same degree is the early film industry's translation of great literature to the screen, nor what were popular films concerned with issues directly affecting immigrants, the working poor, victims of corrupt politicians, and the like, including stories about white slavery, drug addiction, and alcoholism.

The undereducated working poor and the politically disenfranchised were often victims of corporate and political manipulation and abuse. Alcohol- and drug-laced tonics, sweatshop employment, unsanitary conditions where the poor bought their food, and similar problems were occasionally revealed in newspaper "muckraking." But the broad popular awareness of these issues often came from the movie industry.

For example, there were films with titles such as *The Reform Candidate* and *Capital versus Labor.* One of the better-attended films in many of the hardscrabble towns was one with the unlikely title (for today's audiences) of *The Molly Maguires, or The Labor Wars in the Coal Mines.* Important social issues were discussed in films such as *Votes for Women* and *Suffragettes' Revenge.* The movies challenged the social norms of the Victorian era, a time when class distinction and exploitation were common, women were disenfranchised, and criticism of the existing society was considered inappropriate.

Perhaps it was only in the new phenomenon of movies that men determined to reform government could get elected and successfully challenge the corrupt sitting officials. Perhaps it was only in the movies that factory bosses could be forced to cease treating their workers like expendable cattle. Perhaps it was only in the movies that the exploitation of the poor—in sex, on the job, in housing, and in social opportunity—could be challenged and beaten by the determined "everyman." But when the movies graphically depicted problems in one community to the nation at large, the depiction also provided hope. The exploited poor discovered they were not unique, and with this awareness often came the courage to challenge those in power.

Today the subject matter of the early silent movies seems corny, the emotive acting rather humorous, the dialogue periodically flashed on the screen both heavy-handed and a bit melodramatic. But in the beginning there were no mass-market alternatives. People went to the movies and found themselves entertained as well as inspired. Films were subversive, delightful, and educational, depending on the subject matter, and in any given week, in any small town or large city in America, all three types of movies were likely to be shown.

The popularity of the new films grew rapidly. In 1907, in New York City alone, an average of two hundred thousand residents per day spent five cents each to go to the movie houses everyone called nickelodeons. That figure doubled each Sunday when workers were home with their families. That same year, throughout the United States, ten times that number of people were likewise spending their nickels.

Each success led to new entrepreneurs opening nickelodeons until there were ten thousand such places nationally in 1910. These usually were not in the theaters that existed for stage productions. Many of the screens were in crude structures, thrown up to take advantage of the interest in films, or in the midst of other businesses. Some small towns had general stores where an unused room was converted to an area housing a projector, screen, and chairs. Or the local nickelodeon might have previously been a storage room. Unlike burlesque, vaudeville, and theaters showing plays, these were locations that had not been used for entertainment. Yet despite the crudeness of so many settings, even the most slapdash nickelodeon had a draw never before seen in the country. Couples on dates went to nickelodeons. There were single shop girls, tired from their workdays, who knew they could safely enjoy a film alone without being considered a harlot or hit upon by a man seeking a date.

Men took their wives and children, but they also stopped by on their way home from work. Children went alone, with friends, or with families, depending on how much money they could save, beg, or borrow.

Again, using New York City as an example, most "decent" hotel restaurants banned single women from dining. Some clubs were so against women that they banned wives accompanying their husbands during the week. New York's nickelodeons had no such pretensions. They were neither sexist, racist, nor discriminating among classes. In theory, though rarely in practice, an Astor or a Vanderbilt daughter could drop by and enjoy a film alone in the midst of cooks, cleaning women, taxi drivers, and others. The cinematograph, the technical but rarely used name for the new moving images, was the great leveler of its day, though most were attended by people who had to work for a living, not those who relied on inheritance for their wealth.

Nickelodeons took advantage of a society where most people worked long hours at least six days a week. They opened early in the morning and stayed open until late at night. A piano player or organist supplied musical accompaniment to the silent movies, and there was no set show-time. The movies ran continuously, allowing customers to drop in any time they had fifteen or twenty minutes to spare. Most came for the films. A few dropped in to enjoy the music. Always the entertainment was varied and often important.

The men who founded the new production companies came from many parts of the country. The four Warner brothers got their start making chase films in daylight on vacant lots. The films were shown in whatever space they could rent. A sheet tacked to the wall served as a screen. Chairs borrowed from an undertaker served as seats, except when a funeral was in progress. Then the audience stood.

Other pioneers had come from businesses where they understood specialty product sales. Samuel Goldfish (later called "Goldwyn") had sold gloves. Louis B. Mayer had bought and sold rags. And Adolph Zukor had sold furs from a loft in Chicago. All of them were used to selling products to people who frequently had no need for what they were selling, an expertise they used with the new film industry.

These men and their employees had created Hollywood. In 1913 Cecil B. DeMille was working from a barn when he made *The Squaw Man*, an early feature film. His makeshift studio at Selma and Vine streets was at that spot solely because he got on the wrong train from New York. He had planned to establish his studio in Tucson, where there were an average of thirty-seven hundred hours of daylight each year and he would have little need for elaborate lighting to expose the extremely low-sensitivity photographic film of the day. Instead he got on a train going the northern route, and when he reached Flagstaff, 6,907 feet above sea level, an early blizzard showed him that outdoor shooting would be impossible. He asked the conductor which stop was next. When the conductor said Hollywood, DeMille decided to see what that portion of California looked like. He never went back to his original destination.

By the time Joe Kennedy was ready to make his move in Hollywood, his personal accomplishments in the business world made him a desirable player. One of his earliest but little-known businesses was the Columbia Advertising Agency, the company that invented product placement advertising now commonly used in motion pictures, on television shows, and even in some video games.

Product placement was first accomplished through the use of posters that promoted vaudeville acts, including those that preceded the showing of a movie. Vaudeville houses used painted backdrops for their acts. These were usually street scenes showing various nonexistent businesses. Joe arranged for companies to pay to have their business names and logos added to the backdrops. It was a unique form of advertising more effective than newspapers in the eyes of the companies that used it, though not preferable to outside billboards. Because many communities were eliminating billboards or reducing their placement, the vaudeville backdrop advertisement was warmly embraced.

There was not much money to be made in backdrop ads, but they showed Kennedy's originality and willingness to try new ideas. They also served as part of his transition to working with the film industry.

Kennedy never went to Hollywood to be an innovator, though at times innovation (as well as deception) was a key to his success. He went to Hollywood to make money, a fact that let him ignore the high principles and high ideals of those production companies that favored using great literature as the basis for their stories. These were the companies whose films ranged from biblical epics to the dramatization of books used in college English classes. Often they were expensive to produce—far costlier, for example, than a chase comedy with the Keystone Kops or the Tons of Fun. It took longer for such literature-based films to make money, and their primary markets were upscale theaters in larger cities with diverse populations. Since the vast majority of Americans still lived in rural areas, the studios were not making the gross Kennedy felt they could. An epic film might play only two or three days in small-town American theaters, while a chase film or slapstick comedy might last a week or longer in those same nickelodeons. Since the lowbrow entertainment also was cheaper to make, Joe decided to work for high profits, not the creation of what were defined as quality films.

Joe's idea was to concentrate on what, in fiction, would be classed as popular genre categories. This meant love stories in which a young woman with neither money nor family position marries a man who is handsome, wealthy, and prominent in the society from which her family was previously excluded. This also meant stories about gangsters and firefighters, about cowboys and police officers. Everyone liked action, adventure, romance, and comedy. Why not stay with the broadest possible market instead of worrying about the serious side of some of the moviegoers?

Cities such as New York, Chicago, and Boston could fill nickelodeons with all types of pictures. Joe wanted to focus on small-town Main Street theaters where simply made formula films could make a man rich, something FBO also had discovered. That was why FBO was known for films such as *A Poor Girl's Romance*, *Rose of the Tenements*, *The Bandit Son*, and *Hook and Ladder No. 9*. More important, they were producing these films when the novelty of motion pictures was over and people were becoming discriminating in their choices. It was no longer enough for images to be on the screen; stories and stars were what mattered.

Joe Kennedy arrived in Hollywood almost a generation after the era of slapdash movies. The community had become a reasonably well-established business region when he took the train cross-country to California. Filming was done in custom-designed buildings on carefully planned lots. Streetcars carried workers, supporting actors, and stars alike, and houses had been built for people of all incomes. There were restaurants and specialty shops. It was obvious that the area had once been largely agricultural, but most of the farmers had sold out, retiring or moving away so the growing population base could be housed in new developments.

The popularity of the films could be seen in the obscene amount of money available for actors who became stars. Charlie Chaplin, for example, had been making $150 a week as a British clown. It was excellent money for the day, but could not compare with his rise to $10,000 a week in the film industry. Mary Pickford matched Chaplin's money and was given half the profits from every movie she was in.

Yet while money was rolling in to the studios, their businesses had been developed without careful planning. Success and failure were not always understood. The former often could not be replicated, and the latter often could not be avoided.

There were several problems Kennedy identified within the industry. Theaters were in demand, but many of the studio heads built more than they could afford. They were filling the seats, though they had not planned on a realistic cash flow. In addition, salaries were often too high for the projected returns, and everyone was counting on the exceptional picture to save them.

D. W. Griffith probably was the most often cited name when it came to unrealistic hopes. He had created the nation's first "blockbuster" with his *Birth of a Nation*. The actual production process had been a nightmare, and Griffith, perpetually short of cash, was considered a pathetic joke as he pleaded for financial aid to finish the film. However, Griffith's critics also saw that over the next fifteen years he grossed $18 million from the film, a remarkable sum well in excess of costs. This led to the myth among studio heads that each movie that was overbudget or too highly priced for one set of backers would ultimately yield the riches of *The Birth of a Nation*. None of them did.

The financial situation at FBO was overwhelming only to men in an industry that was not used to the creative financing that would seem routine to a man whose background included both banking and the stock market. The British owners had reached a crisis where they needed short-term financing and could only find an offer that would require them to pay a rate of 18 percent per annum. They did not know where else to look.

Joe Kennedy handled the short-term financing by creating a new entity called Cinema Credit Corporation, which issued stock to raise money. Freddie Prince, owner of the Chicago Union Stockyards, the business that fronted the issue of a $500,000 loan, purchased much of the stock. Kennedy took the loan and parlayed it into a $500,000 line of credit at four different banks. (This was the forerunner of creative financing approaches created by attorney Ted Raynor and others in which a movie or block of movies is presold to investors so there is no risk of loss by the studios. The film *Urban Cowboy* was the first to be created in that manner, and that was several decades in the future.)

The management team Kennedy created was a combination of the aides he always kept around him—Ed Derr, who served as treasurer of FBO, and the ever-present John Ford, Eddie Moore, Pat Scollard, and Charles Sullivan. All were intensely loyal to Kennedy. All put their private lives on hold whenever their boss wanted them. And all of them were amoral enough to go along with anything Joe tried to do, no matter how questionable.

Next Joe added the one man who actually knew movies, William Le Baron, to be the production chief. Joe knew how to create a business for making and distributing movies in a manner that would have low, controlled costs and high profits. Le Baron knew how to make the pictures themselves.

Joe's idea of profitable moviemaking involved the creation of more films at lower cost. Paramount's Jesse Lasky liked to think of the industry as having three markets. There were films that were so important to society that the production companies were lauded for their efforts in creating them. These were known as "road shows," in contrast to the "Rialto specials," popular market films that would stay in a theater for a few days, a few weeks, or however long the public desired. And then there were the cheap action films that were the delight of the small towns but that stayed for only three or four days before moving on. They were movies for people who liked to attend films frequently and were always eager to experience the next production, not savor a "classic" several times over. What Lasky did not say was that without the lower-budget movies bringing solid, albeit short-run returns throughout the country, Paramount and the other studios would be in financial trouble.

Joe Kennedy had no interest in quality work unless it could be made inexpensively for the popular market. In 1927 Joe, in an interview with a reporter, was told, "You have had some good pictures this year."

Joe replied, "What the hell *were* they?"

The cynicism was well deserved. Joe Kennedy was not trying to make cinematic history any more than the writer of a romance novel expects to have the book studied in great literature classes a hundred years in the future. In 1926, the first year Joe owned FBO, he set a $30,000-per-week budget for the one film his studio made every seven days. By contrast, the most famous movies of the day—*The Big Parade*, *Ben-Hur*, and others—often cost their studios close to $700,000 each, with production spread over many weeks. Such films could make studios rich beyond their greatest expectations when they succeeded. However, a failure ate up a major portion of working capital.

At the same time, Kennedy recognized that there was a growing market for certain actors that required spending unusual sums of money. The most famous was the horse Silver King, one of the earliest animal stars, and his cowboy hero, Fred Thomson.

The story behind Silver King is actually the story of one of the twentieth century's most interesting women writers. Frances Marion was enamored with the film business and began writing for it from the industry's earliest days. The silent-movie scripts were loosely created by contemporary standards, the writer devising the framework for a story that had no dialogue except for boxes of writing inserted as appropriate to help the viewer understand the visual action. When World War I began, she longed to be the chronicler of what was taking place and switched to journalism long enough to cover the European theater of war.

While Frances Marion was writing about American soldiers at war, she met a ruggedly handsome man with a Ph.D. whose academic career as a college professor was interrupted by his desire to serve his country. The man's name was Fred Thomson, and he fell in love with the writer. They were married in 1919 and used the money she had saved from her highly successful career to travel over Europe for eight months.

It was while the couple was in Ireland that Fred became obsessed with a gray stallion he purchased and named Silver King. The wealthy and adventurous had cars, but American transportation still relied primarily on the horse, and neither Fred nor Frances thought his purchase an odd extravagance. However, as Frances watched Fred gently taming the animal and teaching it tricks, she realized that her husband would make a perfect Western movie hero.

At the time, the cowboy hero was king of the low-budget movies that men such as Joe Kennedy were producing. Real ranchers and former lawmen were being paid to act in films. Tom Mix was the classic, and stories about him always stressed the injuries he had sustained over the years, both working the ranch and fighting with real bad guys. Thomson, who had never been a cowboy, looked more authentic than the rest.

Frances wrote a scenario for her husband, sold it, and the two of them gave Silver King top billing. It was a brilliant move, and Thomson became the most popular movie star in America. Each year ten thousand different distributors paid to show Silver King/Fred Thomson movies in the theaters they represented. It was the reason why Joe Kennedy signed Thomson to a contract guaranteeing him $15,000 a week, half the budget he normally wanted to maintain for each complete film.

Joe's support of the highly successful Western film led to a national craze that was unexpected by the other studios. Joe had rightly reasoned that while films made for a sophisticated or specialized audience would not do well in much of the country, those movies made for what today the industry calls "heartland America" would do well in major cities. Thomson's 1926 movie *The Two-Gun Man* was proof.

The Western was a morality tale concerning a man—Thomson—whose home and cattle were stolen after his father's death. The story was about revenge and fit the sensibilities of a nation steeped in religious ethics. It also was a good action picture, and the combination led a distributor to risk showing it in New York. Actually, the risk was minimal, since Kennedy did not charge a fee to prove that Manhattan residents would like it. When the theater was jammed with "sophisticates" night after night, the Western suddenly became a national staple.

Joe was unable to keep Thomson after the initial contract expired. Paramount Pictures offered the "cowboy" far more money and greater production values to make a switch when his FBO arrangement ended in 1928. Joe couldn't beat Paramount that year, but he was able to steal cowboy actor Tom Mix from Fox.

While Joe was establishing his small but profitable studio operation, he made yet another attempt to gain respect in Boston. He decided to introduce the business side of the film industry, both as it existed and its potential for the future, to business students and professors at Harvard.

In 1927 the movie industry in its entirety was the fourth-largest business in the United States. There were 21,000 theaters and an investment of $1.5 billion. In addition, more than 60 million Americans made a weekly habit of attending films. On an international scale, while the United States was producing only 20 percent of the world's wheat necessary for survival, it produced 80 percent of the world's movies. Yet none of the major colleges or universities were looking at the industry as having important careers for its graduates. The business majors had been bypassed by entrepreneurs lacking formal education, and now that there was a need for professional business management, the colleges had no courses to prepare their students for what would become some of the highest-paying jobs in the nation.

Joe Kennedy understood that the working class was becoming increasingly sophisticated through the movies and radio while the elite, holding these media in disdain, were hurting themselves with their lack of awareness. Hollywood was an important business, and he arranged to have a series of talks for Harvard's three-hundred-member Graduate School of Business Administration class. Also in attendance were various faculty members and a number of undergraduates. As far as can be determined, no other school in the nation offered this information, and they all realized that they were having a unique experience.

The lecture series was an odd one, at least as far as Joe was concerned. Exactly what was said is known because the talks, which began on March 14, 1927, and ended on April 28 of the same year, were collected in a book that Joe "edited" and had published. It is called *The Story of the Films as Told by Leaders of the Industry to the Students of the Graduate School of Business Administration, George T. Baker Fund, Harvard University*, edited by Joseph P. Kennedy, President FBO Pictures Corporation.

In the years that followed, Joe frequently bragged about what he did for both the film industry leaders and the business school. Certainly the lecture series was one of the most valuable a student could experience because the men who delivered the lectures, with the sole exception of Joseph Kennedy, had information available nowhere else. Sydney Raymond Kent discussed distributing the "product," a subject he knew well from his position as general manager in charge of distribution for the Famous Players–Lasky Corporation. Jesse Louis Lasky, the vice president of the same company, covered production problems. Will Hays, the man appointed to bring a sense of morality and propriety to the film industry, spoke on "Supervision from Within," the industry's approach to self-censorship. There was an actor. There was a screenwriter. There was a representative from every segment of the industry, each presenting both a detailed overview of his area of expertise and answering questions from students who were likely to be part of the future of the industry. There also was Joe.

Years later Kennedy would brag about his presentation. The implication was that he was a suave, sophisticated businessman and studio head amid a dozen rather crude, albeit financially successful people in the movie industry. The truth, evident by reading the collection of essays, is that Joe brought nothing to Harvard except the men he held in mild disdain who presented their expertise so brilliantly. Yet he always enjoyed giving the book as a gift to special friends and lovers, as though they would be impressed by his name on the jacket and would not actually read the presentation he had made.

The Harvard lectures did help Joe at home. He and Rose had become estranged over his adultery, a subject he knew she would never raise again once she had agreed to her father's orders to return home instead of separating or getting a divorce. Now she was concerned about the alleged immorality of the movie business, even though her father had been an investor with Joe in his early connections to the industry.

The Kennedy family was always impressed with glamour. While Joe never was a fan, though he attempted to bed many a starlet, Rose was so starstruck that she would delight in having the neighbors be aware of Gloria Swanson, one of the most popular actresses of the day, staying with the family in Massachusetts even though she knew Swanson was her husband's lover. The children and some of the grandchildren were no different.

At the same time there were rumblings within the Catholic Church about indecent films and story lines that were not suitable for families. Eventually there would be organizations whose members prescreened films, rating them for Catholics, Protestants, and Jews. But when Joe was headed for Hollywood, official reviews and industry codes of decency had not been invented. Instead, there was only Will Hays, a friend of Joe's and a man who was as corrupt as the industry he was "saving."

Will H. Hays began his public service career as chairman of the Republican National Committee. For an outright bribe of $75,000 and a "loan" of $185,000 that he did not expect to have to repay, both coming from wealthy oilman Harry Sinclair, Hays helped Warren G. Harding gain political office in 1921. Then Sinclair and Edward Doheny arranged to secretly begin utilizing the nearly a hundred thousand acres of government oil reserves in Teapot Dome, Wyoming. In essence, Harding, who also was an adulterer, had an administration that was willing to give up critical national security reserves.

The public image of Hays during the Harding administration was so positive that he was named postmaster general of the United States. During his years with the film industry, he was often called by his former title: General Hays. It was an affectation that Rose Kennedy adopted, eventually calling both her husband and her sons by whatever position they had last attained. Joe Kennedy, for example, would always be known as "the ambassador," even though he would not warrant the title for more than two decades prior to his death.

Hays, during his Harding cabinet years, seemed above reproach only because he was less disreputable than others in the administration. He also was involved with high-profile concerns that genuinely mattered to him, such as stopping the mailing of pornography. However, his past with the Republican Party and his questionable actions bringing Harding to power led to a Senate committee investigation into bribes he may have made prior to being appointed to the cabinet. Hays assured the senators he was telling the truth, though his answers were different during three different interrogations. Everyone knew he was lying. Everyone knew he was comfortable in the shadowy world of bribery. Yet his political connections were too powerful for him to be disgraced.

Later, when working in Hollywood, Hays occasionally utilized men who were allegedly moral leaders to review films he knew might be controversial. To assure that the studios had their product approved, he bribed the reviewers. The money was paid in the form of salaries and honoraria, but almost everyone involved knew the rating check was rigged.

Hays, who was happy to leave the potential for exposure in a Washington targeted by reformers, began his tenure as president of the Motion Picture Producers and Distributors of America when it was experiencing a number of crises. Not only were many of the films considered inappropriate, but also several of the major stars were being discovered in divorce, sex, and suicide scandals. The newspapers headlined every lurid detail, and thirty-six states, Massachusetts most prominently among them, introduced censorship laws that would prevent many movies from being shown.

Will Hays was brought in to fight the new censorship regulations. His strategy was to rid the industry of those men and women who had no intention of changing inappropriate behavior, then create an organization that would be seen as protector of the public morals. As long as Hollywood was working for the good of the American people, the states would be likely to stop trying to legislate movie censorship codes that made film distribution increasingly difficult.

It was in Massachusetts that Joe and Will became friends. Hays needed to beat the Massachusetts law as part of his goal of showing that the industry was handling the problems that had led to state censorship. He wanted filmmakers to be viewed as responsible citizens who would assure that there would be no further scandals.

The onscreen problems came from such films as the Triangle-Keystone comedy *The Mystery of the Leaping Fish*, starring Douglas Fairbanks playing the perpetually stoned detective Coke Ennyday. He seemed to be celebrating a subculture that encouraged cocaine and alcohol abuse. In another instance of moral laxness, D. W. Griffith frequently added orgy scenes to his religious movies, for how else could he show how bad a city such as Babylon had been?

The personal lives of some of the actors and directors were even more titillating. Roscoe Arbuckle, an overweight plumber with the dexterity of a dancer, was renamed "Fatty" when Mack Sennett discovered him. He went from unplugging the director's drain to starring in a series of comedies. He became so popular as a hapless foil, often with Mabel Normand, that he went from being paid $3 a day to $5,000 a week in four years, then was hired for still more money by Paramount Pictures.

Fatty may have had trouble with girls onscreen, but his private life was filled with sex and alcohol. When model turned actress Virginia Rappe died from injuries after a wild party attended by Fatty, he was charged with rape. The witnesses were drunk, and the "proof" did not match the evidence. Ultimately the jury realized that Fatty's only crime was to be famous and present at the party. They acquitted him of all charges, but the press reaction destroyed his career and condemned all Hollywood nightlife. The incident added fuel to the backlash against the film industry that was growing among religious organizations. While movie attendance had not diminished, there was a fear among production company executives that the still-new medium might be condemned.

Hays was hired to correct the image, reduce the problem, and stop the state censorship laws. The greatest challenge was in Massachusetts, where the law was strongest. Fortunately, Joe Kennedy was willing to assist him in the fight, working behind the scenes and assuring Hays a victory over the local censorship.

Hays understood that initially his office, which was in New York, then moved to Hollywood, would be a rubber stamp for the "reforms" planned by the producers. This meant that sin still could be shown in all its forms, but that in the end, virtue would triumph. It was the concept Cecil B. DeMille used to make his biblical epics a success. The bulk of the movies could be filled with violence and sexual excess as long as, in the end, the hand of God destroyed the evil, and the virtuous characters triumphed. Titles also were changed to no longer be suggestive. And many studios decided to stop creating films based on novels that were considered salacious because of their content—adultery, especially involving the clergy; interracial romance; and the like.

There were other targets for reforms. Women still smoked cigarettes in films, not yet acceptable behavior for "nice" girls in polite society. Men still carried hip flasks, defying Prohibition. And while the mores of the nation also were changing, and women in the larger cities were ignoring the strictures of the past, the newspapers were blaming the movies for inspiring rebellious youth. Hays needed to make filmmakers avoid the subtle counterculture messages of such movie images.

Eventually Hays would demand other changes in screenplays and the way films were shot. A list of rules—the Hays Code—would be created after the stock market crash, and stars were expected to sign contracts with morals clauses. Their private lives were expected to be above reproach, a ridiculous suggestion for most. Some would still be caught in scandals. Most signed the clauses, however, living as they pleased, though letting the studio publicists create idyllic lives of purity, virtue, and monogamy that were carefully choreographed, then photographed for fan magazines. The newspaper and magazine reporters and photographers assigned to cover the movie industry were so delighted to have any direct access to people they, like everyone else, admired that they were willing to go along with the charade.

Rose Kennedy was torn between the moral outrage expressed by many Catholic leaders and her own love of the films Joe eventually brought home to show his family. Having General Hays looking out for the industry was enough for her to justify the inherent goodness of Joe's endeavors. And the fact that his FBO pictures were mostly action/adventure films starring cowboy heroes and recently retired athletes further comforted her. She could pretend that her Joe was in the forefront of the new Hollywood, a concept that was played up by the fan magazines.

On December 11, 1926, *Motion Picture World* announced the well-known banker's more active involvement in the film industry. The implication was that he was encouraged to come to Hollywood by industry leaders to further the efforts of the New York–based Hays to clean up the industry. "General Hays wanted his friend to come into the motion picture business because he regarded him as . . . a man who, in his business ideals and concepts as in the fine character of his home life, would bring to the industry much that it has lacked in the past," *Motion Picture World* explained.

But Joe Kennedy was no more a moral force than his friend newspaper publisher William Randolph Hearst, who lived openly with his mistress, actress Marion Davies. Hearst and other major publishers of the day could dramatically influence public opinion, and their gossip columnists had a love/hate relationship with the movie industry. The columnists thrived on access. They needed to be near the actors, the nightclubs, and the power players. At the same time, without the columnists and reviewers, a film or an actor's career could live and die with a single picture.

Usually there was an elaborate dance between the columnists and members of the entertainment industry. The studio publicist carefully invented an actor's love life, hobbies, and related matters. Dates and marriages might be arranged, especially if the man played leading roles. Seemingly everyone in the industry knew who was drinking, doing drugs, and having sex with whom, but as long as the scandals were minor and the columnists were provided access to the stars of the day, most of the stories were never filed with the papers.

Joe was assured positive coverage by the Hearst papers whenever his films needed a boost. He was a friend of Hearst and a closer friend of Marion Davies.

There would be two sides of Joe Kennedy visible in Hollywood. The better known was the man who would seduce, flaunt, and financially abuse the most popular movie star of the day. But the more important was the man who would create an empire that lived on long after he left the industry. That side of Joe Kennedy made his move in 1928.

To understand the change in the world of entertainment, it is important to know that vaudeville was the leading public diversion in the nation in the two decades at the start of the twentieth century. Theaters were in every community, and the entertainers put on two shows a day throughout the year. As movies began to capture audiences, some of the theaters showed both films and live vaudeville acts, the owners pretending that the movies brought in crowds who stayed because of their love of the live singers, dancers, comics, and other acts. The delusion became obvious in 1926, when only half a dozen major vaudeville houses remained in the United States. (Vaudeville on a small scale was not dead, but the elaborate theaters had been converted entirely for film.) In 1927, when Will Hays was the Hollywood presence in New York, only one major vaudeville house offering only live entertainment remained in the city.

There were other changes coming, especially the effort to link sound and film. Numerous inventors and electronics experts tinkered with creating talking pictures, though the systems that seemed most promising were the Kinetophone, the Phonofilm, Vitaphone, Movietone, and Photophone.

A sound-and-picture peep show invented by Thomas Edison, the Kinetophone, was the first to drop from the ensuing battle. Despite the small size that hid most of the flaws, the Kinetophone's picture was considered quite poor. However, the viewer, who heard the synchronized sound through headphones, was delighted with whatever was playing. Eventually Edison decided that neither his system nor any of the others would ever be successful. He urged the abandonment of talking pictures as impractical on a national scale.

But Edison was shortsighted. Dr. Lee DeForest eventually led the way with projected films when he took his Phonofilm to New York's Rivoli Theater on April 15, 1923. This time the picture was excellent but the sound was poor. All that saved the picture was the fact that it was essentially a filmed series of vaudeville acts featuring some of the top performers of the day, including Eddie Cantor and Sissle & Blake. Possibly he hoped the public would be familiar enough with the routines to be able to figure out what was said. But the Phonofilm process was being constantly improved, and by the following year Dr. DeForest was able to present a better sound film. This time it was an original story called *Love's Old Sweet Song*.

Warner Brothers was involved with the Vitaphone process. It was a sound-synchronizing system for either music or voice, and one of the outside investors was William Fox, the president of Fox Film Corporation, who did not want to miss out on any of the more promising new technologies in case his own Fox-Movietone system proved to be a failure.

Fox was open with his actions. Other producers were not. In December 1926, the heads of most of the major studios got together because they could see that sound might be the wave of the future. They recognized that the electronics for the competing systems were different. A film made using one system could not be shown using projection equipment from another system. Each theater would adopt a system based on any number of factors—the most frequently used distribution firm, the types of film being offered through that distributor, and the quality of any system used by area rivals. Silent movies were profitable, in part, because they could be shown anywhere. Sound motion pictures, if not standardized, would greatly reduce everyone's income.

Not as open as Fox, producer Adolph Zukor was part of the group that was looking to standardize production, but he also sensed that Warner Brothers had the right idea with Vitaphone. Zukor owned the six-hundred-theater chain known as Paramount Publix Theaters Corporation. He secretly offered to convert all his theaters to show Warner Brothers' products, knowing that he might be able to show only their sound pictures. It was the deal that Warner Brothers needed to combat decreased revenue and rising expenses. Instead of taking it, though, Warner Brothers insisted upon more money than Zukor was willing or able to pay. He quietly returned to the other producers, agreeing to ignore Vitaphone without admitting he had tried to jump-start the technology.

While the different companies were working on sound, another innovation was creating havoc in the nation: radio. KDKA, in Pittsburgh, became the first radio station in the United States, in 1920. By the time crude sound pictures were possible, the public was gaining increasing access to radio throughout the nation. Live orchestras, singers, comedians, and others performed at no cost beyond the building or buying of one of the new radio receivers.

David Sarnoff entered the world of talking pictures through the new medium of radio. He was the general manager of Radio Corporation of America (RCA), and in 1927, the year after Zukor was leading the way in having motion picture producers unite, he founded NBC.

NBC—the National Broadcasting Corporation—was a network of twenty-five stations from New York west to Kansas City that could all carry identical programming. Sarnoff liked the idea of making radio a free music box with an ever-changing array of live musical programs. Whole orchestras would be gathered in studios to play for the listeners. The early years of such programming were so popular that many thought radio would eventually replace both motion pictures and most reading material. Then came *The Jazz Singer.*

The Jazz Singer had been created with the improved Vitaphone process and was enormously successful. At the same time, William Fox's Movietone idea was being expanded to include newsreels. A motion picture show would have everything from a talking story to musical presentations with opera singers and symphony orchestras, to whatever news of the day could be filmed. By the end of 1927, the Movietone process had shown everyone from Italian dictator Mussolini to Charles Lindbergh after his solo flight across the Atlantic. The future was clear, and Movietone was in the forefront.

A personal challenge for the producers was the cost of incompatible sound reproduction systems. Rival standards were not likely to survive. Converting movie houses to sound was an expensive process. Would theaters have a single type of projection equipment and be limited to the films produced in that sound format? Would theaters have to add projectors so they could show any movies they knew would have local appeal? Would cities be divided in the way theaters received films so that one house showed only Vitaphone while another showed only Movietone?

The one fear everyone shared was that they would have to fight for their audiences anew. For years each production company had gained audiences based on the appeal of the talent they had under contract. Handsome men and beautiful women engaged in romance and murder, adultery and cattle rustling, train robberies and football games, singing, dancing, and just about every other aspect of the real or imagined human condition. There always was music that accompanied the silent films, and when dialogue or some other explanation was needed to help understand the visual story, writing would appear on the screen. The voices of the actors were known only through the imagination. With sound, many stars would lose their following because of the poor quality of their voices.

Ultimately many actors would have to be fired despite previously bringing millions of dollars in box office revenue to the studios. Likewise, talent who had been in scenes without being featured would have to be given star buildup if their skills warranted promotion. And new actors would have to be found and marketed. There would be a period when revenues might decrease. There would be a time when loyalty to the pictures of a popular actor would not be developed. The potential expense was enormous, yet sound was inevitable no matter what Thomas Edison and, briefly, the pessimistic Harry Warner believed.

Adding to the concerns was the foreign market. Silent movies were a universal language. Talking movies would have to be dubbed into the languages of the countries where they were shown. Again this was something new, another problem to be surmounted at who knew what additional expense.

David Sarnoff knew nothing about Adolph Zukor's overture to Warner Brothers to establish a theater/film production connection with his Paramount Publix Theaters Corporation. However, he independently concluded that there would have to be industry links.

Sarnoff also was concerned about the potential for Photophone, the talking-picture concept developed by his RCA in March 1928, to become the dominant system. That was why he decided to talk with Joe Kennedy, a man to whom he was introduced by Louis Kirstein, the head of Filene's Department Store.

The Sarnoff/Kennedy relationship was an odd one. Both were from immigrant families and had known the bias that can linger against the sons and grandsons of those who came from abroad. Sarnoff was a Russian Jew, someone Kennedy would normally have held in disdain.

However, he was different, more sophisticated than the men who left the rag trade to create the current motion picture industry. Sarnoff saw concepts and dreamed of making them a reality. Joe Kennedy was adept at the mechanics dreamers could not master without his sound grounding in business. Sarnoff envisioned a radical change in the film industry, with RCA being dominant. Kennedy saw himself getting very rich by helping change an industry.

It was October 1927 when the first business arrangement between Kennedy and Sarnoff was consummated in New York City. Sarnoff agreed to have RCA buy a stock interest in Kennedy's FBO for $400,000. Then Kennedy went off in search of a theater chain to add to the new organization.

Joe Kennedy owned enough nickelodeons to understand that among the finest potential movie theaters were the hundreds of either unused or underused vaudeville theaters that had once been part of the Keith-Albee-Orpheum (K-A-O) chain. The chain was involved with a deal with Pathé-DeMille, but the films they were getting seemed too costly. John Murdock, the president of the merged companies, wanted to find a way to get films made for less money. Joe Kennedy, whom he approached early in 1928 after realizing Kennedy was looking for an investment, was the answer.

Once again Joe became a stock manipulator. Earlier in his career he had manipulated stock to save Yellow Cab. Now he was looking at handling mergers and acquisitions within the film industry. He had Lehman Brothers, the bankers for Pathé-DeMille and K-A-O, work with Elisha Walker, his friend and the president of Blair and Company, to buy enough Pathé-DeMille and K-A-O stock so they could move Joe Kennedy into a consulting position for the companies. The fee would be $2,000 per week, and Joe would not be limited to spending all his working time with the merged businesses.

The Harvard lecture series paid off for the first time. Expected opposition from Cecil B. DeMille never came because DeMille was still delighted by the prestige of being a lecturer whose words were enshrined in Kennedy's book.

Others were not thrilled. Joe worked with Murdock to buy out Edward Albee in preparation for firing the man. Murdock, as part of his rise to the presidency, was given a stock option that he sold to Kennedy. Then Joe offered Albee $4.2 million—$21 per share for two hundred thousand shares that were selling for just $16 on the open market when Kennedy made his deal. Albee was delighted to be rich when moved out of his company, though Joe managed to profit far more than Albee when he had friends manipulate the stock to $50 a share three months later. Albee was not resentful of the deals, but he was shocked when Kennedy pronounced him worthless as an executive and had him resign. Albee was so crushed to be forced out of the business he loved that he died shortly thereafter. Joe next acquired Pathé-DeMille from Jeremiah Millbank through the efforts of Elisha Walker. The company was in the process of converting to sound, and Joe needed to save money to cover the cost. He began reducing salaries and cutting personnel, an action that frightened Cecil B. DeMille, who sold his stock and moved to MGM. Since his last picture for Pathé-DeMille was the religious epic *King of Kings*, Joe was not sorry to see him go. The religious film had been a box-office success, but its production cost of $2.5 million was so outrageous for the day that Joe wanted no further epics of such magnitude.

Suddenly Kennedy was wealthy beyond his expectations now that he had moved his business focus to the West. He headed three companies—FBO, K-A-O, and Pathé. He had extensive stock options, and though the stock market stumbled a bit in mid-1928, it recovered in a few days and Kennedy was never hurt.

Next came a surprise involvement with Joe's old firm of Hayden, Stone as Kennedy continued his efforts to expand his power. Several theater owners had combined to create their own production company, First National Pictures, in an effort to better control the fees they were being charged by other producers. Now, a little more than a decade later, while Joe was consolidating FBO, K-A-O, and Pathé, Stanley Rossheim of the Stanley Company of America had purchased First National Pictures and was using Hayden, Stone to reorganize the company.

Joe was less interested in the production company than he was in its roster of stars under contract. They ranged from actress Colleen Moore to cowboy star Ken Maynard. More important, most of them had skills that would enable them to transcend the problems of sound pictures.

Joe made his move by becoming an "adviser" to this fourth company for a fee of $150,000 a year. This was a massive sum of money for any executive of the day, and the idea that it would be paid to a man who was actually working for it only a small portion of his time was outrageous. Worse in the minds of industry analysts was the fact that the contract, which extended for five years, gave him the right to buy a 25 percent interest in the company. He would be in charge of production. He would control distribution. He would essentially be moving toward total ownership.

While outsiders were shocked that such a ridiculous action could take place, insiders did not tolerate the greed. The board of directors for First National refused to approve the contract.

The reasons ultimately given for the decision varied with the stockholders. It was clear that few people were comfortable with the way Kennedy ran FBO film selections and with his attitude toward productions. They had not seen an improvement in his actions when he added Pathé and K-A-O.

Temporarily frustrated, Kennedy returned to New York, telling Rose that he was going to Europe on the *Île de France*. She was to meet him there so they could travel to Biarritz and Deauville. He did not mention that he was also taking J. J. Murdock so the two men could finish their business. RCA was looking to buy control of FBO at the same time that Joe was equipping both that company and Pathé with the RCA Photophone.

What went unsaid to Murdock was that Kennedy was working behind the back of his investment partner, Guy Currier. On August 6, 1928, apparently with Currier's knowledge, FBO released *The Perfect Crime*, a silent film to which sound was added. This was not the sophisticated combination of sound and picture that would be possible in a few years. This was a silent picture with as many inserted sounds and voices as possible. It was crude even by the limited potential of the day, and certainly not the test picture for FBO's Photophone venture with RCA.

Recognizing that releasing pictures like *The Perfect Crime* could hurt the corporate image, two months later, in October 1928, David Sarnoff announced that RCA had taken control of FBO, creating RKO (Radio-Keith-Orpheum). It would be a $50 million wholly owned subsidiary, with Joe being paid $150,000 plus being able to option 75,000 shares of K-A-O stock for negotiating the deal. Joe also would stay involved with Pathé.[1]

Currier was furious. He made a substantial profit from the relationship, but he felt he should have been involved with all deals, sharing in all income. He felt Joe had enriched himself at his partner's expense. What Currier did not realize was that Joe had a tendency to take advantage of anyone—friend or lover—who let him become intimate with his or her financial affairs. And among those he would eventually cheat was Gloria Swanson, arguably the most famous actress of her day.

10

SEDUCED AND BETRAYED

IT WAS THE MOST FAMOUS SEDUCTION SCENE OF THE 1920S, THE Palm Beach hotel scenario laid out after the fact by the "star." The story might even be true. As Gloria Swanson described the night of her undoing by Joseph Kennedy,[1] she was on her bed when the maid came in with dresses to consider for a party the following evening. The dresses were left, and the actress started to doze, not realizing that the door was unlocked and Joe Kennedy had entered, apparently as the maid left the room.

As Swanson related the story, Joe came at her like a man so sexually driven he could not stop himself until he had intercourse with her. "He just stood there, in his white flannels and his argyle sweater and his two-toned shoes, staring at me for a full minute or more, before he entered the room and closed the door behind him," she wrote. "He moved so quickly that his mouth was on mine before either of us could speak. With one hand he held the back of my head, with the other he stroked my body and pulled at my kimono."

Swanson continued, explaining that she had known from their first more or less innocent kiss on the train that they would end in bed together. She discussed the fact that they were both married, both had children, and neither had any intention of leaving his or her spouse. Yet she also knew that she would allow Joe Kennedy to do whatever he desired, no matter what problems arose.[2]

That Gloria Swanson should fascinate Joe Kennedy was perhaps inevitable. She was little different from Rose Fitzgerald, though raised without the constraints of the Catholic Church and the public scrutiny brought on by Honey Fitz's political position. She was a woman of passion who delighted in sensuality, the freedom to do what she wanted with whomever she desired, and a love of material possessions, not very different from Rose when Joe first came to know her. The difference, beyond the radically different adult life paths the women followed, was

134

that Rose was too intelligent and too well educated to let herself be financially raped. Gloria, by contrast, was naive enough to be trusting, and every man who handled her financial affairs, including Joe Kennedy, took advantage of that naïveté.

The Gloria Swanson the public was permitted to see on the screen was little like the woman in private life. Part of her success was her appeal to both men and women of the day. She was tiny—just five feet, one inch tall, flat-chested, and with sticklike legs. The size 2½ shoes she wore were no bigger than a child's, yet women across America demanded the same size from frustrated shoe salesmen. She was stunning, her teeth flawless, her smile radiant, her hair perfectly coiffed. Financially successful at a young age, Gloria spent more than $11,000 a year on clothing and in excess of $755 on shoes when she was twenty-three. More than $26,000 went for perfume, makeup, and a staff of hairdressers, a manicurist, a masseuse, and others catering to her hedonistic whims. Her cars included a Cadillac and a Pierce-Arrow, the two most expensive autos of the day. Yet somehow she never seemed a threat—her characters were never aggressive manhunters—even though men found her desirable. It was as though all women saw themselves in Swanson. If they could only be so rich (her $230,000-a-year salary was raised to $7,000 per week by the time Joe Kennedy met her), they would look and dress exactly as she did. That was why they emulated everything they could learn about her fashion taste. She was not going to take their men, as a vamp might do. She was the girl next door, just richer, famous, and luckier.

Gloria Swanson also was titled, at least with the husband she had gained prior to being seduced by Joe Kennedy. The couple had met in Paris in 1924. She was twenty-five and a veteran of thirty movies who was about to make a joint French/Hollywood film, *Madame sans Gêne*, in Paris.

The film companies assigned Adolphe Osso to manage Gloria's stay so she would have no problems with sightseeing, the fans who constantly mobbed her, transportation, or anything else. He arranged for a translator, escort, and someone to work on her wardrobe.

Language translator James Henri Le Bailly de la Falaise, marquis de la Coudraye—"Hank" to the French-impaired such as Gloria—was ironically of both French and Irish descent, the latter on his mother's side. His great-grandfather died at the guillotine during the French Revolution. His father was a career soldier who taught at France's St.-Cyr Military Academy, and his mother was the daughter of cognac distiller Richard Hennessy. The family home was a grand estate in Brittany that the family could ill afford to maintain. However, the title assured him a place in society that enabled Gloria to be escorted among the rich, the powerful, and the glamorous.

Henri was technically a paid escort, but his intelligence, wit, and courtly manners quickly made him something more in Gloria's eyes. She also learned that he was a war hero, a volunteer commando, and a man who had known the sadness of lost love when his beloved wife committed adultery.

In December 1924 Gloria Swanson learned the two most important details of Henri's life. First, he had never seen a Gloria Swanson film, though the mobs she encountered seemed to indicate he might have been the only man in all of Paris who could make such a statement. And second, he had no money. He could offer her nothing of a material nature at the same time that her excessive spending exceeded even her lavish income.

For Gloria, however, Henri seemed perfect. She was working her way through lovers and marriages that would eventually extend from actor Wallace Beery to No. 6 (and last) husband, nutrition and health guru William Dufty. There also would be various assorted lovers, abortions, and two children—a daughter and an adopted son. Henri would be No. 3 and the first man she would have kept were it not for her pesky little habit of adultery.

Gloria had been through more exciting men than Henri, but often they were alcoholic, violent, and involved with the film industry. They were shallow, possessive, melodramatic, yet wildly exciting for a young girl. Now, older though just out of adolescence, she found Henri's courtliness, his sophistication, his refusal to drink, his lack of a history of wives and lovers, and his absence from the film industry to be the most desirable traits she had ever encountered in a man. She knew that she might stray from the man when he proposed marriage to her, but Gloria Swanson had long before separated sex from marriage. If she strayed, she strayed. In her mind, Henri would be her last husband. As a result, she returned to Hollywood as the marquise de la Falaise de la Coudraye. She also had what would have been a scandalous secret.[3]

Gloria had no intention of buying a husband she had not pretested. Henri performed as hoped, and Gloria found herself in Passy, France, two months pregnant. The Hays office's growing morals code and the attitude within the nation were such that the moment she gave birth and the public counted back to see the date of conception, she would be finished as an actress. The studio writers could publicize marriages effectively. Romances could be hidden or downplayed to casual dates.

The March 28, 1925, photo was taken in New York's
Ritz Carlton Hotel after the arrival from France of
Gloria Swanson and her new husband, the marquis de la
Falaise. It would be during this marriage that she would
commit adultery with Joe Kennedy, then be shocked that
her husband would leave her when she decided he was a
better spouse than Joe was a lover. (Cleveland State
University Library, Special Collections)

But a baby was forever. Jesse Lasky was considering the possibility of
luring Gloria for a new contract that would cost him $1 million a year.
The mere hint of pregnancy would result in her banishment from the
industry. Since Henri had no money, and neither could see themselves
as regular working people, taking home less each week than they might
spend together on breakfast at the Hôtel Crillon, where they were first
introduced, an abortion was necessary.

Gloria Swanson was a woman who had started in the movies when
the companies for which she worked saw her only as a sex object. She
had been in slapstick comedies and she had been in suggestive pictures
such as *Don't Change Your Husband*. She had been born on March 28,
1899, in Chicago, sharing infancy with the movie industry. She was raised

an army brat. Her father, Joe Swanson, worked for the War Department and was placed in charge of transportation while the United States was building the Panama Canal.

Gloria, through the efforts of her mother, Addie, began singing and acting in various theaters in the cities where they lived. At eight, she performed in Key West, Florida, after meeting such theater people as Frank Hayes, an actor recovering from tuberculosis, and his daughter, Venice Hayes, who was a New York theater actress. Four years later, in San Juan, Puerto Rico, where the Swanson family was transferred, she was in the play *The American Girl*. This also was the city where the Swansons saw their first motion pictures.

By the time Joe Swanson returned to New York, it was 1914 and movies were being made in studios in several parts of the country, including Chicago, where Gloria and her mother visited Gloria's Aunt Inga. Aunt Inga was a liberated woman just before the era of flappers and vamps. She smoked, an outrageous act, and worked as a private nurse for wealthy families. She was an independent woman who took her niece to see F. M. Anderson and George K. Spoor, partners in Essanay Films, with divisions in Chicago and San Francisco. The former handled mostly urban films. The latter was in the Niles Canyon area, where Westerns and other period films could be shot.

Gloria loved watching the movies being made. The Chicago division worked from Argyle Street, making two-reel comedies. The director always needed pretty faces, athletic bodies, and a willingness to do anything for a laugh. Something about Gloria intrigued him, and he arranged to have her return the next day to appear in a picture. Since Aunt Inga was a friend of George Spoor, Gloria's mother thought there was no harm in it.

The first role was a walk-on in a wedding scene. Gloria gave the star a bouquet of flowers and was paid $3.25 for the work. It was as much for an hour as an adult might earn for a day.

Gloria did not realize that she was, in essence, auditioning for what would prove to be a career. The director was able to establish several points immediately. First, Gloria was pretty. At fifteen her physical appearance was more woman than child, and she was dazzling. However, she had the enthusiasm and energy of a child, the willingness to do anything requested of her. (Star Wallace Beery was wearing a dress in order to play a fat maid. Although considered a skilled actor, and at thirty he had enjoyed a distinguished stage career as well as working in films and as a race car driver, at Essanay he was "Sweedie," the immigrant Swedish maid who was a caricature of all that was stupid.) Gloria, though tiny, had a figure so good that she seemed to photograph taller. She could play opposite all leading men, from the tall Beery to those who might be only a few inches taller than she was.

Swanson became a stock player earning $13.25 for shooting schedules that lasted four days, and $20 when she had to work a full six-day week. She was still a minor by law (girls became "adults" at seventeen), but costumes and makeup made her look older.

Gloria's first break came when she auditioned to be Charlie Chaplin's foil. The man who dominated American comedy had been with Mack Sennett's Keystone Company. When his contract expired, George Spoor determined to bring him to Chicago. Sennett offered Chaplin the then unheard-of amount of $1,000 a week, wealth beyond dreams in the Hollywood of the day. Spoor increased that by half, and Charlie Chaplin, earning $1,500 per week, went to Chicago and began working to find a female foil.

Gloria's test was less than successful. She later commented, "All morning I felt like a cow trying to dance with a toy poodle. Moreover, I knew after one hour that I didn't want to spend the next month or so trying to be cute and elfish, so I made very little effort and finally told him I just didn't see the humor in many of the things he was asking me to do."

Gloria returned to the anonymous roles she had been playing, then prepared to move to Los Angeles when her father was again transferred and her mother felt the family should no longer be separated. She was sixteen years old, still a minor, but with experiences almost no teen had ever enjoyed. She was part of the film industry, experienced, and reasonably skilled. She also had contacts to rejoin the industry, the most important being Wallace Beery. (Her contract was meaningless when she left Chicago. She was being paid weekly, and Essanay was not in southern California.)

The one aspect of Beery's life that Gloria and her family did not know was his penchant for young women. He had been banished from Chicago to California for relations with a minor, but with Gloria now new to the area, vulnerable, inexperienced, and almost old enough to be legal, Beery pursued her. He would become her first husband.

Beery had taught Gloria everything she needed to know about the dark side of the film industry except how to handle an adulterous lover like Joe Kennedy. Gloria, her career on the rise, was paid $100 a week to star in two-reelers opposite Bobby Vernon. At the same time, Beery's career was in a decline, and he was being paid only $50 a week by Mack Sennett until he proved himself worthy of the salary at which Gloria started.

Jealousy and alcohol climbed into bed with Beery and Gloria their first night together after eloping. She was a virgin who was ready for anything except violence. He wanted to enter her and dominate her. There was no foreplay. There was no gentleness. He forced himself on her before she was ready, then fell asleep by her side. In the morning, when she could finally look at herself, she was bruised, and both her body and the sheets were bloody.

Joe Kennedy, who would be Gloria's lover during her third marriage, was similar to Beery in many ways. What little gentleness he displayed was usually the result of what he had learned in restraining himself during his courtship of Rose. He was capable of the same sexual violence in the name of "love," but he undoubtedly sensed that his world would be shattered if he caused the popular daughter of Honey Fitz such discomfort.

The first meeting between Joe and Gloria Swanson was in New York's Barclay Hotel. It was November 1927, a time when New York was between its seasons of romance and bleakness. A month earlier, with the wind racing along the rivers bordering Manhattan Island, the trees of Central Park were richly colorful, the residents seemed to walk at a more leisurely pace, and it was hard to find a couple not walking hand-in-hand. A month later, after the first snowfall, the wind moved the snowflakes like razors being hurled randomly throughout the city. Heads were bowed and covered with hats and scarves. The cars, trucks, and buses left sludge where pristine white had previously fallen, and romance was conducted inside coffee shops, nightclubs, and similar locations. But November was a time of bare trees, of springlike warmth followed by winter chills, all within hours. Rain could turn to snow, creating ice slicks that seemed to run from one end of Manhattan to the other. And the excited children who would fill the streets with their parents in the days between Thanksgiving and Christmas were not yet to be seen.

November was an easy time to conduct business because the city provided none of the distractions that would be there in weeks. Bob Kane, Paramount Pictures' studio manager and friend to both Joe Kennedy and Gloria Swanson, may have recognized this fact when he asked the two to get together. He also may have simply known that Gloria was in some sort of trouble and that Joe Kennedy was a man who might be able to help. Joe was looking to improve the quality of the pictures his new businesses were seeking to produce, and he had talked with Kane because Paramount, along with MGM, had the most experience among the major production houses. Gloria, having risen to star status, might be beneficial to Joe. And the salary she could command from Kennedy's productions would help reduce or eliminate the star's debts.

Gloria Swanson had returned to California from Paris in a manner guaranteed to get the attention of every producer in the industry. The coverage of the event also would titillate every one of her fans who read Hollywood gossip columns and magazines about the stars. Before leaving for Hollywood, the newlywed cabled her boss, Paramount's Adolph Zukor, with this message: "Am arriving with the Marquis tomorrow. Please arrange ovation."

Adolph Zukor complied.

The party at Paramount was as carefully orchestrated as any motion picture. Work on all films was stopped for the day, though all employees were enlisted in what amounted to a major production. Flowers were ordered by the hundreds, and extras were dressed as flower girls. They were told to curtsy as though royalty were passing, tossing their bouquets as though she were being honored as the most beloved star of all time. There was partying everywhere, technicians as well as actors enlisted for the day. But always the partying was meant to laud the marquise.

The entire event was nonsense and everyone knew it, but Gloria was well enough liked that most of the people did not mind. The in-house performance was different from the normal workday; it was fun. Gloria got to show off the extremes of the industry to Henri, and publications throughout the nation were sent photographs they also pretended were news.

Whether or not Henri was impressed with the show at Paramount, the staff that served Gloria and the home she owned amazed him. There were four secretaries catering to the every whim of someone whose work kept her confined to the set. When she went home she could take an elevator rather than having to climb the steps in her two-level house. The master bathroom was made from black marble to provide a contrast to the gold bathtub and sink. (There were five bathrooms in all in the twenty-two-room mansion at a time when just two bathrooms in a home were considered the height of luxury.) Four butlers managed the house and all entertainment, and when she wanted to create a dinner party, her theatricality extended to hiring liveried foot-men to stand behind each seated guest, catering to any whim. It was a lifestyle of squandered money, her success wasted in a sea of excess.

Joe Kennedy's first contact with Swanson was impersonal, one of several signatures on a June 10, 1927, telegram criticizing her plan to produce the controversial story *Sadie Thompson*. She was challenging the moral boundaries of the movie industry, and Joe had joined fellow producers in expressing moral outrage.

The *Sadie Thompson* controversy began when director Cecil B. DeMille first fashioned Swanson's image as a sexual being through rather daring images and suggestive movies. A careful study of frames from the film *Male and Female* shows that her bare breasts were briefly flashed in a bathroom scene. The use of such images was rare, though, DeMille preferring to hint at sex through titles such as *The Affairs of Anatol*.

Paramount's producers often knew firsthand that Gloria's mild raci-ness on the screen was greatly exceeded in her private life. When her second husband, the one before Henri, sought a divorce, he named Para-mount executives who had been her lovers, to increase his chances to be free. The executives were able to keep the list from going public, and the divorce was based solely on the lover of the moment, a man named Marshall Neilan, the highest-paid motion picture director of the day.

The controversy began when Gloria sought independence by join-ing United Artists, a company founded by Douglas Fairbanks and his wife, Mary Pickford, along with Charlie Chaplin and Joseph Schenck, the administrative head of the company. It was Schenck who taught the star about finance, including the need for insurance and friendly physi-cians who would make certain she passed her physicals before each filming. He also made clear that as an independent, Gloria would no longer have an entourage provided by a studio. She was in for a much more difficult life than she had known in the past, and the rewards, though potentially far greater than her $7,000-per-week salary, also could be offset by severe losses if the company failed. The alternative would have been to create a company that hired her separately as talent. There would be a guaranteed paycheck that would continue as long as the company had money, and if the company failed, her personal loss would only have been her investment in the business. She decided to go for the greatest wealth, knowing she would always be either rich or poor, depending on how the films fared at the box office. She was a hard worker, and Gloria Swanson Productions, a subsidiary of United Artists, was involved with two films by the time she met Joe Kennedy.

The first Gloria Swanson film was *The Love of Sunya*, a critical success that had taken nine months to make. The problem was that similar films were made in six weeks, and while Gloria had the luxury of added time to improve the quality of what she did, she quickly learned that time meant money, and the more a picture cost, the longer it would have to be shown to recoup the production expenses and begin making profits. Worse, most of the extra expenses would not have existed had Gloria been willing to work from her home in Hollywood with experienced personnel instead of trying to make her headquarters in New York.

Gloria, Henri, and their two children, along with a staff of twenty-one people, realized the unrealistic nature of working from New York and returned to Beverly Hills in March 1927. There she would pick her next project, and for a woman concerned about finances, it probably was the worst possible choice.

Somerset Maugham was one of the most popular writers of the day. His works were considered classics that would live well beyond his lifetime, and several of them were being turned into plays. There was little censorship of stage plays except public indifference. As a result, a steamy short story named "Miss Thompson" had been successfully converted to a play called *Rain* by writers John Colton and Clemence Randolph.

There were few actresses aware of *Rain* who did not covet the role of Sadie Thompson. It was one of a character of power and depth that was richly challenging to a dramatic artist. It also was scandalous.

First there was Maugham himself. He was bisexual, and it was known that his lover at the time he had gained critical and financial success for *Of Human Bondage* was a twenty-four-year-old man named Gerald Haxton. The difficulty was that Maugham met his lover when his wife, Syrie, was pregnant, adding to the scandal surrounding his name.

In November 1916 Maugham and Haxton traveled by steamship to Hawaii together to look at the Iwilei prostitution district of Honolulu. Among the other passengers were the Reverend and Mrs. J. J. Mulqueen, medical missionaries returning to their mission in the Gilbert Islands, and a prostitute known as "Miss Thompson." Unlike the image of the prostitute as victim, Maugham realized that Miss Thompson was unrepentant and seemed to enjoy entertaining the crew in her cabin each night. When all the passengers were subjected to health quarantine in Pago Pago, Maugham and Haxton were placed in a cabin next to Miss Thompson and a lover she took to pass the time. The sound of their pleasure coupled with a noisy rainstorm led him to begin writing a story.

Maugham developed his work in pieces. He began with an overview of the concept, then worked on the plot and dialogue until he had what would be published as "Miss Thompson." He saw no reason to change the character's name, since both women were (would be) unrepentant prostitutes. However, he did create a totally fictional missionary, because the couple he met on the steamer was as outraged by the whore as he and his lover were.

To understand the outrage that greeted "Miss Thompson" after it was converted from one of the short stories in the 1920 book *The Trembling Leaf* to the stage play *Rain*, you need only read Maugham's initial outline of the play. It read: "A prostitute flying from Honolulu after a raid lands at Pago Pago. There lands also a missionary and his wife. Also the narrator. All are obliged to stay there owing to an outbreak of measles. The missionary, finding out her profession, persecutes her. He reduces her to misery, shame, and repentance. He induces the governor to order her return to Honolulu. One morning he is found with his throat cut by his own hand. She is once more radiant and self-possessed. She looks at men scornfully, exclaims, 'Dirty pigs!' "

The stage play was different from the story. A military man was added, and when the missionary, who obviously fell under the sexual spell of Sadie Thompson, kills himself, Sadie and the soldier become lovers. The play ends happily for Sadie, sailing off into the sunset with yet another man.

Almost every motion picture producer in the nation wanted to create a screen version of "Miss Thompson" or the stage play *Rain*. It would be controversial. It would shock the audience. It would broaden the base of moviegoers. It would generate its own publicity. It would fit nicely with the postwar looseness gripping the nation. However, the major figures in the industry were all part of the Association of Motion Picture Producers and Distributors of America, and they had agreed to follow "The Formula," the concept created and defined by Will Hays. This meant that at least 85 percent of the members had to agree on the appropriateness of a story for filming. "More than 150 books and plays, including some of the best-sellers and stage successes, have thus been kept off the screen," Hays related proudly, stressing that this was not censorship. He noted that although films had been made that were not approved, some approved films probably should not have been, but most of the time "The Formula" worked for the good of society.

Gloria Swanson Productions was not a member of the association. She did not have to submit a story for approval. Nevertheless, she began looking at the story to see if it fit anything the association would condone.

The original screenplay was conceived to include both profanity and the minister. Swanson decided that they could eliminate the profanity and make the missionary "Mr. Davidson" instead of Maugham's "Reverend Davidson."

The only part they knew they could not get over was the fact that the heroine was a whore. The Hays Code, a listing of subjects that were taboo, included as No. 17 "The sale of women, or of a woman selling her virtue."

Henri and Gloria invited Will Hays for lunch, where Gloria raised the issue that, though she was not yet a member of the producers' and distributors' association, having made only one film, she did not want to violate their standards. She talked about a short story (unnamed) that had a fanatical missionary as the lead. She said she wanted to make it, knew that the man could not be in the clergy, and wondered if it would be all right if she changed him into someone who was indeed a zealot reformer but not in the clergy.

What followed was business seduction at its most artful. Swanson asked to use Will Hays's name when trying to persuade the author (unnamed) to let her convert the story to the screen. Hays had no objections, since the one potential problem of which he was aware had been changed. Then she explained who the writer was, and Hays admitted that Maugham often wrote work that could be considered classic. She then confirmed that the Davidson name could be used provided the character was called "Mr." Davidson.

Gloria told Joseph Schenck what she had done. They decided to buy the original short story, "Miss Thompson," and the film rights to the existing stage play, *Rain*. The film rights to the play were available for a standing fee of $100,000, perhaps the highest price ever demanded for a play at the time. However, no one had dared take it.

Ultimately the deal was made through a secret broker who did not reveal the buyer. By then the playwrights were convinced there would be no film made from *Rain*. They agreed to sell the combined rights to the short story "Miss Thompson" and the stage play *Rain* for $60,000, far less than originally desired for the film rights to the play alone. They understood that United Artists would be the owner of record for *Rain*, preventing any other company from filming the play, and that they also would leave it unused, since the firm was a signatory to the code.

Gloria Swanson Productions now officially owned the short story "Miss Thompson," about which there had never been criticism, since no one had thought to buy the rights and create a fresh screenplay. However, when the other studio owners and the writers learned the truth, they were livid. Gloria, knowing she had the legal right to do as she chose, began assembling the film.

NEW YORK JUNE 10, 1927
JOSEPH SCHENCK
UNITED ARTISTS STUDIO
HOLLYWOOD CALIFORNIA

WE THE UNDERSIGNED IN MEETING ASSEMBLED TODAY DESIRE TO VOICE THE STRONGEST PROTEST OF WHICH WE ARE CAPABLE AGAINST THE MAKING OF RAIN EITHER UNDER THE NAME OF SADIE THOMPSON OR ANY OTHER NAME OR THE MAKING OF THIS STORY EVEN WITH VARIATIONS AND CHANGES STOP A YEAR AGO IT WAS AGREED THAT THIS STORY WAS BANNED AND ON THE STRENGTH OF THIS EVERY PRODUCER LAID OFF THE MAKING OF CERTAIN MATERIAL STOP . . . IT WAS FURTHER UNDERSTOOD THAT IF SUCH MATERIAL WAS PRODUCED BY ANYONE THAT MEMBERS OF THE ASSOCIATION IN ORDER TO PROTECT THEMSELVES SHOULD REFUSE TO EXHIBIT THE SAME STOP FOR THIS SUBJECT TO BE PRODUCED AT THIS TIME WILL OPEN UP THE ENTIRE QUESTION AGAIN AND CERTAIN BOOKS AND PLAYS NOW BANNED WILL BE PRODUCED BY THIS ASSOCIATION AND WE WILL LOSE FOR OURSELVES EVERYTHING THAT WE HAVE GAINED IN PUBLIC RESPECT AND CONFIDENCE FOR THE PAST FOUR OR FIVE YEARS STOP AS MEMBERS OF THE ASSOCIATION AND AS PERSONAL FRIENDS OF YOURS WE BEG YOU TO STOP THE PRODUCTION OF THIS PICTURE AT ALL COSTS STOP WE DO NOT BELIEVE THAT ANY INDIVIDUAL MEMBER HAS THE RIGHT TO JEOPARDIZE THE INTERESTS OF ALL THE MEMBERS NO MATTER WHAT THE FINANCIAL GAIN MIGHT BE BY TAKING ACTION WHICH WILL PUT OUR ENTIRE ASSOCIATION AND ALL OF ITS MEMBERS IN DISREPUTE WITH THE PUBLIC OF THE COUNTRY STOP OUR REFUSAL TO PRODUCE SALACIOUS BOOKS AND PLAYS AGAINST WHICH THERE IS AN OVERWHELMING PUBLIC OPINION AT THIS TIME HAS BEEN THE CORNERSTONE UPON WHICH THE PRODUCERS ASSOCIATION HAS BEEN BUILT AND TO DESTROY THAT AT THIS TIME WOULD IN OUR OPINION BE AN ACTION UNFORGIVABLE AND UNWARRANTED AND A DIRECT VIOLATION OF PROMISES WE HAVE MADE THE PUBLIC THAT MATERIAL OF THIS KIND WOULD NOT BE MADE   KINDEST REGARDS FROM . . .

Fifteen producers, including William Fox, Marcus Loew, Abe Warner, Jesse L. Lasky, Adolph Zukor, and Joe Kennedy, signed the telegram. They were all heads of the most powerful companies in Hollywood except Joe Kennedy, of whom Gloria had never heard. She was not involved with backstage financing or ownership machinations. Joe Schenck had to explain Kennedy to her.

Swanson took matters into her own hand. She was livid that everyone was attacking Joe Schenck, since that meant they were not respecting a woman as a producer. She was head of Gloria Swanson Productions and intended to adapt the short story. Schenck was head of United Artists, and no matter what the company's connections with Gloria Swanson Productions, each held rights to different properties and each was accepting the reality of the situation. Schenck would not produce *Rain*. Gloria would produce a cleaned-up version of the short story, omitting the clergy reference, and creating a dramatic product that even Will Hays had approved. It was a brilliant end run around the association.

The only problem remaining was the same one that had always haunted Gloria Swanson since she began working on her own: money. Joe Schenck had developed an ingenious way of financing his friends' pictures. He was on the board of directors of Attilio Giannini's Bank of America, a company that loaned money to Art Cinema, whose president was Joe Schenck. Art Cinema, in turn, loaned money to the members of United Artists to finance their pictures. And United Artists was headed by Joe Schenck. The conflict of interest was enormous. Seemingly no one cared. However, when Gloria went over budget, she had a constant war with Schenck and no other resources for borrowing.

Sadie Thompson went through three different cinematographers. Actors changed. There were problems with technicians and the cost of location work. Staff members were overpaid for the work they were expected to do. Gloria had been brilliant in creating the environment in which the short story could be filmed despite the original opposition, but she would ultimately go into such great debt that she was at risk of losing everything. That did not matter to her, for the picture, when completed, delighted her, and she took it to New York to show distributors. She also made time to meet with Joe Kennedy at Robert Kane's suggestion to see how he could help with her financing.

Swanson was aware that Joe Kennedy had signed the telegram attacking the purchase of the Maugham story. She wanted to be completely independent of him while she heard him out over lunch. Even accepting a free meal from him seemed to give him power, so she made arrangements to handle everything. Before being seated at the table they would share, she had the maître d' place the check on her bill. She warned him that if Kennedy tried to pay, he should be told that the meal was compliments of the management.

Swanson, according to her memoirs, was not impressed with Joe. "With his spectacles and prominent chin, he looked like any average working-class person's uncle. A man of about forty, he still retained a certain boyishness."

It is impossible to know what Joe Kennedy had in mind when he first agreed to meet with Gloria Swanson. The story of the sexual relationship would override all other information in the years to come. And in the end, when it was obvious that Kennedy had taken financial advantage of Gloria's trust and inexperience, it could be said that misappropriating her funds, albeit with her unwitting approval, was his primary goal. In truth, it is most likely that this first meeting was a combination of curiosity and favor for Bob Kane.

Gloria Swanson was both beautiful and the object of fantasy by many women, including Rose Kennedy and the Kennedy daughters old enough to be aware of the motion picture industry. Swanson was a major draw for moviegoing audiences, a fact that always interested Joe in his capacity as producer. And the fact that she was having money problems also made her of interest, for Joe was still learning how poor Hollywood's business practices could be.

Gloria came prepared for a business lunch with the two offers she had been made for her planned third picture. She had gone directly to Bank of America's president for one loan offer, and she had used Joe Schenck, operating in his official United Artists capacity, for the other. What she did not realize was that more could be done for her if she had more information about the pictures.

Joe Kennedy may have known little about the film industry compared with the men he lured to the Harvard conference, but he did understand the business of business. He explained that Hollywood spent money in a manner that was not advantageous. Equipment could be depreciated, costs could be spread over several pictures, and it was possible to consider scheduled showings of movies as income. He explained that the money owed for booked films was no different from accounts payable when selling other products. He taught her how to prepare a proper balance sheet.

As the meal progressed, the business discussion changed to a more lighthearted conversation, as Gloria expected and encouraged. Then, when she thought Kennedy was off guard, she brought up the subject of the telegram attacking her plans for making the now-complete *Sadie Thompson*, as well as her response.

Joe Kennedy claimed that he had not really shared such intense feelings. He felt that he owed the other men a favor, so when he was asked to sign the telegram, he did so. Joe explained that the favor had been related to the Harvard talks, and then asked Gloria's opinion of his films. To his embarrassment, she had never heard of them.

The lunch was a waste. Joe Kennedy was humiliated by not being able to assert himself, either through impressing Gloria with the films he had made or being able to at least treat her to the meal. On her part, the meeting also was worthless. He told her to take the Schenck funding because it was the better deal, something she already knew. What she had hoped for, what Bob Kane had encouraged her to think, had not happened. Joe made no offer to finance her picture.

Gloria began working on a screening of *Sadie Thompson* for the theater chain owners who were based in or near New York. She wanted to be present to answer any questions. She had brought along highly favorable reactions from test audiences, and she was able to explain that there would be no problems with the Hays Office. All questions that could have led to a delay had been handled before and during production. The film would meet no further opposition.

While Gloria was selling *Sadie Thompson*, Joe was working to answer some questions he had raised during the lunch. He had wondered about the European grosses. Not only did the actress not have an accurate figure, she also admitted she did not trust the Paris office of Paramount Pictures, which acted as her distributor. He knew whom to call and had done so, the information to be available the following day.

Joe then explained that the man who was helping Gloria, a Sydney Kent, was in a divorce proceeding and wanted a postponement. Kent's wife was using attorney Milton Cohen. Joe knew that Cohen was Swanson's lawyer as well, and Joe asked her to call Cohen and arrange for him to agree to allow the postponement for Kent.

Just as Gloria arranged to secretly pay for the first lunch she had with Joe, so he wanted to avoid any hint of obligation. He helped Sydney Kent, freeing him from any other favors for checking the grosses. And he canceled any debt to Gloria, who made the call by obtaining those grosses. In the world of Joe Kennedy, it was only right for someone to be in his debt. Seemingly all of his life, he feared being out of control.

The second meeting between Kennedy and Swanson was more date than business. Joe again seemed mildly threatened, this time recognizing that Gloria was a young, self-made woman. She was rich in her own right, having made her money in a new industry far faster than he had done in established businesses when he was her age. He took her to dinner on Long Island using a chauffeur-driven, heated car. Heaters, now standard, were uncommon accessories in those days. To have both heat and a driver was a hedonistic luxury rare even for many of the well off.

The dinner was part romantic meal and part business talk. There was a full orchestra playing music in the background, but no dance floor where awkwardness might develop. Joe brought a corsage, again hinting at a personal relationship. However, once again he failed. As Kennedy learned later, Swanson hated corsages and especially orchids. She also was on a strict diet because her past eating habits caused her intestinal problems. She never said anything to Kennedy and obviously did not care that he ate a large meal.

There were more tests as well. The restaurant was upscale and catered to a customer's every dining whim. Joe said that if Gloria would like some wine, although it was Prohibition, a hidden bottle would be made available, the wine served in teacups to avoid being seen. She declined and he was relieved, since he neither drank nor smoked, the latter being one of Gloria's habits. He never complained about her cigarettes, though, and made certain he was carrying matches. He had not realized that the actress was a smoker when he met her for their first meal together. He had realized his mistake when she took a cigarette, then held it for him to light. She had to accept the light offered by the waiter, a breach of dating etiquette. Joe refused to make the same mistake again.

Filmmaking was the primary subject of the meal, Joe seriously interested in how production might be handled differently in France, where Gloria had made a movie. He then proudly gave her a copy of *The Story of the Films*, explaining how he had brought the producers and other professionals to Harvard.

Swanson recognized that Joe was as devious as she was. His knowledge was greater in many areas, but his methods were the same. He had seduced the Hollywood elite by taking them to Boston, then giving them a bound copy of all the speeches, complete with gold lettering for their names. He had signed the telegram they felt obligated to send to Schenck, with a copy to Hays, concerning *Rain*. He was buying his way to insider status through emotional bribes and flattery, pretending to be outraged where appropriate, becoming involved where money could be made.

It also was during the second meeting that the emotional reason for Kennedy's involvement in Hollywood became evident. Swanson would later remember that Joe constantly talked about the *importance* of the motion picture industry. He had made his early money with readily forgotten films, but he thought that everything from the title of a film to the script to the star and the director should be *important*. He explained that 80 percent of the world's films were American pictures. He talked about the cultural gap that was closed through the movies. He said that anyone with sense could make money in the industry. What mattered was quality, and together with Gloria, that was what they could produce.

Kennedy's ideas and business acumen impressed Swanson. She decided to give him complete access to her business life, starting with all the files in her New York office. She had to return to California, but he would be in touch by telephone until he, too, could get out to the West Coast.

Joe Kennedy discovered how poorly Gloria Swanson's business affairs were being handled. Important matters were not being handled well, and minor matters were taking too much time. As one example, he cited an hour-long conference between her financial adviser and the attorney for Joseph Schenck, both high-priced men. The matter about which they were arguing was the salary of the Cosmopolitan Studios' dressing-room maid. The money in question? Eighteen dollars a week.

There were other examples, all of which Swanson saw as valid. Kennedy said he would handle everything, which he did before returning to California in December. This time he brought the four men he trusted throughout their lives—Derr, Moore, O'Leary, and Sullivan, the same team that had been with him since he worked at the Quincy shipyards. It was their recommendation that the entire company be dissolved and a dummy corporation established. The entire time it would take to handle the job would be a month, a fact that amazed Gloria, who had spent a year establishing her first business. More important, they told her that all problems, from various lawsuits that were nuisances for all successful producers, to legitimate contract issues still in dispute, would be handled. She was to give E. B. Derr her power of attorney, and he would coordinate the handling of everything else.

Gloria quickly discovered Joe Kennedy's secret for success. He understood his limitations, that he was not a particularly intelligent man. The same would be true for at least two of his sons, Jack and Ted. However, he hired the most brilliant staff he could find, made certain they lacked ambition other than to anonymously serve their employer, and taught his sons to do the same.

E. B. Derr, who was to have the power of attorney, was a math wizard who could analyze large sums of numbers in his mind, always correctly.

Eddie Moore, Joe's chief of staff, was skilled in all facets of business and thus could oversee everything with which Joe Kennedy involved himself, no matter how different from previous ventures. Ted O'Leary was a specialist in the liquor business, handling both bootleg and legitimate operations as appropriate. Charley Sullivan handled the complex paperwork that needed to be done. Each was Catholic. Each was married and devoted to his family. And each knew to keep his mouth shut about Joe Kennedy's public and private lives.

As the days progressed, Joe Kennedy found the man to create his first *important* film with and for Gloria Swanson. He arranged for Erich von Stroheim, an arrogant actor turned director, to create and direct a screenplay for the actress. Von Stroheim was a man of both ego and brilliance who was arguably one of the three best directors working in film at the time.

The story von Stroheim created and presented to Swanson should have seemed as odd to her at the time as it does in hindsight. Kitty Kelly, the heroine, is a delightfully high-spirited Irish Catholic convent girl living in a land ruled by a self-centered queen whose sanity is questionable. The queen is betrothed to a prince, but before they can marry, he falls in love with Kitty Kelly. He impulsively goes to her convent, sets it ablaze, and kidnaps the young woman. She is wearing only her nightgown, but he gallantly covers her with his coat before carrying her off to the palace where the queen is living. He thinks he has successfully sneaked her inside where they enjoy a quiet feast at midnight, drinking champagne and declaring their love for one another. But the queen has learned of their presence and bursts in on the couple.

The queen is livid. She assumes from the fact that Kitty Kelly is clad only in a coat-covered nightgown that the couple have been intimate together. Livid despite the fact that the girl remains a virgin, the queen grabs a whip and drives her into the night.

The wedding is off. The prince goes on maneuvers to German East Africa, discovering that Kitty, still a virgin, is running a dance hall previously owned by her aunt.[4] The two renew their devotion, though the happy ending comes only after they are chased through a swamp (exactly by whom was never too clear in the telling, though presumably either enemy soldiers or minions of the queen).

Von Stroheim's odd story would be called *The Swamp*, and he was ready to begin writing the moment he was given the okay.

The entire matter was ridiculous, and even Joe Kennedy must have had his doubts. This was *not* an *important* picture in the manner of a film that addressed a social issue of the day or some other meaningful subject. This seemed a cobbled-together adventure romance that was part impetuous love story, part kidnapping, and part chase scene. What made it "special" was that the director was envisioning it as a vehicle specifically for Swanson, a fact that flattered her into agreeing to what appeared to be an obvious fiasco if not kept to a very low budget.

Joe Kennedy's doubts, or perhaps his self-centered caution, led him to create a contract that should have been a warning for Gloria and Henri. The two partners would split the profits, an equitable arrangement for a success. However, if there were problems with the film, if it lost money, it was Gloria who would have to make up the loss from the money earned from future pictures. Joe would be covered. Joe would have no downside risk.

The business side might have been typical Kennedy, protecting himself at the expense of those who worked with him, but Joe was making a major commitment to his latest affair. In December 1927 Joe rented a home on Rodeo Drive in Beverly Hills. The house, complete with tennis court, was on a street that eventually became the most expensive retail business district in the United States. It was also near Gloria's 904 Crescent Drive estate.

In January 1928, when Gloria and Henri traveled to Palm Beach, they were met by Derr and Kennedy. Joe's assistant took Henri to deal with the luggage. Joe raced to the drawing room, where he could greet Gloria away from any witnesses. There she reported that he kissed her twice, so overwhelmed by passion in crowded quarters that he injured his head on an overhead rack, knocked off his glasses, then fell trying to pick them up. It was a series of pratfalls reminiscent of Gloria's Mack Sennett comedies, and when he finally stood up, his face was smeared with lipstick and his white slacks were smudged with dirt. The lipstick was hastily cleaned from his face, the pants brushed, and no one said anything about his slightly disheveled appearance.

Palm Beach, where Joe maintained a second home, was to be a working vacation spot for Gloria. She and Henri stayed in the Hotel Poinciana, then made the rounds of various social events. The community was home to the rich, powerful, and social elite. It also was extremely segregated by race and religion. Anyone who was white and moneyed was welcome to live there, but a Catholic could not join the dominant WASP country club. The Jews had their own golf club, accepting the reality of the area, and offered to let Joe join. It had previously been the ultimate humiliation in his mind, to be able to play with Jews, whom he despised, and not play with the Florida equivalent of the Boston Brahmins, from whom he still desired acceptance.

The bigotry of Palm Beach was not a concern for him at that particular time. Gloria was. Joe arranged for Eddie Moore to take Henri deep-sea fishing, giving Joe uninterrupted time with Gloria. It was in the Poinciana that Joe famously attacked his lover, their first sexual encounter, which left her bemused and vulnerable. She would not give up Henri, yet she knew that sex would be an ongoing part of her relationship with her business adviser/partner.

The year 1928 was a period of intense change for the Kennedy family. Joe was making his final deals uniting the various film companies. He was escalating his affair with Gloria Swanson. And he was settling the family into what would be their primary residence. This was a 15-room, 9-bath white frame house set on a bluff overlooking Nantucket Sound. It was in the town of Hyannis Port, on Cape Cod, Massachusetts. There were 2½ acres of land, a beach, and a breakwater. There the children would swim, sail, and play both softball and touch football. Always they were to be competitive. Always they were to enter whatever community contests were being held. And always they were expected to win.

As all this was taking place, there were numerous questions about Rose. The Kennedys maintained a facade of family life when Joe was at home. Breakfast in the summer was preceded by 7:00 A.M. calisthenics conducted by a paid instructor. Dinner was promptly at 7:15 P.M. In between came training and competition, the children taught to play to win, to smile through adversity, to be loyal to one another at the expense of friendships, lovers, and spouses.

Rose was a loner, taken to daily Mass, long walks, and regular swims. She talked of making the couple's children their best friends, but the children found her cold. Physical touch was not part of their upbringing, at least not from Rose.

Joe, by contrast, needed close friends. He used his four advisers like a private club. He could count on them for anything, though there is some question about how giving he may have been in return.

There would never be a discussion of Joe's adultery between husband and wife. However, there was a curious discussion with Alice Harrington—the mother of a friend of Eunice, a Catholic, and a neighbor on Hyannis Port—related by author Axel Madsen.[5] According to the story, Rose was asked if she ever showed "iciness" to her husband. Alice Harrington presumably meant that Rose might be so mad at Joe that she refused to have sex with him for a night or two.

Rose, if the story is correct, took the question a different way. "Yes, I have. And I made him pay for that iciness. I made him give me everything I wanted. Clothes, jewels, everything. You have to know how to use that iciness."

The problem with the story is being certain what it means. It is doubtful that Alice was talking about a cheating husband. It is doubtful that Rose was talking about anything other than infidelity. What is certain is that Rose eventually refused to have sex with Joe. There would be no more children after Ted was born and therefore no more need for intercourse. Along the way she seemed to deny him her body whenever she suspected, or perhaps knew, that he was straying. In her reasoning, if she was not having sex with Joe, then he could not be committing adultery.

The cold isolation was Rose's key to survival, probably preceding the Gloria Swanson affair and certainly while Joe and his mistress were flaunting their relationship in front of Rose. She became physically and emotionally distant from her children. She taught them attitudes toward sex and sexuality that seemed to impact on them and cause them to mock their mother.

There was little time for a love affair after von Stroheim received script approval for *Queen Kelly*, the new name for *The Swamp*. Kennedy's approval meant that the payroll would begin and production could start. Gloria would be on the set from morning until night, working on the picture. Joe went to his Palm Beach home to relax. What neither realized was that von Stroheim was so self-centered that he would do anything he wanted.

The original *Queen Kelly*, though a rather silly film with pretensions rather than the potential for greatness, was one that would be approved by the censors. Neither the Hays Office nor state censorship boards were likely to complain. However, once he began shooting, von Stroheim had grand visions. He would carefully light a set, get everyone in perfect position, check the camera angles, then shoot a scene he would almost immediately regret. There would be new writing, new planning, and a different scene. Sometimes it worked, allowing him to both continue the movie and redo earlier work to be certain it came together to make sense. Sometimes it didn't work, in which case he would throw it out and start fresh.

Gloria Swanson was impressed with the first days' filming, work accomplished before she had to start. She attended the rushes, a look at the raw film the day after it had been shot and processed. She would later describe the brilliance of von Stroheim's work, saying, "Every scene was alive with glowing light play and palpable texture. You could almost smell the thin Havana cigars and taste the Viennese coffee and feel the dew on the grass."[6]

The screenplay changes that rolled through his fertile mind were destined to cause yet another scandal if anyone were to see them. In one, a priest who has become respectfully fond of a whorehouse madam gently gives her the last rites as she lay dying in Dar es Salaam. The support of the clergy for a woman who runs a house of prostitution paled by comparison with another scene, which involved the seduction of a girl living in a convent. Perhaps the scene with the clergyman could have been altered so he was seen as making a desperate effort to save a soul. But convent girls were virgins, and under the guidance of Will Hays, they had better stay that way. Von Stroheim was immediately fired.

With twenty thousand feet of film shot and the movie already costing $600,000, Joe decided to see if Gloria's future income could save the picture. He would not take the loss, so he consulted with other producers and brought in Edmund Goulding to finish directing the film. Another $200,000 would be spent, but it was not enough. They would have to start from the beginning, and no one was willing to do that. Ultimately what amounted to a rough edit with no ending was made and the film released in Europe. Some money was recovered, but nowhere near enough to help Gloria.

Not that Joe reminded Gloria of the fine print of the contract she and Henri failed to read. He did not want to end the relationship, and she would not be a willing adulteress if she knew how he had cheated her. Instead, Joe bemoaned the loss, eventually bragging about his problems. He wanted it to seem a badge of honor that he was so rich that he could fail dramatically and continue in the business.

There would be two more movies financed by Joe Kennedy and one last time to flaunt his famous mistress. The first of the two was *The Trespasser*, and it meant more to Gloria Swanson's career than *Queen Kelly* or *Sadie Thompson*. It would be her first talking picture, and neither she nor anyone else was certain how she would sound. It had been several years since she had done live stage, but even her theatrical background could not prepare her for the new, more subtle approach to acting required when the audience could hear you speak. Ultimately there was nothing to worry about. Gloria had not forgotten her early training as a singer. She would make a smooth transition to talking pictures, her career potentially greater than before. She and Joe could move on to create *The Trespasser.*

Despite the suspense implied in the title, *The Trespasser* was yet another story of cross-class love. Marion, a Chicago legal secretary, marries into a wealthy, upper-class family that ultimately wants to have her sent away while they keep and raise the couple's baby. There is a complication in which Marion appears to be compromised by her employer, but ultimately everything works out. Marion is cleared of any stigma, her husband truly loves her, and the couple lives happily ever after.

The Trespasser was carefully planned. A reel of sound film lasted nine minutes. Traditional editing practices created bleeps that would constantly remind the audience that the movie was an illusion, not real life. It was decided to shoot scenes in nine-minute lengths. As many cameras would record each scene as necessary so the same action would be covered from all angles, as well as with long shots, medium shots, and close-ups. There were times that twelve cameras were filming simultaneously, but by working so carefully, production time was drastically reduced. Film was far less expensive than the daily rates of technicians, carpenters, lighting experts, and all the other people involved in the films. The movie was made in twenty-one days, and it proved to be the least expensive Gloria Swanson movie since she had gone independent. More important, the viewing for United Artists' representative in New York went extremely well.

Joe Kennedy had planned to hold the world premiere of *The Trespasser* in New York City's Rialto, the most famous theater in United Artists' chain. A booking conflict meant that they would have to delay the opening, and the incoming cash flow, until November. Joe felt they should start in England if New York was out because Gloria always did extremely well there. *Queen Kelly* was still being worked on behind the scenes, so there would be no problem with Gloria attending. Henri was already in France, so it was a small matter for him to meet her.

Then, when the plans were being confirmed, Joe mentioned one other point. Rose Kennedy had never been to Europe, according to Joe. The three of them would go together; then Gloria could travel on to Paris, get Henri, and the two of them would return to London for the premiere.

Rose had been to Europe, of course. She had traveled when she went to college. After all, the Ace of Clubs limited its membership to women who studied abroad. Rose would want to go to the film's premiere, but she was not lacking in sophistication or experience, as Joe implied.

Gloria Swanson also claimed that Joe told her that she and Rose would have to meet someday. Perhaps that was true if Rose came to visit Joe in Hollywood. But other than such a tourist-style trip, there was no reason why the women would ever come in contact with one another under normal circumstances. Gloria was just another business associate, not unlike the men with whom he worked while still on Wall Street. She was more glamorous and certainly more famous, but that did not warrant a special meeting.

The arrangements Joe Kennedy made were simple. Gloria Swanson called a friend from Chicago, Virginia Bowker, and asked her to accompany her to London. Joe's sister also would make the trip, along with Rose. The size of the entourage apparently was supposed to diminish the chance that anyone would learn the truth about the affair. The problem was that the entourage made the situation all the more conspicuous, especially when Joe had Gloria and her daughter travel to Hyannis Port to spend some time with the Kennedys before leaving for England.

There are several reasons why Joe Kennedy may have brought Gloria Swanson to Hyannis Port with him. The simplest may have been that he wanted her to see his home and meet his family. It is also possible that he took pride in having acquired the two most important women in his world, albeit at different times in his life. He was a collector, and suddenly he had Rose, once the most desirable Irish Catholic girl in all of Boston, and Gloria, arguably the most beautiful and desired movie star in the nation, both under the same roof.

The Kennedy mansion was a living museum. Rose collected dolls, and one room was devoted to them, with special glass-covered shelving displaying dolls from throughout the world.

Joe liked historic relevance and completeness. His holdings included two locks of hair and two plates that had belonged to George Washington. He also bought the collections others had built instead of enjoying the hunt for each desired piece. This was why he had purchased not only antique furniture but also the floorboards of the room in which the New Hampshire Shea family had once placed handcarved duck decoys, cranberry glass, furniture, silver hollowware, and numerous other items. Some of the treasures were displayed. Others were kept carefully stored, sometimes being forgotten with time. The Washington possessions, for example, had been placed in shadow boxes, then stored in a cedar closet, forgotten until found by Rose's assistant Barbara Gibson in 1975.

There also was a full movie theater in the house. Joe delighted in showing the family and their friends first-run pictures and movies not yet released to the public. Often they carried the credit "Joseph P. Kennedy Presents . . ."

And there was Rose. Joe bragged to Gloria that he had proven his love for her by not getting Rose pregnant in the months they had been lovers. He did not say that Rose had cut him off from sex with her because she did not want to face the physical fact of his cheating. Yet he was sensitive enough to his wife that he may have wanted to end any thought that he might be having an affair. Bringing a mistress and her teenage daughter into the midst of his own family may have been his way of defusing a potential problem. No one would do anything so hurtful to his wife. No one would risk the disapproval of the community. Gloria Swanson *had* to be living the life with her beloved Henri that the studio publicists assured the press she was enjoying.

School had started, and Gloria's daughter visited with Pat Kennedy, who was close in age. Her friends had difficulty believing that the child was the daughter of the woman they knew from fan magazines and the movies.

Kathleen had long been a Swanson fan. The Kennedy sisters and Kathleen's friends had turned a room above the garage into a clubhouse filled with adolescent dreams. The walls had movie posters, and they all read fan magazines such as *Photoplay*. They invited Gloria to their private sanctuary and delighted in her signing the wall. The dedication of the fans was obvious when Kathleen learned the truth about Swanson and her father. She immediately became as devoted to actress Constance Bennett as she had been to Swanson. However, she refused to cover, remove, or destroy Gloria's autograph. It was too precious to her.

Rose had long had her way of coping with Joe's activities in Hollywood. She avidly read the stories about Joe and the family in *Motion Picture World*, *Photoplay*, and similar magazines. She delighted in posing with their eight children. She read the glowing captions and the positive articles, all describing the way his family meant everything to him. She clung to the image to maintain what little self-esteem remained.

The one person who had no illusions was Josie Fitzgerald. She had had to deal with Honey Fitz and his women. There were questions about whether Toodles Ryan was one of them, but there had been and were plenty of others. She was almost delighted to discuss the fact that all men were alike, even Rose's precious beloved.

Rose remained steadfast. Her daughters would one day experience divorce and marital disillusionment, though without pretense. Rose pretended nothing was wrong, never correcting Joe when he covered himself in the community by introducing Gloria as "Rose's friend."

At home, Rose remained steadfast to her routine of daily Mass at St. Francis Xavier Church followed by breakfast with her older children. Joe had time alone with Gloria, but not the opportunities for intimacy he was seeking. Finally he decided to take her on a sailboat he had purchased two years earlier, one Joe Jr. and Jack had named *Rose Elizabeth*.

Gloria was reluctant to go on the boat, not because she was avoiding the intimacy she knew would follow but because she could not swim. Joe was an excellent swimmer, though, skilled with the boat, and knew that the weather would make for a pleasant time away from land. The vessel was large enough so they could enjoy themselves on the deck as the boat drifted safely in the water. Assured that she would not be in danger, Gloria agreed.

Jack Kennedy, just reaching his teens, learned of his father's plans and was disappointed that he wasn't asked along. He liked Gloria Swanson. She was a nice lady, nothing like the image he had of a stuck-up movie star. He thought that whatever his father and Gloria might do, they would enjoy having him along to enliven the day. He decided to hurry ahead of them and, when he was out of sight, sneak down belowdecks.

Everything went as Joe had planned. The weather was clear, the water smooth, and Gloria felt safe once they were on the water. The couple kissed with growing passion, then shed each other's clothing to make love. It was some time after this, when Joe Kennedy was making love to his married lover, that Jack climbed onto the deck to surprise them.

The youth was overwhelmed. He had never thought of his parents in an intimate way. Now he was forced to see the blatant sexuality of his father in the arms of another woman. This was no business associate.

Horrified, Jack leaped off the boat and began swimming toward land, his congenital back condition limiting his strength and endurance. Jack could swim only a short distance before tiring and starting to sink below the surface.

Joe, horrified, leaped into the water, swimming to his son and pulling him from the water. Ironically, it would be the same life-saving action that Jack's younger brother Bobby would take, saving one of his own sons on the last day of his own life. No one knows what may have been said between father and son. Gloria Swanson recorded no reference to the incident in her autobiography. Since Jack hated his mother, telling her she was cold and distant during an angry tirade later in his youth, it was likely that he suppressed his rage and confusion. What is certain is that he would grow to be a womanizer himself, seeking so many sexual encounters with so cavalier an attitude that many people came to feel he might have hated most women.

The trip to Europe was less troublesome. Rose prattled on about children and other "women" issues. She was better educated and more sophisticated than Gloria Swanson. However, Rose avoided any confrontation, even when Joe spent all his time focused on the actress and no one else in their party. His one concession to both Rose and propriety was to spend each night in the cabin with his wife.

Ultimately the trip seemed worthwhile. Gloria Swanson was enormously popular in England, and any picture she made would have had a good audience response there. However, in this case the public and the critics truly enjoyed her pleasant voice and the way she sounded in her first talkie. The studio had a hit on its hands, and the couples, along with their guests, prepared to return to New York.

Joe Kennedy was not hurt by the crash of the stock market. He had been looking at finances—his own and his family's—since his seventy-one-year-old father died in May of that year, the will naming Joe as executor. The estate Pat Kennedy had built for himself and his family was a solid one of $50,000 to $55,000. (Multiply by 6 to approximate the contemporary value.) He also had stocks in the coal company and the East Boston banks he had helped to build, as well as a no-longer-valid $25 bond issued nine years before by the Republic of Ireland. Pat had kept his money in his community, investing in the people he had always treasured and always tried to help.

Ultimately it would be obvious that while neither father nor son had ever wanted for money, Joe's fantasy that he would be truly happy the richer he became from a variety of national investments was wrong. Pat Kennedy died beloved in the community, an experience Joe could witness but never duplicate.

Three months later, in August 1929, Joe took a serious look at his own financial situation and the condition of the nation's economy. He had been aware that the stock market was spiraling out of control. He understood the danger of the speculators, of the improbable rise in stock prices beyond normal profit-to-earnings ratios that helped establish legitimate value. However, he did not anticipate the crash, as some have given him credit for doing.

It has been said of Joe that he was getting his shoes shined when the youth doing the shining accurately analyzed several stocks currently in play in the market. According to the story, that was when Joe decided to pull out of the market, claiming that when even a shoeshine boy was speculating, a crash was inevitable. But the story probably never happened, and if it did, it occurred after Joe had made his exit. Joe simply understood the economy, the need to diversify, and the fact that the economy was in for a rapid change. The same situation—albeit not so dramatic as the Great Depression proved to be—had occurred in the last decade of the nineteenth century and in the first decade of the twentieth century.

It is likely that Joe did his initial analysis of the stock market during the time he spent in Florida during the winter of 1928–1929. He was a professional manipulator, so he understood how some stocks could become increasingly overvalued. He also saw syndicates operating in the manner he created, including one by William Crapo Durant, who had made, lost, and regained a fortune, first as founder of General Motors, then with a group of millionaires who had enough of a pool to move a stock anywhere they desired.

Other men made wealthy in the automobile industry also put together bankrolls to manipulate stocks. Unlike the fluctuations created for Yellow Cab, most of the work was meant to assure ever-higher prices.

Kennedy understood that a rising market creates a myth about itself. Instead of investors stepping back and looking at whether the price increases are based on the quality of the business, they assume that if it is rising today, it will rise tomorrow, and if it rises tomorrow, it will rise next week. They know that there is a point where overpriced stocks collapse, especially when manipulators turn profit takers. What they fail to do is stop themselves. They mock those who become scared and remove their money, pointing to ever-growing paper value. Yet it is paper value, based on nothing tangible, and it will drop. The problem is that the longer the run-up, the harder it is for investors to not want to make just another few dollars.

Joe also realized that when a stock was on a rise and a man bragged about his profits, there would be those who deliberately waited to buy in until the stock was a "sure thing." A stock valued at 100 was a good buy, but they made the purchase at 200, shooting the stock to 300, where others felt the need to get involved with the money machine. It was a variation of a pyramid scheme except, in this case, the sinners were the investors, not the leaders of the companies.

Joe Kennedy was a greedy man, but he was not a fool. He liked investing in sure things, whether it was a solid investment, he was in control, or he could skim money from someone else. He sold his holdings rather than waiting for what others thought was the top dollar yet to come. Then he kept his money in cash, awaiting the inevitable though with no idea whether that meant in the short term, in months, or even in years. It did not matter. He was a millionaire many times over, just as he had dreamed. He could afford time. He could not afford a major loss. (Joe began establishing trust funds for his children during these years. They were always designed so he could have access to the money should his world collapse. He wanted to be certain his sons and daughters were set for life only after he protected himself.)

Joe was uneasy when he first learned that the stock market crashed, but he soon realized that it was a major opportunity for him. The value of various properties he had long coveted plummeted to below what should have been fair market value, allowing for previously unheard-of investment opportunities. The movie industry, on the other hand, profited beyond anyone's expectations. Going to the movies had become America's national pastime. It was a way to hide or heal, to escape to fantasy or rekindle the spirit. However it was viewed, people continued spending their money in the theaters. If they had any money left after paying for food, clothing, and shelter, they went to the movies.

The stock market crash occurred between the times that *The Trespasser* opened in London and when it opened in New York, yet the New York opening was a mob scene. Thousands of people were waiting to see both Gloria and the film, creating a serious danger of injury to the star. Joe had to have two of his assistants take Gloria by the arms and wedge her through the crowd. When she entered the theater, the audience was in a frenzy. She received a standing ovation just for being there.

In the end, the critics loved the work as well. They felt that she gave a better performance than she had when they raved about *Sadie Thompson*. She had entered the sound era, brilliantly making the transition, and as Joe soon discovered, the movie industry also survived the transition from a robust economy to the growing Depression.

The relationship between Joe and Gloria was almost over. Joe was looking to finance just one more picture with his mistress, yet he may have become bothered by the relationship after his return from London.

According to Swanson, at the end of 1929, while she was still in Manhattan but Joe had gone elsewhere, Ted O'Leary told her that she was to meet someone at another hotel in the city. This was not unusual. Joe frequently either tried to impress her by introducing her to someone he felt was important, or arranged for her to have a business meeting on the spur of the moment. The latter occurred when he had laid all the groundwork and she was expected to go along with whatever was asked.

The man Gloria was to see turned out to be William Cardinal O'Connell of Boston. The actress was certain the cardinal had never seen any of her films and probably knew little about her. She also tried to defuse the need for a conversation by suggesting that if he was there on business, he should talk with E. B. Derr, Joe's assistant who handled her business affairs.

The cardinal tried to politely explain that Swanson did not understand Catholics, his tone being one of someone who feels that such a situation is an abomination. He said that she should stop seeing Joe because each time they were together was an occasion for sin. He did not come out and say that their relationship was personal and sexual, but it was obvious that was why he was there.

Gloria wanted none of such hypocrisy. She explained that if there was a problem for Joe, then the cardinal should be talking with Joe.

The cardinal said that Joe had come to him for help. He wanted permission to leave Rose and live with Gloria. He did not want a divorce, which would not have been granted, nor an annulment.

The cardinal seemed to think that Joe had discussed his plans with Gloria. He did not realize that she was surprised by the idea. He also did not realize that Gloria would not leave Henri at that stage in her life. She would be unfaithful to him—with Joe and perhaps others—but there was never a thought of divorce.

O'Connell continued by emphasizing that Joe Kennedy was one of the most prominent Catholic layman in America, suggesting, it seemed, that every Catholic and many Protestants were aware of the man, his actions, and how he lived.

Finally Swanson had enough of the situation. She told the cardinal that his talk should be with Joe, not her. Then she left, livid with Joe. However, once back in O'Leary's car, she learned that Joe knew nothing of what had taken place. It was the cardinal's staff who had contacted the cardinal directly.

But is the story true?

One biographer claimed to have done research that revealed no such New York trip for the cardinal. The lack of a record might be meaningful but more likely reflected discretion on O'Connell's part.

The fact that Boston and New York are so close suggests that the trip would not have had to disrupt the cardinal's work schedule in a noticeable manner.

Another biographer, Axel Madsen, interviewed Rose's niece Geraldine Hammon, who claimed to have been present when Joe and his father-in-law began fighting over Joe's adultery. Honey Fitz threatened to tell Rose what he knew, not realizing that his daughter was not naive, just determined to hold the marriage together. Joe, who also did not appreciate what his wife was doing, said that if his father-in-law did speak to his wife, Joe would divorce Rose and marry Gloria Swanson. Neither man understood that Gloria wanted nothing to do with Joe Kennedy as a husband.

The truth is likely to be closer to what Madsen found from interviewing Geraldine Hammon. Talks with people familiar with the couple at that time in their lives, with comments Rose Kennedy made later, and the information found by biographers of both Kennedy family members and of Gloria Swanson seem to indicate the following.

Joe Kennedy had committed himself to Gloria Swanson as his primary though not only lover from 1926 forward. He spent more time away from Rose than with her, though that was not all time spent with Gloria Swanson. They were frequently seen together, and she was the only lover he enjoyed who is known to have been photographed with him. Women he escorted to various Florida nightclubs were never to be photographed by the club photographer, who went from table to table taking pictures and then selling them as souvenirs. Gloria, by contrast, was photographed so frequently with Joe that seeing their picture on a restaurant wall such as that of Musso & Frank's Grill on Hollywood Boulevard was not an unusual sight. But Joe never actually lived with Gloria.

Rose was Joe's first trophy in the game of life that only he was playing. Marriage and staying with the Catholic Church was his idea of faithfulness. Adultery was never a concern. He also realized that William Cardinal O'Connell probably had no illusions about the financial benefits possible from staying friendly with both Kennedys. He would intercede between them only when asked, and then only when a moral stance would have to be taken with either of them.

It is likely that Rose and Honey Fitz went to see the cardinal to have him speak with Gloria Swanson. They knew that further action was useless when it came to Joe. There was some gossip making the papers, but the family knew that the Fitzgeralds were more vulnerable than the Kennedys. Besides, Joe's adultery was always committed away from Rose, her family, and their children (except for Jack's unexpected discovery). John Fitzgerald enjoyed his women where all could see, but few had any interest in using the information against him, at least until the Toodles fiasco.

While all this was taking place, Gloria Swanson learned another side to her husband's character. He may have been quiet, compliant, and lacking in the excitement she brought to everything she did, but he was not a fool. Henri was not Rose Kennedy, determined to pretend that real life was not taking place all around. Henri was a man of deep feelings who refused to be treated casually. He sent Gloria a note telling her that she was to plan a formal separation. Once that was accomplished, she could arrange for the divorce in whatever way she desired. He would not endanger her reputation or career. He also would not stay married to her.

"Henri and I have decided to continue living apart, as we have lived for the last year and a half," Gloria eventually stated to the Associated Press. It was a release she first discussed with Henri because he wanted to be certain that they put out the same story to avoid embarrassing her. "We have found it possible to maintain separate establishments and still be the best of friends."

Gloria was shattered, though it was impossible to feel sorry for her. She had a husband she felt was the best man to come into her life (until the next "best man," and the next, and . . .). She had a lover who was working to enhance her life as a star. And she had great sums of money coming into her production company.

Even as Swanson pondered her personal life, Joe was creating a film for her. He went to Vincent Youmans, a composer, to work on songs Gloria would sing in a new musical, enhancing her career in the talkies. He also hired the husband/wife team of John and Josephine Robertson to write the screenplay, in which Gloria would show all her talents as a comedienne.[7] However, the script was bad, a situation that was embarrassing for all concerned, since Joe had commissioned it and seemed comfortable with it. When too many of his trusted friends and associates agreed that it needed reworking, Joe turned to Pulitzer Prize–winning playwright Sidney Howard, who created the story *What a Widow*.

The story was a simple one. An innocent young woman marries an older man. He is sixty when he dies and leaves her $5 million (approximately $30 million in contemporary dollars).

This was a typical Swanson liberated female character. Why the very young woman married the much older man is unclear, though she had to care for him in what, back then, would be considered old age.

Suddenly she had wealth, no husband, and a determination to live life to the fullest.

The widow leaves Manhattan for Paris. She spends her money, enjoys hedonistic delights, and is pursued by a singer-dancer who performs the Youmans songs, a lawyer from the New York office that represented the widow's late husband, and a Russian violinist.

The new script, much changed from the original, was a competent story and an easy vehicle for Swanson. The only problem was that the mood of the country was changing. Movies might have been doing better than ever as the standard escape from the Depression that was beginning to cripple the nation, but only certain types of films were in demand. Gangster movies came into their own, a genre that quickly dominated the theaters. In addition, musicals were desired, but not just a movie with a few songs and maybe some dancing. This was a time when lavish spectacles filled the screen. Busby Berkeley and, a little later, Hermes Pan brought their wonders to the screen. Fred Astaire, Ginger Rogers, and numerous other young dancers invigorated films, making the stories almost secondary. Lavish production numbers and gangster films dominated the theaters. *What a Widow* seemed a throwback to a simpler time, an easier time, a time that was often only a few weeks in the past for much of the country just beginning to feel the harsh effects of the Depression.

Joe was not ready to admit that *What a Widow* was the wrong picture, shown too late. He informed Sidney Howard that he was so thrilled with the title of the reworked screenplay that he was giving him a Cadillac. And when the car arrived, a thrilled Howard thanked the studio head. What neither he nor Gloria Swanson realized was that Kennedy was busy cutting all ties with his soon-to-be-divorced "beloved." This meant that he wanted no financial obligations in her world. He charged the Cadillac to Gloria's personal account, a fact she learned from her accountant Irving Wykoff, a man outside Joe's control.

Wykoff was a trusted accountant and friend who had been eased from Swanson's life by the Kennedy entourage. However, Gloria still felt that there might be accidental errors. She had Wykoff review her accounts and do the preliminary tax planning. During one of these reviews he caught what both thought was a mistake. Gloria paid for Howard's new car. To both Gloria and Wykoff's surprise, the payment was not a mistake but a deliberate misuse of Gloria's money.

Shortly afterward, Gloria Swanson learned the truth about her life and lover. She had played Henri, the man she thought she truly loved, for a naive fool. She thought that she could enjoy the sexual attention of Joe Kennedy while knowing that when the affair grew boring, inconvenient, or otherwise needed to be ended, Henri would wait for her.

Gloria also was convinced that Joe Kennedy's lustful aggression reflected a level of commitment that went beyond the sensual, even though he never considered a divorce. In another time, in another place, perhaps she and Joe would have been married. That was why she had been certain that he only had her best interests at heart when he took over her finances.

By the time *What a Widow* was completed, several facts were obvious. Many of the gifts Joe Kennedy lavished on his lover had been paid for out of her accounts. He had robbed her in ways so subtle that there was no full determination of how many hundreds of thousands of dollars he had cost her.

Worse, Gloria learned that Joe also had been enjoying the company of actress Constance Bennett, a growing Swanson rival. He had flirted with her, signed her to the studio where he had influence, then passed her off to his friends. Bennett also made the acquaintance of Henri, a man she found as appealing as Gloria had. Bennett approached him at his most vulnerable, eventually marrying him when the divorce from Swanson was finalized. As a result, Swanson had to regularly see Bennett both at work and in the gossip column illustrations, where she was photographed standing with the dapper marquis.

The interlude with Swanson would prove the most dramatic and vicious of Joe Kennedy's life, though it is likely he had no illusions about the woman with whom he wanted to live. She was exciting, beautiful, and comfortably married. She also was earning enough money to keep him satisfied when he siphoned off funds for his own purposes or to pay for loving "presents" when he chose to not spend his own money for his paramour.

However, before Joe Kennedy left the industry $5 million richer than when he started, there was one more deal that was underreported until uncovered by Kenneth Anger, a former child movie star turned filmmaker and biographer of the dark side of Hollywood. The story, told in his second *Hollywood Babylon* book, involved one of Joe's acquisitions, the sixty-theater chain owned by Alexander Pantages. It was the second-largest chain in California, and it made the Greek immigrant extremely wealthy.

Pantages had no interest in selling the theaters. The economy was excellent early in 1929, as far as Pantages knew, and the idea of selling made no sense. He rejected Kennedy's first offer in February of that year, then rebuffed two subsequent offers.

Then Joe started his final effort to gain the Pantages chain with a personal action that was reprehensible and reminiscent of men such as John D. Rockefeller, who was willing to lose money on every gallon of gasoline he pumped when trying to drive a rival from the business. Joe couldn't undercut box office admissions, but he could deny a theater both his films and the films of friends who were willing to cooperate.

The first action took place against the downtown Los Angeles Pantages. None of the studios with which Alexander Pantages did business would provide him with their most successful first-run pictures. He still obtained films to show, but by the time he could have them play, most of his potential customers had seen them, and his business suffered greatly.

The second action Kennedy took is subject to question, some of the accusations based on a deathbed confession allegedly made to the perpetrator's mother, a not-unbiased party.

It said that Joe Kennedy, working with a man named Nicholas Dunaev, decided to destroy Alexander Pantages's reputation. Dunaev was a writer of limited ability and a theatrical agent with a limited clientele. His newest would-be starlet was just seventeen and seemed to be paying his commission in "trade." Her name was Eunice Pringle, and she and Dunaev lived in a low-cost residence motel called the Moonbeam Glen Bungalow Court. The $10,000 Joe Kennedy provided for Pringle to put on a show to compromise Pantages would assure the couple an adequate lifestyle for two years. And to sweeten the plot, Joe was supposed to have promised to put the woman into motion pictures.

The Kennedy involvement was an allegation never proven with absolute certainty. The action by Pringle was something else.

According to Pantages, Pringle was acting as her agent's representative when he first met her. The teenager brought him a short play to read and, hopefully, purchase. Apparently Dunaev and Pringle thought Pantages might be able to help them either produce it or have it turned into a film. Instead, he rejected it as "vulgar."

Again according to Pantages, Pringle returned to the theater after receiving the rejection of her lover's work. She became irate, attacking him with such force that she tore his shirt. Then she clung to his legs until he could get rid of her.

What is certain because of both credible witnesses and information subsequently brought out at trial was that on August 9, 1929, Pringle was in the broom closet of the 607 South Hill Pantages movie theater in Los Angeles. She was wearing a low-cut dress that revealed more of her breasts than was proper.

Suddenly the closet door burst open and Pringle came racing out, screaming to attract the attention of an employee. When he hurried to her side, she collapsed, pointing to Pantages, who also came forward. "There he is, the beast!" she yelled. Then she demanded protection from him.

Pantages was shocked. He knew the girl was trying to frame him, but by then a policeman had been summoned. By the time the girl calmed down, Pantages was arrested for attempted rape.

The trial was a simple one. According to Pringle, the theater owner was kissing her passionately, then lowered his head and began biting her breasts. That was when she had escaped the closet, saw the employee, and was aided by the police officer.

There was no hospital check of Pringle's body at the time she made the accusation, no witness to bite marks on her breasts. No one asked why she was in the closet when the implication was that some sort of relationship had begun innocently, then led to the passionate embrace and improper actions. And no one questioned how Pantages, a physically slight man, could have overpowered Pringle who, despite dressing to limit what someone might notice when first meeting her, had an athletic body. She would have been able to more than hold her own in a fight.

Young ladies were presumed not to be liars in those days, and perhaps that was true. However, Eunice Pringle was young but no lady. Pantages was found guilty and sentenced to fifty years in jail. However, attorney Jerry Geisler appealed. He noted that the judge had ruled Pringle's sex life inadmissible because she was underage.

Geisler pointed out that the living arrangement of Pringle and Dunaev gave a very different picture of the incident. He noted that when all the facts were introduced, it was obvious that there was a conspiracy. Pantages was innocent.

The California Supreme Court sided with Geisler and ordered a new trial, during which Pantages was acquitted. However, the theater owner had been hurt too badly. Joe had offered him $8 million for the chain before the rape charges. After the acquittal, Joe had him sell to RKO for $3.5 million, the highest offer from any source despite the $8 million offer made earlier being a fair value.

In 1933, two years after the acquittal, the twenty-one-year-old Pringle told her lawyer she wanted to tell the truth about what had happened when she set up Pantages. Before she could do so, she became ill with cyanide poisoning. She knew she was dying, and when her mother came to see her, she allegedly made her confession naming Joe Kennedy.

Did Joe Kennedy have the Pringle woman murdered? If he was involved, and if he did promise her a chance to be in films, it seems that completing the bribe would have been simpler than arranging for her to be given cyanide. Or did Joe not trust women the way he trusted men? Did he provide Dunaev with additional cash to get rid of the girl in whom he might have lost interest? It is impossible to know.

Joe Kennedy's California years were a time when he engaged in the most openly vicious actions toward those close to him that would ever occur, but arranging to murder a woman because she was naming him as a conspirator against the theater chain owner seems extreme. Pringle was a known liar and perjurer. Her statements, had she lived, probably would have been dismissed as being similar to the charges leveled against Pantages.

11

AFTER HOLLYWOOD

JOE LEFT GLORIA WITHOUT SAYING GOOD-BYE. IT WAS A COLDNESS spawned from his emotional isolation from all but his closest male friends. He may have attacked her with passion when they first became intimate, but it was the conquest that was the goal.

Gloria Swanson was the most famous actress in Hollywood. She had talent, beauty, and an earnings potential greater than Joe's when only honest business deals were considered. He wooed her, won her (monogamy for Gloria was having only one husband and one lover at a time), and then abandoned her to the wilds of Beverly Hills.

The only difference between wife and lovers for Joe was that a wife was forever, even when the relationship was long dead. A lover was a way station in the pursuit of dreams never quite fulfilled.

Joe's relationship with Hollywood would be longer-lasting than his relationship with various starlets. He had been an unwanted interloper when he first arrived. He was a theater owner, an exhibitor of films who thought he could produce, and in Hollywood most such men were known by a single adjective: bankrupt.

Joe was different. Although what became known as vertical mergers had been used in a few companies here and there, Joe solidified the concept by applying it to a single industry. He also promoted it in ways that made it a path of choice for interrelated businesses. The logic of ownership of all aspects of creating, manufacturing, marketing, and distributing a product seems obvious today. However, it is obvious only because so many businesses have since emulated Joe's approach to bringing together production people, sound manufacturers, marketing, and distribution.

Joe's approach also influenced the way some studios operate today with independent companies that might otherwise be their rivals. The larger studios now give space to independent studios that have their offices on the large studio grounds and may get some rent, parking, and security benefits, but are responsible for their own products, payroll, and some portion of their overhead. Each time the independent company decides to produce a screenplay, the company president presents the project, committed talent, and the like to the larger studio. If the studio likes it, money and other assistance will be provided, assuring a better picture, more expensive picture, and/or a film that can be made faster because the search for financing has ended. If the studio doesn't like it, the smaller production company is told why. They can make it on their own, seeking whatever outside resources are necessary, or they can learn from the criticism, decide it is valid, and look to another project. Everybody profits through gross percentage sharing and interest payments determined on a studio-by-studio basis. The small studio no longer has to fight for survival, and the larger studio is not limited by its own cash flow as to the number of smaller, lower-budget, but potentially profitable pictures it can make.

Eventually other industries, including car manufacturing, experimented with some of the same ideas that Joe brought to Hollywood. The only difference was that as the automobile industry changed, some of the businesses were sold for needed cash, creating an "independent" company that often had only a single customer: the car manufacturer that had originally owned the company that became a supplier.

It is probable that the film industry would have prospered during the height of the Great Depression without Joe Kennedy's involvement. However, the profitability of the companies and the number of smaller film studios that survived owe their greater success to what Joe created before the stock market collapse. This would be why Joe would eventually be recalled to Hollywood to help save giants such as Paramount Pictures, which had fallen so far that there was a chance their names would become film industry trivia questions.

On the personal side, Rose seemed to understand that no matter what Joe had done with other women in Hollywood, he had come home to Bronxville for her. (They had moved to a five-acre estate there at the end of 1928.) He spent his days on nearby Wall Street and his nights in the marital bed, a fact that soon led to Rose's pregnancy with their ninth and last child, Edward Moore "Teddy" Kennedy.

Friends and relatives were surprised. They felt that nine children would be too great a responsibility. They also felt that Rose would never regain her figure, a concern shared with those women who looked on maintaining their prepregnancy appearance as a ritual equal in importance to Rose's daily Mass.

The pregnancy was never a problem for Rose, who was both athletic and obsessive. Her large staff would raise Teddy as they were raising the other eight children. Swimming and long, rapid walks would restore her figure.

There also was a price she extracted from Joe, whether it was for the sex or a reprisal for the nights she was certain he spent in someone else's bed. It was a financial penalty to be paid in the acquisition of clothes and other items she enjoyed. As she explained with her uniquely personal "spin" in her memoir *Times to Remember*:

> During Joe's years in the movie industry he was surrounded daily by some of the most beautiful women in the world, dressed in beautiful clothes. Obviously, I couldn't compete in natural beauty, but I could make the most of what I had by keeping my figure trim, my complexion good, my grooming perfect, and by always wearing clothes that were interesting and becoming. And so, with Joe's endorsement, I began spending more time and more money on clothes. Eventually I began landing on some lists of "Best Dressed Women."

Rose Kennedy never knew quite how wealthy the family had become, nor did she fully understand the extent of the family holdings in her lifetime. She was separated from the poor by layers of paid help and studied indifference. She just knew that when Joe returned to New York, he was engaged in the serious business of making money in the Depression, which he saw as filled with opportunity. He had thoroughly enjoyed the world of West Coast excess, but no matter how rich you became in Hollywood, the power you could wield there was limited in scope and often transitory. Wall Street was where Joe felt himself a master of the game that could lead to national and international influence.

Eddie Moore, a friend so close that Joe's fourth son would be named for him,[1] became the front for an account Joe used for manipulative trading. Joe was provided a desk at the Madison Avenue firm of Halle and Steiglitz, essentially making him a company stockbroker. However, he worked only his own account, the brokerage firm presence giving a legitimacy to his work. In exchange, the company was paid a small percentage of his trades, much like the arrangement for a staff broker.

Kennedy's primary business partner was Bernard E. "Ben" Smith, who had a similar arrangement with W. E. Hutton and Company. However, much of Smith's buying and selling of stock was noticed only if you knew to look at the trades made through friends at both Bache and Company and J. H. Oliphant and Company.

Ben Smith established the parameters for the game he and Joe enjoyed. Smith was a traditional short player, no different from those investors who manipulated high-flying fads such as the initial public offerings of the early 1990s and the Internet business stocks at the end of that decade.

Joe and Ben fancied themselves Wall Street outsiders. Certainly anyone considered a "bear"—making profits on a declining market for a stock instead of counting on dividends or a rise in value—was an "outlaw" to traditional players. A "bear" profiting from short selling deliberately hurt individuals who often were from the blue-blood aristocracy that so troubled Kennedy. They were just another form of Boston Brahmin, the men who controlled access to the desirable country clubs, the prestigious corporate boards, and sometimes even the locations where a man could buy a home to raise his family.

Both men loved the game of making money no matter who got hurt. Both men had an underlying sense of being forever seen, even in their maturity, as the slightly "nerdy" high school student forever picked on by less accomplished but socially acceptable classmates. They were raised Irish Catholic, neither of them smoking or drinking, yet both loving bawdy humor and crude language. The one deviation between the two involved their goals in life. Ben Smith wanted to make money. He hadn't been obsessed with becoming a millionaire by a certain age, as Kennedy had been. He didn't feel the need to show off his wealth, as Joe and Rose did. He just liked making money as an end in itself.

Joe Kennedy was different. There was an anger that stayed just beneath the surface of everything he did. He hated his heritage, yet always wanted the approval of the people he had fled when he moved his family from the Irish Catholic North End of Boston. He was a man who exuded self-confidence yet forever felt himself tested. He dared not lose in whatever game life brought him, and he raised his children to feel the same stressful internal competitive demands. At the same time, he knew that both he and his sons were somehow wanting. He felt compelled to constantly reinvent the lives of family members, to create a myth, much as he had done with the Harvard talks by the film industry giants and the book that resulted from binding them together.

Joe was a manipulator of the stock market and a user of all but the handful of trusted associates such as Eddie Moore who would be associated with him his entire life. He would enter into partnerships for one or another deals, make his money, and move on. Sometimes the deals were legitimate investments. Usually they involved creating the illusion of a stock's change in value so Joe could profit by either selling short or buying low, then manipulating it higher before unloading his holdings.

Joe's schemes were known, and he was under investigation by the U.S. Senate Banking and Currency Committee. According to the records of the committee,[2] in one instance Joe used his own money but Eddie Moore's name to become a partner in Redmond and Company. This was a stock market firm that existed solely to manipulate prices. The company pooled the money of investors, then bought and sold stock in ways that allowed for either making "short" profits or through selling out at a predetermined high point.

In January 1932 Kennedy made his move with yet another new partner, Henry Mason Day. Joe shifted among "outsider" players, seeing a partnership as more of an arrangement for one or more deals than as a business commitment. With Day, Joe was attempting to recoup recent losses from taking part in a group of insider traders led by financier Bernard Baruch. The group had inside information that the Brooklyn-Manhattan Transit Corporation, known to the public as the BMT, was going to merge all of New York's transit systems. At the time the companies were independent, and the investment group bought 150,000 shares of stock, waiting for the rise that would come when the plans were made public. Unfortunately for the partners, the unification of the systems was the only information they had correct. The company was changing to municipal ownership, and the stock was about to become worthless. There would be no soaring profits after the announcement of the change.

Joe tried a different approach, also meant to make a fast profit on a stock's rise, with Redmond and Company and an investment in Libbey-Owens-Ford Glass Company, manufacturer of plate glass. The business was a solid one, and the customers included automobile manufacturers. However, it was not a growth industry. The business was stable and so was the stock price.

The somewhat similarly named Owens-Illinois Glass Company manufactured bottles. With Prohibition coming to an end, the Owens-Illinois Glass Company was gearing up for a massive increase in production and an expected boost in stock value.

The idea for making money was to confuse the buying public. A fairly rapid change in fortune for Libbey-Owens-Ford would arouse suspicions. A check into the company would reveal that the firm was cash-poor and facing the final payoff for a loan. While the company was in no danger of going bankrupt, it did need an infusion of cash.

The Libbey-Owens Security Corporation was created as a holding company to issue 65,000 shares of stock at the fair market value of $26.50 per share. The deal was fairly elaborate, the most important points guaranteeing the manipulators the right to buy another 60,000 shares in three separate 20,000-share blocks at prices of $27.50 per share, $28.50 per share, and $30.50 per share. This meant that the manipulators had a stake in making the stock price rise substantially above both the issue price and the various buy prices coming available in each of three successive months.

The market was rigged on the stock exchange floor by veterans Frank Bliss and floor manager Charles Wright. These two men would be working on the trades, assuring that the initials of the two companies would be confused, and generally doing everything they could during the heat of trading to assure that the Libbey-Owens stock would be purchased heavily. The exact methods are not known, but one approach still in use today is to deliberately confuse the stock letters when making trades. A buyer thinks he or she is getting one stock, and the traders are making a deal in a similar-sounding one.

In the manner of short sellers, information implying that Libbey-Owens-Ford was on the rise was provided to everyone who could influence the stock. The pool buying and selling began in June 1933. A million shares would be manipulated over the next four months. The price rose high enough for the investors to take advantage of the options, then trade solely with profits.

(Seventy years later the scam was still being used. During an interview with a man who made $42 million with similar manipulations before being criminally indicted, he commented that he had learned the trick from old-timers talking about Joe Kennedy.)

There were rumors that Joe was trading both with the pool and outside the pool, though for the same ends. Profits were found to be $395,238 when the Senate committee analyzed the various accounts of the pool traders. Joe's share was $60,805. If Joe traded outside the pool, or if the pool had more accounts than the six located by the Senate committee when examining Redmond and Company records, even more money was made.

Joe Kennedy's entry into politics months before the 1932 election reflected his ongoing desire for power and respect. He had gone to Harvard without making the meaningful contacts he thought would be his. He had purchased a home in Palm Beach, where only the Jews whom he disdained accepted him. He had gone to Hollywood, where the producers' backgrounds were held in even greater disregard by the Brahmins than his own. Then he had taken them to Harvard, given them an audience that would have otherwise ignored them, and helped them be perceived as men of vision and respectability. Yet the producers still would not accept him, even though he had better education, connections, and wealth.

Perceiving that the accumulation of large sums of money was neither emotionally rewarding nor a means to buy his way into the Brahmin elite in all its WASPish forms, he turned to seeking political power, the only area he had not tried. With the 1932 election coming, it was time to see what he could do to enter the inner circle of the nation's political leaders. Not that he would personally run for office. Not then, anyway. Running for office would mean campaigning, community service, and leading the type of life his father had led. He would have to spend two, three, or more years working for the needs of others, then publicizing that fact, to work his way into power.

This was not Joe's style. Rather than seeking and holding office, controlling the man who held the office was more to his liking. And if that man happened to be a former enemy, a man he still held in disdain, so much the better. One such man was Franklin D. Roosevelt.

Whether Franklin Roosevelt hated Joe Kennedy or just found him a pathetic figure of a man is not known. There had been no personal animosity when he "stole" the Argentine ships from Joe during World War I, and there had been little or no contact since then.

Joe's venture into politics combined the deliberate manipulation of Jimmy Roosevelt with the frustrations of encountering Franklin's longtime insiders who held Joe in disdain. Primary among them was Louis McHenry Howe, a self-made character who was a cross between an insightful political strategist and a street bum whose greatest aspiration seemed to be to always have one more pint of booze on hand than his present thirst required.

Howe was a tiny man, barely five feet tall and shorter than Gloria Swanson, of indomitable will and deteriorating body. He treated his asthma and a cigarette addiction by regularly going to the ocean's edge and alternating between puffs of smoke and deep breathing of the moist air. He had a head befitting a giant and the torso of a gnome, with a neck that looked as though it had been extended by an overzealous midwife pulling too rapidly in a desperate effort to get away from a face even Howe felt was ugly.

That Howe married and fathered two children may have had more to do with the rebellion of his wife, Grace Hartley Howe, against her own family than a beauty-and-the-beast form of adoration. Not that Louis had been unattractive when people got to know him in his youth. He came from a background of contradictions and a childhood plagued with so much illness that he spent extensive time reading and writing. His first creative work was published at a young age, and he became a journalist, a business in which his father also found a degree of success.

The father, Captain Edward Howe, lost his insurance business in the depression known as the Panic of 1873. The family moved full time to their former summer vacation residence, Saratoga Springs, where he scraped together enough money to buy the weekly *Saratoga Sun*. He parlayed that position into prominence in the local Democratic Party as well as in the Presbyterian Church.

Louis Howe developed an interest in professional writing through his isolation, reading, and his father's newspaper. He also became fascinated with theater both through the summer companies that played in the community and through the understanding that, as an actor, his appearance no longer mattered. As long as he did not pretend he could be a leading man, he could create whatever person he wanted to be onstage, living out someone else's life and gaining applause for his re-creation. Howe also became an accomplished speechwriter and orator when he realized that he could dazzle large audiences with words he would be too shy to speak in a much smaller venue.

Howe took over leadership of the *Sun* when his father became too ill to continue the business. Later Louis Howe would move on to the *New York Herald*, where he covered the local community.

Howe was known for his intellect and wit when he grew into manhood. Friends eventually overlooked his physical appearance, and, despite poor health, he was strong enough to participate in tennis, golf, and other athletic activities. He was a young man who was fun to have as a friend in those days, the reason Fall River, Massachusetts, heiress Grace Hartley came to enjoy him. Grace had been sent to Saratoga Springs by her domineering mother when the older woman discovered that her daughter was in love with an Irishman, a fate too horrendous to contemplate. What she did not expect was for Grace to delight in the eccentric, unattractive Howe.

Howe had to sell the local newspaper to help make money, then returned as a $10-a-week reporter. There was frequently inadequate income for food, times when Grace and the children went to live with her mother to save money. It was only after Howe joined the *Herald* that their fortunes improved. And when he became the political specialist for the *Herald*, his brilliance as a writer was recognized. He moved on to Albany, the state capital, where he became the most successful political reporter in New York. He was able to find the stories other reporters overlooked. He also met Franklin Roosevelt. It would be twenty years before Howe would be one of Roosevelt's strategists for the presidential race, yet the middle-aged Howe had seen enough politicians to recognize that Roosevelt just might make it to the White House.

By the time Joe Kennedy met Howe, the man had degenerated in all but his political brilliance and his loyalty to then Governor Franklin Roosevelt. The year was 1931, and Howe had forsaken wife, children, and cleanliness. Shirts were grabbed as needed, clean or not. He frequently slept in his suit and infrequently had it cleaned. His neckties were a food archaeologist's delight. And every part of his body seemed to be covered with cigarette ashes. His world was the back room, literally and figuratively, and he knew that his importance as a strategist was such that he need please no one. As long as his work was successful, Roosevelt insiders would tolerate his eccentricities and defer to his brilliance.

The front men for the Roosevelt campaign that had been established in a Madison Avenue office were attorney Frank Walker and actor Eddie Dowling. They made the rounds of business leaders they felt could financially help the Democratic cause through the support of Roosevelt for president. Joe Kennedy was one of the men they visited, not knowing he had already decided to involve himself in politics.

Kennedy expressed interest in Roosevelt and was introduced to Jim Farley, the official front man and eventual postmaster general. Then, after being disarmed by the affable Farley, Joe was taken to meet Howe.

Louis Howe was well aware of Joe Kennedy. His manipulative actions on Wall Street were shocking in light of the nation's economic crisis. Joe seemed to be the epitome of all that was wrong with capitalism. He was a greedy opportunist who took advantage of others through the management of markets. He had profited before the collapse, and he had delighted in scavenging the corpses of businesses in tatters and lives in near ruin.

Howe also did not know the nature of the relationship between Kennedy and Roosevelt. The men appeared to many to be friends. They had a history together that went back to World War I. More important, Joe was rich and had the personal income to fully fund a presidential campaign.

Howe did not understand that Joe coveted Roosevelt's social history and acceptance among the Brahmins. Kennedy hated Franklin for the humiliation he had suffered while working in the shipyard, yet was willing to ingratiate himself in any way necessary to become part of the inner circle. This was why he would cultivate Jimmy. And this was why Roosevelt saw him as an object of bemusement at best, someone to be held in disdain at worst. But Howe knew none of this. He personally hated Kennedy for his business ethics, and feared Kennedy as someone who could displace him as a Roosevelt insider.

The first meeting between Kennedy and Howe was a disaster. Louis pretended to be asleep while Walker talked with Joe. When Louis finally joined in, he said little. After fifteen minutes of being ignored and seemingly mocked, Kennedy left, irate over what had happened. He would not alter his original thinking and seek another candidate to back, though. He was certain that Roosevelt could win the 1932 election, and he needed to align himself with a winner. He would endure Howe if it meant gaining Franklin's favor.

The 1932 presidential election would be one of the most unusual in American history for the Democratic Party, the candidates, and the nation. The Great Depression was a stunning indictment of the business world in ways that had not been seen in the various depressions that preceded it, including the Panic of 1873 that had affected Captain Howe.

First were the numbers. In 1928 Joe Kennedy had realized that corporate mismanagement and unfounded public trust in business listed on the New York Stock Exchange were portending disaster. In 1928, with the economy reaching a precarious level, the gross national product was $97 billion. Four years later, as Roosevelt faced his run for the presidency, the GNP had shrunk to $58 billion.

In 1928 approximately 47,367,000 men and women were considered employable. Only 982,000, or just 2 percent, could not find a job, and even that number might have been lower had the unemployed been able to travel to a different city. By 1932 the labor force had grown to 50,348,000 men and women. Of those, approximately 24 percent, or 12,060,000, could not find work. Worse, it is believed that had they all been able to travel to other cities, as many men and some women did, the number would have been unlikely to change to any significant degree. Seventy years later, following a major stock market decline, business scandals that cost the jobs of more than 100,000 Americans employed by large corporations, and several hundred thousand more jobs impacted by the problems, the region of the United States with the greatest unemployment reported just 8 percent who could not find work. That was only a third of the problem that existed in 1932.

Most of the country's attention was focused on Wall Street and the lives of the very wealthy. Their sudden loss of material goods, homes, and country club memberships led to great drama. Some committed suicide by jumping from their office windows. Some moved into summer residences, burning furniture for heat, living on the largesse of friends or relatives in better shape than they were. A few were lucky enough to have friends such as Doris Duke, the heiress to both a tobacco and power industry fortune who also was a shrewd investor. She was able to maintain her fortune, and she quietly gave money to friends in need so they could maintain appearances while trying to determine where to go next with their lives.

The most serious problems came in smaller communities and rural America. People who hauled goods to retail stores lost their jobs, as did salespeople, since few individuals could afford anything new. Grocers continued to be comfortable because people had to eat, though they chose cheaper food. Often doctors were paid with barter. And thousands of men took to the rails, traveling from city to city in search of opportunities that usually did not exist.

Franklin Roosevelt was seemingly not the man to inspire the masses. He was rich, and his friends were rich. Robert Worth Bingham owned the *Louisville Courier-Journal*. Jesse Straus's business was Macy's Department Store, an institution in New York, later the inspiration for the film *Miracle on 34th Street*, and a business run in a manner that allowed merchandise and employees to be shifted to maintain profitability. Among Roosevelt's other friends were men in politics, manufacturing, and railroads, all businesses where the ownership was not pleased with anyone too liberal.

For eight years the Democrats had aligned themselves with Al Smith, a man of the people. But Smith was able to get rich and keep the money during the Depression. He went from limited means to being able to campaign from a chauffeur-driven limousine. It was not the image for the party, nor did his sentiments inspire the average voter struggling to pay for food and shelter.

By contrast, Roosevelt had come to understand that the United States was fundamentally flawed. The world of business had proven itself to be corrupt, out of control, and unwilling to use common sense. The ramifications of the stock market crash were affecting the arts, agriculture, and every other aspect of the economy and life. Radical ideas were

necessary. The president could not be a man beholden to friends, especially if the friends had more money than brains.

Joe Kennedy understood that the mood of the nation was shifting
and that Roosevelt was better equipped than Herbert Hoover or any
other Republican to make those changes necessary to rebuild the country. He also felt that the public was going to respond. He wanted Roosevelt to owe him a favor, and he started through his most common method
for ingratiating others: he gave money. He loaned $50,000 to the Demo-
cratic National Committee, a sum he did not expect to see returned.
Another $25,000 was given directly to Roosevelt. Kennedy also did some
traveling to raise money, using the wealthy Bill Danforth's private plane
and pilot. Danforth, like Kennedy, had made the bulk of his money
through short selling and certainly contributed to the crisis that brought
down the stock market. Yet he, too, saw that Roosevelt was the only
answer to the crisis.

Kennedy had no intention of giving any more credit to any other
contributor than necessary. He understood that the more money he was
perceived as giving to the Democratic Party and/or directly to Roosevelt, the more he would ingratiate himself. Every time a large contribution was given to him anonymously, a not-uncommon practice of the
day, Kennedy would place the money in his personal bank account.
Republicans supporting the Democratic Roosevelt, men who did not
want to admit how little the Depression had affected them, and others
seeking privacy all were relieved by Kennedy's actions. However, instead
of keeping records that he could privately turn over to Roosevelt as he
sought future money, Kennedy made certain that Franklin, Howe, and
others close to the governor saw only checks with Kennedy's name.
They presumed that the money had come directly from Joe, and with
each contribution they felt they owed him all the more.

By spring, as the summer 1932 Democratic convention approached,
the key to the selection of the candidate seemed to rest with Joe's longtime friend William Randolph Hearst. The publisher controlled the
convention votes from Texas and California. They were officially pledged
to John Nance Garner for the first ballot. Everyone knew the candidate
would not be chosen then, that Garner would lose the first go-round,
and that Hearst could then pledge the same delegates to someone else.

The most likely candidates would be Al Smith and Franklin Roosevelt, and the division within the party was such that the eighty-six votes
Hearst controlled were critical. Both Smith and Roosevelt had few connections with Hearst, and consequently nothing to call on to gain the

upper hand. The one man who did have some influence was Joe Kennedy, who was just at that time trying to avoid an investigation into the practices that had made him rich.

Kennedy's most pressing problem was keeping a low profile during the April 1932 hearings of the Senate Banking and Currency Committee. The committee understood that Joe Kennedy and his ilk who had utilized pooled money and price manipulation had caused part of the destruction of the stock market. The hearings were meant both to expose what had taken place and to shame some of the leaders. For their part, the senators needed laudatory headlines to keep their own jobs, for the crash had occurred on their watch.

Joe's desirability as a witness and a target for the probe was diminished by his work with Roosevelt. It would be easy for him to say he had changed, that he had seen the wrong in the actions that had made him rich. He was a Democrat, a man who cared for the average citizen.

Fortunately for Joe, though no one suspected he was anything more than a self-centered, money-grubbing isolationist, there were better targets. John J. Raskob made the greatest headlines. He had been chairman of the finance committee of General Motors, a man who encouraged every housewife to place at least $15 a month in the stock market to make their families rich, and a longtime Republican.[3] Raskob switched his allegiance to Al Smith, strengthening his backing as Smith sounded more and more like a dedicated capitalist. Raskob went so far as to change party affiliation, becoming head of the Democratic National Committee.

Raskob's change in party affiliation based on the altered ideology of Smith seemed to help him with the Senate. He answered questions with self-deprecating humor, avoiding the fact that he regularly participated in pools that drastically affected the value of the stock he urged the average person to buy. He had frequently done business with J. P. Morgan that resulted in unearned financial benefits as a way of being thanked. Yet, before the evidence was revealed to both Raskob and the press, he was quoted as saying, "[S]trange as it may seem, I really know nothing about the Stock Exchange."[4]

The hearings were never about change. They were more about headlines in an election year. As long as facts about pools, raids, and short selling were revealed, no one cared who made headlines. Raskob was sacrificed to the Senate wolves. Joe remained protected through his association with Roosevelt. And William Randolph Hearst remained the problem within the party, the reason Joe was dispatched to see his longtime friend.

Joe Kennedy was the ideal man to see Hearst. Kennedy was a Roosevelt backer, but he had kept his wealth through the crash, believed in avoiding international involvement, and had been a success in the one business where Hearst had failed—making movies. This was an especially sore point because Hearst had wanted to buy a career for his lover, the one area where he felt he had failed to give her everything he could afford. He never recognized that she did not care about that, even when the depth of her love became obvious to those who had seen her as a gold digger. In a little-known incident in the multimillionaire publisher and businessman's life, he had once come close to bankruptcy at a time when the public thought him beyond financial cares. Davies, who had been a skilled investor in real estate, offered to give him more than $1 million from money she had earned if it would help him. Nothing was to be paid back. She loved him, and this was the one place where she could help him. (He didn't take the money.) Yet Hearst never could make her a star.

Ultimately several decisions were reached when Kennedy and Hearst met. Hearst controlled eighty-six votes pledged to Garner, a power that would stop Smith on the convention's first vote for a standard-bearer. Then Hearst would release his California and Texas delegates from their first-ballot pledge and have them give their support to Roosevelt.

The Republicans were the first to meet in Chicago, the site of both major-party conventions that year. Herbert Hoover was nominated for a second term the Republicans knew he would not win. The party leaders knew that many incumbent politicians had kept their offices because they felt the public believed them when they said that Herbert Hoover still could save the country. Abandoning Hoover meant admitting they were wrong.

Next came the Democratic convention, where Kennedy worked to gain all the postelection favors he could. He had met with Hearst. Now he worked constantly behind the scenes, from arm-wrestling delegations whose vote he could influence, to running errands. No job was too small. No job was too difficult. And when Louis Howe was near, Joe quietly disappeared so as not to be seen as trying to win over Roosevelt.

The first ballot was closer than anyone anticipated. Hearst went back on his promise to Joe and refused to release any of the votes he controlled for the second ballot. Instead, a dark-horse candidate was introduced—Woodrow Wilson's former secretary of war Newton D. Baker, who said he was willing to be drafted as his party's nominee.

Baker was a valid choice. He had the background and experience. He also had been connected with the League of Nations, an organization Hearst hated. Hearst thought that Roosevelt was an isolationist and Baker an internationalist, and he was determined to stop Baker whenever necessary. That was when Joe went to Hearst and explained that either the publisher use the votes he controlled to back Roosevelt, or Baker would win the nomination on the next ballot. Hearst gave his support to Roosevelt.

Joe Kennedy felt he had been successful. He had persuaded Hearst to make his move earlier than the publisher intended, and he had forced him to take what he knew Hearst considered the lesser of two evils. However, far more credit should have been given to Howe and others whom Joe ignored.

For whatever reasons he may have had, perhaps including a last fling, he decided to call Gloria Swanson and brag of his accomplishment. She was married again and a new mother. She was temporarily in England, and she now hated Joe for all he had done to her. Still, he had to brag, had to impress her, perhaps had to make her beholden for one last time in bed. Whatever the case, knowing she would never accept his telephone call, especially since it was the early hours of the morning in London, he got hold of Gloria's mother, Virginia, a Chicago resident. He brought the woman to the hotel, then placed a call to Gloria that she later described in her autobiography.

It was four o'clock in the morning London time, just 10:00 P.M. in Illinois:[5] " 'I read about your baby,' " he shouted when Gloria answered. If the words were as she remembered them, it was an odd way to start the conversation, and odder still that Swanson's mother didn't say something first. " 'We just had one, too [Edward Moore "Teddy" Kennedy]. We named him after Eddie Moore. That isn't why I called.'

" 'I should hope not!' I yelled," Gloria wrote. " 'Why did you call?'

" 'Do you know who's here with me, Gloria? The next President of the United States, Gloria! He just won the Democratic nomination. I want you to say hello to him.'

"It was so blatantly opportunistic that I was stunned.

" 'How Dare you?' I shouted.

" 'Seriously, Gloria. He wants to say hello to you. Wait a second while I—'

" 'Don't bother! I don't want to talk to him and I don't want to talk to you!' I slammed down the phone.

"By then Michael [her fourth husband] was wide awake and so was the baby.

" 'Who was that?' Michael demanded suspiciously.

" 'The next President of the United States, presumably. But I hung up on him.' "

Later Virginia would cable her daughter to apologize for awakening her but that she had done so because Joe begged her to call. "She said he wanted me to know that if I needed help financing the new picture, he stood ready. She also said Joe had told her to tell me he had been promised a Cabinet post, probably Secretary of the Treasury, if Roosevelt went on to be elected in November."

The relationship between Joe Kennedy and Franklin Roosevelt was a symbiotic one after the election. Each needed the other. Each hated the other. Joe was certain he would be rewarded in some way, perhaps with a cabinet post, when Franklin was elected president. Roosevelt had no intention of doing anything other than using Joe, uncertain of his full value and seemingly caring only that Kennedy not hurt the campaign.

Joe's relationships with men of wealth and power were obviously important to Roosevelt. These were men who had no interest in the average American. These were men who had little sense of the nation and the crises that existed and continued to grow. These were men who wanted to keep the United States away from international affairs, and who, like Kennedy, often thought that politicians and political concepts did not matter. Nations and forms of government rose and fell over the centuries. Business was always of value, and business must remain unfettered.

Joe Kennedy, an isolationist, was a go-between, a man who could talk with both sides on the issue of the economy. Consequently, Roosevelt asked him for suggestions for his speeches on economics and for help when discussing the failings and dangers of Wall Street. And in listening to Kennedy, Roosevelt began formulating ideas that would become major innovations after he took office.

For example, Roosevelt realized that it was necessary for Wall Street to be honest. Stock could no longer be sold solely to make money for the issuers, a common situation before the collapse. Financial statements would have to be prepared, and they would have to be accurate and available to the public. To assure that this took place, Roosevelt decided to promote legislation that would create what we now know as the Securities and Exchange Commission. It would be a watchdog organization that would protect the American public, penalizing only those who were, in essence, committing fraud.

Raymond Moley wrote FDR's speeches. He understood how to weave the candidate's new ideas into a form that could be sold to the voting public. Although he did not consult with Joe Kennedy or even

Louis Howe, the influence of both men on Roosevelt meant that many of their ideas would ultimately make themselves into the campaign.

In the fall, soon after the convention, Joe was asked to join the campaign train with both Franklin and his son Jimmy. The railroad covered the United States in a grid that allowed Roosevelt to be seen and heard in small towns and big cities several times a day. Speeches could be refined on the move, jokes dropped, added, or constantly repeated, new ideas tried in locations where there would be strong newspaper support or such isolation that if no one liked them, only the local citizenry would hear them.

Kennedy seemed to come to genuinely respect Roosevelt as they traveled together. He seemed to realize that Roosevelt would be an effective president at worst, and the Republicans would be ineffective at best.

Although Herbert Hoover did not cause the Great Depression, he was seemingly at a loss about what to do to fix the problem. The stock market collapse had been inevitable and would have occurred on the Democrats' watch had they won the White House in 1928. But Hoover compounded concerns because he had no concrete plan other than not to let those who still had money lose any of what they had kept.

Roosevelt needed to reverse what Hoover could not, and toward this end Joe Kennedy was one of the people he felt he could consult. However, Joe wanted more. He was desperate to be accepted into Roosevelt's inner circle. He wanted the power. He wanted the prestige. He wanted to thumb his nose at the Brahmins while standing with his arm around the most powerful Brahmin of them all. Joe could not accept the fact that he was only one of dozens of important men, each with special expertise, who helped bring Franklin to power. He did not understand the importance of a seemingly disreputable man like Howe, refusing to look beyond the filthy clothes and disheveled patches of remaining hair to see the brilliant strategist. That Joe Kennedy only saw himself would be demonstrated in the days after Roosevelt was elected president, yet not reported for twenty-eight more years, when the October 1, 1960, column of nationally syndicated columnist Drew Pearson described a party held in Coral Gables. Harry Doherty was the host, and the event was held in a hotel he owned—the Miami Biltmore. The guests included seemingly everyone of political importance who had supported the Roosevelt campaign, including Boston's prominent ex-mayor and his wife—John and Josie Fitzgerald. According to Pearson, when Eddie Dowling was waltzing with Josie, she shocked him by exclaiming, "Isn't it wonderful! My son-in-law Joe Kennedy has made Franklin D. Roosevelt President."

The arrogance and transparency of Joe Kennedy, coupled with the fact that no one involved with Roosevelt trusted the man based on his past, assured that any rewards for him after the election would be fought. The comment of his mother-in-law clinched a deliberate snub by the new administration. As the president's cabinet and inner circle were being defined in the weeks before the inauguration, Joe Kennedy emerged as the man no one wanted.

The expected call from FDR did not come. In March 1933 Joe Kennedy decided he could no longer live like the most popular girl in a high school class waiting for someone to ask her to the prom. Too much time had passed, and he was not going to miss the dance. He contacted Roosevelt, praising his fledgling administration and passing on supposed praise from others for the quality of his appointments. It was clear he wanted to be the next. Instead, he received a letter that stated, in part: "[W]e are all keeping our fingers crossed and hoping to get in some real work while the temper of the country and the Congress is so pleasant. Do be sure to let us know when you are going through Washington and stop off and see us."[6]

Roosevelt was comfortably wealthy in his own right and had worked an accommodation with Eleanor that seemed to leave them happy together. As time passed, when she took up an independent career as a writer, she willingly let Franklin edit any of her articles that might cause embarrassment to him.

The only area of intense disagreement between Eleanor and Franklin, aside from his having a mistress, was over their oldest son, James. Jimmy was a ne'er-do-well opportunist in his mother's eyes. A youth lazy enough to try to play off his father's connections, and willing to use his father's influence to get whatever he sought in the business world.

12

THE OUTSIDER COMES IN

JOE KENNEDY NEVER UNDERSTOOD THE WAY HE WAS VIEWED BY the Protestant elite when he tried to emulate their lives. In his forties, he had earned a fortune greater than most of them had inherited. He had personally kept his presence within the Catholic Church to a minimum, downplaying his Irish Catholic heritage the way his mother had taught him when she suggested he call himself "Joe," omitting his last name. He had knocked on the doors of their country clubs, dues in hand. He graduated from Harvard and would send his sons to the same bastion of social introductions. He had ingratiated himself with Roosevelt by explaining the corruption that led to the stock market collapse, but never stopped playing the games he taught the candidate to deride.

The difference between Joe and those he emulated was that men like Franklin Roosevelt achieved power through their efforts to better the lives of others. They had power drives. They enjoyed the prestige that comes from success, and they enjoyed whatever boost their privileged backgrounds might have given them. But ultimately when they were called to develop ways to fix the crises facing the nation, men like Roosevelt rose to the challenge without regard to personal cost or criticism.

Joe Kennedy never could see why Roosevelt and those around him didn't want him to join their inner circle. He was perceived as a man for whom greed and self-interest colored all decisions. Just the idea of his currying favor with Roosevelt while taking part in ongoing stock market manipulation was beyond comprehension to those closest to the president-elect.

To make matters worse for Joe, he played the role of "pure" campaign supporter so long and so well that the Roosevelt staff was able to use his words against him. An example was a *Boston Globe* interview that would be quoted on November 3, 1932. The story was meant to be about a man who was raised in Massachusetts, made a fortune, and now was part of the entourage of Governor Roosevelt as he ran for office. Joe stated: "There is nothing I want. There is no public office that would interest me. Governor Roosevelt asked me to go with him on this trip and I agreed to accompany him."

Kennedy added, "I have heard it said that Roosevelt is indecisive. I certainly have never seen anything indecisive about him. Roosevelt is a glutton for work, but he is one of the easiest men in the world to advise with. He keeps his mind open so well that it is a pleasure to work with him. I do not think he is the greatest man in the world, but I do know he would accomplish things."

The *Boston Globe* material was belied by Josie Fitzgerald's comment during the victory party. However, the Roosevelt staff knew that Kennedy could not make a fuss about how they treated him after the election. They not only had the self-effacing quote as ammunition, but they also knew that he would not embarrass himself publicly by saying he had only supported Roosevelt to gain prestige for himself.

Joe didn't go public, but still he felt he had to take matters a step further. At first he sent Roosevelt a series of flattering telegrams, including one from a convent, where he noted that the mother superior had said "since your Inaugural, peace seemed to come on the earth; in fact, it seemed like another resurrection. Mortal man can pay you no higher compliment."

Then he began criticizing the president-elect's ingratitude to William Randolph Hearst, a man who had been uneasy about supporting Roosevelt in the first place. In this lack of gratitude, Joe was given a harsh lesson that while money can make an individual powerful in the world where he or she exerts an influence, such as Hollywood, it cannot buy respect. It cannot buy friendship. It can only buy access, and even that is often limited.

Before the inauguration, Joe thought he might be named secretary of the treasury. He did not understand that a man who had made a fortune pool trading even after the stock market crash was not going to be placed in a position of responsibility for the nation's money. The reality was that he wasn't considered because he couldn't handle the job, but rather because the president would be attacked for considering such an appointment.

The only position for which the new administration considered Kennedy was treasurer of the United States. His name would appear on all paper money, he would make ceremonial appearances, but he would have no real power or authority. And even this position went to someone else.

At first Joe Kennedy wanted to strike back at Roosevelt. He felt himself used, even though he had put himself in the position he was in.

He thought about suing the Democratic National Committee for the repayment of the loan he had made, even though his original expectation had been that there would be no cash reimbursement, just an appointment of status.

Indecisive about suing, he tried to bribe FDR's speechwriter Raymond Moley to embarrass Roosevelt. Moley was not a wealthy man. He was a professor at Columbia University who was one of a group of academic advisers that became known as Roosevelt's "brain trust," and a man truly close to the new president. Moley was about to become a major adviser to the president, and whatever financial arrangement was made, it would be inadequate for the standard of living Moley would be expected to maintain. Public service was not financially rewarding, as Kennedy pointed out to Moley, and Joe proposed soliciting a fund that could be used to underwrite Moley's expenses. In that way the sacrifice would be lessened.

But Moley had no intention of becoming financially beholden to Joe Kennedy. He also knew that if he accepted the money, he would be vulnerable to either blackmail or public disgrace. Instead he thanked Kennedy and told him that if he, Moley, ever needed a loan, he would consider his "friend" Joe.

Finally, Joe decided that he had to try to win the president's favor through Franklin's favorite son, James "Jimmy" Roosevelt. Jimmy's position in the president's emotional and professional life stemmed from the 1924 Democratic Convention, where Franklin's speech for candidate Al Smith had been greeted by thunderous applause, more for him than for Smith. It was a stunning comeback after the polio he had suffered that had threatened to end his political career. His appearance as a vigorous man recovering from a debilitating illness was in large part achieved through the efforts of Jimmy, who stage-managed his movement to the podium so that few realized his physical limitations.

When Franklin returned to Warm Springs, Georgia, where he spent extensive time undergoing therapy, he accepted the fact that he would never recover the ability to walk. He only wanted to be able to plan his life so he could find the means to do whatever he desired without scaring people, looking like a freak, or falling down. If that meant traveling with Jimmy and scouting ahead wherever they went, so be it. From then on, instead of using crutches, he practiced a technique involving using a man on one side—a human "crutch"—and a cane on the other. Then he followed the same balance-and-swing movement until he found the method that was best for propelling him forward without his dropping to the floor.

Oddly, it was not Jimmy who was used for the new phase of walking. It was Elliott, then eighteen, who practiced with his father. And once the two had their walking act where their bodies responded to one another like a practiced team, Franklin taught Elliott to look up and out at the audience, to smile, to appear as he would if accompanying his father without the older man being disabled. They moved like two close friends, father and grown son, working the crowd, happy to see others, neither seemingly aware of the other as they walked.

The act was enormously successful. Franklin again introduced Al Smith as the Democratic candidate in 1928. And while Smith was the standard-bearer, his lack of success did not matter. Franklin Roosevelt was viewed as heroic, virile, a leader whom disease had failed to stop. More important, with Governor Smith running for the presidency, Franklin Roosevelt was able to go after the governorship of New York in his own right.

The problem of the paralysis and Roosevelt's ability to govern had to be resolved to achieve his own ambitions for the presidency. There were rumors that even if Franklin won—and that seemed likely because his popularity was dramatically on the rise—he would resign after the swearing-in. Lieutenant Governor-elect Lehman would take over, and Roosevelt would retire from public life.

The predicted Roosevelt strategy never took place. Instead, a special touring car was created for Franklin to show how healthy he was. A steel bar was mounted on the back of the front seat. Roosevelt would ride in the back, as was normal for a candidate. He could wave to the people and stand to make speeches. The fact that Franklin stood only by holding the bar and pulling himself erect was never noticed. To the masses, Franklin Roosevelt stood when and where he so chose, addressing them, shaking hands, and acting like every other candidate.

Similar ruses were used in auditoriums. There were few elevators, and he often had to give the illusion of greater mobility than he actually had. There even was a time when he used the metal railing of a narrow inside fire escape staircase like a gymnast's parallel bars. He reached the top without assistance, his muscles aching, his face covered with sweat, and no one any the wiser.

Elliott may have been the son Roosevelt used to practice more elaborate "walking" techniques, but Jimmy's efforts in 1924 and his subsequent devotion to his father's needs created a special father/son bond. Joe Kennedy, as an insider who had been allowed to travel with Roosevelt enough to realize his physical limitations, understood Jimmy and worked to seduce the youth.

In 1933 Jimmy Roosevelt was clear about his personal ambitions when not working with his father. He had attended Harvard for the social connections, married, and settled in Boston, where he would create a base for running for governor of Massachusetts. This was the same goal that Joe had for his oldest son. There was talk of each man looking to the 1940 term. Joe floated the idea that Jimmy would be governor in 1940 and Joe Jr. would seek to have the office in 1944. Where Jimmy might be at that time was left unsaid, though presumably some higher office, such as the Senate.

Jimmy also intended to make money through investments and the insurance business. The latter seemed an easy way to wealth because he knew that wealthy business owners, including the fathers of some of his Harvard classmates, would be happy to give him their business. They would assume that buying insurance from Jimmy was giving them access to the president, and Jimmy apparently did little to discourage this idea.

One of the early customers was Henry Ford, whose company was suffering greatly from the Depression. There were thirty-two Ford Motor Company assembly plants operating full time in 1928. By 1932, when Ford vigorously opposed Franklin Roosevelt's presidential candidacy, there were just six assembly plants still functioning. However, it was known within the Roosevelt administration that at least some of the Ford assembly plants could be reopened. Because the business would be less profitable with more than the half dozen plants operating, such a move would be counterproductive if profits were the sole concern. But the reopening of even some of the plants would imply the start of a national recovery. Cars were luxury items. People could walk to jobs or take public transportation. New cars meant more people working and more workers receiving higher pay. The Roosevelt presidency's first term would be greatly boosted.

Henry Ford's assistant Harry Bennett, who knew that Ford was ill, brought Joe Kennedy into the insurance effort. Joe developed a plan in which Franklin would send a telegram asking about Henry Ford's health. There would be restoration of some manufacturing through increased production and the opening of more plants. At the same time, Ford would pass insurance business to Jimmy's firm.

The plan worked. Plants were activated, men returned to work, and the image of a recovering economy boosted support for Roosevelt's various programs for the nation. Franklin acted, not for his son but because Edsel Ford had donated one of the swimming pools used for the treatment of polio in Warm Springs. Jimmy was grateful to Joe Kennedy for trying to include him in the deal, but claimed his firm never received any insurance business from Ford. Whether he did or didn't, Jimmy came away from the incident viewing Joe as a close friend. As a result, that same year, with Prohibition about to be repealed, Joe and Rose, and Jimmy and Betsey Roosevelt traveled to Great Britain.

Their 1933 British trip was for pleasure for the two wives, business for the two men. The rumor, denied by Jimmy, was that Joe promised Jimmy a partnership in liquor importing franchises he was obtaining for himself. The franchises were hotly contested because anyone who gained them stood to make large sums of money. Joe knew that the presence of the president's son in the meetings with the distillers would assure his being given the business. The only question was whether Jimmy believed he would be a partner.

Despite Jimmy's denials, it seems that Joe led Jimmy to believe that there would be a financial reward for coming to the business meetings. Both Eleanor and Franklin Roosevelt were certain such an arrangement was made. They both knew that Kennedy was using their son, and they disliked him for that.

It is also possible that Jimmy lied to save face. He certainly did not have the knowledge of the liquor import and distribution business that Joe had and could not have gained any of the business on his own.[1]

According to one story, Joe maintained his friendship with Jimmy by telling him that he couldn't make him an active partner because he was the president's son and such a business arrangement could be used against his father. Consequently, it was for the good of Franklin that Joe would have to find some other way to show his gratitude.

What is certain is that the liquor importing business was placed in the hands of a company called Somerset. Joe arranged the stock so that he held 2 percent and his family held the rest. Although much like trust funds, these were not meant solely to ensure a life of leisure or to help free them from worry as they dedicated themselves to low-paying public service. Instead, he knew that being somewhat of a business gambler, it was possible that he might make a mistake or be victimized by a business partner. The trust funds holding the Somerset money could be tapped to start business life anew. And if all went well, it would be the children who withdrew the money over time.

Somerset itself created a number of scams. Gordon's gin was so popular that by 1934, with Prohibition lifted, Somerset was moving 150,000 cases a year. Haig & Haig routinely sold a third more cases. Five years later, the Distillers Company, parent of British Haig & Haig, discovered that Somerset was deliberately hoarding cases of the liquor. Stock was being warehoused instead of distributed in order to increase the selling price to retailers. Since Joe's commissions and other benefits came from the amount he imported, the hoarding necessitated more imports and a subsequent financial advantage.

There were other scams alleged, some of which had first been developed for the movie industry. Movie theater owners were often forced to rent films they did not want to run in order to get features they knew would draw large audiences. Somerset forced retailers to buy larger quantities of cheap rum they did not need in order to be able to get the Scotch they could sell. Those who balked at the arrangement found their Scotch shipments to be less than they needed, not shipped in a timely manner, or otherwise withheld to some degree as a penalty.

That Christmas Jimmy Roosevelt and his wife stayed with the Kennedys in Palm Beach. Joe asked when he was going to get his appointment to something of substance. Jimmy promised that the matter would be handled soon, and he took it up with his father when he returned to Washington. Joe again was rejected, though in a nicer way. January 1934 was when Roosevelt's first treasury secretary, William H. Woodin, resigned, and the president replaced him with Henry Morgenthau Jr. Joe Kennedy was sent a letter from Raymond Moley acknowledging a talk with Jimmy about the position, and that seemed to mollify Joe for the moment. Jimmy was working for him, and if Jimmy couldn't eventually influence his father, no one could.

Roosevelt signed the Securities Exchange Act on June 6, 1934. The Committee on Banking and Currency had long before held hearings on the stock market manipulations of financiers whose names were synonymous with wealth, power, and corruption. Joe Kennedy, who had avoided public exposure and national condemnation solely because of his work on the Roosevelt campaign, had earlier had the nerve to write: "For month after month, the country was treated to a series of amazing revelations which involved practically all the important names in the financial community in practices which, to say the least, were highly unethical. The belief that those in control of the corporate life in America were motivated by honesty and ideals of honorable conduct was completely shattered."[2] Now it was time for the hypocrites and the true believers to come together and create the new Securities and Exchange Commission (SEC).

The original intent of the various laws that were developed in response to all the factors that led to both stock market manipulation and the 1929 crash was to prevent a repetition of such practices. The SEC would be a commission of five, with the authority to make the new laws mandatory. But by June 1934, the SEC had become a body that could create the standards and priorities by which it would operate. This meant that the first commissioners would establish the parameters of the agency's work regardless of the intent of the new laws.

The role of chairman was the most coveted position because it was presumed that the chairman would guide the way in which the oversight was handled. Roosevelt did not have a chairman in mind, but he had two men who made clear they expected the position. The first was Ferdinand Pecora, who had just finished leading the Senate investigation into the stock market crash. The second was Joe Kennedy.

Pecora was a liberal who hated Kennedy, hated the leaders of big business and Wall Street whose greed and manipulation he had learned firsthand during the hearings. He knew the activities that came before the October crash. He knew that Joe Kennedy was a man who was as guilty as anyone he had called before the congressional committee. The problem was that he had not called Joe Kennedy. Joe had never been asked to testify. The extent of Kennedy's actions was unknown by the vast majority of Americans.

Pecora might have been the better chairman, but Roosevelt was uncomfortable with the man being more than one of the commissioners because his background did not give him an intimate understanding of the stock market. He would be a commissioner, and it was believed he would defend the public interest. He would not be allowed to lead, however.

The problem with Joe Kennedy was that he was a thief in Roosevelt's mind. In addition to his dislike for the man, he was increasingly upset over Kennedy's use of Jimmy to further his personal wealth.

Raymond Moley disagreed. He felt that Joe, who would definitely be one of the commissioners, also should serve as chairman. Joe knew the world of the Wall Street manipulator. He had made large sums of money and overseen large numbers of people. He understood business and finance, and it would be hard for a manipulator to get past a man who had mastered that skill, plying it both before and after the stock market crash. Besides, Moley pointed out, Roosevelt owed Joe Kennedy. Vast sums of money had been raised for the campaign. In addition, Joe was ambitious. There were rumors of his being interested in political office one day, and if that proved true, a man with his ego would only aspire to the presidency. He needed to be given a position of prestige, if only to reduce the danger he posed as a rival should he ever decide to take on Roosevelt.

Not all of Roosevelt's cronies agreed with Moley. Frank Walker, Roosevelt's principal fund-raiser, tried to talk Joe Kennedy out of being the chairman. He met with Kennedy night after night, walking with him, discussing the situation, pointing out the serious opposition. He did not speak for Roosevelt, but Joe understood that Walker was reflecting concerns that had been brought to the president's attention.

On June 30, 1934, the matter came to a head. Roy Howard, head of the Scripps-Howard newspaper chain, was in Washington with Raymond Moley. Howard hated Joe Kennedy, recognized him to be a crook, and was outraged that he was to be rewarded with the chairmanship. He decided to use his newspapers against the appointment, but he had time to use only one—the *Washington News*. He went to the paper's office and wrote an editorial against Kennedy's appointment. He also made clear that he would have similar editorial attacks in all his other papers.

Joe Kennedy was outraged. He had long seen the manipulation of events created by his publisher friend William Randolph Hearst. He had not expected to bear the brunt of the attack.

That evening, an angry Joe Kennedy met with the president; financier Bernard Baruch, who supported Kennedy; and Raymond Moley. According to Moley, Roosevelt did not look at any of them. He had a piece of paper with a list of the five names of the men he had nominated to the commission. He noted that the first name was Joe Kennedy's, and Joe would be the chairman, a five-year appointment.

Moley understood that Kennedy needed to be ready to deal with the attacks that were certain to come. He also knew that Roosevelt needed an extra comfort level about the appointment and how Joe would handle the criticism that would be forthcoming. Moley asked Kennedy to reveal anything in his background that might create a problem for the president. In his book *After Seven Years*, Moley noted: "Kennedy reacted precisely as I thought he would. With a burst of profanity he defied anyone to question his devotion to the public interest or to point to a single shady act in his whole life. The president did not need to worry about that, he said. What was more, he would give his critics—and here again profanity flowed freely—an administration of the SEC that would be a credit to the country, the president, himself, and his family—clear down to the ninth child."

The public concern about the new commission became evident when the announcement of the appointment was made on July 1, 1934. It was the day Adolf Hitler faced a revolt from among his early followers for leadership. Brown Shirts fought Brown Shirts, and those who were not murdered were sent to the Dachau concentration camp. The image of Hitler as a comic fool who had managed to head a defeated country was instantly eliminated, yet it was Joe's appointment that mattered to many of the reporters.

Joe had never had to deal with truth, and he seemingly did not wish to start. He wanted to control the hostility, accepting the fact that his financial maneuverings would become public. He wanted to rewrite history, and toward this end he began calling in favors where he could.

The *New Republic* voiced the most prevalent reaction. "Had Franklin Delano Roosevelt's dearest enemy accused him of an intention of making so grotesque an appointment as Joseph P. Kennedy to the chairmanship of his Stock Exchange Commission, the charge might have been laid to malice. Yet the President has exceeded the expectation of his more ardent ill wishers."[3]

The *New York Times* handled the story of the appointment differently from the *Washington News*, noting that Joe had been increasingly away from the public eye after the 1932 election. The paper wrote that the appointment came as a surprise, but nothing more negative.

The story Joe spread was that he was definitely controversial, that he had no intention of going into government service, but that Roosevelt thought differently. He wanted to reward him with the chairmanship of the SEC, not just a commission membership. It was Joe, the story continued, who had to decline to protect the president from criticism, but Roosevelt would hear none of that. Roosevelt understood the sacrifice Joe would have to make, the problems that could arise, yet he would have no one else.

The media test of the fiction came when Joe was interviewed for a *Boston Post* article that appeared on July 1, 1934. The Boston paper was not one that intended to laud Kennedy on the front page. There was too much news the editors felt was important that day. However, it did show Joe's media influence.

Headlined "Big Sacrifice for Children's Sake/Joseph P. Kennedy Accepts Securities Exchange Control Job against Will, but Seeks Public Service Legacy," the story stressed that Joe was concerned that his children would be pleased that he went into public service to benefit them and the country at a time of great turmoil. "Having almost everything

Joe Kennedy was appointed chairman of the National Securities Exchange Commission, whose role was to protect the public from investing schemes of which he had been a master. The July 2, 1934, photo shows Kennedy seated between Ferdinand Pecora and James M. Landis. Standing behind them are George Mathews (left) and Robert Healy. (Cleveland State University Library, Special Collections)

else, he wants to leave a name known for public service as well as business success. This is what made him accept a position he did not want. Of course, he was at the mercy of the world's super-salesman, Franklin D. Roosevelt, but even at that, he resisted one call but succumbed to the next when the President pointed out the need for his services. That desire to leave an honorable, unselfish name, which has been the moving force behind so many men of unusual abilities, was what made him give in and agree to go to Washington to take over the job which, at its best, looks like a thankless task."

Part of the sacrifice Joe had to endure was the renting of a place where he and Eddie Moore, his constant companion in business and public service ventures, could live. The house they rented was in Maryland on land that overlooked the Potomac. It had twenty-five rooms, including a hundred-seat movie theater in the basement. The master bedroom had gold-plated fixtures, and the original cost of the place, called Marwood, had been $500,000.

Marwood was a little like San Simeon, Hearst's castle and monument to adultery. Marwood's original owner was known as a playboy, and the house was a gift to the showgirl he loved. However, unlike Hearst, the owner of Marwood married his beloved. By the time Joe was in Washington, the place was for rent.

Joe told anyone who asked that he needed Marwood because it was the only place big enough to hold Rose and their children on those rare occasions when they all came to visit. The truth seems to be more that the location was isolated enough for Joe to enjoy his latest girlfriend and impressive enough to assure stories that reminded the public just how successful he had been before going into public service. He also used the location for male-only dinners where the more prominent guests were invited to spend the night.

Roosevelt met with his cabinet to announce the appointment, and Secretary of the Interior Harold L. Ickes made notes in his diary concerning what was said. He wrote that he felt that the president considered Joe a good choice, since he had taken his money out of the market, invested in government securities, and understood all the dirty tricks. Joe would do well if only to please his family.

Pecora remained the last obstacle to Joe's success. Pecora said he was going to resign from the commission the same day all five commissioners gathered to meet the press, to gain maximum publicity. He was going to denounce Roosevelt for choosing Kennedy, and he was going to be specific about why Kennedy was no good. Both he and Joe went to their respective offices, each preparing for the other, while attorney James Landis, one of the men who drafted the bill creating the SEC, desperately went between the two.

It took two hours for Pecora to agree to stay on and not attack either Roosevelt or Kennedy. Joe also understood the risk he was facing, a risk far greater than he faced with any of his affairs.[4] He immediately began deferring to other members of the committee, telling the press that he had much to learn from them and was looking forward to the opportunity. It was the type of statement they all needed to hear.

The one point seldom made is that the commission did not have to choose Kennedy. By law the commissioners had to vote among themselves. The reality was different. Roosevelt appointed each man to a term of from one to five years. Joe's was the longest, the signal that he was the person to be selected. The fight among them, especially the near revolt of Pecora, could have created a major scandal. But such was the power of persuasion of the president of the United States that Franklin

Roosevelt could make his decision, have it announced, and have the commissioners rubber-stamp the action.

As the initial verbal violence subsided, Joe approached each of the men who had fought him and asked, privately, "Why do you hate me?" For those used to the subtle machinations of both business and politics, it was a question that caught them off-guard. No one spoke his mind, and soon Arthur Krock was writing glowing articles that told about Kennedy's commitment to protect the public. Krock, who was on the Kennedy payroll to supplement his pay from the *New York Times*, also began shaping the Joe Kennedy biographical myth.[5]

Kennedy, on the commission then, claimed that he would serve his full term, but he made clear to Roosevelt that he wanted only the prestige. He would take one year before resigning, and that year would be spent organizing the operation. It was the one skill he truly brought to the commission, an ability that even Pecora lacked.

Roosevelt gave Joe a free hand to act despite recommendations from various influential members of the administration and the president's supporters. No one other than Joe, who understood both business and the stock market, was in a position to stop such subtly manipulative practices as short selling.

Kennedy recognized that the SEC chairman had power that would be lacking in other appointments. He would be shaping the rules for the way America did business. He also would be revealing the weaknesses he had previously exploited, including the difference between investing for rapid buying and selling and investing in carefully selected stocks to be held for the long term. He also said that the nation needed to feel confident that if a business was well planned and well run, it should be given the opportunity to grow and would not be vulnerable to speculators who cared only about quick profits.

Business leaders welcomed Joe's remarks. They knew that Kennedy was not a reformer. Most of the men drawn to Roosevelt's New Deal legislation were people who were concerned about the nation but clueless about big business. Even those who had some understanding had no influence among the leaders of major corporations. Only Joe Kennedy was in a position to call the president of any business, no matter how large, and demand to speak with the comptroller. Only Joe could understand what the company was really doing, when to back off, and when to attack.

Joe organized the SEC much like any business he had taken over. He maintained his close friends on his personal payroll, bringing Eddie Moore along to Washington to work on SEC business. The only snag was that Moore could not have access to the confidential documents his boss needed him to review unless he worked for the U.S. government. That matter was resolved by making him an 88-cents-a-year man. (Eddie was hired for $1 a year just before government workers had to take a 12 percent pay cut, the difference between the fee set when hired and his first year's check.)

By fall, the New York Stock Exchange agreed to work with the rules created by the SEC. These were not perfect. That became clear recently, almost seventy years later, when short players and speculation again dominated the market, creating "prosperity" for millions before plunging the economy into recession, wiping out 401(k) retirement plans, and ultimately sending corporate executives, stockbrokers, and others to jail. Yet even in the boom and bust years of market manipulation spread over the century, at no time has the economy been shattered in the manner of the Great Depression. Joe Kennedy's commission assured that speculators and manipulators still could profit, but not in the same way and not with impunity.

A number of now little-known stock exchanges quietly stopped operating because of the SEC. The Boston Curb Exchange disappeared. The California Stock Exchange went out of business. Exchange after exchange that had been created solely for market manipulation ceased operating.

Joe also ended initial public offerings that were designed to benefit insiders rather than investors. One example he cited when explaining his work to reporters involved a firm that was about to float an initial public offering (IPO). The bylaws of the corporation stressed that the business's policies would be controlled by a majority of the stockholders present at meetings. He immediately saw that there was nothing requiring stockholder notification or adequate lead time to assure large numbers of stockholders. The company was planning to play an insider's game. Joe told the firm that he would approve the IPO only if the policies had to be decided by a majority of all the stockholders.

One of the other innovations of the SEC, though not one that was exclusively Joe Kennedy's, was a new restriction on short selling. Joe said that short selling could not take place until after a stock rose in value. In Joe's mind, this made the manipulation less desirable and protected the company. The fact that short selling could begin the second day after an offering did not bother him.

In truth, the change in the rules affecting short sellers was not Joe's original idea, but the result of a series of suggestions from leaders of the twenty different stock exchanges that existed after the SEC put its rules into effect. Joe adopted the idea as his own, knowing that some speculation would be ended, but for the big-money players like himself, manipulating the market became more interesting. Anyone still could do with an initial public offering what Joe had done for Yellow Cab when he saved its stock.

Penalties for fraud also were put into effect. The manipulation of the stock market had not changed things as much as Joe later would give himself credit for having done, but there were penalties severe enough to protect the country from a repeat of the Great Depression.

Change came both rapidly and slowly, a seeming paradox that actually made sense. Businesses began issuing bonds that did not follow past procedures by which they had gone through a syndicate of investors that demanded a relatively high percentage for its efforts. Pacific Gas & Electric, Swift & Company, and several other businesses came forward in ways that showed their confidence.

At the same time, the efforts were far too few to bring about change without federal programs. Public works projects, the backbone of the National Recovery Act, the Works Progress Administration, and other New Deal programs of Roosevelt, were obviously necessary. Although there was direct relief for the poor in the form of checks sent to each person in need who qualified, direct relief was meaningless for recovery. While a man could feed his family with a relief check, a public works project could lead to a full-time job, an earned check even if indirectly from the government, and a future in a trade when the economy recovered. The federal government had to invest in average citizens through programs for the arts, construction, and other areas of the economy. Even Joe Kennedy, who had thought that the way to save corporate America was through corporate America, came to agree with the importance of public works projects. Still, corporations underwrote bond issues that increased by almost $2 billion in the one year between 1934 and the implemented SEC rules of 1935, a fact that showed the nation was improving by measurable increments.

Despite his work on the SEC, Joe could not win the public relations war no matter how hard he tried. Conservative businesspeople thought Joe had sold out to the liberals he hated. Roosevelt's ardent supporters thought Joe was deviously pushing Franklin into a more probusiness stance.

No matter what the criticism, Joe Kennedy worked intensely hard. It was as though he were again trying to prove something to an unknown critic whose approval he could never fully achieve. He hardened his stances against Roosevelt, telling the president what he thought about economic policies in language that was often crude and always direct. At the same time, he was circumspect, using a street approach but basing what he said on enough documentation so there was valid reason for his disagreements. Ultimately Eleanor encouraged Joe to keep it up because she felt yes-men too often surrounded Franklin.

Roosevelt finally made Joe take a break from Washington and return to his family's home in Palm Beach. In a memo dated February 19, Roosevelt wrote, in part: "[I]n view of the sleepless nights and hectic days of the Chairman of the S.E.C., in view of his shrunken frame, sunken eyes, falling hair, and fallen arches, he is hereby directed to proceed to Palm Beach and return to Washington six hours after he gets there." The message was deliberately continued on a second sheet of paper that read: "and AFTER TEN INTERVENING DAYS HAVE PASSED BY (FOOLED AGAIN)." (Emphasis in the original.)

The vacation was the beginning of the end of Kennedy's initial public service. By spring of that year he was looking for ways to resign. Roosevelt, who knew he would be leaving, was now impressed with his organizational ability and suggested Joe act as a consultant looking at the proposed public works programs the administration wanted to inaugurate through Congress. Joe realized that such a role would put him in the middle of administration insiders who were constantly at odds over such matters, and he knew it was time to leave the SEC.

There would be one more crisis before Kennedy left. The Senate Committee on Audit and Control was looking into what was called the Wheeler Resolution. This would have led to an investigation into railroad financing and the issue of having publicly owned railroads. James F. Byrnes, the committee chairman, wanted Joe to testify as the member of the Roosevelt administration most knowledgeable about corporate financing and the impact on stock.

The problem was a minor one in Roosevelt's eyes. It was one that any member of the administration should have been able to handle without consultation. But Joe was afraid to act without Roosevelt's approval, a fact that further diminished him in the president's mind. "I very definitely am on the spot," Joe wrote, in part, to the president. "I am to be asked whether I think an investigation should be made— what can possibly be accomplished and what I think may happen to the value of securities in the stock market. In other words, it looks like I am on the spot. Have you any opinion? I can go on my own and do the best I can unless you have some angle—it occurs to me that there may be some political angle to this investigation. Shall I go or have you any suggestion?"

A disgusted Roosevelt told Kennedy what he felt the SEC chairman should have known—don't testify unless you have to do so. Then he commented: "The trouble with Kennedy is you always have to hold his hand."[6]

In May 1935 a U.S. Supreme Court decision ended the National Recovery Act. The NRA was the cornerstone of Roosevelt's economic policy, and suddenly everything had to be redone. Instead of leaving office, Kennedy allowed himself to be elected to a second one-year term as SEC chairman. (Kennedy's term as a commissioner was five years, but the chairman had to be elected annually.)

The reelection came in July, the same month that Tom Corcoran and Ben Cohen, the two men who helped Roosevelt with his legislative initiatives, suggested that the SEC take control over the utility companies. Investigations had revealed that owners of utilities were often creating interlocking corporations that increased profits and inflated stock values while hurting the delivery of power.

Kennedy sided with the utility companies in opposition to such a takeover. He sent a letter to the head of the Senate Interstate Commerce Committee, whose members were leading the investigation. He explained that the bill, as written, gave too much power to the SEC and too few guidelines to be certain it would work. There were various forms of holding companies undergoing criticism for not being in the "public interest," Joe wrote, but there was no definition of "public interest." Everything was so vague as to risk greater problems with the current abuses by the companies themselves. He felt that limited government was best in the issue, a reversion to his thinking before he became a part of the government.

Congress was delighted to have an administration insider attack the administration. The Utility Holding Company Act did pass Congress, but it dramatically diminished the power that was originally to be given to the SEC.

Finally, with the new act in place and the SEC working within its strictures, Joe felt that everything he could do as an administrator there was complete. "To discontinue my official relations with you is not an easy task," Joe wrote to FDR early in September 1935. Joe was forty-seven years old and had returned to Washington after spending Labor Day with his family in Hyannis Port. "Rather it is one involving genuine regret assuaged only by the privilege of your friendship."

The resignation letter continued, "You know how deeply devoted I am to you personally and to the success of your administration. Because of this devotion, after retiring from the post of Chairman of the Securities and Exchange Commission, I shall still deem myself a part of your administration."

Two weeks later Roosevelt sent a formal acceptance of the resignation, praising Kennedy for what he had achieved. And, in truth, Joe had been successful. He accomplished what others felt he could not, and though there was plenty of room for abuse even with the stock exchanges operating under the SEC regulations, no longer could the country be manipulated into a depression. The nightmare that led to the collapse of Wall Street would not happen again. Public confidence in business investment was slowly on the rise. Joe Kennedy had truly been an important part of U.S. history.[7]

13

THE CONSULTANT

BEING THE CHAIRMAN OF THE SECURITIES AND EXCHANGE COM-
mission benefited Joe more than he imagined. He had entered public
life as a scoundrel, a man known to be dishonest for everything from his
bootlegging to his stock manipulation. He left public life with his reputation restored. In the eyes of the public, he had become a leading business expert, a loving family man, and an individual who could be trusted
to work with companies in crisis and restore them to health. Joe Kennedy had become a consultant.

The first client for the consulting business Joe inadvertently entered
was David Sarnoff. Radio Corporation of America's stock structure was
a business nightmare, with one form of common stock and two forms of
preferred. There were dividend obligations so unrealistic that they had
never been met in the best of times. And the men on the inside of the
corporation who were theoretically charged with doing something to
correct the problem were so busy arguing among themselves that nothing was happening. A good company with an excellent future was about
to be destroyed, and that was the reason Sarnoff sought the man he saw
as a dispassionate expert, Joe Kennedy.

Sarnoff and Kennedy both understood that RCA was poised to be a
dominant player in electronic media, including television, an older idea
than radio but one that had taken longer to become technically feasible.
The market would be limited for television at first. It was expensive,
unlike radio receivers, which could be made with little more than coiled
wire, a crystal, and earphones, and television programming had not yet
been determined.

Knowing that television probably was an important future entertainment medium and being able to achieve it when currently in crisis
were not the same. Joe Kennedy asked for a fee of $150,000 to fix mat-
ters, a price Sarnoff willingly paid. (Joe absorbed a $30,000 accounting
fee to handle the paperwork from the sum he was paid, but still he took
home more than twenty times the income of a successful blue-collar
worker.) He arranged for the elimination of one of the classes of pre-

ferred stock through low-interest bank loans. The second preferred stock would be eliminated through the creation of a new preferred stock that would be exchanged for the old. Eventually that new preferred stock would be added to the common stock, eliminating preferred stock entirely.

The technical side of the stock restructuring did not really matter. What was important to everyone was that the common stock would actually pay dividends with the new plan.

The reorganization was introduced at the 1936 annual meeting of RCA stockholders. Sarnoff called for an approval vote, and 98 percent of the stockholders qualified to approve the new plan did so. They had never received a dividend under the old system, and they hoped that Joe's reorganization of the studio structure was more than smoke and mirrors. To everyone's delight, in 1937 a common share of RCA stock paid twenty cents in dividends.

Paramount Pictures, seeing the turnaround at RCA, contacted Joe Kennedy next. The company had declared bankruptcy and been restructured. The new plan, though working, left the company in danger of financial devastation. The restructured company was too large, too ill conceived to be profitable for long.

In April 1937 Joe Kennedy joined Paramount as a special adviser. He brought in a team of financial experts he had used both at the SEC and when working in the film industry. They first looked at the business structure itself, the way the corporation had been created and how it was being run, but found few problems in that regard. Instead, as Joe learned when he spent weeks looking at the filmmaking process itself, Paramount was making the same mistakes he had seen when he was advising Gloria Swanson. Paramount Pictures had let the production people run amok, running up as many needless expenses as von Stroheim had done.

First there were the shooting schedules. The tighter the shooting schedule, the fewer days of production necessary to complete a film, and the lower the cost. It was basic business, yet Paramount's producers and directors were shooting twice the scenes they were using in the finished films. Each setup and take ran $14,500 on average. Each scene required an average expenditure of $29,000, double what it should have cost.

Paramount's directors had been given godlike powers. If a director alienated a critical star, he or she would remain angrily off the set for hours or days. If a director alienated a crew, they would either fail to work or dramatically slow down. If a director wished to go from idea to idea, wasting money on film stock that should not have been shot, no one said anything.

Joe's answer was to fire the arrogant directors and replace them with people who would do the work more efficiently. The director of a film was expendable. Cast and crew were not. Even if a director could make a film better than his replacement, slightly increasing the box-office take, it was not enough to warrant keeping him if he was the cause of some of the problems. The waste in film stock alone came to $7 million a year.

Joe's scathing report ran fifty-four pages, and he demanded that Paramount's president, just ending the first year of a five-year contract, release the information to the public. Kennedy was convinced that the men who headed the company and hired him to do the work would keep the report secret. They knew that it revealed them to be at fault, not the business structure of the company. He did not want to be a hero in the business world because of the SEC and RCA, only to go back to being the goat because Paramount Pictures failed to follow his recommendations. However, the men refused, and Joe released it to the press himself. He wanted to be certain that if the company went under, it was not perceived as being his fault. The record would show that he had warned them of every meaningful problem.

The results of going public were remarkable. The president of Paramount Pictures was immediately fired. Barney Balaban, who had been heading one of the profitable theater divisions of the company, was given the $150,000-per-year job.

The board of directors also was changed, though more slowly. In less than a year, ten directors were either let go or given new positions of lesser power and influence.

Finally, because of the importance of Paramount Pictures as a business in Hollywood, and the unusual problems that had led it into, out of, and almost back into bankruptcy, the company was about to be investigated by a congressional committee. The legislators wanted to determine why corporate restructuring had failed and whether there was criminal or civil wrongdoing. Instead, because of the Kennedy report identifying so much of the information the committee would otherwise seek, the leader of the committee agreed to hold off action.

This time the fee was "only" $50,000, plus $24,000 for the men who assisted Kennedy with the business structure analysis and $5,000 for expenses. And again it led to more consulting contracts.

William Randolph Hearst was in trouble. Truth be told, William Randolph Hearst always was in trouble. The publisher was a man to whom no one ever said "no." Who else in public life had ever decided to leave his wife, boldly take up a new life with his mistress, and glorify both actions? The wife was left in a New York mansion to which he occasionally paid a highly public visit. He did not divorce her. She did not try to divorce him. She wanted for nothing, yet would have wanted for nothing even if they had divorced.

Hearst had money, of course. He made $15 million per year from his newspaper empire, his insurance company, and his other holdings and investments. If a newspaper wasn't profitable, such as the *New York American*, which cost $1 million per year more to operate than the advertising and newsstand revenue, he allowed it to continue operating as long as he enjoyed what it was doing.

And Hearst bought "toys"—antiques, collectibles, anything he desired. He bought on impulse as he traveled, had everything shipped to his home, then unpacked little of it. It was as though it were enough for him to acquire. He didn't need to use or display his acquisitions.

Accountants and financial advisers constantly warned Hearst that he had great wealth but was approaching even greater spending each year. He refused to change, demanding that they handle matters, and often they were either able to do so or heroically made the attempt.

Finally the crunch came. Hearst was in danger of losing everything. He shut the *New York American*, and Marion Davies came to Hearst with an offer. As mentioned earlier, she had earned large sums of money in her own right, and she said she would give it all to Hearst.

Hearst, deeply moved, turned to Joe Kennedy instead of Marion, hoping he could keep his beloved from making such a sacrifice while retaining what he had acquired. Joe was paid $10,000 a week to restructure the Hearst empire. He was successful, though he never cured Hearst's excesses. He simply modified them enough so the publisher would never again be at risk of losing it all.

Joe made another offer during this time. He had come to understand the power that comes from being a publisher. He saw that information could make or destroy a career. The one business he had not entered was publishing, and with Hearst in trouble, he hoped he could acquire the successful Hearst magazine division at a fraction of its value. He told Hearst that he would pay him $8 million, though the publisher, having talked with the wealthy Armand Hammer, had the sense to turn Kennedy down. The proffered amount was a fraction of its value.

In the summer before the 1936 election, Joe relaxed in Hyannis Port with his family. His son Jack was sickly as usual, though looking to college. Joe Jr. was already attending Harvard. Rosemary was growing into a flirtatious teenager. And all the children were reaching a point where they could not be fully ignored. He did not realize it, but Joe was about to reenter government service, an action that would take the family into the most dramatic period of all their lives before the children left home to raise families of their own.

14

OF FAMILY AND AMBITION

WHEN JOE CAME HOME IN 1936, ONE OF HIS NINE CHILDREN WAS a preschooler and one was at Harvard. There had been photographs taken of the family over the years, images that filled the pages of numerous magazines around the country. Joe always was smiling. Rose always was smiling. The children were obviously enjoying the experience. And always the impression was the same—here is a man who delights in his sons and daughters. Here is a couple who dote on house and home.

The doting parents idea was all a myth. The children coveted Joe's presence because it was so rare. Rose would later be seen as a liberated woman because she so often led a life apart from her husband, traveling without him and sometimes staying in separate hotels in the same city. In truth, Rose had grown to despise the man she married. As for the children, she had long before abdicated the emotional, nurturing side of parenting to the paid staff.

That Joe Kennedy was the focus of his children's desire for attention is without question. The letters saved in the John F. Kennedy Library and elsewhere show that. No matter where he went, no matter what he did, the Kennedy children seemed to want to be a part of his world, to always have his approval. The trouble was that winning that approval often meant seemingly having to sublimate who you were, a situation that became a crisis for both Rosemary and Kathleen.

"Daddy was always very competitive," Eunice Kennedy Shriver once commented. "The thing he always kept telling us was that coming in second was just no good. The important thing was to win—don't come in second or third—that doesn't count—but win, win, win."

The children were professionally trained in athletics, not because they were world-class competitors but because Joe could afford such an extravagance. The Kennedys were never particularly athletic, with the possible exception of Joe Jr. Former classmates of Joe's sons used to laugh at the way they behaved when engaged in routine dormitory competitions. Many of the members of the pickup teams had played serious high school sports and were in college on partial athletic scholarships.

Yet the Kennedy boys felt they had to lead, even when they were the least skilled players in what, to the others, were meaningless games meant to get some exercise and pass the time.

The calisthenics instructor was hired to provide general fitness. Other instructors were hired for other sports, such as sailing. When the children competed in regattas sponsored by the Hyannis Port Yacht Club, they were grouped by ages. Joe, Jack, and Rosemary were on one boat; Kathleen and Eunice, the strongest competitors in the family, were on another with their sister Pat. In 1935, the best year for the family, most likely because they were delighted with Joe's presence for once, the oldest six children won a total of forty first, second, and third prizes in the seventy-six races held that summer. Bob, Jean, and Ted watched from the side, too young to participate.

The problem with the way the Kennedy children were raised was that the competition extended to everything. Although the children were quite different in health, physical abilities, and age, they were expected to compete with one another when together. Even as adults, when the family would have their touch football games, each had to win against the other. It was only when an "outsider" joined them—and that included spouses such as Peter Lawford and Joan Kennedy—that the family members joined together, working against the others. The siblings lived their lives as though seeking Joe's approval for their aggression against each other and the outside world.

Joe's presence was desirable for another reason as well. The children feared their mother, who often punished them by striking them with wooden coat hangers. Barbara Gibson, Rose Kennedy's assistant during the last years of Mrs. Kennedy's functioning life prior to the stroke that robbed her of all ability to speak or care for herself, witnessed one such event with the adult Eunice. She was not whipped, of course. Those punishments were long over. Only the fear lingered.

In the incident, Barbara Gibson and Rose Kennedy were in the attic, unwrapping a silver sauceboat Joe had purchased in England during World War II. Eunice had been told to come to the house so she could help, but what Rose really wanted was to *sell* her the sauceboat for $4,000. Eunice, like all the siblings, was a millionaire, though nowhere near as rich as their mother. However, she balked at having to buy something her mother considered an heirloom but that Eunice really didn't want to purchase. Since Eunice knew she would not be able to leave unless she bought the silver piece, she wanted to at least check it against a master list of silver pieces her mother maintained. The list was of items she and Joe had accumulated, some quite valuable and some of lesser quality. Eunice argued with her mother, insisting her mother show her that this was the silver piece worth the $4,000 being demanded.

Barbara Gibson recalled, "The three of us, heads bent over the list, were intent on determining which pieces fit the description of the expensive one, when Eunice started to disagree with her mother. Rose then stood upright and, eyes blazing, said, 'Eunice, be still!'

"As Rose calmly went back to the list, Eunice immediately closed her mouth, turned, and walked over to the corner of that small room, and stood with her arms folded in front of her. It was as though Eunice had returned to early childhood, the punishment so ingrained from so many repetitions that now, when she was of an age to be a grandmother herself, it was automatic. This fear of her mother remained intense until long after Rose was helplessly debilitated by a stroke."[1]

The children had no sense of their mother's intelligence, no understanding of the sacrifices she felt forced to make. Ironically, as the children and grandchildren grew to adulthood, it was the Kennedy women—both wives and blood relatives—who were the brightest. Joe's grandson John Kennedy Jr. would have to take the bar exam three times, while his sister, Caroline, took it only once, then followed with a coauthored book on the application of the Constitution to everyday life (*In Our Defense: The Bill of Rights in Action*, written with former classmate Ellen Alderman).

A third-generation Joe Kennedy, son of Robert Kennedy, became a congressman whose career was cut short by temper tantrums and inappropriate behavior with women while he was married. Joe's sister, Kathleen Kennedy Townsend, was a highly respected innovator, first in the field of education and then as lieutenant governor of Maryland. Even among the wives, Joan Kennedy was a classical pianist of note, and Jacqueline Bouvier Kennedy far outshone her husband, Jack, with her knowledge of art, history, and language. But it would be the Kennedy males who mattered, and for years, when one of the brothers was running for office, the Kennedy women were expected to scurry about like industrious little mice, doing whatever was necessary to get out the vote. Worse, they learned that they were to expect infidelity from the men, often enabling it, such as when Pat Kennedy Lawford let her brother Jack use the Lawfords' Beverly Hills home for California rendezvous.

Following the thinking of the day, Joe was responsible for the education of the sons—Joe, Jack, Bobby, and Teddy—while Rose was responsible for the education of Kathleen, Rosemary, Eunice, Pat, and Jean. This did not mean that Joe discussed his work with them or that Rose helped them with their schoolwork, church catechism, or even took them swimming, part of her daily exercise program. Rather it related to the selection of boarding schools and colleges they would attend. The couple had little interest in the unique personalities of any of their children while growing up. They only wanted them to do what would bring credit to the family, and that almost always had to do with winning all competition.

Joe Kennedy was unique among the early-twentieth-century business moguls in this regard. Joe Kennedy desired wealth solely to gain power and access to power in the manner he thought the Brahmins respected. Culturally this was a time when philanthropy was reaching its zenith, foundations were being established to carry on a family name in a manner more respected than the behavior of the dynasty's founder, and sons were educated to preserve the wealth coupled with social consciousness. Andrew Carnegie endowed the free library system. John L. Severance created a symphony hall. Doris Duke had such secret causes as suddenly impoverished society friends, poor southern black churches, and isolated Appalachian communities. The Astors and the Vanderbilts were involved with the arts.

There was the Rockefeller Foundation, the Ford Foundation, the Nobel Prize. Every famous name had a cause, a means for helping others, and the perpetuation of a family identity through good works despite what may, in part, have been a reprehensible series of business or personal activities by the patriarch. Not Joe Kennedy. All spending during his lifetime appears to have been totally self-serving—a tax dodge, the preservation of reserve capital to take him through bad times, and the like. He helped extended family members gain educations, and the staff was fairly paid, but the idea of using money to fund meaningful social causes, spur change, underwrite critical research, or even preserve great works of art was beyond his thinking. Even Rose, who often said that "To whom much is given, much is expected," seemed to think in terms of enduring the pain life can offer instead of working on the boards of charitable or cultural institutions, as would other wealthy spouses.

Hyannis Port summers, during which Joe was obsessed with the discipline and competitive spirit of his children, did not lend themselves to charitable thought. The family focus was always on beating others. The community had boat races for the children. They had swimming competitions for the children. They had a schedule of events meant to keep the kids occupied and happy, no parents taking the winning or losing of the different age group competitions particularly seriously—

except Joe Kennedy. Not only did Joe expect each of the nine children to win in their age groups for any event in which they competed, but also the Kennedy boys and girls were considered outcasts among their siblings if they failed to take first prize. The children thus competed indirectly against each other, knowing Joe would be angry with any son or daughter who came in second, or worse. He encouraged those children who won their events to taunt their less successful siblings.

Jack, the second son, had the greatest problems with Joe's expectations because his older brother, Joe Jr., was a natural athlete, while he had a genetic back problem and a poor immune system. The health of the children did not matter when they felt challenged by one another, though. Joe Jr. was the gifted son. He easily excelled academically, athletically, and socially. Yet Joe had a desperate desire for his father's love, and he felt he had to earn it by besting Jack in ways that could become vicious.

Author John Davis, a cousin of Jack's wife, Jacqueline, described a race between the two oldest Kennedy brothers the family members were still talking about long after the boys had grown into manhood. Each got on his bike, then made a circuitous route back to the starting point to see who could get there first. They were traveling as fast as they could, heading toward one another, each determined to prove that the other was "chicken" and would turn away from a head-on collision. Neither did. They smashed into each other, each the "winner," though Jack had to go to the hospital for twenty-eight stitches.

At the same time, each child was responsible for teaching proper behavior to the next youngest. Joe, the oldest, was expected to discipline Jack for any transgressions. Joe also would use Jack to relay a message that something was wrong to the next oldest, and then to the next and the next.

Joe's mixed feelings about his expected roles led to extreme bullying while he was growing up. Touch football games could become personal, Joe Jr. slamming the football into Jack's stomach as they worked on plays together. The bullying and the show-off attitude became worse each time Jack was sick and Joe Sr. was in town. Jack was frequently ill with his back problems, jaundice, or something else, and Joe Sr. would spend extra time with him if he were present. To Joe Jr. the illness was just a ruse to get their father's attention.

Jack's illnesses ultimately affected everything he did. His back was slightly curved, and he was constantly in pain as he grew to manhood. Today there would be surgery and, possibly, the use of growth hormones. In the 1920s and 1930s, medical science could do nothing. Worse, once

Jack reached full height it was too late to do anything except provide him with painkillers.

Joe Jr. was the athlete and the scholar. Jack was the withdrawn reader. But Jack lacked the intellect to enjoy more than the story.

Joe Sr.'s "writing" related to his world as a business executive. His sons, by contrast, would one day be presented as knowledgeable about history and current events. Jack's reading material when growing up consisted primarily of novels, the same interest he would have in the White House. As president, he was a voracious reader of Ian Fleming's James Bond novels, for example, and the White House press secretaries would explain that he was seeking relief from the stress of the day and the more serious reading that dominated his life.

Jack, like his brother Joe, attended the elite Protestant private school Choate. It was as hostile to its handful of Catholics and Jews as Harvard had been when Joe Sr. attended. It was strong in academics, though that was not a concern for the Kennedys, even though Jack needed all the help he could get. He seemed unable to retain much of what he read, and he lacked the ability to take in multiple ideas about the same subject, then analyze them in a way that would warrant a fresh conclusion. His spelling was atrocious and would remain so at least into his marriage. Papers he wrote during his late teens and early twenties show him making more mistakes with spelling than his sister Rosemary, for whom the myth of mental retardation was created. Ultimately Joe had to use the influence he had been gaining with Harvard starting back when he held the conference on the motion picture industry. Power and money from an alumnus mattered more than the abilities of a rich man's child, the only reasons Jack was allowed into Harvard.

The oldest Kennedy children were into young adulthood before Joe and Rose seemed to discover their unique personalities and how they meshed with their interests. The growing maturity of the daughters also led to Kathleen's unwillingness, when she was sent to the Sacred Heart convent in France, to accept as strict an education as her mother had received. But Kathleen was not the type of young woman to adapt to any forced, structured environment, and the French nuns, less strict than those in Holland, were unable to break her spirit.

Kathleen had been willing to stay in Europe as long as Jack also was there. The two had become close on the trip over on the _Île de France_. Jack was going to spend a semester at the University of London, and traveling back and forth to France would be easy. But Jack became ill once again, having to return to the United States for a stay in Arizona to fight the jaundice that ravaged his body's immune system. Kathleen, denied the freedom of her brother's presence (Joe Jr. and Kathleen were not yet close), refused to stay at Sacred Heart. Her parents transferred her to a more liberal convent school, in Neuilly, a community just outside of Paris.

Freed of the strictures of the Sacred Heart school, wealthy beyond imagination, and anxious to experience all of life, Kathleen took advantage of the turmoil, the art, and the society of Europe. She went to Rome to meet the Pope and stayed to hear a speech by Mussolini, one of many uniting the people for the war that was coming. Kathleen skied in Switzerland and went to art exhibitions in Rome. She came alive to the world in ways that her father admired yet did not fully understand.

Rose came to visit her daughter in April 1936 and discovered a sophisticated young woman who also liked to visit stores filled with items only those with unusually large bank accounts could afford. They traveled to the Soviet Union to attend a party put on by the U.S. ambassador, William C. Bullitt. Then they went shopping. Spending money on clothing and accessories was not just a pleasure, it also was a bonding experience.

The relationship between Kathleen and her mother, as well as the relationship that would shortly develop between Kathleen and her father, would be the most important any of the children would experience except for Rosemary and Teddy. The former would be a negative one. The latter would be unique to Rose, who saw in Teddy the same aggression, amorality, and charm that her father had used when seducing both women and the city of Boston.

Kathleen was the liberated woman her mother would have been had the pressures from her father, the convent school, and Joe's abuses not radically altered Rose's naturally gregarious personality. Kathleen was a bright woman who would soon get a job on a Washington, D.C., newspaper before moving permanently to England. She had a curious mind, compassion for others, a willingness to follow her heart despite the times she went against some of the teachings of the church, and eventually would not let so minor a matter as her lover's marital status interfere with her happiness. She became close to her father when he realized he needed her advice in matters related to her younger sister, Rosemary, but that was a few years ahead. This trip was solely a time to bond with Rose, mother and daughter touring together as friends, a unique situation among the Kennedy women. The child Kathleen whom Rose had virtually ignored had become the woman Kathleen to whom Rose could finally relate.

When the children returned to the United States, Jack and Joe stopped being competitive with each other. Joe was a junior at Harvard, with all the knowledge, experience, and friends of an upperclassman. He was thinking ahead to a political career, and his father was encouraging him to consider a run for governor of Massachusetts in 1940 or, more likely, 1944. Joe Sr. knew the importance of the Kennedy/Fitzgerald families' names, knew he could get the support of both Honey Fitz and, if he was careful, Franklin Roosevelt. Joe also had enough money to bankroll his son beyond the wealth of any likely rival. It was a combination of political assets that could beat a more seasoned politician.

Jack stopped competing with his older brother because he no longer could do so. He was six feet tall but weighed only 149 pounds, little of which was muscle. He did try out for the football team at Harvard to please his father, but a ruptured disk ended all realistic participation in competitive athletics except swimming. He had improved greatly since the day he had jumped from the yacht after watching his father begin a sexual encounter with Gloria Swanson. However, Jack had no endurance, and though he might have been competitive in short-distance events, he was never strong enough to go a full practice session without suffering from exhaustion. From then on, all photos of Jack engaging in family games were taken in a way to disguise the intense, debilitating pain he was experiencing.

The one child whose life was being inadvertently guided toward disaster was Rosemary. Joe and to a lesser degree Rose were experiencing increasing frustration with Rosemary's growing into womanhood. She did not share in the family's competitive drive. She did not share in her mother's sense of the importance of Catholic ritual. And she did not learn school lessons in the manner of the other Kennedy children.

Joe Sr. felt that a Kennedy could not be a unique individual with strengths, weaknesses, and desires that did not meet his standards. He was like the wagon train master in one of the Westerns so popular in his day, drawing his family into a protective circle. Each was interdependent on the other and would never think of self if that violated the standards of the group.

Rosemary knew she was not on a wagon train. Rosemary did not care whether a Kennedy was liked or disliked. Rosemary had nothing to prove and no interest in reinforcing her father's view of the world. In a family of leaders, she was the one follower. In a family being placed on center stage, she was the lone member of the audience. Increasingly Joe assumed that such uniqueness meant brain damage or mental illness, and since both were viewed as family stigmata, he dared not seek the counsel of someone who might provide a healthier perspective.

The children were raised in isolation from "real world" circumstances as much as possible. There is a classic note Jack wrote to his father in which he asks Joe to send him newspapers and magazines to read "because I did not know about the Market Slump until a long time after." He was referring to what the rest of the nation considered the Great Depression.

Rose was equally in the dark about the extent of her own wealth, though she was aware of the stock market crash. She knew she was rich enough to go on buying trips to Paris whenever she liked, yet she periodically thought she should save money by putting off needed repairs or not keeping a house staff on salary when she and the family were away for a few weeks.

Rose also became eccentric about managing her time. She began to use small pieces of paper on which she would make notes she wished to remember. Since she feared losing track of the pieces of paper, she obtained a quantity of straight pins, then would pin each note to her dress. At any given time, on any given day, her dress of the moment would have as many as ten pinned-on notes.

Rose drilled the children, especially on the catechism of the Roman Catholic Church. This was most important to her when her oldest sons were in Choate, since it was connected with the Episcopal Church.

In addition, Rose believed that her children should know the facts of history. She constantly quizzed them about the names, dates, and locations of important people, places, and events throughout the periods of history she thought they should know. This carried over to the children's friends, who quickly learned that a visit to the Kennedy family home was like being on a radio quiz show.

Joe, by contrast, expected the children to be able to discuss current events. He did not care how naive their opinions might be. He wanted them to be aware of what was going on in the world and to be able to argue any position they took.

Joe took a similar attitude toward religion. He saw no reason for ritual. He preferred that the children be obedient to his leadership and aggressive toward others in whatever form that might take.

Joe also insisted on punctuality for the children and any overnight guests. A child who was late to the dinner table would not eat that night. Only Jack escaped such a fate because of his scrawny, sickly body.

He was the one child who would have a meal taken to him if banished to a bedroom. However, Jack knew not to push his good fortune very far. He dared not deliberately be late on a regular basis, or his siblings would be openly outraged by the special treatment.

Guests were given a schedule for meals and again denied food if they did not meet it. Every bedroom had a clock, so no one could claim he or she did not know what time it was. The couple had a heavy turnover in domestic help because the undisciplined children dumped their clothing, towels, and other various possessions wherever they so chose, knowing a staff person would pick up after them. The maids felt the burden was unfair, that the children of privilege were being abusive, and they regularly quit. Joe was terrified that the cook would feel the same burden, so he set hours for serving. Breakfast was at 9:00 A.M. on days when there was no school, for example, and if anyone complained, Joe stated, "If the cook leaves, I'm following right after her."

When Rose ran out of local staff people, she took to driving to agencies in surrounding communities to find new help. Eventually she found she could not mention the size of the family without being turned down. Barbara Gibson was told one story where a new maid was informed that Rose had five daughters and one son. The maid was comfortable working with girls who, other than in the Kennedy family, always had been less trouble. That was why, at the first meal being served, only Joe Jr. was present along with his sisters. However, at the second meal Jack was added. Bobby came to the third meal. It took two days before the maid realized the exact size and nature of the Kennedy family, though Barbara did not know how long the maid tolerated the results of the deception.

Joe Sr. constantly ordered the children to strive for success. Eunice went so far as to combine religious ritual with aggressive competition one summer. She made her sailboat crew say the rosary with her before competing in each of fourteen races held the same week.

Rose often tried to imply that the children were only encouraged to do their best. However, the children remember the humiliation when they had to tell their parents that they lost.

Kathleen, who was not as attractive as Rosemary, was made more beautiful by her aggressively outgoing personality. Kathleen bowed to the authority of her parents, and she also got involved with the lives of others. She was nosy enough that she eventually worked as a newspaper reporter, but she also cared about others. Eventually she would be the one Kennedy whose presence was truly welcomed in England by the social elite.

As Joe spent time with his family following his Hollywood adventures, he began seeing the future for his oldest children. Most indications were that Jimmy Roosevelt might run for Massachusetts governor in 1940. Four years later, with Joe Jr. "seasoned" and Jimmy ready to move on after two terms (the Massachusetts governor was elected for two years at a time), Joe Jr. would pursue the same position.

Jack would go to Harvard, but beyond that, his future was unclear. Joe Sr. would stress that he would be going into politics, but it was not until the war years that the idea of Jack being groomed for the White House would become either a given in family planning or a joke Jack shared with his friends. Certainly the stories of such a run are found only in letters from friends, while a number of men connected with Roosevelt knew that Joe Jr. was being groomed for governor, presumably after Jimmy Roosevelt's attempt for that office.

What bothered Joe Sr. during the time he was at home was that Rosemary was becoming a young woman. He saw her indifference to family rules, church rituals, and all the other values meant to rein in the children as they grew older. He saw her emerging sexuality. He saw her independent spirit. There was much of her mother's spark, at least when Rose was coming of age, and Joe feared what that might mean with an adolescent like Rosemary. Soon he would act on those concerns.

The one area where Rose and Joe found a comfort level with each other was in politics. Rose understood that Joe's work for the 1932 election had been the action of a man buying position in the new government. The contributions to Roosevelt and the Democratic Party were no different from ward heelers buying votes for local office. Subtle corruption was something she and her father had engaged in for years. It was a world with which she was familiar, a world she could support with an insider's knowledge and experience. For the moment, though, Joe would not involve his wife. As he had four years earlier, Joe would work in areas where he had expertise.

Joe Kennedy's value in the 1932 election had been his ability to put Roosevelt in contact with business leaders who would otherwise be hostile to him. Joe also liked fronting for Roosevelt—meeting with the press and talking up the candidate. Often his actions were self-serving, but Franklin did not mind. Joe served a useful purpose, even though finding ways to reward him could be a nuisance.

Roosevelt realized he had problems with Joe when Kennedy and Jimmy went to Europe to set up the liquor distribution business. Franklin was aware that there was a good chance that Jimmy had been promised an estimated 25 percent of the action ($250,000 per year based on Joe's estimated $1 million-per-year earnings from the end of Prohibition until the sale of the business in 1946), then was cheated out of it with the excuse that such involvement would hurt his father's presidential campaign.

Joe did bring Jimmy indirectly into the liquor business in a way that would not cause the Roosevelt family embarrassment. He helped the young Roosevelt become president of the National Grain Yeast Corporation of Belleville, New Jersey. This was a business that made a key ingredient in liquor, and the end of Prohibition assured the company's success. Unfortunately, the position of president was not just a title. Jimmy had to do the work, something he either ignored or was not capable of doing. Either way, he failed at the job and was thrown out six months after he was hired.

Now, with the 1936 election coming, there was increased tension between Kennedy and Roosevelt because of Kennedy's dealings with Jimmy at the same time that Rose was encouraging Joe Sr. to get more involved in the political arena. The result of Rose's nudging was Arthur Krock's first ghosted book for Joe Kennedy, a volume titled *I'm for Roosevelt*. There is some question as to whether Krock was paid for his endeavor. He was offered $1,000 a week for the writing, the job lasting five to six weeks. However, there is some indication that Krock did not charge Joe, gaining benefits in other ways later. By Krock's not charging for the writing, Kennedy could claim that he alone did the writing.

The need for the book became apparent after groundwork he had laid for a return to government service after finishing his consulting work failed. He had sent Missy Le Hand, Roosevelt's secretary, the message, "I'm fairly free now of any business activities, and so if he thinks I can be of any use to him, please let me know." Nothing happened.

But there was a way Joe could ingratiate himself with Franklin. Roosevelt had sent him a list of fifty major businessmen who might be sympathetic to the New Deal. It was a far shorter list than the Republicans could put together to support their efforts. Joe's job was to try to gain contributions, but he decided to do more. He decided to have Arthur Krock of the *New York Times* write the story of why a businessman, Joe, saw Roosevelt and his policies as the only way to move the nation forward.

The resulting book was an analysis of the nation's economy and the troubles of the world. It showed how Joe, a conservative businessman, could find himself forcefully in the president's corner for reelection. Given the newfound respect Joe had achieved thanks to his work with the Securities and Exchange Commission, the book made a difference among conservative Republicans. But not only did Joe have nothing to do with it, other than the use of his name, it also would be a vehicle for a future power exchange meant to jump-start what Joe thought would be his oldest son's political career.

There was no great philosophical statement in the book. Joe was never a great thinker, and Krock tried to make certain that the book read in the manner Kennedy spoke. Instead, it was a very public endorsement by a man who seemed to represent everything the Republicans embraced. It also was a statement decrying the excesses of Republicans who practiced the same business principles as Joe had long done himself. It was almost as though he were declaring that he got rich with the Republicans but that their way failed the country. Roosevelt, who also was wealthy, had founded programs of public service that could restore the economy. The only exception involved a handful of tax proposals, but that was a minor disagreement.

Joe's one important statement in the book was his endorsement of national planning to assure the future success of the country. The social and economic order required a strong central government, something the Republicans had fought for years. He said that either there would be regulation of daily life to support the social order, or there would be a dictatorship bringing the nation under control.

In the book Joe claimed that he had no political ambitions for himself and his family. He related his support for Roosevelt and strong government to being the father of a large family.

Krock became active in other ways, ghosting articles for Joe in a variety of business-related publications as well as the *New York Times Magazine*. Joe began talking about the social obligation brought about by having money and power.

Ironically, Joe was now talking in the same manner as his father. Patrick Kennedy truly believed what Joe was professing in print and in interviews, but not living in his own life. That was why he died comfortable rather than rich, beloved instead of tolerated, admired for his deeds and not his flashy excesses. But Joe never placed his statements into personal action. He understood that the wealthy had to work for the greater good of society. He professed the need in his book. Yet he never did it himself.

There are other stories about the book, all thirdhand yet persistent enough to be mentioned. One tells that Joe was allegedly being investigated for income-tax evasion based on an arrangement he had with one or more people in the Vatican.

Contrary to what many non-Catholics think, the Vatican is not like a glorified church or an American cathedral. It is a political entity, an independent city-state or small town (as of 1929) within Rome, and there are far more people involved in a wide variety of occupations—accounting, law, maintenance, security, investment, and so on—than people realize. The Pope is not the chief executive officer in the manner of a corporate CEO. Much takes place of which he is not aware, since his primary role is as spiritual leader for all Catholics. Thus in the twentieth century, as in the centuries preceding, there has been corruption by individual Catholic leaders working for the Pope but acting illegally without the Pope's knowledge.

Joe Kennedy had contacts in the Vatican who allegedly created or participated in financial scams. Earlier it was noted that Joe was not actively involved with the local churches where Rose worshiped each day. He did, according to stories circulated by several different sources, arrange a money-laundering and tax-evasion scam with someone connected with the Vatican.

In 1936 Joe allegedly was looking at an income-tax-evasion charge based on a $1 million contribution to the Vatican. The allegation of close friends who supposedly knew the scam was that Joe arranged for an actual contribution of $500,000. He gave $1 million, received appropriate receipts, and deducted that sum from his income tax. Then his cohort in the Vatican returned half of the money. Joe got $500,000 tax-free to use as he so chose, a $1 million tax deduction, and the Vatican benefited by the $500,000—all that had been promised.

Later Joe allegedly laundered money for Jack Kennedy's presidential campaign in the same manner. The problem with these stories is that the sources are not primary. One was Morton Downey Jr., who said the information came from his late father, a big-band singer specializing in Irish tunes and making $12,000 a week as one of the stars of radio in the 1930s and 1940s. He was the one close friend Joe had who was not connected with his business inner circle. The only time Joe and Downey

Sr. did business together was when Joe arranged for a personal loan so Downey could buy into a New Haven, Connecticut, Coca-Cola bottling company. Downey was the voice on many Coke commercials, and both men knew that the investment could not fail.

Another source was a courier or bagman interviewed by author Peter Maas, a specialist in stories about organized crime. Maas learned of the laundering in regard to Jack's election campaign funding.

Even a friend of Joe's who was a writer for the *Chicago Tribune* heard the story about the Vatican gift from Postmaster General James Farley. Yet the information always came thirdhand. Still, Joe had been saved from an investigation into his stock market manipulation by campaigning for Roosevelt. Having a book prepared to support the president as a way of avoiding an investigation into his taxes would make sense.

Fortunately for Joe, Roosevelt felt the need to reward him for what he did—fund-raising. This time the prize also was in line with Joe's background. The Merchant Marine Act of 1936 established the Maritime Commission. In February 1937 Joe was asked to be its chairman. It was a logical appointment, given his history with Fore River, yet Joe balked. He admitted to Roosevelt that he was making large sums of money and wanted to continue doing so. "If it's all the same to you, let some other patriot take it on the chin for a while. There's a lot of money to be made in the market. I'd like to skim off my share of the profits," Kennedy related.[2]

There was only one post that Kennedy wanted, and that was secretary of the treasury. However, Roosevelt persuaded him to take the commission position because of the challenge. The act required the commission to handle a vast array of claims and mail contracts before July 1. There was little doubt that Joe could handle the work, though it meant seven-day weeks and a commitment much like he first gave to the saving of Yellow Cab.

What Kennedy did not realize was that he was going to become the administration's scapegoat in a very dangerous situation. Roosevelt had won the 1936 election, but he could keep the job only with the support of both labor and management. The problem was that the docks were alive with controversy. Not only did management and labor have disagreements, rival unions were striving to represent the same workers. Strikes were called so regularly that the industry was losing millions in work stoppages.

Everything came to a head when the crewmen aboard the USS *Algic* went on strike in September 1937, a year in which various strikes had cost the industry 1 million man-hours of work.

The *Algic*, a U.S. government ship, was in the port of Montevideo when the local workers were on strike. The crew had no grievances but felt the need to support the locals. Joe, furious, ordered the arrest of the fourteen ringleaders after the ship returned to Baltimore.

Joe Curran, the general organizer of the CIO's National Maritime Union, was also furious. He already hated Joe for suggestions Kennedy had made for improving the training of merchant seamen. Joe's reasoning was that they were "second class" and could not be trusted to provide first-class service when working the merchant vessels. Curran had been a sailor before he went to work for the union and resented Kennedy's arrogance. The jailing of the seamen was the final insult, and Roosevelt knew to keep away from the controversy. Joe had made the judgment call, and as Roosevelt told his maritime commissioner, if the decision was wrong, Kennedy would bear the blame.

While Kennedy was facing his unusual set of problems, he tried to relax at the twenty-fifth reunion of his Harvard graduating class. The vast majority were successful Republicans who hated the New Deal, hated Roosevelt, and thought their arrogant classmate was ripe for ridicule. To get revenge, one of the classmates, an attorney named Ray Wilkins, later a Massachusetts Supreme Court justice, wrote songs to accompany a play, *In the Good Old Maritime*, by humorist Robert Benchley.

The sketch began in a room where a secretary sat at a desk covered with telephones. This was supposed to be the outer office of the Maritime Commission, and the secretary was frantically telling every caller that no matter what their clocks said, it could not be nine o'clock in the morning because Mr. Kennedy hadn't arrived yet.

After a couple of minutes of the secretary telling every caller that his clock was off, "Joe Kennedy" walked in. The actor was Edward Gallagher, who had found his financial success in the railroad business. He wore spats, gloves, and a bowler hat as he came in twirling his cane. "Get me Franklin at the White House," the actor said, sitting at a second desk and propping up his feet. Then he took the telephone and said, "I'm here, Franklin. It's nine o'clock. You can start the country." Immediately there were intense sound effects mimicking factory whistles, truck horns, and similar indicators of blue-collar commerce.

Other jokes in the sketch included a mock report indicating that Joe planned to alleviate all problems with the class of 1912 by putting them all on the government payroll at $10,000 a year.

Joe was not happy with the joking, and he was booed when he tried to give a brief talk about the New Deal and the economy. The men had mocked the bootlegger, the Joe Kennedy they remembered from the time when he supplied them with illegal alcohol for a previous reunion. They did not realize that he was fighting to achieve a sense of dignity he thought could come only from being more sober about all aspects of life. He did not understand that these might have been men who held him in enough respect to create the show. He never returned to another Harvard reunion.

The year ended no better for Joe. He had to go before the House Merchant Marine Committee and tell them that the act they had passed and he was supposed to administer had been a mistake. Most ships were in disrepair, with only a single new ship being built since he assumed the chairmanship. Worse, some of the men who understood the merchant marine were leaving for other jobs, and some cabinet posts were becoming vacant, but Joe made clear to Franklin Roosevelt that he wanted Henry Morgenthau Jr.'s job at Treasury.

The stock market was doing poorly at the end of the year, a fact that Joe thought might give him leverage. But Roosevelt knew that Joe was a man who would not work with the president if he were given the job he coveted. He would want to run Treasury his own way, something Morgenthau never attempted. Roosevelt would only appoint someone he could work with, and that was not Joe Kennedy.

As the midterm of Roosevelt's second four years approached, Joe found himself in a better position. Louis Howe had died, and Jimmy Roosevelt had become his father's gatekeeper. Writing in March 1938, Secretary of the Interior Harold L. Ickes noted: "Jimmy has his father's ear at all times. When the President is tired or discouraged, Jimmy is at hand to say what may be influential. Jimmy has no political ideals, he is not a liberal, and he is trying to make a place for himself in public life. Joe Kennedy's influence has been bad too. It was Kennedy who dissuaded the President from appointing Lowell Mellett as Kennedy's successor on the Maritime Commission. Kennedy was afraid that Mellett would settle the labor difficulty which he had not been able to settle, and so he persuaded the President to appoint a stooge of his own."[3]

Ickes's bias was obvious, though there was some truth to what he said. Kennedy had stepped into a nightmare that was not going to be resolved in a few weeks or months. He had brought order to the controllable chaos of paperwork. He had brought his volatile temper to areas where quiet negotiations were preferable, though he was known to be skilled as a negotiator when he was not emotionally involved.

But Jimmy did have his father's ear, and Kennedy did have Jimmy. Not that Joe liked the young Roosevelt. His business failures and his inability to control his sexual wanderings offended Joe. He felt that Jimmy, like himself, should have more discretion. Instead, Kennedy once said that Jimmy was "so crazy for women that he would screw a snake going uphill." Yet in a letter to Jimmy and Betsey sent in January 1937 he said, "You know as far as I am concerned you are young people and struggling to get along and I am your foster-father." The letter, saved in the Roosevelt Library in Hyde Park, was yet another example of the subtle manipulation of Jimmy that Franklin understood and hated.

Joe also had worked to convince other members of Roosevelt's entourage that he was someone they should help. His Palm Springs, Florida, home became a winter resting place for Missy Le Hand; Bishop Francis J. Spellman, then of Boston and later archbishop of New York; Harry L. Hopkins of the Works Progress Administration; Arthur Krock, who was increasingly using editorials and articles in the *New York Times* to help Kennedy and his ideas; and, of course, Jimmy and Betsey Roosevelt. That was why Joe decided to put in his bid for a new position in the government—ambassador to the Court of St. James.

The opening occurred not for political reasons but because of a death. Robert Worth Bingham, appointed the ambassador to Britain in 1933, was a wealthy Louisville, Kentucky, newspaper publisher. He had the international relations awareness to hold the position, and he had the wealth to support the expense. The annual salary was $17,500, with an added annual expense allowance of $4,800. The elaborate receptions that were to be held were enough to use that much money and more every few weeks. Every ambassador needed to be at least a millionaire and willing to expend six figures out of pocket every year. Bingham had been delighted to do so until he took ill in London, was rushed to Johns Hopkins Hospital in the United States, and turned in his resignation when it became clear he was dying.

Joe Kennedy's name came up for consideration even before Joe decided to make an effort to gain the ambassadorship. He was an extremely wealthy man who could handle the expense of London with ease. He understood international trade. He understood shipping. He was skilled as a negotiator in areas that mattered between the United States and Britain. And it was believed that Joe would be able to act as an accurate witness to what was taking place in the country.

In Franklin's mind, an ambassador did not make foreign policy. An ambassador represented the government's interest, noting the political, social, and economic conditions that could affect the relationship between the two governments. An ambassador acted as an unbiased reporter of the inner workings of the nation to which he was assigned. Joe, known for collecting and sharing gossip, could handle the task.

There was one more issue: Roosevelt owed Kennedy, and a payoff could not be put off.

Joe Kennedy's wealth had made him an insider with people the president had reason to fear. Henry Luce, founder of publications such as *Time* and *Life*, was looking to the 1940 election as a way of gaining a political position for himself. He hated Roosevelt, backed Secretary of Agriculture Henry A. Wallace, yet seriously considered Joe Kennedy a man who might be all right in the Oval Office, at least if he would back Luce for a cabinet or other high-level position. He eventually ran a *Life* magazine story featuring the likely candidates to replace Roosevelt in 1940. Joe Kennedy's picture would be included.

Roosevelt had concerns about sending Joe to London. There were rumors of war in 1937, and Roosevelt had no idea if Joe could handle the necessities of the crises that were occurring in Europe. Before Franklin talked with Joe about the post, the president decided to replace his commerce secretary, Daniel C. Roper. Business was again in trouble, and Roosevelt wanted to be known for aiding the recovery of the economy, not for being on watch during a second stock market crisis. Joe Kennedy would actually be an ideal commerce secretary, and the post was high level, public, and excellent for the man's ego.

Secretary of State Cordell Hull also liked the idea of moving Joe to the Commerce Department. He found Kennedy a crude man with no sense of propriety during their first talk together. According to author Joe McCarthy,[4] Hull and Kennedy discussed the furor over the appointment of Hugo Black as an associate justice of the U.S. Supreme Court, a position given for life. Justice Black, one of the more liberal members of the Court during his years on the bench, had a secret past. He had been a member of the Ku Klux Klan in his youth, a fact that was released only after the appointment.

There were and are a number of unresolved questions about Justice Black. Was he a man who had been a fool in his youth, learned a better way to think and live, and yet always carried the unpleasantness of his early membership as part of his background? Or was he a man who could objectively look at the Constitution no matter what his personal bias? Whatever the circumstances, he had just joined the bench and was too new to evaluate.

Joe Kennedy mentioned to Franklin Roosevelt and Cordell Hull that his friend Arthur Krock felt that Black should have mentioned his past to Roosevelt the moment the appointment arose. According to the story McCarthy related, the president asked Joe what he said to Krock.

"I said to him if [glamorous movie actress] Marlene Dietrich asked you to make love to her, would you tell her you weren't much good at making love?"

Krock was shocked. The joke, minor by today's standards, was quite bawdy in 1937. It would be totally inappropriate in England, where sex scandals were frequent but gossip about them was still impolite. And while Roosevelt laughed, he realized that Kennedy was probably inappropriate for the Court of St. James. He decided to push for Joe to become secretary of commerce.

When Franklin sent his son Jimmy to talk Kennedy into the Commerce Department position, Joe was thinking about becoming ambassador to the Court of St. James. It was then that Joe had Jimmy return to his father to arrange the meeting in the Oval Office. That would be the meeting where Kennedy's desperation for the ambassadorship would be revealed in his willingness to do anything, including the humiliating act of dropping his pants, to get the post.

No one but the three men present would know of Joe Kennedy's low self-esteem and desperate desire to be ambassador to the Court of St. James. And before Franklin could again change his mind, Joe had Arthur Krock break news of the as-yet-unannounced appointment in an article in the December 9 *New York Times*.

Joe Kennedy had received what, by then, had become his greatest dream. It was to prove a period of endless nightmares.

15

"THE AMBASSADOR"

THE PEOPLE OF GREAT BRITAIN THOUGHT THEY WANTED JOE KEN-
nedy as the ambassador to the Court of St. James. It was 1938, and Germany was obviously rearming. The German air force was being built into
what some observers considered the finest in the world. Adolf Hitler
was solidifying his political support, continuing to murder or jail his
enemies, and obviously expanding his power both within and beyond
Germany's borders.

The British knew they were being threatened by political forces
that made their isolated island nation much like a small Florida coastal
city resting in the path of a hurricane whose ever-building wind velocity
was becoming increasingly destructive. The United States, ill equipped
for the type of manufacturing commitment necessary to either fight a
war or support one, was nevertheless perceived to be the one nation
that could help England in a significant way. It was an illusion, but one
that led to fear among enemies and the desire for support from friends.

Franklin Roosevelt was critical to London, and it was assumed that
the new ambassador to the Court of St. James would be a man who had
the president's ear and respect. No one in Britain knew that the president privately had said to Henry Morgenthau, "I have made arrangements to have Joe Kennedy watched hourly—and the first time he opens
his mouth and criticizes me, I will fire him."

Joe seemed to have understood instinctively how tenuous his new
position was likely to be. Harvey Klemmer, his aide at the Maritime
Commission who would be accompanying him to England as a combination speechwriter and publicist, quoted his boss as saying, "Don't go
buying a lot of luggage. We're only going to get the family in the *Social
Register*. When that's done, we come back and go out to Hollywood to
make some movies and some money."

There were other plans as well, none related to the affairs of state.
Irish Catholic Joe Kennedy was going to use his new position to get
subtle revenge against the Brahmins he hated with an irrational passion.
What Joe did not expect was that his new, very public position opened

Stanley Reed, Associate Justice of the U.S. Supreme Court, swears in Joseph P. Kennedy Sr. as ambassador to the Court of St. James. President Roosevelt is looking on. (Cleveland State University Library, Special Collections)

his life to serious examination by media on both sides of the Atlantic. Journalists were anxious to tell the colorful story of the disreputable character who had risen so high.

Henry Luce's *Fortune* was the first to attack. A staff writer had created an objective profile of Kennedy, a fact that meant the piece would reveal the ambassador's dishonesty, his philandering, and all the other traits that made him so hated within Washington.

Today the article would have run before the subject knew what it said, the way most publishers avoid what is called prior censorship. Kennedy would likely have declared the piece to be false, brought a massive libel suit, and then quietly dropped the legal action later, when the dismissal would not gain headlines. In 1937 publishers like Henry Luce let the subjects of their articles review the text well before it was published. They felt the subject had the right to object to any mistakes, perhaps adding information to make the text more complete.

Kennedy read the material, found it accurate, and exploded. He showed Luce that he could afford to buy Time, Inc., and would do so if the article wasn't killed in its entirety. There would be no lawsuit. He would not expose himself to the humiliation the mirror to his life would provide. He would simply buy the company, fire the publisher, fire the writer, and have yet another weapon to use against his critics.

Luce agreed to stop the original article, and the two men became friends. Then the publisher had another writer start the research process anew, eventually writing the "facts"—all positive and without mention of women such as Gloria Swanson.

The initial problem with Luce was barely resolved when Joe again encountered what he thought was a personal affront against a successful man whose only flaw was being Irish Catholic. The incident occurred when he watched the Harvard-Yale football game of 1937. Joe Jr. was a senior player who, like his father in baseball, had not earned his letter. He had to get in the game, the most intense rivalry of the year, to be eligible.

Joe Jr. entered Harvard a superior team player to what his father had been a generation earlier. He made the freshman team and had the potential for starring until he broke his arm, putting him out for the season.

As a sophomore, Joe Jr. looked as though he would overcome the inexperience of missing a year's practice and play to become a star. Then he was tackled, sustaining a knee injury serious enough to finish him for the season. Sports medicine was not yet a specialty, and the knee was treated by physicians who mistakenly thought the injury would heal with time and rest. It didn't. It was much more serious than that, and he needed an operation the following year.

Dick Harlow, the coach of the Harvard football team, had been hired because the president and the alumni, including Joe, wanted a winning team. The coach was to show favoritism to no one and was to disregard the pedigrees of the youths who played on the team. The players for every game were to be selected based on their proven skills against the type of opponent they might be facing on a given week.

The night before the Harvard-Yale game in which Joe Jr. needed to play to get his letter, either Joe Kennedy or someone close to him, most likely Eddie Moore, called Coach Dick Harlow at his office. He was asked if Joe Jr. would be playing, to earn his letter sweater.

Harlow was livid, and his anger intensified when a second call was received that same night. He had no intention of being bullied.

The next afternoon the Harvard team was one touchdown in the lead with six minutes remaining in the game. The players knew that it probably would be impossible for Yale to score. They also knew that tradition would have the coach let a number of benchwarmers onto the field so they could earn their letters. Among those who had yet to play was Joe Jr.

Joe Sr. watched from the stands. He no longer cared about the score. He had been forced to use bribery and deceit to earn his letter. He wanted his son legitimately placed on the field. If the boy was no good, if Joe Jr.'s failings resulted in Yale scoring a tying touchdown, he did not mind. He just wanted the coach to call his son to play.

Coach Harlow ignored eight seniors who needed to get off the bench to play in a game and earn their letters. One of them was Joseph P. Kennedy Jr.

Revenge, of sorts, would have to wait until England.

The British had lost the Revolutionary War and the rematch War of 1812, but American socialites deferred to England as a superior society. Just as Rose Fitzgerald had elevated the status of a handful of Boston's Irish Catholic women through her Ace of Clubs, so a handful of the Brahmin young women attained a superior status by being presented to the queen. Each year a small handful of American debutantes would be presented in court through the intercession of the U.S. ambassador. The king and queen did not mind because their roles in life involved handling rituals, and the country often benefited by developing improved relations with the girls' fathers, often powerful business leaders.

Joe planned to have his daughters presented to the queen, then end the privilege of presenting American debutantes. Not only would Rosemary, Kathleen, Eunice, Pat, and Jean be able to say they had been the last Americans to be presented to British royalty, they also were young women of Irish descent. He could think of no greater vengeance for what he fantasized his family had suffered over the years.

As journalist Frank Kent commented in a letter to Joe, "That neat little scheme you cooked up before you left . . . to kick our eager, fair and panting young American debutantes in their tender, silk covered little fannies, certainly rang the bell. A more subtle and delightful piece of democratic demagoguery was never devised."[1]

There was no worse time in history to send a man so concerned with vengeance and publicity to a country that was about to be forced into a fight for survival. *Time* magazine covered the casualness of Kennedy's move into the thirty-six-room London embassy in Grosvenor Square. The building was a gift of industrialist J. P. Morgan, and Joe liked to sit in his office, his feet on the desk, as he talked with the press. "You can't expect me to develop into a statesman overnight," he was quoted as saying in a March 14, 1938, article, two weeks after his arrival. He was new to London, having delayed his voyage by six weeks because Rose had suffered an attack of appendicitis, a problem that led to surgery that, at the time, was still considered potentially life-threatening. She fully recovered and was planning to join him when the article came out. "Right now the average American isn't as interested in foreign affairs as he is in how he's going to eat and whether his insurance is good. Some, maybe, even are more interested in how Casey Stengel's Boston Bees are going to do next season."

Harold Ickes was livid. The world had changed dangerously, and though Joe may have been right that the average American did not seem to care, he was not the average American. He was part of the government, a man who had to get involved, whose intelligence-gathering abilities and reaction to changing events would influence millions of lives in the near future.

Joe was performing his "good old American boy" act on the same day that Adolf Hitler sent his army into Vienna and announced that Austria and Germany were one. The German leader also made clear that he was going to bring Czechoslovakia into the Third Reich.

There were and are many questions about the extent of knowledge concerning the mass extermination of Germans and others as Hitler was expanding his hegemony over central Europe. It was known that mass arrests of Hitler's political opponents were taking place. The growing isolation of Jews, Communists, and pacifists, among others, was being reported. But the extermination programs—the "final solution"—were not yet common knowledge. Diplomats and religious leaders were aware of crises developing, but the extent of the plans and the growing use of concentration camps for both work and death were not yet widely known.

Much of the criticism would come with hindsight. Arianne Ritschel, the half sister of Joseph Goebbels' wife, Magda, discovered after the war that at least some of Germany's giant furnaces used to cremate millions of Nazi victims had been made in England. The implication was that the British knew and perhaps were aiding the Nazis in some manner. The allegations were nonsense. Many people, including historians, are uncomfortable with the idea that the horrors of the damned could be happening without people outside the country being aware. What is often overlooked is that Hitler took control of the media before he took control of those he hated. He convinced the public that since the government was so good, certainly the best it had been for years, there was no reason to criticize it. The public agreed, and soon it was illegal to criticize Hitler in the media.[2]

Germany also was helping the Spanish government in its bloody quelling of civil war, Italy was attacking Ethiopia, and Japan was moving into China. The world was in turmoil. Rape and murder by soldiers had become commonplace, and in the United States, one of the issues of Roosevelt's first term had been profiteering by arms manufacturers and dealers, along with international bankers, as they worked to benefit from the Great War.

Congressional hearings indicated that it was believed that these profiteers had tricked the United States into entering what would soon be known as World War I. In response the country had become increasingly isolationist at a time when it was going to need to become involved in Europe and Asia.

Congress had passed the Johnson Act of 1934 followed by the Neutrality Acts of 1935 and 1936. If the president declared a country to be in a state of war, no weapons and munitions could be shipped to that country. Americans, whether through banking, business, or from their personal wealth, could not make loans to governments fighting a war.

Worse, Britain was rapidly heading toward being the first line of defense against those who would change the political structure of the Western world, yet Americans were increasingly anti-British. The Brahmins still delighted in the pomp of Buckingham Palace, but the average American, worried about the losses suffered in the Great Depression, found something ridiculous about the British obsession with pomp, ceremony, and the maintaining of wealthy figureheads in the form of the monarchy. Ironically, Kennedy probably was a satisfactory ambassador for many Americans who would have applauded his candor had they known he referred to the queen as "a cute trick." Those who understood the changes in the world and the dangers being faced recognized that the ambassador was the wrong man for the times.

Harold Ickes wrote, "[A]t a time when we should be sending the best that we have to Great Britain, we have not done so. We have sent a rich man, untrained in diplomacy, unlearned in history and politics, who is a great publicity seeker [Kennedy was the first U.S. ambassador to take along a public relations man to represent him to the press] and who is apparently ambitious to be the first Catholic President of the United States."[3]

Roosevelt first realized his mistake when Joe had been in England just eleven days. After Hitler's takeover of Austria, Joe said, "The march of events in Austria made my first few days here more exciting than they might otherwise have been, but I am still unable to see that the central European developments affect our country or my job."

Compounding this inanity was a later comment: "I am sure I am right that none of these various moves has any significance for the United States, outside of general interest."

In hindsight, many have noted Joe Kennedy's anti-Semitism. As support, they cite the fact that when he was a consultant to Paramount Pictures, he told the board of directors that President Roosevelt was worried about anti-Semitism in America, in part because the movie companies were owned by Jews. He said that Paramount should be owned by a non-Jew, then suggested that Roosevelt wanted Joe to be that person. However, when one of the board members, Edwin Weisl, a partner in a Wall Street firm and a leading Democrat, checked the story, he found that Roosevelt was not aware of the ownership of Paramount Pictures, much less Joe Kennedy's being touted as the new owner.

The entire issue of anti-Semitism came to a head when Joe went as ambassador to the Court of St. James, but whether he was truly anti-Semitic is not clear. There are several questions that have to be raised.

First, there is the issue of Joe being raised a second-class citizen in the eyes of the people he most wanted to impress. Joe witnessed bias against both Catholics and Jews growing up. It is common for the people trying to assimilate into a community dominated by one group to adopt the biases of that group. This has been frequently seen in New York City, where Korean greengrocers adopted a biased attitude against African Americans when they realized that racial hatred seemed to be a characteristic of the white culture dominating where they lived and established their business.

A similar pattern existed in communities where one ethnic or racial group moved in, then was replaced by a new population. In cities such as Cleveland, Irish moved in and were the hated ethnic group. Police patrols considered the Irish to be the leading crime problem and named the vehicle they used for larger-scale arrests on Friday and Saturday nights the paddy wagon. However, when Italians moved in, Irish were assimilated and Italians became the distrusted group. Then came East European Jews, for whose sons going to jail in the 1940s became almost a rite of passage. These were followed by African Americans from the South seeking both freedom from open racial violence and a chance to work in the booming steel mills.

Each time the new immigrants became the target of hatred, bias, and isolation, the previous group, sometimes still excluded from the mainstream but still on a higher social order than those who came after them, joined the attacks. Irish hated Italians. Irish and Italians hated Jews. And all three groups hated African Americans.

Why? Apparently because subconsciously, adopting the dominant bias made them feel a part of the country, the culture, or the neighborhood.

Joe Kennedy almost certainly adopted the bias of the Brahmins to be like the Brahmins. He also felt that his ideas were so important that the only criticism he could possibly receive would be the result of Jewish media influence. Joe's granddaughter Amanda Smith noted that in the spring of 1940, Kennedy told her grandmother Rose that Walter Lippmann, a more prominent staff member of the *New York Times* than his own man, Arthur Krock, "hasn't liked the US Ambassador for the last 6 months. Of course the fact that he is a Jew has something to do with that."[4]

In June 1938, when Joe Kennedy met German ambassador to Britain Herbert von Dirksen, he left von Dirksen with the belief that the United States, at least in the person of Kennedy, understood the plight of Nazi Germany. Von Dirksen felt that Joe Kennedy understood why the Germans wanted to get rid of the Jews, though in fairness it must be said that it is not clear if Kennedy understood what that meant. Within the Third Reich itself there was often a different understanding among the leaders concerning what should be done with the Jews. For example, Heinrich Himmler, head of the SS and overseer of all the concentration camps, was not quoted as making anti-Semitic remarks until 1941. He did not hold the rabid hatred of Jews that Hitler and Goebbels espoused. However, he did see Jews as inferior beings who should be removed from Germany and placed in Palestine. During the period when he was expressing such ideas, Himmler seemed to want to use Palestine as a holding area for Jews. Some would be breeders because their strength and intelligence, and that of their offspring, could be used to serve the superior Aryan race that would be running Germany. Others would be sterilized, then worked until old age or ill health caused them to be of no further value. Killing, at the time he was expressing these ideas, seemed more like the humane culling of herds of work animals that had proliferated without proper attention to the best breeding stock.[5]

Unlike Himmler, German ambassador von Dirksen shared Hitler's desire to destroy the Jews, and he had full knowledge of the intention of the concentration camps. He later related that Kennedy told him that getting rid of the Jews was not harmful to the Nazis. It was "rather the loud clamor with which we accompanied this purpose. He himself understood our Jewish policy completely; he was from Boston and there, in one golf club, and in other clubs, no Jews had been admitted for the past . . . years." Joe allegedly added that there was little anti-German sentiment in the United States except in the East, where the majority of America's 3.5 million Jews were living.

The information concerning the conversation was first published in the *Boston Globe* on July 17, 1949. The article also quoted Joe Kennedy as saying that the story told by von Dirksen was "poppycock."

Did Joe say what he was quoted as saying? Most likely. The difference is that Joe Kennedy had no idea of the degree of horror experienced by Jews during World War II until after the war was over.

Joe did understand that Jews were being hurt in Germany. He understood that homes and possessions were in danger. He understood that there was a shift in power and economics. He also felt that the Jews were responsible for some of their suffering through actions they should not have taken.

There has been some indication that Joe was familiar with the writing of Brooks Adams, brother-in-law of Henry Cabot Lodge, who propounded that there is a time in history when a particular race reaches a level of achievement where it is no longer functioning effectively and a more violent, barbaric race must take over. This is why a dictator is almost always stronger than a democratically chosen leader: because the dictator uses personal power instead of consensus.

In Adams's view, England had been engaged in high living too long. The well-educated Germans with their superior armed forces would be the logical next governing force in England.

Joe Kennedy had several concerns that would have made him sympathetic to Adams's views. He did not want his sons to go to war any more than he himself had wanted to be in the military. He also believed that all governments have finite lives. The British monarchy had had a thousand-year run. Perhaps it was time for National Socialism to take control.

Some observers have felt that Joe Kennedy did see himself in Adams's theories. Accordingly, he could have seen that the Brahmins had grown soft, making the aggressive capitalist the perfect person to take power.

In the mix of all this Joe was hoisting trial balloons for a run for political office. Von Dirksen invited Joe to come to Germany to see for himself what Hitler was doing. When Kennedy indicated an interest, the information was forwarded to Germany's ambassador to the United States, Hans Dieckhoff.

Ambassador Dieckhoff was a far better student of the American mood and government concerns than Joe. He realized that Ambassador Kennedy was almost certainly *not* speaking for Roosevelt or the Roosevelt administration. He also understood that Joe had political ambitions, a belief confirmed with what may have been a trial balloon in the popular *Liberty* magazine issue of May 1938. An article by Ernest K. Lindley discussed Joe Kennedy's possible run for office, explaining the ambassador's intelligence, drive, and successful accomplishments. The article and/or the idea of Joe as a candidate soon reached other newspapers. The German government's intelligence analysis of the information was the same as Roosevelt's. Joe Kennedy was acting as a lone wolf, not someone who was leading the U.S. government into a stance of appeasement.

Franklin Roosevelt had said that Joe was being watched hourly. That was an exaggeration, but he had prepared his staff to fight back. White House press secretary Stephen Early utilized the *Chicago Tribune*'s Walter Trohan to send a message.

Trohan was an odd mix of Kennedy friend and anti–New Dealer. He also was a professional and was willing to go with any good story, provided it was accurate, even if it hurt someone he liked. On June 23, 1938, a front-page story in the *Chicago Tribune* was headlined "Kennedy's 1940 Ambitions Open Roosevelt Rift." It was a warning shot by Roosevelt's followers against Joe, letting him know that the White House was on to him. It also stressed a high-level, unnamed source (the president himself, speaking through Early) who made clear that Joe Kennedy was a selfish, self-serving individual. The fact that Joe was allegedly representing his government's position, not his own, as ambassador was understood. The criticism was severe, especially coming through the writing of a friend, and Joe knew it.

Joe tried to rewrite history through a different journalist, C. L. Sulzberger, who was profiling the ambassador for *Ladies' Home Journal*. He expressed the fiction that he had never thought about the ambassadorship, was shocked by its offer, and certainly had no political ambitions.

Sulzberger, though planning a mostly positive piece, could not tolerate the falsehoods. He expressed his disbelief in Joe's claim not to be seeking the presidency, then cross-checked with Arthur Krock, who had not been forewarned to deny such ambition.

Kennedy, livid, went to the publisher and arranged to have Sulzberger's piece edited so that nothing offensive would remain. Then Krock continued to use his position with the *New York Times* to paint Joe as a populist, a man who felt that government service was a high calling and that government officials deserved respect. He also noted that Joe Kennedy turned down an honorary degree from Harvard, the latter an interesting bit of fiction he knew would not be challenged. Harvard never offered him such a degree, nor, at the time, did Trinity College of Dublin. The latter effort was actually made by Joe through the U.S. ambassador to Ireland, John Cudahy. Joe thought that being Irish and being able to represent the United States to Ireland's old enemy England meant that he should be honored immediately after reaching London. The college officials thought otherwise.

Roosevelt also realized that Kennedy, who seemed pro-Hitler at times, may actually have been profascist, not pro-Nazi, that Kennedy found comfort in the idea of a ruling elite for the government. This would mean a committee of powerful individuals, presumably run by Joe as chairman (at least in Roosevelt's mind), who would reduce the power of the legislative branch.[6]

Joe Kennedy made a poor presentation upon arrival in England, though not because he was ignoring conventions in his choice of formal dress. He ignored the fact that there had been other ambassadors who maintained American-style clothing when meeting with royalty, and always without criticism. Where Joe was viewed with bemusement was with his flamboyant self-importance. He was the first ambassador to bring along his own publicist/writer whose job it was to keep his name in the newspapers, magazines, and on radio.

Joe also abused government largesse for officials working abroad. The State Department had to ship three cars to England for Joe; the family's two dogs (both of which would be quarantined for six months, as was standard for all dogs brought to the island); speechwriter Harvey Klemmer; publicist Harold Hinton; nine children, though in stages (Joe and Jack remained at Harvard, where Joe graduated later that year); governesses for the children; cooks; and fourteen trunks of their clothing and other possessions. Joe spent his own money to bring Eddie Moore; "Ding Dong Jack" Kennedy (no relation), whom Joe had employed at RKO; and Arthur Houghton and James Seymour, both friends from Hollywood. The men had small salaries from the government and larger sums from Joe.

Rose was in charge of the ambassador's residence, including the staff of twenty-six full-time and twenty part-time employees. She also held the gatekeeper's role for American socialites. If she wanted to follow the tradition Joe was about to end, she would receive personal visits, letters, and telegrams from socially prominent families throughout the United States. Each would be a plea to allow the family's debutante daughter to come to London to be presented to the queen. Usually more than two thousand young women would express a desire for the honor. The ambassador's wife would make the decision concerning the twenty who would be allowed the honor.

Rose was suddenly in the same position relative to the Brahmins that she had achieved with Boston's Irish Catholic society when she created the Ace of Clubs. It was a position she did not mind losing as a result of Joe's declarations. Her daughters would meet the king and queen, then the tradition would be ended, and the Brahmins be damned.

There were two primary ceremonies welcoming the Kennedys in their new position. The first had Joe, wearing white tie and tailcoat instead of the customary knee breeches, meeting with King George VI four days after he met with Neville Chamberlain, the prime minister. The king was waiting in Buckingham Palace, not St. James' Palace, which had been built by King Henry VIII and to which the first U.S. ambassadors had been sent. Joe presented his credentials, the two men talked for a few minutes, and then the simple ceremony was over.

The entire matter should not have been important enough for more than a mention in the press and a handful of words in history books about this period. Instead Joe had to make clear that he was deliberately flaunting convention.

Many ambassadors had quietly not worn the knee breeches for reasons that were personal. They were accepted in the court because they wore what would be considered their most formal attire for the country they represented, as did Joe. But hot-tempered, equally embarrassed Joe was being goaded by Roosevelt. Franklin knew that Joe was bigoted against homosexuals, so he made comments about how Joe would be a "knockout" in breeches, according to Grace Tully, one of the president's two secretaries.[7]

Joe had already quite viciously criticized his office in the embassy. He noted to Jimmy that he had a "beautiful blue silk room, and all I need to make it perfect is a Mother Hubbard dress and a wreath to make me Queen of the May. If a fairy didn't design this room, I never saw one in my life."[8]

Kennedy had received more attention for his athletic prowess a few days earlier. He went to the Stokes Poges golf course in Buckinghamshire, where the second hole was 128 yards. Joe struck the ball and to his astonishment (and his sons' later disbelief) achieved a hole in one.

The athletic achievement was the type of diversion appreciated by the British. The *Sunday Observer* ran a contest for poems that told about the achievement, and in a number of speeches Joe added the line, "I am much happier being the father of nine children and making a hole in one than I would be as the father of one child making a hole in nine."

The one problem that arose during this early period in England had to do with protocol. A deference to royalty was expected of the am-

On March 16, 1938, U.S. Ambassador Joseph Kennedy is shown leaving the American embassy to present his credentials to the king at Buckingham Palace. He is wearing formal evening clothes, as had others in the past, rather than the customary knee breeches for which he believed himself to be too bow-legged. With him are Lieutenant Colonel Raymond E. Lee, Military Attaché; Captain Russell Willson, Naval Attaché; Herschel V. Johnson, Counsellor of the Embassy; and Sir Sidney Clive, Marshal of the Diplomatic Corps and escort to the palace. (Cleveland State University Library, Special Collections)

bassador. Whatever happened during a meeting with the king or queen was to be reported first from the palace. It was a tradition Joe knew nothing about.

The meeting with the king had lasted just thirty minutes, and nothing of substance had been said. However, there was a mutual respect in the ambassador's wearing formal clothing and the king dressed in the dramatic uniform of an admiral of the fleet. Then, after the foreign envoy left—in this case Kennedy—an announcement of what had taken place would be placed in the court circular.

At no time was an envoy to discuss what the king said, but Joe told reporters that the king was looking forward to meeting his children. It was not a serious error, but it mattered to the British.

Roosevelt adviser Harry Hopkins was worried about Kennedy's actions and attitude. It is not certain if he acted on his own or on the president's orders, but he sent at least one letter to a British official alerting him to the fact that no matter what else Joe might be, he also should be considered a slick operator.

The British did not understand what Hopkins meant. Kennedy was careful in how he handled himself, only once revealing his hand openly. That was when he was in the United States in April 1941 and checked with the State Department to see if it was legal for him to engage in personal business transactions while ambassador. He was informed that the practice violated a law Congress had passed in 1915. Joe did not say he had been speculating in the stock market the entire time he was in London, something he had done through John J. Burns, who worked from Joe's New York office. Either the officials questioned overlooked what Joe had asked or felt that he was thinking of doing something in the future, not pondering the past. Author Seymour Hersh was able to obtain transcripts from an interview with Harvey Klemmer when Joe was dead and Klemmer was dying from cancer.[9] That interview included a story in which Klemmer mentioned a joke Joe pulled where he talked about being at a dinner with a Jew. Kennedy made clear that the stock market was going to drop, and he had ordered Burns to sell. Kennedy allegedly watched the man become increasingly uneasy, then leave the table to sell his own stocks. Only then did Joe reveal that the market was on an upswing and he had ordered Burns to do more buying.

The far less reputable action on Kennedy's part was to use Klemmer's contacts from the Maritime Commission to set aside critically needed cargo space on merchant ships sailing from England to the United States. This was used to ship as many as two hundred thousand cases of whiskey at a time to Kennedy's Somerset Importers, drastically reducing space available for shipments to rival importers.

Later it would be revealed that British Intelligence did not trust Joe Kennedy, tapping his telephone and keeping him under surveillance. Those closest to Joe also were occasionally checked, including having their cars or apartments searched when deemed necessary.

Questions remain about who wanted Kennedy checked. The British came to both hate and distrust him. Hopkins and others around Roosevelt did alert men of similar importance in England about Joe being a loose cannon. However, it is not clear whether Roosevelt was directly involved.

Given what has been discovered in recent years from declassified files, there is a good chance that Roosevelt stayed out of the matter. He needed Joe Kennedy neutralized as much as possible. Keeping Kennedy the ambassador to the Court of St. James delighted Rose and the family, a fact that encouraged Joe to remain in the position instead of resigning and challenging Roosevelt for the presidency. The balance of maintaining Kennedy in a position of importance while trying to work around him and his seeming profascist and pessimistic outlook created difficulties for both governments.

The British fears about Kennedy were well grounded, as the United States learned when the March 19, 1938, *New York Times* published Joe's first speech as ambassador. Kennedy had wanted the speech to show Americans that he was not a party to the British thinking concerning the United States and an impending war. He went so far as to ask Secretary of State Cordell Hull to delay a speech in the United States that would have been covered in the same newspapers. Joe considered what Hull, who represented the United States to the world, had to say to be less important than what he would say. Hull ignored the arrogant request.

The speech was shocking. It should have been the type of innocuous address that would stress the unity of the English-speaking countries without actually committing to any agreement. Such "feel good" speeches were traditionally expected, since the serious negotiations had to take place in secret.

More important, given the era and what is known today, Hitler had been only tentatively feeling his way to world domination. He had rearmed his country in 1935 after denouncing the Treaty of Versailles, which had disarmed Germany following what was still known as the Great War. He had moved troops into the Rhineland. Yet he also made withdrawal plans if Britain and France had resisted the occupation. A strong speech by the U.S. ambassador pledging support for Britain would likely have been seen in Germany as a warning shot to prevent further action. Hitler might have seen Joe as sympathetic, given the German ambassador's reports, but it would have been clear that the country Kennedy represented did not share such appeasement ideas or friendly concerns.

Tragically, the prime ministers of England had already given an indication that appeasement was their preferred route. Stanley Baldwin had won the prime minister's position in 1924 as a conservative, then lost to James Ramsay MacDonald in 1929. When Baldwin regained power as part of a coalition government in 1935, he felt that the peace issue would put him in power. Neville Chamberlain's coalition succeeded MacDonald's in 1937, and Chamberlain felt he had a mandate to aggressively pursue appeasement.

Chamberlain was a man from the blue-collar working world of Birmingham, a steelmaking center so heavily polluted that sun-blocking clouds

of waste in the air made noon seem like nightfall. Chamberlain understood that the men of his community had been the front-line fighters of
the past. They were sickened by war and wanted him to treat international relations like a business negotiation between labor and management. As long as everyone could gain something, he was certain that
war talk would be defused. He naively stated, following his first meeting
directly with Hitler, "I had established a certain confidence, which was
my aim, and on my side, in spite of the hardness and ruthlessness I
thought I saw in his face, I got the impression that here was a man who
could be relied upon when he had given his word."[10]

Foreign Secretary Anthony Eden was outraged by Chamberlain's
naïveté. Prior to Joe Kennedy's arrival, secret correspondence between
President Roosevelt and the prime minister indicated that Franklin
understood Hitler's tentative move toward domination. He did not
know that a united front would have caused Hitler to pull back. He
only sensed that a united front could stop further aggression.

Roosevelt's message, sent in January 1938 and unknown to Kennedy, said that Roosevelt would act as a peace mediator with France,
Germany, and Italy. He would not challenge Hitler. Instead, he would
make clear that the United States had aligned itself with the various
democracies seeking to restore peace. The implication was that the
United States would help form a coalition that would fight any further
aggression, though the words would be carefully phrased to imply that
peace was the primary concern.

The United States was isolated enough from the rest of the world
and progressive enough in the manufacture of industrial products that
the impression was of a nation at its peak of strength. In truth, the military was one of the weakest forces among the Western nations, and the
ability to produce the guns, planes, and other equipment needed for
war was almost nonexistent. However, since the image would be consistent, Chamberlain's acceptance of Roosevelt's diplomatic help might
have stopped Hitler where he was, delaying or ending the chance for a
world conflagration. Chamberlain refused and Anthony Eden resigned
in disgust, infuriating Winston Churchill, who recognized that the
United States had to be dragged into the impending conflict. Appeasement meant the end of Europe as it was known.

Joe Kennedy arrived in England believing that as long as international business was not interrupted, the world would find its own form
of stability. Governments would come and go. Business was what moved
society. He also felt that talk of war was premature, and that when or if
war happened the United States should decide what to do—not before.

Joe's first speech reflected this. He wanted to tell the British what Americans thought, though where he developed the fantasy that he spoke for the masses is not known. He was a man who kept his own counsel when he should have been representing the president. He also was a man who had lived in isolation from the vast majority of Americans.

Joe explained that the U.S. government was not about to commit itself to any single course of action. He said that some government leaders felt that the United States would not fight unless directly attacked. He said that others were convinced the country would not remain neutral if war broke out in Europe. Then he explained that both ideas were mistaken.

Kennedy, in private correspondence to isolationist leaders such as Idaho senator Joseph Borah, had stressed that there should be no American involvement in a European conflict. Years later Joe claimed that he had been against economic devastation and the horrendous loss of life that a world war would bring. He did not address the loss of lives that preceded the war and then continued throughout as Hitler ran extermination camps and Russia's Joseph Stalin killed millions of his own people. He never said that an awareness of the death camps would have brought about a different moral stance. He seemed almost as oblivious to the world condition after it was revealed as he had been when few Americans fully understood what was taking place.

Joe had a brief break from criticism when Rose and five of the children arrived in mid-March, much to the amusement of the British press. Part of the attention came because the family was different—"The U.S.A.'s Nine-Child Envoy," according to one paper. Other reporters were amused by five-year-old Teddy trying to figure out why their father was treated with formality. Kathleen, now called "Kick," was having her debut that year and delighted in everyone she met, everything she saw. As for the others, the family provided a respite from the serious problems that were looming in Europe.

For Rose, England seemed overwhelming. She had been abroad, of course. She was a sophisticated woman with all the privilege that money could buy. Yet everything had changed with Joe as ambassador. It was as though she had entered a fairy tale where she was the star. She had responsibilities, but only in theory. Any task she did not wish to handle would be taken care of by a member of the staff. She had to learn the protocol of royalty, but it was because she would regularly be in the midst of royalty. She would not be one of the wealthy American tourists

Ambassador and Mrs.
Joseph P. Kennedy Sr.
arrive in Port Washington,
New York, from Europe on
December 6, 1939. Joe told
reporters that the British
government did not have
the "slightest belief" that
the United States would
become involved in the
European war. (Cleveland
State University Library,
Special Collections)

standing outside the castle, hoping for a glimpse of the king or queen
from afar. She would be the one riding in the limousine, swiftly moving
past the guards, a welcome presence, a regular visitor, a woman who
would be expected to converse wittily, charmingly, and appropriately.

The reality of where the family had come dawned on the couple for
the first time during an overnight visit to Windsor Castle on Saturday,
April 9, 1938. They arrived alone, a maid and valet having been sent
ahead to the U.S. embassy to bring the clothes they would wear.

The American guests were placed in a suite once the private chambers of Queen Victoria, an irony not lost on the couple. It was Victoria,
who ascended the throne prior to the American Civil War and who
would remain there into the twentieth century, who continued Britain's
anti-Irish policies. She had perpetuated the hatred and oppression that
their relatives endured even after their grandparents came to the United
States. Now they were using her rooms as honored guests.

There were a bathroom and two bedrooms, one with a canopied bed
set so high off the ground that a step stool was placed on one side to aid
the person preparing for sleep. The furniture and washstand were gold
and white damask.

It was not the serving staff that showed the couple to their bed-rooms. Their escort was Brigadier General Sir Hill Child, and when they were told to dress for dinner, a liveried servant presented them with a tray containing two glasses of sherry.

Joe changed into a black suit with red collar, standard clothing for the House of Windsor. Rose wore an elaborate gown, expensive jewelry, and a diamond-encrusted tiara. When ready, both sat by the fireplace, sharing perhaps the most romantic and exciting moment of their adult lives. Not since their marriage, when Joe had lusted for both Rose and her heritage, and she had wanted the tall, handsome, virile Kennedy boy, had they been so close. Years later, speaking separately and often about the experience, they both remembered Joe turning to her and saying, "Rose, this is a hell of a long way from East Boston."

A second escort came to take the couple to the ballroom so they could enter at 8:20 P.M. Exactly ten minutes later the royal couple entered. Queen Elizabeth wore a Winterhalter-style, rose-pink gown with opalescent trim. She wore a double-stranded necklace, a tiara, and a blue sash of the Order of the Garter across her body. Both Joe and rose bowed and curtsied, respectively, to King George VI and his wife.

The dinner seating arrangements were carefully prepared. King George VI was placed between Rose and the wife of Prime Minister Neville Chamberlain. Queen Elizabeth was between Joe and the prime minister.

Rose had been unsure what to talk about. However, when she real-ized that Princess Elizabeth, who would eventually ascend the throne, and Princess Margaret Rose were the same ages as the Kennedys' Bobby and Jean, she lapsed into a discussion of parenting issues.

The king was in charge of the evening. He and Elizabeth had developed a subtle series of signals they used when it was time to leave the table and adjourn to separate rooms. The problem that night was that the flowers were longer than usual and angled, making the sig-nals impossible to be seen. Rose was bemused by the king's frustration, though eventually the queen went to a drawing room through which the bowing men passed on their way to an adjacent area to speak with the king.

Only Lord Halifax among the dignitaries stayed with the queen, and he did so to handle proper procedure. Each wife had a specific social standing. That evening, the wife of the ambassador from the United States was the most important spouse and thus the first to be taken to the queen for an exclusive fifteen-minute conversation. It was a ritual that assured that all the women had time with the queen.

The queen seemed to recognize a kindred spirit lost in the protocol of the royal family. She took Rose aside and taught her how to speak on such formal occasions, how to dress, and what deviations were permitted. Rose did not have to call her "ma'am," for example, because Rose, though fluent in two languages, could not correctly pronounce the word as expected. She also taught Rose to bend her arm and hold it away from her body when having her picture taken because the angle gave her a trimmer image in any photograph.

Rose also was told to wear brightly colored clothing and a hat that did not cover her face. She would stand out in a crowd.

Queen Elizabeth was not the inane monarch her conversations with Rose might have indicated. During dinner she aggressively discussed the world situation with Joe. She listened to his fears of war and international involvements, then explained that she shared his fears. She also could see that with the United States united with Britain, violence might be avoidable. The world was facing dictators, and Britain needed to do so from a perceived position of strength.

The events continued through the next day. The king and queen attended Anglican (Church of England) services along with all their guests except the Kennedys. The ambassador and his wife went to a Roman Catholic church. This was not considered an insult to the royal family. Their concern was that everyone attend the church services of their choice. The only insult would have been if the Kennedys had not gone to church.

Lunch that day was with the prime minister in addition to other dignitaries. Rose worked Chamberlain in the same manner she had once handled Boston dignitaries of importance to her father. She discussed the interests he shared with Joe, reminding him of their similarities. She knew that such awareness could eventually lead them to understand their commonality. Later Joe was upset with Rose for what she had been saying. He did not realize that it may have been helpful.

More important, as evidenced both by comments made later by those who were meeting and working with the Kennedys, and statements made in memorandums, letters, and the like, the Kennedys were out of their element. They were ill equipped for the tasks expected of them. They brought to England rigid visions of the world created by circumstances very different from what they were facing.

Rose Kennedy was a master of cutthroat city and state politics. She understood the effective way to run a smear campaign, to bribe voters, to organize a registration drive and get people to the polls. She also saw the world through her studies in convent schools where the nuns were isolated, history was skewered by the stated (and evolving) beliefs of a single faith, and to be right with God required a certain amount of isolation. Her only other international experience related to shopping.

Rose knew couturiers. Rose knew how to make an appearance. Rose constantly took advice that would help her present the best appearance as her body changed with childbirth and age.

Rose had no sense of changing entangling alliances, of nations moving in and out of relations with one another, establishing the frameworks for war or peace. Rose had little sense of the thinking of various cultures, even though the treatment of the Irish Catholics in Boston, if fully understood by her, could have given her a sense of compassion toward the downtrodden and a comprehension of some of the international concerns. Instead, Rose saw everything from the perspective of either a paranoid victim who had risen atop her detractors, or someone so determined to do the right thing in the eyes of others that she never accomplishes anything that truly matters in the world.

Joe was no better. Angry, self-centered, amoral, and determined to gain personal attention instead of achieving change that might benefit the world, he was neither adaptable to the world situation nor seemingly capable of understanding it. By contrast Franklin Roosevelt, also an isolationist in the early 1930s, moved with the changing world conditions, the gradual development of the United States as a world power in the manner that others mistakenly believed it already had become, and the need for working with Stalin in the 1940s. Roosevelt's successes in life, of which Joe was always jealous, were results of flexibility and pragmatism, neither of which characterized Kennedy.

Worse, Joe Kennedy had no grasp of how changing international relations could affect the United States. He seemed to take as a personal affront the way the American stock market was being negatively impacted by Chamberlain's decision to appease Hitler by not standing against the invasion of Czechoslovakia.

Joe also expressed the belief that the United States was overreacting to Hitler's statements about the British and the Jews. He felt that Hitler was acting in a manner that would help the Germans rise from the ashes of military loss and disarmament following World War I. He seemed to believe that when Hitler focused the nation's anger against the Jews and the British, the average German worker was given an incentive to work harder. After all, he had risen to a position of wealth and power because of his hatred of the Brahmins. Sometimes having a scapegoat can be motivational, and he saw nothing wrong with that.

Rose Kennedy was slightly more sophisticated about what she was hearing. She knew that as ambassador, Joe's public pronouncements could have an impact on people in the United States. She worked to understand what was taking place through talks with people she met wherever she had to go. What she did not consider was that she was only meeting the economic and social elite. She had little conception of the lives, the concerns, and the future of the masses. Still, she came to see herself as a representative of the United States in a manner similar to but apart from Joe. She decided she needed a makeover, not through learning the lessons of history, the political and social concerns of the nations, or anything of value. Instead, she concentrated on voice lessons to reduce or eliminate her Boston accent, and regular guidance on clothes and makeup.

Michael Scanlon, the protocol expert for the U.S. embassy in London, and his wife, Gloria, took on the task of re-creating Rose Kennedy as she desired. Michael handled the voice lessons. Gloria took Rose and Kathleen to Paris for a selection of proper gowns for meeting the queen.

Kathleen, too, was in the midst of a variety of activities. She had graduated from convent school, enrolled in New York's Parsons School of Design, then dropped out to spend time in England. Rosemary was placed in a Montessori School that actually proved the most beneficial form of education tried for her. The British teachers understood dyslexia even though they hadn't identified it by name. The less structured Montessori method, originally developed in Italy, proved perfect for a young woman who was at once intelligent and learning-disabled.

Eunice, Pat, and Jean were enrolled in yet another Sacred Heart boarding school, this one just outside of London. Bobby and Teddy, thirteen and six, respectively, stayed back in the United States, attending a day school and cared for by servants.

The four oldest Kennedy children came alive in England as they never had in the United States. They were near adult in age, able to care for themselves, and suddenly in a world that offered them unparalleled freedom. No longer did they have to compete with each other or please their parents. They could be themselves, and each found joy in his or her way.

It is somewhat ironic that in the months that followed, Rose, who seemed to think that her handling of her family was similar to the manner of the WASP elite, was rebuked by Queen Elizabeth. The incident occurred during an embassy dinner on May 4, 1939, long after the first two daughters had been presented to the court and all the children had made their presence known in the country. As Rose later commented to Barbara Gibson, the queen "asked me if I got up in the morning to see

Ambassador to the Court of St. James Joseph P. Kennedy Sr. sits with his sons, Joe Jr. (left) and Jack in this 1939 photo. (Cleveland State University Library, Special Collections)

the children off, and I said I used to in what I called the good old days, but that now I was usually up late at nights and rested in the mornings. To my astonishment and humiliation, she said she usually got up, half-dressed, to see her children and then went back to bed again."

Rose's inattention did not hinder Rosemary. She realized that she could learn in an environment that adapted to her disability. The school did whatever it took to help a child, teen, or adult taking classes, including having the person nap, regardless of age, if such a respite made studying easier. Each student was watched to see at what time of the day the person learned best; then classes were structured around that period.

Soon Rosemary was teaching younger children in the school to read and write. She reinforced her skills by using her mastery to help those who had not come so far. She was not on the staff, though it was her mentoring of the younger students that may have given the family the idea for one of the lies that would be told later.

Kick delighted in the freedom from the strictures of church schools and parental demands. She loved both the pomp of royalty and the down-to-earth demeanor of many in the elite. She did not feel the need to be special, as her mother seemed to do. Rather she saw this as a different culture in which to participate, yet with a base of normal people in unusual circumstances and extraordinary times. She was as flippant as her father, calling the royal couple "George and Lizzie," but she did so with love, not with the disrespect Joe made clear he held for the British system of government.

Rosemary and Kathleen, along with a handful of other seventeen- and eighteen-year-old debutantes, were carefully groomed for their presentation before the queen. The preparations for the presentation were elaborate. The Vacani School of Dancing was among those teaching the daughters of the elite how to bow. Rose also took lessons since, as an American, she had not studied curtsying when she became a young woman in society.

The curtsying lesson idea sounds foolish until you see the gowns. These typically were floor-length and with long trains. It was easy to walk up the fabric and fall to the ground. A woman meeting the queen on such a formal occasion would be expected to walk across the floor, then kneel on her left leg, her back kept straight, all the time smiling, holding flowers, and generally being in danger of making a fool of herself. She had to learn to give her gown a slight kick with her foot to keep it away from her shoes as she walked.

Rose chose Molyneux, the most respected designer of the day, to prepare the gowns both she and Rosemary would wear. They were white, and Rose's gown, which she would later wear to Jack's inauguration as president, had white lace with silver and gold beads embroidered on it. Rosemary's gown had white net with silver trim.

Kathleen showed her independence by buying from Lelong's of Paris. This was a white net gown with silver croquettes. It also was a bit of a scandal.

Molyneux was simply where you went to buy the gown to be worn when meeting the queen. Lelong's . . . well, Lelong's was expensive. Lelong's was as respected a design house as Molyneux. The same woman who could afford Molyneux could afford Lelong, and the queen really didn't care. But Lelong was a bit of a rebel, and it seemed to take a rich American to carry it off. Fortunately, everyone realized that Kick was just being herself, and she did look lovely. However, if she had been a British debutante, she would have been subject to negative gossip by her peers.

One of the reasons Kick felt she could be playful and independent was because she already knew she was welcome in the country. She had gone to Cliveden when she first arrived, a social coup easily the equal of her mother's going to the palace.

Cliveden was the summer home of Lady Nancy Langhorne Astor, the Virginia-born wife of Waldorf Astor, the first woman member of Parliament despite having been born in the United States. She was also famous for having parties in which she mixed men and women from the elite among those in business, politics, or the arts. Comedian Charlie Chaplin might dine with Edward VII on one side and George Bernard Shaw on the other.

Equally important, Waldorf and Nancy Astor were rich. Cliveden was a small community of four hundred acres and staffs for different aspects of the lifestyle. Thirty men and women were employed to do nothing but see to the wants and needs of the Astors and whoever they had as guests. There were dozens more employees handling every possible need of the estate. There were the usual coachmen, butlers, and maids, full-time carpenters and electricians, and men tending to the herd of dairy cows.

Lady Astor and her friends were viewed with both awe and suspicion. They were perceived falsely as being at the center of the pro-Nazi movement in Britain. They were seen as being convinced that Hitler would win and the government of Britain would be forcibly changed to National Socialism.

It was Claud Cockburn, publisher of *The Week*, who was the Astors' severest public critic. He was a left-wing writer who was convinced that the Astors and their friends, whom he dubbed "the Cliveden set," were conspiring to help Germany. He did not see them as sabotaging the nation, but as being pro-German. When Joe Kennedy occasionally visited Cliveden, he was vilified in both the American and British press.

Kick did not care about any of this. She referred to the duke of Marlborough as "Dukie Wookie." She made comments she knew were permitted precisely because she was an American, raised in a different culture. Yet Kick respected the society and understood when to stop joking.

Kick had another advantage. She had difficulty showing emotion. She was a very private person. She had been raised with so little intimacy with her parents that she had grown comfortable being devoid of emotions.

The wealthy British elite were raised to show reserve at all times. They could be publicly stoic in the face of disaster, stoic in the face of success, stoic in loss, and stoic in love. They were actually far more emotional about one another, especially in the privacy of an intimate relationship, but they were taught to show none of their feelings to outsiders.

Kick, who felt she had no strong emotions about relationships, fit in perfectly.

Part of the stoic image came from the social mores of the day. British debutantes were consciously bred with all the planning of champion show dogs or fine horseflesh. They were livestock whose pedigrees were well known and impeccable. They were selectively mated to produce the next generation of elite males.

British debutantes were virgins. Abstinence from sex before marriage was the one part of their upbringing that was treated with great seriousness. The idea that a young woman could be so overwhelmed by love that she would go to bed with a man who aroused her prior to marriage was not a consideration. This was the end of an era where a debutante who was known to be "damaged goods" or "secondhand goods" could forget a future of happiness with the right man.

The debutantes lived with rituals. They were carefully trained and dressed. They attended schools that would teach them the skills they would need to oversee an estate, have dinner with royalty, and raise children exactly like themselves. They attended social events that were planned for each season. There were social rituals in which a girl and her mother would meet for tea with another properly raised girl and her mother so that one woman's daughter could invite the other woman's daughter to one of the coming-out dances.

Once again Rose Kennedy was delighted. This was an even more snobbish world than that of the Boston Brahmins. She had created the Ace of Clubs to ease the pain of Protestant elite rejection; now she was the person in charge of the ultimate Protestant young woman's triumph—being presented to the queen. Rosemary and Kathleen had become the type of young women she had once hoped to be. (Eunice, Pat, and Jean would have their turns when they got older.) Perhaps even better, Rose was doubly honored by standing with them and controlling who else would be in the room for a similar experience.

Ambassador and Mrs. Kennedy would have been expected to appear at the court presentation of debutantes even if they had no daughters present. It was part of the ritual of the position, and Molyneux made certain Rose was ready.

The hairdresser styled Rose, Kathleen, and Rosemary's hair so the tiaras would fit properly. Jewels had to be attached correctly. There were shoulder-length kid gloves that had to fit like a second skin.

In photographs and comments recorded by the men and women who were present, it is obvious that Rosemary was the most beautiful of the three Kennedy women. Rose was in her late forties, a handsome

This photo of Rose Kennedy and her daughters Kathleen "Kick" (left) and Rosemary as they prepare to leave for their presentation at the first court of the season at Buckingham Palace belies the myth of Rosemary's retardation. She was the most beautiful of the Kennedy sisters, as vibrant and filled with life as the others, just not sharing their closeness and competitive nature. (Cleveland State University Library, Special Collections)

woman who looked at least ten years younger. Kathleen had the same spark that had captivated the Cliveden set, but Rosemary was set apart. She had come to respect herself, to recognize that she was intelligent, only needing to learn differently than her brothers and sisters. She loved England, loved the idea that this was her special night. And though there would later be family comment about how worried they were, how she seemed to trip once, then regain her balance, the statements strike one as a way to justify the horror that would befall her.

The only detractor in all this was Joe. As usual, he wore his black tailcoat, white tie, and long trousers, the only diplomat present not in the formal knee breeches considered proper for the court. He and the family were unaware that, in the eyes of some of those present, his dressing differently from the others upstaged his wife and daughters. He called attention to himself when his appearance should have been so benign that he faded into the woodwork.

The next day a writer for the *Evening Standard* who had witnessed the event viciously commented: "Mr. Kennedy's desire to shield himself from the charge of 'flunkeyism' achieved the somewhat paradoxical result that the only trousers at last night's court were those worn by himself and some of the less important waiters."

The ceremony was carefully choreographed with the look of a painting come to life. The king and queen entered the ballroom at nine-thirty in the evening. As soon as they were settled, each debutante would be checked by the court usher. He would then have the lord chamberlain announce each young woman in turn from his position at the entrance to the Throne Room.

There was a red carpet in the Throne Room, and discreetly on the carpet were small gold crowns in key places. These were place markers identical in purpose to those used on stages. Each girl would walk to the first crown, stop, smile, curtsy, take three gliding steps to the right, curtsy, then continue moving rightward to the open door. She was not to look toward the door. She was not to turn her back to the king and queen.

The rest of the setting looked like something that Joe might have funded for a Hollywood movie. First were the men known as the Beefeaters, elite mace-carrying palace guards—if your palace was in the sixteenth century, when they were organized. They wore red tunics with puffed bloomer pants. Each had a black felt hat with one feather, white hose, and a small white ruff. They stood in line from the grand stairway through the anterooms and on to the ballroom. Liveried footmen were everywhere to help with whatever was necessary. Finally there were the diplomats and their wives, positioned wisely—not by order of importance to Britain but rather by the length of time they had worked in the country.

When the evening was over, Rose, the mother of two daughters presented to royalty, and the wife of the American ambassador, was suddenly in demand. The most prominent women in England needed her approval.

Joe and Rose gave their own party for their daughters in 1938. Years later there would be the implication that everyone, especially Kathleen, covered for Rosemary's problems. The truth was that Kick covered for no one. Rosemary was given her own escort, a youth known as "London Jack" to keep from confusing his name with that of the Kennedys' second-oldest son. But the escort seems more to reflect either Rosemary's shyness or the fact that she was becoming too flirtatious. Whatever the case, she was content with a single escort for the evening, while Kathleen enjoyed the company of many men.

Kick was actually the more conservative of the two sisters. She was aware of the infidelities of her father and did not want to be hurt in the manner of her mother. She saw the way her brothers had begun treating girls and worried that no man could be monogamous. She liked the attention of men but had no plans to become seriously involved with anyone, perhaps ever.

It was July 18, 1938, when life changed for Kick and, indirectly, for the Kennedys. She had been going to nightclubs and other taboo locations, treating London like a home she would never leave and into which she had to assimilate as quickly as possible. She had met many young men, some of whom had become friends. But on July 18, she attended a party so massive that it seemed inevitable that no one could develop a relationship with anyone present.

The party, at Buckingham Palace, was hosted by the king and queen. The size of the palace can best be placed in context when it is understood that there were twelve thousand invited guests in all. There were also a much smaller number of individuals from among that mass who enjoyed a private tea. Among those guests were all the debutantes of the year, along with young male members of royalty. One of those was a man who was expected to be a future suitor of Princess Elizabeth, then twelve years old.

The relationship between young Elizabeth and the older, tall, lean William "Billy" Cavendish, the marquess of Hartington, future heir to the title of duke of Devonshire, was not something arranged or to be arranged by their parents. The idea that such a relationship was in the future came from various royalty-watchers. These were people who studied the lineage of the privileged classes, their ages, and the expectations that would be placed on them as adults. There was no commitment by the parents. Instead, given the way debutantes and female members of royalty were raised for the proper marriage with the properly educated male of appropriate lineage, outsiders could tell which men would be most eligible for which girls when they reached marriageable age.

In the case of Billy Cavendish, the one person who would be the right number of years younger, the right background, and the right upbringing would be Princess Elizabeth. At the same time, it was also understood that she might not like him when she reached adulthood. She might never consider him an appropriate suitor, and he also might choose to reject her.

Kick knew nothing about a future relationship between Billy and Elizabeth being the talk of royal-watchers, nor would she have cared had she known. He was a nice young man who was as quiet as Kick was outgoing. She was drawn to his seeming depth of wisdom that kept him from engaging in the sometimes inane chatter of the young and the rich. He was drawn to her ease with others that enabled her to go from person to person, talking with strangers as though she had known them for years. Kick and Billy talked for two hours, then Kick went to Compton Place, Eastbourne, to meet his parents and attend the horse races the following week.

Billy's parents were charmed by Kick. They liked her instantly and understood their son's interest after only two hours of conversation. She was vibrant, friendly, and open. She also was Irish Catholic.

Billy's father hated the Catholic Church in the same irrational manner that Joe Kennedy hated the Brahmins. At the same time, all of them understood that Kick's religion did not matter. Billy and Kick weren't dating and had no intention of dating. They were just friends, with all the limitations that implied. None of them imagined that anything more would happen between them.

Just as Joe ignored Rose's sense of politics and business when they were newlyweds and she had much to offer his growing career, so he paid no attention to his daughter's experiences with the Cliveden set and the youth who would bear the brunt of war. The one Kennedy who came to understand what that would mean was Kick.

Joe had never had firsthand experience with the military. War was an abstract, a complication for international business, and an experience only a handful of his classmates would have in all its horror. Wealthy Americans usually avoided fighting in wars. During the Civil War a man could buy his way out of going into the army, and many did. Others hired men of lesser standing to go in their place.

Great Britain was the opposite. In England, wars were fought by the elite. To have power and wealth was to be assured that you would do battle when the country so demanded. No one Kathleen met, no one with whom she was friends, had families untouched by war. Everyone had a father, uncle, older brother, and/or some other male relative who had gone into combat. They had moved hand-to-hand against the enemy. Some had been killed, others shot, bayoneted, or gassed. They returned in shock, maimed, recovering from wounds, or physically unscathed, yet guilt-ridden that they had not been killed when so many of their friends had not returned at all.

Lord Moran, the man who became Churchill's physician, documented perceived acts of heroism during World War I. He found that the men who survived seemingly selfless actions against overwhelming odds to save friends were actually men who had become depressed by battle. They were suicidal, taking actions that not only frequently saved the lives of their friends, but that often so shocked the enemy that they surrendered.

Churchill thought such heroism was the best and bravest within humanity. Lord Moran showed that the men, most of whom were from the upper classes, had been so shattered by the realities of battle that they had used a fight against all odds as a method they hoped would end their own lives.

Kick's friends understood all this. They also understood that it was their turn next. They would be fighting Hitler. They would be taking to ground, sea, and air to stop Britain's enemies. And they would come back forever changed if they were lucky enough to survive at all.

The men and women who so enjoyed Kick understood that her father was a dedicated isolationist. They also gave him credit for being more powerful in his influence with President Roosevelt than he actually was. That was why they joked with their American friend that when Germany unleashed the first air raid, one of them would shoot a member of the Kennedy family, then claim it was done by Hitler's soldiers. Joe Kennedy would become so irate, according to this fantasy, he would have to force America into war to avenge his family's honor.

Kathleen Kennedy understood her friends' feelings. She was becoming so sensitive to the way they were thinking that she was increasingly estranged from her family. How estranged was apparent from the September 30, 1938, entry Rose made in her diary. Prime Minister Neville Chamberlain had not opposed Hitler's annexation of Czechoslovakia, and Rose wrote:

"We all feel that a new psychology for settling issues between countries has been inaugurated and that henceforth war may be out of the question.

"Chamberlain's words, from Shakespeare's Henry IV: 'Out of this nettle, danger, we pluck this flower, safety.' The result of the Munich settlement, he said, would be 'Peace in our time.'"

Joe Kennedy was relieved. Franklin Roosevelt was livid. Kick and her friends wanted to weep. Many among them would pay with their lives, the price for the short-term impression of successful appeasement.

16

THE WAR YEARS

MONITORED CONSTANTLY, FOLLOWED, ALL THE TELEPHONES IN THE U.S. embassy tapped by British Intelligence, Ambassador Joe Kennedy seemed to the British to be in denial about the realities of the world condition. The British did not understand American politics, and had they comprehended Franklin Roosevelt's perceived dilemma about the 1940 election, they might have found reality even more unsettling than their belief that Joe represented the thinking of the president himself. Still, as long as they believed that he was a surrogate for the president, what he expressed both privately and publicly was critical information when trying to anticipate what actions the United States might take as war became inevitable. It would not be long before they finally recognized that Joe was a loose cannon by any government's thinking.

For Joe Kennedy it was not enough to be in one of the most important listening posts in the Western world as countries moved into position for conquest and war. His primary pursuit still was making money. And toward this end he kept a close eye on what was taking place in U.S. business.

Joe believed that businesspeople had no interest in politics and that the public was concerned chiefly with jobs, money, and their daily lives. He could not understand how the stock market could fluctuate with news of what was happening in Germany, Italy, France, and England, yet it did, and it did so with a consistency that could be plotted. He saw which announcements about relations among the various countries jockeying for power changed the market for good or for bad. Then he began investing in the market based on announcements he knew would be forthcoming. He bought before there would be a rise in price, and he sold before the prices would drop. He was almost 100 percent accurate in his bets.

Proof of Joe's market activity has never been released. However, many diplomats who were neutral toward Joe, including Baron Erik Palmstierna, Sweden's ambassador to London, all told the same story about his actions. In addition, Jan Masaryk, the Czech statesman who headed the Czechoslovak government-in-exile in London, alleged that Joe manipulated Czech investments based on British prime minister Chamberlain's actions. He estimated that Joe made 20,000 British pounds profit based solely on the turmoil in Czechoslovakia during this time.

Joe also openly arranged aid for the American film industry, using his position as ambassador to handle the matter. Such intercession on the part of a business was inappropriate but not all that unusual. Years later Kingman Brewster Jr., a former Yale president, would do the same as ambassador to the Court of St. James, involving himself in concerns on the part of Margaret Thatcher and General Motors about a new car being built in Ireland by former GM executive John DeLorean. Special-interest actions during peacetime are one thing, but during a period when there are preparations for war, other concerns take precedence.

The U.S. neutrality laws limited what could be shipped to England, and officials from both countries were looking to find ways around it without being in overt violation. A barter arrangement sent rubber to the United States and American cotton to Great Britain. The United States also shipped fruits, such as apples, pears, and raisins. All of these required critical cargo space that Joe wanted used to carry film.

Prior to the war, Britain had been a major importer of American films. The desire for such pictures continued because the movies provided an escape from the pressures of living with the knowledge that, at any moment, bombs might be falling from Nazi warplanes.

There was a set fee for each film shipped to England, in the same manner as American industry theater rentals. Joe could see that by forcing higher prices for the films when the demand was so great, his friends would prosper. He also saw that the more films the studios could ship in cargo holds, the sooner the films could be shown, and the more money could be made. He ignored the fact that his actions reduced space for future survival essentials.

The British were quietly enraged. They thought Joe was acting for the film companies because that was what Franklin Roosevelt wanted. They did not want to hurt relations with the United States based on something not yet critical for survival. For the moment they were willing to tolerate what they thought were the warped priorities of the American president. They did not go over the ambassador's head to check if he was acting appropriately or independently.

Kennedy returned briefly to the United States in June 1938 to watch Joe graduate from Harvard. He had planned to be honored along with his son, receiving a special degree for his achievement as ambassador to the Court of St. James. Harvard officials did not see Joe's importance in the same way he did. Among their alumni, "just" being a U.S. ambassador was not an adequate achievement. The men were frequently rich enough to be able to gain such an appointment, and there were many ambassadors among their older classes. Joe was told he would not get an honorary degree, though the trustees did not want to alienate a man who might endow the school with a few million dollars in the future. They allowed him to spread the fiction that he had been offered the degree and then turned it down.

That June Joe used his respite from London to attempt to move toward increased political power through personal duplicity. Newspapers throughout the country carried Joe's words from a press conference in which he stated, "I enlisted under President Roosevelt in 1932 to do whatever he wanted me to do. There are many problems at home and abroad and I happen to be busy at one abroad just now. If I had my eye on another job, it would be a complete breach of faith with President Roosevelt."

Faith had been breached, of course. A number of reporters had been carefully nurtured (and sometimes bribed) by Joe to begin speculating on his political future at that time.[1] The *Boston Post* spoke of Joe Kennedy as one of the men best able to handle any matter, political or economic. Writers for the *New York Daily News*, a paper beloved by working-class New Yorkers, declared that Joe was the man *Roosevelt* wanted to succeed him. The *Washington Post* discussed the fact that Kennedy was likely to become the first Catholic president. And articles appeared in magazines discussing everything from his "faultless" taste in clothing to his willingness to toil in obscurity for the good of others.

None of the descriptions matched how Roosevelt and the British government viewed the ambassador. However, a few writers for national publications were able to bring forth the truth. The original Sulzberger article for the *Ladies' Home Journal* came close. The July 2, 1938, *Saturday Evening Post* ran writer Alva Johnson's exposé of James Roosevelt, the most vulnerable of the president's family members and the one who could be tied directly to Joe Kennedy. The piece, titled "Jimmy's Got It," included the statement "Jimmy has helped Kennedy to reach the two great positions he now holds—that of Ambassador to London and that of premier Scotch-whiskey salesman in America."

Kennedy focused on the "Scotch-whiskey" statement, claiming that while he was ambassador, he was not the "premier" salesman. It was a matter of semantics worthy of President Bill Clinton who, some sixty years later, would be caught in a consensual sex scandal with a White

House employee and explain touching the two admittedly enjoyed was "sex" depended upon how someone defined "sex."

Joe Kennedy told reporters, "I suffered by knowing James Roosevelt. If the rest of the *Saturday Evening Post* article is no truer than the part about my connection with James Roosevelt, it's all a lie."

It wasn't, of course. However, what made the article so important was that it was the first serious look at the illicit dealings between Kennedy and the young Roosevelt. Joe could not kill the story or have it altered. And the magazine, one of the oldest in America, had a large readership in all parts of the country. Yet Johnson's *Saturday Evening Post* piece foretold the beginning of the end of Kennedy's presidential power drive, even though the writer, the publisher, and Kennedy himself did not fully recognize this fact.

Kennedy returned in August to London when it became clear Hitler would march into Czechoslovakia. Joe feared both war and economic devastation. He decided to give a speech that would present his views, and though he did not see why Roosevelt would care, he properly requested clearance by the State Department. Top personnel would review the speech and tell him what needed to be changed.

The speech Joe submitted contained these words: "Perhaps I am not well informed of the terrifically vital forces underlying all this unrest in the world, but for the life of me, I cannot see anything involved which would be remotely considered worth shedding blood for."

Roosevelt mocked that section of the speech and also ordered its removal, calling it the "I can't for the life of me understand why anyone would want to go to war to save the Czechs." The president was livid when he talked about it with his longtime friend, business partner, and current secretary of the treasury, Henry Morgenthau. These conversations added to the tensions between Joe and Roosevelt's advisers because Morgenthau was Jewish.

Morgenthau was not unique in following a faith that was held in disdain by many in the White House. The wife of Secretary of State Cordell Hull, who had his own aspirations of becoming president, also was Jewish, though her religion was a closely guarded secret because of his political goals. The more obvious the attacks on the Jews, and the more Joe Kennedy seemed to be defending the German attitude if not the actions of which Americans were aware, the more difficult it became for the White House staff to remain objective. Events in Europe did not help Joe's image, either.

Austria was annexed on March 13, and two weeks later Hitler began orchestrating pro-Nazi rallies in and around Czechoslovakia. On April 26 all German Jews with assets exceeding 5,000 reichsmarks had to be registered. On June 14 Jewish businesses also had to be registered, and the more important ones were expected to be sold immediately to approved Nazi companies ranging from banks to IG-Farben—for prices lower than fair market value.

July 6 saw the banning of certain types of Jewish business activities, followed by laws restricting the activities of Jewish doctors and lawyers. The men in the Roosevelt administration had no idea that Jews were being put to death or that extermination was becoming official policy. They did see a culture being destroyed, the lives of individuals suddenly restricted for no reason other than their being the object of hate.

As always, Joe remained blissfully unaware of the impression he was making both in England and with Roosevelt. He began sending letters to friends and meeting with reporters from the Hearst newspapers, expounding on his thinking. The remarks showed little sensitivity to the world situation or the concerns of family members of those in areas facing persecution. He did not grasp the fact that he needed to always work through the State Department. It was as though Joe were making his own foreign policy.

On September 10, 1938, Kennedy sent a diplomatic dispatch to Secretary of State Cordell Hull. He stated, "The British secret information is that Hitler is prepared to march, and with that in mind, preliminary steps were taken with the Admiralty yesterday. The opinion of the British is still that there are three alternatives for Hitler: (1) to stir up trouble in the Sudeten area and march in to put down bloodshed (2) try to get public opinion on his side by calling for a plebiscite and (3) to march and bomb Prague."

Kennedy made clear that the British felt that Hitler should be stopped at once. British government officials were making feelers to determine a possible American response. They were hoping to learn from Joe if the United States would forcefully help stop Hitler if he advanced into Czechoslovakia.

Joe told the British that while he did not know, he felt that the American people would see any act of British aggression related to Czechoslovakia as a British problem. Supporting a battle would not relate to American interests. The fact that the French felt that the Germans could be stopped, and that a coalition of Britain, France, and the United States could bring an end to the encroachments, did not matter.

Kennedy was unaware that Roosevelt was working regularly and in quite a different manner with British ambassador to the United States, Sir Ronald Lindsay. The president had been backing Chamberlain's appeasement of the Nazis when the prime minister felt it necessary, but Roosevelt also wanted the British to understand that he did not want to see compromise with the Germans. There was a point where Britain could yield too much, a point that was about to be reached.

On September 12, 1938, one of the most photographed and chilling Nazi rallies took place in Nuremberg. The carefully orchestrated gathering featured a thousand swastikas, each carefully lighted. Thousands of supporters stood before Hitler as he spoke, his words carried to the crowd by loudspeakers and to the Czech people by radio.

Hitler's speech addressed the supposed Czech government's treatment of the Sudeten Germans, a group about whom many Westerners knew little. German migrants entered Bohemia and Moravia in the twelfth century, settling there and dominating the Czech population when the Habsburg rule began by the sixteenth century. The Czech people flourished during the next three centuries, increasingly demanding autonomy from the Sudeten Germans, who had become a minority. Finally, in 1919, the Paris Peace Conference established the borders for the new country of Czechoslovakia, with a capital in Prague, where a combination of Czechs and Slovaks shared power. The minority Sudeten Germans, considered an arrogant people by their neighbors because of their expressed belief that they were racially superior, no longer had authority over anyone.

The majority of the Sudeten Germans busied themselves in the textile mills that employed most of the people in the community. They also entered politics, establishing several different parties when they could not agree among themselves what they desired. Some believed in National Socialism and demanded total autonomy. Others wanted to be treated like an independent state, allowed to have their own government and police.

The Great Depression brought a new crisis for the Sudeten Germans. The Japanese had been developing their own textile industry, operating mills that produced a lower-cost product. With money scarce internationally, price became the major concern for consumers, and the Sudeten mills closed. The majority of the community was suddenly out of work.

Konrad Henlein rose to leadership in the Sudeten German Party and developed close ties with Nazi Germany in 1935. Czechoslovakia's president, Eduard Beneš, was simultaneously working to strengthen the entire country through mutual protection alliances with France, Romania, the Soviet Union, and Yugoslavia.

Hitler saw Czechoslovakia as a test. The nation was an independent country with military alliances that might come to its aid if attacked.

The nation also had a definable minority with German ties who could be used as justification for seizing land. He decided to position himself as the "savior" of an oppressed people and see who would call his bluff.

The relative strengths of the countries that predictably would be involved seemed a good test for Hitler. France was potentially the most troublesome ally of the Czech government. The nation had a population of 40 million and could mount a formidable army. Germany had a population 75 percent greater, though, and had more modern equipment. The German air force—the Luftwaffe—had 200 more aircraft of recent construction than the 2,600 planes held by France, Britain, and Czechoslovakia combined.

Czechoslovakia also had its own defense forces along the German border. The 205,000 men in 15 divisions were well trained but had older equipment than Hitler's army. He also had a total of 70 divisions at his command if he needed to use them at the front.

The only unknown was Italy, and in May 1938, the Italian government agreed not to interfere with any military action Germany felt necessary to aid the Sudeten Germans.

Britain prime minister Chamberlain sent Walter Runciman, a wealthy member of Parliament, to negotiate with the Czechs and the Sudeten Germans, in direct opposition to Eduard Beneš's wishes. Impressed by carefully staged National Socialist rallies, Runciman bought into the myth of the oppressed Sudeten Germans. He made clear that if Hitler acted on their behalf, the Crown would take little or no action.

Then came the September 12 Nuremberg speech in which Hitler denounced the Czech government's attitude toward the Sudeten Germans. Hitler did not say what he planned to do but instead focused on achieving "justice." It was met with thundering repetitions of *"Sieg heil! Sieg heil! Sieg heil!"*

For the first time Joe Kennedy saw enough of the future to realize that there would be war and that it would involve England. He began thinking about sending Rose and the children home. Chamberlain, as much in denial as Kennedy had been, decided to personally go to Germany to assure the peace. He had no intention of rattling sabers. He knew that the German army was better prepared for war than the British, who were still building up their defenses.

While Chamberlain made his pilgrimage to make peace with Hitler, others in the government felt that a strong opposition was needed, even if it led to war. Lord Halifax, for example, went to see Joe Kennedy to learn how the neutrality act might affect England. Could the United States begin supplying shipments of arms and supplies?

Kennedy would not commit to anything other than Chamberlain's approach. Czechoslovakia should allow self-determination for the Sudeten Germans, a rather vague concept that meant separation for the Sudetenland without formally breaking up the country. Hitler, by contrast, appeared to be talking about Germany occupying the territory on which the Sudeten Germans were living. The French and English arguments were meaningless in Hitler's mind. Chamberlain realized it would be necessary to tolerate some form of occupation, no matter what that meant. Czechoslovakia, as it had been created, was to be sacrificed in the name of peace.

On September 18 the matter appeared settled. Representatives of France came to London, where it was agreed that Prague would be ordered to give to the Reich any areas of the country where Germans comprised at least half the population. The alternative, the French understood, would be a war in which 40 million French would risk death to maintain a government under which 7 million Czechs were dominating 3.5 million Germans.

The Czech ambassador to France, Stefan Osusky, stated, "My country has been condemned without a hearing."

On September 29, 1938, Chamberlain and Hitler met in Munich to sign an agreement that ceded 16,000 square miles of what had been Czechoslovakia to Germany. England and Germany had become friends. War had been avoided—or so the British prime minister and his supporters wanted desperately to believe. But in Washington, Franklin Roosevelt knew that war was inevitable, and he began to formulate a strategy that would include the complete destruction of Hitler and his followers.

In London, a delighted Joe Kennedy was the guest speaker at the British Navy League's annual Trafalgar Day dinner on October 19. He told the shocked audience: "It has long been a theory of mine that it is unproductive for both the democratic and dictator countries to widen the division now existing between them by emphasizing their differences, which are now self-apparent. Instead of hammering away at what are regarded as irreconcilables, they could advantageously bend their energies toward solving their common problems by an attempt to reestablish good relations on a world basis."[2]

He also stated, "It is true that the democratic and dictator countries have important and fundamental divergences of outlook, which in certain areas go deeper than politics. But there is simply no sense, common or otherwise, in letting these differences grow into unrelenting antagonisms. After all, we have to live together in the same world, whether we like it or not."[3]

Earlier Joe had alienated himself from the then Czech ambassador to London, Jan Masaryk, when he commented on Chamberlain's agreement by saying, "Isn't it wonderful? Now I can get to Palm Beach [for a vacation] after all."

The speech outraged Roosevelt. Other nations thought that the president might be using Joe to spread the word that American policy had changed.

Joe was certain that he had made no mistakes. He felt that there was a conflict of political ideologies and nothing else. Joe allegedly privately suspected that the Nazis might take control of both England and the United States. This apparently did not worry him, though. He seemed to see it as inevitable progress.

There was no way for Joe to buy the press after this mistake, especially since he had told the truth as he saw it. The *New York Post* noted that Joe seemed to be suggesting that "the United States make a friend of the man who boasts that he is out to destroy democracy and religion."

In an apparent effort to reduce criticism hurled against him, Joe began spreading the word that he and Chamberlain were working on a resettlement arrangement for German Jews. He said that they would seek money from private individuals, concerned organizations, and governments to help Jews leave Germany. The Kennedy Plan, as this was known, would look to one or another country to plan for Jewish resettlement.

The problem with the Kennedy Plan is that it did not exist. It was all talk. Instead, a program had been developed at the Évian Conference on July 6, 1938. Washington attorney George Rublee of the Intergovernmental Committee on Refugees brought together the ambassadors from thirty-two nations for a meeting in Évian-les-Bains, France. Joe was not included. The Évian Conference determined that relocation probably would be best to Africa and/or South America, the two areas with the landmass and the likelihood of being able to effectively absorb thousands of men, women, and children.

Years later Joe would seem to understand that he had to vindicate himself for his failure to participate in the resettlement question. He decided to write his memoirs—never published—with his longtime friend and Securities and Exchange Commission associate James Landis. Those members of the Kennedy family who want to see it as a document of record have used the manuscript to vindicate Joe. Those who see it as a rewrite of history have used it to condemn Joe. Either way, it presents the spin Joe wanted used when historians looked at his career during the Roosevelt administration.

The manuscript "quotes" Roosevelt as saying that he felt that the root cause of the world's troubles over the previous nine years had been economically based. Joe claimed Roosevelt also stated that the United States was determined to stay neutral in any war that might take place. He allegedly wanted the country kept apart from any involvements in Europe. The United States would show no obvious favoritism to those liked and those disliked. Thus Joe, with all his talk, had simply done his proper job on behalf of the president.

The quotes found in the unpublished Landis manuscript may or may not be accurate. They may or may not be based on diary notes Joe made of the conversations immediately after they happened. They certainly do not reflect State Department documents and other material from Roosevelt's secret negotiations with the British that bypassed the ambassador.

During the Roosevelt administration recording devices were used in the White House for the first time. These were secret; only the electronics experts and the official who had them installed knew of their existence. Some recordings were kept; others were destroyed, though transcripts were maintained. It is possible that, while Joe's discussions definitely were *not* recorded, he may have felt that the making of as exact notes as possible was important.

If Joe did make notes that were accurate, it is possible that Roosevelt's instructions to his ambassador concerned maintaining neutrality. More likely the issue was Joe's handling of matters versus official policy to be formulated and executed by the president and the secretary of state using intelligence from the ambassador and others. But assuming such orders were given for whatever reason, Roosevelt's foreign policy and attitude toward war were constantly evolving. He was endlessly looking at the world and reassessing what was taking place. He watched with a historian's knowledge and a skilled politician's eye. He never intended for there to be a singular course of American action regardless of changing world events.

For careful observers, there was a major clue to Roosevelt's thinking about Munich and Hitler. The day after Chamberlain signed the Munich Pact, Winston Churchill denounced it from the floor of the House of Commons. Roosevelt wanted Churchill's voice heard by Americans, so he arranged for him to address the United States through a coast-to-coast radio hookup. Churchill clearly stated the anti-Hitler sentiment:

"We are confronted now with racial persecution, religious intolerance, deprivation of free speech, the conception of the citizen as a mere

soulless fraction of the state. To this has been added the cult of war."
Churchill detailed Hitler's actions, and then said that preparation for
resistance was not the same as deliberately unleashing a war. He said
that all nations must come together to guarantee peace through a
united front. "We need the resolute and sober acceptance of their duty
by the English-speaking peoples and by all the nations, great and small,
who wish to walk with them. Their faithful and zealous comradeship
would banish from all our lives the fear which already darkens the sun-
light to hundreds of millions of men."

Joe's views had been further reinforced by meetings with Charles
Lindbergh, the isolationist pilot who had become a folk hero for his lone
crossing of the Atlantic Ocean. In Joe's world of heroes, a man who had
achieved success in any dramatic field was someone he respected, even
when the person was talking outside his area of meaningful expertise.
This was certainly the case with Lindbergh, who had no background to
judge politics, war, or the course of history. Instead, he was a skilled pilot,
an aviation innovator, and an inventor who focused on finding a way to
remove and safely store the organs of individuals undergoing surgery.

While Joe Kennedy made a number of statements concerning Lindbergh's revelations about the Luftwaffe and Germany's ability to conquer the world with their aircraft, Joseph P. Kennedy Jr. wrote the best
assessment. He was twenty-three years old, living at the U.S. Embassy
in Paris, and he sent a note dated October 1 to his father.[4] Joe Sr. had
arranged for his son to serve a two-month stint under Ambassador Bullitt so he could learn more about the world than he had learned in college. Rose was delighted because she was able to shop at Cartier's for
jewelry when visiting her oldest son. Joe Jr. wrote:

> Met Colonel Lindbergh for dinner and he impressed me a great deal. He
> is modest and shy, and neither smokes nor drinks. His interests however
> are nearly completely wrapped up in his artificial pump and flying. He
> has a small house on an island off the coast of Brittany where he lives
> quite apart from the world. You can walk to shore only at low tide. He
> also can walk to Cavels [sic] Island at low tide.[5] He is terribly outspoken
> against the newspapers and says that they keep him from living in Amer-
> ica. He thought that Chamberlain had pursued the right course during
> the present crisis: and had the greatest of praise for the German air fleet.
> He said that they would have completely wiped out all the cities in
> France and England. He felt that to destroy the culture of Europe for the
> sake of an error made in the Treaty of Versailles was ridiculous. He said
> that Russian aviation was hard to figure out because that had moved com-
> plete factories from America and it was hard to discover their own work.

He is doing some work with the ministry here. He feels that for France
to import planes weakens her own industry.

Joe Jr.'s succinct evaluation of Lindbergh's thinking matched Joe Sr.'s
understanding as found in numerous discussions and memos. It also revealed the naïveté of both Kennedy men. Instead of observing the world
situation from the unusual vantage point of participant/observer with
access to extensive information denied others, Joe Sr. relied on sources
such as Charles Lindbergh. Yet Lindbergh made clear that he had physically and mentally cut himself off from ongoing news of the day. He
had become focused on the medical sciences, ignoring all else though
being against war. Yet whenever anyone talked about the quality of the
German air force, he or she seemed to be equally naive, usually referring to Lindbergh's evaluation. And as history repeatedly showed in the
months to come, Lindbergh was wrong.

Joe also was swayed in his thinking during this period by his belief
that Chamberlain was warmly welcomed in Germany. He mistook choreographed celebrations by a once-vanquished people preparing for
conquest to mean support for the idea of continuous peace. He felt that
these peace-loving citizens would influence Hitler to go no farther.[6]

The desperation of the Jews and the failure of both plans became
evident on November 9, 1938. Hitler had achieved all the support he
needed to openly destroy the Jews.

For years there would be stories that the German people were often
naive about Hitler's actions. There would be true stories of righteous
Christians who hid Jewish families and/or helped them flee the country.
These Christians were subject to death for their actions, but they did
not care.

But as studies conducted a generation after the war have shown, most
Germans of the era seemed not to care. Their sense of nationalism and
racism were such that they actively or tacitly supported the Nazis. They
moved into the homes of Jews who had been sent to work camps or
death camps. They took the possessions of Jews. And some participated
in violence against Jews as they were isolated from the mainstream society in preparation for their removal.

The proof of the hatred that should have alerted the world was the
night of November 9–10, 1938. Most of the six hundred thousand Jews
in Germany were already living in isolated ghettos, easily cut off and
subjected to violence.

The justification for what would become known as "the night of the
broken glass," or *Kristallnacht*, was the action of a seventeen-year-old

boy. He had watched his father be forced into a boxcar on a train that would ultimately be part of the deportation of ten thousand Jews to Poland. Many of the men suffocated when they were crammed into the boxcars. Many others became ill from the vomit and the stench of dead bodies. Still others survived, only to be murdered or to die slowly from a combination of overwork and undernourishment. The boy, emotionally overwhelmed, killed the third secretary of the German embassy in Paris.

"Obviously" the Jews had to be taught a lesson for the actions of a lone, distraught seventeen-year-old with no political affiliations. As night came on November 9, the Nazis engaged in "spontaneous" demonstrations of their own "anger" throughout Germany. Women were grabbed and raped. Windows were smashed so stores and homes could be looted and vandalized. Thirty-six people were killed and another twenty thousand arrested, either for fighting back or the greater "crime" of being both Jewish and alive. Two hundred synagogues were set ablaze, along with an unknown number of homes and shops.

This was not a hate crime or local terrorism in the manner of the Ku Klux Klan and White Citizens' Council actions against African Americans, Jews, and Catholics in the South during the several decades following America's Civil War. This was war fought internally, a systematic destruction of groups of people spread throughout the nation. No one was kept safe. No one was isolated from the horror. Everyone experienced the hate. Everyone would remember the night. The message was clear. To be Jewish in Germany was to be a noncitizen, someone less than human, someone whose existence would be destroyed through the loss of possessions; home; freedom; and, in the end, life. More important, it was an event made known to journalists and the officials of other governments, unlike the still-secret death camps.

And once again, Joe Kennedy either did not wish to understand beyond his agreeing that the Jews were the source of many of their own problems, as he stressed when talking with the German ambassador, or he was afraid of what he learned. Either way, he continued to argue against war.

The Christmas holidays approached, and Kennedy returned to the United States to meet with the president before spending his vacation with Jack in Palm Beach. Rose and the other children were in St. Moritz, skiing. He had developed two ideas for handling the world. The first, the Kennedy Plan for resettlement of the Jews, seemed something that could be accomplished. He knew wealthy Jews, and he assumed they would raise the $50 million to $100 million he estimated would be necessary to relocate Jews from Germany. He never expressed concern about the moral issues of what was happening. He never talked about the horrors of Jews being forced from homes they may have owned for generations. The Jews were the problem, so the removal of the Jews would be the solution. Hitler would have no one to hate. The Jews would be safe elsewhere. And the world would continue to do business as usual.

The ambassador was not reacting to the issue of refugee ships or Jews who were being deported. He was concerned with those Jews still living in Germany who were beginning to be isolated. He seemed to feel that even those not yet at risk should be removed.

The other idea he had was to divide the world into sections, where the largest and strongest would dominate. There would be the Americas, which would be handled by the United States. Territory might be defended as far as a thousand miles in all directions, a not too difficult task, since the distance comprised little more than water, Canada, and Mexico. Other countries that would have their own territory included Britain and France, Germany, Russia, Japan, and China. They would develop interrelated businesses where appropriate, and self-sufficiency where that would serve them best. Trade, barter, and currency would all be worked out within each area, and always there would be peace.

The 1938 Christmas holiday was a period for reflection. Kennedy had never understood his position with Roosevelt, the way he was perceived in London, and the concerns other nations had about his pronouncements. He did not realize that he could not look on world affairs as just another business venture to be mastered. He did not understand that even when he shared some of the same biases as the German leadership, their hatred went much deeper, their actions knowing no boundaries of decency, morality, or humanity. He did not realize that they were taking advantage of him in his position as ambassador to the Court of St. James.

Also, Kennedy did not realize how little Roosevelt respected his ideas. He valued Joe's business experience. He felt he had done a good job with the Securities and Exchange Commission. He also understood that a man who is forever looking out for himself can serve no one else. Where Joe fancied himself an innovator, Roosevelt often saw a fool.

In January 1939 there were secret hearings in Washington regarding the appeasement issue and the changes the United States would have to make to accommodate to the realities of Hitler's moves. Ambassadors

Bullitt and Kennedy secretly testified in Washington. The hearings bolstered Roosevelt's growing recognition that the United States would have to get involved with providing arms and money, though where that might lead was still uncertain. Total isolation was not going to be possible.

Joe considered leaving the ambassadorship instead of returning after the winter break. Likewise Roosevelt thought about ridding himself of the man. But the president needed Joe to stay where he was, to be out of politics in the United States. For his part, Joe Kennedy had an ego that made him uncomfortable with the idea of leaving a post when the business or his reputation was in trouble. He liked to leave at the top, to take credit for all the good that was taking place, knowing that the truth would come out later, when few people cared. He was not on top in England. Not just yet, and possibly not ever. He needed to find a way to leave that would imply that a greater opportunity was the reason. Whatever else happened in the world he could either claim was partially of his doing or he could take credit for delaying the horrors the nations might endure.

As Joe mused over his circumstances, he decided that he could leave government service in June. He wanted to be "forced" to return to the United States to accept an honorary degree from a prestigious university. Then he would find that there were so many pressing business and family concerns that he would have to resign. It would be a departure he could live with, if only a school would cooperate.

Harvard had refused Joe an honorary degree. He had Arthur Krock explore whether Princeton might be more amenable. It wasn't. As with Harvard, the school felt that a mere ambassadorship was not an achievement warranting such an honor.

Word was then slipped to columnist Drew Pearson that Joe was looking at an offer from the brokerage firm Morgan Stanley. Pearson was told that being the ambassador to the Court of St. James was costing Joe $250,000 of his own funds. Even if the figure was exaggerated because of his family's extravagant spending, his private outlay was extremely large. Although he could well afford to continue for life if he so chose, to the average American the figure would be shocking and more than justify leaving government service.

Roosevelt's suspicions that Joe Kennedy had a tendency toward fascist thinking were proven accurate in correspondence sent to the president on March 3, 1939, following Joe's return to London. Joe explained that he believed that to defend the United States there would be a need for taxes and the control of society that would erode and possibly end democratic society there. He said that fighting totalitarianism required adopting a totalitarian approach to government. Civil liberties would be lost.

While history disproved Joe's theories, a careful reading of his son's 1961 inaugural address shows that Jack came to share or at least parrot some of his father's thinking. The famous "ask not what your country can do for you but what you can do for your country" phrase, read in context, indicates the new president suggesting that some civil liberties might have to be abandoned if there was a conflict. The height of the Cold War had many of the same tensions as the time of the Munich pact, and father and son both believed that some freedom could or would be lost in order to triumph in warfare.

And still Joe Kennedy believed that Hitler would not act. In April he told Cordell Hull, "I'm just as convinced that he [Hitler] doesn't want to fight as anybody else is, but I'm not convinced as to how he can save his own situation for his own people." He continued to see the matter as economic, though in this case the problem was one of Hitler having to switch Germany from a wartime economy, with full productivity, to a peacetime economy, where war plants would be idled or temporarily shut while converted to other uses.

Joe did not leave government service in June, as he had contemplated. His position was no longer one where he felt he could leave. Instead he was being sidestepped, ridiculed, or ignored by the administration at every possible moment, yet he seemed certain that he could regain his perceived former glory. All that stood in his way was the State Department, but Roosevelt was fully aware and approving of State's actions.

In May, for example, Joe continued his efforts to talk with high-level Germans by planning to go to Paris to have dinner with James Mooney, head of General Motors in Germany. The guest of honor was going to be a man who was involved with the Krupp family of armament manufacturers and a close personal friend of Adolf Hitler. Joe would have a chance to talk with someone who was at such a high level that, as he saw it, he could almost be in negotiations with the Führer himself.

Kennedy asked permission to attend. He said that the meeting would be kept secret and he'd be able to report back on whatever he learned. However, the State Department's Sumner Welles recognized that Kennedy's "secret" talks, his private musings, and other actions with which he had been involved had a tendency to make their way into at least the Hearst newspapers. The man could not be trusted to keep his mouth shut, especially if he thought he could influence others to his way of thinking. Joe was denied permission.

Joe did not fully understand what was happening until June when, at his suggestion, the king and queen visited the United States. The royal couple was given permission to come, but others handled all arrangements. Joe would remain in London. The British ambassador to Washington worked out the full itinerary with President Roosevelt. Kennedy was blatantly bypassed, a departure from usual procedure.

While Joe was seeing his ambitions destroyed and his image eroded, Rose and the children were delighted with their new lives. Rose busied herself with the minutiae of protocol, not all that different from what she had handled in Boston for her father. The dignitaries were different, of course—royalty, the archbishop of Canterbury, leading government figures—but each fit a known pecking order no different from the streets on which Honey Fitz pressed the flesh and passed the bribes.

Rose also worked on decorating the embassy interior, including the library. She loved the respect she received, the power she was given, and the deference her husband had long abandoned.

Joe Jr., at twenty-three, was part intensely curious and part obnoxious spoiled brat. He became the eyes and ears of his father, gathering intelligence through visiting embassies and hot spots throughout Europe. His initial trip to the Paris embassy, where he met Lindbergh, lasted three weeks. Then he moved on to Berlin, The Hague, Leningrad, Moscow, Prague, and Scandinavia, studying each country, analyzing each government. Each impending crisis was carefully anticipated—and all in a total of sixteen *days*. Worse, Joe Sr. seemed to actually feel that his oldest son's work was of importance.

Next, Joe Jr. turned to international banking. This time his father should have been troubled by his son's arrogance. Joe Sr. had spent eighteen months as a bank examiner at the start of his career. Joe Jr. spent a total of eight days in two banks and a brokerage house, all in London, then had the audacity to believe he had mastered the basics. Worse, his father did not disabuse him of his notion.

Joe Jr. then decided to go to Spain, a country he knew something about, since he had completed an honors thesis on aspects of the Spanish Civil War. The problem was that violence was continuing even though the war was officially deemed over. The Communists and leftist remnants of the Loyalist (republican) government still held a sizable portion of territory. Franco's Nationalist government had taken two thirds of the land and been declared the victor, but violence continued. In addition, the Communists were battling the liberals, so it was impossible to know where a tourist might be safe from both declared and undeclared battles raging within the country. Joe Jr., taking the trip as the ambassador's son, would be a more likely target than the average tourist. Joe Jr. eventually obtained a regular passport, went as a conventional tourist, and managed to see areas that would otherwise have been denied him. He acted when both his parents were busy elsewhere, alerting them only after he arrived in Spain.

The one nonpolitical event, at least as far as the impending war was concerned, that involved the entire family occurred that February while Joe Jr. was in Spain. Eugenio Cardinal Pacelli, who had visited the United States two years before, staying with the Kennedys in their home, was elected Pope Pius XII. His predecessor, Pope Pius XI, had died, and Pacelli was likely to become a critical influence during what seemed to be the inevitable world war. He would be the spiritual head of the Catholic Church, and as such of great importance to Catholics in France, Germany, Italy, and elsewhere. More important in the minds of the Kennedy family, a second meeting with the man who had risen to the top within the church would be the greatest social coup they could achieve. Even Protestant Boston would look up to the couple who was present when their "friend" was elevated to the papacy.

The public story of what happened was quite different from the truth. Joe Sr. understood how important the event was to Rose, but neither he nor his oldest son were interested in the coronation. Joe quietly wired Joe Jr. in Madrid to tell him that if he felt himself safe, he should stay where he was. The event was not that important.

Rose had been traveling in Egypt when she learned of the death; the election; and the coronation, which was held on March 9, 1939. She rushed to Rome to meet Joe, who arrived with their other children then in Europe, his close friend Eddie Moore and Moore's wife, Arthur Houghton, governess Elizabeth Dunn, and nurse Luella Hennessey. They traveled by private railroad car, and when Rose met them, Joe lied and said that their oldest son was regrettably unable to get there from Madrid.

There were forty nations sending representatives to the coronation, including the Catholic aristocrat the duke of Norfolk, who represented the British government. Irish prime minister Eamon De Valera was there, and France sent Paul Claudel, a statesman who also was a noted poet and writer. However, Joe wanted to make the biggest impression by having his black limousine decorated front to rear with small American flags, but none could be found in Rome at the last minute, forcing him and his entourage to travel anonymously.

Some seventy thousand people attended the Mass in St. Peter's Basilica, the Kennedys seated in pews directly before the altar. The next morning the family met privately with the new Pope, and two days after that, the Pope gave Teddy, then seven, his first communion.

There was no question that the new Pope was fond of Joe, Rose, and their children. Joe easily could have maintained an important presence with the Vatican throughout the war years had he been so inclined. As it was, Rose Kennedy was declared a papal countess, and Joe was given the Order of Pius IX. The latter was typically reserved solely for heads of state and the highest officials in any government. Joe, as an ambassador, should not have been so honored, but an exception was made.

What the family neglected to mention in the retelling is that the whole family had no right to be present where they were on the day of the coronation. Joe Kennedy had been personally asked by Franklin Roosevelt to attend the coronation. He almost certainly could have arranged for Rose to be by his side. As for everyone else, that was another story.

"I was later in the John F. Kennedy Library where Cardinal Giovanni Battista Montini, later to become Pope Paul VI, had provided a taped remembrance of the day for the oral history collection," Barbara Gibson later told this author in preparation for a biography of Rose Kennedy. "A transcript of that interview noted:

" 'It happened that the ambassador of the United States to London, Mr. Kennedy, father of the dead president, was charged by his government to represent the United States at the ceremony, and indeed he arrived punctually but bringing with him five children, who proceeded to occupy places that were reserved for the members of the official mission, with the result that the arrangement of places was altered; and when there arrived the Italian minister of foreign affairs, Count Ciano, the son-in-law of Mussolini, he found his seat in the gallery of the official missions was occupied and he began to protest, threatening to leave the Basilica and to desert the ceremony. The situation was immediately resolved; but there remained in our memory the procession of the children of Ambassador Kennedy.' "

Cardinal O'Connell, the man who had married Rose Fitzgerald and Joe Kennedy, and the emissary of Rose when she wanted Gloria Swanson to leave her husband alone, also was present in Rome. He, too, was livid but said nothing that day or in the weeks to come. Between the favors done for him by Joe Kennedy and the obvious friendship the family enjoyed with the new Pope—his boss—he chose to complain privately, never challenging the couple's actions.

The one Kennedy who was beloved in England was Kathleen. She had come to know Billy Cavendish in ways that were both meaningful and ironic.

Billy was physically appealing—six feet two and one-half inches tall and in his early thirties. He was tall for his generation, so tall that he was embarrassed and had adopted a slight stoop to make himself look shorter. Despite his age, he was a graduate student in history attending Trinity College in Cambridge. He was officially the marquess of Hartington but was generally referred to as Billy Hartington. He would become the duke of Devonshire, a member of Britain's ruling elite and extremely wealthy.

The irony was that this deepening friendship was between Kathleen, great-granddaughter of a persecuted Irish immigrant, and Billy, a descendant of William, the first duke of Devonshire and a member of the Anglican Church, who had led a rebellion against the Catholic king James II. Since then the Cavendish/Hartington family had been known for their anti-Catholic bias as well as for the cold-blooded marriages of the men. Each male descendant of William sought a bride of wealth so that the marriage would increase the riches of the Cavendish/Hartington line. Breeding did not matter, only money, until the family had so much money that the youngest men, such as Billy, stopped seeking women based on their bank accounts, jewels, and real-estate holdings. If Billy married the most impoverished young woman in London, she would move among his London mansion, his Derbyshire estate, and his other holdings. Even Kathleen, a millionaire through the trust fund Joe established for each of his children, was relatively lacking in material goods by the standard of Billy's male ancestors.

Billy also was at such a level in the world of British royalty that only the king and queen and their immediate family commanded more respect. Fortunately, the royal family did not share the Cavendish bigotry against the Irish Catholic Kathleen. She was endearing herself to both Billy and the royal couple. She also was falling in love with Billy, something she had once considered impossible.

Eunice remained in England for her coming-out party June 22, 1939, though she was bitter about not having the pomp that Rosemary and Kathleen had enjoyed. With war inevitable by then, the parents of the debutantes knew that their sons and nephews would soon be taking up arms. British socialite families understood what Eunice did not. This was likely the last party some of them would attend. None of them would be celebrating during the war. All efforts would either be focused on defense of the island or on supplying the forces in Europe. This was not a time for pomp, elegance, and pretentiousness. This was a night to party!

Eunice went to Paquin, the appropriate couturier for that season, to get her peach-colored dress. The royal family wore brightly colored clothing in order to be identifiable from a distance. Eunice's choice was based on how she felt she looked, not a wish to make a statement.

Eunice had discovered men in much the manner that Kathleen had enjoyed them before settling on Billy Hartington. But where Kick was aggressive, Eunice was shy. Kick filled her dance card by moving to the men with whom she wanted to dance. Eunice stayed with other young women, waiting to be asked. The fact that she was somewhat awkward and did not feel comfortable even in designer wear added to her hesitancy to mingle when she was sitting without a man.

The dance was timed around twenty-minute sets for the musicians. Unlike the events of Rose's youth, boys did not sign the card by the dance. Instead, they signed for the twenty-minute blocks of orchestral music. Then the musicians would be silent and there would be a break between sets for the couples to better get to know each other or to switch partners without embarrassment. If a girl was not asked for a set, there was a resting area in sight of everyone where she could sit with other debutantes. Sometimes young men approached one or another of the seated young women. Sometimes the young women sat only with each other during the twenty minutes of music.

Eunice's frustration with the lack of extreme formality her older sisters had known was compounded when the orchestra began playing the new line dance called the Big Apple. It was the latest craze in casual clubs as well as paying homage to the United States. It also was a dance that delighted the duke of Marlborough, who went to the floor and began leading the line dancers. Once he was dancing, Eunice realized that her pretensions of formality and proper behavior were for another era. The nation was on the brink of war. The formal splendor of the past was a show that would not be repeated, perhaps ever again. Instead, it was time to enjoy a more casual, more emotional experience than her sisters had known.

The Kennedy family began to see that the seeming love affair they had with the press was over when they faced criticism for handling the aftermath of the Germans torpedoing the British passenger liner *Athenia* on September 4, 1939. Four days earlier, the inevitable had happened. Germany marched into Poland, and Britain declared war on Germany. For Britain, the attack on the ship was the first violent action of what would be an increasingly deadly war.

The unarmed *Athenia* was taking fourteen hundred passengers between England and Canada. A dozen Americans, along with another hundred men, women, and children, were killed in the blast. Everyone else had been rescued by other ships and were being taken to Scotland. It was 3:00 A.M. when James Seymour at the U.S. embassy took word of the incident. He immediately alerted Joe.

Britain and the United States were outraged at Germany. The German high command pretended shock. Instead of accepting the blame, German propaganda minister Joseph Goebbels expressed his own outrage at the British, whom he accused of deliberately attacking their own ship to foment trouble. By the German "spin" on the story, the British wanted to whip up sentiment against Germany so they would have an excuse to attack. Knowing full well that no U-boats (German submarines) were in British, Canadian, or U.S. waters, or the international waters in between, the British had deliberately attacked their own vessel, Goebbels charged.

The implication of the "spin" was greater than the immediate situation. It implied that there could be other attacks in the immediate future, including on the evacuating Americans.

The passengers were terrified when they arrived in Scotland. They wanted the U.S. fleet to form a protective convoy to take them to their respective destinations. In addition, the nine thousand Americans who were living in or visiting England had to be evacuated. They were in danger of direct attack, something Joe came to fear so much that he began sleeping in locations in the country other than the embassy. He was ridiculed for his cowardice, especially when Queen Elizabeth refused to leave Buckingham Palace and the surrounding city during the harshest of the German air raids. She insisted on being with the citizens, experiencing whatever fate might befall London, rather than fleeing to preserve her life if the danger became too great.

Joe Sr., Joe Jr., Jack, James Seymour, and Eddie Moore joined together to handle the evacuations of Americans. Joe Sr.'s responsibility was in Scotland, to explain to the Americans how they would be cared for and evacuated. Detractors say that Joe was afraid to go because the Germans might attack the same people again. Others say that the number of Americans in England warranted his thinking of them first.

Whatever the case, the Americans in England had a system in place for helping them. There was no one in Scotland until Joe arrived there.

Once again giving too much credit to members of his own family, Joe sent Jack to Scotland. He was a twenty-two-year-old college student who looked younger than his years.

On his father's orders, Jack explained the situation they believed was taking place. Germany and England were at war. Germany and the United States were not. *Athenia* was a clearly marked British ship. The people going to America would be traveling on the clearly marked American liner *Orizaba*, and there would be no danger.

Whether or not Jack was right, the liner made the crossing safely, and Jack received praise for his accomplishment. However, despite the fact that the trip had been successful, the idea that a boy was handling the ambassador's job did not set well with those close to the incident.

On September 11 Joe Kennedy moved to end the evolving war. He had decided, in the week following the attack on *Athenia*, that the British government could not survive a war. He sent a message to Roosevelt that further alienated the president: "It seems to me that this situation may crystallize to a point where the President can be the savior of the world. The British government as such certainly cannot accept any agreement with Hitler, but there may be a point when the President himself may work out plans for world peace."

Joe Kennedy was ready to abandon any country and any government to avoid violence. He was scared, and he had no sense of the reality of the conditions of the world as the Nazis moved forward in conquest. The outraged Roosevelt understood this and had Secretary of State Cordell Hull write him:

"The President desires me to inform you, for your strictly confidential information and so that you may be guided there without divulging this message to anyone, that this Government, so long as present European conditions continue, sees no opportunity nor occasion for any peace move to be initiated by the President of the United States. The people of the United States would not support any move for peace initiated by this Government that would consolidate or make possible a survival of a regime of force and aggression."

With war approaching, Joe Kennedy decided to have his family return to the United States. Three of his daughters had been introduced to the royal family. Kathleen had been so accepted in British society that she was a member of many committees, including that for the 1939 Derby Ball. Joe Jr. had been educated in affairs of state. And Rosemary, the one daughter who would remain, was thriving in the Montessori program. Since the school was in the countryside, away from cities that would be under attack, he knew she would be safe. He also realized that there was nothing for Rosemary in the United States except a growing number of suitors, the potential for inappropriate behavior, and an educational system that failed to understand her learning problems.

Most of the family adjusted to returning home. Joe Jr. did not. He became intensely angry for reasons that were never determined.

Young Joe had always been arrogant, belligerent, and inappropriately aggressive with some of his siblings, especially Jack. At the same time, both he and Rosemary had long been surrogate parents for Teddy. They were gentle with him, nurturing him, both playing with him and teaching him. Teddy and his sister Jean were the two children having the most obvious difficulty with childhood and their parents' lack of emotional substance, but for some reason, Joe Jr. and Rosemary "adopted" him.

Years later Teddy talked of going to fifteen schools in his twelve years of elementary and secondary education. He talked of never having an assigned bedroom. He was endlessly shuttled from place to place, often with his father in one city, his mother in a second, and Teddy in a third, only the oldest two siblings acting as constant, loving presences.

Joe's anger seemed directed at everyone other than Teddy and Rosemary. He entered Harvard Law School, doing so poorly that he was in danger of flunking his first year. He spent much of his free time at school talking about his whirlwind trip to Spain, as though he had learned everything there was to know about the revolution. He would become livid when anyone dared to argue with the "facts" as he felt he knew them.

Joe Sr., with his usual overkill, hired a tutor for his son to help him with his legal studies. The tutor, who was undoubtedly handsomely paid in money or special favors, was Massachusetts Superior Court judge John H. Burns.

Kick and her friends had been the first to notice Joe's angry side in England, though in a more subdued way. There would be times when Kick was dating one man or another, and she invited her brothers Jack and Joe to accompany them. The dates were mildly scandalous in that she was playing the field, something that shocked many males who were doing the same but expecting each of the women to be faithful. However, she was not having sex or leading anyone on, while Jack, in his letters to his friend Lem Billings, was claiming to be as sexually active as he could get females to agree to be intimate with him.[7]

Joe Jr. never acted out in the manner of the men whom Kick and her female friends dubbed NSIT—Not Safe in Taxis. These were the ones who wanted to touch as much of a woman as they could, seemingly keeping score of the intimate areas they explored. They would begin their kissing and fondling in taxis, where such activities would be allowed, with the understanding that there would be a big tip for the taxi driver if he played along; thus the designation NSIT.

Instead of being aggressive toward anyone, Joe Jr. would go into himself when turned down. He would become sullen and withdrawn. Kick and her friends ignored him at those times, though such moods obviously failed to help him get dates.

The girls who normally would have been part of Joe's Boston area social circle were as uninterested in the angry youth as Kick's friends in London were. He took to going to New York City nightclubs such as Roseland, the Stork Club, and the Plaza, where he could meet somewhat hardened older women who were mildly desperate and as lacking in discrimination about their escorts for the evening as young Joe.

For her part, Kick considered attending Sarah Lawrence College when she returned to the United States. It was an experimental school perfect for her temperament, and she seemed to have the intelligence necessary to be successful. However, admission required that a young woman had achieved high marks in a school with excellent academic standards. The convent schools she had attended did not meet the criteria. There would be no exception made for a daughter of wealth, power, and privilege.

The answer was Finch. Finch was a cross between a junior college and a finishing school and where a student was judged by her bank account, not her report card. Some of the girls who attended Finch were not very bright. These were the ones who considered average grades to be honorable achievements for intensely hard work. The others—and Kick probably was one of them—were extremely bright, easily handled the coursework, but had rarely or never applied themselves before. Both types were educationally nurtured to bring out their best.

Rose also began talking before women's clubs, whose members invited her to tell them firsthand about British royalty. The 1930s was a time when the worlds of the wealthy and the powerful were as much of interest as the world of movie stars would be a decade later. Heiress

Doris Duke, for example, traveled around the world on her honeymoon and was involved with a succession of men who always were in the news. Teenage girls would avidly search their local newspapers for stories about her that they could clip and save in scrapbooks, just as Kick and her friends had done with stories about Gloria Swanson. To be able to listen to someone who was from a rich and prominent family tell about what really happens in a castle—there was no more exciting series of meetings any of the club members could imagine.

Joe Kennedy visited the United States regularly, but his return to England in 1940, after three months away, was very much against the wishes of the British. They were tired of the bigoted, naive, buffoon of an American ambassador, whom they had begun to realize was more likely speaking for himself than for the president. He was finally being criticized for his words and deeds quite apart from Roosevelt. For example, on March 8, 1940, journalist Harold Nicolson wrote in the *Spectator:*

> He will be welcomed, as fitting, by the large and influential Anglo-American colony in London. He will also be welcomed by the native or unhyphenated rich, who hope that he may bring with him a little raft of appeasement on which they can float for a year or so longer before they are finally submerged. He will be welcomed, of course, by the bankers and the isolationists, by the knights and the baronets. He will be welcomed by the shiver-sisters of Mayfair and by the wobble-boys of Whitehall. He will be welcomed by the Peace Pledge Union, the Christian Pacifists, the followers of Dr. Buchman, the friends of Herr von Ribbentrop, the Nuerembergers, the Munichois, Lord Tavistock and the disjecta membra of former pro-Nazi organizations. A solemn gladness will even crown the brows of M. Maisky, ambassador of the USSR. Few envoys, on returning to their post, can have received a welcome of such embarrassing variety.

At the same time, Joe was tired of Roosevelt. He decided that he would back the Republican opposition in 1940, and toward this end began talks with Henry "Harry" Luce.

Luce did not agree with Kennedy about appeasement, but Kennedy's threat to buy out the magazines had led to a gradual respect between the men. In part as payback, and in part because he hated Roosevelt, Luce began making Joe and his family familiar faces in his magazines. Joe Kennedy appeared twice on the cover of *Time* during the time he was chairman of the Securities and Exchange Commission. He appeared

Two former enemies finally gained mutual respect when
Joe Kennedy was named ambassador to the Court of
St. James. Joe is shown with father-in-law John Fitzgerald
on the latter's seventy-seventh birthday, February 11, 1940.
(Cleveland State University Library, Special Collections)

on *Fortune*'s cover when it ran the adulterated story about his life. Beginning at the end of 1937, *Life* had begun running pictures and stories
about all the Kennedys.

Luce ran stories lauding Joe Kennedy for being a great Democrat, a
concept that meant he was bringing business efficiency to an administration Luce thought was otherwise less than competent. Joe was seen
as pragmatic about business and politics, just the sort of man who could
work among New Dealers without being corrupted by them.

In 1940 Luce realized that Joe Kennedy was close to coming home
to endorse the Republican candidate for president, Wendell Willkie. The
Willkie candidacy had not come easily. The convention delegates voted
six times before they chose him, and his campaigning was not impressive.

Joe's supposed reason for supporting Willkie was that he had seen the German White Book, a collection of Polish secret documents that had been captured and then made public. Kennedy's reading of the documents indicated to him that Roosevelt had pushed the Allies into war, and he was livid. He worked out an arrangement where he would return to the United States, flying into Queens, New York. There Harry and Clare Luce would meet him. They would drive him to the Waldorf Hotel, then take him to a radio station where he would have a national hookup. Joe would announce his support of the Republican.

It is difficult to know what Luce thought about the impact of such a declaration. Certainly the press would see it as a rift in the Roosevelt administration. However, by that time journalists had come to realize that Joe was not Roosevelt's fair-haired boy, that there was little love lost between them, and that they strongly disagreed with each other about events unfolding in Europe. The change might not be shocking so much as a situation to which writers could point when attacking the president.

Joe saw things differently. He had become an Irish Catholic legend in his own mind. He was convinced that by switching to Willkie, he would bring 25 million Catholics to the polls, where they would throw out Roosevelt.

The idea that Joe was seen as a Catholic leader, or that the Catholics would follow Joe's political preaching, was nonsense. But it also was a possibility that Roosevelt dared not overlook. Willkie himself had been given much of his support by Luce, who also had suggested that he would be willing to use his magazines to back Joe Jr.'s political ambitions.

Luce had already shown Joe Sr. that he could be generous with support of pet projects, including Jack's first book, *Why England Slept*. The book was deliberately titled to play off Winston Churchill's book *While England Slept*. But where Churchill was an experienced diplomat, a government leader, a historian, and a skilled writer, Jack Kennedy was a college kid with a senior thesis his father decided to promote.

Exactly who wrote what in the book has long been the subject of debate. What is known shows much about Joe Kennedy, Arthur Krock, and Harry Luce, with their various machinations and currying for favor.

First there was Jack's background. Like his older brother, he was given a whirlwind tour of the trouble spots of the world. He, too, sent messages to his father. But what did professionals think of all this? In his *Memoirs, 1925–1950*, George Kennan, the American chargé d'Affaires in Lisbon at the time of Jack's whirlwind visits, said, "His son [Jack] had no official status and was, in our eyes, obviously an upstart and ignoramus."

During Jack's first two years at Harvard his grades were average. He was viewed as an undisciplined student without original thoughts. By his junior and senior years, though, Jack seemed to find himself. He had strong grades in political science, a natural for a youth raised talking politics with his Grandfather Fitzgerald and his mother. He did so well that it was suggested that he could graduate with honors if he wrote a strong undergraduate thesis.

Joe Kennedy was delighted with his son's prospects at Harvard. He hired a personal secretary to help Jack prepare his paper, eventually a work of 150 pages compared with the normal 70-page manuscript expected. It was going to be titled "England's Foreign Policy Since 1731," but was changed to "Appeasement at Munich."

Jack concluded that democracies move too slowly in times of crisis. This was why Hitler was able to gain military power while England was too slow to rearm in the face of the impending threat. A democracy was unable to think as far ahead as a dictatorship.

Like his father, Jack stated that the Munich conference, with its illusion of peace, bought time for rearmament. It also was a concept that had proven inaccurate by the time Jack was writing his paper.

Neither Jack nor the youth's short-term personal secretary could complete the thesis by the March 15, 1940, deadline. Joe ultimately arranged for five stenographers to work on the project, assuring it met the deadline.

The readers' response? The thesis was "badly written." They said it was interesting and intelligent, but they recognized that it was exactly what Jack's older brother had commented when their father asked him to read it—"it seemed to represent a lot of work but did not prove anything." Still, Jack was told the paper would be designated *cum laude* plus. How much influence Joe used to achieve this is unknown.

Joe Sr. had his book on the film industry that evolved from the Harvard lectures he coordinated but to which he added almost nothing. Jack would have his senior thesis published at the same school. As he wrote to his son, having a book "really makes the grade with high-class people [and] stands you in good stead for years to come."

How many people were involved with converting the poorly written thesis into a book is still open to dispute. There was at least one "editor" hired to do the serious writing. Arthur Krock was enlisted, but even he had his limits of toadyism. He bluntly told Jack to rewrite it, presumably giving him some more appropriate lessons in history. To his credit, Jack did the work.

Krock expected to be openly involved with the book by writing the authoritative foreword. He undoubtedly knew Joe's plans to buy enough copies to get the book national attention, and the foreword would both help Krock's own reputation and assist his effort to become editor of the *New York Times*. Instead Joe asked Henry Luce to do it. Luce's publications were more widely read and politically powerful on a national level. Joe also was trying to manipulate Luce so that Kennedy was always owed a favor.

The two men had obviously come to a mutual understanding concerning who could more effectively use money to stifle dissent when Joe had the *Fortune* article rewritten. But Joe wanted more subtle power, especially after the two became friends. They disagreed about world politics, and Joe wanted Luce firmly on his side. Krock was angry about the Luce foreword, though he was too well paid, too comfortably aided in his own career, to say anything that might damage his relationship with Kennedy.

Harper & Brothers, one of the most respected New York publishing houses, was sent the book, and the editors promptly sent it back. The ideas had proven nonsense in light of recent world developments.

Infuriated, Joe decided that the book would be a best-seller. He arranged for the book to go to Wilfred Funk, Inc., where the editors were supposedly most impressed. The truth was that they were impressed with the men who were behind the book. Harry Luce had agreed to write the foreword, the greatest coup Joe achieved. Reading the reviews, the foreword is singled out far more than anything Jack wrote. In addition, Joe likely made clear that he intended the book to be a best-seller even if he had to nurse the sales with a few purchases of his own. He ultimately bought thirty thousand to forty thousand copies directly from the publisher, then stored them in Hyannis Port.[8]

Joe Sr.'s efforts on behalf of Jack's thesis were emotionally shattering for Joe Jr. He knew that his father had tried to help him with a book of his own well before Jack's. The effort had begun after Joe Jr.'s trip to Spain. The problem was that the arrogance of a naive youth and the wealth of an indulgent, ambitious father could not match reality. No one cared. The events in Germany had long eclipsed the situation in Spain. Worse, as Joe Jr. tried to put his thoughts on paper, he realized he had nothing to say. He knew little of the history, had seen none of the fighting, had talked to neither leaders nor the general populace. He was a brash young man who tried to turn a few days' sightseeing, coupled with opinions based on assumptions, into a treatise someone might buy.

War hero Joseph Kennedy Jr. (left) and actor Peter Strauss who played him for the television movie *Young Joe: The Forgotten Kennedy.* (Cleveland State University Library, Special Collections)

The problem was that Jack accomplished what Joe Jr. could not. Worse, Jack was able to utilize his father's letters and papers as resources, something Joe Jr. also had not been able to do.

The days passed, and Roosevelt kept Joe out of the United States as much as possible. When it was obvious that Joe was going to come out for Willkie, Roosevelt played his trump card: He brought in Rose. She adored Eleanor and would not tolerate her husband's betraying Roosevelt for Willkie just because it would mean that Harry Luce could obtain a cabinet position if Willkie won. Rose and Joe's relationship remained one of intense mutual respect. The sexual commitment issues would never be resolved, but the family was still intact, Joe continued to be treated with deference in the capitals of the world, and Rose's opinion of him still mattered to Joe. She ordered him to do nothing to hurt Franklin, and he respected her demands.

In August 1940 Joe learned that his power and influence had been undermined once again. Intelligence reports indicated that Operation Sea Lion—the invasion of Britain—was being planned by Germany. France had fallen to Germany, and the British began building their coastal defenses in preparation for attack. In the meantime, there was vicious fighting in, on, and over the oceans. The Nazis were using a combination of aircraft and submarines to sink as many British ships as possible. They knew that the British Isles were not self-sustaining, requiring a constant flow of supplies the Germans hoped to interrupt.

British destroyers were traveling constantly to protect their ships, but the Germans were sinking the ships at a terrifying rate. One hundred put out to sea at the start of the war. Slightly over half that number remained in July. Churchill contacted Roosevelt, asking him to send "destroyers, motor-boats, and flying-boats." There was no time to wait. Without them Britain would be lost.

Roosevelt realized that he had to find a way to work around the need for special congressional legislation. The Senate was presumed isolationist. The various laws in existence did not allow the president to handle matters firsthand. Finally he sought the advice of a group of lawyers he trusted both to remain silent about what they were doing and to find legal loopholes.

The answer was ingenious. Britain owed the United States money from World War I. There was no way they could pay the bill, so the lawyers suggested that Roosevelt "demand" that all Western Hemisphere territories of Great Britain be made available as U.S. military bases. Then they would be given ninety-nine-year leases for both the army and the navy, though to be fair, the United States would send Britain fifty World War I destroyers.

Roosevelt told Joe Kennedy a little about what he was doing, but he did not let Joe handle many of the negotiations in London. Most of the work was done in Washington with Lord Lothian, a friend of Kennedy's who had been appointed ambassador to the United States.

Joe was furious. He had spent extensive time on Lord Lothian's estate where, in the latter part of 1938, many of the guests had favored Chamberlain's actions. However, by early 1939 Lord Lothian and his friends recognized that appeasement was nonsense. Joe's friend went to Washington at the same time the ambassador was excluded from Roosevelt's inner circle. Kennedy's inability to understand the full international situation left him no longer part of a group of people he once thought were friends.

There were compromises to be made. Could the vessels be surrendered if Germany overpowered the navy? Did so much land have to be traded for outdated equipment that, though effective, was no match for the newer armaments of the German navy?

Ultimately Churchill "gave" his "old friend" Roosevelt bases in Bermuda and Newfoundland. He "traded" the fifty ships for the other locations. And Joe Kennedy, an outsider, acted like a petulant child because he knew the details only after everything was finished.

On August 28 Roosevelt had to send Kennedy this message: "The destroyer and base matter was handled in part through you and in part through Lothian but the situation developed into a mapping proposition where the Army and Navy are in constant consultation with me here and the daily developments have had to be explained verbally to Lothian.

"There is no thought of embarrassing you and only a practical necessity for personal conversations makes it easier to handle details here."[9]

The message did not calm Joe. He accepted the fact that much had to be done in Washington. He also was convinced of his importance in London, especially his belief that he perceived the reality of how the British were thinking and their misunderstanding of Washington's stance. He did not know that Roosevelt was constantly involved with secret talks, developing ways to work with the British and nurture what would eventually become the Allied forces.

On August 29 Joe Kennedy weighed in on the part of the agreement between Roosevelt and Churchill. The businessman in him noted that the Americans got the better of the trade. He was especially pleased with a clause that assured, in the event of the defeat of the British Isles, whatever remained of the naval fleet would be sent to Canada. He failed to see that the simple maneuver of the two leaders assured that the United States would never again be seen as neutral. Churchill grasped this from the start, never telling the ambassador that Roosevelt had given the German government the right to attack the United States or its ships, personnel, and assets abroad.

The news in the United States was mixed. A few critics were outraged over the seeming end to isolation. Most editorial writers looked at the deal as Joe had done, though. The United States had gained territory both vast and important, much like what had been accomplished by forward-thinking presidents of the nineteenth century when they took land from France, Spain, and elsewhere within what became the borders of the continental United States.

On September 7, one year after England entered the war, the Germans launched three air raids against the country. The first target was the Royal Air Force. Once it was destroyed, as Hitler was certain he could accomplish, the invasion of Britain would begin.

The attacks against London caught the city of 7 million people off guard. For twelve hours the bombers worked to destroy the waterfront. Some of the raids occurred in daylight, others at night. The flames from fires raging out of control from the daylight raids guided the planes after dark.

The work was not over, though. For almost two months the raids would continue. Two hundred planes a night.

Joe was as surprised as anyone. He found himself slightly exhilarated by what was happening, as though he were experiencing a taste of the "glory" of warfare he had missed in World War I.

The staff of the American embassy was told to spend each night in the countryside because the raids, other than the first, were mostly carried out in the dark. Joe led the retreat by going to his home in Windsor Great Park, much to the derision of the British, whose queen remained in London every day of the Blitz. However, although Joe was safe from the bombing, a German Me-109 was shot down by a British plane, the crash occurring close enough to Joe's home that he could see the pilot in the cockpit of the descending aircraft. He was also close enough to an exploding bomb while being driven in a car that the concussion from the blast flipped the vehicle onto the sidewalk, scaring him but not causing injury.

Kennedy had mixed emotions about what was taking place. He had compassion for the people of London who carried on despite lack of sleep and, often, loss of their homes. The shelters to which everyone went at night were often cold and damp.

As for the Luftwaffe, Joe believed that the worst was being saved, that they had seen no more than one in twenty of the German fleet of bombers. He did not know that the Luftwaffe was possibly more worn out than the public. He only saw the economic cost to the British, the loss of production, and the likely conclusion that they would go under long before they could rebuild. He felt that Churchill, whom he blamed for triggering the Battle of Britain, was the wrong man to lead the people. In one dispatch he wrote:

> I cannot impress upon you strongly enough my complete lack of confidence in the entire conduct of this war. I was delighted to see that the president said he was not going to enter the war, because to enter this war, imagining for a minute that the English have anything to offer in the line of leadership or productive capacity in industry that could be of the slightest value to us, would be a complete misapprehension. It breaks my heart to draw these conclusions about a people that I sincerely hoped might be

victorious, but I cannot get myself to the point where I believe they can be of any assistance to the cause in which they are involved.[10]

Ironically, when the German government got word of Kennedy's attitude, they were surprised. By then they realized that he did not view things in the same way as the British, who were far more optimistic despite the nightly hell of the Blitz. In fact, visitors to the city found that the people were delighted to awaken each morning, to embrace life, and, more important, to embrace whatever was left of London each day.

Joe returned to the United States that October. He had lost whatever momentum he may have had in pursuit of whatever acclaim he thought he could ride to take him gracefully out of the ambassador's position and back into money, politics, or whatever his next dream might be. He reluctantly supported Franklin Roosevelt for president because he had failed to build on the slight advances he had achieved for his own ambitions. Worse, his seventy-seven-year-old father-in-law was inadvertently gaining the positive press with Roosevelt that Joe tried to buy.

The 1940s was still in the era of whistle-stop campaigning. The candidate would use one or more private railroad cars to travel across the country. He would stop in small towns ("whistle-stops") and big cities, sometimes having the car placed on a siding while he remained for a few days, sometimes giving a speech in the station from a platform at the back of the car. Either way, there would be a speech, the embracing of local political leaders, campaign donors, and other supporters, then a moving on.

Joe Jr., Jack, and their grandfather John Fitzgerald went to meet Roosevelt while he was in Boston. Honey Fitz had done extensive traveling in South America, and Roosevelt had been there as well. The president greeted the popular ex-mayor by shouting, "Welcome, *Dulce Adelina!*" as he embraced the tiny Fitzgerald. He then explained that he had traveled to the same areas in South America as Honey Fitz but after the older man had made an appearance. In each community the people had a band to honor the president by playing what they thought was the national anthem. However, instead of "The Star-Spangled Banner" they would strike up "Sweet Adeline," which, in Spanish, was *"Dulce Adelina."* The president said that the people of the various countries were certain that "Sweet Adeline" was the national anthem. *"Dulce Adelina"* was the name the president jokingly used for Honey Fitz from then on.

No one other than Roosevelt and Honey Fitz knew if the story, related years later by then-senator Jack Kennedy, was true. What was certain was that Roosevelt genuinely liked the man, and Boston liked any friend of their beloved ex-mayor.

Joe Sr. had to give a pro-Roosevelt speech that day in the Ritz-Carlton Hotel. Honey Fitz organized the event, and the press that turned out was always favorable to the old man.

Joe said that he was pessimistic about the future, that he felt democracy was finished in England. The only reason to supply aid was to gain extra time for the United States to fortify itself. He explained that England was fighting for self-preservation, not one government or another. And then, according to Louis Lyons, writing for the *Boston Globe*, "It's all an economic question. I told the President in the White House last Sunday, 'Don't send me fifty admirals and generals, send me a dozen real economists.'"

The anger, viciousness, and stupidity of the ambassador became even more evident when he began mocking Eleanor Roosevelt. He talked of her having sympathy for everyone she met, a trait that actually had made her the most beloved first lady in the nation's history. Joe complained, "She's always sending me a note to have some little Susie Glotz to tea at the embassy."

The speech was Joe Kennedy's last hurrah. The press was turning strongly against him, and he had intense opposition in the one area where he had achieved a certain amount of continued respect: Hollywood.

On November 26, 1940, columnists Drew Pearson and Robert S. Allen wrote about Joe's views in the *Boston Evening Transcript*. They gave three specifics that were later confirmed by screenwriter Ben Hecht, who had been leading Hollywood writers, producers, directors, and actors in finding ways to fight Germany's fascism. According to the columnists, Kennedy felt that:

1. England, although fighting heroically, faced overwhelming odds, and the United States might as well realize that England was virtually defeated.
2. The United States should carefully limit its aid to Britain so as to gain time to become fully armed, in order to be in a better position to do business with the Axis victors.
3. Hollywood producers should stop making films offensive to the dictators.

Hecht, in his autobiography *A Child of the Century*, noted that he discovered that Kennedy had been meeting with the primarily Jewish heads of studios. "They told me that Ambassador Joseph Kennedy, lately returned from beleaguered London, had spoken to fifty of Hollywood's leading Jewish movie makers in a secret meeting in one of their homes. He told them sternly that they must not protest as Jews, and that they must keep their Jewish rage against the Germans out of print.

"Any Jewish outcries, Kennedy explained, would impede victory over the Germans. It would make the world feel that a 'Jewish War' was going on."

Roosevelt demanded and accepted his resignation within days. By 1941 Joe would be suggesting that the United States should develop a barter arrangement with the Nazis rather than going to total war on behalf of the British.

Joe Kennedy had worked in a manner he thought would be lauded. The British, by contrast, finally felt comfortable expressing their outrage over his outrageous and often inappropriate actions.

One of the first writers to attack after the ambassador resigned was A. J. Cummings of the *London News Chronicle*. Acting on his own in an effort to control the news coming from England, Joe had arranged for Hollywood production companies to edit out any interviews that were contrary to Joe's beliefs. Cummings was one of the men who had been interviewed on camera, made statements Joe felt were inappropriate, then had his appearance removed before American theaters carried the newsreels.

Cummings was finally able to vent his rage to a reporter for the *New York Times*. In an article that not even Krock could modify or kill, the December 7, 1940, paper quoted Cummings as saying of Kennedy, "While he was here his suave, monotonous style, his nine over-photographed children and his hail-fellow-well-met manner concealed a hard-boiled business man's eagerness to do a profitable business deal with the dictators, and he deceived many decent English people." It was not a career epitaph any man would want for posterity.

Joe and Rose retreated a bit, ridding themselves of the New York estate and dividing their time between Palm Beach and Hyannis Port. At the same time, their older children were preparing to be involved with the military and life in wartime. It was a new lifestyle that would ultimately prove emotionally and/or physically shattering.

Kick was the first of the children to find success in a business, though not one she ran or wanted to run. Kathleen was oblivious to her father's fury with the way he was being treated. She had no compassion for his beliefs about government. Her Billy had gone to war, serving with the British Expeditionary Force defending the Maginot Line in late 1940. There was a chance he would die, and she insisted on personally returning to England to be closer to him. There would be leave time, if he lived, and she wanted to be able to spend it with him.

All her British debutante friends were getting jobs in war-related activities, and before she had to leave, Kick thought she might join them. It is humorous to note that though they all were serious about the war effort and all understood that many would be killed, wounded, or permanently impaired, they were still rich young women with a sense of style. Some actively sought military service, not because they wanted to be as close to the battlefields as possible but because they loved the way the women looked in their hats. Others sought factory work because the uniforms were flattering to their figures. And some joined the Red Cross, an activity that would take them in the midst of whatever horrors awaited the country and the troops, though still with nice clothing to wear. Kick had no idea what she would do, but her parents' attitude toward her desires was not what she expected.

Joe and Rose were livid. Joe hated the British all the more. Rose did not want her daughter in danger.

Kick had mentioned that she was interested in journalism, a career her lack of specialized education would allow. She was genuinely interested in people, willing to listen, and delighted in learning their personal stories. Joe thought a job on a newspaper would be good for her and keep her from thinking too much about England. He asked Arthur Krock where she should go, and he suggested the *Washington Times-Herald.*

The *Washington Times-Herald* was unique in the nation in that it was the first paper to have a female publisher/editor. Eleanor "Cissy" Patterson was the granddaughter of Joseph Medill, owner of the *Chicago Tribune*, and sister of the founder of the *New York Daily News*. However, unlike the papers of her grandfather and her brother, Patterson's paper had almost no influence in the city in which it was published.

Kick was serious about the newspaper, even though several on the staff knew she was likely to be one of the Arthur Krock debutantes. He was notorious for helping the daughters of the rich and powerful by getting them entry-level positions on the paper in exchange for whatever favors might one day come his way.

Kick was different in her attitude, though probably not her abilities. She wanted to be respected as a newspaperwoman, not known as Joe Kennedy's daughter. She rented an apartment affordable on her salary, and since she often had to attend important social functions, she hid her mink coat in a shopping bag whenever she needed to go from work to an evening affair. She wore a cloth coat affordable on her income, an annual sum that was about the same as her father spent for the mink. She also wore clothing that matched that of the other girls.

The ruse was more successful than Kick intended. She worked as an assistant to Executive Editor Frank Waldrop, then transferred to working with John White, who handled the gossip/profile column "Did You Happen to See?" Finally she moved on to being a theater and motion picture critic with a bylined column. However, one day while she was still a new hire, she had to return to the office in the midst of heading to a diplomatic reception. She was seen wearing an expensive dinner dress and mink coat by a handful of women employees who thought they knew the score. Kick, that happy, aggressive, hardworking woman, was moving faster than perhaps she realized. By day she was a reporter, and as they were certain they had deduced, by night she was either a kept woman or an extremely high-priced call girl.

Caring for their new colleague, the women took Kick aside the next day. They talked with her about maintaining her independence, about self-respect, about making her own way instead of relying on the largesse of men. They had no idea she was wealthy or the role her father had been playing in the U.S. government.

Rosemary was the first to fall victim to Joe Kennedy's frustrations and fantasies. She had been thriving in England, but he did not want her to stay. Neither she nor Kick was worried about the German attacks against Great Britain. Kick wanted to stand with the British people in the manner of their beloved queen. Rosemary wanted to stay in the countryside, both working and learning in the Montessori School. Joe would have none of that. The two daughters were forced to return, and Rosemary was bitter.

Exactly what was taking place in 1941 played out beyond the public eye. Certainly Rosemary was angry and rebellious. She was still in late adolescence, and she had been forced from the first place where people understood her disability.

There is one family story about Rosemary becoming violent with Honey Fitz during the summer of 1941. This rather vague tale involves Rosemary kicking her grandfather as he sat on the porch of the Kennedy home in Hyannis Port, Massachusetts. Given the detail provided for so many critical areas of the family's life, the lack of information about something so serious seems to indicate it is family myth.

What appears certain is the following. First, Rosemary was dyslexic. Retardation was never an issue except, perhaps, in the family's misunderstanding. It is even possible that Rose considered a learning disability to be the same as retardation, because there were few sources of factual information to provide a better understanding.

Joe Kennedy was concerned with Rosemary's becoming a woman. Since Kick had access to John White, who had written about surgical procedures to control extreme mental illness, Joe asked her to help him gain information.

Given the culture of the time, it is impossible to know what Joe thought of the surgical procedure. This was a period when little was understood about mental illness, and even less could be done for it. In the extreme, straitjackets were used to prevent an individual from using his or her hands to do harm to oneself or others.

The only meaningful drugs were sedatives, and they did not deal with a problem. They simply rendered a violent individual unconscious for a few hours while risking damaging the person's heart and lungs. Padded cells were used when someone was striking out at others but not a danger to himself or herself. There were no pharmaceuticals that could alter a person's mood or serve as a biochemical restraint.

Prefrontal lobotomy was a way to alter the mind without disfiguring the body. Dr. Robert Eiben, who was part of the Boston area medical protocol committee in 1941, explained: "That's the area of the nervous system that is not developed in the newborn, and all of the growth that takes place in the first year or two years of life is the growth of the anterior portion of the frontal lobes, and the anterior portion of the temporal lobes. The anterior portion of the temporal lobes [is involved] more in retentive memory, and the anterior portion of the frontal lobes [has] a lot of relationship with learned motor activities, and the development of a lot of the behavioral patterns that evolve, that newborns, toddlers, and so forth are just not capable of. These areas mature and these connections are made, and the attempt is made to sever these connections; they obviously will not be so graceful in their ambulatory efforts and are just dull in their social adaptive responsiveness."

Boston was a community with strict standards for when a prefrontal lobotomy could be done and when it could not. Dr. Robert Eiben understood prefrontal lobotomy and the need to use it only in the most extreme cases. He discussed men and women locked in back wards, unable to function at all. They might be extremely intelligent, as shown by earlier behavior, but something had gone wrong with their minds. Eventually they were useless to themselves and society, sitting, staring, unable to communicate. For some of these an extreme measure such as prefrontal lobotomy was appropriate because there was nothing else to be done. They would often recover enough to go out in society, to work, go to school, and function. They were not as bright or as out-going as they had been, and often they would eventually lapse back into almost autistic behavior. But for a few weeks, months, or years they could live their lives outside a locked ward. Given that nothing else worked at that time, the operation was tolerated.

The Washington, D.C., hospitals involved with prefrontal lobotomies at the time, St. Elizabeth's and George Washington School of Medicine, had lower standards than Joe encountered in Boston. Apparently he learned of the procedure through reading John White's articles and/or talking with the reporter. All the hospitals were attempting to practice the best possible medicine, but some were more willing to tolerate experi-mentation than others. Dr. Eiben was conservative, as were the other medical professionals who ruled on Rosemary. Dr. Walter Freeman and Dr. James Watts, the pioneers in the Washington, D.C., area, were more liberal with their application of the procedure.

A team consisting of Freeman and Watts did the surgery on Rose-mary. They were the most experienced surgeons in the world with this procedure, having accomplished approximately one of every five pre-frontal lobotomies tried at that time. All but one of the procedures had been done on patients older than Rosemary and closer to fitting the Boston protocol. Allegedly none of their work had achieved the desired outcome, though the patients had been so extreme, the effort seemed valid.

There are two stories about what happened with Rosemary, both provided by Rose. In one the decision to perform the operation was made jointly by Rose and Joe. She was out of town when the operation occurred, but this was not unusual, even with her daughter going in for major surgery. They had discussed the matter before and agreed to the procedure.

The other story is that Rose had no idea of what Joe planned. Joe did what he felt was best. A half century later Dr. Eiben remembered only Joe, but that did not mean the couple failed to discuss the matter. The complete emotional separation between the two did not occur until after the operation occurred and was a failure. And years later, when Rosemary at last came to visit the family, Rose sadly talked with her assistant Barbara Gibson about what "we" had done to her.

The problem with trying to find the truth is that the results were horrendous. Rosemary went from being an attractive young woman with a good future to being a five-year-old child in a woman's body. There was no reversing the procedure. There is no way to alter her condition with today's medical knowledge. She will die with the mind of a five-year-old.

Joe had to acknowledge what happened. He had done the research. He had taken Rosemary before the medical protocol committee in Boston. He had taken her to St. Elizabeth's Hospital.

But there was more, something horribly strange with the aftermath. Apparently Joe contacted Archbishop Richard Cushing about where to hide Rosemary. She would not come home, even though he could well afford whatever long-term care she might need and could thrive in the midst of family. Instead, she was rushed to St. Coletta's School in Jefferson, Wisconsin, where the nuns were skilled in this type of long-term nursing care. Then nothing more was said.

Rosemary disappeared. Over the next twenty years there is little evidence that Rose ever visited her daughter. There is no evidence that friends or outside family members asked about Rosemary. Rose seems to have assigned Eunice the task of being a liaison, though even that is subject to question in the first few years after the operation. Certainly for everyone other than Eunice, Rosemary was a nonperson. She was home one day and gone forever the next.[11]

How any of this psychologically affected the family is uncertain. Kick certainly could have deduced what happened, but her heart and mind were on England.

As for the others, the one child who seems to have become terrified by the loss was Teddy. Rosemary meant more to him than anyone else as a child. She was the nurturing mother he never had. At his age it appears that he may have seen Rosemary rebel against her father, then suddenly be made to disappear. The trauma must have been overwhelming and may have been a cause of his inability to emotionally commit to a woman, as well as his adult abuse of food and alcohol.

There would eventually be several official family versions of the Rosemary myth. The first story came out in 1939, though it was not the type of cover-up spoken later. She was not as public a figure as her sister, so the family admitted that she was slow to learn in school. The implication was that she was not very bright rather than that she had dyslexia, for as one member of the British press wrote: "She is the quieter of the older girls, and although she has an interest in social welfare work, she is said to harbor a secret longing to go on the stage."

It is doubtful that Rosemary mentioned the theater, because such an interest does not appear in her diary. She was starstruck, both with political leaders and Hollywood celebrities, a love shared with her siblings. She was also becoming increasingly interested in boys, a fact that made her parents nervous. They both realized how aggressive Rose had been with a much stricter upbringing in more conservative times. Rosemary was likely to engage in premarital sex and what to Joe and Rose would be inappropriate relationships. Ironically, it was the seemingly obedient second daughter, Kathleen, who would ultimately do all the things they worried Rosemary might try.

Later, in 1953, the *Saturday Evening Post* ran an article in mid-June. Titled "The Senate's Gay Young Bachelor," it described Rosemary as a "schoolteacher in Wisconsin."

Then in 1958, when Jack Kennedy had unofficially been running for president for more than a year, Joseph Dineen interviewed most of the family, though not Rosemary, for a book titled *The Kennedy Family*. He wrote: "In large Catholic families, it is commonplace that at least one child shall have a 'vocation,' a divine call to the priesthood, the Christian Brothers, or a women's religious order. All of the Kennedy children loved rough-and-tumble sports except Rosemary. She cringed and shuddered at violence of any kind; she was a spectator, but never a participant. Unlike her siblings, she shunned the limelight and was shy and retiring. It was inevitable, perhaps, that she should study at the Merrymount [*sic*] Convent in Tarrytown, New York, and devote her life to the sick and afflicted and particularly to backward and handicapped children.

"She is the least publicized of all the Kennedys. She prefers it that way and her wishes are respected."

And in the October 11, 1960, issue of *Look* magazine, Rosemary was identified in a photograph as "a victim of spinal meningitis, now in a Wisconsin nursing home." The closest anyone came to the truth would eventually be the *Palm Beach Daily News*. On Sunday, July 22, 1990, an article by Chris Romoser stated, "As the children matured, it became apparent that Rosemary was different from the rest. When she was diagnosed as mentally retarded, Joe. Sr. decided to send her to a special boarding school near Milwaukee. Mrs. Kennedy was said to have been crushed when her oldest daughter went away. To the public, however, no disappointment or despair ever was voiced."

Joe Jr. would be the second to suffer for his father's actions, though in Joe Jr.'s case the damage was emotional. Perhaps he was the weakest of the Kennedy brothers. Perhaps he was suffering from depression, his sullen withdrawals from others actually mood swings. Perhaps he was so desperate for his father's love and approval that he became filled with self-loathing each time he felt himself beaten by one of the others. Whatever the case, Joe decided to enter the navy. He had been in the naval aviation cadet program during his last semester at Harvard. Upon graduation he joined the U.S. Naval Reserve in June 1941. He was a seaman second class and stationed at Squantum Naval Air Facility near Boston.

Joe Jr. also had the strongest sense of military service within the family. When war was declared and he became skilled in working with aircraft converted to makeshift missiles, he volunteered for Top Secret duty that put him in great danger. He did not discuss his actions with his family. He sought neither articles by his father's friends nor a book of his exploits. He seemed to find a cause in which he believed, one where he didn't have to prove himself special. All he wanted was to do his job, serve his country, and, in so doing, earn the respect of his father. He did not realize that for Joe Kennedy Sr., any good deed accomplished in silence and shadows might as well have never been attempted.

Jack likewise wanted to join the navy, though no one knew why. He also may have felt the desire to serve the country. He may have been influenced by friends who were entering the service. He may have simply been competing with his brother Joe. Regardless of the reason, he had no business putting on a uniform. In 1941 Jack was a physical wreck, too weak to make his way through the rigors of basic training, much less active duty in a war zone.

Jack's health had declined dangerously the previous year. He had spent a portion of 1940 in California, where it was hoped the climate and lack of pressure would enable him to heal his ulcers and other problems. It also would enable him to lie out in the sun and chase girls who, he hoped, would appreciate his catching them.

Recognizing that a certain amount of boredom might take over, Jack arranged to audit classes at Stanford Business School. He wouldn't have to meet the grade requirement or other background needed for admission. He wouldn't have to take tests or meet any of the school's standards. He would go when he wanted, sitting out of the way, making notes if he chose or just listening.

The Kennedys never could let their family members be human, and that meant that illness and/or physical frailty could be embarrassments.

Jack's problems did not affect his intellect and should not have been concerns for his future. However, even after his death, Rose and the biographers either approved by or working with family members often created a myth for this time. Rose said that he spent a semester studying "economics, finance, and business," implying that these were formal courses of study benefiting his future. Author James MacGregor Burns told of Kennedy attending six months of business school at Stanford, again indicating a formal course of study. The truth was that he spent only three months, and his class attendance was sparse enough to assure failure if the courses had been taken for credit.[12]

Jack was classified 4-F, physically unfit for military service, when he returned to the East. Perhaps Joe felt that being in the service would look good on his son's record, much like having a book to his credit. Whatever the case, Joe called Captain Alan Kirk, the director of the Office of Naval Intelligence, whom he had known in England. Kirk had been involved in the investigation of the sinking of *Athenia* and been more impressed with Jack's abilities than the passengers. A deal was worked out in which Jack would be assured of passing his physical exam no matter what it showed about his health. The physician would be a doctor connected with the family, no further checks or genetic information needed.

Once allowed to enlist, it is not known if Jack endured all of basic training, though Joe arranged for his son to have help with exercises that included strength, weight gain, and developing stamina. He was stronger going into basic than when he had his physical, and everyone was careful to ensure he avoided injury that might have killed him.

Captain Kirk, who ranked high enough to place any recruit in any job area he chose, would then give Jack a desk job. Jack also received an ensign's commission, something his older brother had yet to earn through his serious, legitimate efforts. Finally Jack was assigned to work in the intelligence division, analyzing the Japanese buildup in forces and the strategic planning for the U.S. military in the Pacific. It was September 1941, three months before the attack on Pearl Harbor.

Jack Kennedy was one in a line of paper-pushers with an inadequate background to do a job few people in government realized needed to be done. He had a uniform, a security clearance, and little knowledge of Southeast Asia. He did not speak, read, or write Japanese. He had no knowledge of Japanese culture and history. He could not have and had not studied their writings or religion. Had he received all the reports and understood them, he probably still could not have anticipated the problem that would erupt in what President Roosevelt called "a day which will live in infamy."

While Joe Kennedy was attempting to pick up the pieces of a shattered career, find a way to make himself richer, and deal with the Rosemary crisis that led him to be permanently estranged from his wife, Rose was focusing on Kick's career. Rose regularly wrote family letters that often were hurtful in their bluntness. Teddy, who ironically became her favorite child and frequent companion when he became a U.S. senator, was often ridiculed for being fat and clumsy (e.g., "I think he has put on the ten pounds which he lost at Riverdale." "I am afraid he is getting too fat as he now weighs about 105." And about his learning to dance the conga, she wrote the family, "He only fell down once last week, so he is improving."). When Kick gained her first important assignment at the paper, her mother wrote, on February 16, 1942:

> Kathleen has been transferred to the Play Department; that is, she has a column and is giving her opinion of plays and pictures. I am a little confused as to whether it is both or one, but anyway, that is the general idea. My suggestion would be that she have a nom de plume. My second suggestion would be that she have a decent picture taken, but she and her father seem to think both of these matters are okay. She is quite thrilled at the idea of people watching for her column and I am quite crushed to think that my three or four children got into print with works of their brains and I was never allowed to edit one little word. I believe it is the Bible which says—"The twig cannot be greater than the root from which it has sprung."

There was a more serious concern about Kathleen, one that would cause Joe to endanger his sons. This was Inga Arvad, a woman who was probably the first serious romance in Jack's troubled life. Inga was a sophisticated twenty-eight-year-old woman of the world, an ardent American immigrant who had previously been involved with the Nazi Party in her native Copenhagen, Denmark. She was educated in Brussels, London, and Paris, where she became a beauty contest winner and had a short-term marriage to an Egyptian diplomat. The Nazi connection came when she began working as a freelance writer for a Copenhagen newspaper that had her interview Adolf Hitler. Her beauty matched the Aryan ideal, and she was welcomed into the inner circle of the Nazi high command, where she was given interviews and access to Hitler during the 1936 Berlin Olympic Games.

Arvad's problems seemed to stem from the impression in Denmark that she had joined the Nazi Party and her failure to denounce the Nazis after *Kristallnacht*. However, the Nazis horrified her, especially when they asked her to move to France as a spy. Instead there would be one more brief marriage in Denmark, an affair, and a move to the United States, where she enrolled in the Columbia School of Journalism, where Arthur Krock was a consulting professor. Then it was on to the *Washington Times-Herald*.

While all this was taking place, Ensign Kennedy began sharing an apartment with his sister Kick. This inevitably led to his meeting Inga when she and Kathleen became closer.

Jack and Inga were an unlikely pair. He was younger than her twenty-eight years, well traveled, and with the opinionated nature of the naive. She was tall, beautiful, truly sophisticated, and completely uninhibited in all her actions, whether in public or in the bedroom. They dated, were intimate, and they exchanged letters that he kept.

Joe understood his son's attraction to Inga Arvad and knew that the youth might marry her. He would be a fool not to know. She was beautiful. She was intelligent. Allegedly she was as uninhibited in the bedroom as Gloria Swanson had been. Inga also was a foreigner, divorced, and as far as he was concerned, a former Nazi. The marriage might be ideal for his son's libido and maybe for a partnership in life. But it would be the kiss of death for any political office after the war, and it would bring disgrace to the Kennedy family as they tried to prove themselves better than the Brahmins, who had the good taste to hide their more controversial politics.

While the relationship deepened, Joe Kennedy arranged for Inga's apartment to be placed under intense surveillance. It is uncertain whether this was done through personal resources or through J. Edgar Hoover, who always was delighted to comply with any request from someone in power whom he later might blackmail. Certainly Hoover kept as many records as he could on Joe and his family, something he found most useful when Jack became president and wanted to fire him. When Jack, through his father's mob connections, confronted Hoover with information on his private life, the director matched the information with material ranging from Inga Arvad to trips Jack took to Cuba before the revolution.

It was March 1942 when Joe arranged to have his son assigned to active duty at sea. The threat of the twice-divorced Arvad was just too great in his mind. He arranged for Jack to captain a PT boat, a terrible situation for someone with his back problems. The navy would never have tolerated the situation had anyone known. Instead, Joe remained silent to assure that Jack would be separated from Inga. Although they remained friends until her 1947 marriage to cowboy star Tim McCoy, on March 11, 1942, she wrote a letter accepting what she realized was inevitable:

"A human breast to me has always been a little like a cage, where a bird sits behind. Some birds sing cheerfully, some mourn, others are envious and nasty. Mine always sang. It did especially for a few months this winter. In fact it sang so loudly that I refused to listen to that other little sensible creature called reason. It took me the FBI, the U.S. Navy, nasty gossip, envey [sic], hatred and big Joe, before the bird stopped."

It is no longer possible to know what anyone was thinking when sending Jack Kennedy into war. Joe Sr. was angry with the president, angry with the nation for being at war, angry with the British for fighting the Nazis, and angry with the doctors whose work on Rosemary had resulted in yet another embarrassment. Joe had lived half a century, obtained wealth seemingly beyond avarice, gained respect in Hollywood, become a noted business consultant, and traveled the world. He had thumbed his nose at descendants of the royal crown who had wreaked havoc on his ancestors. He had known the heights and depths of achievement, notoriety, and family, yet nothing was working, and his children were blindly going wherever he led.

PT boats were arguably the least safe of all vessels assigned to any sort of combat role during World War II. They were made of plywood and carried three thousand gallons of gasoline. Each PT boat was given torpedoes that were among the smallest and least effective available. Some were so bad that they exploded while traveling through the water before reaching their target. Others struck the vessel they were attacking, then bounced harmlessly off the side.

The radios for the PT boats had been used in airplanes that were decommissioned or needed better equipment. Sometimes they failed to work. At other times they would have signal drift, the frequency changing uncontrollably in the midst of a transmission.

The three engines were not properly sealed against water damage.

The men assigned to captain the PT boats were not the best and brightest in the navy. Often they were spoiled, rich boys, some dedicated to their country's war effort, some seeking adventure, and some failing to get the type of desk job that Jack was leaving. They were chosen for one reason: their wealthy families owned cabin cruisers, sailboats, or other vessels approximately eighty feet long. The eighty-foot PT boats handled in much the same way.

The problem with the captains was that the ones who had enjoyed family yachts were usually competitive. The PT boats were lightly and poorly armed, inherently unstable, though more maneuverable than larger vessels. They were primarily used for nuisance attacks, several vessels hiding in wait, then moving in and out, shooting at a ship that hopefully could not quickly respond before the vessels had escaped. Yet the captains were youths who had often been taught to compete, not cooperate. They often tried to be heroes or, as in the case of Kennedy, ignore the other PT boat captains when on a mission.

None of the men selected to be captains of PT boats was in particularly good shape when he entered the training academy at Northwestern University's Midshipmen's School. Jack started a special back-strengthening program three months before he had to report on December 2, 1942. The muscle strengthening was meant to help him avoid corrective surgery, though the doctors did not know he was heading for active duty. Sailing in any form was dangerous for him. The idea that he could handle the physical demands of leadership was outrageous. The navy seemed to know this as well. That was why he was asked to stay back and teach others.

Instead, Jack, with his father's help, got himself assigned to the Solomon Islands in the South Pacific. The posting assured that he would see combat, as his father well knew. It was a situation that raised serious questions that have never been answered.

Joe Jr. was deeply troubled by his younger brother's going into the midst of war. At that moment he was involved with critical but safe reconnaissance flights out of Puerto Rico. He traveled in PBY-4 gull-wing aircraft, a task that lacked any hint of danger. This would change, but Jack's opportunity to see combat, something Joe Jr. desperately wanted, again seemed like his father's favorite son getting special privilege.

Joe Sr. had destroyed one child, Rosemary, with his intervention, and the PT service almost destroyed a second child while costing the lives of two men on Jack's vessel. It was July 1943 and the Americans had not been able to seal a passage through the Solomon Islands the Japanese were using to ferry supplies. The concern was the "Tokyo Express," the route the Japanese supply ships were taking from their bases on the Shortland Islands and Bougainville to Kolombangara. The Tokyo Express involved supply ships escorted by cruisers and destroyers. The navy decided to use a pack of unreliable PT boats to stop the Tokyo Express. Each vessel was at risk of breaking down. None of them had much striking power, but a pack of them together just might be able to do what larger, less maneuverable vessels had not.

On August 1, 1943, fifteen PT boats were moving about the Pacific like a pack of hounds chasing a fox on an English estate. Jack Kennedy and his *PT-109* had been with the group only a couple of weeks, having just been transferred to Lumbari, an island near Rendova off the coast of New Georgia in the Solomon Islands.

The route allowed the Japanese to hold the area known as Munda, from which they could dominate New Georgia. So far they had managed to hold off the Ninth Marine Battalion and the army's Forty-third Division. It was hoped that the highly maneuverable PT boats could begin doing some damage to the Japanese ships.

That night the PT boats spotted their prey, four troop- and cargo-carrying Japanese destroyers, just as the vessels spotted them. Lights were played on the water by the Japanese vessels. Guns were fired. The fourteen more experienced PT boat captains had learned to work together, taking evasive action, then regrouping for an angular attack from which they could strike and flee before the Japanese could respond. Jack, on *PT-109*, was the only captain who did not work with the others. He fled, joining two other PT boats after the attack. They watched as the Japanese destroyers reached shore in Blackett Strait, unloaded men and equipment, then hurriedly started to return. It was 2:00 A.M.

Jack was expected to have his crew on full alert. One of the men, who had been assigned watch duty, was night blind, though Kennedy did not know that. The boats frequently traveled without radio because the commander thought that silence was best. Still, radio could be used in an emergency, and it was not normal procedure when Jack pulled his radioman off duty to come over and talk with him. Four crew members had been sent to rest, two of them sleeping. There were three good engines, and all of them were critical for the fastest attack, maneuvering, and escape actions. Jack left only one in gear despite squadron policy to the contrary. It was a combination of circumstances that added up to dereliction of duty.

It was the Japanese destroyer *Amagiri* that created the nightmare. It was heading back to sea, with *PT-109* directly in its path. The wake of the vessel was on Kennedy's starboard bow, and there was plenty of time to take evasive action. Otherwise *PT-109* would be accidentally struck.

Jack and his crew were unaware of the impending danger. The other two PT boat crews began calling *PT-109* by radio. They tried frantic efforts to signal. Nothing worked. *Amagiri*, oblivious to the PT boat, sliced it in half.

Lieutenant Commander Hanami, the skipper of *Amagiri*, later gave a different account of the incident. He stated:

> It was August 2, 1943, that my destroyer was on her way to her base at 30 knots. That night it was cloudy and squally, so that our visibility was very poor. As we had confronted with U.S. PT boats on our way to Kolombangara, I ordered our men to take their offensive positions and keep watch especially.
>
> At about 2:30 A.M. we discovered an enemy boat bearing at about 10 [degrees] right, 800–1,000 meters from us. In a moment I took it for PT boat and planned the heading straight for her, which we thought the best tactics. I ordered the helmsman, "Ten degrees turn! PT boat heading," and made our destroyer face to the PT, which was bearing as before (I think it did not discover our destroyer at that time). In an instant we crashed into her and cut her in two. She went past by and sank down near our stern, flaming up.[13]

Later, facing a possible court-martial, Jack would claim that he had been aware of *Amagiri* and that he was turning his boat to go into full attack. The idea sounded heroic. Even if it had been true, it was a maneuver that went against all training. The vessels had to work together or take evasive action.

The second mistake was in not following orders. The military always planned for the worst. It trained the men on how to prepare for rescue whenever a mission went wrong on land, on sea, or in the air.

Jack Kennedy's surviving crew members were to fire a flare gun into the air the minute they hit the water. Jack felt certain that the flare gun also might bring Japanese who would kill the men under his command. Violating training, he planned to wait until daylight.

The PT boat burst into flames, instantly killing two men and leaving Patrick McMahon so badly burned that he could neither swim nor hold on to floating debris. There was no life raft, Kennedy having replaced it with a 37mm gun that he never had time to shoot. Fortunately, when the fire burned out, the gun's mounting plank was large enough for the men to use as a flotation device that kept them alive.

The men should not have had their vessel struck, and Kennedy should have followed procedure, but once in the water there is no question that he and two other crew members acted heroically. They kept those men who were living but too weak to save themselves afloat until they reached land. Kennedy used his teeth to hold McMahon's life jacket. Then, with the strongest helping the weakest, they spent the next four hours staying afloat while slowly moving to safety on an atoll approximately three and a half miles from where the boat went down.

While all this was taking place, Australian Army lieutenant Arthur Evans was working from a hidden observation post on the Kolombangara volcano. He saw the ramming and the fire, then made the radio contact needed to start the rescue on the landmass where they found safety.

Kennedy and the other men had been trained to stay in one place in circumstances such as they were encountering, then make themselves visible to aircraft. Instead of following the training, Kennedy ordered his men to hide each time a plane was near. Again he did not consider the fact that the danger from not being rescued was greater than the slight risk that a Japanese plane might be the spotter.

That night, at 8:00 P.M., he knew that PT boats might be in the area. He went to a section of the atoll called Ferguson Passage and tried to swim out to where he could find someone. The effort so exhausted him, he nearly drowned before he could return to land.

The following day Lieutenant (j. g.) Kennedy again went out, this time ordering one of the crew, Barney Ross, to come with him. When Ross realized he was going to reach a dangerous level of exhaustion, he returned to the atoll.

On the third day the men moved to another, more visible nearby island, where there was enough food and water to sustain them. Kennedy again ordered Ross into the water. The other men, following their training, were able to link up with natives who helped them.

It took a week for the crew to be fully reunited. Joe Kennedy was alerted as a courtesy. It also was clear that there would be an official inquiry and probable court-martial, something that would destroy Jack's future.

Joe contacted Arthur Krock, and suddenly there was a *New York Times* story that Joe Kennedy's son saved ten crewmen in the Pacific. According to the early, controlled press release, Jack had spotted the destroyer speeding toward his PT boat. Too late to avoid a direct encounter, the crew was summoned to general quarters and prepared for a torpedo attack. The calamity was inevitable, but they were not going down without a fight. Tragically, they were struck before the torpedo could be launched.

There was talk of a Silver Star until the men being pushed by Joe to honor Jack rebelled. Joe was a close friend of Undersecretary of the Navy James J. Forrestal. But the undersecretary was not in the midst of action where men truly were acting properly, heroically, and often suffering horribly every day. Jack Kennedy was a failure, not a hero.

Jack was awarded a lifesaving medal to appease his father. The commendation did not mention the fact that had he acted properly, the lifesaving rescue probably would not have been necessary.

Joe next contacted Jack's friend John Hersey, a Pulitzer Prize–winning writer who was working for the *New Yorker* magazine. He told Joe's version of what happened in the Pacific, turning Jack into a hero and making the incident seem unavoidable. Then the article was condensed in *Reader's Digest*. Eventually there would be a book and then a movie. The created heroism of *PT-109*'s skipper would help propel him to national attention.

Joe also worked with the Boston newspapers. An artist re-created the daring rescue at sea, a technique Joe learned from his friend William Randolph Hearst, who had used the idea to start the Spanish-American War. He sent artist Frederick Remington to Cuba to paint scenes of the violence and horror experienced by the people who were facing a developing war. The artist wired the publisher that nothing of the sort was happening. Hearst did not care. He wired back that Remington should send the (false) pictures and Hearst would start the war.

The Boston pictures "re-created" the seven days of horror and heroism. Then Joe Kennedy was hailed as the "father of the hero." And in the midst of this, Joe Jr. was forgotten.

Joe Jr. may have been a lot of things in his brief life, but in the military he had discovered patriotism, dedication, and courage. He volunteered for the Aphrodite Project, a desperate effort to counter the German government's successful development of the V-1 rocket "buzz bombs."

Desperate to counter the missiles, they invented a modified unmanned plane to drop from a larger aircraft and attack by remote control.

The remote-controlled plane, a PBY-4, would be loaded with explosives. One man would be inside until the plane could be maneuvered within probable striking distance of the identified V-1 missile launch site. Then a last-minute hookup would turn the aircraft into a time bomb aimed at the target site. The pilot would bail out and could be safely on the ground when the remote-control plane struck and exploded.

Two branches of the service participated in the attacks against positions in different sections of France. The army air force targeted one V-1 launch site, and the navy air wing, to which Joe Jr. belonged, targeted the second.

The army attacked first. Its plane went off course, because of unexpected wind changes, failure to properly control the plane remotely, or too premature a launch. This left the second site and the navy's attempt, to be handled by Joe Jr. This was a volunteer assignment, a fact his family knew nothing about, including when he had briefly taken leave to return home and hear his brother feted for heroism both men knew had not occurred.

Joe Jr. listened to the way his father handled the aftermath of the sinking and how he had manipulated the facts to keep his fool of a brother out of the brig. Jack was no hero. If there was a hero in the family, it was Joe Jr., though he would not violate the trust he had been given by saying anything about the work he was doing.

During the visit Joe Jr. and Joe Timilty, a friend of the elder Kennedy, shared a room. Timilty later said that when Joe Jr. thought he was asleep after the dinner honoring Jack, he heard the youth crying in frustration.

Joe Jr. knew that the Aphrodite program was dangerous. He had volunteered because, like other navy men involved with dangerous missions, he felt that he should take greater risks than those men who had wives and children. Still, if everything was handled correctly, the risks should have been minimal.

The mission was scheduled for August 12, but it was not a high priority. It could have been handled later. There was no critical window of opportunity. There were two planes being used at two sites, and one had failed. Others could be modified for future tries. However, with luck the navy's target would be eliminated.

On August 11, 1944, electronics officer Earl Olsen found that there were circuit problems on the plane. Possibly it meant nothing. However, if it was serious, switching from manual flight of the plane to automatic controls could accidentally detonate the explosives, killing Kennedy. Olsen said that it was up to Joe whether he wanted to take the chance because Olsen would need only a few hours' time to make all the corrections.

Whether or not the danger was stressed, the fact was that it was Joe's judgment call. He decided when he would go up. He decided whether to delay the flight by twenty-four hours. The target would still be there. The V-1 problem would still need to be taken out.

From all accounts that could be reviewed, the facts seem quite simple yet shocking as yet another of the myths created by the Kennedys. Joe seemed certain he would die by going up before Olsen checked the wiring. He had a girlfriend named Pat Wilson back in the United States. He told others he wanted to call her, to say good-bye, but that was not possible. Instead, he wrote a will and divided his possessions among his friends.

The top officers for the Aphrodite project were uncertain what to do with the information from Olsen and the desire of the pilot, Joe Kennedy Jr., to go up. He was an experienced pilot, well trained for the mission. He knew how to jump from the plane and had practiced in England. There was no reason why he couldn't succeed if everything was working, and Olsen could not say for certain that the pilot wouldn't make it. They decided to let Joe make the choice, and he took off at 6:00 P.M.

It was Sunday, August 13, 1944. Joe, Rose, and most of their children were in their Hyannis Port home. It was a hot day, and the children were going to compete in a sailboat race. Only Jack would watch from shore, his body too battered for any physical exertion.

Joe, tired, decided to take a nap before the race began. As he slept, two priests drove to the house and told Rose that her son was missing in action. Then they asked her to awaken Joe so they could speak to him.

Only the briefest of information was exchanged. Joe had not known about the secret mission. He had not known about his son's courage. And he did not realize the stress that caused him to go up that day. All that mattered was that twenty-eight minutes into the mission, at the time when the electronic switching would have been activated, the plane blew up in the sky. There was no sign of a parachute. There was no indication that Joe had gotten out of the plane.

Shocked, Joe Sr. gathered all his children onto the back porch. He gave them the news, then told them to carry on as before, including competing in the race. To the family's credit, the siblings have talked about competing that day, not trying to hide what, to outsiders, seems a rather cold and distant reaction. What they have not said, probably did not remember, was whether they won.[14]

The other victim in all this is rarely recognized this way. "Teddy" Kennedy, one of the most influential legislators in the United States despite keeping a little boy's nickname, was twelve years old and suddenly alone. The older brother and sister who had served as surrogate parents were gone. They had disappeared from his world, and the knowledge that one was dead did not mean anything.

The final victim of the war years was not so influenced by Joe as the others had been. If anything, she was encouraged to act independently until her new lifestyle caused a further schism between her parents.

Kathleen returned to England to help with the war effort. Americans had to make do with rationing and grieving. The British were dying, their island nation under attack. She could not stand by and ignore them.

The romance with Billy became so intense that Kick explained to her father that the only concern she had was with her religion. She was a devout Catholic. She was in love with an Anglican. Being in love was not a sin, yet she knew that the Catholic Church frowned on marriage outside her faith.

Joe talked with Archbishop Francis J. Spellman of New York to see if the couple could marry in a ceremony in a Catholic Church building. They could not. Thus they decided to have a civil ceremony in England. Joe Jr. was still alive and able to attend, since his launch site was in the London area. Other family friends also were present. The date was May 6, 1944, and in ten minutes the couple felt they had grasped the happiness each had always sought, while Rose, who remained in the United States, became convinced that her daughter was literally going to hell.

For one month the couple was able to both enjoy the moment and plan for the future. They honeymooned at Compton Place in Eastbourne. They knew the intensity of wartime marriage, something experienced by many of their friends and acquaintances. Then Billy had to return to duty to be part of the Normandy invasion that began on June 6, 1944.

Kick decided to return home to Hyannis Port to see her family while Billy was on duty. She was Lady Hartington when she arrived, and on September 10 she learned she was a widow. Rose considered the death of Billy to be God's punishment for her daughter's marrying outside the Catholic Church, a fact she tried to convince Kathleen to believe. When Kick returned to England, the country she considered her home, Billy's sister commented on the overwhelming stress Rose had placed on Kathleen. "I never met anyone so desperately unhappy in my life. I had to sleep in her room night after night. Her mother had tried to convince her that she had committed a sin in this marriage, so that in addition to losing a husband, she worried about losing her soul."

And so the war years passed. Joe had everything he thought he wanted and nothing he expected to receive. He had lost much more than his reputation, of course. He put Jack in a life-threatening situation when the youth was unfit for any military service, much less one in which command judgment was critical. Joe Jr., overwhelmed by the false hero,

Rear Admiral Felix Gygax, commandant of 1st Naval District, presents the posthumously awarded Navy Cross to Joe and Rose Kennedy as a result of their late son's heroic actions during World War II. (Cleveland State University Library, Special Collections)

seemingly took his own life. And the beloved Kick's radical new lifestyle created a nightmare for Rose, and Kick herself had become a tragic, lonely, guilt-ridden figure.

As for Rosemary, no one can say whether Joe would have gone ahead with the surgery had he known the outcome. No one can say whether a protected child living in a woman's body was better in his mind than an independent woman with no sense of what being a Kennedy meant. What is certain is that he had no more contact with her than Rose, paying the bills for her care, leaving her with a trust fund, but destroying any semblance of the life she otherwise might have led.

Joe Kennedy had walked with kings and presidents. He had changed Hollywood, only to have the studio heads hate him more for his seeming anti-Semitism than they once lauded him for saving their companies and making them rich. Joe had enjoyed sex with movie stars and other beautiful women, yet the woman closest to him throughout the years went from worshiping him to respecting him to hating him perhaps as much as she once desired him for every dance and every free moment of their young lives together. He had far surpassed the achievements of his father-in-law, then watched when Roosevelt favored the eccentric old man to the "obviously" superior ambassador. And Joe had money. He could travel anywhere in the world, do anything he desired. But there was nowhere he really wanted to go now that the war was over, at least not for pleasure.

The only thing left seemed to be politics, and since his own career was shattered, he looked to Jack to be a surrogate for himself, someone around whom the entire family would rally. The Kennedys still would have their day, whatever that meant. Power would be regained and become greater than before, no matter what favors Joe had to call in and no matter how disreputable those he planned to use to help him.

17

ADRIFT

THERE WERE TWO STAGES IN THE LIFE OF JOSEPH P. KENNEDY. THE first was the era of rising power, influence, and rapidly increasing wealth. Had Joe died in place of his oldest son, obituary writers would have established a legend around his name greater than that of such contemporaries as Henry Ford and William Randolph Hearst, and their records were considerable. Ford died a man honored for innovations in automobile production whose creation helped end the isolation of rural America. Hearst revealed the power of the media conglomerate and the way the press could influence the political course of a nation. Yet both were radicals held in disdain for their private lives—Ford for his isolationism and virulent anti-Semitism, Hearst for his flaunted adultery. Both men died with the good lauded, the bad ignored, and biographers telling abridged stories in books meant to inspire the young in the manner of the Horatio Alger stories, where hard work and determination overcome all obstacles.

Had Joe Kennedy died during World War II, he would have been known for being a bank president, for helping run Fore River Shipyards, and, later, for being appointed to the Maritime Commission. He would have been lauded for turning his knowledge of investing into service as the first commissioner of the Securities and Exchange Commission. And he would have been most highly praised for ignoring personal gain to help his nation in the difficult days just prior to formal involvement in World War II. There would have been discussion of the Hollywood years, focusing on the creative use of mergers and acquisitions to modify the industry as it moved from silent films to talkies. And any writer who dared to hint at his liquor industry business would likely have made oblique reference to Joe as an "importer."

Rose would have reveled in the minutiae of Joe's death. The funeral would have been led by every Catholic dignitary of any importance in the United States and certainly would have warranted an emissary from the Vatican. She would have traveled after the funeral and been welcomed in England, France, and other nations of the world in a manner he had never been received after his time as ambassador. The leaders who saw her would have talked about the greatness of her husband and embraced a woman who had suffered the loss of a son in war and a husband in public service.

Instead, Joe lived to see his original hopes and dreams shattered. He would not run for political office because he could not. He had been exposed too often in the foreign press. He had made too many enemies among increasingly powerful American newspaper columnists such as Drew Pearson. He had attacked the leaders of the Hollywood studios long after they felt they needed his expertise, and they were ready to counter with their own accusations about his failings. The only friends he retained were his closest associates and men both inside and on the fringe of organized crime.

Information about Joe in the period of transition from public figure to backroom manipulator—roughly 1945 through 1960—has come in ways that preclude anyone knowing the full truth. Instead there is a mosaic of stories from sources who were around him during this time. Chauncey Holt, the man who worked as Meyer Lansky's Miami, Florida, accountant immediately after the war, remembers Joe drinking, dining, and gambling in Lansky's Colony Club. Always there was a woman. Always Joe avoided having his picture taken by the club photographer who moved from table to table, snapping portraits for couples desiring a memento of the evening. And always there was tension between Kennedy and Lansky, with whom he had been at odds during Prohibition.

In the 1950s Lansky had gained national notoriety when Tennessee senator Estes Kefauver electrified the nation with televised hearings into organized crime. Kefauver moved from city to city, revealing the dark underbelly of corruption throughout the nation. He exposed everything from mob influence in Texas to the figures who were the earliest investors in the creation of Las Vegas. Meyer Lansky arranged for the assassination of his close associate Benjamin Siegel (known as "Bugsy" outside his hearing) after Siegel and his girlfriend Virginia Hill skimmed or misspent more than $500,000 from the money set aside for the Las Vegas Flamingo Hotel's construction. Kefauver's investigators revisited the case four years after the fact, not getting an indictment but titillating the nation with a group of colorful, often violent characters.

That the Kefauver hearings were televised was something so new that most Americans lacked television sets. Instead, movie theaters throughout the nation rented, borrowed, or purchased the largest receivers they could find, setting them up side by side for viewing.

The Kefauver committee did not subpoena Joe Kennedy, and it is not known if he should have been. However, a number of businesses he

owned, and the men who fronted for Kennedy, were identified in the
hearings. It was obvious to Joe that the less reputable business ties had
to be reduced to avoid too much scrutiny of his family as his sons
moved into public careers of their own.

The most important revelation in the hearings concerning Joe came
when it was reported that Kennedy had hired Connecticut attorney
Thomas J. Cassara to head Somerset Importers in 1944. Cassara seemed
the perfect man for the job. He had a long history in ownership and
management of Miami Beach hotels and obviously understood all aspects of the hospitality business. What made Joe nervous was that it was
noted during the hearings that Cassara was not actually the investor in
the hotels. Instead he was the front man, doing the work of a number
of organized crime figures who supplied the money, made the profits,
and presumably took the skimmings.

Chicago-based Cassara was placed in charge of Somerset, and in the
following year, 1945, Joe bought the Merchandise Mart, arguably the
most important investment in his portfolio. It was the largest building
in the world at that time. When built just fifteen years earlier, it contained a block-long speakeasy. There is no evidence whether Kennedy
had money in the former Prohibition drinking palace, but he was
believed to have owned or have invested in two saloons near the Merchandise Mart. Gambling and prostitution were rife in the area. Some
of the East Chicago Avenue police district officers were allegedly either
paid off or ordered not to make arrests by supervisors who were on the
take. Every businessperson in the area, presumably including Joe Kennedy, made monthly payments to assure smooth operations.

Cassara worked relatively unnoticed until he was shot to death in the
Trade Winds nightclub in the East Chicago Avenue area. Then it was
learned that one of his business partners was Rocco DeStefano, perhaps
the key to the Kennedy/Cassara linkup. DeStefano was a first cousin of
Al Capone, with whom Joe was connected for liquor deliveries during
Prohibition.

The Cassara shooting also may have been meant to be taken as a
message by Kennedy. However, this was an era when the mob settled
disputes among its own, and Joe was not known to be in the middle of
any mob problems. More likely he saw that growing mob violence could
lead to public exposure of mob-connected businesses. Worse, he knew
that at the time there were FBI documents being developed that linked
organized crime figures with Kennedy, though such documents would
not be available to the public until long after his death.

In 1946, because of these concerns, Joe sold the liquor business that had netted him at least $1 million a year. The sale was to such upstanding citizens as Longy Zwillman and Joe Reinfeld. Reinfeld, the lesser known of the two, was the Prohibition era alcohol supplier to New York mobsters such as Waxey Gordon. Abner "Longy" Zwillman headed all rackets in New Jersey. When he was in partnership with Reinfeld, he also was known as a member of the Mafia ruling commission. Although most people think of the five families of New York, he made his deal with Joe when he was in partnership with Frank Costello, Tony Accardo (head of the Capone family when Capone went to jail for income-tax evasion), Joe Adonis, Jake Guzick, and Meyer Lansky.

There was another reason for Joe to sell. The Massachusetts Democratic Party knew that Jack was going to make a bid for Congress. The youth was going to be positioned as a war hero, the debilitating condition sometimes evident when he made appearances readily connected with the war. He had been to Harvard. He had been around the world. He would be hard to criticize, even by a more experienced candidate.

Instead of attacking Jack, supporters of opposition candidates were looking to embarrass him by revealing allegedly disreputable actions by his father. Joe learned this, making reference to his fear of both the opposition and the media in a July 31, 1946, letter to Sir James Calder, chairman of the Distillers Company. Among the allegations Joe expected to be raised was that he supported the loans to England in the early days of the war solely to gain the Haig & Haig franchise. Joe claimed that as the father of a congressman, and by implication still an important person in the U.S. government, any support Jack might give England over Russia could be construed as the son acting for his father's benefit. Joe wanted the public to see Jack's stands as reasoned, not based on a business deal.

The only mob-connected business in which Joe kept an interest was racetrack investment. He bought 17 percent of Miami's Hialeah Racetrack in 1943, later selling it for a profit. He also tried to buy Boston's Suffolk Downs but was not the high bidder.

Joe's racetrack ownership would not be a problem for Jack. Organized criminals understood that it was a cash business that could easily be rigged to launder money when desired.[1] However, so were restaurants, and no one ever faulted someone for becoming a restaurateur. J. Edgar Hoover, the most respected lawman in the nation, was regularly photographed at racetracks, dutifully staying at the $2 winner so no one would suspect he was a heavy gambler.

The most serious problem facing the Kennedys was reestablishing the family name in Massachusetts. Joe had turned his back on his father's prominence, seeking to create a life in New York, Palm Beach, Hollywood, and Chicago. The newspapers told of the former local man who made movies and bought the Merchandise Mart, but that was quite different from his creating business opportunities in the state where he was raised.

The visceral reaction against Joe was evident in 1945 when Massachusetts governor Maurice J. Tobin asked Joe to head a commission that would look into establishing a state department of commerce. Joe was to travel throughout the state, looking at the wool mills, the shoe factories, and the other businesses that dominated the area. He was to consider how the end of the war would affect such industries as the shipyards. He was to try to decide what could be done to save the state from economic disaster.

No one doubted Kennedy's capabilities. The problem was his purchase of the Merchandise Mart. The building, twenty-four stories tall and with ninety-three acres of retail and office space, was well known throughout the nation. The purchase seemed like a major commitment to the city of Chicago, creating the impression that Illinois, not Massachusetts, would be where Kennedy's heart and money relocated after the war.

The brilliance of the Merchandise Mart purchase was not understood. Marshall Field and Company built the structure for $30 million. Joe paid $12,956,516, approximately $8 million less than the owner desired.[2] A mortgage for $12.5 million was borrowed from the Equitable Life Assurance Society with a total cash outlay of approximately $1 million.

But there were other factors in the Merchandise Mart deal, ones that further complicated the situation. In 1941 Joe learned of Manhattan real-estate broker John J. Reynolds's work for Archbishop Spellman and other wealthy real-estate holders. Spellman, like Catholic Church leaders around the country, had all regional church property in his name as the highest church official in the city. Without such authority, the buying and selling of church property would have to involve the Vatican's officials as well as local church leaders, complicating all real-estate matters. Instead the property was in the archbishop's name, so a single signature could authorize a transaction. Reynolds was one of the fortunate real-estate experts who brokered what often were multimillion-dollar deals. The commissions made him wealthy.

Joe was planning to sell his twenty-room mansion in Bronxville, New York, so he could declare the family's Florida home as the permanent residence. Florida had no income taxes or inheritance taxes, and Joe did not care where he lived.

Reynolds showed Kennedy the potential for making money in Manhattan real-estate sales even without such clients as the Catholic Church. The 1920s and 1930s had been a time of extensive construction in the city. The Depression and the war years had driven the value of holdings to a point that seemed to be the base for a new real-estate boom. This was still an era of low rents, of families living comfortably in large apartments despite modest means. Yet all the reasons people desire Manhattan real estate—the access to shopping, entertainment, recreation, and the like, and all within a short distance of one another—made it obvious that prices would rise.

Joe established two holding companies in New York: Ken Industries and the Park Agency, Inc. The latter was the headquarters for the family fortune. The Park Agency handled trust funds, allowances, and any problems for his sons, daughters, and, eventually, grandchildren that could be taken care of with a check. Eventually he would place his son-in-law Steve Smith, the husband of Jean Kennedy, in position as the head of the Park Agency, essentially passing the mantle of most powerful male in the family to a trusted outsider. But for the moment, Joe was firmly in charge of his real-estate destiny, working with the trusted advice of Reynolds.

Joe was never greedy, at this time never concerned with assessed value. He wanted to know what he had to pay and what a relatively quick resale could bring. For example, on Madison Avenue and Fifty-first Street, just behind St. Patrick's Cathedral, was a $1 million property known as the Fahnestock mansion. Joe ignored the assessed valuation and convinced the owners that a low-priced sale was better than perhaps waiting years for another buyer. He convinced them to sell the mansion for $250,000, then resold it for $200,000 more. Both sales were far below what the mansion was supposed to be worth, yet Joe saw that if he could almost double his money, there was no reason to hold the property.

Larger properties led to greater profits, though for different reasons. Usually the buildings were rented for amounts that could be substantially raised with a new lease, or there were high vacancies that would have occupants after the war. The late 1940s and early 1950s saw an explosion in corporate headquarters, advertising agencies, photography studios, design studios, and numerous other businesses that had previously not existed or been too small to be meaningful. The baby boom helped retailers, and the city began to prosper in ways that drove up the value of buildings. Property on Lexington Avenue did especially well for Joe. One building, at Fifty-first Street and Lexington, eventually was resold for six times what he paid; another, at Forty-sixth, went for almost triple. He also did well on parcels of land in the other boroughs and office buildings in the more popular suburbs.

Joe learned to treat real estate like margin stock buying. He would borrow most of the money for a building at a rate that was close to prime. The rental income on the building would be planned so it exceeded prime by enough of a percentage to make a substantial profit over the interest rate on his loan. Frequently he would pay only 10 percent out of pocket.

Joe then engaged in price gouging and the manipulation of existing tenants. He never bought a building unless he saw how it could make money for him. For example, in the case of the Merchandise Mart, the executives at Marshall Field bemoaned the fact that a third of the property was rented by government agencies. The lease agreement was extremely low, but the space was full. Marshall Field personnel decided to sell, taking a loss on the building, because they were certain that when the government agencies moved out, there would be massive amounts of vacant space.

Kennedy recognized that he had the luxury of time that Marshall Field did not. The property had no other serious investors looking at it, and all of them were concerned with the government leases. Joe decided not to buy until he had arranged for new tenants.

For seven months Joe aggressively sought tenants who would pay substantially more for rent than the government after Joe bought the property, the government leases expired, and the agencies moved out. He made the purchase only when he knew there were confirmed new tenants willing to pay higher rents when he took over the property.

The transition for the New York properties was never so smooth. Joe had a tendency to force existing tenants to either pay substantially higher rents once their leases ran out, locked in for five years with only Kennedy's holding company able to cancel the lease at the end of two years, or leave. Frequently rents were doubled, and the price gouging became serious enough to lead to an investigation by the New York City Council. The focus was a West Side loft building purchased in 1943, the year before the inquiry. Reynolds handled the matter for his partner, explaining that Joe Kennedy should not be smeared, that Joe Kennedy knew nothing of the building or the transaction, that John J. Ford of Boston, who was operating on behalf of a trust fund for the Kennedy children, had conducted the purchase and rent arrangements. The idea that any purchase or sale would be made with Kennedy money without Joe being aware was nonsense. However, no one from either side could prove that the Ford story was only partially correct.

The Kennedy modus vivendi with tenants led to the now-famous rent control laws that protected and sometimes still protect New Yorkers from outrageous rent raises (and ultimately brought them some of the greatest real-estate bargains in the country). Joe did not worry about it. He sold the property that had been under scrutiny, walking away with $1 million profit.

The most outrageous arrangement Joe Kennedy made came many years later, with a small building he owned at 70 Columbus Circle in Manhattan. According to Kennedy, the property had a 1956 valuation of $1.1 million. His appraisers came up with the price for tax purposes, and his lawyers demanded that the city accept the private appraisal so Joe would not pay too much in taxes.

In the months that followed, all the buildings in the immediate area were valued for purposes of condemnation to clear the land and build what would become Lincoln Center for the Performing Arts. A new private assessment was made, and suddenly the 70 Columbus Circle property had an assessed value of $1,750,000, more than six times the value of all the surrounding properties. The Kennedy building was the last parcel needed, and it was finally acquired for $2.5 million.

There was opposition to the transaction, but the payment was upheld. The state Supreme Court ruled that Kennedy's greed and attempt to avoid taxes had nothing to do with the real value of the building. He never explained why the selling price was radically higher than those for all similar buildings acquired.

His involvement in New York real estate, netting him an estimated $100 million in ten years, and his growing real-estate empire in Chicago, where it made national news, evoked attacks against Joe Kennedy as someone who did not care about Boston. They raised valid questions, especially since Joe was openly pessimistic about the Massachusetts business climate. He did not want to buy property that might benefit the state but was of poor quality, vacant and without prospects for leasing, or otherwise a bad deal.

As to John Ford, the "fall guy" in the New York investigation into Kennedy's rent gouging, he was the quiet front man for much of Joe's holdings. He looked after everything from the movie theaters Kennedy owned to the trust funds for the family members. He was in charge of issuing checks for various family personal and political activities. However, he acted only with Joe's full knowledge and review of all records.

Joe had made his start in Boston, trying to become an intimate of the power elite. Failing in his efforts, he turned his back on the city. Now he was forced to return, and the people in Boston who were indifferent to Joe Kennedy were also the ones most important to his son Jack. These were young men and women, fresh from the war, and often from families who owned successful businesses their sons would eventually take over.

The men and women coming home from World War II recognized that they were the first generation born in the twentieth century to move into politics. In their minds they had come of age in a time more modern than their parents understood. They had been tempered by war. Now they were marrying, having children, entering careers. Some also had families who were long active in politics, if only as fund-raisers and campaigners, and these were people who could be of value for a new, young candidate. Jack Kennedy was one of their own, and though they saw him as a lightweight, someone without a meaningful understanding of social needs and world affairs, he was still one of them. They would support his running for office where, presumably, he would grow in knowledge and skill.

Joe began the process of getting Jack known within the city. In April 1945, with Jack rail-thin, often sick, and showing the first symptoms of what would be diagnosed as a slow-acting form of leukemia, Joe arranged for Jack to be cochairman of a second economic survey of Massachusetts. Joe knew that it did not matter what the committee's findings might be. If Jack and the others thought the economy was solid, that there was enough business to take up the slack in postwar manufacturing demands, he would look like a hero capable of leading the area with his insightful knowledge of the future. If Jack and the others thought the economy were failing, that unemployment would rise dramatically, that the area was in crisis, the problems would not be blamed on him. Instead, his insight would assure that he knew what to do to make changes. His image could not suffer no matter what was taking place.

Next Joe and his father-in-law, Honey Fitz, began working with Congressman James M. Curley of the Eleventh Congressional District. They hated the man but knew he had ambitions outside of Congress.

He wanted to be mayor of Boston, and that was something they could help him achieve. Between Honey Fitz's connections and Joe's money, Curley ran for the position and won, leaving his congressional seat open.

Not that Congress was the only choice. Massachusetts governor Maurice Tobin was running for reelection in 1946, and he needed someone on the ballot running for lieutenant governor. This was a state where each man ran alone, so the party affiliations did not matter. A Republican could win one position and a Democrat the other. Tobin was a Republican and favored for reelection, but he was likely to leave office partway through his term. One of the state's U.S. senators was dying, and when he did, Tobin was looking to take the position for himself. The lieutenant governor would move into the top spot according to Massachusetts law. At that point Jack would gain a position that, at twenty-eight, he might have been considered too young and inexperienced to achieve through the election process.

The problem with Jack running for lieutenant governor was that Massachusetts politics was cutthroat war. Honey Fitz experienced the viciousness when Toodles brought him down. The Republicans would find any scandal they could to attack Jack if he tried for too-high-a-profile office, as lieutenant governor would be. They would likely use his poor judgment as a PT boat skipper, along with anything else they could get. He would likely lose, ending a political career that had yet to begin.

The final decision to keep Jack out of the lieutenant governor's race was ironically made by Joe Kane, a man who had been brought in to help with strategy. John Fitzgerald hated Kane, the brains behind James Curley's 1913 campaign against himself. They had gone to Kane because Honey Fitz recognized the wisdom in such Kane statements as "In politics you have no friends, only coconspirators."

The Eleventh Congressional District was a different matter. It was arguably of greater importance, but it was lower in profile and did not concern the entire state. However, it carried with it such national prestige that Rose Kennedy thought it would be better for her son to start lower and work his way up from local politics or the state legislature like her father and Joe's father had done before him.

Joe Kane, John Fitzgerald, and Joe Kennedy all agreed that Jack should aim higher than Rose wanted for that first race. They carefully analyzed the state, the places where Jack might have appeal, and recognized that the Eleventh Congressional District was the one place where Jack could have success. This was because the seat would be open only if Curley won the general election for mayor, and then a special election, always assuring a low voter turnout, would be held for the House seat.

Both the Republicans and the Democrats spent most of their money in the regular election, where Curley won the mayor's seat and kept his House seat. Many of the men who might have opposed Jack for Congress decided to try for other offices in case Curley stayed in his House seat. Jack came into a new race with fresh money and a new name.

Oddly, the success of the campaign required a degree of vision, not usually a strong point for Joe. By planning how to take the office in advance, the entire Kennedy family was hitting the streets in February 1946, their first goal being winning the Democratic primary to be held on June 18.

The other important concern was the demographic makeup of the Eleventh Congressional District. It was an area the eighty-three-year-old Honey Fitz knew well, an area old P. J. Kennedy would have instantly understood. The people were blue-collar and often of limited education. Their sons had, for the most part, been in the infantry— "cannon fodder"—and many of the older women were gold star mothers (women given a gold star to put in their windows to show that they had lost a son in combat).

Joe Kennedy made the initial move on behalf of his son by bringing together youths who had been through some of the same experiences. He paid for the Joseph P. Kennedy Jr. Veterans of Foreign Wars Post. They first met in the Puritan Hotel on Beacon Street, a strategic location. It was near the Harvard Club. It was near the neighborhoods where Jack would have to campaign. The sons of blue-collar families would be pleased to meet in so nice a location, and the sons of the more well-to-do also would feel comfortable in such surroundings. The VFW post would bring together a broad spectrum of backgrounds, money, and influence.

There were a dozen men at first, including Edgar Grossman, who worked in his family's successful printing business after returning from the war. He also was a longtime active member of the Democratic Party. All the youths attending that first meeting were unwitting pawns for Jack, the post's first commander, and Joe Kane. It was Kane who created what would be the slogan first used in 1946, "The New Generation Offers a Leader," and the idea was brilliant. Kane was sixty-six at the time and did not live to see the full impact of what he started, but many of the men connected with the campaign credit the slogan with ultimately keeping Senator Ted Kennedy in office.

The impact of the emotions behind the slogan was evident while interviewing Democratic leaders, both current and retired. They repeatedly made derogatory remarks about Teddy, today one of the most powerful men in the Senate. Yet before and after joining the Senate, he also was an embarrassment. He was known for overeating, womanizing, drinking too much, and being responsible for the death of a young woman who had worked for his brother Bobby's presidential campaign. Teddy was regularly in the supermarket tabloids, exposed for one irresponsible act or another. And there was a rumor among staff people that a deal had been cut where the senator would give at least one tabloid periodic stories, often working against him, in exchange for their not printing other true stories that might force him from office. Yet he always maintained the support of his constituency.

"He's our only link with that era," several older leaders of the Democratic Party told me, referring to the heady times when they won the war, married their sweethearts, started families, and proudly began their adult lives. "He reminds us of the hope and promise we felt with Jack." "If we vote him out of office, our generation becomes as meaningless as we once thought the men in power were when we came back from war." And in Massachusetts Jack was the first to take the lead.

June 17, 1946, was the day the first large political move was made in anticipation of the primary election just twenty-four hours away. For several weeks a number of other men had talked about and/or campaigned for the Democratic Party nomination for congressional representative. These included such politically experienced individuals as the mayor of Cambridge. Then came June 17, a regional Charlestown holiday commemorating the Battle of Bunker Hill. Veterans would be marching, and Joe Kane arranged for the Joseph P. Kennedy Jr. VFW Post to be part of it all.

"Every other veterans' organization came in full regalia with hats, uniforms, color guard, flags, sometimes a band. This group appeared without trappings, without anything fancy. In fact, they were told what to wear and everybody was asked to wear dark trousers, black shoes, white shirts, a simple tie, and no conventional military hats. Not military at all. You'd never know what they were except that there was a little banner identifying them," said Grossman.

"And we marched the full route—I think it was two or three miles—Jack was up at the head of the line, and it was not in a military formation. It was a loosely jointed military formation. We were in rows, but not keeping step. But we made a nice appearance.

"It was the new look. A fresh wind was blowing. And John F. Kennedy led this fresh wind.

"It was refreshing."

It also emphasized the message Kane wanted them to project. They were the new generation, born in the twentieth century, tempered by war, and ready to take command.

There were other ex-GIs using a similar approach around the country. Several men made their political moves at this time. Richard Nixon, Joe McCarthy, and George Bush Sr. were politicians who came from this same generation and tempering experience.

Jack never was a campaigner, never an aggressive individual. His grandfather could walk into a room filled with strangers and give them the impression that they were people he had been waiting to meet his entire life. He became a part of them, if only for a minute, warmly shaking hands, commiserating about any loss, sharing their joy over any celebration, and understanding any problem they related.

Most Boston politicians were similar to Honey Fitz. They understood the need to create an image that would take them to victory.

Jack was different. As Edgar Grossman, also a combat veteran, noted, "Jack never had, in my opinion, the desire, the ambition, the intestinal fortitude, the stomach, for a political campaign. He was a quiet, laid-back, somewhat introverted person, seemingly kind, gentle, and hardly one that you'd expect to get into the dirt which politics in general, and Massachusetts politics in particular, are duly noted."

There was a joke told after Jack began his political career that he was the only politician in Boston who attended a wake only if he actually knew the deceased.

Joe understood a little of what his father-in-law had accomplished by personality, competence, and bribery, and he created his own variation. Sometimes the money he ordered spent was subtle. Host a gathering to introduce the candidate to your friends and neighbors in an area that was either against Jack or unpredictable, and Joe would see that you were paid $100 for "expenses." Families could count on another $50 each if they would help at the voting places on Election Day. The money was paid even if they did not show up as expected. Joe knew how they would vote, and that was all that mattered.

Joe Kane also made certain the candidates understood the potential to make money. There were ten people in the primary. In addition to the Cambridge mayor, there were two Joe Russos. One Joe Russo was a popular city councilman. The second Joe Russo was someone Kane located and hired to go on the ballot to confuse the voters and diminish the power of the Russo name to draw votes away from Kennedy.

At least one of the ten candidates other than the second Joe Russo was being paid $7,500 to run. If it looked like Jack would do best competing in a crowded field, the man would stay in the race. If it looked as though the fewer people running in the primary, the better, the man would drop out.

One of the candidates was a woman from Somerville who also was a veteran. Major Catherine Falvey of the Women's Army Corps wanted to go to Washington. More important, she had lived in the area for years, absent only during army service. Jack had been gone from the area since he was eleven, and he had never voted there. He knew none of the residents and had yet to join the Democratic Party of which Falvey was a longtime member. (Jack had to join a minimum of twenty full days before the primary, a deadline he made with only days to spare.)

Joe wasn't certain what to do for Jack other than having an open checkbook to support all good ideas and necessary bribes. Rose later commented, "Joe was wise in the fields of national and international political affairs, but his interest dwindled as the political unit grew smaller. Events at the level of district, city, town, and ward left him progressively bored. Particularly in Boston. It was a life he had left long ago without regret."

But having an open checkbook was important, since Joe looked on Jack as a product to sell. He hired an advertising agency. Joe hired writers to create press releases that would remind the voters that his son was a war hero.

In contrast, Rose took to the streets. She knew there were three different images she could portray, each chosen for the specific audience.

First, she was a gold star mother who would be talking with many other gold star mothers. She had experienced the same loss they had. She knew what it was to grieve and never fully heal. She could speak from the heart, then move to the surviving son, the one running for public office and needing their support.

Second was the variation on the gold star mother. This was the woman who was proud of her son who was going from war to peacetime community service.

Third, she was Honey Fitz's daughter. John Fitzgerald may have been many things to these people, but everyone knew, either firsthand or from their parents and grandparents, that Honey Fitz took care of the community. He found people jobs. He was present for their pain.

He celebrated their weddings, the births of their children, the healing of their sick. He also did his share of campaigning for his grandson. In the end, Rose and her father bore the brunt of the active campaign, each moving among different constituents to be certain as many people were reached in the Eleventh Congressional District as possible.

Both Rose and Honey Fitz tried to take Jack to gatherings. Honey Fitz amazed everyone because he still remembered names. He had a facility for people that was extraordinary, and it was not unusual for him to introduce Jack to a roomful of people the old man had not talked to in decades, then have him say each one's name in turn as Jack shook his or her hand.

Rose went on a different route. Jack was seriously ill, and even when he was fairly strong, there were days when his flesh was discolored. She knew she would have to set up gatherings for her son, then plan how to handle matters if he could not show up himself.

The answer was Coffee with the Kennedys, using imprinted paper cups prepared by the Grossman family's printing business. They were run a little like Tupperware parties. Several women would come together to meet the candidate and his mother. They would talk, share coffee and tea, and be encouraged to have their husbands also vote for Jack.

Rose and/or several of her daughters always would be present. Jack would show up when he was healthy, stay away when he was not. Rose understood that these women were mothers and sisters with whom she could share "intimate" secrets of her love and pride.

The attitude was: "Jack's so busy, he overscheduled himself. He's rushing to get over here, but he's rushing to get over there. Rush. Rush. Rush. So much energy these young people have. It must be the rigors of the war. He starts early in the morning and goes nonstop until late at night. I don't know how he gets along with so little sleep, but when you care as much as he does. . . . I'm just glad he's so healthy."

The truth was that Jack was no more than twenty or twenty-five years from death. His body was almost constantly racked with illness and/or pain. It was only the assassination that saved the country from learning the truth earlier than it did. Jack's doctors did not expect him to survive past the first year of his second term. The medical treatment available at the time also was potentially deadly, slowing the body's decline rather than healing the ailments. For the moment he could still find prolonged periods when he could be fully active, and Rose lied about those hours or days when he was too overwhelmed to be in public.

Rose's work came during an odd period in history. Women had long had the vote, but Rose had seen that they did not exercise that right in proportions that could influence politics. In 1946 Rose focused on reaching the Eleventh Congressional District women who would influence their husbands. Some were registered or would be registered to vote before Election Day. Others just told the registered men in their lives what they expected. She was relieved to find that the Eleventh Congressional District was one where, though few women voted, they still voted more frequently than men. Many of them also credited Honey Fitz with giving them patronage jobs in their youth when they could not yet legally vote. If the old man had given them a hand when he had nothing to gain from it (ignoring the fact that fathers and brothers could vote), the women would reach out to the Fitzgerald grandson just starting his political career.

By the time Jack was running for president, Rose would go farther. She would organize a national voter registration campaign for women who, though enfranchised by law, disenfranchised themselves by inaction. Joe spent money. Rose handled the grassroots organizing that assured success.

Rose arranged for her daughters to participate in the campaign. Jean, in her first year of studies at Manhattanville College, which Kathleen also briefly attended, left school to help. Pat went from graduation at Rosemont to the streets of Boston. Even Eunice, who was working for the State Department helping former German prisoners of war, returned home from Washington, D.C.

Kick and Jack were close enough that she was anxious to return to the United States to campaign, but Rose would not tolerate it. Undoubtedly she was still angry about Kathleen's marriage to a Protestant, but there was also a practical reason to keep the American royalty out of the homes in the area. Joe Kane wanted a carefully orchestrated image because it was possible that Major Falvey could be the greatest threat to Jack's ability to get votes.

Catherine Falvey was a thirty-five-year-old attorney who had served at the war crimes trials in Nuremberg. She also had been in newspapers, on radio, and in newsreels played in movie theaters throughout the country. She also had served two terms in the state legislature. Jack could not match the quality she brought to the race. With such meaningful competition, Rose knew she had to build an image for Jack that would resonate with the voters.

Joe Kennedy had never paid attention to the men and women who came begging for help at his father's door. Rose had observed everything and everyone. She understood that the working-class, largely Irish Catholic Eleventh District women, often had lived hard lives of work, sacrifice, and the glimmer of hope that their sons would have a better life than they did. They wanted to see someone who understood what they felt. They wanted to see someone who could show them a better tomorrow was possible. And they would support an Irish Catholic youth—little more than a boy no matter what wartime hell he had endured—if he could be a role model for their own surviving sons. They liked the image of Rose living a life of glamour resulting from years of her husband's hard work, yet both Joe and Rose coming from what they imagined were backgrounds similar to their own.

Each day that there was a Coffee with the Kennedys, Rose, dressed in expensive clothing she had previously worn in England, went to the house chosen for the gathering. First there would be a theatrical entrance. If Rose was coming with her daughters, she made certain to arrive a few minutes after they did, entering alone, a small, stylish, articulate woman dressed in her finery. She talked about what it was like to be in the palace, to see, touch, and speak with the queen. She did not talk about being a gold star mother, but everyone knew that she was the mother of a large family, that her oldest son was dead, and that despite that, she had risen to a level of wealth and respect. Kathleen did not fit. It was one thing to talk about royalty, to be the fantasy of the working poor who might one day be able to be in the same room with someone so important. It was quite different to be royalty. Kick's presence would make evident how estranged the Kennedys were from the world of the congressional district Jack said he wanted to serve.

Rose understood that the women would vote for Jack and encourage their fathers, husbands, brothers, and sons to do the same because Jack represented the embodiment of their dreams. Jack was the boy who would benefit from his parents' hard work and sacrifice. Jack was the boy who would elevate the family in a way once thought impossible. Jack was the son living the life they hoped to have their sons experience. Or so they fantasized.

While Rose got the votes, Joe continued planning how to influence the election with his wealth. He arranged for an article to appear in *Look* magazine the week of the primary. Now long out of business, there was a time when three magazines—*Look*, the *Saturday Evening Post*, and *Collier's*—vied for attention in many, many homes. Each held an eclectic mix of fiction and nonfiction, humor, and always features about people who were important by virtue of being written about in the magazine. Sometimes they were individuals who were household names. Sometimes they were strangers whose first touch of fame came through the article. All of them reached a national audience, and for *Look* to have a Jack Kennedy story meant that the boy must be "somebody" special.

Look also was partially a picture magazine in the manner of *Life*, then a weekly companion to *Time*. *Look* had images of Honey Fitz, Joe, and Jack, stressing the continuity of public service. It was in *Look* that the writer stressed that Jack had taken up the mantle of his older brother, Joe Jr. The implication was that he was going to Congress for love of family, to honor the dreams of a youth whose life was tragically cut short in wartime.

The magazine was a national one, which meant that the vast majority of the readers did not know Jack, could not have voted for him if they wanted to do so, and probably would not remember who he was a week later, when the next issue reached the stands. This was a calculated decision. Joe hoped that the families who read *Look* in the Eleventh Congressional District would think that if Jack was important enough to be in a national magazine, he must be far better qualified than they realized.

Joe also arranged for the printing and mailing of ten thousand copies of one of the articles he had assured would be favorable to Jack. Yet for all the cost and all the effort, Rose made the greater impact.

Two days before the march that the VFW post seemed to dominate, Rose made her dramatic move. She rented Cambridge's Commodore Hotel ballroom, had Joe wear his formal clothes, and she and Eunice dressed as they might have in England, though without jewels. Jack was present—scrawny yet handsome. Some of the women saw him as a boy who had been through the hell of a war and now needed a loving mother to fatten him up. They understood that Rose was doing her best, but they felt the urge to help, one mother to another.

Other women saw a handsome lad returning to wholeness. He was rich, well educated, politically on the move, and they had lovely daughters who would make perfect wives.

The gathering had the formality and planning of a convoluted fairy tale. Jack was to be Cinderella, the "nobody" who would become beloved by the kingdom of the Eleventh District. The town's people became the royalty, specially chosen to come to the ball.

Rose obtained the names and mailing addresses of every registered voter. Eunice was assigned the task of making certain that thousands of invitations were personally signed and mailed. There was no dress code, other than for the Kennedys, and no one was to be excluded. A woman who cleaned toilets was as welcome as the wife of the CEO of a major corporation.

There may have been no dress code, but if a woman was going to a ball as an honored guest, the least she could do would be to dress with dignity. Every formal-wear shop in the surrounding area was stripped of garments. Rental places were emptied of everything they had and could locate from other shops farther out. It was alleged, though possibly not accurately, that some storeowners found they did more business that one day than they had done for all combined special events—weddings, proms, and the like—the previous year.

The ballroom was designed to hold fifteen hundred people, and it was always jammed that night. If one person stepped outside, one of the hundreds waiting to get in would take his or her place. There were traffic jams, and all city business came to a halt in the immediate area. Worse for Mike Neville, the local mayor and himself a candidate for Congress, the event was being held in his town, in the hotel he relied on for his own events.

No one could remember ever seeing anything like this campaign stunt. Men like Joe knew how to buy votes, where to spread their money, whom to bribe and when to do it. But a party for every registered voter in the district was beyond their comprehension.

For the first time since she married Joe Kennedy, Rose was in her element. She had learned from her father, then created her own innovations based on her understanding of the community. She had helped her father take office. She would help her son do the same.

On June 18 the Eleventh Congressional District voters went to the polls. Some went once. Some went many times. This was an era when Catholic priests joked about their cemeteries being the location for large numbers of "active" voters.

Joe undoubtedly bought votes. Rose certainly would encourage a voter to show loyalty by casting a ballot as many times as possible. But so did most of the other candidates and their supporters. The process was thoroughly corrupt, as the running of the two Russos most blatantly revealed.

Ultimately what mattered was that Jack won, and his relative achievement—40 percent of the votes cast in a ten-candidate field— probably was an accurate reading of the relative votes. Most likely almost every candidate used dishonest means to about the same degree. The vote count was undoubtedly inflated, though the percentage win probably was close to the truth.

Joe, shocked by what he knew was his wife's victory, learned another lesson the day after the election. John "Honey Fitz" Fitzgerald, an old man Joe once thought was a useless joke, sat down at the telephone with a list of the hundreds of party workers who had helped Jack's campaign for even a few hours. He called each one, personally thanking them. Each person called was given a chance to say whatever he or she desired. It took several days, but no one was overlooked.

The Eleventh Congressional District was now "owned" by a twenty-nine-year-old, inexperienced, scrawny youth. He was so young-looking that when he went to Washington in January 1947, fellow congressmen glanced at him in his polished shoes, dark trousers, pressed white shirt, and tie, then told him to which floor they wanted to go. They thought he ran the elevator.

But Jack had won the vote, and the only value Joe Kennedy had been was to earn so much money he could essentially hand Rose a blank check to pull off the biggest political coup Massachusetts had seen in at least a generation.

Joe never said if he minded. There were bigger stakes to come, and it would be with those elections that the man who had once been an intimate of members of organized crime would return to the more vicious aspects of his roots.

There was tragedy in the midst of triumph, a foreshadowing of the Kennedy future. Kick had returned just once to the United States, in 1946 when Jack ran for Congress, only to find that her mother wanted nothing to do with her. Jack was ordered to ignore his sister, and even the church would not let her receive the sacraments when she attended services.

Overwhelmed by the rejection, Kick returned to England, where she became friends and then lovers with Peter Milton. Milton, also known as Lord Fitzwilliam, was perfect in every way except one—he was married.

Milton filed for divorce, and in 1948 the couple knew they would be married as soon as it was legally possible. Joe Sr. was in Paris on business, and the couple had plans to fly to Cannes in a private plane. Kick wanted her father to meet her fiancé, and Joe was delighted. She said that they would come to Paris when they were finished in Cannes. However, when they were preparing to leave for the Cannes-to-Paris flight, the weather had gotten bad. Rather than miss their appointment, the couple decided to fly into the storm.

No one ever determined if the pilot was inexperienced for the weather conditions or the plane was not equipped to handle the storm they encountered. All that was certain was that there was a crash and the lovers were killed.

Oddly, Rose was a friend of Kathleen's mother-in-law, a woman she called Moucher, and remained so despite what Rose imagined to be a blot on her daughter's soul. Rose would continue to write to her over the years, even after Kick died. But while Kick was buried in the William Hartington family's Devonshire estate of Chatsworth, Rose refused to attend the ceremony. She claimed she had to have a hysterectomy. She also claimed to others that Kick had died in Switzerland at a party attended with "friends." She would never acknowledge the plane crash or the rendezvous with Joe. She was convinced that Kick died outside the state of grace, her soul in hell, and thus she would not grieve.

18

THE RACE FOR THE SENATE

PERHAPS IT WAS THE WAY ROSE HANDLED THE PARTY THREE DAYS before the congressional special election of 1946. Perhaps it was the way Honey Fitz worked the telephones after the win, setting up for the next election instead of resting from the first. Whatever the case, Joe Kennedy finally recognized the Fitzgerald brilliance, and Honey Fitz understood what Joe could buy.

Jack Kennedy campaigned intensely for the November election, though it was not the harsh battle of the primary. The Eleventh District was Democratic, and he took just under four of every five votes cast in the general election. Joe personally spent an estimated total of $300,000 out of pocket. A week after Jack was the congressional representative-elect, the financial statement he filed indicated that he had neither publicly collected money for the campaign nor spent any money from such outside sources. There was no place to ask about a wealthy father's contributions.

Joe also had called in favors for Jack during the general election. He had long laid the groundwork for his son's move to power. Some time in about July or August, Joe contacted William Randolph Hearst, who owned the *Boston American*. Then, two months before the election, Cambridge mayor Mike Neville's name disappeared from print in that paper. It did not matter what the news story might be. Mike Neville had become a nonentity. There were no editorials against him. There were no news stories mentioning his name. And all efforts to buy advertising space were rebuffed. It was exactly the treatment Hearst gave Orson Welles following the release of *Citizen Kane*. This time it was just one paper, not the Hearst chain, and the action was a favor for a friend.

Still, the victory primary belonged to the strategy of Rose.

Joe could not bring himself to show respect for Rose, but he could at last align himself with her father. The two of them began analyzing the next meaningful race for which Jack soon would be eligible.

Honey Fitz understood that moving up in power had little to do with ability and everything to do with appearance. His grandson was an indifferent congressional representative who could move along his father's trail of ambition though was unlikely to have ever gone very far without pushes from others. At the time he lacked the heart of an inveterate campaigner.

Jack's indifference was not proof that he was serving out Joe Jr.'s "right" by birth order. The problem with trying to understand his attitude toward politics and life at this stage in his growth has more to do with the myth the family has desperately sought to make his legacy than the truth of his life.

Jack Kennedy was an intensely shy young man, frequently debilitated by pain, and more comfortable with books or a handful of close friends than he was being a public servant. He had never lived in his congressional district. He had not gone to school with the young men who shared his wartime experiences, then returned home to blue-collar jobs in the area in which they were raised. He had no sense of how changes in the manufacturing world were affecting the area or what he should be doing to help his region of the state.

Even the camaraderie of veterans was slightly hollow for Jack. He had more in common with men such as Ronald Reagan, whose background in the entertainment world led to their assignments to make training films and propaganda. Army Air Force captain Reagan served at the Hal Roach Studios, often called "Fort Wacky." He never flew farther than Catalina Island, and he spent each night in bed with his wife, Jane Wyman.

Jack, like Reagan, was expected to serve Stateside. But in Jack's case, his perceived indiscretion with Inga Arvad caused him to be inappropriately assigned to sea duty. He had legitimately gone into combat, though he was too young and inexperienced for the leadership expected of him. He had been through hell, endured great terror and grief, and been further debilitated by the experience. Yet that was different from the blue-collar boys of his district who frequently had been cannon fodder of the military, front-line infantry fighters who often had survived hand-to-hand combat only through the grace of God.

Jack enjoyed the pursuit of women and leisure more than the pursuit of power. There were men in the freshman class of the Eightieth Congress who were comfortable seeking power at seemingly any cost. Both Representative Richard Nixon and Senator Joseph McCarthy, the latter a Kennedy family friend who occasionally dated Eunice, wanted power, fame, and to manipulate the media. Jack had no such ambitions. He was an obedient son.

At the same time there was a touch of the theatrical about Jack Kennedy. He was handsome, enjoyed the company of movie actors he met both when recovering in California and through his brother-in-law Peter Lawford, and came to enjoy the use of television for debates and direct communication. He had less of an intellect than others who sought office, and he had no burning issues to resolve. Yet that could be said for some of his fellow congressional representatives as well as some of the members of the Senate. The same career with a different family might have been objectively viewed as a modest success, his stance on issues typical of the conservative nature of wealthy white politicians of the era.

Jack was assigned to three committees that guaranteed high-profile news stories no matter what he did. One was the District of Columbia Committee, which ran the area that was a mix of government offices, including the White House and Capitol Hill, shops, hotels, restaurants, and residences. In any other part of the nation, the district would have been a traditional city. Congress provided what passed for oversight, and Jack was on the committee. He had little work but great local attention, something even Joe's money could not buy.

Jack also was on the House Veterans' Affairs Committee and on the House Committee on Education and Labor. Veterans were constantly gathering in Washington, seeking help with readjusting to civilian life. And the literacy rate of Americans had been a national scandal since before World War II. Any public image of helping his fellow veterans or of showing concern about education kept the names and photos of members of the relatively minor committees, as the representatives rated them, in the papers.

The work that came from Jack's office seems to have been mostly done by his secretary, Mary Davis. Her efforts on his behalf would fit with Joe's teachings about locating and using a staff.

Joe recognized that he himself was not as intelligent as others. He also realized that no one noticed who did the work for a project. The person who held the titular responsibility for the achievement was the individual remembered.

Joe had been effectively on his own in England, not willing to consult with historians, military experts, and others who truly knew the people, the culture, the times, and the reasons behind what was happening in Europe. The men he trusted were from business. They were transplanted to London because that was their job as Joe defined it, and he was paying the bills. It was the one time he had not used experts in the field in which he was working, and the result had been his being shown to be both shallow and naive.

By contrast, because Joe utilized brilliant businessmen appropriately in his other endeavors, Kennedy was given credit for having more than street smarts and an innovative mind. He took acclaim for every triumph and had someone else take the fall for any glitch.

Recognizing that his sons were not great intellects, he taught them to hire the best minds they could find to do the actual work for them. This might mean drafting bills, writing speeches, researching problems, and ultimately taking care of constituents when necessary.

Mary Davis was the first such secretary Jack utilized as an adult, though he had witnessed the results of his father using men such as Arthur Krock and John Hersey to give him literary authority and the image of a hero. There would be others, including Evelyn Lincoln, who understood that she should do everything in her power to protect Jack. The only person to whom she was to defer was Joe.

Joe did not disparage his son's lack of dedication to mastering the affairs of the nation and the world. For the moment, image would be as good as substance. He also saw that Jack was becoming enamored with the background his father had created for him. From the embarrassed youth who mumbled something about the Japanese sinking his boat, he was growing into a hero in his own mind. As the years passed, he increasingly began telling a story of heroism at sea, not of an accidental sinking or a mistake that cost the lives of two men and nearly got him a court-martial.

Having established his son in Congress, where he needed to mark time before moving higher, Joe returned to two passions. One was making money, and toward this end he added oil company investments because of the depletion allowance.

Joe first entered into groups backing oil exploration, a risky business at best, though one filled with tax advantages. Joe bought the Arctic Oil Company and went into a partnership with Raymond F. Kravis, a petroleum engineer from Tulsa who owned Roytex. The two companies—Arctic and Roytex—had previously been a single business known as Transwestern Royalty Company, a spin-off of the San Antonio, Texas, firm of Transwestern Oil Company. The corporate structure was a complex one involving oil exploration, oil drilling, and royalty interests, as well as a combination of liquidation and holding of differing assets. Advisers such as Jim Landis had carefully analyzed the industry, and once Joe understood the business fully, he began purchasing oil and gas companies.

By the 1950s Joe would have a number of holdings in Texas, such as Mokeen Oil Company, Suttron Producing Company, and Kenoil. Tom Walsh of New York's Park Office, the location overseeing all of Kennedy's affairs, handled the financial dealings and the tax concerns.

Joe's investment would prove extremely important when Jack ran for president in 1960. There was a need for Texas money and Texas support. Oilmen, whose contributions were greatly needed, convinced themselves that the Kennedys were such heavy investors in oil that they would never allow the depletion allowance to be cut.

The second passion he returned to was women. With Jack in an "easy" congressional seat—no primary or general-election opposition in 1948 and five opponents in 1950, when the combined vote for the opposition represented a fifth of Jack's vote—Joe could relax. The marriage to Rose was long over except in name. They worked together for the sake of their children, especially since Rose understood how to achieve the political power Joe coveted for his sons. But sexual relations were finished, and the friendship they had once enjoyed had slipped away with the years, ending with the loss of Rosemary.

Joe's philandering ranged from movie stars to his personal secretary. The longest relationship during this period was allegedly with Janet Des Rosiers. She was twenty-four years old when Joe hired her in 1948. She was skilled in secretarial work, bright, and had held jobs of importance with both a law firm and for the clerk of the Worcester, Massachusetts, Superior Court. She also was a good-looking woman whose photos are reminiscent of Rose at the same age.

The relationship between Kennedy and Des Rosiers turned intimate in December 1948. She was living in a two-bedroom West Palm Beach home, a short drive over a bridge to Palm Beach. As with Gloria Swanson, Joe allegedly was the aggressor. He also understood that if she was amenable, she was someone who would be constantly available.

Joe was a philanderer, but he also was a man who liked routine and convenience. Whenever he was in a place he considered home, he would establish a pattern for meals, exercise, reading, thinking, and doing business. Des Rosiers always was available as his unmarried assistant. She was expected to travel with him when truly necessary for business. She was expected to be present in his homes. There also were times when she allegedly stayed with Joe while Rose was traveling.

Des Rosiers was especially welcome because she was a relative innocent. She had never had a serious relationship with any male before Joe.

She had never been seduced. She had never been cared for. And now a rich, powerful man who was legitimately her employer, using her for work that needed to be done, also was sharing a larger part of his life. There was no extra money to make her feel cheap. There was no sense of being a mistress. He made certain that there were two hotel rooms when they traveled. The same was true with his New York apartment. No matter how intimate they might be, most of the nights were spent in separate bedrooms.

For Des Rosiers, the relationship with Joe was a physical and emotional experience that became quite special, according to statements made to author Ronald Kessler while researching for his book *The Sins of the Father*. For Joe it probably was business as usual. Men and women who knew him during this period talk of one or another mistress, kept women, or intimate friends. It was as if Janet were his female best friend and Joe had intimate visiting privileges, but Joe was not committed to her in any way. Often he was seen with other women in clubs.

The ritual nature of Joe's days and nights also seemed to give Rose a comfort level. She could see him working. She could see him exercising. He was so predictable, she could avoid thinking about the fact that they were apart much of the time, or that the boats he owned were ideal places for seduction. Rose also had come to believe that all important men have affairs and that a relationship with a secretary was inevitable. A secretary was often the most intimate woman in a businessman's life, the one who was present for triumphs and failures, and for the work that led to the moment when the outcome would be discovered. She did not think about the fact that a wife should be fulfilling the same role.

Perhaps the philandering filled another need. Joe was too rich and too famous to fade quietly away to backroom deals and politics. Instead, with his hatred for Roosevelt and the New Deal greater than when he was a presumed insider, Joe began making speeches and having articles published under his name that were intensely conservative.

In 1945 the man who was investigated for his rent gouging of businessmen in the New York buildings he owned began talking about the dangers of socialism. He complained about people coming into government who thought that the state, not the individual, should assume the burdens of life. He wanted a free economy without restraint, ignoring the fact that he had recently showed that the extremes as he sometimes practiced them could be as destructive as state control.

Joe then began railing against the British. Harold J. Laski of the British Labour Party was declaring that capitalism was dead in much the way that Joe had declared that the British monarchy was finished. Joe noted that twice in the previous thirty years the United States, a capitalistic country, had been needed to save Britain.

Harry Luce gave Joe space in the March 18, 1946, issue of *Life* magazine for an article titled "The U.S. and the World." Joe, ever the pessimist, was convinced that World War III was likely if the United States demobilized too quickly. He wanted the nation to be powerful enough to attack anyone who threatened U.S. interests, at the same time having the world divided into alliances so the United States would not have to fight alone. In his mind there should be an alliance of European nations much like the Allied forces, close ties to Nationalist China, and a strong American defense. He felt that the United Nations would prove to be worthless and that the United States had no business getting involved in the affairs of other nations, though to what he was referring is unclear. He may have been speaking of the rebuilding of Germany and Japan. He may have been speaking of attempting to influence other governments. Whatever the case, he stressed that the one area of concern was the Soviet Union. He felt that it should be given limits of behavior, and if it exceeded them at all, the United States should attack with all its forces.

Joe Kennedy's conclusions may not have been reasonable in the changing world, but his concerns about how the United States should use its power were valid. Before World War II the United States was militarily weak. The country could ill afford the support it gave England at the beginning of the war and certainly could not have protected its territory had the United States been attacked. By war's end the United States had become the world's most powerful nation.

Kennedy was right in recognizing the danger from the Soviet Union. Russia was on the march and soon would dominate much of Eastern Europe. Many experts felt that the thinking in the Kremlin was more dangerous to the United States and the stability of the world than Hitler's actions in the 1930s. Joseph Stalin was known to have murdered at least 20 million people, and the Russian gulags—concentration camps— were both well known and widely feared.

But how could the United States best fight communism? Joe gave his answer in the *New York Journal-American*, one of the Hearst papers. On May 25, 1947, Joe stated that the best defense against communism was prosperity. It was an odd reasoning. "America with its matchless resources, its skills and abilities, has merely to continue to be the land of free enterprise which our forefathers made it in order to attain a lasting prosperity inspiring to the dejected peoples of other nations who

are striving to escape political serfdom and attain national independence." He wanted tax relief at home. He thought the Marshall Plan
bringing aid to badly damaged nations abroad was wrong. In his view,
many of the nations were so wrecked that any foreign aid was meaningless. On June 13, 1948, the *Journal-American* again gave him a voice, at
which time he said, "To sink billions of dollars into countries which can
produce nothing that matters to us, that in the end turn Communist, is
merely to waste our strength."

Critics felt that Joe was saying that the United States should do
nothing to challenge the spread of communism. They saw communism
as the politics of a desperate people. They felt that by using the nation's
wealth to help desperate people in other nations, their populace might
be saved from such a takeover. A few went so far as to call Joe a coward
who justified inaction as a moral stance.

During this period Joe seemed to project his own feelings on the
nation. He was both somewhat of a loner and very much alone. He saw
the United States as a friendless nation, powerful, wealthy, and besieged
by others who wanted to take but had nothing to give. The nations that
sought American military aid or intervention were too lazy or too
uncaring to defend themselves.

To achieve proper ends, the United States, according to Joe, should
get out of every country where there was no compelling U.S. interest
for staying. He wanted to protect America from communism if the system tried to cross the Atlantic, though at the same time he was comfortable with its growth. He stated that the more people who had to
live under communism, the greater the likelihood they would revolt
against the system and its leaders.

Joe stressed that he was not an appeaser with the Communists when
he said he was willing to let their numbers grow. He wanted the government to withdraw from what he felt were unwise commitments. He
also continued to harp back to Chamberlain's action, reminding everyone who would listen that Chamberlain bought time for England. As
with Jack and *PT-109*, Joe Kennedy had repeated the same lie to himself so often that he had come to believe it.

To Jack's embarrassment, his father was vilified once again. Newspaper columnists pointed out that Joe Kennedy had once wanted to give
the world to the Nazis. With his recent speeches and writing, the writers
felt it was clear that he had now decided to give it to the Communists.

Sadly for Rose, none of this mattered. She and her relationship with
Joe had become a matter of curiosity for some, of ridicule for others.
There was no great romance ground tragically into the dust of life's

happenstances. As the couple entered their sixties, all that mattered was power. Honey Fitz had defined the target for the next important election before his death in 1950. Joe Kennedy, Rose Kennedy, Joe Kane, and the family members and sycophants were about to focus on the 1952 election for Senate and the candidate to beat, Henry Cabot Lodge Jr.

Jack had never been much of a congressman. He is most remembered for minor actions, such as bolting his party to vote for the Twenty-second Amendment, limiting the president to just two terms. The Democrats were expected to support the party line against such limits, since they would have prevented Franklin Roosevelt from being elected to serve four terms. Jack went with the Republicans as a way of avenging his father.

Jack also was a fiscal conservative who talked about welfare while being against deficit financing. He felt that the national budget was a disgrace. He was in favor of higher taxes to assure a balanced budget.

Overall Jack, like others seeking to eventually move to higher office, felt that his position in the House had no meaningful power. Jack seemed to share his father's views on many subjects, but his father did not try to influence his vote. Neither man seemed to think that Jack's positions mattered.

By 1951 Jack was looking to gain a higher profile for a run for Senate while Ted, a freshman at Harvard, was facing the repercussions of a scandal. Ted, never a very good student, was earning a C− in Spanish. He was an adequate football player but good enough so he thought he could make the team. The problem was that he expected to flunk his Spanish exam. He could not play if he did not pass, so rather than miss being on the varsity, he paid a friend to take the exam for him. Both were caught. Both were quietly expelled from Harvard, the university officials handling the matter so it would bring no public embarrassment to the families.

Ted was allowed to return two years later, after serving in the army. It was presumed he had matured, and though he was never again caught cheating, there was an angry edge to him. A member of the rugby team when they played against the New York Rugby Club, he was hot-tempered throughout the match, engaging in three separate violent fights before being expelled from the game.

Harvard let Ted graduate but did not want him to return for law school. Instead he went to the University of Virginia Law School in Charlottesville. There he liked to play in pickup football games, insisting always that he be the captain. Sometimes he was tolerated. Sometimes the other players, some of whom had been top college stars courted by the pros, walked away in disgust or deliberately roughed him up on the field. But the original expulsion never was mentioned, never known until ten years after the incident, when the Boston papers became aware of it.

Something about Ted's freshman year expulsion bothered Joe in ways that brought forth a desire to help others. In July 1951 there was an exam cheating scandal at West Point in which a hundred cadets were expelled. Joe learned about it at the same time that the University of Notre Dame was using Father John Cavanaugh to try to persuade Joe to contribute the money for a graduate school. Joe did not pay for the graduate school, but he did offer to pay the cost for sending all hundred West Point cadets through the college—room, board, and tuition.

Agreeing to pay the bill if needed for everyone, Joe had Father Cavanaugh approach the expelled students to offer them a second chance. Twenty-one of the youths applied after being assured that their religion did not matter, only their willingness not to repeat past mistakes. Ultimately thirteen arrived, their education paid for by a "secret" donor.

But the donor did not remain secret for long. In September the story was "leaked" by Joe himself to the *New York World-Telegram.* The gifts were genuine and the youths were delighted. Only the idea of donor humility did not exist.

Joe dealt quietly with Ted's problems, but he helped Jack put a more positive spin on his career that same year. Joe underwrote a six-week tour of Europe for his son in February 1951. Jack's primary itinerary was to visit the members of NATO—the North Atlantic Treaty Organization. Joe arranged as many contacts with leaders as would let themselves be used by the public relations people who were hired to promote the tour. Jack called the experience a fact-finding tour and was given courtesy time, heavily publicized, before the Senate Foreign Relations Committee.

No one knew what "facts" Jack had been seeking on his trip. He had no committee assignments or other work for the House that would warrant a tour. If he won the Senate seat he would again be a freshman, in that body, even though he would have six years of congressional experience. However, the Kennedy publicists made the trip "important," while Joe's picking up the tab assured that no one could claim a misuse of government funds. And Jack did separate himself slightly from his father, concluding that the United States should be more involved internationally instead of following Joe's strict isolationist ideas.

In October, to add additional luster, Joe sent Jack, his brother Bobby, and his sister Pat to Israel, India, and Vietnam, a country that still was under French control. The calculated move proved to be a failure. Jack Kennedy was seriously ill. His adrenal glands were failing from his Addison's disease, and his temperature rose to 106 degrees. He was rushed to the military hospital in Okinawa. Desperate to save his life, the army doctors used long-distance telephone to talk with Jack's physicians in the United States. They worked out a treatment regimen of hormones and penicillin that saved his life. However, he would never again be truly healthy enough to handle the full rigors of public office.

The illness on the second trip was covered up as much as possible. No one thought Jack was seriously in trouble. It was just one of those incidents that could happen to anyone when traveling in a foreign country.

Jack was able to hide his weakness when he returned. As a congressional representative and as a senator, the demands on his time were within his control. He could choose to fill his days with endless meetings, greeting constituents, and the other minutiae of being a politician. Or he could arrange personal downtime when staff people would handle the work and others would be given the impression that the resting Kennedy was actually hard at work somewhere else. His father was willing to pay any additional staff costs, and that also helped hide the truth.

The real concern in 1952, as Honey Fitz had expressed before his death two years earlier, was that Henry Cabot Lodge Jr. offered the state all the character traits Jack lacked but needed to seem to have. Lodge, like Jack, was a Harvard graduate whose family was wealthy. He had first won the Senate seat in 1936 at age thirty-four, just old enough to have experience in life and the community. As a U.S. senator, Lodge would have been able to ignore World War II. He was draft-exempt, yet he realized that he could not let the men of Massachusetts risk their lives in battles the Senate supported while he stayed safely in Washington. He resigned his seat and enlisted, going into combat and winning several honors, including the Bronze Star.

Lodge returned to the civilian world in 1946, determined to regain his Senate seat. He had served the people well his first two terms. His military record had been excellent, and he had fought alongside the sons of some of his constituents. There was no reason not to return him to office. Any Democratic Party opponent was perceived as having no chance against Lodge in 1952, especially since his activities transcended party lines. He was a liberal Republican and reached out in quite personal ways to every constituency. He was fluent in French and used it when speaking with the French Canadian constituency. A growing Italian community caused him to take along his sister-in-law, who spoke fluent Italian, so she could translate for him.

This was an era when ethnic groups were often at each other's throats and politicians rarely reached out among the various communities within their concern. Lodge went everywhere in the state, making certain he showed respect by having someone with him who spoke whatever language he did not.

Jack Kennedy was almost a nobody who had done little. The people of the state were discerning. The Republicans believed they would look at the histories of each of the two men and do the sensible thing—vote for Lodge. What the incumbent senator did not expect was a vicious, cutthroat campaign orchestrated by Joe Kennedy, a man who saw no need to limit what he spent on behalf of his son. Lodge also did not realize that he was vulnerable that year, something Honey Fitz instinctively understood years earlier, and others saw in hindsight but few could anticipate.

Joe Kennedy began planning the political strategy for Jack's run by analyzing the other meaningful Democratic Party contenders. The strongest Democrat who might seek the Senate seat was Massachusetts governor Paul Dever. He had already won statewide office, and in a race against Lodge, the party would prefer someone already in power greater in reach than a single congressional district.

Joe Kennedy went to Dever with an offer the governor could not and did not refuse. If Dever ran for another term in office, Joe would be happy to blend Jack's Senate campaign money with Dever's gubernatorial race needs. The implication was that there would be an open checkbook, and though Jack would accept and spend contributions, the unlimited funds Joe planned to use could be hidden from Dever's books as well.

Lodge seemed to have the edge over Kennedy when the League of Women Voters arranged for a debate between the two men in Waltham, Massachusetts. Lodge was older, distinguished, and had the look of someone a movie director might have cast for the role of a senator.

Jack was handsome and younger. He also was surprisingly relaxed—because he knew his father would be secretly helping him with aspects of the debate.

Lodge thought he could handle a routine debate. He did not pre-pare to go on the defensive. He assumed that whatever questions arose, he could speak from experience, knowledge, and/or belief.

Jack was told to look forceful. He would make a point by pounding his fist for emphasis or aggressively gesturing at his opponent. The emphasis actually meant nothing. Often the answer was innocuous. It did not matter. He came across with the image Joe Kane had developed.

As the debate went on, Joe Kennedy sat in the balcony, where he could see and hear everything but remain relatively unnoticed. He made suggestions on appearance, questions to ask, statements to make, and how to recover from unexpected challenges. Two runners went from the floor to the balcony, passing Joe's notes to his son.

Joe was not that well versed on Lodge but was able to rely on what became known as the "black book," a notebook Representative Ken-nedy's aide Ted Reardon had prepared on Lodge's record. Politics had been vicious in the past. Politics had involved lies and innuendos, per-haps since the earliest campaigns. But Joe had an idea that had not been tried in a campaign, and it left Lodge unprepared.

Thanks to Joe's use of the "black book," Jack would be able to detail everything Lodge had not done or had done in a manner that could raise questions. He would ignore all the good.

The first step was to examine Lodge's attendance and voting record. Lodge and Kennedy were frequent no-shows on the floors of their respective houses. Worse, by partisan standards, Lodge's voting was inconsistent. These facts were irrefutable.

What went unsaid was that Lodge worked hard for his constituents. He missed votes, but rarely a crucial one for the nation or the state. And the inconsistent record was inconsistent only if he was the type of person to vote a strict party line. He was someone who voted his con-science after studying the issues, and that did not always mean he would side with one party or the other.

Lodge easily would have destroyed Jack had he been prepared to put Kennedy's record to the same scrutiny. Lodge had expected the debate to be a discussion of issues, the type of discourse both he and Jack might have had in their respective Harvard days. Instead he was thrown on the defensive, with no details to move into attack.

The other "failing" for Lodge was the same "failing" Joe had seen in Roosevelt. Lodge was an isolationist before World War II. He had be-come an internationalist after the war. He changed with the realities of the times. He was not rigidly constricted by ideology, but acted based on world events. Jack liked to use the isolationist Lodge as a bad example when speaking with internationalists, ignoring that eventual change. And he did the reverse when speaking before a group of isolationists. During the debate, Lodge was so thrown that he did not mention the fact that he left the Senate to serve during World War II. He had had the courage to risk his life for his changed beliefs even though he did not have to do so.

Finally there was the issue of anticommunism. A study of the records of both candidates indicates that when it came to issues such as China, Lodge was the more aggressive anti-Communist. Again Jack ignored his own voting and speech record to attack an underprepared Lodge.

Jack won the debate according to the media and would continue to win such events in the future.

Joe Kennedy had been right back in 1927. How a man is perceived—as an author, a statesman, a business leader, an aggressive youth, or anything else—means more than the substance. At first this was obvious on a local level. Votes were won and lost based on image within the venue where they were heard—a town hall meeting, a school auditorium, and the like. Later, and 1952 was the start, the electronic image mattered.

For many years the news media had consisted solely of newspapers, magazines, and motion picture theater newsreels. By 1952 television was becoming an important part of the entertainment business. Television receivers were still expensive, and much of the country was considered "fringe"—locations with poor reception. But television was developing a new way to perceive a candidate. Suddenly it was possible to see the person as he or she talked, to be seduced or repelled by the person's appearance, gestures, and other tangibles of limited importance in reference to issues.

In the years to come, including the presidential debates that would take place between John Kennedy and Richard Nixon, it would be obvious how much image mattered. Anyone reading a transcript of the debates or listening to an audio version only would know that Jack Kennedy routinely lost. He was never as well prepared. He was never as knowledgeable. Yet those who watched the debates, who saw the aggressive body movements, were almost entirely convinced that Jack won. The image of the man meant more than the meaning of his words.

The one person outside of Joe's control who helped inadvertently was Bobby. He had married Ethel Skakel two years earlier, and by chance she was well along in her second pregnancy on September 23, 1952. She gave a speech on behalf of her brother-in-law that day, then went into labor, giving birth to a son named after his grandfather and uncle—Joseph P. Kennedy II. (The proper form of address should have been Joseph P. Kennedy III, since there had been a "junior." With his uncle dead, the couple decided to stay with the II designation.)

The news media delighted in the birth coming on the day of a campaign speech. The reporters also gave coverage to the subsequent baptism by Archbishop Richard Cushing of Boston. The future cardinal's presence had nothing to do with the campaign, but the Republicans perceived it as an implied Kennedy endorsement that would weigh heavily on Catholic voters.

Joe rented an apartment at 81 Beacon Street in Boston, then began following Honey Fitz's strategy of getting volunteers who could be separated from others, made to feel special, and hopefully would be more dedicated. Each volunteer was called a "Kennedy secretary," a title that made the person seem like a true insider. It was an idea that worked so well, when the "Kennedy secretaries" began seeking names for nominating positions, they came back with 262,324 signatures. State law required 2,500.

Joe and Rose analyzed how the voters would react to each of them and where one or another would be a liability. Rose was as anti-Semitic as Joe, but she had never been in a position where her feelings were publicly known. She would regularly go to Jewish gatherings, especially where any Kennedy would do. When Jack went, he would note that his voting record in Congress was never anti-Semitic. He always explained that he was the one running for the Senate, not his father.

Polly Fitzgerald, Rose's aunt by marriage to Edward Fitzgerald, coordinated the statewide gatherings that were the equivalent of Coffee with the Kennedys. She worked with women who were rich and usually apolitical. None of them cared whether Jack Kennedy won the election. These were women who were impressed with "stars." Each gathering would be visited by Rose Kennedy, usually wearing her finery, who would be speaking as the wife of the former ambassador to the Court of St. James. Invariably she would be greeted with tables set with expensive linen, the finest silver, and all else that comes with having an honored guest.

There also were thirty-three gatherings around the state, each being by invitation marked "reception in honor of Mrs. Joseph P. Kennedy and her son, Congressman John F. Kennedy." These were in addition to the Coffee with the Kennedys meetings. The invitations went to the elite in the state who wanted to have the enjoyment of famous people feted in their homes.

Jack did not fully understand the speech he was expected to give each time he spoke with his mother, but the words came from her efforts to understand the electorate, and she would eventually take them nation-wide. He routinely opened the gathering of women who came to one of his Great-Aunt Polly's receptions with this comment:

"In the first place, for some strange reason, there are more women than men in Massachusetts, and they live longer. Secondly, my grandfather, the late John F. Fitzgerald, ran for the United States Senate thirty-six years ago against my opponent's grandfather, Henry Cabot Lodge, and he lost by only thirty thousand votes in an election where women were not allowed to vote. I hope that by impressing the female electorate that I can more than take up the slack."[1]

The speech, like so much of the strategy Rose followed when seeking votes for her son, was brilliantly layered. First, Jack was acknowledging the importance of women and the fact that, together, they had power.

Today this is not meaningful, but the speech has to be understood in the context of the times. Women were considered second-class citizens in some parts of the nation. Education for women was encouraged, but they were expected to graduate with their "M-R-S" (Mrs.) and devote their "career" to raising children. And movies and television shows typically showed women as less intelligent and less capable than men.

Suddenly a young congressman, a bachelor, was telling women that they mattered. He was telling them that they needed to exercise the right to vote. He was telling them that his own family had been hurt by the failure of a system that discriminated against women. John Kennedy was telling them that they mattered, and no one else had the foresight to say that. Jack was speaking as though he not only respected the power of women but also was not afraid to ask to utilize it.

Finally there was the mention of Honey Fitz. Women did live longer in Massachusetts, and many of them remembered Jack's grandfather. For some, this made Jack part of a legacy on both sides of his family. For others, this was a reminder of an old-time politician who had truly cared.

Jack Kennedy, with his mother orchestrating, was creating an image women wanted to help. And everywhere the women related to Rose, a gold star mother, the wife of an ambassador, daughter of a mayor, mother of a congressman . . . the list went on and on. No one could claim to have reached greater heights of money or power. No one could claim to have been better traveled and to have met more heads of state. Few could claim more tragedy, and none could claim the combination of wealth, power, and loss she had endured. In addition, in cities like Boston, where wealthy elite lived, she knew when to stop campaigning in the traditional sense, sit down, and start sharing gossip about which Paris shops had the nicest dresses.

Rose added television to the effort. She put together a "Coffee with the Kennedys" morning show, perhaps the first "infomercial," with the product being her son. She knew that morning shows were popular with women. Some were taking breaks from various chores. Others would have set up ironing boards and were watching as a diversion while working.

The show was call-in. There was a toll-free line, so viewers could ask Rose the secrets of rearing a large, successful family. She took to television the way she previously had handled the streets of Boston for her father. She told of her little boy growing into manhood. She talked of Jack's picking blueberries and teasing little girls. She spoke to each person in the manner of an intimate friend, the way you would if you and your neighbor were hanging laundry in the backyard, chatting over a low fence.

Then there were the Kennedy sisters, each wearing a flared skirt with "John F. Kennedy" embroidered on it. This was not a family of sibling rivalry. This was a family where the girls spoke with one voice, and that voice always was in favor of their brother.

Joe next arranged for a tribute to his sons meant to tug at the heart-strings of every parent who had lived through the anguish of World War II. It was an outrageous exploitation of tragedy, but Joe was rarely a compassionate man. Nine hundred thousand copies of an eight-page publication titled *John Fulfills Dream of Brother Joe, Who Met Death in the Sky over the English Channel* were printed for distribution by mail and in person. There were pictures throughout, including Bob's new baby—Joseph P. Kennedy II.

The crass exploitation worked, perhaps because it was so outrageous. Henry Cabot Lodge Jr. had never encountered anything like Joe Kane's coordinated attack, the lessons adapted from the late Honey Fitz's strategizing, and Joe Kennedy's use of money.

No one had ever experienced a television show selling a candidate's mother and sisters to the women of the state. No one had ever sent out a tabloid exploiting a dead son, a newborn grandson, and a living son whose record was so limited, he probably should not have been on the ballot.

Years later, Jack Kennedy would be on the defensive about the 1952 election. He would talk about how he had laid the groundwork for three years prior to running. He would become angry with people who said his father bought the election. He did not talk about the money spent for television and other uses. He also did not talk about the cost of his mother's effort after she understood the demographics of the state.

There was one other expense that Joe had to run up during this period. He needed a newspaper endorsement, and this time the Hearst backing was not enough. Instead it would cost Joe a short-term loan of $500,000.

The story has two sides to it. The truth seems to be rather straight-forward. Joe Kennedy had been offered a chance to buy the *Boston Post* sometime in late 1950 or early 1951. The paper was essentially the voice of the Democratic Party, but its partisan editorial stance was not the reason Joe was offered the business. The paper was losing money, and the loss would benefit Joe, giving him tax advantages he could utilize.

Joe had toyed with buying media properties, but at this stage in his life the idea of being in newspapers, magazines, radio, or television did not appeal. He wanted to stay with the stock market, real estate, and his son's political career.

John Fox was the man who bought the *Post*. He was a millionaire, though not on the scale of Joe Kennedy. The Fox money came from a combination of New York real estate and oil and gas speculation. He was the type of investor who was willing to bet everything rather than holding back a few million dollars in case he made a mistake, as Joe Kennedy had done with his children's trust funds, which he could tap if needed.

Fox wanted to have a conservative Republican voice. He pragmatically backed Ohio senator Robert A. Taft in seeking the Republican nomination for the presidential race. Not only was Taft a conservative, but also Lodge was managing the campaign of General Dwight D. Eisenhower, giving the war hero the aura of a liberal.

Joe Kennedy, a Taft backer, alerted all delegates to the Republican National Convention in Chicago that he had opened a campaign office for Jack in Parlor B of the Sheraton Plaza Hotel during the convention. Jack, thus seen as a conservative, would gain the support of Independents for Taft.

Joe also provided financial backing for Adlai Stevenson, the liberal Democrat who ran against Eisenhower. Allegedly Joe was a Taft man who backed Stevenson because, when younger, the candidate had worked for Joe at the Securities and Exchange Commission. In truth, Joe wanted to be certain that Jack had the backing of conservatives and liberals from both parties.

In the midst of all this came Fox, with his newly purchased paper, a new editorial policy that cost him readers, and growing financial problems. Fox had his assets for "play" in the form of highly salable Western Union stock. He sold his shares to buy the newspaper, his timing such that he lost a small fortune when he couldn't take advantage of a substantial price rise that occurred immediately afterward.

Fox needed some interim capital—an estimated $500,000 for sixty days. He could not get the money from a bank. He never truly had collateral for anyone. However, he was given the money by Joe Kennedy right after he had the *Boston Post* declare its support for Jack.

One story of the loan is that there was no connection with the endorsement, that it was a coincidence. Three weeks before the election, when Fox was preparing the endorsement, he was asked by conservative Republicans not to come out for Lodge. The reasons are unclear, though apparently they had to do with the senator's moderate track record. Fox allegedly alerted the Lodge campaign that he could not back the incumbent unless he was asked to do so by proven conservative Senators Joe McCarthy or Robert Taft. Not only did neither man call Fox, when he tried to reach McCarthy, who was traveling in Seattle, Washington, the request apparently was ignored.

The day after learning that McCarthy was too busy to come to the telephone to speak with him, Fox endorsed Jack Kennedy for U.S. senator. Supposedly Joe Kennedy actually wept when Fox told him what he planned to do. The grateful Joe told Fox that if he could help him in any way, he would. The loan was mentioned. The loan was provided. The loan was paid back, albeit late.

Both the money and the endorsement are beyond dispute. However, the one place the story falls apart is with the dramatic, tear-filled meeting.

Joe Kennedy was sixty when his son ran for senator. He had spent his entire adult life being certain he was beholden to no one. He had long followed the organized-crime concept of being certain that others always are in your debt. There seems little question that the loan was based on the endorsement no matter how much the Kennedys tried to deny it.

To the credit of the people of Massachusetts, Jack almost did not win. The race was so close that at midnight the vote seemed likely to go for Lodge. The Kennedy family felt certain Jack would be victorious, whether because they were optimists or because they had hired more people to vote frequently than the other side, if indeed such cheating existed. All that is certain is that the morning after the election, Jack Kennedy was the new junior senator from Massachusetts. The final tally on November 4, 1952, was 1,211,984 votes for Kennedy and 1,141,247 votes for Lodge. Jack had won by 70,737 votes.

19

JOE AND JACQUELINE

THE STORY OF JACQUELINE LEE BOUVIER HAS BEEN DISTORTED BY time. The image of the White House years of Jack and Jacqueline (*never* Jackie, not even to her friends) Kennedy was always carefully orchestrated. Both were lovers of the arts. They adored one another and their children. They were devoted to each other and uncomfortable when they had to be apart.

There were photo sessions with Caroline and her pony. There was John-John, who was never called by that nickname despite the press, playing under the desk in the Oval Office.

This was a family of youth, love, and vigor. "Grandfather" Dwight Eisenhower had governed America. Both Harry Truman and Franklin Roosevelt were viewed as remnants of the previous century. Now there was a new generation, born in the twentieth century, tempered by war, and ready to lead. Or so Joe Kane would have it.

The truth was both greater and less than the myth. Jacqueline Lee Bouvier was a woman of boundless hope and shattered illusions. She also had the courage to protect those she loved most, to pursue a life that led to her being held in disdain, yet never destroyed, by people who were desperate to maintain myth over reality.

Her father, John Vernon Bouvier III, known as "Black Jack Bouvier," lived the dashing, sexually active, and ultimately self-destructive life to which Jack Kennedy may have partially aspired but never achieved. Some called John Bouvier "Black Jack" because of the bluish-black tone of his skin caused by a lifelong illness. Most thought the nickname was apt because he reminded them of a pirate hero in a romance novel where the heroine is kidnapped, then discovers love in the midst of an almost violent assault. In the fantasy of such novels, aggression is lustful passion masking deep love, and the woman's decreasingly loud cries for help and curses of disdain hide her overwhelming desire. Such books have nothing to do with real life, yet if a man had to be cast in the role of such a muscular, handsome, devilish antihero, Black Jack would have been the man.

Bouvier had made millions in the stock market and was an ardent Republican who hated both Franklin Roosevelt and Joe Kennedy. His greatest outrage at the two men reached its zenith when he was selling short at the time Joe Kennedy, formerly notorious for the same technique for building wealth, took over the SEC. SEC rules changes cost Black Jack $43,000 in the stock market in 1935. Livid, he told his daughters that Franklin Roosevelt, impetus behind the SEC, was another name for Satan.

Jacqueline was born on July 28, 1929. Her mother, Janet Lee, was sixteen years younger than her father, and Black Jack's losses, coupled with his reckless spending, womanizing, and alcohol abuse, meant that the couple was in financial trouble. He started in a downhill financial slide and would eventually die poor by the standards of his youth, though able to afford a relatively large Manhattan apartment and one full-time employee.

Jacqueline's maternal grandfather, James Lee, also was rich and could have helped the Bouviers. However, he hated his daughter's choice in first husband and decided to get back at his daughter for marrying the disreputable Bouvier. He cut off his granddaughters without a cent.

Janet Bouvier handled matters her own way. She divorced Black Jack, desperately trying to survive on his monthly payments of $1,050.

The income was a dramatic comedown for Janet. However, to put this in perspective, middle-class families consisting of two adults and two children were considered quite comfortable with a $200 to $250 per month *gross*. Being just four times better off than "normal" people did not fit Janet's plans or desired lifestyle. That was why she quickly sought another rich husband before the curse of normalcy became ingrained.

Janet Lee Bouvier married the wealthy Hugh Auchincloss, owner of Hammersmith Farms. He was eastern aristocracy as cold-blooded in their concern for social pecking order as the British had been. At least Janet was born into money and raised with it. The only difficulty was the fact that the Lees, the Bouviers, and the Auchinclosses were all Catholic, a religion that frowned on divorce. There were ways around such problems, annulments being more readily available for the generous rich than for the working poor. However, Janet did not care what the church thought about her lifestyle, and Hugh was just happy to have Janet.

Hugh Auchincloss took Janet's daughters, Jacqueline and Lee Bouvier, into his homes in Newport and Southampton, raising them as children of privilege. Lee blossomed at a young age. Jacqueline was one of those

Jacqueline Kennedy, both as First Lady and as a child. She is shown during happier childhood times with her parents, Mr. and Mrs. John V. "Black Jack" Bouvier. The image was taken during the summer of 1934 at the Annual Horse Show of the Riding and Hunt Club at Southampton. (Cleveland State University Library, Special Collections)

young girls who never looked quite right in terms of dress, body shape, and normal development. She was either ridiculed or ignored, and never a part of the "in" crowd. However, she was extremely intelligent, with a flare for journalism and publishing that would rarely be recognized until later in life. Her intellect took her to Vassar and for study at the Sorbonne. She won *Vogue* magazine's Prix de Paris contest in 1950 with a prize-winning essay. She also was debutante of the year when she had her debut.

Though Jacqueline grew into a beauty, her sister had been beautiful seemingly since birth. Jacqueline was brighter and worldlier. Lee was the prettier one. Jacqueline was the smarter one. She became painfully shy and withdrawn, though when she chose to challenge those who tried to put her down, she could surprise them with a tart tongue and a steely resolve.

When Black Jack divorced their mother, Janet Lee Bouvier, the girls were essentially abandoned to their mother for long periods of time. Black Jack and Janet separated for six months, tried to get back together, then bitterly fought through the divorce. Black Jack's lifestyle did not leave room for growing daughters. Instead, he would arrange to show up, taking them to expensive restaurants and giving them treasured gifts. They grew to think of love as something experienced with loneliness, absence, then excess attention and money. Rather than seeking commitment as a sign of love, Jacqueline became comfortable with the idea that a man will alternate between periods of indifference or absence and periods of sexual aggressiveness and intense involvement, and the giving of expensive gifts.

Hugh Auchincloss hated his wife's first husband. He raised the Bouvier girls in his world of privilege, yet forced their biological father to supply some of the luxuries expected of girls of the family's social standing. When Jacqueline, hating the college, fled Vassar to study abroad, it was Black Jack who footed the bill, even though he and his sisters were gradually selling all their possessions and Hugh could well afford his stepdaughter's travels.

Jack Bouvier had come to see his older daughter as the most important person in his life. The cost for the European trip was not seen as a sacrifice because Jacqueline spending a year away from the Auchincloss influence offset the financial difficulties.

Jacqueline immersed herself in language study in Grenoble, then moved to Paris to continue her education. She stayed in a boardinghouse run by the widow Countess de Renty, whose husband had died in a concentration camp.

The one unusual experience was a trip to England during a break from her studies at the Sorbonne. There she visited a woman she knew to have been her father's sweetheart during the war. The woman was married, with fraternal twins who looked so much like Jacqueline that she realized they were her half brother and half sister. Black Jack later confirmed the fact.

The reality of her other family was shocking. When she married into the Kennedy family, she feared that her father's indiscretion would eventually create a political risk. The story did not come out during the presidency. She did not know that Joe Kennedy, her future father-in-law, had led a more scandalous life that was well known in political circles.

After Jacqueline returned from Europe, Black Jack Bouvier finally had the opportunity to spend more time getting close to his daughter. Since she did not wish to return to Vassar, he suggested that she come live with him in his apartment at 125 East 74th Street in Manhattan. "Poverty" for Black Jack was a relative term. His daughter would have her own room, privacy, and the housekeeper who cared for him.

Janet Auchincloss adamantly refused. If she wanted a different school, she could go to George Washington University in Washington, D.C. Jacqueline would not spend any meaningful time with her father.

The first man to seriously look at Jacqueline Bouvier as a wife was John G. W. Husted Jr., a New York stockbroker. He was a poor man by the standards of her family—just $17,000 a year, or enough to live a reasonably upscale life in one of the nicer apartments of New York. His father was a highly successful banker, and his future would provide Jacqueline with a comfortable life, though not with the type of money that had long surrounded her. More important, the dating relationship would regularly bring her to New York, a situation that delighted her father. If she married Husted, she would be living in Black Jack's world, not the estates of the Auchincloss family.

In the years that have passed, many critics of Jacqueline have said that the reason she did not marry Husted was money. Her stepfather was earning more than $100,000 a year, a massive sum in the early 1950s. Even Jack Bouvier, whose 1951 income was a fraction of what it once had been, was making $45,000.

The problem with focusing on Jacqueline's supposed greed is how long the relationship lasted. Husted took Jacqueline to meet his parents. He bought her a diamond and sapphire engagement ring. She knew what he did, where he came from, and what he could afford at that stage in life. There was even an engagement party generously thrown by Hugh and Janet Auchincloss, during which discreet inquiries into his finances were begun.

Hugh and Janet realized that they needed to get Jacqueline away from John. They sent both sisters, Jacqueline and Lee, to Europe. When they returned, they had had so much fun mocking the pretensions of tourists, wealthy locals, and various eccentrics that they wrote what amounted to a book about what they had done: *One Special Summer*. It also included drawings by Jacqueline. However, instead of trying to publish it, an achievement that would have impressed Joe Kennedy, they placed everything in a series of scrapbooks and gave them to their mother. Over time it would be lost, then rediscovered, and published in 1974 by Delacorte Press.

Being withdrawn and sensitive to others was a blessing when Jacqueline decided to enter journalism. She was comfortable asking questions, taking pictures, and learning about a variety of subjects. Her first job was with *Vogue* magazine, the leading fashion publication of the day. Then she went to work for the *Washington Times-Herald*, earning $42.50 a week. Her situation was more like that of Inga Arvad than Kick.

Jacqueline had already paid her dues, had a stack of clippings of her stories, and was able to operate a Speed Graphic Camera (the standard press camera that used a flashbulb the size of a 100-watt lightbulb, and 4x5 film). Among her other assignments, she became the "man on the street" who went out and asked a question that was deemed important for the day. She took down the answer, took a head shot of the person, then ran the most interesting one in the paper twenty-four hours later each day. The idea was to make the publication a "must read" for the broadest possible readership, and it was hoped that whoever was photographed would alert family, friends, and coworkers, some of whom would buy the paper.

Jacqueline met Jack Kennedy at the end of his years as a congressman. Fellow journalist Charles Bartlett, who had them both to dinner, introduced him to her in May 1952.

What happened next is subject to interpretation according to the bias of the biographer. There are those who look on Jacqueline as a calculatingly cold woman who followed her mother's thinking, seeing Jack Kennedy as excellent husband material because his father was rich. Later, they argue, when she realized that Jack was a philanderer, Joe bought her off.

Part of the problem with understanding Jacqueline is the tendency to connect her too closely with the greedy, self-centered Janet Auchincloss, who felt that there was nothing wrong with looking out for oneself through marrying money. Black Jack Bouvier was a philanderer who seemed to use his money to buy his daughter's affection. Hugh Auchincloss was comfortable with the idea of marriage for capital gain. And Joe Kennedy was willing to do anything, pay any price to assure that his son achieved the nation's highest elected office.

What is often ignored is that Jacqueline was a woman of passion, independence, and great humor. She left John Husted because she couldn't handle the unbearable family pressures, but she did so as a young woman in the final throes of adolescence. Money never was a factor in the decision as far as can be determined, though it was the cause of the pressure used against her.

Years later there would be stories about prenuptial arrangements with her second husband, Aristotle Onassis. Overlooked was the fact that Jacqueline had come to hate the United States, to fear the violence. There is a famous picture from the assassination in which she is seen climbing toward the back of the car in which the Kennedys were riding, reaching out to grab bits of flesh and brain that had just exploded from Jack's head. She arrived at the hospital covered with blood and gore.

She had experienced a horror beyond imagination, and Onassis, a long-time friend, offered her a chance to protect her small children from further harm. The financial arrangements, quite minor and routine in Onassis's world of billionaires, assured that her children would be protected. And in her final years, after her second husband's death, her married lover would move into her apartment in Manhattan. It was an unheard-of arrangement for someone like Janet and quite different from what would be expected of someone spending her life in search of ever greater wealth.

Jacqueline's relationship with Jack was one of young love. Her detractors and those individuals who want to keep Jack Kennedy as the patron saint of all that was good in the 1960s like to talk of her coldness. The implication was that she could take sex or leave it, that it was somehow distasteful because it was not neat and orderly. One especially vicious comment was that she was too fastidious for sex.

At the same time, those who knew the couple recognized Jacqueline as a woman of subtle sexuality. She was sensual with Jack, her jokes and his responses indicating a couple where the physical side of marriage was both desired and fulfilled. Certainly there was an inner lustiness that drew other men to her after Jack's death. Aristotle Onassis did not buy a trophy to put on a shelf, and she did not suddenly become an escort for hire. And no man throws away his reputation and provides incontrovertible ammunition for his wife's potential divorce lawyers by moving in with a lover who is cold, calculating, and uncaring. Yet Maurice Tempelsman, the man who lived with her until her death, put himself at risk of losing everything for love.

Jacqueline accepted Jack Kennedy without conditions. She did not know he was an unrepentant womanizer. She did know of his constant pain from the genetic condition and serious damage of World War II. She knew of his life-threatening illnesses. She knew he was debilitated; there would be times when she would share in the stresses of political campaigns so he would not have to bear the physical burden alone. She never loved the Kennedys as a group the way others marrying into the family did, like Ethel, Bob's wife, or tried to do, like Joan, Ted's spouse. But she loved Jack and was not intimidated by Joe, the two characteristics that could have meant great long-term happiness.

Jack always was far from attentive to Jacqueline. He stood her up, was late, and generally seemed not to care about her. However, as time passed and the relationship deepened on both their parts, she watched him become the junior senator from Massachusetts. She realized he had an unusually busy schedule in a world just enough different from that of a congressional representative that he had to take extra time to learn. She never considered that he might not particularly care for her beyond being a casual friend. She never considered that Joe Kennedy had ordered his son to get married in order to move into higher office. A handsome young bachelor was sexy to women when they were considering voting for a senator, or so Joe believed. A bachelor president meant that there was something sexually or emotionally wrong with the man. As Joe saw it, Jack's career would dead-end in the Senate if he didn't pursue someone, and since Jacqueline seemed to love him, she was perfect. She also had the type of class he had seen work so well when Rose put on one of the more sophisticated Coffee with the Kennedys events.

Hatred for Jacqueline within the Kennedy family was intense. Eunice, Jean, Pat, and Ethel all ridiculed the way she wanted to be called by her given name, not "Jackie," as the nation would dub her. They would talk about "Jack-Lean, rhymes with Queen." They called her "the deb." And this from young women so snobbish that they would have done anything to have the opportunity their two oldest sisters had had to be presented in the Court of St. James.

Jacqueline accepted Jack's sisters and sisters-in-law as "the rah-rah girls." She found ridiculous their desperate attempts to win at everything they did. She played touch football at the Kennedy compounds when she had to do it, but she had no knowledge of the game and no sense of what to do. Also, she did not care. She stopped attempting to be part of the group after the sisters deliberately threw her to the ground, where she broke her ankle.

Jacqueline's relationship with Rose was another area of speculation. The two women did not particularly care for each other, but Jacqueline watched her future mother-in-law with curiosity. She came to understand the woman who had been Honey Fitz's de facto "first lady" of Boston. She witnessed the giddy, girl-like delight in life that Joe Kennedy first saw when they were dating. She also saw the rigid, seemingly emotionless woman who greeted Joe and the children when they gathered together. It was privately, when there was no reason to act in the straitlaced manner she adopted for family get-togethers, that the spark that was Rose came through.

Had Jacqueline stayed an outsider, the two women might have become friends. Both of them treasured many of the same values. Both of them believed in making a home for husband and children. Both of them entered their marriages with a desire to be nurturing helpmates. However, once she married Jack, she saw Rose almost exclusively when the family was present, and the stiffness that separated the two women was rigidly in place.

To her credit, Rose tried to warn both Jacqueline and Ethel, the first two women to marry Kennedy men, that they might experience philandering or allegations of adultery, as both she and her mother had endured. She told them about the anonymous letters and telephone calls. She told them about the stories that might come in the press and from the gossips. She wanted them to understand that the life of a woman married to a man in politics was quite different from normal married life. While she was right in some ways, it was as though she were justifying what she had endured by characterizing it as ubiquitous rather than the cruel choice of uncaring men.

Rose also was somewhat of a joke to her, just as the older woman was to her staff. No matter how much the employees showed respect to Rose, and she was always "Mrs. Kennedy," even in the privacy of their work area, the woman had become a caricature in private.

First, there were the notes reminding her of the day's appointments and planned activities pinned all over the clothing she wore at home so she looked a little like a living Day-Timer. Jacqueline loved fine cloth-ing, and in this her mother-in-law was a kindred spirit, but she never considered turning it into a cloth memo board. That was why she was amused to watch a woman with a wardrobe costing more than most people spend on all the houses they might own in a lifetime walk around home with notes pinned everywhere.

Then there were the "frownies."

Somehow Rose came to believe that she could eliminate facial frown lines by attaching a piece of cloth tape to whatever area was in danger. She called the small pieces of tape "frownies." Barbara Gibson men-tioned that when Mrs. Kennedy was about to travel to a place like Paris and felt the need to look especially good, she would walk around the house with hair curlers, taped pieces of cloth on her face, and the ubiq-uitous notes pinned to her dress. The family said nothing, either out of fear or respect. Jacqueline saw no reason to keep her opinions to her-self, though she never insulted the woman who would become her mother-in-law. She was the one Kennedy (or soon-to-be Kennedy) with discretion.

Frank Waldrop was the one coworker at the *Washington Times-Herald* who was openly uncomfortable with Jacqueline's choice for marriage.

He knew Jack Kennedy, knew that Jack was not only twelve years older than Jacqueline but also a seemingly unrepentant womanizer. He tried to warn his reporter away from the senator-elect, but he eventually received an invitation to the wedding. He would later say that he assumed she was marrying for money, with the Kennedy nuptials restoring the family fortune that Black Jack had tossed away.

The one person who did know what was going on was Evelyn Lincoln, who would remain Jack's executive secretary for the rest of his life. She fielded the endless stream of telephone calls, an estimated half of which were women trying to reach him. The women ranged from movie stars to housewives, and many of them had been with Jack in bed or would willingly find themselves there in the future. Evelyn recognized that Jack's impending marriage was Joe's idea and that Jack was far from committed to the idea of having a wife in any traditional sense.

Ultimately nothing would stop Jacqueline's commitment and Jack's need to be wed. On September 12, 1953, the marriage the nation seemed to have been awaiting took place. Joe had used his relationship with Harry Luce to assure that the couple had been photographed for *Life* magazine.

Life had become the most trusted publication in the nation for news photos. There is nothing published today that can match the impact and importance of *Life* then. It had brought the nation still images of the world at war. It told the story of recovery and of new dangers in the world. Its photographers covered everything from celebrities to science, the poverty and violence of some inner-city neighborhoods, and the private lives of the ultrarich and ultrafamous. It was the picture magazine of record for the nation, providing information available from no other source. And anyone who appeared on the pages of *Life*, or ideally on the cover, was automatically "important" just by being shown. The mediocre congressional representative who had become senator-elect by a squeaker election was suddenly a national figure.

Life was planning to run an article titled "The Senate's Gay Young Bachelor." Joe had set the parameters for the material, but it was a valid story as far as anyone knew. Jack was rich, young, handsome, and presumed to have been a war hero. The magazine had a large readership among single females who, along with their mothers, presumably would be interested in such a man.

Jack delayed announcing his engagement so the *Life* story could run first. Then, in July, Jacqueline was introduced. She was shown on a boat with Jack, as well as looking at photographs of both the Kennedys and the royalty they had known.

Then, bored with the pretense of being happy about a marriage his father insisted on, Jack went to Europe with friend Torby MacDonald. He sent his fiancée a postcard.

The wedding was a Joe Kennedy production, a fact that horrified Janet Auchincloss. She and Hugh had the wedding at Hammersmith Farm, and they expected the affair to be large but private.

Large it was. Joe Kennedy invited everyone who could influence his son's career in any way. The entire U.S. Senate, including spouses, was asked to come. There were movie stars, producers, and directors. There were business associates and people Joe knew from his days as ambassador.

The wedding was held in Newport's St. Mary's Roman Catholic Church, Archbishop Richard Cushing presiding. Every pew was full. Three thousand spectators gathered outside. The unofficial wedding photographer was a man from the *New York Times*, and reporters for that paper covered the event. Joe chose a Saturday, a traditional wedding day but, more important in his mind, because it was the second-slowest news day of the week and he could be certain of getting his son's nuptials on the front page of the *Times*.

Two trucks brought quality champagne to the reception for twelve hundred of the couple's nearest and dearest friends who gathered at Hammersmith Farm. The cake was five tiers. The Pope had sent a blessing. Only major heads of state were missing, though undoubtedly not for lack of effort on Joe's part.

The one dark moment came because Jacqueline made the mistake of thinking that she mattered on her wedding day. She was a traditionalist and contacted her father to give her away. He was thrilled; Jacqueline was elated; Janet was livid.

Black Jack Bouvier had been in an emotional decline in the previous couple of years. Just when father and older daughter had come to an understanding about life, the marriage vs. the parent role, and the other issues that had first caused estrangement, the older man was spiraling downward. He was in his early sixties at a time when such an age was considered old for a male. He had been an alcoholic. His body was ravaged, and he had come to hate what he had let himself become.

To compensate, Black Jack gave up alcohol. He wanted his daughter and some semblance of a life more than he wanted to drink. Yet he was only in the earliest days of recovery when his daughter was getting married, and as Janet well knew, he was a weak man without a support system.

Janet realized that the marriage of his beloved daughter would be stressful for her ex-husband. She also knew that his love was too intense for him to go to the hotel bar or a bar in the neighborhood to "celebrate." He would stay in the hotel room to ensure sobriety. That was why she arranged to have room service deliver his favorite liquor directly to the room.

Black Jack could not resist a few sips to prepare him for the marriage. Then he took a few more sips to prepare him for seeing his ex-wife. More to deal with Hugh Auchincloss.

An hour before the wedding was to start, Janet had Black Jack's hotel room checked, since he hadn't shown up at the wedding. To her delight and their daughter's horror, he was passed out, too drunk to be roused. It was one of the most vicious rejections of her feelings and desires her mother had ever shown. Jacqueline understood that her father would never have deliberately sought alcohol prior to her wedding. After the honeymoon, Jacqueline sent him a long letter forgiving him, further bonding the two in ways denied while she was growing up.

There was one other thought that came to mind for Jacqueline when she discovered her father was drunk. She wondered what would happen on her honeymoon.

The night Black Jack and Janet were married, they stayed together in the hotel. The next day, after boarding a cruise ship, the new husband found an interesting woman and went to bed with her, leaving his wife alone. Frightened, Jacqueline asked Jack if he would do such a thing to her. Unlike her father, Jack was faithful, at least during that most intimate of times.

Jacqueline did gain one friend with her marriage—her father-in-law. Joe watched the wedding preparations unfold. He watched how the family treated the young woman. He watched how she viewed the family. He realized that they both had the same inner strength, or so he believed about himself. She also had Rose's desire to make a pleasant home for her spouse. Jacqueline's only failing was politics. She did not see the importance of selling your soul for public office. Her world was one of ideas, the arts, and music. She was a fluent speaker of foreign languages. Her sisters-in-law thought of her as a snob and worried that she would ultimately be a liability. But her sisters-in-law had been raised to believe that the pursuit of public office by a Kennedy male required 100 percent support by the Kennedy women.

Joe knew that Jacqueline had the "class" that Rose exuded when working Coffee with the Kennedys and similar gatherings. His daughter-in-law was not a street fighter, but neither was his oldest surviving son. Bobby inherited those traits. Instead, she was someone who genuinely loved her husband, who could be worked, albeit gently. She might do far less than the Kennedy sisters, but the appearances she made would be far more effective.

Jack and Jacqueline settled into a home next to Joe and Rose. Rose came to admire her new daughter-in-law's sense of interior design and art. She felt that the young woman was adding glamour to the family, something that had been lacking since England.

Jacqueline proved to be the wife Joe Kennedy thought she would be. During their first year of marriage she was often seen attending sessions of Congress, watching her new husband give speeches. She also felt completely lost in understanding what was happening in the world, and to change this, she enrolled in the Georgetown University Foreign Service School.

Jacqueline was twenty-four when the couple married. She was uncomfortable in large social events and with strangers in whom she was supposed to pretend to be interested because they were somehow important to Jack's career. Fortunately Jack was similarly withdrawn, the result of his longtime illnesses and injuries. They stayed home together most nights when he was in town, and when they attended social gatherings, it usually meant being with just one or two other couples they knew well or wanted to know.

The intellectual ability of his wife caught the Kennedys off guard. Joe wasn't certain what to make of it, but Rose was rather delighted. Jacqueline had a tendency to play the helpless woman, incapable of effective decision-making. This image was exaggerated by her total disinterest in sports, the focus of Kennedy family competition. No one considered that she had lived abroad, was fluent in several languages, and was taking the same training diplomats are given just so she could stay abreast of the Senate's work. She also wrote, and when Rose saw one of her poems, as skillfully written as that of any professional, the image began to change. But ultimately Jacqueline's intellect came out in the one area of competition she enjoyed—the game of Categories, where vast knowledge of often obscure areas of life—Italian Renaissance writers, for example—was necessary to win. Jacqueline proved unbeatable, including when the Kennedys thought it would have been diplomatic to graciously lose, such as when playing with prominent international politicians or area church leaders.

Instead of saying that she was proving something to her husband and in-laws when she undiplomatically won, Jacqueline feigned innocence. She was known to softly say that she thought the Kennedys loved competition.

More blatant would be Jacqueline's loving way of letting her father-in-law know she saw through his character and accepted him anyway. Among other gifts, she painted a watercolor of a crowd of Kennedy sons and daughters, standing on the beach, looking out over the water. She added the caption, "You can't take it with you. Dad's got it all."

With Jack as senator, Joe felt the need to begin being seen as a philanthropist—as long as it didn't cost him very much. A Catholic hospital for handicapped children was funded, in large measure, by a check for $650,000 from the Joseph P. Kennedy Foundation. Jack was president of the foundation and photographed turning over the money to Archbishop Cushing. Not only did Jack have nothing to do with the money, there also is some question as to how much actually came from Joe's earnings and how much involved outside donors whose checks were funneled through the foundation so that only the Kennedys would get the credit.

Joe handled a new physical education building's dedication at Manhattanville College the same way. The school was naming the building after Kathleen, and they expected Rose to give a speech. However, the twenty-five-year-old Ted was being groomed to enter politics. He was ordered to make the speech in his mother's place.

The speech was handled effectively. The youngest Kennedy, who always had difficulty handling small groups, was skilled with large crowds. He also impressed one senior, Joan Bennett. She had planned to skip the meaningless speech and reception until it was made clear that all students would attend, names being checked off, and failure to go would warrant a demerit, a serious offense for a senior. When Joan learned that the names would be noted only at the reception, she skipped the speech to work on a term paper, then attended the reception, where she and Ted found that they wanted to see each other again. Joan already knew some of the Skakel family, one of whose members, Ethel, had married Ted's older brother Bobby. Casual dating led to a marriage proposal, and all because of the image Joe wanted his sons to project.

It was the summer of 1954 when Joe's earlier insistence on Jack going to sea during World War II almost cost him his son. What began as a way to rid the youth of an unwanted lover ended in his coming close to death and nearly destroying his back.

Jack's spine had become progressively worse in the previous few years. The genetic problem had been horribly aggravated by the ocean turbulence when he skippered a PT boat, and later when the vessel was sunk. By 1954 Jack was suffering from what some thought was malaria but more likely was connected with a drug reaction with the symptoms of slow-acting leukemia. He had adrenal insufficiency, frequent fevers, and pain so intense that he was often in mild shock and could no longer walk without crutches. Dr. Sarah Jordan of the Boston Leahy Clinic explained to Jack that the best doctors could do for him would be to perform spinal fusion surgery. She also explained that the worst doctors could do for him would be to perform spinal fusion surgery, because the operation carried a high risk of death.

Jack's pain was so great that he felt there was no alternative. He would not continue living in agony, walking on crutches. He would fight for life, and if he didn't make it, the peace of death would be better than the hell he was enduring.

Jack underwent surgery in Manhattan's Hospital for Special Surgery that October. The procedure was a double fusion of spinal disks, and Jack was so horribly weakened that last rites were given. Jacqueline, Joe, and Rose were twice called to his room for what might be his last minutes of life.

Recovery was slow. Jack had to lie on his back in a darkened room for week after week. Finally, when it was felt that he could be protected from injury during a trip, Jack was flown to Palm Beach for Christmas. Instead of healing faster, the problem seemed to be continuing. A second operation was performed after Jack was flown back to New York in February. Once again the staff thought he would die. Once again Joe, Rose, and Jacqueline were present when a priest came to administer the last rites.

The second operation was the key. Jack would survive, though recovery would be slow. He was flown back to Florida, where he was bored, bedridden, and encouraged to participate in a project that would ultimately be awarded a Pulitzer Prize for biography.

Exactly what happened is uncertain, though enough facts are known to understand the phenomenon that came to surround the release of a book called *Profiles in Courage*.

Joe Kennedy may not have loved Rose, but he did admire her. In Joe's mind it was Rose who was courageous. Part of his attitude came from recognizing what she endured from him and the people of Boston when she was growing up a mayor's daughter. She had learned when to fight back. She had learned when to remain silent. She had learned when

In a rare image of three adults who were uncomfortable with one another, Joe Kennedy walks with his daughter-in-law Jacqueline and her mother, Mrs. Hugh Auchincloss. The picture was taken January 17, 1955, in Palm Beach, Florida, where they were attending the opening of Hialeah Racetrack. The then senator's wife and her father-in-law put aside such pleasures in the years that followed as Jack became a contender for the presidency. (Cleveland State University Library, Special Collections)

to seek revenge and how to do it in a way so subtle others would not know, something she eventually did when Joe was dying.

Part of Joe's praise for Rose came from how she handled the family when there were losses. Joe was a man who withdrew from life when it became too emotional, leaving Rose to cope not only with her own grief but also with the remaining children. He also had a bad stomach, ulcers, and various intestinal problems all his life, and though these discomforts might be understood in a different context today (e.g., allergy and/or bacteria), at the time they were believed to result from intense emotional stress. A person with an ulcer was often viewed as being weaker than a person undergoing the same stress who had no physical problems.

Jack's fight for survival in the midst of horrendous pain struck Joe as courageous. Joe realized that both his second-oldest son and his wife were people who showed courage in the midst of problems that would overwhelm others.

Joe was right about his son's courage. In hindsight, though, the question must be raised as to why Joe repeatedly used his influence and money either to force Jack into inappropriate actions or to not stop him from behavior that would be debilitating. Joe knew that Jack's back could not safely handle sea duty, yet in his anger over the Inga Arvad affair he helped place Jack on a PT boat. Jack's back was assured of getting far worse, perhaps leaving him in a wheelchair, just by constantly being on the ocean. There was a chance Jack would see combat. There was no chance he could handle the ocean.

Likewise Joe knew that his son was not able to handle the rigors of a national campaign. This was driven home most blatantly when his European travels left him hospitalized. If the presidency had been about leadership and selfless giving, Jack could have held many positions in the private sector, using family money and his intellectual abilities for others. Yes, Jack was courageous in fighting through the pain and exhaustion. Joe ultimately seems to have been an exploiter of that courage rather than a nurturer of his son's physically unhealthy political career.

Harold Russell, who lost his hands in an accident during World War II, learned to live with hooks operated by shoulder movements, and went on to win two Oscars for his role in *The Best Years of Our Lives*, discussed Jack Kennedy. Russell had leadership roles in many organizations for disabled veterans dating back to the years of Harry Truman. He worked on the President's Committee on National Employ the Physically Handicapped Week and on the Disabled Veterans Committee. He worked with Jack Kennedy and realized what had been kept hidden from others about his health.

Russell was shocked, but he also believed in the attitude of Dr. Henry Viscardi Jr., founder of Abilities, Inc., whom he quoted in the second of his autobiographies, *The Best Years of My Life*.[1] "Attitudinal barriers are far more detrimental than architectural barriers will ever be. And you're not going to change this by passing some law. I don't believe any individual ever climbed to a position of dignity and responsibility because some federal law mandated it. I think any disabled person succeeds because somebody loves him and is willing to help him make the necessary sacrifice. Harold Russell without his hooks and without his good articulate voice and personality would be far more severely handicapped than the person who doesn't have arms."

But this didn't apply to the history of Jack Kennedy's medical problems and the drugs he took much of his life. Harold Russell lost his hands, but once he was trained to use hooks, he was no longer on medication, no longer limited by his body. Franklin Roosevelt could not walk, but for his first twelve years as president he was a vibrant man, his mind clear, able to handle any crisis, and far more astute than many of his colleagues. Ronald Reagan had early-stage Alzheimer's and a tendency to fall asleep during some of the cabinet meetings. However, current understanding of Alzheimer's is such that we know it is unlikely that Ronald Reagan was ever mentally impaired as president.

Jack Kennedy was different. He was ruled by pain and the drugs meant to counter that pain. He took "vitamin shots" from New York's Dr. Max Jacobson, neither knowing nor caring that they were heavily laced with amphetamines and that he was at least psychologically dependent on them. He reasoned that if the drug helped him feel better, there was nothing wrong with taking it.

Sleep often came only with the help of Tuinal, a drug to which his brother-in-law Peter Lawford was so addicted that he kept bags of syringes for injecting himself with a drug normally taken in pill form. Among the side effects of the drug are prolonged drowsiness, confusion, dizziness, hypotension, and depression. There was at least one brief period when Kennedy had to be given an extremely strong antidepressant over a forty-eight-hour period, quite probably to counter the side effects of the Tuinal.

Kennedy's Addison's disease may have been triggered in the 1930s when he began taking the then new desoxycorticosterone acetate (DOCA) to treat his many ailments. The treatments he was enduring caused a decrease in granular white blood cells, a situation that led to the diagnosis of leukemia. Today, with new medical knowledge, it is likely that Jack did not have a slow-acting leukemia but rather a drug reaction that created the same symptoms.

Jack's periodic jaundiced coloring—sometimes described as yellow and other times as golden—was similar to Lawford's coloration at death. Lawford's body was so damaged by the Tuinal and other drugs he took that not only was his skin jaundiced, but also his cell walls were so weak that his veins could no longer hold in the blood.

Kennedy's situation was never quite as bad, but his back frequently locked so that he could bend neither forward nor back. His White House physician, Janet Travell, whose training was as an internist and pharmacologist, frequently walked a few paces behind with a syringe filled with procaine to instantly inject through his clothing if he froze.

The medications—and often there were eight different drugs used throughout the day that his secretary, Evelyn Lincoln, knew about—might or might not be a problem. Jack was predictably unable to handle all the physical demands of the White House. He could not handle the mental demands of the White House at some times and on some days, none of which were predictable.[2]

Jack obviously was in pain during the period he was recovering from surgery, and he turned to reading because there was nothing else for him to do. It was then that the idea of exploring the lives of leaders who also showed courage in the face of adversity began to evolve. Jack, as senator, had access to the Library of Congress, the nation's repository for all books published each year. He had his assistant Theodore C. "Ted" Sorensen start gathering reference works from which he selected leaders to be profiled and the stories he wanted to use. Then Sorensen did the initial writing, handing the material to Jack for final draft.

There were others involved. Gertrude Ball, Joe's secretary in New York, later told author Ronald Kessler that both James Landis and James Fayne did some of the initial research, which she then typed and sent to Florida.[3] By her account the book was being researched and the early writing done just before Jack's second New York surgery rather than during the recovery.

Harper & Brothers published *Profiles in Courage* on January 2, 1956. It was a collection of stories about leaders in crisis—John Quincy Adams, Daniel Webster, and others. The stories were readable and focused on moments in the lives of the subjects that were both important and memorable.

Joe's handling of *Profiles in Courage* was different from Jack's earlier *Why England Slept*. The later book had a valid concept, a collection of stories of people of courage coming at a time when the United States still remembered World War II and had just finished the experience of a humiliating two-year "peace action" in Korea that ended with a fragile treaty, not a victory. A book about leaders who had to triumph over adversity written by a senator who was perceived to have been a war hero was a suitable product for Harper & Brothers. No one expected the volume to be particularly successful. It was not based on original research in archives and/or collections of the subjects' writing. However, by coming out in January, a time when book buyers are willing to read something fairly serious to pass the dark nights of winter, it was expected to make a little money for everyone.

Joe Kennedy began buying copies in enough bookstores to have the book become a best-seller. He was not concerned with whether anyone actually read *Profiles in Courage*. He was only concerned that the public view Jack Kennedy as a second-time, best-selling author.

Kennedy used no personal papers or other material of the subjects that would be available in specialized libraries, the Smithsonian, the National Archives, or elsewhere. Instead the basic research was done with generally available publications, and for the type of collective biography he was doing, such secondary, limited research is standard. The books that result routinely win no honors because they add nothing new to what is already known. However, they may be fun to read and successful with the public.

Jack Kennedy probably wrote the final draft of his book. The subject information came from other authors. Staff personnel did the research. Assistants handled the early drafts of at least some of the chapters. Ted Sorensen was acknowledged as research assistant and was paid $6,000 for his efforts. (If the publisher paid an advance for the book, and both the payment of an advance and the size will vary with each book, a $6,000 advance in 1957 would have been considered excellent for this type of book. Thus it is possible that Sorensen received the full amount the publisher paid to the "author," and there is nothing wrong with that if it happened.) But Jack spent considerable time reading the stories of the people profiled, reading the notes and drafts made for the book, and eventually reworking the final draft for consistency.

Was Jack Kennedy an author in the sense that he did all the research and writing himself? No. Was Jack Kennedy an author in the sense that he did any original research, coming up with ideas and approaches that were fresh and new? Certainly not, nor did he claim such activity. But was Jack involved with the creation, development, shaping, and other aspects of the book, including some phase of the writing? He was. It also is the reason why the family so vehemently insists that to claim *Profiles in Courage* was a ghostwritten book—anonymously written in its entirety by someone else—is nonsense.

Joe decided that Jack Kennedy should have a Pulitzer Prize as he moved toward receiving his assignments as a junior senator. The right position in government would assure a high media profile, something Jack needed as quickly as possible to satisfy his father's ambitions.

The Pulitzer Prize, awarded annually in several fields of literary endeavor, was decided by a committee after receiving recommendations from panels of judges distinguished in the fields for which the prize is awarded—biography, play writing, fiction, and so on. To be "nominated for a Pulitzer Prize" can simply mean that a book was submitted to the Pulitzer Advisory Board. The judges may find it abominable trash, but technically it is still "nominated."

The judges recommend a handful of books to the committee. Then the members of the Pulitzer Advisory Board, often past winners, make the final selection. In theory these are people who have achieved the highest honor and understood what was involved.

By 1956 the Kennedy family had decided that Jack should make his move for president in the 1960 election. The Pulitzer Prize would be the ultimate achievement, and toward this end Joe sought the help of Arthur Krock, a man who had been an Advisory Board member in years past. Krock lobbied the twelve men who made the final decision for 1957.

There is no proof that the Pulitzer Prize was given for reasons other than merit. However, even Jack recognized that a book that was not original scholarship was not one that should win. Worse, when trying to explain the committee selection of *Profiles in Courage* as the most outstanding biography written in the previous year, J. D. Ferguson, the president of the *Milwaukee Journal*, made one justification. He stated that what influenced him was that his twelve-year-old grandson had read the book and was deeply influenced by it. This was a book that had never been mentioned as a contender by the preliminary judges. This was a prize meant for a book created for an adult readership. The idea that Ferguson would make such a comment and the eleven other judges would suddenly agree in unison that the book deserved the prize is beyond credulity.

Sadder than the co-option of the judges was Jack's reaction. The book names Theodore Sorensen as someone who worked on the project. Yet when thanking the Advisory Board for the prize, and later when talking about the accomplishment, it suddenly became a solo endeavor. Jack never did give credit to those who assisted him. Truth, as it had been and would continue to be for Joe, was an elusive entity.

Coupled with Jack's positioning as a scholar was another maneuver. Dwight Eisenhower would be coming off two terms in office, and his vice president, Richard Nixon, would be the logical candidate for the Republicans. The Democrats would want someone to run against him whose politics would appeal to a broad range of voters. Tennessee senator Estes Kefauver was an experienced man who was considered the front-runner for the nomination, but Joe felt he could boost Jack's image with some inside maneuvering.

Senate majority leader Lyndon Johnson determined committee assignments and had planned to give Senator Kefauver a position on the

Foreign Relations Committee, a critical assignment for someone who was seeking greater power. However, even when a member might be incompetent, he or she would gain national attention. The members were perceived to be the most familiar with the world at large and often were invited to give speeches around the country. The position, coupled with the press manipulation that had accompanied the wedding, would begin to make a national figure of a man Massachusetts Democratic Party members considered a "lightweight."

Joe worked with Johnson behind the scenes to assure the appointment. It is not known what strings were pulled, financial arrangements made, or other inducements used. Certainly the choice of Lyndon Johnson as the vice-presidential nominee when Jack took the party's nomination over Estes Kefauver was connected. Jack was rewarded with Johnson's backroom influence, his experience, and his power among southerners, while Johnson was rewarded with what the family expected to see as the majority leader's own ability to run in 1968.

20

THE RUN FOR PRESIDENT

JACK KENNEDY DECIDED TO DECLARE HIS INDEPENDENCE FROM HIS father by deciding when he would make his first move for the White House in 1956. The rebellion was a minor one, but Joe was concerned because he knew such a run was destined for disaster.

The incident occurred because Eunice Kennedy had married Sargent Shriver, a lawyer who was involved with Democratic politics. Shriver was in Chicago when he learned that Adlai Stevenson, the Democratic Party's choice for president in 1952, was looking for a running mate for the 1956 election. Shriver thought Jack could take the vice-presidential slot on the Democratic Party ticket. He and Jack were both naive enough to believe this was a career boost even if he ran and lost.

Joe knew that the idea of running with Stevenson or anyone else that year was nonsense. Eisenhower was a war hero who was credited with restoring economic prosperity. He was unbeatable. However, instead of explaining all this to Jack, he assumed the youth was concentrating on his committee assignment and his book, not seriously considering a run for higher office. It was only when Jack openly discussed his plans that Joe explained the realities of politics to the youth.

President Eisenhower was the army general credited with coordinating the downfall of Adolf Hitler. He was beloved by the men who had served under him, a genuine hero, and as president had been plunged into the Cold War and faced the Korean War, the increasingly aggressive Soviet Union, and the Suez Canal crisis. In addition, the economy was booming. Stevenson may have been a good man and a popular Democrat, but Eisenhower's popularity transcended both parties. He was a Republican because the Republicans tapped him first to run on their banner. Had the Democrats gotten him first, the outcome probably would have been different.

Joe worried about more than Jack's inevitable loss if he ran with Stevenson. He also was concerned that the loss would be blamed on Jack's Catholicism and make it more difficult for any other Catholic in the future. Yet whether or not there truly was a "Catholic issue" at the time remains a question about which contemporary political analysts still argue. This is because by the 1950s, anti-Catholic feeling in the United States had long been dissipated.

Catholicism was the largest Christian denomination, frequently blue collar, and changing radically leading up to Vatican II. Where the leadership had once been conservative, appealing more to Republicans, increasingly there was a liberal movement within the church as a whole.

Catholic politicians had not been singled out for attack. Joe Kennedy had suffered some angry assaults in the media and on flyers, including when Jack ran against Lodge, but the attacks were based on his perceived anti-Semitism, not that of his son. The nation as a whole seemed to have reached a level of maturity where the voting public was more concerned with a candidate's attack ads than they were interested in the candidate's religion. For this reason both Jack and Rose appeared before Jewish groups, but Joe stayed away.

Supporters of Henry Cabot Lodge Jr., acting without the candidate's permission, also had spread flyers about Joe's anti-Semitism when the race became close. Lodge denounced the smear campaign, and the issue was not brought up again. The win was so close, it is possible that there was a backlash vote *for* Jack, who seemed to have the most openly clean, albeit less honest, campaign of the race.

Certain regions, including sections of West Virginia, had a strong anti-Catholic bias. However, such pockets of hostility also included those who hated Jews, Italians, and anyone they thought to be connected with the Mafia. Catholics weren't singled out, and candidates of any background could get elected if they were generous in helping the voters through hard times. A man might hate a Catholic, but a bribe or other support would turn him into a liberal.

Joe tried to explain to Jack the reality of all he was facing, and asked his son to stay out of the battle for the vice presidency. Neither Jack nor his brother Bob would listen. They worked the 1956 convention crowd, trying to gain delegate support against the other contender, Estes Kefauver. Jack came surprisingly close, especially since the next rush of national publicity he enjoyed would not be until the following year. Nevertheless, as Joe had hoped, Jack lost.

Jack was allegedly both sad and angry about the loss. However, he quickly came around to Joe's thinking. By the time he was interviewed by Bob Considine for the May 5, 1957, edition of the *New York Journal-American*, a Hearst paper, a chastened Jack Kennedy indirectly apologized to his father by speaking about the election and what would have happened if Joe Jr. had been alive and present to run with Stevenson.

"Joe was the star of our family," Jack related. "He did everything better than the rest of us. If he had lived, he would have gone on in politics and he would have been elected to the House and Senate as I was. And, like me, he would have gone for the vice-presidential nomination at the 1956 convention, but, unlike me, he wouldn't have been beaten. Joe would have won the nomination." There was a pause before Jack added, "And then he and Stevenson would have been beaten by Eisenhower, and today Joe's political career would be in shambles and he would be trying to pick up the pieces."

A larger problem for Jack was his decision to fly to France to vacation with Florida senator George Smathers and Jack's father immediately after the convention. Jacqueline was pregnant with their second child, the first having miscarried the first year of their marriage. She was lonely and miserable. She understood Jack's need to work the crowd and spend time away from her immediately before the convention, but once over, she expected him to be by her side. She did not know that the men had several women with them.

Jacqueline went to stay with Hugh and Janet Auchincloss in their Newport residence. It was there that the baby was stillborn after she underwent a cesarean section. She was in critical condition, and a priest was called to issue the last rites if necessary.

Jack had to be contacted at his father's villa in Cap d'Antibes. Joe ordered him home, and he spent the next two weeks by Jacqueline's bedside. Only after the press drifted away did he leave to campaign for Stevenson's election. At the same time he quietly declared that he would be making his own move for the presidency in four years.

Joe Kennedy knew his son lacked the experience in leadership and domestic and international affairs to be the type of statesman the American public expected to be in the White House. He also understood that it was the perception of the president and not the reality that mattered. A loyal, skilled staff, including media experts, could put the correct spin on any gaffes and come up with appropriate tactics to handle any genuine crisis.

In a sense, Joe's own career had been partially filled with smoke and mirrors. He had long been an extremely public figure engaged in high-profile activities that were often counter to what others thought were proper. His actual crimes, especially during Prohibition, may have been hidden, but his lack of business ethics was well known. He had hired reporters to give him better coverage with their papers, but he couldn't hire everyone, and there were those who would not lie when writing about his activities.

Jack was something else. He had made only one very serious error—his dereliction during the *PT-109* incident—that had left a paper trail, to be discovered only well after his death. Nothing else was likely to be held against him because his professional life was lacking in controversy. Even the fact that both Jack and Bob were involved with the McCarthy committee and its hunt for Communists did not matter. The times were conservative, and the anti-Communist right had gone so far as to make even the most bullheaded reactionaries look moderate. The John Birch Society, named for a soldier who was killed by Communists when he became belligerent rather than surrendering his rifle, declared Dwight Eisenhower and his brother Milton to be Communists. They felt the White House had become an arm of the Soviet Union, and their "bible," the *Blue Book of the John Birch Society*, outlining the death knell of democracy, looks more and more ridiculous as the years have passed and their "facts" have been shown to be nonsense.

Interviews with men who had been with Jack since they joined their first VFW post together all talked about how they had first learned in 1958 that Kennedy was being nationally groomed for the White House. They had worked on his campaigns. They had voted for him. They considered themselves old friends who knew him well. And they all said the same thing: "We were shocked. He was a lightweight in Massachusetts. No one took him seriously."

The difference between Massachusetts and the rest of the country was familiarity. The members of the state Democratic Party knew what he had and had not accomplished, as well as what had been done by those who came before. On a national basis, he was a scholar, a best-selling, Pulitzer Prize–winning author, and a member of the Senate's Foreign Affairs Committee. He had traveled the world, fought to save the nation, and been injured in combat. He was handsome, a devoted husband, and a man who cared about the future. Indeed, he *was* the future.

Jack and Ted Sorensen began traveling from state to state throughout the country at the end of 1956. They wanted to find the men and women who would be key delegates at the 1960 Democratic national convention. Jack was known from his close fight with Estes Kefauver, something that made more of an impression than if he had won. He seemed to be a comer with a growing constituency within the party. No one would ask about his leaving Jacqueline or not working for his constituents during the time on the road.

Joe Kennedy began working with the media, having proven to himself how important the press could be. The popular women's magazines, including the slightly upscale *McCall's* and the solidly blue-collar yet highly respected *Redbook*, were the first to begin profiling Jacqueline. She was the perfect candidate's wife because she was brilliant, sophisticated, well traveled, multilingual, knowledgeable, young, beautiful, and genuinely humble. Her shy, quiet demeanor won over interviewers, and their stories won over the public.

Joe opened his wallet, not for bribes but to pay for skilled personnel in those many months before the convention. Joe understood something that few others did: the best people money can buy are available only when the money is available, and traditionally that has been when the candidate has the nomination. Even when the campaign comes down to two candidates, one from each party, and the original core group of supporters swells in numbers and skill levels of both volunteer and paid staff, the very best wait until after the election. They feel they can financially afford to go only with the winner.

Joe began financing a campaign staff of individuals so skilled and in demand for high-level government and private sector service that they normally would be available only after an election, not during the race. Jack would have top people working full time to make him president in 1960.

There were several key states and key cities based on population. There also were key players. Mayor Richard Daley of Chicago was one. Charles Buckley, less well known nationally than Daley, was the Democratic boss of the Bronx and key to taking New York. Some were public officials. Some were behind-the-scene players. Actor Peter Lawford, who had married Pat Kennedy, worked the Las Vegas area as well as Hollywood connections.

Perhaps the most important entertainment industry connection was Frank Sinatra, who had long supported the Democratic Party. He became involved with Jack Kennedy through their mutual relationship with Lawford, jokingly called "first brother-in-law" after the 1960 election. But Sinatra would have been involved with the Democratic Party candidate no matter who he might have been.

Sinatra came to politics in 1944. He was no stranger to that world, his mother, Dolly, being one of the most influential people in New Jersey politics. She worked hard for candidates, yet was not above using blackmail when she needed someone's special help. For years she was a respected abortionist at a time when abortions were backroom surgeries usually performed on desperate women by men and women with limited skills. Women routinely became infected, sometimes sterile and sometimes dying after an abortion. Dolly had a better safety record than most. She also noted which women were pregnant by which politician, business leader, mob member, or the like. She never asked them for money beyond the fair price for her services. She never took advantage of the situation, always showing compassion for the woman. But if, a few years later, she needed a favor, the man being asked knew it was not wise to say no. Dolly's memory was too good.

Frank was too busy trying to become successful as a singer to care about politics other than what he overheard when he lived with his mother, a woman who was master of the backroom deal. Eventually she was enlisted by Joe to help his son Jack, just as Joe eventually would quietly assist Sinatra with business deals. But it was actually 1944, long before Jack Kennedy was in politics and when Frank was a successful big-band singer, that Sinatra first became involved with the political arena. That was the year restaurateur Toots Shor introduced Frank to Franklin Roosevelt.

Frank Sinatra was emotionally seduced by Roosevelt, as so many others had been. Here was one of the world's most powerful individuals— friendly, articulate, intelligent, caring—and confined to a wheelchair, unable to walk. The obvious struggles he had endured, the worlds he had conquered, and the sheer lust for life that defined Roosevelt moved the youth who had made his own way out of Hoboken, New Jersey. He donated $5,000 to the Democratic National Committee, then made recordings for fund-raisers that had tremendous appeal for young voters. He said, "I'd just like to tell you what a great guy Roosevelt is. I was a little stunned when I stood alongside him. I thought, 'Here's the greatest guy alive today and here's a little guy from Hoboken shaking his hand.' He knows about everything—even my racket" (i.e., singing).

Sinatra began mobilizing Hollywood for Jack, but he was a dangerous choice, and Joe kept a tight rein on his actions. Sinatra was involved with the mob for more innocent reasons than Joe Kennedy. Sinatra was raised on the streets of Hoboken, where some of his neighbors were low-level soldiers in various organized-crime groups. When he became a singer, it was organized criminals who owned or controlled many of the clubs. Sinatra worked with them or he didn't work at all. The real problem with Frank Sinatra was that he was a liberal. The Kennedys were not. To be a liberal in the Cold War was to risk being labeled a Communist.

Frank and Peter Lawford were part of what they called the Clan and others called the Rat Pack. The latter actually was the name of a group that included Sinatra and some friends who all lived in the Holmby Hills

area of Los Angeles. They smoke, drank, played cards, and made fun of
others. When Humphrey Bogart, the founder of the Holmby Hills Rat
Pack, died of throat cancer in 1957, the group dissipated. Then Frank
began spending time with Peter and Pat Kennedy Lawford, Sammy Davis
Jr., Joey Bishop, and Dean Martin. Peter, Pat, and Dean were considered socially acceptable wherever they went, but not the others. Sammy
was black and Joey was Jewish. However, Frank didn't give a damn,
even though hatred was so intense that Sammy's life was threatened and
Frank had to fight to get both Joey and Sammy the same quality rooms
on the same floor he was on when the five of them made appearances.
They were all paid the same. They all worked together. The draw was
the act involving their combined efforts. Yet the hotel managers often
tried to separate them so that other guests would not be "offended."

Jack Kennedy had been careful about not offending anyone. He
voted for a civil rights act, and then supported an amendment from
southern senators that effectively rendered the bill almost neutral. He
denounced those critics who tried to connect him to the anti-Semitic
remarks of his father, reminding them that he was his own man. The fact
that he may have had similar feelings did not matter. His critics always
backed off when he demanded that his father's independent statements
not taint him.

Now he was faced with the problem of Sinatra, a man who could
help get him votes and could hurt him because of his mob friends. Sinatra also was trying to help Jack relax in a way that made him vulnerable
to blackmail.

Justice Department files for the late 1950s revealed Kennedy's endless stream of women whenever he would stay at the Sands Hotel, where
the Clan performed and where Frank had a piece of the action. It was
safer for Kennedy when Peter and Pat let him use their Beverly Hills
home for his various rendezvous.

Beyond his own, he needed to avoid the perceived indiscretions of
friends if he was going to protect himself from fallout over criticism of
their activities. For example, Sammy was in love with May Britt, a white
woman from Sweden. Davis was drawn to beautiful women and never
thought about their color. Britt came from a country where there was
no race hatred. Together they were a dangerous liability for Jack.

Then came Sinatra's decision to produce the television movie *The
Execution of Private Slovik*. The story was a simple one that had been
largely forgotten. During World War II, soldiers in the armed forces of
all the armies in combat occasionally deserted. However, only one American, Eddie Slovik, was ordered executed by General Dwight D. Eisen-

hower. Whether or not he later regretted the decision, it was a blight on Eisenhower's record.

Sinatra wanted to tell a good story, and any embarrassment it might cause the Eisenhower administration was not his primary concern. Where he did take a stand was in his choice of screenwriter. He hired the brilliant Albert Maltz, one of ten writers who had been blacklisted as Communist sympathizers in 1948 when the House Un-American Activities Committee was conducting investigations into Communists in all fields of endeavor. Richard Nixon had been a part of the House committee, but the hiring of Maltz was not done to hurt a Republican. Sinatra felt that it was time to end the blacklist. It was destroying lives for no reason that endangered national security, and he felt Maltz was the best writer for the job.

It is difficult to understand the action Sinatra took in the context of the day. The *New York Post* saw Sinatra as heroic for taking an overdue stand against a needless blacklist. However, the rival *New York Mirror* condemned him for using an "unrepentant enemy of the country." Since Maltz had never been accused of spying for the Soviet Union, attempting to overthrow the U.S. government, or even creating movies that were anti-U.S., the extreme reaction was outrageous. Even the *Los Angeles Examiner*, a paper whose staff well understood the film industry, editorialized that Sinatra's movie could become a vehicle for Communist propaganda.

Leaders of the Catholic Church told Joe Kennedy to ditch Sinatra from the presidential campaign. General Motors threatened to withhold advertising money to any network that showed the film, and other large corporations agreed that they would also join a boycott.

Sinatra understood when it was time to back off, even though his critics were wrong. He paid Maltz the agreed-upon $75,000 for the film, then hired another writer. Sinatra also began keeping a lower profile.

The one exception was in the state of West Virginia. Sammy Cahn had written a song called "High Hopes," a recording of which had been quite successful for Sammy Davis Jr. Cahn changed the lyrics, making it into a campaign song for Frank to record. The new version had such lyrics as:

K-E-double-N-E-D-Y,
Jack's the nation's favorite guy.
Everyone wants to back Jack.
Jack is on the right track.
And he's got HIGH HOPES
High apple-pie-in-the-sky hopes.

Joe had the record installed in jukeboxes throughout West Virginia. Then a Kennedy aide went from tavern to tavern, paying each owner $20 to play the record as much as possible.

West Virginia was one state Joe had targeted for buying as much influence as possible. It was perceived to have some of the most corrupt public officials in the nation. Teamsters Union organizer, arsonist, and "slugger" Alan Friedman claimed to have bribed officials in both politics and law enforcement to help his brother-in-law, future Teamsters Union president Bill Presser, put gaming machines in private clubs that already had gambling equipment from other sources. The politicians and law enforcement officers allegedly asked Friedman about Presser's religion and ethnic background, and though they weren't happy to be working with a Jew, they went along with the deals as long as no Italians were involved. Uniformed officers went into clubs in a number of cities, confiscated the gaming machines that had been installed, then replaced them with Presser's. It was only when they realized that Bill was mob-connected that they rebelled.

How votes were to be bought was never discussed. Joe learned which middlemen to use and had the money distributed through them. The Sinatra record was meant to help sway the minds of voters who might not receive the largesse that was supposed to assure victory.

Jack had another advantage. Joe arranged for one of his corporations to buy a $300,000 custom-fitted Convair aircraft, which he then leased to his son's campaign for $1.75 a mile. This was far below the real cost of operation, but because the plane was part of a family business, the law did not consider it a campaign contribution. In addition, Joe funded voter polls, direct-mail ads, newspaper ads, the use of radio and television, and anything else that could reach a potential voter.

By contrast, Democratic rival Senator Hubert Humphrey went into debt to use television for ads and traveled by bus. He already owed $17,000 for campaign expenses when he entered the West Virginia primary.

On June 27, 1960, Selig Harrison had an article in the *New Republic* that stated that the command post for all Jack Kennedy's political efforts "has been Joe Kennedy's office in the Kennedy owned building at 230 Park Avenue. One can only imagine how many open-dated blank checks have been given to strategically placed individuals to help Kennedy get where he is. How many of these checks, if any, call for repayment by Kennedy as President, no one can foretell."

The second point Harrison raised was that, though Jack and Bob would deviate from their father's plan, Joe always had worked to let no one feel a Kennedy was beholden to him or her. He did the favors, sometimes years earlier, and though there might be cash payments involved or some other form of remuneration during the campaign, essentially the other person was repaying Joe. According to the article, he was calling in markers.

Harrison was only partially correct. The money was critical, and the Kennedy family was by far the wealthiest family in the history of the United States to have its patriarch devote all his wealth toward political ends. At the same time, other wealthy candidates had been willing to spend their own money, and in the years to come men such as Ross Perot, with an estimated $4 billion, would enter the race for president. What made the Kennedys different was that Joe utilized everyone from Honey Fitz, prior to his death in 1950, to men such as Ted Sorensen to help create strategies, craft speeches, develop an image, and otherwise create what might be considered the perfect candidate. It was the strategy—it was how the money was spent—that made the difference. Someone with lesser tactical ability spending greater sums of money probably would not have done so well.

In the midst of all this, Kennedy had one last campaign for the Senate, in 1958. The defeated Lodge did not try to make a comeback. The Republican Party recognized that Kennedy was too strong to challenge in a meaningful way. Oddly, the Massachusetts Republican Party leaders did not see Jack as unbeatable. Quite the opposite. The problem was that the forthcoming presidential election was far more important to the state party. The money was best saved for 1960, when there was a chance to keep control of the White House and assure a Republican-dominated Congress.

The Republicans ran a token candidate, Vincent J. Celeste, a man who lived on the top floor of a tenement. He had first challenged Jack in 1950 and made Kennedy wealth the focus for what proved to be a noncampaign. Celeste was a working-class man, thirty-four years old, and sincere in his anger, but he lacked serious issues to attract the voters. However, Joe orchestrated Jack's campaign as intensely as if it mattered. Joe knew that winning against a weak opponent would be of little interest in the state and less interest elsewhere unless he could gain a lopsided victory and the numbers would warrant stories in newspapers throughout the country. By the time Joe finished coordinating a campaign executed as though it were critical for political survival, Jack amassed 874,608 votes more than his little-known opponent. The win was to be expected. The numbers generated headlines.

During this same period, the self-created tragedy of Joe's life became evident in a way that might have forever altered for the better a more introspective man less afraid to evolve as he experienced life.

For years Joe thought that if he could acquire the houses, the cars, the clothing, the influence, and everything else enjoyed by those whose respect he desired, they would view him with awe. He failed to realize that the men whose approval he wanted were not in a race to check off the most items on some fabled acquisition list that, when completed, would assure a life of unprecedented esteem. Worse, Joe's greatest pain came from his years at Harvard decades earlier.

Joe Kennedy was not shunned at Harvard solely because he was Catholic. Instead, he had done everything in his power to assure that he would be an outcast. His money-earning scams, his bribes of classmates, his stealing the Harvard/Yale baseball game ball, and his use of family connections to put pressure on classmate endeavors requiring city government agency assistance had all assured a lack of acceptance.

Joe also had been arrogant about athletic competition while making little effort at academics. Then he had tried to get the school to honor him over men who had achieved greatness in endeavors that benefited others, not just the Kennedy family, as the ambassadorship had done.

A different man might have attended class reunions, accepting the deserved (and sometimes undeserved) ridicule for his past, admitting to his immaturity, and started fresh. Then those who had rejected him based on such matters as his religion would likely have become less hostile, perhaps even friendly. He might have made some business alliances or been sought after for advice. He might have put the past behind him and spent his later years in the company of men who shared more in common in life than their perceived differences.

Instead, Joe built an emotional wall to protect himself from the past, made it thicker with each reminiscence, then came to fear the presence of the men he had once tried so hard to please. The ridicule he experienced when he joined the SEC had stayed with him for almost two decades. Yet always he was lonely. Always he longed for the masculine companionship he saw other Harvard men enjoying with one another.

Joe took an apartment on Boston's Beacon Street while preparing Jack for the 1958 Senate reelection campaign and coordinating the national effort for the run at the presidency. He wanted to be someplace where he would have a low profile and not become an issue in his son's campaign. What he did not know was that the apartment building also was the address of Raymond S. Wilkins, chief justice of the Massachusetts Supreme Court, and the former Harvard classmate who had written part of the show that was used in the last reunion Joe attended. Wilkins had no idea that Joe was offended. He seemed to think that the humor was a tribute in the manner of a "roast." He also realized that Joe did not recognize him when he saw him in the apartment building so many years later.

Wilkins invited Joe to his suite, and soon Kennedy and the judge's wife were friends as well. Then Wilkins called Oscar Haussermann, a successful Boston lawyer and also a former classmate. The two men realized that Joe was intensely lonely. They recognized that he seemed to see himself as an essential liability in Jack's reelection campaign. His money and his contacts were helping his son gain the lopsided victory that was needed. At the same time, the issue of his money and his past speeches could cost Jack votes. The seat Jack held was safe, and he would be returned to office, but when every vote counted to give Jack the greatest possible landslide, Joe could not be around, since his presence might offend.

Haussermann and Wilkins apparently also understood Joe's fears and emotions about Harvard. Certainly they knew that Joe had been shunning their regular gatherings of former classmates. They also were aware that he had earlier attended the Boston Latin School Class of 1908's fiftieth-year reunion, making clear when invited that he wanted nothing to do with similar celebrations for Harvard.

Haussermann began calling classmates of Joe's from the Harvard Class of 1912. He selected those men who had never harbored ill will in the manner Joe was certain had existed. These were men who had enjoyed their classmate, though Joe had been too blind to realize it.

The classmates were invited to gather in a private dining room in the Boston Union Club. There they could eat, drink, and talk about the past and about those aspects of personal and professional life that everyone of their generation was likely to experience.

There were approximately a dozen former classmates in all at the Union Club when Joe made his appearance. He was frightened, but when he quickly realized that they simply enjoyed each other's company and had genuinely missed his presence, he was deeply moved.

The evening was one of the most enjoyable Joe Kennedy had had or would have again. It also was the last time he was known to have let himself be vulnerable to others in so emotionally meaningful a manner. Tragically, instead of reflecting on his life and risking reaching out to others in the future, he left the gathering to return to the world he felt was safe. He continued the familiar role of strategist, banker, and attacker against all who would stand in the way of his achieving the dreams that proved so unsatisfactory in their reality.

*   *   *

Perhaps because of the dinner, perhaps because of the usual pressure and bribes, and perhaps because having someone politically connected and rich on its side always was good for a school, Jack was elected to Harvard's Board of Overseers. Joe used his son's position to inspire other Kennedy supporters. He stressed that if a Catholic could be elected to the Harvard Board of Overseers, no other office would be such a test.

Joe also handled most of the media contacts for Jack. Publishers and writers who could be convinced to produce favorable articles were given special access. In addition, Jack and Ted Sorensen, the latter working as his speechwriter, would travel the nation so Jack could give talks. By 1958 the senator's office would have at least a hundred requests for interviews each week. Yet if you asked those requesting exactly what Jack had done in the Senate, the programs he advocated, the bills he sponsored, the national stances he had taken, they would be hard put to think of any. Jack Kennedy's job, as carefully shaped by his father, was to run for president. His work in the Senate had to be squeezed in only as absolutely necessary.

Joe's concerns about Jack's image as husband and father ended in November 1957, when granddaughter Caroline was born by cesarean section. This time Jack was present at the birth, and this time he genuinely seemed to care that Jacqueline had given him his first child.

The couple's relationship was otherwise strained, though to what degree is impossible to know. Too many of the people who worked for the couple told different stories and ascribed different meanings to the same events. To some, Jacqueline was lazy and self-absorbed, someone who spent most of her time by herself and seemed obsessed with both her appearance and constantly remodeling the couple's first home. Others saw a lonely woman deeply hurt by her husband's well-known affairs. She had the money to hire a staff for everything, including Maud Shaw, who was Caroline's nanny, and Jack delighted in the well-run household, where there was order to everything except the continuous redecorating.

Jacqueline also was careful to involve herself in the 1958 Senate race, proving to Joe that no matter what stress she and Jack were under, his daughter-in-law would go along with the Kennedy program. She lacked Rose's campaign experience, yet she instinctively understood how to present herself. She wore little jewelry or makeup. Her hairstyle was simple and easy to care for. And her clothing always included hats and white gloves. Everything about her indicated both class and respect for the voters who began flocking to meet her. Joe realized that whenever the couple were together, twice as many people would come out than when Jack went alone to the same areas.

December 1958 brought an unexpected crisis the candidate needed to handle. Minnesota senator Hubert Humphrey was already in trouble as he campaigned hard for the Democratic nomination for president in 1960. He had one of the most liberal records of leading senators in the nation. He had a compassion for others seemingly lacking in Jack. And he had a relaxed, friendly manner that belied the intensity of his beliefs and his desire to campaign. Humphrey's opposition was the only serious onslaught against Jack at that time, but it was not his greatest problem.

In the years since her husband's death, Eleanor Roosevelt had come into her own as a writer, speaker, and voice for liberal politics. In the past, as a president's wife, she always had to be concerned about Franklin—what he thought, what he was planning, how what she said and did might impact on his reelection campaigns. She had let him edit her writing before it was sent to the editors of the magazines, newspapers, and others in the media as she freelanced her work. With his death, she could speak her mind.

Eleanor always had despised Joe Kennedy. She saw him as a man of few moral principles. As for his son Jack, he was someone she felt would not or could not take a stand on anything. The only time Eleanor noticed a hint of compassion was when he and Jacqueline made a trip to rural West Virginia, a horrendous world of poverty unlike either had encountered elsewhere in the United States. Depending on where they traveled, they found isolated communities suffering from every physical and social ill—from malnutrition, lack of plumbing and contaminated water, to incest and birth defects. Many children died before reaching their teenage years, and many thirty-year-old men were aged beyond their years.

The horror of rural West Virginia had been a concern of Eleanor's for two decades. But where Eleanor actively worked to improve the lives of the people she encountered, including trying to arrange help long after she left, the Kennedys were not disturbed enough to return other than for political reasons.

Eleanor began writing about Jack in her column, considering him young and charming. She also stressed that he was too much under his father's thumb, and she had always hated the self-serving Joe. That

On January 12, 1960, hours after announcing his candidacy for the Democratic nomination for president of the United States, Jack Kennedy met with Eleanor Roosevelt for a self-serving photo opportunity. She seems to be endorsing the strong candidate as he gestures meaningfully during a conversation at the Brandeis University campus. Eleanor Roosevelt was extremely wary of the youth, not trusting him because she despised his father and felt that the son would be just as bad. (Cleveland State University Library, Special Collections)

December Eleanor told an interviewer that only Humphrey had what she called a "spark of greatness." She stressed that Joe was trying to buy the presidency for his son and probably had paid representatives throughout the country. She also felt that Jack had never stood up to Joe McCarthy when the senator was spewing hate and attacking people for being "Communists" when he had no proof of such involvement.

Joe was frightened by the power of Eleanor Roosevelt. She had become a successful writer since leaving the world of politics. She was intelligent, compassionate, articulate, and thoroughly honest. Some people hated her, but more people loved her. No one questioned her sincerity even when they disagreed with her beliefs. As a result, he knew he had to neutralize her, and toward that end he asked Jack to invite Franklin Roosevelt Jr. to dinner. The younger Roosevelt was close to his mother in ways Jimmy was not. To the Kennedys' dismay, Franklin Jr. also understood the purpose of the dinner. What shocked him was Jack's inability to make an effective case. Instead the young senator came across obsessed with his position and his problems. Roosevelt considered him politically immature and had no intention of saying anything kind about Jack to his mother.

Jack, by contrast, encouraged comparisons between himself and Roosevelt's father. He implied that he was his own man to those audiences fearful of his father's seeming anti-Semitism and isolationism at a time when the Middle East was volatile and Israel was constantly threatened by outside forces. He worked to separate himself from his father, as though he were both enlightened and someone who understood the New Deal, seeing where it still could benefit the nation. In New York, a crucial state with forty-five electoral votes, the *New York Times* found that many in the large Jewish community were fearful of Kennedy being like his father. However, by Election Day the forced separation of father and son in the minds of the voters was successful enough so that many within New York's Jewish community were ignoring Joe and saying that Jack reminded them of Franklin Sr. It was an idea that would have horrified the rest of the Roosevelt family, but it was effective politics.

The situation in West Virginia has been discussed repeatedly. The gambling machine information came from men such as Alan Friedman, who was long involved with businesses where cash could be skimmed. Others talked about political corruption. Since it was rare for anyone to be indicted on any political corruption charge in West Virginia, the truth is somewhat elusive.

Allegedly during the years after World War II and going into the 1960s, a number of key officials were taking money to assure that elections would be won, businesses used, vending machines installed, or whatever else was desired. The corruption allegedly reached the top— the governor's office, the state police, and the like. The problem is that no one interviewed knew if it was true. They knew that cash changed hands. They knew that results were achieved, whether the removal of one company's vending machine and the replacement by another or an election being swayed through bribes. There was always a middle person so that no one could say, "I handed the briefcase of cash to governor so-and-so." It was always, "He took the briefcase of cash for the governor."

Was West Virginia "bought" by Joe Kennedy? Yes. Who was corrupted? No one but the men involved know for certain.

Joe's methods were numerous. One of them was discussed by a number of writers, including Peter Maas and Ronald Kessler.

Joe wanted to be able to benefit from tax breaks on his deals, as he had in the past. In a variation of his earlier schemes, he allegedly made arrangements with Archbishop Cushing—now also a cardinal—to donate money to the Boston Archdiocese of the Catholic Church in a way that gave him a tax deduction and untraceable working capital. The arrangement involved the collection of all donated money in all the Catholic churches in the archdiocese on a particular Sunday. The sum would be totaled, then Joe would write a check to the archdiocese for that amount plus many thousands of dollars more. He might give $250,000 when the archdiocese collected $225,000, as an example. Whatever the case, the check would go to the archdiocese, and the cash would go to Joe.

This resulted in two benefits. First, the Catholic archdiocese retained all the money offered plus an extra donation from Joe Kennedy that otherwise would not have been made. Second, Joe received a deduction for the full amount of the check, setting the cash aside to use as he pleased. No one was hurt, yet Joe had essentially laundered money he could pay under the table. There were no records that could come back to haunt him, and the church did nothing illegal. The leaders reported the gross income received. The parishioners had their own legitimate deductions. And Joe had working capital otherwise not available to him without disclosing its use. He also had a deduction that would not be challenged by the IRS because he was in an income bracket where such a donation would not be out of line.

Part of the problem with West Virginia was the anti-Catholic bias that permeated the state. In a poll taken before the primary, Jack Kennedy led Hubert Humphrey 70 percent to 30 percent. When the people learned that Kennedy was Catholic, many expressed concern to the news media that Jack would be under the control of the Pope. The next poll showed overwhelming support for Hubert Humphrey solely because of the religious issue. Humphrey was then able to develop a volunteer organization consisting of men and women who were politically savvy and those individuals they recruited.

Joe Kennedy knew that the state was pragmatic in its hatred, and he did not want Jack or anyone from the staff trying to reason with the people or talk about issues.

Instead he had his people seek out each of the political organizers and offer $150 to have the person switch allegiance to Jack. Each person who volunteered to work for the organizer on the Humphrey campaign was offered $20 to do the same work for Jack. And when poverty is so great that most people had to hunt, fish, and trap to have adequate food, even $20 was a little like winning the lottery.

The anti-Catholic sentiment remained strong enough that Rose Kennedy chose not to go into West Virginia to campaign for her son.

Eventually, when Kennedy won the primary and even those who were against him personally rallied behind him as the party candidate, Franklin Roosevelt Jr. agreed to sign an endorsement of Kennedy that would be mailed to every registered voter in the state. Roosevelt's father, when president, had fought to give the miners the right to organize, bargain collectively, and eventually earn a living wage. Life was still hard by the time Jack was running for president, but it was easier than it had been.

As a further reminder of and connection to the late president, Joe arranged for the mailing of the endorsements to come from Hyde Park, the Roosevelt home area. It was a subtle addition to the mailing of basic campaign literature, but it mattered to the people receiving it.

In those areas where Rose felt she could campaign, she addressed the papal influence question directly. She explained that the Vatican was in Italy, and that Italy was a predominantly Catholic country. Yet it was obvious over the years that the Pope had no influence whatever in Italy's governmental affairs. The same situation was true with the White House.

Rose also explained that there was no Catholic voice. Catholics had never voted as a bloc and often were at odds with one another.

When Joe sent staff into the same areas, he did not waste their time by having them try to persuade the locals that the little-known Senator Kennedy was the better, more compassionate man. He had them spend money.

The money Joe was spending should have been an issue within the Democratic Party because West Virginia had become a blatant area for buying support. Hubert Humphrey was rightfully livid, yet there were no laws against what Joe was doing. At the same time, questions about the character of Jack and all his family were being raised by people who could hurt the senator. Finally, during one gathering in New York as the general election approached, Jack went on the offensive with humor. "I got a wire from my father," he announced. "Dear Jack: Don't buy one vote more than necessary. I'll be damned if I'll pay for a landslide."

Jack did beat Humphrey in the primary, and the win seemed to both startle and please Joe. The elder Kennedy was still a virile man, athletic, sexually active with a variety of women, and with acquaintances at the top of political power and business leadership. His son was a scrawny, sickly young man with a handsome face, growing self-confidence, yet no meaningful achievements of his own. Suddenly Joe realized that the boy was going to go all the way to the top. Jack was going to be the first Kennedy president of the United States.

While Jack and speechwriter Ted Sorensen were effectively using humor, comics who were mocking the family were considered risks.

The most unusual story from this time concerns Mort Sahl, a stand-up comic who began his career in San Francisco at a club owned by Enrico Banducci called the hungry i. There were no humorists like Sahl in the early 1950s, though his irreverence and focus on the actions of politicians were reminiscent of Will Rogers. Sahl felt it was his job to criticize the incumbent, whoever that might be. For example, one of his jokes about President Eisenhower was that he had ridden into the White House on a white horse, but four years later, only the horse was left.

Sahl delighted in tweaking the ultrawholesome image of then vice president Richard Nixon, talking about his quiet evenings at home with the children where he is reading the Constitution while his wife, Pat, is knitting a flag.

It was Nixon who became an early fan of Sahl's as he gained increasing attention, first in San Francisco and later in jazz clubs around the country. At the time there were no comedy clubs as such. Much of Sahl's work came from clubs featuring jazz music, then extremely popular. *San Francisco Chronicle* columnist Herb Caen, arguably the most influential writer in the city, and comic Steve Allen, then dominating late-night television, promoted Sahl and gave him extensive exposure. Nixon had the maturity to see the irreverent sense of a Will Rogers, never mean-spirited or one-sided. The vice president suggested that he begin taking on all politicians equally, and soon he was telling jokes about all of them.

In one routine, Sahl created a series of television shows that would star the various Republican and Democratic politicians who were making a move for power in the 1960 election. He said, "How about *Leave it to Beaver* with Senator Kennedy? Leave it to Eager. I have a good opening shot: Senator Kennedy coming in with a slingshot and going to the refrigerator for some peanut butter and milk and jam.

"Offstage voice of family: 'What did you do today, Jack?'

" 'I got a haircut and talked with some people. Got along with them pretty well.'

" 'Have you thought about what you want to be, Jack?'

" 'I want to be president.'

" 'We know that. We mean when you grow up.' "[1]

During one appearance Sahl said, "We've finally got a choice, the choice between the lesser of two evils. Nixon wants to sell the country, and Kennedy wants to buy it." It was the same type of humor that Kennedy had used in a self-deprecating manner, and Joe Kennedy loved it. Joe went to Sahl and hired him to write jokes that could be used during the campaign.

Sahl did not stop his own brand of humor, and Jack loved the independence of his wit. Joe accepted it grudgingly during the campaign. For example, after the first debate between Jack Kennedy and Richard Nixon, Sahl said that Kennedy and Nixon both lost.

"If I wanted to help someone running for president, I think I should endorse the guy running against him. I think that's how I could be the most help."[2]

Jack Kennedy delighted in Sahl, but his father became increasingly uneasy. As it became obvious that Jack might win the presidential election, he stopped tolerating the sexual banter and schoolboy-type jokes they shared from the early days of their friendship through the start of the 1960 campaign. He made clear that when Jack was elected, he would be "Mr. President." Friends would have to watch their language. They would have to watch the topics of their discussions. It was as though Joe perceived the achievement to be one of such importance, the human side of the winner had to be suppressed. There also was the attitude of the person who has never escaped the memory of childhood taunts and ridicule.

Joe was increasingly like the trim, handsome man who once was shunned and ridiculed when he was an obese loner, plagued with acne. No matter how the adult might have trimmed down, shaped up, and become handsome, the mirror of his mind still reflects the unattractive "late bloomer" for whom each day is a struggle to pretend that the taunts and name-calling did not hurt. Through Jack he might achieve something greater than he had been able to accomplish, yet it also was Jack who should not have been the first Kennedy to hold the office. Once again Joe was the loser. Once again he feared the reactions of others.

With Sahl, Joe's irrational feelings would come to a head after the election. Sahl explained that he always felt his job was to take on the incumbent. He had no party loyalty. He felt that someone who deserves accolades should be lauded. He also felt that someone who deserved to be shown to be pompous, foolish, or out of line also should be talked about. He knew that Jack Kennedy enjoyed his constant humanizing of the man who had become president when Joe finally sought retribution. A mutual business associate of Peter Lawford warned him that the "old man" wanted Sahl to back off.

Sahl traveled the nation, but his home base was always San Francisco's hungry i. When the warnings came, he talked with Enrico Banducci, who had received the same warning from the same person. Sahl said he asked Banducci what he should do, and the club owner said he should continue doing his act as he saw fit. He could not imagine what pressure might be brought.

Not long after this, Banducci said that he walked into his office and found his secretary holding a piece of paper and crying.[3] The letter was from the government, demanding a payment of $490,000. It was far more money than Banducci had or could raise. It also had to be an error. He was an honest businessman who carefully reported his business's income, paid all taxes, and kept current with debts. He said that it was obviously a mistake, that the sum must be $490 or $4.90. He told her to call the agency that sent the letter and have them correct it. She said that she had called and that it was right. Two months later the hungry i was closed. Evidently, Joe Kennedy had his revenge.

While Mort Sahl was an irritant for Joe, a very serious question during this period was Jacqueline. No one is certain what she knew or when she knew it. She understood that she was not loved in a manner that honored the marriage vows. She recognized that Jack was having affairs, though it is not known if she knew with whom. She and her brother-in-law Peter Lawford were close friends, yet he and Pat were letting Jack use their Beverly Hills home for some of his assignations.

The problem was more serious than Jacqueline realized. Jack's affairs had become an issue of potential control through blackmail. Everyone from organized criminals to FBI director J. Edgar Hoover wanted to control Jack Kennedy. They wanted to know that he was compromised so that they would have influence when he took office.

Hoover had been involved with the family the longest. He had known he "owned" Jack in March 1942 when, according to Ronald McCoy, Inga Arvad's son, speaking with author Anthony Summers, his mother and Jack realized that Hoover was tapping their telephones. "Jack was furious. Through his father or through Arthur Krock, he knew everybody, so he and Mother [Inga] went to see J. Edgar Hoover. Hoover told them his investigation showed she was *not* a Nazi spy or did anything for them. So Jack asked Hoover if he would give them a letter saying she wasn't a Nazi spy. Hoover said he couldn't because if he gave her a letter and then she went out and started working for them tomorrow, his ass was on the line."[4]

In 1951 the FBI began what amounted to overt surveillance. A four-person resident agency was opened in Hyannis Port. The community was so small and the nature of the crimes routinely being investigated by the agency of such a nature that there was no reason for it to be there other than to assist the family of the ambassador, the congressman, and the others. Actually, it was the office from which the agents were expected to file reports on the Kennedys.

Always Hoover was concerned with Jack, his father, and his brothers. Joe was as close to a friend as existed within the Kennedy family, but that was a relative term. The relationship between Joe and the director was like that of two chess players whose personal greetings are cordial but whose board play is cutthroat.

J. Edgar Hoover was not the only person trying to protect his power. Jimmy Hoffa was battling Bobby Kennedy who, in 1959, was the chief counsel for the Senate Labor Rackets Committee (later called the McClellan Committee). The committee not only investigated the Teamsters Union, the results of the committee's investigation became yet another Kennedy book—*The Enemy Within*, written by Bobby with John Seigenthaler.

The Teamsters Union was the strongest and wealthiest union in the United States. Whereas the railroad had been one of the nation's largest employers of men in 1945, the growth of the suburbs reduced the importance of rail in American life and boosted the need for truckers. Everything from groceries to fuel suddenly had to move by truck. Teamsters Union membership soared and its pension fund increased to $4 billion, an amount that made it a major player when real-estate developers and others needed multimillion-dollar loans.

Most of the members of the Teamsters Union were honest, as were many of the leaders. Even Jimmy Hoffa was honored for his efforts to improve the wages and benefits of working-class Americans. Yet the money available for corruption, whether to buy the support of political candidates or to assure kickbacks from developers, assured that even the most dedicated also were often dishonest. Some, including Jimmy Hoffa, Bill Presser, and Alan Friedman, also were working with members of organized crime. And with Bobby destined for an important role in a Kennedy presidency, the Teamsters wanted whatever information they could get to neutralize the brothers if Jack won.[5]

With the corruption, the hatred of Bob, and the desire to continue business as usual, some of the corrupt Teamsters leadership[6] eventually hired private investigators, such as the West Coast's Fred Otash, to arrange to wiretap the Kennedys and their acquaintances. They wanted to catch them in compromising circumstances to use as blackmail whenever they were threatened with criminal action. Some of the wiretaps and listening devices were placed in the Los Angeles area homes of women known to be friends or lovers of Jack, based on his past trips to California.

During this same period, members of organized crime, often using the same wiretap experts, were rigging hotel rooms in casinos where Jack came to watch the Rat Pack perform. Sinatra and Lawford would arrange for women to be sent to his suite, not knowing that he was being recorded. Beautiful women were constantly available, and Kennedy used poor judgment in his response.

The Kennedy family did not realize how this might affect their actions in the White House, though some organized-crime experts consider the Jack Kennedy years to be the ones where the mob had the greatest influence. What is certain is that J. Edgar Hoover blackmailed Jack. He knew that the Kennedys wanted him fired. They had chosen William Parker, the innovative chief of police for the city of Los Angeles and the man for whom its headquarters would eventually be named, to take over the FBI. They thought they could get Hoover to quietly resign when he knew they had access to the photographs taken of the director with his lover, Clyde Tolson. They would express appropriate regrets for his loss, have him feted for his many years of service, then be done with him while Parker reconstructed the bureau into a more efficient, less insular agency. Unfortunately, Hoover had access to images and sound recordings of Kennedy with a myriad of women other than his wife.

Perhaps the most important liaison, both in terms of what Jack gained and the potential for blackmail, came on February 7, 1960, when Nick Sevano, Frank Sinatra's on-again, off-again manager for twenty-three years, was sitting in the Sands Hotel with two women who were talking about getting into show business. Frank was there, and when Jack Kennedy came in, he was obviously taken with one of the women, Judith Campbell (later known as Judith Campbell Exner). She was a beautiful brunette who also was known as a "starfucker." This is a derogatory term for a woman who is so enamored with both show business and the persona created by an entertainer that she seeks to become a part of his life, if only for one night. Some of these women hang out in clubs, waiting for the main act, getting an introduction, then going to bed with the star. They acquire experiences with famous men the way Joe was figuratively putting notches on his bedpost each time he had an eager though forgettable starlet, in the manner of a Wild West gunslinger notching the weapon's handle for each bad guy he shot.

Judith Campbell was different. She enjoyed longer-term relationships, more like the rock music groupies of the 1960s. They would be spread among two or three powerful men, but they were sustained over time.

In Judith's case, as discussed in her autobiography *My Story* (with Ovid Demaris) and her extensive interview with Kitty Kelley for the February 29, 1988, issue of *People* magazine, she was sexually available to several men. These included Frank Sinatra and mob boss Sam Giancana, along with Jack Kennedy when the senator expressed an interest in her.[7]

It is doubtful that any man successfully ran for the presidency with so much working against him. Jack's good fortune was that his father laid the groundwork for his son as a product, and the people who wanted to secretly use him could not benefit until he was in power.

For Jacqueline there was an overriding issue rarely discussed. She was at risk of getting a sexually transmitted disease, and the idea was terrifying for her.

Jacqueline also was an unknown in the political process. She was a woman who exuded sophistication and breeding, hunted foxes, and was a skilled equestrienne. Her voice was soft, refined, and quite different from the rather raucous Kennedy sisters, who so enthusiastically worked the nation for votes. She came into a room shy, quiet, obviously out of her element, and uncomfortable pushing herself onto others, a trait much like that of her husband in his early days of campaigning.

Allegedly the public was as uncomfortable with Jacqueline as she was with them. This was why the Kennedy sisters did not want her around at times. Yet they also were faced with the paradox that most female reporters and many of the men in the media were taken with Jacqueline. For eight years there had been Mamie Eisenhower, the nation's grandmother, a long-suffering woman who had endured the absence of her husband as he fought the war. She had a middle ear condition that often made balance difficult and that led some observers to see her as an uncontrolled alcoholic.[8] Before her was Bess Truman, a stay-at-home housewife type suddenly elevated to first lady by the death of Franklin Roosevelt. Both women were long past the age when the latest style of clothing mattered to them.

Jacqueline was different. She was the woman many of the female reporters would have been if they had come from her background. And though she was quiet, she had not become the inquiring photographer by lacking aggression when she needed it.

There have been stories that Jacqueline was seriously thinking of divorcing Jack before he took office. Allegedly Joe offered her money to stay, and more money if Jack brought home a sexually transmitted disease. However, it is doubtful that she was as mercenary as is routinely alleged.

Jacqueline had seen what happened with her parents' marriage. She was a woman of breeding, education, and infinite curiosity. Her father was dying without being able to help her financially. Her mother, Janet Auchincloss, did not seem the type of woman to finance her daughter's crisis. And Janet had married a man who delighted in giving Black Jack Bouvier's daughters nothing in the way of financial support.

Worse, a divorce would cast Jacqueline in the role of the villain. Jack Kennedy was seen as a war hero, devoted husband, and father. If she had gone public with Jack's womanizing, it is doubtful that anyone would have believed her. It is more doubtful that anyone would have published the information.

Typical was what happened with columnist Walter Winchell when he was in Los Angeles to cover the 1960 Democratic national convention. Jack arranged for a sexual interlude with a woman who lived in an apartment owned by his friend Jack Haley Sr. Several reporters caught him sneaking out of the building, though he managed to convince most of them that he was there to see his friend. Winchell was the one exception. He was able to learn what Kennedy had been doing and thought it was a great story.

Winchell got the details, then rushed to the telephone to call his editor in New York. He explained that the senator had been having an affair. He gave the time, date, location, and name. Then, to his amazement, the editor expressed shock, not delight. Senator Jack Kennedy was a married man, the editor reminded Winchell. It was wrong to embarrass a married man. There was no doubting Winchell's fact-checking. Such stories just weren't to be published.

Later the Kennedy family would try to defuse the information. Jack had rented an apartment on North Rossmore Boulevard near the Los Angeles Sports Arena so he could get some rest, they said. When he was seen sneaking down the fire escape, he was simply leaving to be with his parents away from the prying eyes of reporters.

And Jack did go to see his parents, who were staying in the Beverly Hills mansion of Marion Davies. She was eleven miles from the Biltmore Hotel, where room 8315 had been converted to the Kennedy for President command post. Joe wanted to avoid being seen as a manipula-

tor, though Marion arranged for the installation of a battery of telephones for him to use to control the action from her poolside.

Jack won the Democratic Party's nomination, much to the bemusement of some of the Republican observers. They understood what was
happening with Joe. They recognized the older man's ruse of hiding out
and manipulating strategy from behind the scenes.

Throughout the early days of the campaign there were numerous,
endlessly repeated Republican jokes, such as "In America, any boy can
grow up to run for president, especially if his father has four hundred
million dollars." Also there was:

Jack and Bob will run the show
While Ted's in charge of hiding Joe.

There was even a Republican bumper sticker ridiculing the large
family's maneuvering throughout the country: "Be Thankful Only One
Can Win." What they did not say was that they would have used similar strategy if Richard Nixon's campaign could have been manipulated
in the same way.

There were two other important people during this period. One was
Lyndon Johnson, the man chosen for the vice-presidential spot on the
Democratic ticket. He had been a powerful behind-the-scenes player in
the Senate, a man who understood the game in the manner of Joe Kennedy, whom he hated. (Johnson once commented about Joe's prewar
record by saying, "I wasn't any Chamberlain umbrella man.")

The Texas senator was a former poorly paid schoolteacher who became extremely wealthy and powerful through ways as devious as those
of the elder Kennedy. He, too, was a womanizer. But Johnson brought
important additions to the ticket. Southerners respected him, yet he was
a genuine liberal in areas that mattered. He believed in the civil rights
movement that had begun in the national political arena with the 1948
Democratic Party platform. He spoke to blocs of voters who would not
give Jack a chance any other way.

The second critical person was Jacqueline, who was emotionally
shattered by her husband's philandering. She knew that if she did not
make her financial deal with Joe, in whom she took great delight, she
would have been vilified by her father-in-law and his minions should
she seek a separation or divorce. She understood that Joe was a rogue in

the manner of her own father, whom she adored. She also understood that, unlike Black Jack, Joe would cold-bloodedly destroy any person who stood in the way of his son's becoming president, in the family or a married outsider.

The deal struck with Joe would protect her. She admired Jack. She believed in his ability to lead. She was willing to trade a few years in limbo for his triumph and financial security when it all came to an end. In the meantime, she intended to protect her daughter, and later her son, John Jr., from the influences of the Kennedy family members she found so destructive.

Peter and Pat Lawford also struck a bargain, though theirs was not financial. He was a well-paid actor. She had her trust fund.

Peter had never adjusted to the Kennedy family, though he adored Jack and the two became close friends. Peter had once worked as a parking lot attendant for a property Joe Kennedy owned in Florida. There were two other youths on Peter's shift, both black, and the three used to play cards when there was nothing else to do. Joe caught them, and while he did not mind the card playing, he was not pleased with Peter's socializing. He was even less pleased with the fact that Peter was an aspiring actor whose family was from England. He certainly never expected to have the man as a son-in-law.

Peter and Pat had a highly destructive lifestyle. She enjoyed playing cards until late at night. Peter, if working on a film or television show, had to be up early. His wife encouraged him to take sleeping pills so he could get to sleep quicker after a night's activities. Then came stimulants to enable him to work, and alcohol to relax. They both knew that the marriage was over. They both knew that they would need to divorce. They also knew that since both loved Jack, there was no way they would do it at a time when it might hurt him in office. That was why they explained to him that as soon as he took the oath of office for his second term, they would divorce.

Ultimately everyone was living a lie for Jack, and Joe was pulling all the strings.

Rose, who might have been horrified to hear the talk of divorce, ignored everyone in order to put her son in office. The Democratic Party noted that, in 1960, there were an estimated 3 million women who were registered voters and *not* expected to turn out at the polls. She knew that their votes could make the difference, so she began organizing gatherings with women on a national scale.

Jack ridiculed his mother at first. He understood what had worked fourteen years earlier in a single election district. He did not think it would still work. Then he began studying the demographics provided by the Democratic Party's research. In 1960, registered women voters far outnumbered registered male voters in Massachusetts. However, male voters far outnumbered the women who actually went to the polls. This was true for both parties, and it appeared to be a consistent situation in most states. Yet both the Republicans and the Democrats virtually ignored women. They focused almost exclusively on bringing out the male vote. Except Rose. She began a drive to get women to the polls that, in part, became a model for some of the 1964 work with formerly disenfranchised blacks.

While Rose was handling the living, others were handling the dead. The first clearly identified deal was the one made to assure Jack's success in the West Virginia primary. Payoffs were effective, of course, but it always helped to have more votes for your candidate than there are registered voters. It was the tried-and-true method of nineteenth-century Boston politicians. A century later it was still a good idea.

According to authors Sam and Chuck Giancana, writing in *Double Cross*, Joe, Jack, and Sam Giancana (the mobster; the coauthor is Sam's nephew and namesake) had an agreement concerning West Virginia. Using Skinny D'Amato, the manager of the Cal-Neva Lodge in which Frank Sinatra and Giancana were investors, Giancana alerted the Kennedys that West Virginia would be taken care of provided Joe Adonis was allowed back into the United States. Adonis, as powerful on the New York board of mob families as Lucky Luciano, Carlo Gambino, and Louis "Lepke" Buchalter, was a multimillionaire from business investments. He also was a murderer, engaged in prostitution, and had been in bootlegging, gambling, and most other crimes the mob enjoyed. Then, on January 3, 1956, the government had accumulated enough charges against him to deport him to Milan, where he maintained his wealth, a hedonistic lifestyle, but a desire to return to the power he had known in New York. Joe and Jack allegedly said that the matter would be handled when Jack was in the White House. Instead, Adonis remained in Italy, living in great luxury until his death in 1972.

The story has some problems for researchers. D'Amato allegedly was able to bring $50,000 in cash for use in West Virginia, too small an amount to be meaningful. He then made the mistake of bragging that he had moved money to help Jack win in the state. This was caught on an FBI wiretap after Jack was in office, and the information was provided by a gleeful J. Edgar Hoover to an irate Bob Kennedy.

Bob knew that the best way to defuse a politically embarrassing story was to create a situation where the person telling the truth would not be believed. He indicted D'Amato for failure to file a corporate tax return for his club. D'Amato actually had no profit, so filing was not necessary. It was clear that if the case went to court, D'Amato would be exonerated. It was equally clear that if D'Amato told what he had done for the Kennedys, he probably would not be believed. The false charges would seem truthful, and the true allegations would come across as vengeful lies.

Jack Kennedy was indirectly linked with the mob through intermediaries such as Judith Campbell Exner and his brother Bob. A portion of Exner's story that she was a courier between Kennedy and Giancana has been confirmed. In the *People* magazine interview with Kitty Kelley in 1988 Exner mentioned that ten meetings were set up between the two men, but there has been no independent confirmation that they met directly.

Stories about Bob Kennedy are more problematic, since they come from sources who are credible, were present, and yet were never introduced to the alleged mobster by name. Joe Naar, a longtime friend of Peter Lawford, mentioned during an interview for a biography of the late actor that he, Peter, and Bob Kennedy had been in Las Vegas before the election. Bob excused himself to meet with a man referred to as "Mr. Match." Naar said that he later saw a picture of Sam Giancana and realized that "Match" and the mobster were one and the same.

Most interesting were comments made by the late private investigator Fred Otash when discussing his life for a planned autobiography. During the interviews he mentioned the impending divorce of Peter Fairchild and his wife, Judy Meredith. Fairchild was a restaurateur, Meredith an actress. Fairchild was Otash's client, and he had allegedly found numerous instances of adultery, including with "Dean Martin, Jerry Lewis, Frank Sinatra etc., etc. etc." One of the men who was not named was Jack Kennedy, presumably enjoying the woman when he was a senator and hanging out with the Rat Pack. (Otash was able to document Jack's presence, though his name was not included in the original filing.)

Mobster Johnny Roselli, who eventually would be murdered after visiting Otash in his Florida apartment, asked to meet Otash at the Brown Derby Restaurant. He said he was acting for the attorney general—Bob Kennedy.

The meeting with Roselli was held in the presence of two FBI men. Roselli explained that Fred was in trouble because he was about to name

John Kennedy as a corespondent. Roselli said he was representing Jack Kennedy.

Otash, a former Los Angeles Police officer who specialized, when possible, in members of the mob, was outraged. He believed Roselli was telling the truth. He also was enough of an idealist to be shocked by the relationship between the president and a criminal, and enough of a realist to be scared. He could have any manner of problems in the manner of Mort Sahl and the hungry i. However, it was in his nature to put on a public show, so he told Roselli he would not cooperate.

There would be a handful of other meetings, one of which allegedly included Sam Giancana. Otash explained that Judy Meredith was adamant about wanting $100,000 from her ex-husband to go quietly into the night. He said that Peter Fairchild had been hurt so badly by the adultery that he wasn't going to pay her anything. Fred had the proof that she had been having sex with numerous men, and he planned to present all their names to the judge when they went into court. Jack Kennedy would be among those named.

The matter was handled quietly. Fred and his client were in the judge's chambers with the amended Fairchild divorce papers naming Jack Kennedy along with all the other men he felt he could confirm as Judy's sex partners. Before the divorce could proceed, someone entered with a check that was handed to Judy's lawyers. She was satisfied and stopped fighting for the divorce.

There would be more. Robert Kennedy received an FBI memo from J. Edgar Hoover on February 27, 1962. It explained that there was wiretap proof that Judy Campbell had been making telephone calls to both the White House and Sam Giancana. Since Bob was by then making the fight against organized crime a priority of his administration, the director wanted to reveal that he was on top of all that was taking place.

So what was going on as the election approached? As near as can be determined, Joe Kennedy had laid the groundwork for mob involvement in obtaining votes through the assistance of key leaders of organized-crime families. Joe supplied the money. The mob supplied the contacts and the organization, and they were responsible for the grassroots bribery.

The mob activities were paybacks to Joe for various favors done over the years. As always, Joe made certain that everyone approached was already beholden to him for past favors. He let Jack in on what he was doing, though not the groundwork laid. He probably did the same with Bob, though that is uncertain.

Frank Sinatra also claimed to be in the midst of all activity. He did involve himself with both sides, but not as a go-between. He seemed to have made promises to Giancana about the contacts he had with both Joe and Jack Kennedy. Sinatra seemed to have said he would act on behalf of Giancana to get favors and stop some of the Justice Department's activities. However, apparently he never did anything. Certainly wiretaps by the FBI, eventually declassified, indicate that Giancana believed Frank had done nothing.

"I was sitting with Frank when Evelyn Lincoln [Jack's secretary] called for the old man [Joe]. You could hear him talking in the background, telling her what to say," said Nick Sevano, Sinatra's manager for twenty-three years. "Joe Kennedy was telling him that with Jack president, he couldn't keep up a friendship with a man openly involved with the mob. Frank had to choose between the mob and Jack Kennedy.

"This wasn't a choice for Frank. He had been raised on the streets with the mob. They were his childhood friends. We understood about politics. We could see that Jack couldn't be seen with Sinatra if Frank was going to be with the mob, but Jack wasn't important. Frank was loyal to people, and his friends in the mob had been helping him his whole career.

"We didn't know if Jack had him call or if this was the old man's idea. Joe was telling Evelyn Lincoln, Jack's secretary, what to say so it was probably Joe's idea."

Joe's request was well in line, given that the election help of Sinatra and his mother had been a payback to Joe for prior help. Sinatra had developed an ABC television variety series in 1957. The deal was worth $3 million, and for tax purposes, Sinatra had the payment deferred so the money would come to him annually for several years. The IRS allowed the taxes to be figured over the time agreed upon with ABC, but the contract had a clause that required Sinatra to get all the money if the series was canceled.

The series ended the first year, the victim of poor ratings. The money was still going to come over several years, but since the series existed only during a single tax year, the IRS demanded full payment, penalties, and interest totaling more than $1 million.

Frank and his attorney, Mickey Rudin, went to Joe Kennedy for help. Joe arranged for Sinatra to have the tax burden reduced to just $65,000. He was happy to do it. Sinatra would owe him a favor when he needed it most, to use Hollywood and mob contacts for Jack's election.

Joe's utilization of the mob was no different from the patron/client arrangement used in Sicily by men who formed the base of the American Mafia. Joe had done favors for which repayment was expected whenever demanded. He called them in to help his son win the presidential election.

Jack misunderstood this, or his father did not explain the rules. He seems to have made deals on his own, taking advantage of the mob's friendship, never realizing that each favor granted was a favor expected. He acted independently of Joe, only Frank Sinatra knowing what was happening. Yet Frank did not talk to Jack about all this, as Giancana discovered later, according to FBI wiretap transcripts.

Joe Kennedy's use of the mob was actually similar to other concepts developed for the election. Jack understood that his academic credentials could be challenged. He was already utilizing his father's approach of hiring the best minds to handle the work. It was a natural for him to adopt the "Academic Advisory Committee" created by Ted Sorensen as a way to counter critics of Jack's intellectual attainments. The committee was to be reminiscent of Franklin Roosevelt's "brain trust."

Sorensen brought together some of the most respected intellectuals of the day—John Kenneth Galbraith, Seymour Harris, Arthur Schlesinger Jr., and others. Each was known as a professor, and/or intellectual, and/or author of note. They were hired to put together a series of papers on public policy that would help Jack gain critical insight into the nation and the important issues of the day.

The value of the group was questionable at best. Real social concerns were understood more on the grassroots level than they were in academia. There were international experts who had spent their lives studying the culture, history, politics, and languages of different countries and regions. But the men selected were considered among the best and brightest, and if not wholly important, they were certainly impressive. The fact that most of the papers had little relevance to the needs of someone moving toward the presidency did not matter.

Whoever could help Jack win the election was going to be a tool for Joe. Some, like members of the mob, had been primed with favors done, waiting to be repaid. Some, like the intellectuals, were paid for their time and effort. Some, like the entertainers, were delighted with access to a world they could never otherwise experience.

Jacqueline, believing in Jack's presidency though recognizing the problems that would forever plague their marriage, was another tool, helping through radio and television appearances. She was seven months pregnant with John Jr. and could not comfortably travel. However, Joe was keenly aware of how closely members of the media were scrutinizing the men running for president. He had influence with some papers, most notably the Hearst chain, but he had personally experienced independent reporters breaking an embarrassing story. He and Jacqueline wanted to avoid Jack having the same experience because of his callous behavior during her second full-term pregnancy. He had been a junior senator in 1956, and the incident of the stillbirth while he was on vacation had gained enough press to be found in newspaper clipping files. Jacqueline's failure to provide an active role in 1960 could be negatively connected with the past.

Jacqueline began making television and radio appearances, as well as radio recordings in the four languages in which she was fluent. She also wrote a newspaper column in the manner of Eleanor Roosevelt's "My Day." Always Jacqueline made clear that she felt her job was to create a smoothly running household so her husband would have a happy, secure environment from which to go forth and be effective in government service. She never mentioned the work of her secretary, Mary Gallagher, or her live-in nurse, Maud Shaw. She wanted the nation to think that she handled all this herself, respecting Joe's concern that she and Jack come across like the helpful, friendly couple next door.

In the end, the election was most often image, and image seemed to fail both candidates. There were presidential debates for which both men were well prepared. However, in the first debate, when the vice president had been sick with a viral infection until shortly before the day they were to meet, Nixon underutilized makeup, and the lights exaggerated his five-o'clock shadow. His cheeks were jowly and his beard looked almost sinister. Worse for Nixon, Kennedy, whose face had gained a seemingly healthy fullness from the cortisone he used, appeared healthier than usual.

Nixon was the better-prepared debater, but only when it came to the facts. For actual debate technique, Joe and the other advisers his son used had him prepare in the studio prior to the men coming together. For example, Jack stressed that under Eisenhower and Nixon the United States had fallen behind the Soviet Union in the production of intercontinental ballistic missiles (ICBMs). He referred to the alleged problem as a "missile gap." It was a lie.

Beginning in 1956, when aviation technology coupled with new developments in camera lens design created the U-2 high-altitude spy plane, the U.S. government knew that the Soviet Union was lagging behind the United States in ICBM production. Jack was briefed on this fact, but more important, Joe had been part of a civilian Central Intelligence Agency oversight committee for six months during that first year of surveillance flights. He was aware of the relative strengths of the two countries and made certain his son knew. The problem was that there was no way for the American public to hear the truth at a time when national defense was based, in part, on the overkill theory.

Throughout the Cold War, the great fear was of a nuclear war. Two relatively small atomic bombs had been dropped by the United States to end the war against Japan. As long as only the United States held so fearful and proven a weapon, Americans felt they were safe from foreign powers. Then the Soviets exploded their own nuclear device, and a new way of thinking evolved. The country with more nuclear weapons and more missiles capable of taking them into the heart of enemy territory would triumph. War would not break out as long as there was overkill capacity. This meant that a first strike by one country would be met by a massive retaliatory strike by the other country, followed by retaliation from the first, more retaliation from the second, and so forth unto total annihilation. A missile gap meant that Russia would have less to lose attacking first, and the previous administration would seem to have failed the public.

There was no way Nixon could adequately defend himself against such charges. He could not release top secret information to the public because he would be giving the Soviet Union knowledge about how American intelligence was operating and what its limitations might be.

Despite the false allegations about the "missile gap" and the fear it created, most of those hearing rather than seeing the first debate felt that Nixon had won (Kennedy was the clear victor in most people's minds only if they heard *and* saw him, not when they only heard or read his words). Plans were immediately made to give Jack extra preparation prior to the second debate.

Both candidates were offered studio time with their own personnel to rehearse. Nixon, seemingly the more knowledgeable, refused. He arrived at the studio just nine minutes before the fourth debate and less than a half hour before the third. Kennedy, by contrast, was ordered to use all the rehearsal time he could get. Nixon arrived ready to go on the air. Each time Kennedy had spent the previous seven hours practicing how he would look as much as what he would say.

Kennedy had refined the use of body language—facial expressions, aggressive gestures, and the like—to seem like the more knowledgeable individual, coming on strong and confident because he was right and

Nixon was wrong. Most of the television audience thought Jack won the debates because of the image he projected, not the reality.

Nixon was moderate to liberal on many social issues but came through as being conservative. Kennedy was the opposite, yet many voters felt he would be the more liberal if elected, concerned with social change for the lowest Americans.

Both families were supportive. Both families—Richard and Pat Nixon with their two daughters; Jack and Jacqueline Kennedy with their daughter and soon-to-be-born son—were emotionally appealing. And in a sense, the comment that comic Mort Sahl made after the first debate—"they both lost"—befit the election returns. Jack Kennedy received 49.7 percent of all the votes cast. Richard Nixon received 49.6 percent of all the votes cast. Neither man appealed to half the population.

Perhaps there should have been a recount. The margin of victory was such that it was within probable statistical error. So few votes separated the two men that it was conceivable that recounts could lead to alternating winners each time.

There were allegations of vote fraud from the start, though these were kept quiet because it was presumed that both parties had played dirty. Few thought that Jack and the Democrats were any dirtier than Richard and the Republicans. Still, for many years Joe was credited with the deals that placed his son in power even though, in hindsight, high officials in both parties stated that without Rose's voter registration and get-out-the-vote campaign work, Jack would have lost. She brought an estimated 3 million new voters to the polls, all of them presumed to be Jack Kennedy votes, and they are certain that without her efforts, the Republicans would have emerged victorious.

The election was so close that it was still uncertain on the morning of November 9, 1960, the day after nearly 69 million Americans had cast their ballots. The family members, gathered at the Hyannis Port estate, had gone to bed at different times, Bob, the campaign manager of record, having stayed up the longest, not seeking sleep until dawn. It was not until midmorning that Richard Nixon conceded. Then the family came together to pose for photographs, and at noon they went to the Hyannis Port Armory, already surrounded by television cameras, where Jack gave his acceptance speech. For the first time in weeks he made certain his father was standing beside him.

Still, there was bitterness. In an interview with *Life* magazine writer Hugh Sidey for the December 19, 1960, issue, Joe said, "I didn't think it would be that close. I was wrong on two things. First, I thought he would get a bigger Catholic vote than he did. Second, I did not think so many would vote against him because of his religion." He was convinced that Jack would have swept the nation had he been an Episcopalian.

21

THE VIEW FROM THE TOP
IS ALWAYS DOWN

No matter what the previous relationship had been, the moment a man sits behind the White House desk, from then on it is "Mr. President."

— Statement made to both family and friends during conversations following the election

Jack doesn't belong any more to just a family. He belongs to the country. That's probably the saddest thing about all this. The family can be there, but there is not much they can do for the President of the United States.

— Quote in the *New York Times*, January 8, 1961

IT WAS THE IMAGE OF JOE KENNEDY, NOT THE SUBSTANCE, THAT lingered after the election. First, there was the sense of a controlling force behind the scenes. Rumors abounded that Joe had one or another real-estate agent looking for a Washington, D.C., home for him and Rose. The truth was that the couple had no intention of moving. Joe talked with his son as many as several times a day during the first year Jack would be in office, but the conversations were not about politics or government. The closest they came to such an arrangement was when Jack asked his father to suggest names of men who could serve as secretary of the treasury. Joe, whether for emotional reasons or to give his son the chance to find his own way, did not.

Joe did insist that Jack give Bobby the position of attorney general. He knew that there would be times when Jack would need someone extremely close to advise him, and Bobby was much like himself. They were both tenacious. They both carried grudges long after others had forgotten the minor slight that led to the original disharmony. And both could be ruthless in their dealings when they thought that was the way to succeed. Having Bobby as attorney general would give Jack an adviser who was a younger version of their father.

The other two appointees supposedly connected to Joe's recommendations were Robert S. McNamara for secretary of defense and Dean

Rusk for secretary of state. However, it was Bob's appointment, given his very limited legal experience, that caused a backlash of resentment, including privately among family friends.

Joe probably meant what he said about Jack's need to have someone close with whom to work. Certainly Bobby had proven his skills during the election. However, it is believed that Joe had another ambition for Bob.

The most powerful position in the U.S. government is not the office of president. The presidency is in an elected position with a term of office of four years and a maximum two-term limit to serve. The president can wage war and exert tremendous influence throughout the world, but the long-lasting impact, other than devastation that might result from miscalculation or international conflict, is limited.

By contrast, the U.S. Supreme Court is where the nation is shaped. The justices of the Court are appointed by the president, approved by the Senate, and in office for life. Their selections of cases to be heard as the ultimate appeal, and the decisions they render based on their interpretation of the Constitution, can shape the nation for generations. And the most important position on the Supreme Court is that of chief justice, who will have the greatest influence on the shaping of the American government and society for as long as he or she serves, and often far longer.

Joe, when responding to critics of Bob's abilities, stressed that he felt his lawyer son, who had never tried a case in a courtroom, was similar to Attorney General Harlan Fiske Stone. What went unsaid was Stone's last "job" in government—chief justice of the U.S. Supreme Court.

It no longer mattered what Joe meant, though. He was right about the job of president of the United States distancing the leader from family. There was closeness with their father, but as the Kennedy brothers became comfortable in their new roles, they wanted no interference. Each day Jack Kennedy had the opportunity to be briefed about events happening throughout the United States and throughout the world. He was seeing what all the ambassadors and State Department officials were thinking. He was privy to the various activities of the CIA and, to the degree that Hoover would share anything with any president, the FBI.

Jack began studying Richard Neustadt's book *Presidential Power*, learning the difference between real and implied power and how to use them both. He carried over his father's disdain for many in big business. He had far less social conscience than he was given credit for having, but he had achieved something beyond fantasy. Everywhere he went there were Secret Service agents to protect him, aircraft at his disposal, people to bring him food or drink, to whisk him anywhere in the world. His staff hid his womanizing. His children could come and go within the Oval Office.

Joe Kennedy was a man of another generation, another era. Joe Kennedy remembered two major wars. His son the president had fought in one and learned about the other as a history lesson. Joe Kennedy had helped with the creation of the talking-picture industry. Jack Kennedy had experienced three-dimensional movies and the ultrawide-screen Cinerama. Joe Kennedy had an affair with Gloria Swanson. To Jack, Swanson was an old woman. He liked to play with Marilyn Monroe.

There also were critical issues related to Cuba. Jack Kennedy had spent extensive time in Havana, enjoying the nightlife and the women when he was senator. Joe Kennedy had been interested in backing Fidel Castro's revolution on the assumption that Fidel would continue the gambling that his predecessor, Fulgencio Batista, had allowed.

Batista had long worked with men such as Meyer Lansky, a long-time enemy of Joe's from Prohibition days. Others who benefited were Carlos Marcello of New Orleans and some of his employees, including Jack Ruby, and Tony Accardo of Chicago. Joe thought that if Castro won, he might have a piece of the Havana action. Even when he learned that Castro hated what gambling, prostitution, and liquor had done to the people, he still felt triumph of a sort because Lansky and others were no longer welcome.

It is not known for certain that Joe provided Castro with money in the early days of the revolution. Others, including the late Jimmy Hoffa and the late Bill Presser, were alleged by Presser's brother-in-law, Alan Friedman, to have given money to both sides. They wanted to be certain they would be welcome to participate in business deals no matter who won.

Joe was almost certainly not involved when Jack decided to back revolutionaries attempting to retake the island during what became known as the Bay of Pigs invasion of April 16, 1961. The attack involved fifteen hundred men who had been trained and armed by the Central Intelligence Agency to retake their island home. Ultimately indecision by Kennedy and his advisers, coupled with a failure to provide the expected support, led to disaster and world embarrassment for the new president. Only Joe was encouraging, telling his son he was pleased with his having to face a personal crisis so early in his administration so he could learn from it and grow. He also stressed that the fault was that of the CIA, an organization he had come to hold in disdain.

In September 1961 Joe Kennedy was posed with seventeen of his grandchildren. They are (left to right): Front Row—Sydney Lawford, Robert Kennedy Jr., Michael Kennedy, Maria Shriver, Courtney Kennedy, and Mary Kennedy. Middle Row—Timothy Shriver, Victoria Lawford, Kara Kennedy, Caroline Kennedy, Robert Shriver, and Kathleen Kennedy holding John F. Kennedy Jr. Back Row— Joseph Kennedy, David Kennedy, Stephen Smith Jr., and Christopher Lawford. (Cleveland State University Library, Special Collections)

* * *

Joe Kennedy did not discuss the matter with his sons, but his body was in decline even as he tried to reassure Jack about the Cuban situation. He had been feeling ill, and the doctors had diagnosed vascular system problems. Joe was told to take anticoagulants to reduce the chance of a stroke. It is uncertain if he bothered to have the prescriptions filled because, even if he did, he never took any medication.

On December 11 Joe arrived in Palm Beach to spend the winter. He had been fighting a head cold and frequently felt tired and a little dizzy. However, Jack, Jacqueline, and their two children were visiting, and he enjoyed his son's company.

On December 19, still feeling poorly, he and Jack entered a limousine to take the president to the airport so he could return to Washington. Caroline joined them, sitting on her grandfather's lap. She, her mother, and her brother would be staying for Christmas when the various siblings who could come, along with twenty of Joe and Rose's grandchildren, would be present.

Joe returned home with Caroline, playing with her before setting off for the Palm Beach Golf Club on North Ocean Boulevard. Ann Gargan, his niece by his wife's late sister, was with him, and the two always enjoyed each other's company.

Joe admitted he wasn't feeling well just before he teed off to play the back nine holes. He thought it was the lingering cold and managed to keep his mind on the game until he was approaching the sixteenth hole. He had been walking, enjoying the modest exercise the game provided when a player did not use a cart. Then he realized he had to sit down immediately.

The caddie raced to get an electric cart, then drove Joe back to where Ann's car was located. She took him home, and as he went to his bedroom, he told her he didn't want a doctor. He just wanted to rest.

Ann immediately alerted her aunt Rose, who had been out shopping. The Gargan children and a few of the other children idolized Joe and Rose. Joe paid for their educations, expecting neither loyalty nor a life dedicated to the pursuits expected of a Kennedy. In return, they cared about him in ways that were constructive. However, they also saw the couple as head of the family and all-knowing in matters of importance. Ann felt she had to talk to Aunt Rose even before a doctor was considered.

Rose asked her niece if Joe had been able to walk into the house, and Ann said he had, though he required her help. Rose dismissed any problem with the statement that Joe just needed rest.

Rose had lunch, then looked in on Joe, whose face had become ashen. She decided that a doctor should be called, and the physician immediately recognized a crisis. An ambulance was called, Joe was placed inside, and Ann went in beside him. A motorcycle escort raced them to St. Mary's Hospital where, upon arrival, the chaplain administered the last rites as the physicians prepared Joe for tests and whatever else might be necessary.

While Rose was called to tell her Joe might not survive, radiopaque dye was injected into the main artery of his neck. Then a high-speed X-ray unit was used to record how the dye flowed through the vessels of the brain. It was found that Joe had had a stroke on the left side of his brain, paralyzing his right side. Technically it was a thrombosis of the left cerebral hemisphere. Practically it meant probable death.

Jack Kennedy received the news at the White House. He immediately announced his return to Palm Beach and ordered *Air Force One*, the presidential jet, to take him, Bob, and their sister Jean Kennedy Smith back to Florida.

Rose saw no reason to interrupt her routine. She left the house for the golf course, playing her special method for moving quickly. She took three balls and played all three at once, moving through three holes to achieve her version of a nine-hole game.

The eccentricity had developed in Hyannis Port. Joe paid the greens fees for both of them, but he did not tell her, she did not ask, and they never played together. Rose decided to avoid the greens fee so she would arrive with three balls, sneaking onto the fifth hole as though she had been playing through. Then she would play her three balls on the sixth, seventh, and eighth holes before sneaking off. She felt she had achieved the equivalent of nine free holes each day that she played. No one ever "caught" her because there was nothing to catch. She was current with what the family owed, though she did not know it. And the game was so much fun, she often played three balls and three holes in Palm Beach.

Rose, knowing Joe was near death, had no intention of letting the man who had become an annoying housemate, not lover or husband in any traditional sense, interrupt her routine. She left the golf club and went swimming. Then, when she felt she had had adequate exercise, she showered, changed her clothing, and allowed herself to be driven to the hospital. The police, alerted that she was coming, closed the roads to let her driver move swiftly to her husband's side.

The irony of the stroke was in Joe's appearance. Half a century earlier he had allowed surgeons to give his daughter Rosemary a prefrontal lobotomy that had gone poorly. Her mind had been nearly destroyed, but more obvious were changes in her face and body. Joe, like his daughter, now had partial facial paralysis, a tendency to drool, a partially crippled body, and the inability to make intelligible statements. The obvious external damage Joe Kennedy had sustained was exactly the same as that of the child he had hidden away for five decades.

22

AND THEN THERE WAS . . .

JOE KENNEDY LIVED. WHEN YOU HAVE MONEY, PRESTIGE, AND ARE in a hospital wing that has a plaque dedicating your room and the section of the building in which it is located to the memory of your oldest son, heroic methods are used. Patient survival rather than quality of life is the only concern.

Perhaps a patient of lesser stature would have been treated less aggressively. Perhaps a patient who had not walked with presidents and kings would have been kept comfortable but allowed to die when his body said it was time.

Not Joe Kennedy. Not the father of the president of the United States, the attorney general of the United States, and a third son poised to make his name in the U.S. Senate. Heroic methods were used for such a man, but Joe Kennedy never spoke an intelligible word again.

The family tried to put a positive spin on Joe's loss the way they had with Rosemary. They couldn't pretend that Joe was a teacher. He was too public a figure to decide in his seventies that he wanted to join a religious order of married brothers working in isolation though visited regularly by his loving wife.

The lies were simpler ones. He was getting better. He was regaining his speech. He was walking. He was talking seriously with his sons. He was sharing jokes.

Richard Cardinal Cushing of Boston visited Joe in the hospital, then told the press that he said, "Keep up your courage. You're going to be all right." And in his story, Joe said, "I know I am."

But Joe had not spoken since the stroke.

Son-in-law Steve Smith, Jean's husband, would later tell of Joe being driven to his New York office to check on his business ventures after he left the hospital. "He comes in and listens to business, and don't worry, if he wants to say no to something, he can make himself known."

Joe was present in his wheelchair, but Joe had not spoken since the stroke.

* * *

The Kennedy daughters began to fall apart without the leadership of their father, whose physical presence was no longer imposing. They had been raised to be intensely competitive, and without Joe's focusing the direction for their aggressiveness, they turned on each other. They argued over clothing and over the staff. Only Jean, the youngest, avoided such behavior.

Rose suddenly had to look at the household budget for the first time, and she had no idea what she was seeing. She knew she had money, but she did not know that if she spent $1 million a year for the rest of her life, she would hardly make a dent in the family fortune.

It was after his stroke that Joe was found to have been generous to those who worked loyally for the family and expected his staff to follow suit. Rose knew nothing of retirement concerns, Social Security, home equity, and the like.

The Kennedy children had long enjoyed a governess known to everyone as Mamselle. When the children became adults, Mamselle was made the family's cook. She was in her seventies when Joe had his stroke. She lived with her sister in a small condominium, and her health was deteriorating. However, retirement, which obviously was necessary, seemed impossible because she lacked adequate income.

Joe's grandson Christopher Lawford realized what was happening and told his mother, Pat. She went to Tom Walsh of the New York office, who agreed to create a supplemental pension for Mamselle from Rose Kennedy's accounts, as Joe had created them. Mamselle received $200 a month in addition to whatever else she had counted on. It was just enough to live the rest of her live with dignity instead of being hungry. She was extremely grateful, yet Pat could not let her thank her mother because Rose would have been outraged.

Ann Gargan tried to take over the care of her uncle Joe. He never spoke, but he did begin a certain amount of physical recovery. His right brain was unaffected by the stroke, and he was able to learn to use his left side to handle some of the basics of daily living. He had full motor skills for feeding himself with his left hand, for example, but Ann felt he had led a full life helping others. She felt it was time for him to be helped instead of fighting to stay in control.

Ann had compassion but not the knowledge to understand that a stroke victim has to fight to regain full use of whatever skills remain. Otherwise the person becomes more severely disabled until death. That

Following Joe Kennedy's stroke, his niece Ann Gargan was an almost constant companion. Behind Kennedy is Richard Sagura. (Cleveland State University Library, Special Collections)

was why the family hired Rita Dallas, R.N., trained in rehabilitation, who would work with Joe both in his homes and in Horizon House, a Pennsylvania treatment center where he finally learned to walk with great effort and assistance.

But there was nothing that could be done to help him recover the ability to communicate.

Suddenly Rose was in charge of the family. The use of notes pinned to her clothing was something appropriate when raising children. Now that they were grown, she substituted one large diaper pin. All the day's notes would be placed on the pin. Then she would pull them off, one at a time, as she handled whatever matter had been noted. She took great pride at wearing a noteless pin at the end of each day.

Rose was determined to keep costs under control. She did not visit Joe in his rooms. He was in the hands of the nursing staff, and she wanted nothing to do with him. The staff would do the hard physical work of cleaning him, dressing him, and constantly exercising his body to minimize permanent loss of motor skills. The shifts were long and tiring, and the staff regularly drank coffee to keep alert.

Rose had no idea what a pound of coffee might cost. She had heard that the price of coffee was going higher, so this was, to her, an obvious place to economize. She informed Rita Dallas that the nursing staff, therapists, and others tending to Joe were to be allowed a single cup of coffee each per shift. The nurse, knowing that Rose had no interest in seeing her husband, moved a hot plate to the nurses' station Rose never visited. Unlimited coffee continued to be secretly available.

Joe's isolation was more complete than he realized. Rita Dallas insisted that the couple continue what she thought was a normal relationship for Joe. The Kennedy family mythmaking had been so complete that it seemed as though Rose was avoiding Joe because she felt he could not bear her sadness or would be embarrassed by the drooling. Rita knew it would be best for Joe, and presumably for Rose, to return to their "habit" of always being together when he was home. First Rose began taking her dinner with Joe. Then Rita Dallas asked her to have breakfast with him.

Rose endured the last years of Joe's life by planning for his death. She bought her mourning clothes and packed them wherever she traveled, always ready to rush home to play the grieving widow. She also planned for her life after his death.

The staff, Jack, and Bob tried to re-create life as it had been. Each day Joe's secretary would come for dictation. Joe used the telephone with his left hand, calling the White House, calling his New York office, calling wherever he felt he was needed. He would talk. Notes would be taken. Agreeing comments would be made. And not one word would have been intelligible. No one knew what he wanted or what he was saying. Even when Joe was forceful, it was impossible to know if he was angry, concerned, or simply being affected by the emotional roller coaster that routinely follows all strokes.

The breakfast ritual was made more difficult because of Rose's attitude toward paid staff and family. Joe Kennedy was comfortable with men and women from all walks of life. He wanted loyalty. He wanted honesty. He did not care about a person's background when he or she worked for him, just what the person could do. And in the case of the personnel hired to help with the children, he made certain that their manners, their personal hygiene, and their eating habits were beyond reproach. Then he encouraged them to eat with the family, knowing the children would watch them and, presumably, try to emulate them.

Joe was master of the home established in England when he was ambassador to the Court of St. James. Rose was in charge of Hyannis Port and Palm Beach now that Joe had to be wheeled everywhere and could not articulate his feelings. He would sit at the breakfast table with Ann and Rose, Rita Dallas forced to hover in the doorway, knowing that at any moment she would be needed, and trying to be as close as possible to protect her patient.

Rose always read the morning paper, speaking aloud any item she thought might interest Joe. She was diminutive. The paper was large. And one morning, as she read, Ann Gargan slipped under the table, positioning herself where only Joe could see her. Then she began imitating all of her aunt Rose's gestures, knowing the two were estranged and that Uncle Joe would appreciate the mockery.

Joe began laughing, a difficult situation for a stroke victim. His body shook uncontrollably, and suddenly he was out of control, laughing, weeping, and nearly falling from the chair. Ann grabbed him, holding him, upset by what she felt she had done. Rita Dallas, familiar with such reactions in stroke victims, had raced to his side to tend to her patient. And Rose looked up, too late to see the cause, certain she was responsible, but of what and why she did not know.

Jacqueline was the most comforting to Joe. She would touch him when she saw him, something he lacked from anyone other than the paid caregivers and Ann Gargan. Part of his body was deformed from the stroke, and his right hand looked gnarled. One morning Rita Dallas found the hand wrapped in a scarf to hide its appearance. She did not know which family member had done such a thing, but she realized how depressing it must be for Joe to realize his appearance was upsetting. Yet Jacqueline saw nothing, kissing the deformity when she visited as though passing a Continental greeting from one sophisticate to another.

Joe Kennedy may have been debilitated and silent, but his influence was still felt by the youngest member of the family. Ted Kennedy had no interest in politics and knew that a campaign could be personally embarrassing. He was too weak to fight his father, whose last pronouncement before his stroke was that Ted would run for the Senate.

Rose, seeing no other path for the grandson of Honey Fitz, who died in 1950 but was still an integral part of her life and thinking, decided to make Ted a senator. Her efforts were not as elaborate as they had been for Jack, but they were intense. Her political instincts were far superior to those of her children.

The *New York Times* attacked Ted Kennedy because the editors, none of whom were from the Krock era of loyalty to Joe, felt that the

Kennedys were trying to create a political dynasty. It was obvious that Ted was too young and ill-prepared for so important a job as senator. It was equally obvious that the family was concerned only with having the best Kennedy for the job.

Rose recognized that the *Times* article need not be challenged. She understood the opposition and fought it with humor. "I agree with those of you who are opposed to my son, or at least I can understand. Jack was 'too young,' as I recall. So was Bobby 'too young.' But they're doing pretty well, aren't they? Matter of fact, I wanted Teddy to go into the church. But the trouble was that he wanted to start out as a bishop."

There were other factors that helped Ted win that first election, in 1962. Some voted for him because they liked Jack and this was Jack's brother. Some voted for Ted because they felt that, though he would be a freshman senator, he would have the clout of the White House behind him, enabling him to do more for the state than anyone else who was running. And some voted for Ted because they felt that Rose made sense, that Ted was running because he was ready to run and age had nothing to do with ability.

Rose began making more frequent visits to the White House where she was given the Lincoln Bedroom. Because she did not want the public to forget who she was and from where she had come, she was always quite vocal about the fact that the Lincoln Bedroom was not as nice as Queen Victoria's private chambers, where she also had been a guest.

Rose and Joe were in Hyannis Port in November 1963. She had abandoned care of Joe to Ann Gargan, Rita Dallas, and the nursing support staff. She could handle death. She could not handle weakness in herself or others. Joe was on a steady decline, no longer capable of making a sound.

Jack had stopped by the month before, kissing his father on the forehead before boarding the helicopter that awaited him. The morning of November 22 was beautiful—cool, yet sunny and pleasant.

Rose went to Mass, had breakfast, then was driven with Joe in the station wagon so they could view the last of the colorful foliage remaining on the trees. Joe could only handle a short ride, or Rose could only tolerate a brief time with her husband. Whatever the case, Joe was returned home, and Rose went out to play golf.

Joe napped after lunch, and Rose decided to go to her room to rest. Ann Gargan, listening to the radio, was told to turn down the sound when she informed her aunt that there was a bulletin about the president being shot.

Rose was oddly unaffected by the first report. Jack had been dying prematurely from the time he was born. Over and over again he had been in the hospital. He had been given the last rites so often, there were members of the family who knew the words as well as those of the Mass. The news reports did not indicate that Jack was seriously hurt, and though Rose was upset, she assumed that she would have been notified if the incident was serious. She did not realize that everything was happening so swiftly, there was no time to do anything except rush Jack to the hospital and fight to save his life.

A few minutes after Rose went to her room, Bob called with more details. Not long after that, Jack was dead.

The next telephone call was from Lyndon Johnson, the newly sworn-in president of the United States.

If ever there was a nonpolitical moment in the lives of two of the most aggressively political families in the United States, it was the telephone call from Lyndon Johnson. The Senate majority leader turned vice president turned president through an assassin's bullet was rumored to be as dirty in his politics and business dealings as Joe. Lyndon was linked with Carlos Marcello, a man who hated the Kennedys because Bob had arranged to have him deported to Guatemala as a means of harassing the man. Joe was linked with Sam Giancana. Lyndon and Joe were masters of manipulation and the acquisition of power. Each had made trades to achieve where they had come. And now Lyndon Johnson was facing a reality no one anticipated because the incident was so rare.

John F. Kennedy was dead, killed by a sniper during a motorcade through the narrow streets of Dallas. Lyndon Johnson, still in shock, had to call the man's parents to tell them their son was dead. He was a father who could understand such a horrendous loss. He also was the person taking their son's job in a way no one had ever imagined could happen.

The situation for Johnson was especially hard because the shooting happened in his state. This was "home" for Lyndon, and in a sense, Jack was his guest. He was responsible for taking care of the man, and with the death the "failure" was obvious. At that moment all the posturing, all the infighting, all the politics ceased to exist. Lyndon Johnson was in shock, at a loss for words, yet knew he had to reach out to Rose and, if possible, Joe.

Lady Bird Johnson got on the line next. Unlike her husband, she got along well with Rose. Their talk was brief, yet Barbara Gibson said that Rose never forgot Lady Bird's words: "We must all realize how fortunate the country was to have your son as long as it did."

* * *

It is not certain when Joe was given the news. Rose refused to tell him, and she refused to let Ann Gargan say what happened. She wanted his doctor to come from Boston, and she wanted more of the family gathered when the news was broken. She also wanted Eunice, the daughter previously made responsible for Rosemary, to tell him.

Exactly what happened is not known. There have been too many stories, though this time the different tales probably come from everyone being in shock too great to think clearly rather than an effort to hide the truth.

Eunice arrived after checking on everyone involved in the shooting, including the wounded Texas governor John Connally. One story has the family getting through the day, then going to 7:00 A.M. Mass at St. Francis Xavier Church the next morning. Breakfast followed, though Rose kept the *New York Times* where Joe would not see the headlines. Finally, after their father's first therapy session in the family's heated swimming pool, Ted and Eunice broke the news.

Another story was that Eunice and Ted went to see him. Eunice began babbling about Jack, an accident, and heaven. Finally the two children embraced their father, Ted saying, "Dad, Jack was shot," and Eunice saying that Jack was dead.

Rose recalled the incident only slightly differently, adding the presence of Ann Gargan and the doctor.

Joe sat up in bed, was given a sedative and the paper, and read the story. He finished, swept the paper to the floor, and lay back down to sleep. Then the staff took the American flag that daily flew from a flagpole in front of the house and lowered it to half staff.

Joe did not attend the funeral. He was strong enough to be wheeled there, but he stayed at home, watching on television with Father John Cavanaugh, the former president of the University of Notre Dame and a longtime friend. He could not express his grief. Only a longtime friend could understand the depth, the shattered hopes, the pride turned to despair, so he was comforted as he endured the unthinkable.

The Kennedys thought that the death of Jack and the deteriorating condition of their father also would mean his loss would soon take place. They did not understand that their family's story was unfolding like a Greek tragedy. It was as though Joe were the mortal who sought to be like the gods, only to reach the pinnacle of achievement just long enough to understand that all he had achieved would be stripped from his existence.

First, on June 19, 1964, there was Ted Kennedy, flying in a private plane with staff member Ed Moss, Indiana senator Birch Bayh and his wife, and their charter pilot. The plane crashed, killing Moss and the pilot and leaving Ted with a severe back injury. His body was immobilized before he was rushed to the hospital, an action that saved him from becoming a paraplegic.

Then there was Bob, assassinated in Los Angeles as he fought to become the 1968 candidate for president on the Democratic Party ticket. And again, in 1969, Ted Kennedy was back in the headlines when he left a party drunk and drove into a river, killing Mary Jo Kopechne, a passenger in his car.

The details of the deaths and scandals are not important. Each has been covered in dozens or hundreds of books. Each is a part of other people's histories.

On November 17, 1969, just five days short of the sixth anniversary of Jack's death, Joe Kennedy began to die. Jacqueline was there, widowed, frightened of the violence she had witnessed, and hating what the country had done to her family, yet loving the man who had caused her both pleasure and pain in the manner of her own father. Ted also was present, uncertain of his feelings, yet determined not to leave the room except when necessary. He brought a blanket with him, curling up as best he could so he could doze on the chair.

If Joe could see his life as others would come to view it, the memories must have been painful. He had fought his way out of Boston. He had spent his life hating the people he wanted to emulate, desperately seeking acceptance in all the wrong places.

Had Joe chosen to work with Rose as a business partner in his numerous endeavors, had he looked for ways to convince her that her attitude toward sex was misguided, he could have known the joy he unsuccessfully sought in an endless chain of unsuitable lovers. Had Joe chosen to ignore his detractors, he would have nurtured his children to follow their own dreams rather than destroying them by binding them to his own. Had Joe avoided politics or worked with those who thought as he did, he would have escaped embarrassment even when the unfolding events of history proved him wrong. Instead, Joe Kennedy sold his soul in all the wrong places for all the wrong reasons. He had gained the world, and in the eight years between helplessness and death, he had seen it all fall apart.

On November 17, 1969, with the eighty-one-year-old Joe Kennedy near death following a heart attack, newspapers around the nation printed images from the three most prominent stages of his public life. The image on the left was taken in 1937 after Joe was named ambassador to the Court of St. James. The middle image was taken in 1961 shortly after his son Jack was elected president. The image on the right was taken in 1967, several years after the stroke from which he never fully recovered. (Cleveland State University Library, Special Collections)

Joe Kennedy had made one son a hero and lost another son who truly was heroic. He had sought the White House for Jack, only to watch him spend each day in sometimes constant agony, exhausted, and saved from dying from his illnesses only through death by an assassin's bullet. Bob had followed Jack to the Senate, then was cut down on his run for the presidency. Ted delighted in womanizing like his father, then accidentally killed someone with whom it was believed he was planning to have sex.

Rosemary, Joe's most beautiful daughter, had her life shattered by a prefrontal lobotomy, the physical damage caused by the botched operation mirrored in Joe's own appearance after his stroke. Kathleen, the beloved daughter and willing adulteress, died in a plane crash on her way to see the one parent who approved of her unconventional lifestyle.

Joe was like King Midas. In the end, all he retained of what he had long coveted was his money. Everything else had been wrested from his grasp as he lay helpless, cared for almost entirely by strangers.

At 9:00 A.M. on November 18, Joe's vital signs began deteriorating rapidly. Rita Dallas and the doctor alerted the family, who would gather over the next hour and a half.

Ted was present, never having left the bedside. Pat, divorced from Peter Lawford, arrived next, followed immediately by Eunice and Sargent Shriver. Jacqueline literally ran barefoot into the house, knowing that taking the few seconds to put on shoes might prevent her from being present as he passed from life. Joan joined her husband, Ted, and Steve Smith arrived, along with Ethel.

Rose went swimming.

Rita Dallas constantly monitored Joe's vital signs until she was certain from her experience that he would be dead in minutes. It was 11:00 A.M., and only then did Ted get his mother.

Rose placed a rosary in Joe's hand, shutting his fingers around it. Eunice began the Lord's Prayer, stopping after the first line so each Kennedy sibling and their mother could say a few words.

Seconds later Joe Kennedy, eighty-one, breathed his last.

The funeral was an oddly subdued affair, as though no one were certain quite what to do about Joe's death. The Doane Beal and Ames Funeral Home arranged to pick up the corpse and prepare the body for a funeral the following day. That night Father Cavanaugh celebrated a special Mass at St. Francis Xavier Church on Boston's South Street. And the next day Cardinal Cushing, assisted by New York archbishop Terence Cardinal Cooke, handled the funeral.

The surviving Kennedy children and his twenty-eight grandchildren were present, as were longtime friends. Ted Kennedy read the eulogy. Cardinal Cushing quoted Joe's words, "My ambition in life is not to accumulate wealth but to train my children to love and serve America for the welfare of all people."

Outside, in pouring rain, an estimated five hundred mourners stood watching, though whether they were there because of the loss of Joe or to see the family that achieved the status of being America's version of royalty is impossible to know.

The obituaries were routinely favorable. Some spoke of Joe's humble beginnings, ignoring the power and relative wealth that P. J. had achieved and from which his son so greatly benefited. Some spoke of his business accomplishments, his international experiences, and the unusual family he raised.

The newspapers also reported on his wealth. By the time of his death there were complicated financial arrangements meant to assure that children and grandchildren would never have to work. His sisters received $25,000 each. Rose was directly given $500,000 along with property worth another $1 million. Much of the $400 million went to the Joseph P. Kennedy Foundation, and unknown sums had already been provided to family members, often in the form of property.

For the public, the most valuable assets were the Joseph P. Kennedy papers, the records of his years in business and politics. These were secreted away. Some went to the Kennedy Library, where they have been made available to the public only in small quantities. Others went to the New York office. Still others were occasionally called "lost." However, the family's efforts to keep the myth in front of the man were limited because too many others made notes. Diaries, information in the Roosevelt Library, the papers of mobsters whose families were honest and wanted to set the record straight after a notorious family member's death all have been revealing information over the years. Likewise, former family employees such as Barbara Gibson have been invaluable in bringing out information that has not always been comfortable in the closed society that is the family Kennedy.

And in the end there was the life lived, the life desired, and the story that blended the two in an admixture of truth and fantasy. Joe Kennedy walked with kings and lowlifes. He was a brilliant business innovator yet made the bulk of his wealth through a corrupted system he would later be asked to try to fix. He was a man so fixated on tomorrow that he often failed to grasp today. In death, others looked at Joe Kennedy and said he had had the world. Sadly for Joe, it had not been quite enough.

NOTES

1. Mr. Ambassador

1. It was only after both Franklin and Eleanor had died, long after the public knew about Lucy Mercer, that Jimmy discussed seeing his father in nightclothes, sitting in his wheelchair, Lucy on his lap.

2. James Roosevelt, with Bill Libby, *My Parents: A Differing View*, p. 208.

3. This is a story of questionable authenticity, as will be explained later. However, it was a story Joe told with some frequency. Even if the incident did not occur as Joe claimed, those who knew both men realized Joe told it to place Franklin in the worst possible light at that time.

2. Coming to America

1. The Massachusetts Bay Colony established an elaborate civil administration under a governor and with private-citizen involvement in the form of 118 freemen. However, the law always was based on "God's will" as interpreted by the clergy. It was considered to be the work of the devil if anyone argued with the conclusions of the clergy.

The hatred of Goody Glover's Irish Catholic history was such that whatever the children claimed about her was obviously true. Among the records that Cotton Mather maintained, he found that the children sometimes "would be deaf, sometimes dumb, and sometimes blind, and often all this at once. One while their tongues would be drawn down their throats; another while they would be pulled out upon their chins, to a prodigious length. They would have their mouths opened unto such a wideness, that their jaws went out of joint. . . . They would make most piteous outcries, that they were cut with knives, and struck with blows that they could not bear. Their necks would be broken, so that their neck bone would seem dissolved unto them that felt after it . . . their head would be twisted almost round; and . . . they would roar exceedingly." (David D. Hall, ed., *Witch-Hunting in Seventeenth-Century New England*, pp. 267–269.)

Martha Goodwin, during her time with Cotton Mather, knew that she could better her position by flattering him. She had a chance to enter his study while still, in his mind, possessed. Martha pretended that the devil could not enter. "There then stood open the study of one belonging to the family, in to which, entering, she stood immediately on her feet, and cried out, 'They are gone! They are gone! They say that they cannot—God won't let 'em come here!' adding a reason for it which the owner of the study thought 'more kind than true' and she presently and perfectly came to herself, so that her whole discourse and carriage was altered into the greatest measure of sobriety." (Charles W. Upham, *Salem Witchcraft*, p. 306.)

Later, Cotton Mather had Martha taken to his study in front of visitors so they could watch the transformation from angry, possessed teenager to angelic child praising her host's piety. She would often make her body deadweight, forcing others to carry and drag her to the study.

As a historic side note, some "possessed" citizens were actually physically ill. In the book *A Fever in Salem*, there are several explanations given for what occurred. Some of the "witches" may have been trying to use one or another form of "magic" to tell the future or influence the actions of others. Some were mentally ill. But what seems to be certain is that many of the "possessed" or "afflicted" were actually suffering from physical illness.

The most logical culprit was an epidemic of encephalitis lethargica, whose symptoms, recorded during a pandemic in the period 1916 to 1930, matched those in Salem. Martha Goodwin's unusual symptoms directly match those well recorded during the fifteen-year pandemic of encephalitis.

2. The Authorized Version of the Bible, also known as the King James Version, was first published in 1611. It was meant specifically for Anglicans and Puritans and may have been the Bible Cotton Mather used. He may also have used the Geneva Bible, which was the standard Bible used by the Puritans prior to the King James Version. The 1602 version may have been taken to Boston, and the book itself continued to be published until 1640.

3. Boston Town Records, 1772, pp. 595–596, cited in James B. Cullen, *The Story of the Irish in Boston*.

4. At least one reference has been found that states that Bridget Murphy and Patrick Kennedy traveled on the boat *Washington Irving*. According to this story, the couple met and had a chance to get to know each other during the voyage. Allegedly this is where they became friends, perhaps falling in love.

The preponderance of evidence indicates that Patrick Kennedy preceded Bridget Murphy to Boston and was introduced to her through mutual friends.

5. Also spelled "Joanna" by some biographers. It appears that "Johanna" was the correct name, since Patrick and Mary named their daughter after his mother, Johanna.

6. There was an irony to these first deaths. Patrick's firstborn son was also the first of three John Kennedys to die, the other two being his grandson, assassinated as president, and his great-grandson, killed in a plane crash. Patrick's death occurred on November 22, 1858, which was 105 years to the day that his grandson was shot.

4. The Barkeep's Boy and the Politician's Daughter

1. The story has been told many times, but the original interview was conducted by Richard J. Whalen for his book *The Founding Father: The Story of Joseph P. Kennedy*.

2. Many biographers have tried to find a way to show that Joe Kennedy had a brilliant mind. In truth, few of the Kennedy men, from Joe through his grandson, John F. Kennedy Jr., had great intellect. Rose Kennedy had her father's brilliance, and several of the Kennedy women, including Caroline Kennedy Schlossberg and Kathleen Kennedy Townsend, would have high IQs and extensive personal intellectual accomplishments.

3. There are several different stories about Joe Kennedy's courtship with Rose, his sexuality, and his family attitude toward sex. The Kennedy family usually is the source for information that seems to indicate Joe was a virgin when he married and that the Kennedy men of his day were too involved with business and politics to enjoy much intimacy with their wives. However, Joe always seemed to delight in sex. His idea of monogamy meant having sex with one woman at a time. He would later tell one of his mistresses that she could judge his "faithfulness" to her by the fact that his wife had not gotten pregnant during their affair.

4. The story of the cigars wrapped in dollar bills came from Barbara Gibson, Rose Kennedy's assistant for the last ten years of her life prior to the stroke that rendered Mrs. Kennedy unable to speak until her death. Barbara spoke of being with Rose immediately after she had given a speech in support of her son Senator Ted Kennedy during his last run for the presidency. She told Barbara that politics was much easier in her father's day, when the two of them would simply go to the polls and hand men cigars wrapped in dollar bills. Presumably many of the men made substantial sums of money by voting as many times as possible that day.

5. Newspaper freelancers were called stringers because their work output was literally measured against a length of string. First the published work would be cut into column lengths, then pasted one beneath the other. Then the string would be stretched along the length. Finally the string would be measured to see how many column inches the freelancer had contributed. He or she would be paid a certain number of cents per column inch as determined by the string. The total was his or her paycheck.

6. Harvard's president established the social pecking order when he first ranked the members of the freshman class. A wealthy Protestant from an elite family was at the top. Wealthy, elite Catholics and Jews always would be less than the lower-income Protestant from a family whose name would not regularly appear in the society columns. Joe Kennedy was reasonably important as an Irish Catholic because of Pat's prominence, but that still placed him in the unenviable position of nearly last in all activities.

One of the ways to move up was to become prominent within the right social club. Social clubs dominated Harvard and offered a slight opportunity for a man to move up in the caste system among his peers. This would not change how he was seen at Harvard, but it would give him the opportunity to marry into a more prominent family and obtain privilege from a youth's business leader father he might otherwise not have met.

The first step to club membership was to be chosen for what amounted to a preclub club. This was Delta Kappa Epsilon (DKE), commonly known as "Dickey." In Dickey a sophomore would be in a waiting club from which the youths were evaluated by upperclassmen.

Joe made Dickey because of freshman baseball and his friendship with two highly desired athletes. What he failed to realize was that the friendships and his athletic prowess that first year would not take him all the way to the elite. He was good enough for DKE. He was not good enough for anything more, as he learned when his friends were chosen and he was not.

The following year Joe made his move by again calling positive attention to himself when he volunteered to be part of the Junior Dance Committee. However, it would not be until he coerced his way into getting a letter sweater his junior year that he would finally join a club. It was in his senior year, and while Delta Kappa Epsilon had members who were among the Protestant elite, he was still among the lower ranks of prestigious organizations. Worse, by joining his final year there was little time to try to achieve lasting friendships he could use in his adult business and personal life.

7. There are three stories told about the bus route. The second story, usually told by writers who are Kennedy family friends, is one in which Joe shrewdly tricks the mayor. According to this story, the two Joes bought the tour bus they had taken themselves. It was one that retraced the route Paul Revere rode when he traveled from Lexington to Concord in a desperate race to alert the colony that the British regulars (soldiers) were out. As they learned the history of the area, they heard that the bus owner was going out of business. They spent $1,200 to buy the bus, half in cash and half in payments that came from their working the bus over the next season. The bus was renamed *Mayflower*, then Joe went to Mayor Fitzgerald to get the license to operate from South Street Station. According to this story, which does not mention the police commissioner, Joe thought Honey Fitz would give the youth the license to keep him in the mayor's debt. He fantasized that the mayor would want to have Joe owe him a favor such as not seeing his daughter, Rose, and when Fitzgerald granted the two Joes the license, he was looking forward to Joe's being obligated. Instead, Kennedy and Donovan felt no obligation, as they ran *Mayflower* as the exclusive South Street Station tour bus. During the two tourist seasons, according to this story, they netted $10,000. The quite different details of this story are most likely inaccurate, the type of Kennedy family myth that has elevated Joe's reputation from a self-centered, greedy man who occasionally had his scams backfire to someone of brilliance and sophistication who made few mistakes.

The third story has Mayor Fitzgerald helping the two Joes by increasing the bus operating fee for the boys' rival. According to this story, the boys earned a net of $5,000 for approximately two months' work. However, this story requires the belief that Honey Fitz, so protective of Rose that he sent her to Blumenthal, would help the young man he wanted out of his daughter's life.

It is a stretch to think that Honey Fitz might act to win favors or to pay back Pat Kennedy. It is a greater stretch to think of him helping Pat's son at that time.

8. Quote of Rose Kennedy taken from p. 162 of *"Honey Fitz": Three Steps to the White House* by John Henry Cutler.

9. It was traditional for the wealthy to establish organizations to do good works with their money. John D. Rockefeller started the Rockefeller Foundation. Henry Ford started the Ford Foundation. Doris Duke established the Duke Charitable Trust, but privately, long before the organization created at her death in response to the wishes in her will, she was anonymously giving expensive organs to low-income black Baptist churches in the South. She also provided money to an Appalachian community she visited with Eleanor Roosevelt during Franklin's presidency.

10. There is probably only one accurate source for the little-told story of Joe's generosity. This is the interview with O'Meara conducted by author Richard J. Whalen for his book *The Founding Father.*

5. Scandal and Marriage

1. There is only one source for this story, one that had not been heard by Rose's assistant Barbara Gibson or other people close to Rose contacted by this author. However, in interviews conducted by Laurence Leamer during his research for his book *The Kennedy Women,* the story was told to him. It may be truthful, a dirty little family secret, or it may be apocryphal, a story told to show the strength of Rose's feelings about her two quite different men.

6. The Adventure Begins

1. Quote from Amanda Smith, ed., *Hostage to Fortune: The Letters of Joseph P. Kennedy,* p. 5.

2. A week before Joe was able to get Powell to intercede for him, he sent his own letter to District Draft Board 5. This explained his appointment to the job at Fore River and his duties. He listed eight different responsibilities, ranging from handling the compensation insurance to the incorporation of the plant railroad to handling a variety of contracts with the Boston Elevated Railway, Edison Electric, and others. He also noted that he had to spend as much as $1 million a year handling contracts for restaurant accommodations at the Squantum Plant, and he was treasurer of the Mutual Benefit Association. The list was impressive, though it did not result in a deferment. There was nothing noted among his responsibilities that made him valuable to the plant in the manner of his former title of assistant general manager. However, Powell was smart enough or fearful enough to be certain that Joe retained his title so the draft board would continue the deferment. In the years that followed, the family would make much of the Powell telegram. It was noted with pride how

important Joe, not yet thirty, could be to the war effort. The full story was not revealed.

3. Barbara Gibson with Ted Schwarz, *Rose Kennedy and Her Family: The Best and Worst of Their Lives and Times*, p. 54.

4. The problem with the Kennedy family myth was that too many people would come to know a different Rosemary from the one presented to the world. There would be family stories about her physical violence toward her Grandfather Fitzgerald and others, though there never were any witnesses. There would be stories about her learning problems and mood swings, though again there was no proof. Many years later, when researching for the book *Rose Kennedy and Her Family*, this author located the last known Boston doctor to examine Rosemary before Joe sent her to St. Elizabeth's Hospital in Washington, D.C., where procedures were being done regardless of need. That doctor, then in his nineties, his body failing but his mind so sharp that he was still teaching, discussed Rosemary's case. He had been on the protocol committee that examined her for possible surgery. He stressed that there was nothing wrong with her. The surgery desired by Joe was completely unnecessary for so physically and emotionally sound a young woman. In addition, Barbara Gibson was able to obtain Rosemary's diary with entries made until shortly before her operation. Again, it was the writing of a woman coming of age, not someone mentally retarded. In fact, her spelling and grammar were often better than that of her older brother Jack, whose letters from Harvard and from his honeymoon, carefully preserved at the Kennedy Library, seem to show far less ability.

5. *Rose Kennedy and Her Family*, p. 56.

7. Adjusting to Peacetime

1. This story quoted in Laurence Leamer's *The Kennedy Men*, p. 41.

8. Hollywood Beckons

1. *Rose Kennedy and Her Family*, p. 77.
2. *A Child of the Century* by Ben Hecht, p. 479.
3. *The Founding Father:* author interview with banker Ralph Lowell, p. 59.

9. Going Hollywood

1. The time with Pathé was one where Joe abdicated his responsibilities to the company. He was overextended in his business and personal life and felt that he could assign responsibilities to trusted assistants. Occasionally this could be a mistake.

Joe Kennedy was a man who needed to micromanage anything of importance to him. He also was someone who recognized that success came from hiring the best and brightest assistants he could find, then letting them handle all the details of whatever he was involved with. This was a good arrangement as long as his loyalists understood Joe's way. However, in the case of Pathé decisions had to be made with such frequency that the person running the company on a day-by-day or hour-by-hour basis rightfully assumed a free hand. This was the case with Ed Derr, who, though a complete loyalist, seemed to feel that the studio was his reward for learning the Kennedy way of doing business and being willing to handle anything he was asked. The studio was in debt, in crisis, and if Derr didn't handle matters, Kennedy, in his role as chairman, had to get involved. Since he had neither the time to handle the studio nor the inclination to spend the bulk of his business life involved with Hollywood, Kennedy went to David Sarnoff and arranged to sell the studio's production facilities to RKO. In exchange, Pathé would take a five-year hiatus from film production. The problem was that Stuart Webb, acting on behalf of Guy Currier's interests, was told by Elisha Walker, another Pathé director, to not sell stock until Joe, Elisha's partner in speculation with the studio stock, had sold his.

The entire situation became clear. Kennedy had no time for the studio and no interest in it. He did have an assistant who was enjoying the challenge but who had no power if his boss told him to back off. Since Kennedy needed to leave filmmaking, he was speculating on the stock to boost the profits from his personal holdings. As a result, Webb worked around Kennedy, manipulating the business in a manner that assured Kennedy's departure. By early 1930, with Kennedy in Palm Beach presumably counting his money while so many others were lamenting their losses, Webb gained stock control of Pathé, forcing Kennedy out of power. Two months later Kennedy resigned as chairman and announced that he would return to his old business on Wall Street, this time in partnership with Elisha Walker, a former partner in William Salomon and Company, the former president of Blair and Company, and the former banker for Sinclair Consolidated Oil. By the time Joe Kennedy joined with Walker, the latter had merged his Blair and Company with Bank of America, then taken over the holding company Transamerica Corporation, with which Joe would help him. However, Amadeo Giannini disagreed with Walker's approach to Transamerica, forcing Joe to become neutral and his tenure in the industry to be short-lived. Bank of America regained full control of the holding company, Joe retaining both Giannini's friendship for not joining in the fight and Walker's friendship for helping him unload his stock without hurting Transamerica's value.

10. Seduced and Betrayed

1. *Swanson on Swanson*, pp. 356–357.
2. Ibid., p. 357.
3. Ibid., p. 327.
4. There are several versions of this story that pass as "fact," including one where the dance hall is an East African brothel. The scenario discussed here is

based on Gloria Swanson's memoirs and probably is correct. She had chal-lenged the industry standards with her previous film *Sadie Thompson*. She had made a movie from a story that everyone coveted, and she had changed it only enough to bypass the industry self-censorship. Now she was moving to what she fancied was a higher level of storytelling and production with von Stro-heim. He knew the history of Swanson's career. He knew the limitations of the times. And he wanted the money he would be paid. A dance hall might have been a seamy location, but that was quite different from a brothel. It is doubtful that prostitution was ever a thought in the mind of the director when he had his first meeting with Joe and Gloria.

5. Axel Madsen, *Gloria and Joe*, p. 181.

6. *Swanson on Swanson*, p. 368.

7. There is confusion about the identity of the screenwriters. Gloria Swan-son remembered that the Robertsons wrote the initial draft, and it is her mem-ory that is presumed to be accurate. Author Axel Madsen lists a Josephine Lov-ett, a screenwriter who was hired to write what would become *What a Widow*, though originally it had the working title *Purple and Fine Linen*.

11. After Hollywood

1. There is an ongoing myth that Gloria Swanson named her son after Joseph Kennedy, and that myth has led to the belief that the child was Joe Ken-nedy's. The truth was that the boy was born long before Gloria knew Kennedy, and he was named for Joe Swanson, the actress's father.

2. Senate Committee on Banking and Currency, *Hearings on Stock Exchange Practices*, 73rd Cong., 2nd sess., 1934, pp. 6218–6231.

3. In the summer of 1929, with the stock market crash fewer than six months away, Raskob had a ghosted article published in a then bastion of white, middle-income America, *Ladies' Home Journal*. The title of the article was "Everybody Ought to Be Rich."

4. Senate Committee on Banking and Currency, *Hearings on Stock Exchange Practices*, 73rd Cong., 1st sess., 1934, pp. 713, 745.

5. *Swanson on Swanson*, p. 426.

6. Elliott Roosevelt, ed., *FDR: His Personal Letters, 1928–1945*.

12. The Ousider Comes In

1. FBI memorandum in 1955 from Agent Boardman:

A source of unknown reliability advised that James Roosevelt traveled to England just prior to the repeal of prohibition and secured exclusive U.S. liquor rights from the company which controlled almost the entire Scotch whiskey output in England. Due to pressure from U.S. liquor interests, James Roosevelt allegedly transferred these contacts to Kennedy who was reportedly appointed Ambassador to England so he could handle the contracts. It was further alleged that Senator Nye had been advised of the above but was reluctant to act on the information since its disclosure would likely have created disunity while the Nation was at war. In October 2, 1953, the Antitrust Division of the Department requested the Bureau to conduct investigation [*sic*] concerning the important [*sic*] and distribution of Scotch whiskey in the United States, stating that allegations had been received implying that the United States Ambassador to England probably designated the agencies in the United States. It was further alleged that members of the Roosevelt family possibly owned interests in the Somerset Company, Inc., Scotch whiskey importers, formerly owned by Joseph P. Kennedy.

Extensive investigation which was concluded in April 1954 failed to develop any information substantiating allegations or revealing possible antitrust violation.

The information available from declassified FBI files available through Freedom of Information Act (FOIA) requests and the files on Joseph P. Kennedy and others available from the FBI Internet Web pages is inconclusive. However, a number of sources confirm the Haig & Haig and Dewar's Scotch arrangements, including his granddaughter Amanda Smith (*Hostage to Fortune*, p. 109).

2. Michael Beschloss, *Kennedy and Roosevelt: The Uneasy Alliance*, p. 84.

3. The *New Republic*, July 11, 1934.

4. The latest affair, one that would last for several years, was with the wealthy Evelyn Crowell Fay of Great Neck, New York. She was a showgirl who had been married to Larry Fay, a bootlegger and extortionist who was murdered in 1932. Fay was so wealthy, he became one of the society gangsters, a man who threw lavish parties, frequently covered by the press, at which the rich and socially prominent often were present. Joe's indiscretion in his choice of his newest ongoing affair became evident when Walter Winchell's column in the *New York Journal-American* ran a famous blind item that said, "A top New Dealer's mistress is a mobster's widow." The blind items were often little more than blackmail stunts by Winchell. The public loved to guess who was involved, though Joe, with his wife and nine children, never was the subject of speculation. At the same time, Winchell knew that the subject often would come to him as a source of items about others. Joe joined this group of tipgivers, wooing Winchell as he would Arthur Krock, the Washington bureau chief for the *New York Times*.

5. Thanks to Krock, biographers and historians who used the *New York Times* as a primary resource would learn about the "famous" Harvard baseball player. They would learn how he was so brilliant in finance that he was invited to take over Columbia Trust. They would learn about his triumphs at Fore River and in the stock market. And they would learn that though Joe had the

knowledge to be part of a bear pool, he never acted in such a manner because of the people he would hurt. All Joe seemed to need was a mask and a cape—he could have been the nation's first superhero, predating Superman, Batman, and Captain America.

6. Arthur M. Schlesinger Jr., *The Coming of the New Deal*, p. 542.

7. It was during Joe's time as SEC chairman that he started a practice he would carry over with his family. Whenever he or his sons were in the midst of something important, he would try to create a "historic" record that would put a Kennedy spin on a story whose facts might be quite different.

In 1933 the United States went off the gold standard. For the first time in many years the nation's paper money, bonds, and related items were not to be backed by gold. The government was no longer obligated to repay loans in gold despite the fact that when the paper was issued, it stated that gold had to be used. This meant that the value of a debt could vary with the economy. Gold, by contrast, always had been a fairly stable commodity. The price per ounce would rise in bad times and decrease in good times, assuring the holder that his or her money would remain stable. Unbacked currency was not so desirable, a fact that led to lawsuits reaching the U.S. Supreme Court. On Monday, February 18, 1935, the Court issued its decision. Joe Kennedy, wanting to thrust himself into a historic position where he did not belong, wrote a memo to President Roosevelt with the full knowledge that it would be retained and available to be read by future generations:

> From all indications, copies of newspapers attached, the Supreme Court of the United States will today announce the Gold Decision.
>
> I arrived at the office about 9 o'clock and called a meeting of the Commission to see if they had any ideas as to what action should be taken regarding the closing of the exchanges. They all agreed that there was certainly no purpose in closing the exchanges before the decision and that we would have to govern ourselves as to what action we can take when the decision is made. The meeting adjourned then until 12 o'clock, when the Supreme Court was to come in. At 10:30 I called up the President and got Mr. McIntyre, his secretary, on the line, who told me the President was shaving. I asked him if the President had any ideas or suggestions and he said that after talking with him the President would be available, with everything cleaned up, at 12:00, and I could get in touch with him from then on, if anything arose.
>
> The Secretary of the Treasury called me on the phone as to the status of the arrangements at the Supreme Court and I notified him that we had the only line out of the marshal's office, and Judge Burns and Ike Stokes of our legal department would be there. He said Mr. Laylin from the Treasury would go along with them, and he would be with the President at the White House.

At 11:55 Miss LeHand called up, and in a very serious tone announced that since it was a very nice day the President had decided to take a nice, long automobile ride and would return sometime later in the afternoon or evening and was sure that everything would be well handled. I am citing this to show that while the whole world was on the verge of nervous prostration at the possibilities of the Gold Decision, the President of the United States, the one most vitally interested, was not so upset that he couldn't have a little joke, thus demonstrating his capacity to take this along with everything else in stride and to relieve the tension that anyone might feel.

The newspapermen notified me that there was no question about the Decision, as special passes had been issued at 11:45. Judge Burns then called me from the Supreme Court, saying that the Marshal in charge of the Court had a little bun on and everything looked like it was getting started in the right direction. Promptly at 12:00 we opened our telephone lines to the Court and at 12:07 Judge Burns called me and notified me that upon the first case the Supreme Court had decided in favor of the Government. I immediately took up the private line to the White House, connected with line 33, which was the line direct to the President. The phone was answered by Secretary [of the Treasury] Morgenthau, to whom I delivered the first message. He turned the phone over to the President and I relayed the first message from the Supreme Court. About two minutes later Judge Burns notified me that on the second case the Court had decided also with the Government and I then announced this over the line to the President, who in turn relayed it to the group sitting with him at the White House.

The stock market started to rise very rapidly, some gains going as high as ten points. There were 1,000,000 shares dealt in between 12:00 and 1:00. The Chicago Board of Trade closed down because of the volume of orders. I called the President and advised him of all these facts. With a full victory in sight, I called the President to remark on the amazing similarity of the legal point he made in his speech that he had read to me a week ago Sunday, which would have been a classic in American history and which he would have delivered if the Supreme Court had decided against the Government in the Gold Case. He seemed to put his finger on the proper solution of the problem that the Supreme Court should have taken, and in spite of all the guesses that had been made as to how it would be decided, it was on the basis of his outline that the Supreme Court finally determined the fact. I suggested to him that when he wrote his memoirs this speech should find a place somewhere in it. He was in marvelous humor and his only regret was his inability to deliver the speech.

About 2 o'clock Judge Burns notified me from the Supreme Court that the vote was five to four, and that Mr. Justice McReynolds was sounding off in a Fourth of July campaign speech. I relayed that immediately to the President.

Later in the day I called Miss LeHand and assumed that since the victory was the President's, now was the good time to get that week's vacation. She said the President was then in swimming and due consideration would be given to my proposal.

I left the office about 8 o'clock, and the President tried to reach me on the phone. I went to keep an appointment, and called him about 9:45 at the White House from a drugstore. He told me to take the week off, after I had convinced myself that there were no jitters in the stock market.

The memorandum appears meaningless. Joe Kennedy was not involved with the gold standard cases. He had never expressed himself concerning the need to back obligations with gold. He was not connected with the Treasury. He did not help prepare any of the cases that went before the Supreme Court. All he had done was relay information that Roosevelt could have received from anyone he assigned. Yet the chance to serve as messenger boy was so important to Joe that he finished his note with these words:

"I am writing this memorandum because I feel the occasion is a historical one and I feel that the opportunity of being the person to relay this information to the president would be of value historically to my family."

14. Of Family and Ambition

1. Barbara Gibson with Ted Schwarz, *The Kennedys: The Third Generation*, p. 89. The author has interviewed both Kennedy family members and employees over the past twenty years. Some of the interviews were conducted for articles for national magazines. Some were conducted for previous books written with Barbara Gibson, Rose's assistant for the ten years prior to the debilitating stroke that left Mrs. Kennedy alive but essentially nonfunctioning. It was through Barbara Gibson that contacts were made and interviews conducted with staff members ranging from security personnel to nursing help. There also were interviews conducted with friends of members of the family. Always the stories involved the siblings' dislike for their mother, their inability to please their father, and their constant striving for goals they seemed unable to express, even to themselves. One unconfirmed story about Eunice Shriver's hatred was related by Barbara Gibson, who heard it from one of the staff present at the time. "After Rose's first stroke, Eunice insisted that Rose be sat at the dinner table with the rest of the family. Rose would be propped in her chair like a slightly stiff rag doll, five minutes before the meal was served, the exact timing

Rose had once demanded of her children. Her nurse stood at her side to keep her from falling out of her chair. Then, every few minutes during the meal, Eunice would tell the nurse, 'Mother's hungry. Feed her.' The nurse would spoon whatever soft food Rose could handle into her mouth. Sometimes it went down her throat, sometimes down her chin, but Eunice was determined that home life should be 'normal.' " Ibid.

2. *Kennedy and Roosevelt: The Uneasy Alliance*, p. 128.

3. *The Secret Diary of Harold L. Ickes*, vol. 2, *The Inside Struggle: 1936–1939*, p. 340.

4. Joe McCarthy, *The Remarkable Kennedys*, pp. 68–69.

15. "The Ambassador"

1. Laurence Leamer, *The Kennedy Men: 1901–1963*, p. 112.

2. Author interview with Arianne Ritschel Sheppard concerning her life in the Third Reich.

3. *The Secret Diary of Harold Ickes*, vol. 2, p. 370.

4. Amanda Smith, ed., *Hostage to Fortune*, p. 233.

5. The story of Himmler was extensively researched for the book *Walking with the Damned*, the story of Count Folke Bernadotte. Numerous resources exist, including such books as *Himmler* by Peter Padfield (New York: Henry Holt, 1990); and *The Labyrinth* by Walter Schellenberg (New York: Harper & Brothers, 1956); and *"The Good Old Days": The Holocaust as Seen by Its Perpetrators and Bystanders* edited by Ernst Klee, Willi Dressen, and Volker Riess (New York: The Free Press, 1988).

6. At one point Joe was friends with and apparently dating a woman who was connected with Sir Oswald Mosley, head of the small British Fascist movement. It is not known if Joe felt it his job to be acquainted with the dominant political thinkers of Britain as the government was in turmoil, or if Mosley reflected Joe's beliefs. It is assumed that Joe did not realize that the Fascist movement was an insignificant group in England. The domestic intelligence group MI-5 became concerned enough to follow Joe and those working most closely with him who also might be in contact with the Fascists.

7. Grace Tully, *FDR, My Boss*, p. 157.

8. Ronald Kessler, *The Sins of the Father*, p. 154.

9. Seymour M. Hersh, *The Dark Side of Camelot*, p. 86.

10. Keith Feiling, *The Life of Neville Chamberlain*, p. 367.

16. The War Years

1. There are many ways to be nurtured by an important source. Joe understood how one reporter became successful, either within a single paper or in a career that moves the reporter to ever larger markets. He knew it took access. Sometimes this meant sources within a police department so the reporter would

be ahead of others when looking into a case. Such aggression was hilariously captured in this era with the play *The Front Page*, satirizing the cutthroat competition among Chicago newspaper reporters. At other times it meant being connected in some manner to the men and women who were making the news through their positions in government, business, and so forth. Joe saw that as long as a reporter could break important stories through information given by someone high up, the reporter would likely not use a story that would make his or her source look bad. Future access to good stories was worth more than breaking a single scandal. There also were men like Arthur Krock who wanted power. In Krock's case, the desire was to be editor of the *New York Times*. He accepted both cash and influence from Joe Kennedy, the latter seeing an excellent investment if he could move Krock into position as the editor of one of the nation's most powerful papers. And if he couldn't help Krock achieve the top, his efforts along the way, along with the money being paid, assured glowing press with whatever Krock wrote, edited, or could influence.

2. Joe McCarthy, *The Remarkable Kennedys*, p. 79.

3. *New York Times*, October 20, 1938.

4. Amanda Smith, ed., *Hostage to Fortune*, p. 290.

5. Lindbergh is making reference to the island home of Dr. Alexis Carrel, a Nobel laureate for medicine, who was his collaborator on the pump. The mention of "Cavels" island is actually a reference to St. Gidas, the island home of the doctor. The Lindberghs, with the help of the Carrels, bought nearby Illiec Island. These were all small areas, as is obvious from the fact that he could walk from one outcropping of land to the other during low tide each day.

6. One source is Kennedy's personal diary for October 4, 1938. His notations were made three days after he received the telegram from his oldest son. The attitude also was expressed to others. Later he would claim that even if he had been wrong about Hitler's ultimate intentions, the Munich agreement was critical for the British. It gave them a full year to build their defense forces before the first German attack. What he never admitted, though historians have stressed the fact, was that it gave the Germans a full year to build their own offensive and defensive approach before they attacked. He also did not note that the year was so important for Germany's arms buildup that Britain was in a worse position relative to Germany at the end of 1939 than it had been at the end of 1938.

7. Lem Billings always has been a troublesome character in Jack Kennedy's life. What is known without question is that Lem, a homosexual, was Jack's closest friend from the time they were in school together. They came together as roommates during Jack's sophomore year in Choate, and Lem developed a lifelong love for Jack that he spoke freely about. Lem dated Kick for a while, and she thought he was serious about her. She did not know about his being gay. She just knew that unlike the philanderers in her own family and the families of friends, Lem was devoted to her alone. There was no other girl in his life, no other girl he would even look at. She considered his marriage proposal

until she realized that he was in love with Jack, dared not be open with his feelings, and could possibly stay closest to Jack by marrying Kick. She very kindly dropped him as a suitor and put distance to their friendship.

Lem was an odd Choate student—lacking money. His physician father lost his money in the stock market crash. However, Billings traced his pedigree back to the Brewsters of Plymouth Plantation, an impeccable pedigree. Billings was good for the image of Choate and bright enough to earn a scholarship. However, with his bearlike appearance and high, nasal voice, it was obvious that Lem looked and acted in a manner others took as gay. The headmaster did not want Lem and Jack together, but the two were so close that Joe saw nothing wrong with the arrangement.

Allegedly Joe did not care if Jack sexually experimented with another man in the privacy of a closed room. His greater fear was of Jack getting a girl pregnant. He also felt that masturbation was wrong because it was a waste. He was not against a same-sex encounter between male companions in play. And in the case with Lem, who was Jack's closest friend throughout his life, including having a room at the White House, though no official or advisory status when Jack was there, Lem was undoubtedly a blue blood. He was a Brahmin worshipfully adoring a Catholic. If all true, then that alone would have been enough for Joe to turn a blind eye.

Over the years there would be prominent individuals who discussed Jack's alleged bisexuality. They were trying neither to shock nor to ruin the man's reputation. Lem was openly gay, and the Kennedy family knew that. Jack had only a couple of truly intense relationships with women, neither of whom was his wife, and the rest of the time he was a womanizer. Insiders at the Kennedy White House, including brother-in-law Peter Lawford, talked of Jack having as many as two different women a day. They also quoted Jack as saying that he liked to have a woman three different ways before he was done with her. Given that it is the rare heterosexual male who runs through an endless number of women, and that such sex is more a put-down than an intimate act, it is probable that Jack was at least bisexual. It also is probable that Lem was his primary male lover. Author Lawrence J. Quirk, who first worked with Lem Billings on Jack's 1946 congressional campaign, felt that Jack was always on the receiving end of oral sex with Lem. In that way everyone was satisfied and Jack could consider himself a man who had never had sex with another man.

Many years later, Lem Billings would tell the story, perhaps true, perhaps apocryphal, of Jacqueline Bouvier becoming so outraged over Jack's womanizing that she was going to leave him while he was still a U.S. senator. Joe Kennedy, according to Billings' story, offered to give her $1 million to stay with him. "Okay, a million it is," she was said to have replied, "but if he brings home to me any venereal diseases from these sluts, the price goes up to $20 million." Joe was then said to have replied, "Okay, Jackie, if that happens, name your own price. We've got to elect our boy president, regardless of what it takes!" Given the fact that the twice-widowed Jacqueline lived out the last of her life with a wealthy, still-married Jewish man, the story is more likely to be true than the ones about her long-suffering or naive lack of awareness that the family would have preferred.

Whatever the truth, the openly gay Billings was a constant presence and an enigma in the Kennedy saga.

8. The buying of books to create a best-seller is not an outdated concept. Joe used no middlemen for his actions. He paid for the books, and the publisher noted total sales. In more recent times, when best-seller lists are determined by sales in a set number of stores, there has been more subtle buying. The person interested in creating hype will learn, often through a modest bribe, which stores have their sales checked for the creation of the list (as few as five or six copies moving into buyers' hands in the course of a week in smaller outlets was enough to make the book a best-seller in that particular outlet). Then people are hired to go into the stores and buy them in adequate quantity to assure an impact. Sometimes this means a few hundred copies. Sometimes this means thousands. When a movie precedes a book, or when a movie is going to be released and the producer wants the public to know it is based on a blockbuster story, the production company arranges for purchases that boost notice from city to city. Not only is the phenomenon considered news, but also many people buy books specifically because they are on the best-seller lists, whether or not they are interested and whether or not they actually read them. The publicity also promotes the movie at far lower cost than ads. *Why England Slept* ultimately sold eighty thousand copies. Joe Kennedy may have bought half that number. He may have purchased more than that number. And others, including Luce, may have bought some. Certainly the book was nowhere near that successful with the actual buying and reading public, and it is doubtful that many of the readers respected the book, for the same reason Harper & Brothers had turned it down. The realities of the world had surpassed the thinking.

9. U.S. Department of State, *Foreign Relations of the United States*, vol. 3, p. 37.

10. Ibid., pp. 48–49.

11. There are troubling differences with this story and the work of other biographers whose work cannot be discounted. For example, Laurence Leamer tells of Rosemary being sent first to Craig House near the city of Beacon, New York, an hour's drive from New York City. This was an institution for the rich whose family members suffered from anything from alcoholism to schizophrenia. Instead of a locked ward, a mansion had been converted to a luxury prison-type complex, where locked doors and barred windows allowed the violent patients to live in isolated and protected luxury. Everyone else had residences in houses and cottages on the grounds. Supposedly family visits were discouraged as not being in the best interests of the mentally ill, though Rose allegedly visited Rosemary there in 1949. It was at that time that Joe learned of St. Coletta's and arranged the transfer. What is the truth? Each biographer developed special

sources within the family. Each assumes that his or her sources are accurate and unbiased. The story presented in the text of this book is believed to be more accurate than the story presented by a family member who discussed the case with other authors. All that is certain is that the operation was wrong and that the psychological damage to Teddy was extreme.

12. The errors of authors should not be construed as an attack on others or the promotion of this author. The Kennedys have long tried to make certain that they controlled the "facts" in a story. Sometimes this means having one family member act as a primary source, a welcome relief for any biographer or historian. An insider talking is firsthand information. The person also can check information from people who presumably would not otherwise talk with the author. There is no presumption that the person is lying. In addition, there are times when the author checks each statement until he or she is satisfied that everything said checks out. Then the author gets careless or has no reason to keep checking, making a mistake. As an example, when working with the fourth wife of Joe Kennedy's son-in-law Peter Lawford, this author was told a story about the death of his mother's first husband, a colonel who was the aide-de-camp for his father, a British general. His mother was having an affair with General Sir Sydney Lawford and got pregnant by him. When she went to tell her husband, the man, who already knew what had taken place, was distraught and suicidal. Peter told his widow and dozens of people who had become long-time friends by the time he died that his mother's husband summoned her to their quarters. He was standing at the door in full-dress uniform, a shotgun braced on the floor so that the barrel angled toward his face. His feet were bare and he had one toe on the trigger. He saluted his wife, pushed the trigger with his toe, and killed himself in front of her. It was a horror that also was quite possible, many documented cases of such suicides being found in records checks. The trouble was that it was not true. Peter so hated his mother that he made up the story and kept retelling it. Another author, James Spada, who lacked many of the resources I had, dug deeper than friends of Peter's for the previous seventeen years before his death. Spada found that the first husband lived until 1941, by which time Peter was a movie actor. My biography has an error that was checkable, but only by going beyond what I thought was a prudent investigation. Thus the inaccuracy of writers concerning this period should not be considered a reflection on their skill or integrity. It happens to all writers if we work long enough and hard enough on a wide variety of projects.

13. Nigel Hamilton, *JFK Restless Youth*, p. 566.

14. Biographer Doris Kearns Goodwin, writing about the incident in *The Fitzgeralds and the Kennedys: An American Saga*, has a slightly different story. She wrote, "When the priests left, Joe held on to Rose for a moment and then went into the living room to break the news to the others. 'Children,' he said, 'your brother Joe has been lost. He died flying a volunteer mission.' Then, with tears in his eyes and his voice cracking, he said, 'I want you all to be particularly good to your mother.' And with that he retreated into his bedroom and locked

the door." A slightly different story was told by Rose's nephew Joe Gargan and quoted on page 285 of Ronald Kessler's *The Sins of the Father.* He adds, "It was after lunch. They came to the door and asked to see Mr. Kennedy. He said to come up to his room. He came down to the sun room and told the children. Rose was there, and he told her, of course. He probably told her upstairs. They were both distressed, but Jack said, 'Joe would not want us to stay around here crying, so let's go sailing.' The children went sailing."

17. Adrift

1. The idea behind a money laundry is simple. There are cash businesses where the income varies so widely, one location can barely eke out a living for the owner and another, in the same field and possibly nearby, legitimately makes the owner rich. Restaurants are typical of this type of industry. These are low-profit, high-volume locations so numerous that no one ever checks them. If someone goes on a night when every table is taken, carry-out orders are in demand, and there is a line of people waiting to be seated, it is not hard to imagine that the place does the same volume every day. And if the restaurant is half dead, the wait staff standing around instead of serving, and almost no one is eating, who can dispute the manager's statement that it is the first off day the place has experienced in months? The result is that money made from criminal activity is listed as customer payments (the same can be done by exaggerating how much legal betting takes place at racetracks and similar businesses). Some of the money is used for purchasing supplies either from nonexistent companies or from other mob operations that are dummying their books as well. Some of the money goes to the underused staff so they are happy with their pay even when tips are minimal. And always federal, state, and local taxes are properly calculated and paid. The money that is left, all "clean" or "laundered," is legitimate profit from illegitimate enterprise apart from the business that declared it. This is why, in some cities, the mob has had prostitutes working above restaurants, all the income laundered through the restaurant.

2. Information about the deal and the manipulation came from two different newspaper accounts. One was in the *New York Times* for May 14, 1949. The other was in the *Chicago Sun* for January 15, 1946.

18. The Race for the Senate

1. Ralph G. Martin and Ed Plaut, *Front-Runner, Dark Horse*, p. 169.

19. Joe and Jacqueline

1. Harold Russell with Dan Ferullo, *The Best Years of My Life*, p. 164. Also information from extensive author interviews in Russell's Massachusetts home.

2. The first widespread release of information about Jack Kennedy's physical condition came in the December 2002 issue of *Atlantic* magazine in the article

"A Picture of Health" by historian Robert Dalek. He was the first researcher to be given access to some of Jack Kennedy's medical records. However, information about what was taking place was well known before this. The author learned about it from a variety of sources over the past twenty years. The first was Harold Russell as noted. There was a camaraderie of the disabled and suffering when he and other veterans, including Jack Kennedy, got together. They talked freely, and the information was passed to me during interviews conducted about Russell's life. Other information came from the late actor Peter Lawford, who related the stories to his wife, Patricia Seaton Lawford. These were backed by some of his notes and other material that remained in the couple's apartment after his death. And some has been obtained from medical journals and books, including ones found in the Kennedy Library, where files have long been kept hidden or delayed in being put out, but books with some of the same information have been freely placed on the shelves.

3. Ronald Kessler, *The Sins of the Father*, p. 348.

20. The Run for President

1. Quotes from 1989 documentary *Mort Sahl: The Loyal Opposition* produced, written, and directed by Robert B. Weide of Whyaduck Productions.

2. Ibid.

3. Ibid.

4. Anthony Summers, *Official and Confidential*, pp. 265–266.

5. Information on the Teamsters came from a series of lengthy interviews with Alan Friedman and numerous others from this era. These formed the basis for the author's earlier work *Power & Greed: Inside the Teamsters Empire of Corruption*.

6. It must be stressed that the majority of the Teamsters, including the majority of the leaders of the various locals, were honest, hardworking men and women. The Teamsters fought hard to get a living wage for men and women who previously often had to work long hours for low pay and no benefits. The union enabled them to buy decent homes, to have money for retirement, and to send their children to college. Many of the employers had been underpaying, harassing workers, and preventing them from ever getting ahead. The Teamster leadership, known for its toughness, truly helped working people who had been overlooked by civic leaders. At the same time, organized criminals took advantage of some locals, of the wealth of the pension fund, and the like. In working on *Power & Greed* I met men with Damon Runyonesque names such as "Runt" and "The Jew Boy." In the Cleveland region, Bill and Jackie Presser's home local, almost every old leader interviewed—and most were in their mid- to late sixties—eventually went to federal prison for various crimes involving both union and personal actions, including illegal high-stakes gambling.

7. Additional information about what was taking place came from books written by those who were present and by some of their family members. These

include statements by the son of Albert Anastasia; the book *Mafia Princess: Growing Up in Sam Giancana's Family*, by Antoinette Giancana and Thomas Renner; and *Double Cross*, by Sam and Chuck Giancana.

8. The middle ear condition was not widely known. This writer discovered it in 1964 when covering the governors' conference as a freelance photographer. I had punctured my eardrum in an accident two years earlier, damaging the middle ear and having serious fluid loss and balance problems. Among the medications used were two. One came in a small green bottle with a long nozzle for administering to the ear, a traditional treatment that had been used for several years. The other was an experimental medication that my doctor had just been given permission to test on humans approximately six weeks before my injury. I was the first test case and was fortunate. The ear completely healed, though I was told that were it not for the new drug administered within a short time of the injury, I would have had to use the green bottle of medicine for the rest of my life.

Mamie Eisenhower was walking toward the Presidential Suite of the Hotel Cleveland while we in the press gathered outside, awaiting the outcome of a conference among Senator Barry Goldwater, Richard Nixon, and Dwight Eisenhower to see who would tackle Lyndon Johnson for the 1964 race. Mrs. Eisenhower began to wobble, and reporters began whispering that she must have been starting to drink earlier than usual. Then I looked at her hand and she was clutching the small green bottle, identical to the one I had carried. I managed to reach her and asked if she had the ear problem. She admitted that she did, and apparently I was the only person to both spot the bottle and know what it was for.

BIBLIOGRAPHY

Publications

Adams, Brooks. *The Law of Civilization and Decay: An Essay on History.* New York: Books for Libraries Press, 1896.

American Medical Association. "Example of a Patient with Adrenal Insufficiency Due to Addison's Disease Requiring Elective Surgery." *Archive of Surgery* (November 1955).

Anger, Kenneth. *Hollywood Babylon.* New York: Dell, 1975.

————. *Hollywood Babylon: II.* New York: Penguin, 1984.

Barck, Oscar Theodore Jr., and Nelson Manfred Blake. *Since 1900.* New York: Macmillan, 1947.

Beschloss, Michael. *Kennedy and Roosevelt: The Uneasy Alliance.* New York: W. W. Norton, 1980.

Birmingham, Stephen. *Real Lace: America's Irish Rich.* New York: Harper & Row, 1973.

Black, Gregory D. *Hollywood Censored: Morality Codes, Catholics, and the Movies.* Cambridge: Cambridge University Press, 1994.

Blair, John and Clay Jr. *The Search for JFK.* New York: Berkley, 1976.

Bouvier, Jacqueline and Lee. *One Special Summer.* New York: Delacorte, 1974.

Bullitt, Orville H., ed. *For the President: Personal and Secret Correspondence between Franklin D. Roosevelt and William C. Bullitt.* Boston: Windsor, 1984.

Burns, James MacGregor. *John Kennedy: A Political Profile.* New York: Harcourt, Brace, 1960.

————. *Roosevelt: The Lion and the Fox.* New York: Harcourt, Brace, 1956.

————. *Roosevelt: The Soldier of Freedom.* New York: Harcourt Brace Jovanovich, 1970.

Carlson, Laurie Winn. *A Fever in Salem: A New Interpretation of the New England Witch Trials.* Chicago: Ivan R. Dee, 1999.

Ceplair, Larry, and Steven Englund. *The Inquisition in Hollywood: Politics in the Film Community, 1930–1960.* Garden City, N.Y.: Doubleday, 1980.

Clifford, Clark, with Richard Holbrooke. *Counsel to the President.* New York: Random House, 1991.

Clinch, Nancy Gager. *The Kennedy Neurosis.* New York: Grosset & Dunlap, 1973.

Collier, Peter, and David Horowitz. *The Kennedys: An American Drama.* New York: Summit Books, 1984.

Cullen, James B. *The Story of the Irish in Boston.* Boston: J. B. Cullen, 1889.

Curran, Robert. *The Kennedy Women: Their Triumphs and Tragedies.* New York: Lancer, 1964.

Cutler, John Henry. *"Honey Fitz": Three Steps to the White House.* Indianapolis, Ind.: Bobbs-Merrill, 1962.

Dallas, Rita, R.N., with Jeanira Ratcliffe. *The Kennedy Case.* New York: G. P. Putnam's Sons, 1973.

Damore, Leo. *The Cape Cod Years of John Fitzgerald Kennedy.* Englewood Cliffs, N.J.: Prentice-Hall, 1967.

Davis, John. *The Bouviers.* New York: Farrar, Straus, & Giroux, 1969.

————. *The Kennedys: Dynasty and Disaster.* New York: McGraw-Hill, 1984.

Davis, Kenneth S. *FDR: The Beckoning of Destiny, 1882–1928.* New York: G. P. Putnam's Sons, 1971.

————. *FDR: Into the Storm, 1937–1940: A History.* New York: Random House, 1993.

DeBedts, Ralph F. *Ambassador Joseph Kennedy 1938–1940: An Anatomy of Appeasement.* New York: Peter Lang, 1985.

Dinneen, Joseph. *The Kennedy Family.* Boston: Little, Brown, 1959.

Doherty, Thomas. *Pre-Code Hollywood: Sex, Immorality, and Insurrection in American Cinema, 1930–1934.* New York: Columbia University Press, 1999.

Ellis, Edward Robb. *New York City: A Narrative History.* New York: Old Town Books, 1966.

Exner, Judith, as told to Ovid Demaris. *Judith Exner: My Story.* New York: Grove Press, 1977.

Farley, James. *Behind the Ballots: The Personal History of a Politician.* New York: Harcourt, Brace, 1938.

Feiling, Keith. *The Life of Neville Chamberlain.* London: Macmillan, 1947.

Fuchs, Lawrence H. *John F. Kennedy and American Catholicism.* New York: Meredith, 1967.

Gabler, Neal. *An Empire of Their Own: How the Jews Invented Hollywood.* New York: Crown, 1988.

Gardner, Gerald. *The Censorship Papers—Movie Censorship Letters from the Hays Office 1934 to 1968.* New York: Dodd, Mead, 1987.

Gentry, Curt. *J. Edgar Hoover: The Man and the Secrets.* New York: W. W. Norton, 1991.

Giancana, Sam and Chuck. *Double Cross.* New York: Warner, 1992.

Gibson, Barbara, with Ted Schwarz. *The Kennedys: The Third Generation.* New York: Thunder's Mouth Press, 1993.

————. *Rose Kennedy and Her Family: The Best and Worst of Their Lives and Times.* New York: Carol, Birch Lane Press, 1995.

Goodwin, Doris Kearns. *The Fitzgeralds and the Kennedys: An American Saga.* New York: St. Martin's Press, 1987.

Hall, David D., ed. *Witch-Hunting in Seventeenth-Century New England: A Documentary History, 1638–1692.* Boston: Northeastern University Press, 1991.

Hamilton, Nigel. *JFK Reckless Youth*. New York: Random House, 1992.

Hays, Will. *The Memoirs of Will H. Hays*. Garden City, N.Y.: Doubleday, 1955.

Hecht, Ben. *A Child of the Century*. New York: Simon & Schuster, 1954.

Hersh, Seymour M. *The Dark Side of Camelot*. Boston: Little, Brown, 1997.

Heymann, C. David. *A Woman Named Jackie*. New York: Lyle Stuart/Carol, 1989.

Holt, Chauncey. "Memoirs of a Chameleon: Autobiography."

Howard, Brett. *Boston: A Social History*. New York: Hawthorn, 1976.

Ickes, Harold L. *The Secret Diary of Harold L. Ickes*. Vols. 1–3. New York: Simon & Schuster, 1955.

Jacobs, Lea. *The Wages of Sin: Censorship and the Fallen Woman Film, 1928–1942*. Madison: University of Wisconsin Press, 1991.

James, Ann. *The Kennedy Scandals & Tragedies*. Lincolnwood, Ill.: Publications International, 1991.

Kelley, Kitty. *His Way: The Unauthorized Biography of Frank Sinatra*. New York: Bantam Books, 1986.

————— . *Jackie, Oh!* Secaucus, N.J.: Lyle Stuart, 1978.

Kennedy, Joseph P. *I'm for Roosevelt*. New York: Reynal & Hitchcock, 1936.

Kennedy, Joseph P., ed. *The Story of the Films*. Chicago: A. W. Shaw, 1927.

Kennedy, Rose. *Times to Remember*. Garden City, N.Y.: Doubleday, 1974.

Kessler, Ronald. *The Sins of the Father: Joseph P. Kennedy and the Dynasty He Founded*. New York: Warner Books, 1996.

Koskoff, David E. *Joseph P. Kennedy: A Life and Times*. Englewood Cliffs, N.J.: Prentice-Hall, 1974.

Krock, Arthur. *Memoirs*. New York: Funk & Wagnalls, 1968.

Lash, Joseph P. *Eleanor and Franklin: The Story of Their Relationship Based on Eleanor Roosevelt's Private Papers*. New York: W. W. Norton, 1971.

————— . *Roosevelt and Churchill, 1939–1941: The Partnership That Saved the West*. New York: W. W. Norton, 1976.

Lasky, Victor. *JFK: The Man and the Myth*. New York: Macmillan, 1963.

Lawford, Patricia Seaton, with Ted Schwarz. *The Peter Lawford Story*. New York: Carroll & Graf, 1988.

Leamer, Laurence. *The Kennedy Men*. New York: William Morrow, 2001.

————— . *The Kennedy Women: The Saga of an American Family*. New York: Random House, 1994.

Le Beau, Bryan F. *The Story of the Salem Witch Trials*. Upper Saddle River, N.J.: Prentice Hall, 1998.

Leff, Leonard J., and Jerold L. Simmons. *The Dame in the Kimono: Hollywood, Censorship, and the Production Code from the 1920s to the 1960s*. New York: Grove Weidenfeld, 1990.

Madsen, Axel. *Gloria and Joe: The Star-Crossed Love Affair of Gloria Swanson and Joe Kennedy*. New York: Arbor House, 1988.

Martin, Ralph G., and Ed Plaut. *Front-Runner, Dark Horse*. Garden City, N.Y.: Doubleday, 1960.

McCarthy, Joe. *The Remarkable Kennedys*. New York: Dial, 1960.

McTaggart, Lynne. *Kathleen Kennedy: Her Life and Times*. New York: Dial, 1983.

Messick, Hank. *The Mob in Show Business*. New York: Pyramid Books, 1975.

Moley, Raymond. *After Seven Years*. New York: Harper & Brothers, 1939.

———. *The First New Deal*. New York: Harcourt, Brace, & World, 1966.

Nash, Jay Robert. *The World Encyclopedia of Organized Crime*. New York: Paragon, 1992.

O'Connor, Thomas H. *The Boston Irish: A Political History*. Boston: Northeastern University Press, 1995.

Otash, Fred, and Ted Schwarz. "Marilyn, the Kennedys, and Me." 1992.

Parmet, Herbert S. *Jack: The Struggles of John F. Kennedy*. New York: Dial, 1980.

Quirk, Lawrence J. *The Kennedys in Hollywood*. Dallas: Taylor, 1996.

Rainie, Harrison, and John Quinn. *Growing Up Kennedy: The Third Wave Comes of Age*. New York: G. P. Putnam's Sons, 1983.

Reedy, George. *From the Ward to the White House: The Irish in American Politics*. New York: Charles Scribner's Sons, 1991.

Reeves, Thomas C. *A Question of Character: A Life of John Kennedy*. New York: Free Press, 1991.

Roosevelt, Elliott, ed. *FDR: His Personal Letters, 1928–1945*. New York: Duell, Sloan, & Pearce, 1950.

Roosevelt, Elliott, and James Brough. *A Rendezvous with Destiny: The Roosevelts of the White House*. New York: G. P. Putnam's Sons, 1975.

Roosevelt, James, with Bill Libby. *My Parents: A Differing View*. Chicago: Playboy Press, 1976.

Roosevelt, James, and Sidney Shallett. *Affectionately, FDR: A Son's Story of a Lonely Man*. New York: Harcourt, Brace, 1959.

Russell, Francis. *The President Makers: From Mark Hanna to Joseph P. Kennedy*. Boston: Little, Brown, 1976.

Russell, Harold, with Dan Ferullo. *The Best Years of My Life*. Middlebury, Vt.: P. S. Eriksson, 1981.

Saunders, Frank. *Torn Lace Curtain*. New York: Holt, Rinehart, & Winston, 1982.

Schlesinger, Arthur M. Jr. *The Coming of the New Deal*. Boston: Houghton Mifflin, 1959.

———. *The Crisis of the Old Order*. Vol. 1 of *The Age of Roosevelt*. Boston: Houghton Mifflin, 1957.

Searl, Hank. *The Lost Prince: Young Joe, the Forgotten Kennedy*. New York: World, 1969.

Shriver, Eunice Kennedy. "Hope for Retarded Children." *Saturday Evening Post*, September 22, 1962.

Smith, Amanda, ed. *Hostage to Fortune: The Letters of Joseph P. Kennedy*. New York: Viking, 2001.

Sorensen, Theodore C. *Kennedy*. New York: Bantam Books, 1966.

Sorensen, Theodore C., ed. *The Speeches, Statements, and Writings of John F. Kennedy: 1947–1963*. New York: Dell, 1988.

Spada, James. *Peter Lawford: The Man Who Kept the Secrets.* New York: Bantam, 1991.

Summers, Anthony. *Official and Confidential: The Secret Life of J. Edgar Hoover.* New York: G. P. Putnam's Sons, 1993.

Swanson, Gloria. *Swanson on Swanson: An Autobiography.* New York: Random House, 1980.

Travell, Janet, M.D. *Office Hours: Day and Night.* New York: World, 1968.

Tully, Grace. *FDR, My Boss.* New York: Charles Scribner's Sons, 1949.

Upham, Charles W. *Salem Witchcraft.* 1867. Reprint, Mineola, N.Y.: Dover, 2000.

U.S. Department of State. *Foreign Relations of the United States.* Vol. 3. Washington, D.C.: U.S. Government Printing Office, 1940.

Whalen, Richard J. *The Founding Father: The Story of Joseph P. Kennedy.* New York: New American Library, 1964.

White, Theodore. *The Making of the President 1960.* New York: Atheneum, 1961.

Wills, Garry. *The Kennedy Imprisonment: A Meditation on Power.* Boston: Little, Brown, 1981.

Wolf, George, and Joseph DiMona. *Frank Costello: Prime Minister of the Underworld.* New York: William Morrow, 1974.

Special Collections

John F. Kennedy, personal papers and correspondence, 1933–1950, including Inga Arvad letters. John Fitzgerald Kennedy Library, Boston.

The letters and memos of Rose Kennedy as taken in shorthand by Barbara Gibson

The Peter Lawford Files of the Special Collection Division of the Hayden Library, Arizona State University, Tempe, Arizona

The Ted Schwarz Files of the Special Collection Division of the Hayden Library, Arizona State University, Tempe, Arizona

INDEX

Page numbers in *italics* indicate illustrations.